The Pātityagrāmanirṇaya

A Purāṇic History of Some Brahman Communities

Hindu Tradition Series

The Hindu Tradition Series aims to bring together books of the highest academic standard that critically interrogate Hindu tradition in the widest sense. Its focus is on cultural and religious history, including relevant political and social developments. The interaction with other traditions, whether originally from inside or outside the Indian subcontinent, will figure prominently among its volumes.

6

THE PĀTITYAGRĀMANIRṆAYA

A Purāṇic History of Some Brahman Communities

Includes Introduction, The Text of *Pātityagrāmanirṇaya, Sahyādrikhaṇḍa, Skandapurāṇa,* Translation and Critical Apparatus

STEPHAN HILLYER LEVITT

MOTILAL BANARSIDASS PUBLISHERS
PRIVATE LIMITED • DELHI

First Edition : Delhi, 2017

ISBN: 978-81-208-4097-3

<u>*Also available at*</u>

MOTILAL BANARSIDASS

41 U.A., Bungalow Road, Jawahar Nagar, Delhi 110 007
8 Mahalaxmi Chamber, 22 Bhulabhai Desai Road, Mumbai 400 026
203 Royapettah High Road, Mylapore, Chennai 600 004
236, 9th Main III Block, Jayanagar, Bangalore 560 011
8 Camac Street, Kolkata 700 017
Ashok Rajpath, Patna 800 004
Chowk, Varanasi 221 001

MLBD Cataloging-in-Publication Data
The Pātityagrāmanirṇaya:
A Purāṇic *History of Some Brahman Communities*
by Stephan Hillyer Levitt
ISBN : 978-81-208-4097-3
Includes Introduction, Text, Translation, Critical apparatus, Appendices, Glossary, Bibliography and Index
I. Hinduism II. Skanda Purāṇa III. Sahyādrikhaṇḍa
IV. Purāṇic History V. Levitt, Stephan Hillyer

Published by
Motilal Banarsidass Publishers Private Limited
www.mlbd.com • mlbd@mlbd.com

Printed by: Ajanta Offset & Packagings Ltd., Fbd., Haryana

For

Ludo Rocher,

Who Suggested It

FOREWORD BY THE GENERAL EDITOR

It is well known to scholars to Sanskrit literature that being a Brahman carries many obligations and restriction. Much of the extensive literature on Dharma describes these obligations and restrictions in great detail. It is less clear from this literature whether and to what extent breaking these rules has consequences in the real world for transgressing Brahmans. Are these rules mere intellectual play, nothing but a way to mislead the outside world into thinking that Brahmans are entitled to their claimed privileges? Or are Brahmans really expected to live up to these high expectations, at the risk of losing their privileges altogether?

Levitt's *The Pātityagrāmanirṇya: A Purāṇic History of Some Brahman Communities* throws new light on these questions. Though a Sanskrit text, it deals with a number of villages, some of them identifiable in modern India, that are inhabited by "fallen" Brahmans, Brahmans that have lost their exalted state, allegedly on account of transgressions committed in the past. The new status of these fallen Brahmans is that of untouchables.

It is hoped that the publication of this book in the Hindu Tradition Series will invite scholars to pay renewed attention to the sometimes-precarious nature of Brahmanhood.

JOHANNES BRONKHORST

CONTENTS

PREFACE

Since writing my doctoral dissertation in 1973, I have come across Bhasker Anand Saletore's work on the Tuluva *Grāmapaddhati*, which proves to contain eight chapters of the *Pātityagrāmanirṇaya* and the two chapters of the *Mayūravarmākhyāna* which precedes it in the *Sahyādrikhaṇḍa*, among others. While I have not been able to consult his best manuscript of this, I have compared those readings of his in the small amount of text he gave with my text, and have incorporated this information in the Introduction. In those few instances in which this suggested emendations to my edited text of the *Pātityagrāmanirṇaya*, these have been noted in the critical apparatus and in notes to the English translation.

While the amount of text that Saletore gave was not extensive, it demonstrated most forcefully the value of the critical apparatus as formulated here.

I have also consulted for this revised edition another manuscript in the India Office Library, London that I had overlooked earlier. This manuscript (L3), in Malayalam script, proves to contain only one of our *Pātityagrāmanirṇaya* chapters. But this chapter is chapter seven (*Sahyādrikhaṇḍa uttarārdha* chapter 15), which appeared earlier to be possibly fragmentary on account of its brevity. The new manuscript contains two additional verses, and contains appreciably better text for the two *pādas* that appeared to list village names. Also, its readings overall are very good, and support hypothesized emendations to the text made earlier – which is very gratifying. I would like to thank V. Raghavan, who unfortunately passed away in 1979, for pointing this manuscript out to me.

It has been my observation both with regard to the manuscripts of the *Pātityagrāmanirṇaya*, and in the course of cataloguing Sanskrit and allied manuscripts in the collections of the Library and the University Museum of the University of Pennsylvania, that fragmentary manuscripts with sections of text only, such as this latter manuscript (L3), and our manuscripts L1a and L1c, also in the India Office Library, London, contain our better readings. These manuscripts also most often are the less aesthetically appealing manuscripts.

I would as well like to thank Prof. M. Gopal Reddy, Director of Sanskrit Academy, Osmania University at the time, and the staff of Sarasvati Bhavan Library, Sampurṇananda Sanskrit Vishvavidyalaya, Benares for sending me Xerox copy of manuscripts which we had reason to believe might also contain the PGN on the basis of their mention in the respective catalogs, and for trying to track down or tracking down these manuscripts for me. As it works out, a manuscript of the *Sahyādrikhaṇḍa* in the Osmania University Library could not be located, and the manuscript in the Sarasvati Bhavan Library was of something else, plus the first four chapters only of the *uttarārdha* of the *Sahyādrikhaṇḍa*.

When we were editing chapter eleven (*Sahyādrikhaṇḍa uttarārdha* chapter 19), there was one passage that could not be made out. This passage was introduced as are quotations in the legal literature, and so it was understood to be a quotation or group of quotations. These could not be located, though. On looking over the passage again, however, it has been recognized to be just simple declarative Sanskrit. The passage relates to the basis for the origin of some *brāhmaṇas*. This passage has been retranslated here, and annotated anew.

Retranslation, and only very occasionally restructuring of the text, was executed here and there elsewhere as well. And occasionally annotations to the translation have been added afresh or modified. In the main, though, the text and translation have been left as set earlier by myself together with Dr. Ludo Rocher.

In general, the Introduction has been revamped here so as to include not only discussion of Saletore's work, but also the fruits of further research of our own. Also, some points that were not discussed fully and clarified earlier have been discussed more fully and clarified here.

Over the years, I have written several articles on the *Sahyādrikhaṇḍa* and the *Pātityagrāmanirṇaya*:

1977 and 1979. "The *Sahyādrikhaṇḍa*: Some Problems Concerning a Text-Critical Edition of a Purāṇic Text," in *Purāṇa* 19.1: 8-40 and 21.1: 77-79.

1982. "The *Sahyādrikhaṇḍa*: Style and Context as Indices of Authorship in the *Pātityagrāmanirṇaya*," in *Purāṇa* 24.1: 128-145.

1992. "An Origin of Some Brahmans According to the *Pātityagrāmanirṇaya*," in *The Journal of Sanskrit Academy, Osmania University* 14: 1-18.

1993. "Pollution and *karman* in the *Pātityagrāmanirṇaya*," in *Purāṇa* 35.1: 88-105.

In the Introduction here, I have now included some of the points in these articles. Obviously, though, I could not include everything. The reader is encouraged to consult these articles for further information.

In 1976-77, after I had come back from teaching in a short-lived U.S. National Endowment for the Humanities-funded Humanities Program at the University of

Denver – the India course in which was only taught in the second to fourth years (my predecessor in Indian literature and Sanskrit teaching at the University of Denver just for the grant's second year), the course on Ancient Mexico being the only course taught in the fifth and final year of the grant – when I mentioned to a graduate student in Sanskrit at Columbia University whom I had met in their Butler Library that the topic of my doctoral dissertation had been a Sanskrit text treating communities of polluted *brāhmaṇas* of untouchable status in the Karnataka region, he commented, "Leave it to the South Indians!" Nothing could be further from the truth, though. Such groups of *brāhmaṇas* can be found throughout India with surprising frequency. It was originally my intention to publish as a separate article, or to include with this revision of the dissertation for publication, the glossary of approximately 100 such communities of polluted *brāhmaṇas* throughout India that I had abstracted from in the main the various 'Tribes and Castes' volumes compiled during the days of British rule. This was decided against, though, as it might tend to freeze the social positions of these groups. Indian society is dynamic, with social mobility being by groups. Thus Kayasths, for example, a caste of scribes, during the British period raised their status by becoming teachers. While it has proven much more difficult for untouchable groups to do this, I would not want to throw "fuel on the fire" by introducing a compilation of information that might ossify an otherwise fluid situation. The histories behind some such polluted *brāhmaṇa* communities as related in the various 'Tribes and Castes' volumes are referred to in the Introduction here, though, but without naming names.

I might note in conclusion that the material I had wanted to deal with in my doctoral dissertation was on the setting up of villages, following through on work I had done under Dr. Dorothy Spencer on *grāmadevatās*, or village deities of South India (which paper is now, unfortunately, lost). I have now seen reference to such material in architectural texts. Interestingly, it does explain why village *grāmadevatās* are found in South India, but not in northern India. I alluded to this obliquely in my 2011 paper "McKim Marriott's Theory of 'Coded Substance' as an Explanation of Formulaic Turns of Phrase in Certain Vedic and Hindu Prayers, and Its Relationship to Mircea Eliade's Theory of 'The Sacred'," in *Anthropos* 106.1: 49-55 (see pp. 53-54)

Stephan Hillyer Levitt
Flushing, New York
August, 2013

1973 PREFACE TO THE DISSERTATION

In 1966 I approached Dr. Ludo Rocher with a request that, if possible, he recommend a Sanskrit text for me to work on that had an anthropological bent. At the time I was particularly interested in a text which would contain information on the setting up of villages. Dr. Rocher suggested the *Pātityagrāmanirṇaya* as a possibility. I took his suggestion and started to work on the text immediately, but various events made it impossible for me to give it my full attention for a few years.

In the summer of 1971, after having parsed the text as in the edition, having done a preliminary "reading through" and having obtained several microfilm copies of the text in manuscript form, I began to work on the text full time under the supervision of Dr. Rocher. His expert guidance and unusual perceptivity were of tremendous help in dealing with the text. This was particularly so when it came to seeing sense where none seemed to exist, and to showing me that there was no sense where I had forced sense. The observation of William Dwight Whitney that those who slave over *upaniṣads* trying to find some sense in their corrupt texts when in reality none would ever be found until the text was edited critically and all the corruptions which scholars were trying to make sense out of were done away with, was brought home most forcefully.

I worked with Dr. Rocher summer and winter alike, and am extremely grateful for all the time which he afforded me both in the midst of a very hectic schedule and during time which was properly his vacation from teaching. I also add that I am much to the better due to his edifying influence. The text does not treat what I had originally hoped it would treat, but I find its topic and stories intriguing, and believe its readers will find this to be the case also. In addition, the text has interested me in a sizeable group of topically related texts, all of which seem to be equally intriguing and unusual, and important, and for this I also express thanks to him.

It is to Dr. Rocher, who has put out so much in effort, that I dedicate this work.

I should also like to single out for expressions of appreciation Dr. Royal Weiler, Dr. Ernest Bender and Dr. W. Norman Brown.

It was under Dr. Weiler that I first started Sanskrit at Columbia College in 1962. His unique command of Indic knowledge has been a source of inspiration since, and the several conversations I have had with him regarding the work at hand have each added something to it.

The great amount of time Dr. Bender devoted to me as a student at the University of Pennsylvania is greatly appreciated, and what I have learned from him cannot but have entered into my work on the *Pātityagrāmanirṇaya*. I must also thank him for facilitating my receiving the microfilm of the text from the Oriental Institute, Baroda. To Dr. Bender, thank you.

To Dr. Brown I have an especial debt of thanks. During the past year I have had the privilege of being his research assistant. The work done under him has added tremendously to the sophistication of this work – this aside from the sophistication gained previously as a student of his in Indian civilization and Vedic Sanskrit. Most important to me, however, has been the encouragement he has given me during the past year.

There are many others who have helped with specific aspects or points of the work at hand, or who have facilitated the work. These include Miss Khanta Bhatia, Mr. Bernard Ford, Dr. Peter Gaeffke, Dr. Christopher George, Dr. Sanykta Gupta, Dr. Clifford Jones, Dr. Theodore Riccardi, Jr., and Dr. Albrecht Wezler.

I must also give a note of appreciation to Miss K. Blair of the India Office Library, London, Mr. B. D. Velankar of the Asiatic Society of Bombay, Mr. G. E. Marrison of the Department of Printed Books and Manuscripts at the British Museum, and Dr. B. J. Sandesara and Dr. U. P. Shah of the Oriental Institute, Baroda, and to these institutions themselves, for affording me microfilm copies of the manuscripts of the *Pātityagrāmanirṇaya*.

I also extend a note of thanks to Mr. N. C. Sainsbury and the Department of Oriental Books at the Bodleian Library, Oxford, for providing me with a photocopy of a section of the Library's MS. Mill 79, and for giving me permission to use a transliteration of it in the Introduction.

Before closing, I would like to note that there have been times when I considered dropping work on this text for a very unusual reason. From time to time I have been haunted by an anecdote told by the anthropologist Edward B. Harper of a Havik brahman who maintained that untouchables were dirty and degraded because they ate beef. Harper protested and a nearby untouchable working in the Havik's garden was asked if his caste ate beef. The untouchable replied that they had given up eating beef thirty years ago. The Havik was triumphant and said something to the effect of, "You see! I told you they were dirty. They used to eat beef."

Because of the nature of the *Pātityagrāmanirṇaya* I am occasionally plagued by the possibility of similar situations arising should people try to track down the groups mentioned. The cost-accounting of getting on with my degree and my own interest in the text, have, however, over-ruled my moral debates I am ashamed to say.

I sincerely hope that an attitude such as that described by Harper does not enter into future situations which might arise because of the work done here and that my concern is totally unnecessary. I hasten to take solace, and to point out, that at least two great Indians of recent times, Debendranath Tagore and Rabindranath Tagore, were from a *patita* brahman group.

Stephan Levitt
New York City
August, 1973

A NOTE ON TRANSLITERATION

The transliteration system used is that of Sir Monier Monier-Williams (1899), with the following changes: ṛi = ṛ, ṛī = ṝ, ṡ = ś, sh = ṣ. In the transliteration of the *Veda* text in Appendix C, the system of Theodore Aufrecht (1877), from whose text the passages were taken, has been used with the following standardizations to our system: ṛi = ṛ, ṛī = ṝ, ñ = ṅ, ṣ = ś, sh = ṣ, ṅ = ṉ. In quotations and titles the transliteration system used in the work being quoted or in the work being cited has been retained, with the following exceptions: the systems of indicating long vowels has been standardized to that used in the rest of the text; the ç of *The Sacred Books of the East* has been standardized to our ś. In the names of places and peoples the original spelling of the source has been retained, no matter what the spellings might be in an Indian alphabet. In the transliteration of the few Tamil words, the system used is that of the U. S. Library of Congress Processing Department, Cataloging Service Bulletin No. 64 (February 1964).

ABBREVIATIONS AND SYMBOLS

Abbreviations

Aufl..	*Auflage*, 'edition'
E.	East
ed., eds.	edited; editor(s)
e.g.	*exempli gratia*, 'for example'
enl.	enlarged
f., ff.	folio(s), following
i.e.	*id est*, 'that is'
lit.	literally
MA	*Mayūravarmākhyāna*
MS, MSS	manuscript(s)
n., nn.	footnote(s)
N.	North
n.d.	no date
n.s.	new series
p., pp.	page(s)
PGN	*Pātityagrāmanirṇaya*
pl.	plural
pref.	preface
pt., pts.	part(s)
rev.	revised
rpt.	reprint
RV	*Ṛgveda*
Skh	*Sahyādrikhaṇḍa*
Skh.u.	*Sahyādrikhaṇḍa, uttarārdha*
Skp	*Skandapurāṇa*
s.v.	*sub voce*, 'under the word'
syll.	syllable(s)
trans.	translator(s), -ed

u.	*und*, 'and'
verb.	*verbesserte*, 'revised'
verm.	*vermehrte*, 'enlarged'
vol., vols.	volume(s)
vs., vss.	verse(s)

Symbols

° indicates omission of a word in composition with the word at hand.

Daggers around a word or phrase in the text, † . . . †, indicate extreme doubt as to the reading of the text in between the daggers. They are also used around the translations of words and phrases in the translation to indicate that the text at that point is extremely dubious.

Italics are used to indicate an emendation in the text.

Italics are also used for Sanskrit terms which appear as such in the translation or in the Introduction.

Boldface is used for the section numbers of and the section and major sub-section headings in the Introduction only.

§ is used to indicate the section so numbered in the Introduction, e.g. **§5.4**, indicates section **5.4** in the Introduction.

(?) placed after Sanskrit words in the critical apparatus indicates that the word(s) or syllables in question are not or do not make proper Sanskrit.

(?) placed after English words in the translation indicates that there is a question as to whether or not the text should translate as immediately preceding the question mark.

Square brackets around words in the translation, [. . .], indicate an insertion for the sake of clarity.

Square brackets around items in the Bibliography indicate that the information within them is not given in the book or article being listed.

Parentheses around Sanskrit words in the critical apparatus,

(. . .), indicate that the reading or readings within them are clearly derived from the preferred reading and are not significantly different from this reading.

Parentheses in the translation are used around clarifications and around alternate translations.

Three periods, . . . , in the translations and in the variant column of the critical apparatus, indicate that something has been omitted.

In the text, a single period, . , is used to indicate a syllable of text for which it has not been possible to decide on an acceptable reading. Thus, ... , in the text, indicates that five syllables have been omitted.

[?] indicates a syllable or part of a syllable in the manuscript in question could not be read; [? ?] indicates that two syllables, or a syllable and part of another in the manuscript in question, could not be read; and so on.

[-] indicates that a syllable was represented by a dash in the manuscript in question; [- -] indicates that two syllables were represented by dashes; and so on.

˘ indicates a short syllable.

¯ indicates a long syllable.

° and ' , degrees and minutes, are used to indicate latitude and longitude.

C indicates an unspecified consonant.

> indicates that what precedes the sign has given rise to what follows.

< indicates that what precedes the sign comes from what follows.

+ means ‘plus.’

± means ‘with or without.’

= means that what precedes the sign equals, or is equivalent to, what follows.

~ means that what precedes the sign alternates with what follows.

I. INTRODUCTION

1. The Text.

1.1. What the text is about. **1.2.** The location of the text in the *Sahyādrikhaṇḍa*. **1.3.** The *uttarārdha* of the *Sahyādrikhaṇḍa* as presently constituted. **1.4.** The text as a unit.

1.1. What the text is about. The PGN is a series of eight stories which offer us explanations as to how certain communities of polluted brahmans, or *brāhmaṇas*, came into existence. It introduces us expressly to thirteen *pātitya* villages – that is, villages of polluted *brāhmaṇas* of untouchable status, but in the course of its explanation between twenty and twenty-three *pātitya* villages actually are referred to. The first is a village of pregnant *brāhmaṇa* widows who had been expelled from their own villages in an area referred to as 'the thirty-two villages.' The next five are villages established for the sons of these widows. The seventh is a village of a *śūdra* chief which was given to some *brāhmaṇas* after they had sinned at the instigation of the *śūdra*. The eighth is a community of *brāhmaṇas* who devised a crafty but deceitful stratagem in order to obtain an additional paddy field. The ninth is again a village of pregnant *brāhmaṇa* widows, but in this instance the widows have been expelled from various villages throughout the different countries of ancient India. The tenth, and perhaps the eleventh, are one or two villages of *brāhmaṇas*, the people of one of which carried off and raised a lost tribal girl and then married her to a *brāhmaṇa* family of the other. The text is not clear as to whether it was the *brāhmaṇas* of both villages or just of one of them who were excommunicated. The next four are villages which were set up by Mayūravarman of the Kadamba dynasty (beginning or middle of the 4th century A.D.) for *brāhmaṇas* who are referred to as having been established by Paraśurāma at a time when Mayūravarman brought other *brāhmaṇas* from the city of Ballabhī in Gujarat. In the text as we have edited it here, only two of these villages are mentioned by name. The next is a village of *brāhmaṇa* kinsmen one of whom had murdered his wife and her paramour. And the last seven are villages given by a *brāhmaṇa* to seven sons whom he had by a slave girl and whom he had had raised to the status of *brāhmaṇas*. Except for the last seven villages, all may be taken to be located in or near the Sahyādri range of mountains in western India; and more specifically, near the land of the Tuḷus (Tuluva), near Gokarṇa, near Kroḍeśa or within the area of 'the thirty-two villages,' wherever either of these may have been (see **§12.6** below), and, perhaps coterminous with or including at least the latter, the area of the Kadamba empire with its capital at the modern Banawāsi. The villages established in chapter seven (Skh.u. 15) would appear to be in Gorāṣṭra. The last seven are in the Kaliṅga of king Hemamālin who, as noted in **§12.5a** below, cannot be identified yet.

1.2. The location of the text in the *Sahyādrikhaṇḍa*. The PGN comprises chapters 9 to 19 of what is termed variously in the MSS and in DaCunha's edition as the *uttarārdha*, the *uparibhāga*, the *uttarakhaṇḍa*, or the *uttararahasya* of the Skh as it is presently constituted. Preceding the PGN are six chapters which discuss the supposed origins of some of the major brāhmaṇic groups in the area of the Sahyādri range of mountains, one which discusses the mythological origin of the Konkan coast, ending with a reference lauding king Mayūravarman, and one which discusses the introduction by Mayūravarman of *brāhmaṇas* from Ahichatra, or Ahikṣetra, the ancient capital of Northern Pañcāla, and the final establishment of these in the thirty-two villages by his son, here named Candrāṅgada. Immediately following the PGN is a chapter which speaks of *ṛṣis* and Śaunaka gathered together for a sacrifice. A list of contents for the entire Skh and attached *māhātmyas*, as they are given in DaCunha's edition of the Skh, is presented in Appendix H.

1.3. The *uttarārdha* of the *Sahyādrikhaṇḍa* as presently constituted. The integrity of the *uttarārdha* of the Skh is problematic. The PGN begins with speakers who have not spoken to one another earlier in the Skh, and do not speak to one another after the PGN. The *ṛṣis* have spoken briefly in chapters 17 and 60 of the *ādirahasya*, but not to Sūta. Nor have either of the main discussants of the PGN, Śatānīka and Śaunaka, spoken to one another before the text. Following the PGN in DaCunha's edition Śaunaka speaks chapter 20 of the *uttarārdha* and the first eight vss. of chapter 21, and Śatānīka speaks from vs. 9 on. But an examination of the text shows this to be incorrect, and forces us to agree either with the MSS from Bombay (Bm) and the British Museum, London (M) which have chapter 20 being spoken by Skanda and chapter 21 by Śatānīka, who in the PGN asks questions only, or with MS. 3683 (2704) I. in the India Office Library, London (part of L1) which has chapter 20, there the first chapter of the *Rāmakṣetramāhātmya*, being spoken by Sūta. The PGN begins with Śatānīka mentioning an earlier reference to the *pātitya* villages to be discussed. This, of course, does not occur in the Skh, *uttarārdha* or *ādirahasya*. It also begins with the end of a story which is not found elsewhere in the Skh.

Equally perplexing are the chapter numbers given in the Telugu script MS from the India Office Library, London (L2) and in the MS from Baroda (Br). The Baroda MS (Br), which goes only through chapter four of the PGN (Skh.u. 12), numbers chapters 1 to 12 of the *uttarārdha* as 81 to 92 of this section. The Telugu script MS from the India Office Library, London (L2), which contains only the PGN (Skh.u. 9-19), numbers these chapters 88, 89, 90, 191, 192, 193, 174, 175, 194, and 125. The *Devanāgarī* MS from the India Office Library, London gives no chapter numbers at all in its last section (L1c), and in its first section (L1a) leaves dashes for all chapter numbers except chapter two (Skh.u. 10), which it numbers to be chapter 25 of the *uparibhāga*, and the second of two chapters which it inserts between chapters 7 and 8 of the *uttarārdha* and which it numbers to be chapter 20. (See **§6.2 and §6.2b**.) The Malayalam script MS from the India Office Library, London, which contains only one of our chapters, chapter seven (Skh.u. 15), numbers this chapter 36 of the *uparibhāga*.

1.4. The text as a unit. Nonetheless, the PGN does appear to be a unit in itself. The speakers, as noted in **§1.3**, and the manner in which the PGN is introduced, clearly mark it off from the other parts of the Skh. The beginnings of all chapters which introduce discussion of villages after the first two chapters – chapters three, four, five, six, seven, eight, and ten (Skh.u. 11, 12, 13, 14, 15, 16, and 18), are uniform with the one exception of chapter six (Skh.u. 14) and the possible exception of chapter five (Skh.u. 13). The beginning of the latter is too corrupt for us to be able to state anything about it with certainty. We should note that each of these two chapters is in MS. L2 numbered in series with either the chapter before it or the chapter after it. This may be taken to indicate that as far as MS. L2 is concerned, neither of the two chapters are isolated intrusions into the narrative. This standard beginning, spoken by Śaunaka, is '*pātityagrāmam asty anyat*,' (Skh.u. 11, 12), or '*anyad grāmaṃ pravakṣyāmi*,' (Skh.u. 13?, 15, 16, 18) or some minor variation thereof. General locations of the villages in similar phraseologies are also given in the beginning of four of the six chapters with this uniform beginning (three, four, seven, and eight; Skh.u. 11, 12, 15, and 16). We should note that the villages being referred to by one of the exceptions (ten, eleven; Skh.u. 18, 19) are not in the Sahyādri range, and that the other exception is chapter five (Skh.u. 13), the beginning of which, again, is corrupt. The endings of all eight stories, with the possible exception of chapter seven (Skh.u. 15), are also uniform. They all state, in the same phraseology, that one becomes *patita* himself by sight of the *pātitya* people under discussion and that there is nothing more to say. All then add a penance to be performed, though in the case of chapter eleven (Skh.u. 19) the penance is, it seems, to be performed by the people of the story. Chapter seven (Skh.u. 15) is anomalous, perhaps because it is incomplete. It is far shorter than any of the other chapters, being only 14½ *ślokas* in length, and it never really tells a story that focuses on the village referred to in its beginning. Similar phrases and passages in the different stories also mark off the text as a unit. Compare, for example, Skh.u. 9.56 to 9.59 with Skh.u. 13.14 to 13.17b, Skh.u. 12.35 to 12.36b with Skh.u. 14.25c to 14.26, and Skh.u. 14.20ab with 17.14ab. We should note, however, that there is as well one major similarity in the text of the PGN with a section of text elsewhere in the *uttarārdha* of the Skh. Compare the description of the land given in Skh.u. 9.17c to 9.28b with that given in Skh.u. 7.11c to 7.17, for which see Appendix D. The two passages are clearly derived from a common tradition. But what follows in Skh.u. 7 is different enough from everything in the PGN after this description that we may still regard the PGN as a separate unit.

2. Overview of the Topic from an Anthropological Perspective.

2.1. The anthropological framework in brief. **2.2.** The topic of the *Pātityagrāmanirṇaya*. **2.3.** The mentioning of loss of status by *brāhmaṇas* in Sanskrit literary sources. **2.4.** *Pātitya* status and karma in the *Pātityagrāmanirṇaya*. **2.5.** The purpose of the *Pātityagrāmanirṇaya*.

2.1. The anthropological framework in brief. It is often said that Indian social structure places *brāhmaṇas*, the priestly *varṇa*, or social category, on top; the *rājanyas* or *kṣatriyas*, the nobility, next; the *vaiśyas* – landowners, merchants, and moneylenders after that; and the *śūdras* – workers, artisans, and serfs, on the bottom. The *brāhmaṇa* social order gave India not only its priests, but also its thinkers, law-givers, judges, and ministers of state. From the *rājanyas* or *kṣatriyas*, the Indian counterpart of feudal nobility, were recruited kings, vassals, and warriors. The *brāhmaṇas*, the *kṣatriyas*, and the *vaiśyas* were ritually "twice-born". The *śūdras* were not.

Expression of this hierarchy goes back as far as the *Ṛgveda*, the early Indian book containing religious hymns, to *Ṛgveda* 10.90, the *Puruṣa-sūkta*.

One's position in the caste structure is not that simple, though.

In general, among *brāhmaṇas* a household priest is of higher status than a temple priest who bathes and dresses the god. So also, a *brāhmaṇa* who is a gas station attendant is of higher status than a *brāhmaṇa* who farms and who on that account, according to *Mānavadharma-śāstra* 10.83-84 injures the earth and the beings living in the earth with his hoe, plough, etc. (Bühler 1896: 420-421). See the translation of PGN, chapter two (Skh.u. 10), n. 5, for a fuller discussion of this latter point. The *Mānavadharmaśāstra* is the oldest Sanskrit versified law book.

The 16th c. A.D. *Ve<u>ṟṟ</u>i Vē<u>ṟ</u>kai*, a popular Tamil book of maxims, states that *brāhmaṇas*, without reciting the *Vedas* morning and evening, are mere chaff (Levitt 2015: 61 [maxim no. 65]).

When a caste served by a household priest rises in status, just so, the status of the grouping of *brāhmaṇas* from which that household priest comes rises in status. On the other hand, if a *brāhmaṇa* chooses to serve as household priest for a caste that other *brāhmaṇas* will not serve, he lowers his and his family's status.

High ritual status does not necessarily translate into dominance in the villages. In general, which caste in a village is the dominant caste in that village depends in part on ritual rank, but also in part on the numbers of members of the caste in the village, and in part on wealth and land ownership. Different anthropologists propose differing models, depending in part on the circumstances of the villages studied.

The disparity between the traditional Orientalist view of *brāhmaṇa* status as at the top of the social hierarchy and anthropological actuality was recently discussed in Patil (2010). Patil examined infra-brāhmaṇical jockeying for social position within the overall *brāhmaṇa* community in an area of western India through examining five texts, the *uttarādha* of the Skh being one of them. Even within a *brāhmaṇa* community, though, status varies depending on occupation, wealth, and caste affiliations.

Below all other groupings are generally placed the untouchables, or Harijans, today referred to as Dalits.

In Sanskrit literature, untouchables are categorized as *śūdras*. Bhattacharya (1896) categorizes *śūdras* as clean and unclean. Irawati Karve has referred to structural distance between untouchables and other *śūdra* castes, so much so that in Tamil Nadu untouchables were referred to as *pañcamas* 'members of a fifth social grouping (*varṇa*)' (Karve 1961: 48, for instance).

Karve (1965: 6-7) has suggested that the term "untouchable" to describe unclean *śūdras* is an unfortunate term as untouchability is a characterization of the caste system from top to bottom.

> "A few decades back a Brahmin would have been polluted by the touch of any other caste. If he came in contact with persons of other castes he had to take a bath to get rid of the pollution before he could take food. ... Untouchability and pollution are found as well in familial situations like menstruation, child birth, and death. In Brahmin families the main meal was cooked by women after taking a bath. In this state no members of the family could touch them without polluting them" (p. 7).

Untouchability, Irawati Karve sums up, is a feature of the whole caste system and family organization and is embedded in very ancient ideas of pollution and purity.

The Abbé J. A. Dubois, writing in 1806, relates that the further north one goes in India, the less pronounced untouchability is (Dubois 1905: 51-52). He further notes:

> "In very early days ... the separation between Pariahs and the other castes does not appear to have been so marked as at present. Though relegated to the lowest grade in the social scale, they were not then placed absolutely outside and beyond it, the line of demarcation between them and the Sudras being almost imperceptible" (p.52).

And, indeed, Susan Bayly suggests that the structural distance referred to by Karve is a post-Mughal development exacerbated by the British (see Bayly 1999: 30, 65, 190-192, 204-205). In her concluding chapter, Bayly (1999: 371-372) writes:

> "The most dramatic of these changes [by the end of the nineteenth century] was the expansion and rigidification of the pollution barrier. ... [T]he experience of untouchability as a widely shared 'disability' of large numbers of laboring, artisanal and service peoples was in many ways a real if unintentional creation of British rule. ... [U]nder unfavourable British military and land-settlement policies large numbers of twice-born patricians experienced unprecedented insecurities. Such people therefore turned increasingly to the language and usages of purity and pollution in an attempt to subordinate so-called field servants and other labouring groups who had not hitherto been bracketed with

> unclean pollution-removers [= -markers (?)]. In some though not all cases, these moves were reinforced by caste-specific colonial law and administrative practices, and also by the precepts of popular sectarian faiths which taught conformity to the sober norms of a 'civilized' dharmic moral order."

See also Karve (1965: 6) with regard to the word "untouchable" in modern Indian languages not having been used in pre-British times. "The aspect of untouchability was stressed by the British and later by Indian reformists." And see, as well, Levitt (1993: 90-91, n. 6) regarding British rule and the institutionalization of the perceived structural distance between untouchables and other *śūdra* castes.

2.2. The topic of the *Pātityagrāmanirṇaya*. The PGN treats communities of polluted *brāhmaṇas* of untouchable status – *brāhmaṇas* who are *patita*, or fallen in status. These are figured to be unclean *śūdras*. The *brāhmaṇas* so discussed in the PGN are in the Karnataka area.

Such status is not peculiar to Karnataka, or to South India in general. There are many such groups noted in the various 'Tribes and Castes' volumes compiled during the British period as existing throughout India. In these volumes, I have found discussed approximately 100 distinct communities of such *brāhmaṇas*. The volumes consulted were Ananthakrishna Iyer (1909), Ananthakrishna Iyer (1928-36), Crooke (1890), Enthoven (1920-22), Risley (1911-19), Russell (1916), and Thurston (1909). Not consulted was the 1924 *Handbook of Castes and Tribes Employed on Tea Estates in North-East India* as it was viewed this would not add much information. As the area discussed in the PGN is Karnataka, I also consulted the village listings in the available gazetteers for the Karnataka area. These latter were not found to be a very fruitful source for listings of polluted *brāhmaṇa* communities, though the PGN would lead us to suspect otherwise. They do note one such community not noted elsewhere, however, which indicates that not all such groups were discussed in the 'Tribes and Castes' volumes. The gazetteers consulted were Rice (1876), Rice (1897), and Hayavadana Rao (1930).

As noted in the Preface, I have refrained from appending a glossary of such listings out of consideration for the normal dynamics of Indian society by which social groupings can elevate their status. I note here, though, six incidents, practices, and stories that the 'Tribes and Castes' volumes report as having lead to such *pātitya* status in different regions of India, without naming names:

Bengal. According to popular account, a certain *pātitya* community, that is, community of polluted *brāhmaṇas* of untouchable status, became such because their ancestor accidentally smelled food that had been prepared in the house of a Muslim.

Bihar. According to one of several explanations for a certain *pātitya* community being such is that once Rāma, king of Ayodhyā, celebrated a sacrifice and made a great feast to which he invited all *brāhmaṇas* of a certain community. In order to test their orthodoxy he desired them to perform the sacrifice and afterward partake of the feast fully clothed, not merely with a loincloth on, as is the custom among *brāhmaṇas*. Two subdivisions of the larger *brāhmaṇa* community declined to agree to this departure from the established custom, but this community attended the feast and did as the king suggested. For this breach of etiquette they were cut off from communion with the orthodox, and became *patita*.

Punjab. A certain community declares that they were originally *brāhmaṇas*, but lost status by inadvertently drinking liquor that had been placed in large vessels outside a distiller's house.

Madhya Pradesh. It is related that a certain *brāhmaṇa* who was a votary of Śiva had to go on a journey. He left his son behind with instructions to perform the worship of the god at midday. The son had bathed and purified himself when, shortly before midday, his wife came to him and so importuned him to have intercourse with her that he was obliged to comply. It was then midday and in his impure condition he went to the shrine of the god to worship him. But Śiva cursed him and said that his descendants should be *patita*, though he afterwards relented so far as to permit their continuing to act as his priests.

Most of western India. There is a community of *brāhmaṇas* found throughout most of western India, the members of which combine Muslim and Hindu rites. They are considered to be *pātityas* because of this. They receive oblations in the name of Hindu gods from Hindus and in the name of Allah from Muslims.

Kerala. A *brāhmaṇa* community once of high caste was brought to Kerala by one of the zamorins because he wanted to introduce the worship of Gaṇapati. His minister was entrusted with their entertainment, but was so bothered by their fastidiousness and constant complaints about his catering that he secretly mixed fish with their food, causing them to become *patita*.

What becomes obvious in reading the various explanations for *pātitya* status is that at times, what is acceptable in certain areas of India is polluting in other areas. For instance, Sārasvata *brāhmaṇas* eat fish. While they are looked down on in Maharashtra because of this

(Deshpande 2010: 40), they are not *pātityas* because of this, as in the instance of the Kerala community to which reference was just given. They are even said to be of high status by a Karnataka Kōta *brāhmaṇa* whom I interviewed.

2.3. The mentioning of loss of status by *brāhmaṇas* in Sanskrit literary sources. Most of the references to *brāhmaṇas* who are *patita* found in Sanskrit literature are in the legal and lexicographical texts. With regard to such references in the legal texts, see Kane (1930-62). Kane (1930-62/3[=1946]: 614), for instance, notes that the *Devalasmṛti*, as quoted by Vijñāneśvara in the *Mitākṣarā-ṭīkā* on *Yājñavalkyasmṛti* 3.261 and by Aparārka on *Yājñavalkyadharmaśāstranibandha* states with regard to fallen *brāhmaṇas* that "sin is passed from one man to another by conversation (with a sinner), by touching him, by his breath (coming in close contact with one's nose), by occupying the same vehicle (horse) or seat, by eating (in his company), by being a priest, by being his teacher of the Veda or making him one's teacher, or by matrimonial alliance."

We do have occasional reference to such *brāhmaṇas* in literary texts, as well. One, in *Kathāsarit-sāgara*, *taraṅga* 7, vs. 48 (Brockhaus 1839), is spoken by a *brāhmaṇa* visitor who has been mocked by the stupid sons of another *brāhmaṇa* who was away at the time, and who tells the *brāhmaṇa* when he returns that his hospitality cannot be accepted:

> putrās te patitā mūrkhās, tatsamparkād bhavān api,
> tasmān na bhokṣya tvadgehe, prāyaścittaṃ na me bhavet /

Translation:

> 'Those stupid sons are polluted, as is your worship on account of association with them. Because of this I cannot eat in your house. There would not be an appropriate penance (*prāyaścitta*) for me.'

The *Kathāsaritsāgara* was written by Somadeva, a Kashmiri *brāhmaṇa*, between 1063 A.D. and 1081 A.D. (Keith 1928: 281).

See also the study by Warriar (1933) on the *Keralotpatti*.

These references, though, are few.

It might be noticed here in passing, as well, that in the classical Tamil epic *Cilappatikāram* 13.36-43 (Cāminātaiyar 1944: 331) we read, as in the translation of Daniélou (1965: 87):

> "Soon they [Kōvalaṉ, his wife, and a Jain saint] reached a large village inhabited by Brahmins. These Brahmins wore the sacred thread, but were addicted to music and dancing. For this sin they had lost their rank. Kōvalan left his frail wife and the saint in a secure and sheltered place, and, after slipping through hedges of thorny bush, he walked along the road in search of clean water for their morning ablutions."

In the translation of Dikshitar (1939: 191-192):

> "(At that time) they reached a village inhabited by Brahmanas who wore the sacred thread but who were given to music and dancing, having fallen away from the Vēdic life. Kōvalaṉ lodged the holy saint and his loving wife in a harmless place; and crossing a fence of thorns, he passed along a great road in search of water for his morning ablutions."

The *Cilappatikāram* is perhaps datable to the middle of the 5th century A.D. (Zvelebil 1995: 146).

2.4. *Pātitya* status and karma in the *Pātityagrāma-nirṇaya*. Stated in chapters one and two of the PGN (Skh.u. 9 and 10), two linked stories that involve pregnant widows, and in chapter five (Skh.u. 13), also about pregnant widows, is that it is actions in previous lives that have caused the calamitous situations of these women. Similarly, it is a trace of merit in previous lives that has enabled these women to encounter Paraśurāma. Such raises the question of whether karma was viewed as being involved in other of the stories of the PGN. In all instances, fallen status flows naturally from social situations. The pregnant widows, for example, lost their husbands when young and did not have the stamina to commit *satī*. In general, these stories emphasize social situation. The only clue to this question appears in the story of a *brāhmaṇa* who became a minister in chapters eight and nine (Skh.u. 16 and 17), which story is by a different hand than chapters one through six. The portents that this *brāhmaṇa* sees on his way to Vijaya involve fate and destiny; and a similar incident to that which leads to the *brāhmaṇa*'s family's rise to power, leads to their fall. See **§12.4** below. In at least some of these stories, thus, while fallen *brāhmaṇa* status may be caused by situations in this life, it is also the result of karma. Such status not only appears to be contagious, but also to be carried by individuals from life to life. Implied in these stories is a long-term stability of status, both across lives and across generations. Further, one's status appears to be clearly communal in nature. See Levitt (1993) for a fuller discussion of this topic, and see Levitt (2011) for context.

2.5. The purpose of the *Pātityagrāmanirṇaya*. The preliminary words spoken by Śatānīka for chapter seven (Skh.u. 15), found only in MS. L3, imply that the purpose of the PGN is to teach what not to do.

A further purpose would appear to be to maintain social stability and to perpetuate a *status quo*. The text would seem to be an attempt to avoid societal confusion. See chapter four (Skh.u. 12), vs. 2, for instance. This, though, as noted in the Preface, runs against common processes in Indian society by which groups raise their status as a whole. There would appear to be a sub-text here criticizing such happenings.

Such happenings, though, are justified in chapter eleven (Skh.u. 19), vss. 26-33, which story is a later addition, however. See **§10.1** below. A main part of such justification here, oddly enough, seems to be stories found in the *uttarārdha* of the Skh in Skh.u. 1 regarding Citpāvan *brāhmaṇas*, and in PGN chapter one (Skh.u. 9).

See Levitt (1992: 9-13) for a number of examples from Sanskrit literature and from ethnographic sources in which individuals of lower status were raised to *brāhmaṇa* status.

In several texts propagated by different *brāhmaṇa* communities on the west coast of India as discussed in Patil (2010), the different *brāhmaṇa* communities are vying for position *vis-à-vis* one another, and this explains in part their content. I do not think this is the case in the PGN, though – except perhaps in chapter seven (Skh.u. 15), which appears to perhaps discuss Gauḍa Sārasvata *brāhmaṇas*, who Deshpande (2010: 42-45) suggests were the authors of the *uttarārdha* of the Skh – more properly, Skh.u. 1-6. If so, this chapter would be a response to them, but mangled in the course of textual transmission by Sārasvata *brāhmaṇas*; better preserved, in isolation, in a more southerly geographical location (MS. L3) – even here, however, missing perhaps a line.

3. DaCunha's Edition of the *Sahyādrikhaṇḍa*.

3.1. DaCunha's edition. **3.2.** Manuscripts used. **3.3.** The state of DaCunha's edition.

3.1. DaCunha's edition. Mention has been made twice above (**§1.2**) of DaCunha's[1] edition of the Skh. The full title of the edition is *The Sahyādri-Khaṇḍa of the Skanda Purāṇa: A Mythological, Historical, and Geographical Account of Western India. First edition of the Sanskrit text with various readings.* The edition was published in Bombay in 1877 with agents in Bombay being Thacker, Vining and Company, agents in Calcutta being Thacker, Spink and Company, agents in London being Trübner and Company, and agents in Paris being M. Ernest Leroux. It is best, I believe, if we keep in mind, despite their length, DaCunha's comments on his edition, stated on pp. 2-3 of the advertisement (pp. 1-3) at the beginning of the volume:

> "To the text of the Sahyādri-Khaṇḍa have been added almost all the *Mahātmyas* (sic) or legends in connection with the foundation of temples along the Sahyādri range, hitherto unedited, and which are considered to be its supplements.

---

[1] DaCunha's name is listed variously as Joseph Gerson DaCunha and José Gerson da Cunha. As the U.S. Library of Congress has adopted the former version, we use that here, even though the obituary notice for him in *The Journal of the Bombay Branch of the Royal Asiatic Society* (1902), of which society he had been vice-president, gives his name as J. Gerson da Cunha and refers to his wife as Mrs. Cunha.

> "Some of the copies betray the attempt to alter and interpolate, others, to mutilate rather than to circumvent, to which may be added miscopying. All these faults have, however, been controlled by the multiplicity of copies, and the variants (*variae lectiones*) which they supply, given at the foot of the pages where they occur.
>
> "Beyond correcting clerical errors I am not conscious of having taken any liberty with the text. There may have escaped, in spite of the care taken, some incorrections in the MSS., whose copyists have committed numerous violations of orthography; but some allowances, I trust, will be made for me in the novelty and difficulty of the task.
>
> "Of the nature, character, and value of the work I reserve to write in the introductory essay to my translation of the text, which is in preparation."

A translation of the text, along with DaCunha's introduction, never appeared. The edition is very important in that as it is the only accessible form of the Skh, it has been quoted as authoritative by a number of scholars, for which see **§5**. This edition, we should note, is rare in the United States. Emeneau (1935) lists copies at Yale University Library, Columbia University Library, Cleveland Public Library, and University of Chicago Library only. There are also two additional copies at Harvard University Library and there is now film of one of these at the University of Pennsylvania Library. For a bibliography of the publications of J. Gerson DaCunha and a description of his activities see the obituary notice for him in *The*

Journal of the Bombay Branch of the Royal Asiatic Society 20 (1902), and see Moraes (1964-65).

3.2. Manuscripts used. DaCunha used fourteen MSS for his edition. Most came from private libraries. They were listed by him on pp. 1-2 of his advertisement. This list is given here with transliteration for the *Devanāgarī* syllables by which he identified the MSS and for those *Devanāgarī* syllables which appear in his descriptions:

> "Ko., from Cochin. This MS. was kindly lent by Svāmī Bhuvanendratīrtha, the Prelate of the Vaishṇava sect. It contains ninety chapters.
>
> "Ju., from Junnar. This copy was borrowed from Mr. Rahunātha Sharma. It consists of a hundred chapters.
>
> "So., from the Bombay Branch of the Royal Asiatic Society, noted zz-b-14 in the catalogue of its library. It is divided into two sections, the first section containing eighty-eight chapters, and the second thirty-two.
>
> "So., 2. Another copy belonging to the same Society, marked zz-e-31. It is incomplete, consisting of one section only. It is apparently written by a Gujarāthī Brāhmaṇ, who often substitutes sa for śa, ba, for bha, and *vice-versa*.
>
> "Ko., 2., from Kota, a village in the Karnāṭaca. It consists of a hundred and eleven chapters, with several *lacunae*.
>
> "Si., from Sidhāpura, another village in the Karnāṭaca. It consists of one section, its chapters being left undivided in number.

"Ceṃ., from Chempi, also a village in the same district. Several chapters are wanting about the middle of this copy.

"Go., from Gomanta or Goa. It consists of two sections in hundred and eight chapters, and bears the date 1700 A.D.

"Ka., from Kāśi or Benares. This MS. contains a hundred chapters in all.

"Mum., These are five MS. copies collected from several gentlemen in Bombay. Although possessing slight peculiarities of their own, their likeness is very striking, and they coincide to the extent of seeming rather to be copies of copies with errors heaped upon errors. Each of these copies is noted ka, kha, ga, and thus in order.

"With the exception of the MS. Ceṃ., which is written in the Kanarese character, all the others are Devanāgarī. They are, also with one exception, undated."

3.3. The state of DaCunha's edition. It is unfortunate that DaCunha's edition became authoritative for the Skh. There is no way of telling which of the MSS listed were drawn on for which sections of text of the Skh proper and of the attached *māhātmyas*, with the partial exception of the very beginning of the Skh proper. Clearly those MSS of a hundred chapters and over give more text than the Skh proper if, indeed, they give any of the text of the Skh proper. Most may contain *māhātmyas* only. There is no way of knowing. The variant readings which DaCunha had noted in his advertisement to be at the foot of each page were not given after p. 97, the beginning of chapter 23 of the *ādirahasya*. The book is 577 pages. Usually a group of variant readings was given for only one word on a page of text, a page having usually 26 lines of text. This is an absurd situation when one considers what DaCunha had said about the text in his advertisement, and is even more absurd to me due to my experience with just a section of the text. The variant readings which DaCunha does give are also very perplexing as they are noted to come from MSS the abbreviations for which DaCunha did not note in his list of MSS used. In his critical apparatus, what there is of it, reference is made to the following MSS: Ko., Ju. So., Ci°., Muṃ, Ka, Kha, Ga, Gha, Ṅa, Ca, Cha. Ci°. is not noted in his list of MSS used. Muṃ is listed in his critical apparatus together with readings from Ka through Cha. Ka through Ṅa are supposed to constitute Muṃ, and therefore Muṃ should not appear if any MSS through Ṅa are listed. Ca and Cha are not noted in his list of MSS used.

Worse, though, is that whole sections of text do not make sense. Sometimes this is due to the meanings of the words which DaCunha chose to put in the edition. I will use examples from the PGN, but will give the chapter numbers of the *uttarārdha* of the Skh. 9.9cd contains one example of the point under consideration.

tava vāgamṛtaṃ pītvā na vṛttir jāyate kathaṃ /

This translates, 'How is it that proper conduct (!) is not born after drinking the immortality of your speech?' In context, 'vṛttir,' 'proper conduct,' makes no sense. Or, let us look at 9.2cd to 9.3a where, aside from the peculiar sense of the compound in 9.2d, 'destroying the fear of merit and sin,' and the vocative in 9.3a, 'creature,' or 'living being,' there is a grammatical point. There is no finite verb.

ataḥ kathāmṛtaṃ śrotuṃ puṇyapāpabhayārthaṃ /
rahasyaṃ vividhaṃ janman . . . . /

The sentence cannot be translated.

Sometimes it is just one of several grammatical points which make it impossible to translate a sentence. One example is the appearance of an accusative plural neuter of the demonstrative pronoun in 9.12a.

upagrāmāṇi santīti purā yat kathitaṃ tvayā /
tāny ahaṃ śrotum icchāmi grāmāṇāṃ cādhidaivataṃ /

Or, to move to another part of the text, how can one explain the appearance of nominative duals in a list of nominative plurals as happens in 16.10ab?

priyaṅgupāṭalau jambuśālmalyaḥ plakṣavañjulau /

In some cases, the readings given are just not Sanskrit. For example, overlooking the printing error in 10.1a, what is the sense of 10.1b?

kiṃ cakru rathavipreṃdra garbhiṇyārtānitāṃtava /

Or what is the sense of 15.3ab?

ullikhaṃ tatkṣanāḥ kecitkeciddārāmakāriṇaḥ /

Whether or not the state of affairs described here is true for the entire edition we cannot say. Perhaps the readings were good for some parts of the text. But from our experience with the PGN, and with the MA preceding, we must certainly conclude that in refraining from interfering unnecessarily with the text, as DaCunha wrote in his advertisement quoted in **§3.1**, he abrogated his responsibility of editing the text. If no translation of the text was published, this was probably because the text, as constituted in the edition, was impossible to translate.

4. The *Sahyādrikhaṇḍa* and the *Skandapurāṇa*.

4.1. The *Sahyādrikhaṇḍa*. **4.2.** The *Sahyādrikhaṇḍa* as it stands now. **4.3.** The *Sahyādrikhaṇḍa* and the *Jñānayoga-khaṇḍa*. **4.4.** An incomplete list of contents for the *Sahyādrikhaṇḍa*. **4.5.** Sections of the *Sahyādrikhaṇḍa* not included in DaCunha's edition. **4.6.** The Tuluva *Grāma-paddhati*. **4.7.** The relationship of the *Sahyādri khaṇḍa* to the *Skandapurāṇa*.

4.1. The *Sahyādrikhaṇḍa*. It is impossible to state exactly what the Skh treats without first translating it and, given the state of DaCunha's edition, editing the text. As can be seen from the title of DaCunha's edition, DaCunha took it to be a "mythological, historical, and geographical account of western India." Śāstri and Gui (1902: 148), perhaps following DaCunha, note the Skh to describe "the sacred places of pilgrimage in the Sahyādri or western Ghats and along the Godāvari River." As far as I can see from the colophons to the different chapters of the Skh and its attached *māhātmyas*, this is deceiving. Only perhaps part of the *ādirahasya* of the Skh, and the *uttarārdha* of the Skh, the latter perhaps without its last two chapters, can be described with accuracy as a mythological, historical and geographical account of western India.[2]

The main body of the text, the *ādirahasya*, appears to divide itself fairly neatly into four sections, with the first section sub-divided into two parts. We can base this observation on a comparison of chapter titles with one another and on a comparison of chapter titles with the speakers of the various chapters.

The first two sections, comprising 41 of the 62 chapters of the *ādirahasya*, as the *ādirahasya* stands in DaCunha's edition, of course, deals mainly with the *pañcalakṣaṇas*, the five topics that most of the extant *purāṇas* say are to be treated by all *purāṇas*: the creation of the universe, its destruction and renovation, the geneology of gods and patriarchs, the reign of the *manus*, and the history of the solar and lunar races. Few of our *purāṇas* comply with this prescription, though.[3] The topics, as covered in the *ādirahasya* of the Skh are, more exactly, the creation of the world; a description of earth, hell and the seven worlds; some material which is not adequately described in the colophons for identification; the destruction of the world; again inadequately described material, but material which seems to treat gods and rites; instruction on duty and law; and the origin of *kṣatriyas*, the *Pāṭhārīyajāti* (?), and perhaps other groups which cannot be identified from the colophons, this perhaps being local. The fit between the ideal topic coverage of a

---

[2] Rocher (1986: 236) appears to continue this unfortunate fiction: "It [the Skh] comprises a number of local legends relative to the Sahyādri range of mountains, which corresponds to the area of the western Ghats."

[3] See Levitt (1976) regarding the context and actual import of the locution '*pañcalakṣaṇa*' in the *Amarakośa*, where the locution first occurs.

purāṇa that has been handed down by tradition in Sanskrit literature and the actual topic coverage appears to be very close here.

The first section, which covers everything up to the origin of *kṣatriyas*, which begins with chapter 26, is mainly a discourse between Vyāsa and Sanatkumāra. In the first part, chapters 1 through 19, there is only very little spoken by anyone else, and it is likely that there is no direct discourse between any of the occasional speakers. In the second part, chapters 20 through 25, the discussion is mainly between Devī and Maheśvara as related to Vyāsa by Sanatkumāra. Chapter 25, it is to be noted, is a bit anomalous, the speakers being Devī, Mahādeva, a *siddha* and a *brāhmaṇa*, and Rambhā. It is, however, clearly separated from the second section, which begins with chapter 26, on the basis of its speakers; and it clearly falls together topically with chapter 24.

The second section, which contains chapters 26 through 41, is, through chapter 38, exclusively a conversation between Gaṇeśa and Mahādeva, with Viṣṇu, Śaṃkara and Parṇāda speaking only briefly. Chapter 41, which topically would appear to fall together perhaps with the next section, is also spoken by Gaṇeśa. Chapters 39 and 40 are shared by statements from Gaṇeśa, Sanatkumāra, Maheśvara, Vyāsa, Nandikeśvara, and Śaṃkara.

The third section, chapters 42 through 49, is titled for most of its chapters *Durvāsopaniṣad*. It is a discussion between Durvāsa and Maheśvara which appears to be narrated to Vyāsa by Sanatkumāra. Although the title of chapter 49 would appear to indicate that the chapter is not part of the *upaniṣad*, the identity of the speakers demonstrates that it is such. Neither Aufrecht (1891, 1896, 1903) nor Poleman (1938) list a separate *Durvāsopaniṣad*.

The fourth section, chapters 50 through 67, is mainly a discussion between Vyāsa and Sanatkumāra with brief discourse by a large array of speakers: a son, Deveśvara, Devī, Devadeva, Mahādeva, a king, Śilāda, the *maruts*, Īśvara, the *ṛṣis*, Vāyu, Vasiṣṭha, Kārtikeya, the *devas*, Brahman, and Dagdha (?). The topic or topics discussed are not adequately defined in the colophons for us to be able to state what they are.

The contents and structure of the *uttarārdha* have been discussed in **§1.2** and **§1.3.** I might add here that the *uttarārdha*, though it is only 21 chapters long, also seems to be divided into four sections. The first is a discussion between Skanda and Mahādeva or Īśvara. The second is a discussion between Nārada and Skanda as related by Sūta to a *ṛṣi*. The third, the PGN, is a discussion between Śatānīka and Śaunaka related by Sūta to *ṛṣis*. And the fourth appears to be speech by either Skanda or Sūta and Śatānīka, but who holds conversation and what the section speaks of is uncertain.

The different sections of the *uttarārdha* are disjunctive. The second and third sections, for example, are both in their broadest framework related by Sūta to *ṛṣis*. The discourse in the third section, however, does not follow from the discourse in the second; and, in point of fact, the discourse of the third section appears to presuppose a preceding section which is not present here, though both the *ṛṣis* and, inexplicably, Śatānīka do seem to refer back to section two in their opening statements.

A chart outlining the present form of the Skh is given in Appendix H.

We should also note that the various *māhātmyas* attached to the Skh also are not conspicuous for their treatment of the mythology, history and geography of western India. The various chapter titles given for the

Reṇukāmāhātmya, for example, show that the text treats the bestowal of a boon to Aditi, the bestowal of a boon to Reṇukā, the history of the Bhṛgu family, the origin of Paraśurāma, the arrival of Nārada, a discussion on the anger of Jamadagni, the defeat of Rāvaṇa, the death of Jamadagni, the consecration (?) of Jamadagni, and the death of a thousand descendents of Arjuna (?). The coverage clearly indicates something which is broader than just local mythology, just as it indicates that the glorification of Reṇukā is a glorification of her in the broadest terms possible. This, of course, is not to say that local matters may not be touched on. Eggeling (1899: 1370b) gives a brief condensation of the story.

As noted in **§1.2**, a list of contents for the entire Skh and its attached *māhātmyas*, as they are given in DaCunha's edition of the text, is given in Appendix H.

4.2. The *Sahyādrikhaṇḍa* as it stands now. I have noted that as it stands now the Skh proper contains 67 chapters in its *ādirahasya* and 21 chapters in its *uttarārdha*. This amounts to a total of 88 chapters. Of our MSS of the *uttarārdha* and of the PGN alone only Bm, M and K – the latter being a special case – agree with this structure in their colophons. See **§1.3** for a discussion of this. The evidence clearly indicates that the Skh as it stands now, is a late ordering, poorly executed in the *uttarārdha*, at least, of earlier material. This earlier material has been ordered differently a number of times. See Levitt (1977: 19-21) for further discussion of this point. Further, on the basis of a comparison of the different orderings of the Skh.u. with the various readings in the MSS, it can be deduced that while the present Skh.u. was in its formative stages, parts of its text were already corrupt.

4.3. The *Sahyādrikhaṇḍa* and the *Jñānayogakhaṇḍa*. As pointed out in Levitt (1977: 14-17 and 1979b [= Table III]) the *ādirahasya* of the Skh and the *Jñānayogakhaṇḍa* hold many chapters in common with one another, and follow the same format.[4] The main difference between the Skh and the *Jñānayogakhaṇḍa* is that the Skh inserts a large section on *kṣatriyas* of the region in the *ādirahasya*, and inserts a large section on *brāhmaṇas* of the region in its *uttarārdha*. See Appendix H, Table 4. Clearly, work on the Skh must go hand-in-hand with work on the *Jñānayogakhaṇḍa*.

That Madhva wrote a commentary on the *Jñānayogakhaṇḍa* clearly indicates that this text was popular in the Sahyādri area. It may be, though, that the same forces that led Madhva to write his commentary also

[4] Rocher (1986: 235 n. 446) cites Levitt (1977), but fails to note this important point in his notices of the Skh and *Jñānayogakhaṇḍa* (pp. 235-236). For a possibly comparable parallel, note the stories of the baby Kṛṣṇa and a youthful Kṛṣṇa in the second section of the *Harivaṃśa* and the fifth book of the *Viṣṇupurāṇa*, the latter of which closely follows the former. See Winternitz (1927: 552, 445-452), Coleman (2010: 386 n. 1) with regard to the relative chronology of the *Viṣṇupurāṇa vis-à-vis* the *Harivaṃśa*. The *Harivaṃśa*, though figured as an appendix to the *Mahābhārata*, is in actuality a *purāṇa* (Winternitz 1927: 443-444). See also Rocher (1986: 155): "The Brahma° [=*Brahmapurāṇa*] has numerous passages in common with other *purāṇas*: Viṣṇu°, Mārkaṇḍeya°, Sāmba°, and Vāyu°, as well as with the Harivaṃśa, and the Anuśāsana and Śānti *parvans* of the Mahābhārata. In all these cases the Brahma° is reputed to be the borrower." For parallels between Pāli *Jātaka* tales, the *Mahābhārata*, and in some instances such texts as the *Pañcatantra* or *Hitopadeśa*, see Söhnen-Thieme (2009). For parallels between the lexical chapters of the *Agnipurāṇa* and the *Amarakośa*, see Birwé (1976). A number of articles on such parallels are scattered throughout the issues of the journal *Purāṇa*.

led to the transposition of this text to the Skh, perhaps at a date anterior to Madhva.

4.4. An incomplete list of contents for the *Sahyādrikhaṇḍa*. Additional support for these theses may come from what appears to be a partial list of contents for the Skh held in the Bodleian Library, Oxford. The list of contents, which appear on f. 163 verso of their MS. Mill 79, reads as follows:

skaṇḍapurāṇe sahyādrikhaṇḍe sūcīpatram.

2. sahyādreḥ śivālayaṃ kṛtayuge yojanamātraṃ tadardhaṃ tretāyāṃ dvāpare krośamātraṃ kalau ṣaṣti dhanuṣkaṃ.
9. devyā aṣṭatīrthanāmādhyāyaḥ. sahyādriśṛṅge pārvatyā vanaṃ. tatra puṃnāmni jñāta strīrūpaṃ bhaved iti pārvaty uktis. tadā tatra vane iḷa[ḥ] gatas. tadaiva strījātaḥ.
11. aṣṭottaraśataśivanāmāni.
13. sahyādrau udambaramūle mandākinī pārvatyā dṛṣṭā.
14. gaṅgāṣṭakaṃ.
16. śivājā[?]vīsaṃvādādhyāyaḥ.
18. iḷāvṛtāntaṃ.
25. rālātadīnām (?) adhyāyaḥ. 11 prakaraṇaṃ.
33. purā surāsuraiḥ sarvaiḥ kṣi*rāb*dhir[5] mathi*to*[6] yadā kṣīrāmbudhiṃ tyaktvā yayau viṣṇuḥ śivālayaṃ. 1.
36. bhṛṅgiśivasaṃvāde ṣoḍaśapraka[ra]ṇaṃ samāptaṃ.

---

[5] The reading, a misspelling, is '*kṣirādhir.*'

[6] The reading is '*mathitā.*' Apparently the writer, or a scribe, took '*kṣirābdhi*' to be a feminine, which would be a very easy mistake to make.

Translation:

Table of Contents to the Sahyādrikhaṇḍa in the Skaṇḍapurāṇa.

2. The abode of Śiva in the Sahyādri mountains is a *yojana* in the *kṛta yuga*, half of that in the *tretā* age, a *krośa* in the *dvāpara* age, and sixty *dhanuṣkas* in the *kali* age.
9. The chapter named the eight *tīrthas* of Devī. There is a forest of Pārvatī's on the summit of the Sahyādri. Pārvatī said, "Let him with the name of a man obtain a woman's form there." Then Iḷa went to that forest and became a woman.
11. The hundred and eight names of Śiva.
13. At the foot of the Udambara mountain (?) in the Sahyādri range the Mandākinī river was seen by Pārvatī.
14. Eight chapters (perhaps, verses, or any group of eight) on the Ganges.
16. A chapter in the discussion between Śiva and . . . .
18. The story of Iḷā.
25. The chapter . . . . Chapter 11.
33. Once, when the ocean of milk was churned with all the gods and *asuras*, Viṣṇu, having given up the ocean of milk, went to Śiva's abode (i.e., Kailāsa). 1.
36. The sixteenth chapter in the discussion between Bhṛṅgi and Śiva is finished.

As can be seen easily, this list of contents does not tally well with the contents of the *ādirahasya* of the Skh as in DaCunha's edition. Whether or not this is because it represents a different version of the Skh is problematic. It may be a table of contents for an unrecognized section of the Skh. But it should caution us to keep our minds open to the possibility that a different version of the Skh once did exist.

4.5. Sections of the *Sahyādrikhaṇḍa* not included in DaCunha's edition. Eggeling (1899) and Keith (1935) list several MSS which contain chapters from the Skh which are not represented in DaCunha's edition, and several MSS which contain *māhātmyas* which are noted by themselves to be attached to the Skh, or the *uttarārdha* of the Skh, or the *Uttarasahyādrikhaṇḍa*, but which also are not represented in DaCunha's edition.

MS. 3682 (2703) II and III, and some additional material which seems to have been omitted from the catalog in printing, has been examined and is our MS. L1. It contains three chapters that have not been included in the edition. The first two are in our MS. L1a and the third, in the additional material which has just been noted, is in our MS. L1b.

The first begins on f. 145 recto, line 2 and runs through f. 148 recto, line 6. It carries the following colophon:

> iti śrīsaṉhyādrau uttarakhaṇḍe (sic) mayūravarmotpattir nāma - - - dhyāya[ḥ].

The second begins on f. 148 recto, line 6 and runs through f. 151 verso, line 4. It carries the colophon:

> iti śrīsaṉhyādrau uttarabhāge ahicchatrabrāhmaṇanāyanaṃ nāma viṉśodhyāy*a*[ḥ].

The third begins on f. 190 recto, line 6, following, like the first, a text of chapter 7. It runs through f. 195 verso, line 3 and carries the colophon:

> iti śrīsiṉhyādrikhaṇḍe dvātriṉśadgrāmanirṇayakathanaṃ.

MS. 3681 (2730c and d) contains two treatises which profess to belong to the Skh. The first, the *Vānavāsīkṣetramāhātmya*, claims that it constitutes chapters 22 to 26 of the Skh. The second is the *Mayūravarmākhyāna*, which is noted to contain information about Mayūravarman different from that in the edition (= Skh.u. 8).

MS. 3684 (2618a) consists of several sections, with only a very little corresponding to anything in the edition. Part I is the *Rāmakṣetramāhātmya* again. Again, only its first chapter corresponds to anything in the edition. Part II, the *Maṅgīśamāhātmya*, contains six chapters not included in the edition's version of the text. Part IV, the *Śambhugirimāhātmya*, 12 chapters long, is not found in the edition. Similarly, Part V, the *Āmalakīgrāmamāhātmya*, is also not found in the edition. This latter is noted by Raghavan (1966: 146a) to deal with the origin of the Citpāvan *brāhmaṇas*.

MS. 3685 (3702) is of three chapters titled *Kesarakṣetramāhātmya*, and is assigned to the *Sahyādryuttarakhaṇḍa*. There is nothing corresponding to this in DaCunha's edition according to Eggeling.

MS. 3686 (1803) is of 18 chapters titled *Harihareśvaramāhātmya*. DaCunha's edition does not contain this *māhātmya* either.

MS. 6909 is listed as being of the Skh of the *Sanatkumārasaṃhitā* of the Skp, imperfect. Neither the sample of text given nor the titles given for the various chapters after chapter 15 correspond to anything in DaCunha's edition.

MS. 6910, also of the Skh, is listed as starting as does MS. 6909. It contains chapters numbered unconsecutively through 128. No section of DaCunha's edition has so many chapters.

MS. 6911 is of chapters which number themselves as 160 through 165 of the Skh. None of the titles listed are found in DaCunha's edition.

MS. 6912 contains 4 ff. only and is titled on a label *Koṭeśvaramāhātmya.* This title also is not found in DaCunha's edition.

MS. 6914 refers to itself in part as *Grāmanirṇaya* of the *uparibhāga* of the Skh. The text is noted to be different from the PGN. It does contain one chapter found in a more incomplete version in the PGN in DaCunha's edition and elsewhere, though. See our MS. L3 described in detail in **§6.8** below. The chapter titles are not found in DaCunha's edition. These include in the first section of the MS an *adhyāya* numbered 27 of the *Gotravibhāga*, an *adhyāya* numbered 32 of the *Vṛṣotsargavidhāna*, an *adhyāya* numbered 35 of the *Ghaṭaśrāddhavidhi*, an *adhyāya* numbered 13 titled *Lohādityavarṇana*, as well as two *adhyāyas*, 25 and 70, which style themselves *Grāmanirṇaya*, and two *adhyāyas*, 31 and 36, that style themselves *Grāmanirṇaye Pātitye*. It is *adhyāya* 36 here that proves to be PGN chapter seven (Skh.u. 15 as in DaCunha's edition). The second section of the MS contains, for example, an *adhyāya* numbered 190 of the *Śālagrāmakṣetravarṇanam*, and an *adhyāya* again numbered 70 that styles itself *Grāmanirṇaya Lohādityanirṇaye*.

That this list contains chapters which, while in MS they are separate, nevertheless profess to be part of the Skh but are not included in the text as presented in DaCunha's edition, is taken by us to be further evidence that the text as it stands now is a late redaction of earlier material.

4.6. The Tuluva *Grāmapaddhati*. This thesis is supported by still another text which purports to belong to the Skh, the *Grāmapaddhati*. This text is not represented in the MS catalogs consulted by me, but was drawn on heavily by Saletore (1936a). In Saletore (1936b), Saletore discussed the text briefly. He there gave some information on the text not provided in Saletore (1936a), including a general outline of the topics of the twenty-six chapters of his best MS of the text, and promised a detailed publication of the work at some future date. To my knowledge this edition was never published.

Saletore (1936a: 296-297) notes that the text "differs both in style and matter in different parts of the district." The text is primarily in Sanskrit, but contains occasional passages in Kannada. It "begins with portions of the *Sahyādri kaṇḍa* (sic) of the *Skānda Purāṇa* of which it is said to be a part," Saletore (1936b: 116) notes. He notes further that it "contains much legendary matter which is rather unintelligible."

The extent to which the beginning portions of the *Grāmapaddhati* are held in common with the Skh is not mentioned in detail. Saletore (1936a: 23-29) refers to Skh.u. 6 several times. From his description on p. 25 of the contents of a section held in common, however, it is clear that Saletore is referring to Skh.u. 7. Not recognized, it would appear, is that of the first thirteen chapters of the *Grāmapaddhati* as in Saletore's best MS fully ten are in

DaCunha's edition (Skh.u. 7-8, 11-12 , 14-17 + either 9-10 or 18-19), eight of these being chapters in the PGN. The other of these first thirteen chapters, it appears, are identical with two of the chapters not in DaCunha's edition but represented in Eggeling's MS. 3682 (2703) II and III. And it appears to be very probable that Saletore's chapters 14-15, described as "general matters," are either Skh.u. 18-19 or 20-21.

The remaining eleven chapters are described by Saletore as a description of the Hoyyakki and Kāḷagada people, general topics, a description of the Sahavāsi people, a chapter which contains lacunae and ends abruptly, the *Utpattipaddhati*, the *Gokarṇapaddhati*, the *Deśapaddhati*, the *Ahicchatrapaddhati*, the *Deśotpatti-paddhati*, and the division of some houses in various parts of Tuluva.

Clearly, what we have here under separate title is a section of our present ordering of the Skh.u. combined with material not in this ordering.

4.7. The relationship of the *Sahyādrikhaṇḍa* to the *Skandapurāṇa*. Burnell (1880) noted of the Skp that "this Purāṇa apparently does not exist in a definite state, but is composed of a number of detached parts, which are very numerous in this Library." Wilson (1840), in his preface, has noted:

> "It is uniformly agreed that the Skanda Purāṇa in a collective form has no existence; and the fragments in the shape of Saṃhitās, Khaṇḍas and Māhātmyas, which are affirmed in various portions of India to be portions of the Purāṇa, present a much more formidable mass of stanzas than even the immense number of which it is said to consist."

Hazra (1940) has, however, attempted to be more specific. On p. 157 he writes that the present Skp consists of seven *khaṇḍas*, or books, each sub-divided into a number of other *khaṇḍas* or *māhātmyas*. The seven main *khaṇḍas* are noted by him to be the *Māheśvarakhaṇḍa*, the *Viṣṇu-khaṇḍa*, the *Brahmakhaṇḍa*, the *Kāśīkhaṇḍa*, the *Āvantya-khaṇḍa*, the *Nāgarakhaṇḍa*, and the *Prabhāsakhaṇḍa*. The real division of the Skp, though, seems to him to have been into six *saṃhitās* with further sub-divisions, as he states on pp. 158-161. The six *saṃhitās* are the *Sanat-kumārasaṃhitā*, the *Sūtasaṃhitā*, the *Śāṃkarīsaṃhitā* (or *Śaṃkarasaṃhitā*, or *Agastyasaṃhitā*), the *Vaiṣṇavī-saṃhitā*, the *Brāhmīsaṃhitā*, and the *Saurasaṃhitā*.[7] There are as well, he notes on p. 161, a number of *khaṇḍas* which claim to be parts of the Skp even though they are not such properly. These include, among others, the *Ambikākhaṇḍa*, the *Ayodhyākhaṇḍa*, the *Umākhaṇḍa*, the *Kanakādrikhaṇḍa*, the *Tāpīkhaṇḍa*, the *Nirvāṇakhaṇḍa*, the *Paraśurāmakhaṇḍa*, the *Parvatakhaṇḍa*, the *Pātāla-khaṇḍa*, the *Bṛhadbrahmottarakhaṇḍa*, the *Bhīma-khaṇḍa*, the *Bhūkhaṇḍa*, the *Śivarahasyakhaṇḍa*, the *Himavat-khaṇḍa*, and the Skh. Thus, according to Hazra, the Skh, though professing to be a part of the Skp, is such only marginally.

Eggeling (1899: 1369), however, and Śāstri and Gui (1902: 148-149), note the Skh to be a portion of the

---

[7] At variance with everything noted here, Poleman (1938: 68) listed his MS. 1508 to be the *uttarārdha* of the Skp. This, of course, speaks for an entirely different division of the Skp. His listing, however, is an error. MS. 1508 (University of Pennsylvania no. 2357) is actually a MS of the *uttarārdha* of the *Kāśikhaṇḍa* of the Skp.

Sanatkumārasaṃhitā which, as noted above, is professed to be one of the original six sub-divisions of the Skp.

This appears to be one of those matters which, for the present, at least, faith alone can decide. An historical study of the development of the Skp is what is needed, and this can probably be done adequately by collecting all the colophons, first lines and last lines of all fragments and texts of sections of the Skp, and maybe also by compiling lists of speakers for all of these fragments and examining them carefully.

Perhaps of note, Prof. Hans Bakker of Groningen is at present editing the Skp based on Nepalese MSS dated to the 9th c. A.D. These MSS do not contain the Skh (Deshpande 2010: 33 n.).

Regarding the Skp, see also Rocher (1986: 228-237). Rocher, quoting P. V. Kane and M. A. Mahendale respectively (on pp. 228-229), notes "the Skanda° 'is the most extensive of all Purāṇas and poses perplexing problems.' The scholarly literature unanimously considers it not as a single coherent text, but 'only a name to which extensive works, said to be the Saṃhitās or the Khaṇḍas of the original Purāṇa, and numerous Māhātmyas claim allegiance.'"

And see Levitt (1977: 9-12, 35-36 [Table I]) regarding the Skp. Levitt lists the contents of the Skp in its present *khaṇḍa* format (Hazra 1940: 157, referred to immediately above) as represented in the Veṅkateśvara Press edition (Bombay, 1909-11), noting the number of *adhyāyas* and number of stanzas in each sub-section of the edition. It amounts to a total of 1,707 *adhyāyas* and 92,398 stanzas. Levitt (1977: 11) comments, "I give these figures in order to point out that in speaking of the Skp we are speaking of something which is on the order of the *Mahābhārata*, and which perhaps dwarfs it." The

Veṅkateśvara Press edition of the Skp, needless to say, does not contain the Skh.

5. References to the *Sahyādrikhaṇḍa*.

5.1. The reasons for noting the citations here. **5.2.** The citations.

5.1. The reasons for noting the citations here. I have been able to locate several statements which cite the Skh as their authority, and I bring them together here in order to emphasize that they are to be viewed with extreme caution given the nature of the edition and in some cases the nature of the MSS from which they have been extracted. That such caution should be exercised will become even more evident than it should be by this point in **§7.1** and **§7.8** where the magnitude of the differences between the readings in our MSS of the PGN is described. This may also become more evident after looking at the peculiar content of some of the statements attributed to the Skh which have been brought together here. To be kept in mind is the statement of Kane (1930-62/5.2[=1962]: 838):

> "Most of the editions of Purāṇas are based on either a single ms. or on a few mss. collected at random and are not critically edited. . . . Many conclusions therefore, drawn from the current printed editions of the Purāṇas or from mss. of the Purāṇas, must be regarded as merely tentative and are likely to be wrong. What Winternitz said in his History of Indian Literature (English translation, Calcutta, volume I., p. 469) viz. 'that the date of each section, nay, sometimes of each single verse in the Mahabharata must be determined separately' applies with equal (or perhaps greater) force

to the Purāṇas, particularly when one wants to use the section or stanza for historical or comparative purposes."

5.2. The citations. The earliest citations to the Skh precede the publication of DaCunha's edition in 1877.

Mandlik (1875: 99) notes that Saṅgameśvara is one of the principal places noted in such portions of the Skh "as are now accessible." He notes that there are at the end of the *Saṅgameśvaramāhātmya* – an authored text – five vss. quoted from the Skh, and he gives a translation of these vss. This translation is given again on p. 114 in place in a translation of the entire *Saṅgameśvaramāhātmya*. The text itself is given on pp. 110-111. Of interest is a section of Mandlik's translation:

> "There are six holy places – Kuddaleśa (Kudal ?), Dhútapápa, Dálabheśa (Dabhol), Vardhana (Shrivardhana ?), and the great god Rámeśvara. These are the five holy places."

It would appear that either Mandlik's MS of his text was corrupt here or that the text of the Skh used by the *Saṅgameśvaramāhātmya*'s author was corrupt. The author, named Śeṣa, is dated by Mandlik to the reign of a Chalukya king named Karṇa. The vss. quoted in this text, it is to be noted, are additional vss. which do not appear in DaCunha's edition. Also, I have not been able to locate independent references in any MS catalogs to a *Saṅgameśvaramāhātmya* attached to the Skh.

Talekar (1876: 25) quotes the Skh as supplying clear information that Karhāḍa *brāhmaṇas* came originally from Kārāshtra. He cites the location of this country according to the Skh, and notes that it appears that the country was known by the name of its chief town, the present Karhāḍ. It is obvious therefore that the name of the Karhāḍa *brāhmaṇas*, like the names of other *brāhmaṇa* groups, comes from the name of their original country.

Monier-Williams (1891: 271 n.) retells briefly the story given in Skh.u. 1 for the origin of the Citpāvan *brāhmaṇas*. This is quoted by Karmarkar (1944: 111-112).

Bhattacharya (1896: 84) refers to the same story but dismisses its veracity. "Leaving aside legends, the name of Chitpavan given to the Kankanastha Brahmans seems to be derived from the town of Chiplun in the Ratnagiri district." The story is, he maintains, one held about Citpāvan *brāhmaṇas* by other Maharashtra *brāhmaṇa* groups. This generalization appears to be based on his opinion that the Skh "seems to be the work of a Deshastha." No evidence is introduced to support this latter point.

Abbott (1895), in a note, identifies the Nāgapura of a copper plate grant with the modern Nāgāṅv, situated southeast of Alibāg, in the Kōlābā District, not very far south of Mumbai, on the basis of the location given for Nāgapura, or Nāgapuri, in the *Nāgāhvayamāhātmya* attached to the Skh (DaCunha's edition, pp. 505-512; see Appendix H below). Nāgāṅv is substituted by syncope for Nāgagāṅv, or Nāgagrāma, which is the same as Nāgapura.

Betham (1895 and 1897) gives translations of two texts attached to the Skh. Betham notes the first text, the *Mañjgunīpurāṇa*, to be the *Veṅkateśamāhātmya* from the *mahāpurāṇa Sahyādrikhaṇḍa*. This *māhātmya* does not appear in DaCunha's edition. The second text, the *Vanavāsīmāhātmya*, also is not to be found in DaCunha's edition. The translation of this latter text is reported to be of a locally copied legend (p. 78). As noted in **§4.5** above, a MS of this latter text is listed as being in the India Office Library.

Enthoven (1920-22/1: 242-243) refers twice to the *uttarārdha* of the Skh. The first involves a retelling of Skh.u. 1, which as noted treats the origin of the Citpāvan *brāhmaṇas*. This retelling is given as an example of stories about the Citpāvans. The second is a reference to the chapter which treats Karhāḍe *brāhmaṇas* (= Skh.u. 2), and is used as an example of his point that the writer of the Skh was hostile to local *brāhmaṇas*.

Karve (1933: 121-123) also refers to the story of the Citpāvan *brāhmaṇas* in Skh.u. 1. She there places it in context with other versions of the same story in both popular and literary sources. Before introducing the version in the Skh, she warns:

> "It must be borne in mind that the book is notorious for its scurrilous attacks on particular sections of the Brahmin community, the most to suffer being the Karhādas. The part dealing with the Karhādas, the Chitpavans and other castes is regarded as an interpolation in the original text introduced recently (Guṃjīkar, *Sarasvatīmaṃḍaḷa*, p. 145). The story of the creation of the Chitpavans is however similar to the one about other western coast Brahmins given in the Keral Mahātmyam, and it does not seem to be an invention of the writer. . . . It seems, therefore, that the author of the scurrilous attack is not making up a new story but rather putting on paper the popular version of the pithy and brief Purāṇic account in order to make capital out of it for his mud-slinging."

On p. 137, Karve notes that in the Deccan the Skh is said to be recording traditions current in the Malabar region. She cites as her reference for this statement Padmanabha

Menon (1924-37). I have consulted each of the four volumes of this work and cannot find support for it anywhere. On pp. 45 and 51 of vol. 1 (1924), though, Padmanabha Menon does note that part of Skh.u. 7 tells of Paraśurāma making fishermen into *brāhmaṇas* (= Skh.u. 1 ?) and refers to this as a Mahrāṭṭa account. But no evidence is advanced to support this latter point.

Saletore (1936a) draws heavily on uncritically edited MSS of the *Grāmapaddhati*. He also discusses the text briefly in his (1936b) article. Saletore's work on the *Grāmapaddhati* is referred to in **§4.6** above and in **§6.10**, **§7.11** and **§10.2** below. It displays many of the difficulties which devolve from basing conclusions on unedited texts and from basing historical conclusions on a single Sanskrit text without controls of corroboratory evidence from other textual material, and of other textual material which places points of interest in context. One of Saletore's major errors was to consider the text to be of distinctly Tuluva domain.

Saletore was drawn on by Moraes (1941). Moraes here refers to the tales of northern descent for *brāhmaṇa* groups as "the myth of northern descent." On the strength of texts such as the *Grāmapaddhati*, Moraes advances the argument that local priests converted themselves into *brāhmaṇas* and subsequently assumed northern origin as justification for *brāhmaṇa* status.[8]

---

[8] The article by Moraes is referred to by Kosambi (1962: 166), where Kosambi criticizes dismissing the traditions as purely mythical, and by Wagle (1970), the latter referred to below. It has not been possible for me to locate a copy in the United States of the *Transactions of the Fifth Indian History Congress* (1941), in which Moraes' 1941 article "Notes on the Pre-Kadamba History of Goa" appears on pp. 164-174.. No hardcover printings appear to be available. And the microform edition of the proceedings published by the Interdocumentation Center AG in Zug, Switzerland is noted in the various libraries I have

Mankad (1941-42: 207-208) refers to 7.4-7 of the *ādirahasya* of the Skh with regard to the length of the different *yugas*. He makes what might appear to be sense out of the text, noting that it seems to mean that the *kṛta yuga* has 1,000,028,000, the *tretā yuga* 31,200,000 or 1,213,000 years, the *dvāpara yuga* 860,000 years, and the *kali yuga* 828,000 years, but wisely adds:

> "The text here seems to be highly confused and I give it up as hopeless; though the years for the Tretā and Dvāpara are somewhat nearer to their usual figures, the years for the other two yugas are nowhere nearer the mark. Nor is there any scheme in proportion between the yugas."

A large number of citations to the Skh which have been found are in Kane (1930-62/2.1[=1941] and 3[=1946]).

In vol. 2.1 all but one citation are given in a list of castes mentioned in *Smṛti* and *Dharmaśāstra* works from 500 B.C. to 1000 A.D. The citations are all to chapter 26 of the *ādirahasya*, entitled in DaCunha's edition *Śaṃkarajātivarṇana*. The first is a reference to Skh 26.40-41 with regard to Ambaṣṭhas (p. 72). Ambiguous English, however, obscures the content of the reference. The second (p. 73) is a reference to Skh 26.68-69 which is reported to state that an Āyogava works in stone and bricks, makes pavements and whitewashes walls. The third (p. 74) omits the exact reference. It ascribes to the Skh the

consulted as being incomplete, omitting among the early congresses the proceedings of the 1st and 4th - 8th congresses. While the volumes filmed in the microform edition are numbered consecutively, vol. 4 contains material from the 3rd congress, and vol. 5 from the 9th congress.

statement that an Ugra is called a Rajpūta. The fourth (pp. 74-75) is to Skh 26.49-51, which is reported to state that a Karaṇa is the same as a Cāraṇa or Vaitāka, and that the business of a Karaṇa is to sing the praises of kings and *brāhmaṇas* and to study the science of erotics (sic). The fifth (p. 79) is to Skh 26.63-66 which is reported to state that a Kṣatṛ is also called a Niṣāda, and that he is an expert in catching deer by means of nets, that he is a forester, that he kills wild animals, and that he rings a bell at night to remind people of the hour. The sixth (p. 88) is to Skh 26.43 which is reported to state that a Pāraśava is called a *śūdra*, that he is superior to a *śūdra* in status, and that he is to live by the avocations prescribed for *śūdras*. The seventh (p. 99) is to Skh 26.53-54, which is reported to state that a Sūta is inferior to a *kṣatriya* but is entitled to do all the work of a *kṣatriya*, and that he performs the work of a charioteer, tames elephants and rides horses. The citation not in the list is to Skh.u. 10.2-3 which is reported to state that *brāhmaṇas* are divided into ten classes, the first five of which are Gauḍas. The text for this statement is given in a note. I must report that the citation is erroneous: the text given is not Skh.u. 10.2-3. Deshpande (2010: 33-34), which see, gives as the reference for this classification Skh.u. 1.1-4. Deshpande (2010) is referred to more fully in place below.

In vol. 3, Kane's second citation (p. 929) is to Skh.u. 5.64-65, which is reported to state that in the *kali* age one is to avoid performing the *agnihotra*, killing cows, *saṃnyāsa*, offering meat at a *śrāddha*, and raising a son by the husband's brother. The first citation is to Skh.u. 4, in which it is reported to be stated that a *deśa* is made up of one hundred villages, a *maṇḍala* of four *deśas*, a *khaṇḍa* of one hundred *maṇḍalas*, and the earth of nine *khaṇḍas*. Spellman (1964: 136 n.) quotes this latter reference in a brief discussion of the meaning of the word *deśa*, and there notes that the clarification seems to be more for convenience rather than being a reflection of reality.

We also have several references to and retellings of sections of Skh.u. 1, 6 and 7 in Pusalker (1955a). By reporting the gist of major sections of chapters 1, 6 and 7 of the *uttarārdha*, Pusalker is attempting to give the various traditions regarding the creation of the Konkan coast and the origin of the Citpāvan *brāhmaṇas*.

Janaki (1966) refers generally in several places (pp. 69-70, 78, 80, and 81) to material from the Skh. His references to the text are usually from secondary sources, occasionally with the appropriate vss. pinpointed. In a few instances he brings to bear sections of DaCunha's text on to points made elsewhere in Sanskrit literature.

Wagle (1970) refers to stories of the Gauḍa Sārasvata *brāhmaṇas* in the "Maṅgish Mahātmya" of the Skh (in DaCunha's edition, pp. 533-576; see Appendix H below). He views the Skh to have borrowed from earlier sources and to have given its own version so as to provide purāṇic sanction for customs shunned in the original sources. He argues a Maharashtrian origin for the author. In this connection he refers to Bhattacharya's argument referred to above. He also includes the distinguishing points of Skh.u. 1 and 2 about the Citpāvan and Karhāḍa *brāhmaṇas*.

Most recently, Deshpande (2010: 33-45), focusing on accounts of the Citpāvan, Karhāḍe, Padye, and Gauḍa Sārasvata *brāhmaṇas* in the Skh.u., opines that the Skh is a Gauḍa Sārasvata tract as this fish-eating community of *brāhmaṇas* considered to be of low status by the rest of *brāhmaṇas* in the Marathi region is referred to in a positive light in the Skh. In the course of his discussion, he brings in variant accounts of the origin of the Citpāvan *brāhmaṇa* community and publications demonstrating the Gauḍa Sārasvatas' perceived need to distinguish themselves from the surrounding *brāhmaṇa* communities. With regard to the suggestion that the Skh was written by a Deśastha *brāhmaṇa*, Deshpande (2010: 45) notes that "[e]ven granting the dislike for the Citpāvan and Karhāḍe Brahmins on the part of the Deśastha Brahmins, there was no love lost among the Deśasthas for the Sārasvatas, and one would not expect a Deśastha brahmin writing an avowedly pro-Sārasvata text like the *Sahyādrikhaṇḍa*." Deshpande's main focus in this article, though, is a discussion of the classification of *brāhmaṇas* in India into two groups, *pañca-gauḍa* and *pañca-drāviḍa*, which classification is found in the Skh.

Patil (2010) treats the Skh as not being a passive literary work, but together with others to have been actively read, interpreted, and used in various contexts. It emphasizes the Skh's influence on later narratives and its normative status; and it delineates the social realities it sees as being reflected in the Skh, the judicial settings in which the Skh was invoked, and the Skh's politically significant audience. The discussion of Skh passages focuses on the interrelationship between Citpāvan and Deśastha *brāhmaṇas* and between Sārasvata and Karhāḍe *brāhmaṇas*. Patil's discussion on pp. 69-75 gives basis to the claim that the Skh was composed by Deśastha *brāhmaṇas*, which claim she traces to an 1884 Marathi language publication by Ramachandra Bhikaji Gunjikar, p. 145. She also spells out reasons that might as well, though not conclusively, point to Sārasvata authorship of the Skh. Noted on p. 36 is that two MSS of the *Śatapraśna-kalpalatika*, written in 1577 and 1690, mention the Skh; and that the *Koṅkaṇākhyāna*, composed in 1721, refers to the descriptions of regions and *brāhmaṇa* groups described in the Skh. On pp. 184-185, she notes that nowhere does the *Koṅkaṇākhyāna*, a Sārasvata text, refer to the Skh's derogatory descriptions of the Citpāvan and Karhāḍe *brāhmaṇas*. She offers two possible explanations for this: either the poet had access to a different MS of the Skh, or he used an oral version.

6. The Manuscripts Used for the Present Edition.

6.1. Ed. **6.2.** L1. **6.3.** L2. **6.4.** Bm. **6.5.** M. **6.6.** Br. **6.7.** K. **6.8.** L3. **6.9.** Manuscripts which it had been impossible to consult at the time of the dissertation. **6.10.** The manuscripts of the *Grāmapaddhati* consulted by Saletore. **6.11.** The manuscripts used by DaCunha for his edition of the *Sahyādrikhaṇḍa*.

6.1. Ed. J. Gerson DaCunha's *The Sahyādri-Khaṇḍa of the Skanda Purāṇa: A Mythological, Historical, and Geographical Account of Western India. First edition of the Sanskrit text with various readings*. Bombay: Thacker, Vining and Company, 1877. Pp. 576.

6.2. L1. MS in the India Office Library, London. No. 3682 (2703) in Eggeling (1899). 221 ff. 8½ in. x 4 in. *Devanāgarī*. 7-9 lines per folio side. Dated *Śaka* 1729 (= A.D. 1806).

This MS is divided by Eggeling into three sections: I (ff. 1-141), the *Reṇukāmāhātmya* attached to the Skh; II (ff. 142-165), labeled the *Mayūravarmākhyāna* by Eggeling, but actually chapters 7 to 10 of the *uttarārdha* as in DaCunha's edition with two additional chapters not in the edition inserted between 7 and 8, the second additional chapter numbered 20 and chapter 10 numbered 25; and III (ff. 166a-186a), a chapter claiming to be taken from the *Jñānayogakhaṇḍa* of the *Sūtasaṃhitā*, but being partly vernacular. This is not the entire MS though. Eggeling omitted from his description ff. 186b-219. See out L1b and L1c for a description of the contents of these folios. The MS bears the stamps of the East India Company Library and of the Mackenzie Collection, dated 14 September 1825.

Final colophon:

> śake 1729 kṣayasaṃ pauṣava (= pauṣadha ?) 3 taddine asmābhiḥ samūhatvena parameśvarārpaṇakūtaṃ (= °kṛtaṃ ?) śrī /

Translation:

Finished by us on the third day of . . . in the *Śaka* 1729 (= A.D. 1806) as an offering to Parameśvara. *Śrī.*

On the following leaf, toward the lower left, there is written in a different hand the following corrupt (?) statement:

> vudhavāsare tārika 24 phebaravari 14 vāphālapu(perhaps °gu)vadi 11 si / a /

6.2a. L1a. Eggeling's sections II and III (ff. 142-186a of our MS. L1). See description under L1 above.

6.2b. L1b. Ff. 186a-195b of MS. L1. Contains chapter 7 as in DaCunha's edition and two additional chapters not in the edition. Chapter 7 is numbered 19. This section of L1 does not contain the PGN but is included here because it is embedded in two sections of L1 which do contain this, and because some of its readings were utilized for Appendixes D and E.

6.2c. L1c. Ff. 195b-219 of MS. L1. Contains chapters 7 and 9 to 13 as in DaCunha's edition, all unnumbered.

6.3. L2. MS in the India Office Library, London. No. 3684 (2618a) in Eggeling (1899). 46 ff. (paged, in Arabic numerals, 215-308). 9¾ in. x 7¼ in. Bound. Modern Telugu script. 32-42 lines per folio side. Not dated. No colophon.

This MS is divided by Eggeling into five sections: I (pp. 215-226), the *Rāmakṣetramāhātmya* attached to the *uttarārdha* of the Skh, *adhyāyas* 1-10, 20-25; II (pp. 226-242), the *Maṅgīśamāhātmya* attached to the Skh, *adhyāyas* 26 (27 ?)-42; III (pp. 243-258), the *Pātityagrāmanirṇaya*, *adhyāyas* 9-19 of the *uttarārdha* of the Skh as in DaCunha's edition, numbered 88-90, 191-193, 174, 175, 194, 124, 125; IV (pp. 259-276), the *Śambhugirimāhātmya* attached to the *uttarārdha* of the Skh, *adhyāyas* 1-12; V (pp. 276-308), the *Āmalakīgrāmamāhātmya* attached to the Skh, *adhyāyas* 52-70, etc. The MS bears the stamp "Comp's. Library" and that of the Mackenzie Collection, dated 14 September 1825.

6.4. Bm. MS in the Library of the Bombay Branch of the Royal Asiatic Society. No. 1007 (B.D. 226) in Velankar (1928). 266 ff., numbered 1-197, 1-69. 11 in. x 5¼ in. *Devanāgarī*. 8-10 lines per folio side. Not dated. No final colophon.

The MS is of the *ādirahasya* and *uttarārdha* of the Skh. It is stamped in many places as being in the Dr. Bhau Daji Memorial.

6.5. M. Manuscript in the British Museum, London. No. 132 in Bendall (1902). 179 ff. 11½ in. x 8 in. *Devanāgarī.* 22-24 lines per folio side. Dated *Śaka* 1750 (= A.D. 1828).

The MS is divided by Bendall into three sections: I (ff. 2-67), a complete copy of the *ādirahasya* and *uttarārdha* of the Skh; II (ff. 68-115), a copy of the *ādirahasya* only; III (ff. 116-179), described as "supplementary matter, without collective title; analogous to, but apparently differing from, that described above." In the beginning of the MS it is noted that the MS was purchased by Major T. B. Jervis in July 1843.

A final colophon, appearing after section I, e.g. after the *uttarārdha*, reads:

> yādṛśaṃ pustakaṃ dṛṣṭvā tādṛśaṃ likhitaṃ mayā /
> yadi śuddham aśuddhaṃ va mama doṣo na vidyate / 1 /
> śrīr astu kalyāṇaṃ śubhaṃ bhavatu / śrīśake 1750 sarvadhārī nāma saṃvatsare kārtike māsi kṛṣṇapakṣe daśamyāṃ induvāsare idaṃ pustakaṃ samāpitaṃ /

Translation:

> I have copied the book as I saw it. Whether it is a good book or a bad book, it is not due to me. (1) Let there be prosperity! Let there be auspicious splendor! In the holy *Śaka* 1750, the year named Sarvadhārī (= Śiva), in the month of Kārtika, on the tenth day in the dark half of the (lunar) month, a Monday, this book was finished.

6.6. Br. MS in the Oriental Institute, Baroda. No. 327 (9255) in the list of *purāṇa* MSS given by Śiromaṇi (1950). 62 ff., numbered 9-70. *Devanāgarī.* 8 lines per folio side. Not dated. No colophon. The size of the MS is not known as it has been seen by me in film only.

The MS is of the *uttarārdha* of the Skh through chapter 12 only.

Title on last folio verso reads:

iti sahyādrikhaṇḍe brāhmaṇotpatti samāptaḥ (sic) /

Translation:

Thus 'The Origin of the *Brāhmaṇas*' in the *Sahyādrikhaṇḍa* is finished.

6.7. K. No. 5-2834 (*viṣaya* no. *Purāṇa* 464) in the "National Archives of Nepal" in Kathmandu. It is one of four MSS of the Skh or sections of the Skh listed in Parajuli (*Saṃvat* 2020 [= A.D. 1963]), the collection of which is now housed in the "National Archives." Dr. Albrecht Wezler[9] of Tübingen has informed me that it is one of five MSS of the Skh or its sections in the "National Archives," but that it is still the only one to contain the *uttarārdha* of the Skh. 274 ff., divided into three sections: ff. 1-105, ff. 1-70, and ff. 1-99. 34.5 cm. x 16.5 cm. *Devanāgarī*. 13 lines per folio side. Not dated, but recent.

Section 1 is of the *Āmalīgrāmamāhātmya*, and is without a final colophon other than an *adhyāya* colophon. Section 2, also without a final colophon, divides itself into five parts: (a) the *uttarārdha* of the Skh (*adhyāyas* 1-21); (b) the *Reṇukāmāhātmya* (*adhyāyas* 1-40); (c) the *Candracūḍamāhātmya* (*adhyāyas* 1-8); (d) the *Nāgāhvayamāhāmya* (*adhyāyas* 1-2); and (e) the *Varuṇāpuremāhātmya* (*adhyāyas* 1-?). Section 3 is of the *ādirahasya* of the Skh (*adhyāyas* 1-67) and carries the final colophon:

---

[9] I am indebted to Prof. Dr. Wezler for much of the information reported here about this MS. I have seen only one portion of the MS in film, and would not have been able to obtain the necessary specifics about the MS in time to report here without his assistance.

> iti śrīskandapurāṇe ādirahasyasahyādrikhaṇḍe vyāsa-sanatkumārasaṃvāde saptaṣaṣṭitamo 'dhyāya / iti sahyādrikhaṇḍapūrvārdha samāptam / śubham / granthasaṅkhyā 3900 /

Translation:

> Thus the sixty-seventh chapter in the discussion between Vyāsa and Sanatkumāra in the first *rahasya* of the *Sahyādrikhaṇḍa* in the *Skanda-purāṇa*. Thus the first half of the *Sahyādrikhaṇḍa* is finished. *Śubham*! 3900 characters.

6.8. L3. MS in the India Office Library, London. No. 6914 (Burnell 435a and c) in Keith (1935). 81 ff. (ff. 1-48, 91b-124b). 6 in. x 7⅞ in. Bound in book form. Malayalam script. 10-11 lines per page. Not dated, but about 1870 A.D.

This MS is noted by Keith to contain extracts from the Skh, *uparibhāga* (latter portion), in part styled *Grāma-nirṇaya*.

Its first section contains *adhyāyas* numbered 25 (*Grāmanirṇaya*), 26 (no title given), 27 (*Gotravibhāga*), 31 (*Grāmanirṇaye Pātitye*), 32 (*Vṛṣotsargavidhāna*), 35 (*Ghaṭaśrāddhavidhi*), 36 (*Grāmanirṇaye Pātitye*), 13 (*Lohādityavarṇana*), and 70 (*Grāmanirṇaya*).

The second section of this MS (ff. 91b-124b) is not continuous with the preceding section. It contains an *adhyāya* numbered 190 (*Sālagrāmakṣetravarṇanam*), an untitled *adhyāya* the number of which is not clear, an *adhyāya* numbered 70 (*Grāmanirṇaye Lohādityanirṇaye*), and an *adhyāya* numbered 53 (*Pāṇḍyadeśagamanaṃ Yuddhapraśaṃsanam*).

Keith comments that the identification of this MS with the PGN by Aufrecht (1891, 1896, 1903/3: 71a) is erroneous. Note that Aufrecht misprints the MS number as BC [= Burnell Collection] 425. This error is repeated in Raghavan et al. (1988: 24b). This latter reference also appears not to take note of Keith's comment.

Adhyāya 36 of the first section of this MS, ff. 29a-30b, proves to be Skh.u. chapter 15 as in DaCunha's edition. It contains two additional verses not included in DaCunha's edition or in our other MSS of this chapter.

Adhyāya 31 is not in the Skh.u. as in DaCunha's edition.

The MS has no overall colophon.

6.9. Manuscripts which it had been impossible to consult at the time of the dissertation. There are other MSS of the Skh or of sections of the Skh which we know of, but these do not contain the PGN. There are, though, two MSS which it was thought at the time of writing the dissertation *might* contain the PGN, but which it was not possible to consult at the time. These are MS. 136 Eb in the section titled "Epics Etc." in Sharma, Deshpande, Padhye, and Sharma (1964), which catalog covers MSS in the Osmania University Library, Hyderabad, and the MS listed as No. 135 in the *Purāṇa* section (page 238) in the *Catalogue of Sanskrit Manuscripts in the Sanskrit College Library, Benares, with full index* (Allahabad: [19-?]), which library it was eventually determined is now the Sarasvati Bhavan Library, Sampurṇananda Sanskrit Vishvavidyalaya, Benares.

On inquiry, a Xerox copy of a MS was sent me through the good offices of the Director of Sanskrit Academy, Osmania University at the time, Prof. M. Gopal Reddy which was believed to be the MS referred to in their library's catalog, but it proved to be of the *Śrāvaṇamāsamāhātmya* of the *Skandapurāṇa*, *Īśvara-sanatkumārasaṃvāda*. On further inquiry, Prof. Reddy informed me that despite their greatest efforts, they could not locate a MS of the *Sahydrikhaṇḍa* in the library (correspondence dated August 5, 1993).

But a Xerox copy was obtained of the MS in question in the Sarasvati Bhavan Library, Sampurṇananda Sanskrit Visvavidyalaya, Benares. This, however, though its marginal abbreviations indicated it to be the *Sahydrikhaṇḍa*, proved to be a MS of the *Āmalīgrāma-māhātmya*, with its last four chapters being the first four chapters of the *uttarārdha* of the Skh as in DaCunha's edition. The *Āmalīgrāmamāhātmya*, a *māhātmya* attached to the Skh not in DaCunha's edition treats, as mentioned above in **§4.5**, the origin of the Citpāvan *brāhmaṇas* (Raghavan et al. 1966: 146a).

6.10. The manuscripts of the *Grāmapaddhati* consulted by Saletore. The MSS of the *Grāmapaddhati* consulted by Saletore are never mentioned in detail by him. Those mentioned in various places are one from Puttige Maṭha in Uḍipi – numbered 66 – which is referred to as the best MS of the text and is quoted from extensively, another MS from Uḍipi supplied to him by Paṇḍit Veṅkaṭadāsa Ācārya of Uḍipi, two MSS sent to him by Paṇḍit Kṇṇārakuduru Bhaṭṭa Rāmakṛṣṇayya (name reproduced as in Saletore [1936b: 116]), a MS from Mangalore – not further identified, and an old printed edition of the *Grāmapaddhati* published in Mangalore by K. M. Das Prabhu, Publishers, and said to be authored by a certain "Bhaṭṭācārya." After it became obvious that it would be impossible for me to go to India to obtain film of Saletore's Puttige Maṭha MS of the *Grāmapaddhati*, it was decided not to try to obtain a copy of this MS. From my experience, it is not possible to obtain film of a MS in a *maṭha*'s library, or even a Xerox copy; and a handwritten copy – which it also might be impossible to obtain, would introduce changes and new errors.

6.11. The manuscripts used by DaCunha for his edition of the *Sahyādrikhaṇḍa*. Of the MSS used by DaCunha, only one, his So., 2., has been found listed in the MS catalogs consulted. This is MS. 1008 (ZZ. E. 31.) in Velankar (1928). DaCunha's MS. So. (ZZ. B. 14.), which he notes to be in this library, is not listed in the catalog.

7. The Nature of the Manuscripts.

7.1. Ed. **7.2.** L1a. **7.3.** L1c. **7.4.** L2. **7.5.** Bm and M. **7.6.** Br. **7.7.** K. **7.8.** L3. **7.9.** Errors, differences in readings, and unique features of the manuscripts. (**7.9a.** Spelling errors. **7.9b.** *Saṃdhi* peculiarities.) **7.10.** The impossibility of constructing a *stemma codicum*. **7.11**. Relationship of the manuscripts to the Puttige Maṭha manuscript of the *Grāmapaddhati* consulted by Saletore.

7.1. Ed. DaCunha's edition has been used as if it were a MS, for which see **§9.1**. As noticed in **§3.3** above, it is very corrupt. It shares most of its readings with K due to very specific circumstances (see **§7.7**). While, along with K, it appears to be fairly independent after chapter 13 where the only MSS represented are Ed, L2, Bm, M, and K, it is not a very independent MS when L1a, L1c and Br are present. In fact, the way in which it agrees a little with almost every MS combination possible in the earlier chapters would appear to indicate that the MS is conflated.

This might imply that indeed the text it represents is the result of editing by DaCunha, were it not for the fact that the text is so bad. Approximately equal numbers of readings agree with L1a in various combinations with other MSS, with L1c in various combinations with other MSS, and with the combination L2 Bm M Br K as a unit. Slightly smaller numbers of readings agree with L1a and L1c together in various combinations with other MSS, with Br alone, and with Br together with L2. An equal number are also independent, agreeing with K only. Still smaller numbers of readings agree with L2 only, again together with K; with Bm, M and Br, also with K; and with Bm and M alone, but again with K. Of these readings, those with L1c and with L1a and L1c together are preferred invariably; those with L1a are preferred usually; and those with L2 and Br together, and the few with Bm, M and Br together, or with Bm and M alone, are not preferred invariably.

7.1a. Examples of independent readings (readings agreeing with K only).[10]

Preferred: 9.6ab °āpṛcchac chaunakaṃ; 9.8b °karma-†kṛtādaraḥ†; 9.58a hṛṣṭās.

Not preferred: 9.9a °jñaḥ, for °jña; 9.9d vṛttir, for tṛptir; 9.12b grāmāṇāṃ cādhidaivataṃ, for grāmāṇām ādhidaivataṃ; 9.15c °kāmaś ca, for °kāmena; 9.56b °pipāsena pīḍitāḥ, for

[10] The chapter numbers used here and in all the examples given in this section and the next (**§7** and **§8**) are those of the *uttarārdha* of the Skh as in DaCunha's edition and as given in parentheses after each chapter number of the PGN as in our text, translation and critical apparatus. They are not the chapter numbers of the PGN proper as assigned in this edition.

°pipāsātipīḍitāḥ; 9.59b hy aṅga°, for bhaṅga°; 9.67a bhartur, for bhatṛ°; 9.68b tapasvinye, for tapasvinyo.

7.1b. Examples of readings agreeing with L1c.

Preferred: 9.8c °vindaikyaḥ; 9.10d °daivatāni; 9.15b °kṣatra°; 9.18a °juṣṭaṃ; 9.52c devaṃ; 9.60d mṛtaprāyā; 9.65c viśvastā; 9.66a sva°; 9.68c adhairyatvād.

Not preferred: 9.59b paraṃparān (?), for paraṃparāt; 9.71b bhaktir, for śaktir.

7.1c. Examples of readings agreeing with L1a and L1c.

Preferred: 9.1d kathā°; 9.4b gṛha°; 9.8a nirato; 9.15a bhārgavaḥ; 9.52c taṃ; 9.52d vāruṇīṃ; 9.62a dhīrāḥ; 9.65d aśru°; 9.67b lalāṭa°; 9.73b prayayau.

Not preferred: 9.72b taṃ devaḥ, for sa devaḥ.

7.1d. Examples of readings agreeing with L1a.

Preferred: 9.4c tvayaivoktaṃ; 9.6c janmajayasya; 9.53c mandākinī°; 9.55a °mūrtiṃ; 9.56a viśvastāḥ; 9.56c prāpur; 9.59c ākranditāḥ; 9.62b °ātiduḥkhitāḥ; 9.63b kṛpālur (= kṛpāḷur); 9.66b vyāhartum upacakramuḥ; 9.67c avasthāṃ.

Not preferred: 9.9b °kovidaḥ, for °kovida; 9.13b śaṃkaraṃ, for śaṃkara°; 9.52c stutvātha, for natvātha; 9.54d bhāvayet, for bhāvayan; 9.61d °nandanaḥ, for °nandana; 9.62d kīrttayet, for kīrtaye; 9.67a balye, for bālye.

7.1e. Examples of readings agreeing with L2 and K alone.

Preferred: 9.54a mahābhāgas; 9.65b °rasam ivoditaṃ.

Not preferred: 9.53d °parivarjanīṃ, for °parivarjinīṃ; 9.58b upāviśan, for upāga*man*; 9.64b keśaṃ, for kl*eśaḥ*.

7.1f. Examples of readings agreeing with L2 Bm M Br K as a unit.

Preferred: 9.11d yat kathitaṃ; 9.17d °siddhair; 9.56a pūrṇagarbhiṇyaḥ; 9.57a tapasyantaṃ.

Not preferred: 9.1c tava, for bhavan°; 9.2d puṇyapāpa°, for pāyayasva; 9.3a janman, for brahman; 9.4d saṃjñikaṃ, for saṃjñakaṃ; 9.13c svādhīnaṃ, for svavaśaṃ; 9.59c procuḥ, for petuḥ; 9.62a bhūtale, for bhūvane; 9.62d mad abhāyata, for adabhrāya ca; 9.74b °karaṇaṃ, for °karuṇaṃ.

7.1g. Examples of readings agreeing with Br and K alone.

Preferred: 9.5ab tac chrotum; 9.15d †mahendrādrau†; 9.56d navasaṅkhyā navākṛti; 9.63c vācā.

Not preferred: 9.1c mukhendor galitaṃ, for mukhendu-vigaḷat; 9.2d bhayārtihaṃ, for bhavārtihaṃ; 9.8d śiva°, for bhava°; 9.12a tāny ahaṃ, for tad ahaṃ; 9.62a patanti, for yatante; 9.74b saṃtati°, for saṃtata°; 9.74c paṅkajavannūtana°, for paṅkajabhavanuta°.

7.1h. Examples of miscellaneous readings.

With Br, L2 and K together, not preferred: 9.7b °śravaṇe yutaḥ, for °śravaṇotsukaḥ; 9.58a dadarśa, for dadṛśur; 9.68d niyatair, for niyater.

With Bm, M, Br, and K, not preferred: 9.5[1] sūta uvāca, for sūtaḥ; 9.14d ninayed, for nināya.

With Bm, M and K alone, not preferred: 9.17c °yogaṃ, for °yogair.

7.2. L1a. L1a is often a very good MS. The readings of L1a divide themselves between independent readings, which usually were not preferred; readings agreeing with those of L1c, often against all other MSS; and readings which agree with Ed and often other MSS against L1c, many of which were preferred. It also shows several readings, though not many, which agree with Bm and M, and rarely L2 with these. Except where these are only a minor variation of the preferred readings, it cannot be said that they were preferred. L1a also shows occasionally a synonym or a paraphrase which it sometimes shares with L1c (see 9.13c, 9.62a), and in one case shares with all MSS except L1c (see 9.54b). Very rarely only, its readings fall outside this description.

7.2a. Examples of independent readings.

Preferred: 9.5[1] sūtaḥ; 9.69a puṇyaleśaprabhāveṇa; 10.28b viśrutā. Under perhaps mitigating circumstances, 9.59cd petuḥ pādayor bhārgavasya tāḥ.

Not preferred: 9.2a °pute (= °puṭe ?), for °puṭair; 9.7b °śravaṇoditaṃ, for °śravaṇotsukaḥ; 9.8a kṣetre tathaiva, for kṣetratīrthaika°; 9.8c bhava°, for śiva°; 9.8c vindākyaṃ (?), for vindaikyaḥ; 9.11a tadā, for tvayā; 9.66a tatra, for trapāṃ; 9.66a sma, for sva°; 10.3d mudā, for tadā; 10.5a balānāṃ, for bālatvaṃ. Also 9.1d °sāgaḷaṃ (?), for °maṅgaḷaṃ, which might be preferred if the source was clear, but which at present cannot be preferred.

7.2b. Examples of readings agreeing with L1c.

Preferred, and against all other MSS: 9.1c bhavan°; 9.1c °mukhenduvigaḷa (= °mukhenduvigaḷat); 9.2c puṇyaṃ; 9.2d prāpayayasva (= pāyayasva); 9.3a brahma (= brahman); 9.3d vimalāśraya (= vimalā*śa*ya); 9.4d saṃjñakaṃ; 9.13c svavaśaṃ; 9.13c kārayam āsa (= kārayām āsa); 9.55b āreha (= āre*bhe*) japam uttamaṃ; 9.58b upāgamat (= upāga*man*); 9.60a tvayādattā (= tva*dāgatā*) vayaṃ; 9.74b °karuṇaṃ; 10.8a vrātyān; 10.27b tadā.

Preferred, but against the readings of Ed K or Ed Br K only: 9.9a °jña; 9.9d tṛptir; 10.7d nareśvara; 10.25d vartate; 10.41d vidhīyate; 10.43a tantu°.

Not preferred: 9.8d bhavad, for bhava°; 9.11d yad viditaṃ (L1c vaditaṃ), for yat kathitaṃ.

7.2c. Examples of readings agreeing with Ed against L1c:

Preferred: 9.3c addhā; 9.4c tvayaivoktaṃ; 9.6ab āpṛcchac chaunakaṃ; 9.6c janmejayasya; 9.10b tasya deśasya vistaraṃ; 9.11b śrotuṃ; 9.12d jitendriyaḥ; 9.55a °mūrtiṃ; 9.60a brahman; 10.3c viśvastāḥ; 10.3d sutān; 10.25a sīmā.

Not preferred: 9.0[1] ṛṣaya ūcuḥ, for ṛṣayaḥ; 9.9b °kovidaḥ, for °kovida; 9.13b śaṃkaraṃ, for śaṃkara°.

7.2d. Examples of readings agreeing with Bm M or L2 Bm M.

With Bm M only: 9.10d °devatāni (?), for °daivatāni; 9.65d °locanaḥ, for °locanāḥ; 9.68a parityaktā, for parityaktāḥ; 10.2a saṃkṣepeṇa (L1a °ena) pravakṣyāmi, for saṃkṣepeṇātra vakṣyāmi; 10.5d manujeśvaraḥ, for manujeśvara.

With L2 Bm M: 9.1b vimalāśayā, for vimalāśaya; 10.8b tāṃ, for tān; 10.8b piśunās, for piśunāṉs; 10.36b tadā.

7.2e. Synonyms or paraphrases.

9.10a pratāpena (= pratāpeṇa ?), for prabhāvaṃ ca; 9.54d so 'haṃ brahmeti, for haṉso 'ham iti; 9.60c kṛpāsindho, for kṛpāmbhodhe; 10.2b °nandana, °sattama; 10.27b gaṇapatis, for gajamukhas; 10.43a murkhāḥ, for mūḍhāḥ.

7.2f. Miscellaneous.

10.25d, with Br, vimalodakāḥ, for vimalodakā.

7.3. L1c. L1c is the best MS. It shares many preferred readings with L1a, and after the first two chapters, where L1a stops, it continues to display these readings as independent readings. It also shares with other MSS most of their preferred readings. Its readings, when they are shared with another MS or other MSS, fall into the *variae lectiones* column only very rarely. L1c is, though, an extremely independent MS with most of its completely independent readings, for the first two chapters, at least, not being preferred. It must be emphasized that this is not always the case, as in a number of instances these completely independent readings prove to be crucial in deciding the text. One of the main characteristics of this MS is that it often provides us with synonyms or paraphrases which are very helpful in deciding the text. Another is that it often omits lines or sections of text. It also adds lines, but these were not chosen to be included in the text proper as they were considered to be spurious.

7.3a. Examples of readings shared with L1a only.

Preferred: 9.1c bhavan°; 9.1c mukhenduvigaḷat; 9.2c puṇyaṃ; 9.2d pāyayasva; 9.3d vimalāsaya (= vimalā*ś*aya); 9.4d °saṃjñakaṃ; 9.13c kārayām āsa; 9.58a dadṛśur; 9.58b upāgamat (= upāga*man*); 9.74b °karuṇaṃ; 10.4d tān . . . nṛpa; 10.6b cetthaṃ; 10.7b vāṭikāṃ; 10.8a vrātyān; 10.14d °ābdhi°; 10.36a ekam; 10.40ab rājan adrim.

Not preferred: 9.8d bhavad°, for bhava°; 9.11d yad vaditaṃ (= viditaṃ ?), for yat kathitaṃ.

7.3b. Examples of completely independent readings.

Preferred: 9.7b °śravaṇotsukaḥ; 9.53b vihaṃgagaṇa-sevitāṃ; 9.54d haṉso 'ham iti; 9.60d hataśriyaḥ; 9.63a dṛṣṭvā;

10.1b tā vitantavaḥ; 10.3b kvacid vasrād; 10.7d tān 10.9a pravartamānānāṃ; 10.12b dāserān; 10.36b tatrai°; 10.43d rājante; 11.4a kālaṃ; 11.5c kiṃ; 12.1c viprāṇāṃ; 12.2a asākṣi°; 12.2d vismayā°; 12.6c vraihaya° (= vrai*he*ya°); 12.13c kṣapām ardhe; 12.15b sikatām; 13.5c pūrṇa°; 13.6a ākalparahitā; 13.9c no; 13.14c hṛṣṭāḥ.

Not preferred: 9.11b śrutaṃ, for śrotuṃ; 9.12d jitendriya, for jitendriyaḥ; 9.15d mahadrājā, for mahendrādrau; 9.17b kila, for muniḥ; 9.53c mandākinīṃ, for mandākinī°; 9.63a tebhyo, for tāsāṃ; 9.63d narapuṃgavaṃ, for bhṛgunandanaḥ; 9.69a vṛṣaśeśa°, for puṇyaleśa°; 10.3d tu tān, for sutān; 10.4c janayām āsuḥ, for atuḷaṃ prāpuḥ; 10.8b tirākrane (?), for nirākṛtān; 10.8c sevā, for senā; 10.36b yadā, for tadā; 10.40d kukuro, for kuraro; 10.44b °saṃbhāṣayāṃ, for °saṃbhāṣaṇaṃ; 11.2d viśrutaṃ, for viśrutau; 11.4d vedavatāṃ, for vedavidāṃ; 11.12a kurvato, for kurvanto; 11.12b yayur, for ninyur; 12.2c °kaṃ ca, for °karaṃ; 12.7b rājye, for rājñe; 12.24d svair, for sma; 13.9d mamādṛśāṃ, for ca mādṛśāṃ; 13.10c gārbhiṇyaṃ, for garbhiṇyā.

7.3c. Examples of preferred readings shared with manuscripts other than L1a.

With: Ed K 11.5a dvijāḥ, 12.12b dharme, 12.20b °epsitāṃ; Ed Br K 11.5b sabhāryāḥ, 11.19d niścitya, 12.1b koṭiliṅgeśa°, 12.38c śaptvettham; L2 10.6b athāghagāḥ, 12.6a tathā, 12.16d °sarāḥ, 13.25b śāsanāt; L2 Bm M 9.9b °kovida, 9.52c natvātha, 10.43a °mātra°, 11.12c °jo 'tha, 12.6d °hetukaṃ; L2 Bm 12.2b pravadāmi; L2 M 11.8b °guṇādiṣu, 12.13a paraśvaḥ; Bm M 9.68d niyater, 9.74c paṅkajabhavanuta°, 11.8a bhavatoḥ, 12.1a asty.

Except for: Ed K 9.15c °kāmena, 11.11c viprāḥ, 12.25c idaṃ; Ed L1a K 9.61d °nandana; Ed L1a M K 9.13b śaṃkara°; Ed Bm M K 10.7b kurvanti; L1a 9.2a °puṭair, 12.2b °sattama, 10.13b pālayann; L1a L2 10.47a °yogatvaṃ; L1a Bm M 10.42b praśasyate; L1a Br 9.52c devaṃ; L2 9.17c °tapo°, 9.52b °puṭaḥ,

10.50b tathā; L2 Bm 11.20d bata, 13.5b vitantavaḥ; L2 Bm Br 10.1a atha; Bm M 9.2c ataḥ, 10.2c bhārgavasya prabhāvaṃ, 11.7d yuvāṃ, 12.11c niścitya; Bm M Br 11.4d varāḥ; Bm M K 10.14c °mahāprājñaṃ; Bm Br 12.16d āśīr°; Bm 11.3a °saṃpannau, 11.11b dadau; M 9.58b °āntikam,11 14a veda°, 10.37a atra; Br 9.5b icchāmahe vayaṃ, 9.5d cetasā, 10.45d paurohityaṃ, 12.38a grāme; M K 13.25a prakurvantu.

7.3d. Examples of unpreferred readings shared with other manuscripts.

10.4a L1c with Ed Br K saṃjātā, for saṃjātāḥ; 10.46a L1c with L2 Br °karmaṃ ca, for °karmatvaṃ; 12.10d L1c with Bm M °āśubhāṃ, for °āśubhaṃ.

7.3e. Synonyms and paraphrases.

9.10b tad deśavibhavaṃ tathā, for tasya deśasya vistaraṃ; 9.56a avīrā, for viśvastāḥ; 9.57b vaiśvānarasamadyutiṃ, for sākṣād vahniśikhopamaṃ; 10.4d śiśun (= śiśūn), for sutān; 10.10b jagāma, for prapede; 11.4c °madhye tu, for °nilayāḥ; 11.12d aputrā mama vallabhā, for putrahīno 'tha me 'ṅganā; 11.19a tad ākarṇya vacas teṣāṃ, for iti teṣāṃ vacaḥ śrutvā; 12.4c °taskaratvaṃ, for °moṣakatvaṃ.

7.3f. Omissions.

9.14bc, 9.31[1]-9.52d, 11.6c-11.9b, 11.10d and 11.11a, 13.2d, 13.3b.

7.3g. Insertions.

10.12[1], 10.13[1], 12.9[1], 13.2[1], 13.7[1], 13.24[1].

7.4. L2. L2 is a very confused MS. Based on a detailed survey of chapter one (Skh.u. 9), it agrees in its readings with those of Bm and M more than half the time. There is no tendency for this to occur more or less often on the basis of whether or not the reading is preferred or not preferred. A good number of L2's readings are independent of all other MSS except Bm and M, and are occasionally independent even of one or both of these, but in chapter one (Skh.u. 9) with only one exception these are not preferred. A large number of L2's readings (± Bm and/or M) agree with preferred readings of Ed (± Br and/or K), L1c, L1a and L1c together, Ed and L1c together, all MSS together – with the exception of Bm and M and occasionally Br or L1a, and more rarely with preferred readings of L1a – otherwise alone, or of Ed (± Br and/or K) together with L1a. There are however a sizeable number of Ed's unpreferred readings with which L2 agrees (± Bm and/or M), a smaller number of L1c's unpreferred readings with which L2 agrees (± Bm and/or M) and an occasional unpreferred reading of either L1a alone or of L1a together with L1c with which L2 (again, ± Bm and/or M) agrees. Very often L2 agrees with all other MSS against an independent reading of L1a or L1c, or against a reading shared by Bm and M and, very rarely either L1a or Br. After L1a and L1c end, L2 remains as the only representative of the better readings of these MSS but, as is pointed out in this description, its readings represent much that is not to be preferred. I believe that an examination of the critical apparatus for chapters six to eleven (Skh.u. 14-19) reflects the confused situation, but must caution the person who uses the text for these chapters that readings of L2 which would not have been preferred had readings from L1a or L1c been present may have proved to be better than those of Ed and K or of Bm and M in specific contexts, and may have become thereby the 'preferred reading' even though we may suspect that the text should read differently. It is also to be noted that L2 displays certain spelling peculiarities which are probably representative of Sanskrit being written in Telugu script. These are writing '*ru*' as '*ṛ*' as '*cakṛr*' for '*cakrur*,' or '*viśṛtā*' for '*viśrutā*' (see 10.6b, 10.28b); doubling intervocalic '*y*' in gerunds and causative imperatives (see 9.32b, 12.35b, 12.38b); and omitting the intervocalic '*y*' in gerunds of causative stems (see 9.13c, 17.19a). Also, some of the spelling errors it displays clearly indicate that it is derived from a *Devanāgarī* original (see 13.22a, 17.15c).

7.4a. Examples of readings agreeing with Bm and M.

Preferred: 9.2d °bhavārtihaṃ; 9.9b °kovida; 9.9d tṛptir; 9.11a tvayā; 9.11d yat kathitaṃ; 9.12a tad ahaṃ; 9.14a °mudrā°; 9.17b muniḥ; 9.52c natvātha; 9.56a purṇagarbhiṇyaḥ; 9.62a yatante; 9.72b °nidhiḥ.

Not preferred: 9.1c mukhendugalitaṃ, for °mukhenduvigaḷat; 9.2c śrotuṃ, for puṇyaṃ; 9.2d puṇyapāpa°, for pāyayasva; 9.3a janman, for brahman; 9.5ab tat śrotum, for tac chrotum; 9.15a bhārgava, for bhārgavaḥ; 9.59c procuḥ, for petuḥ; 9.61c uddharān, for uddharann; 9.62d mad abhāyata, for adabhrāya ca; 9.71b bhaktir, for śaktir.

7.4b. Examples of readings agreeing with the preferred readings of other manuscripts.

With Ed (± Br and/or K): 9.11d yat kathitaṃ; 9.17d °siddhair; 9.57a tapasyantaṃ.

With L1c: 9.0[1] ṛṣayaḥ; 9.9b °kovida; 9.52c natvātha; 9.54d bhāvayan.

With L1a and L1c: 9.2d bhavārtihaṃ; 9.9a °jña; 9.59a bhaṅga°; 9.61a kim etad idam āścaryaṃ.

With Ed (± Br and/or K) and L1c: 9.10a prabhāvaṃ ca; 9.15b °kṣatra°; 9.60d mṛtaprāyā; 9.71d atandritāḥ.

With all MSS except Bm and M: 9.2c ataḥ; 9.6b °kovidaṃ; 9.9d na; 9.55a hṛdi.

With L1a: 9.1b vimalāśayā (= vimalāśaya); 9.12[1] śaunakaḥ.

With Ed (± Br and/or K) and L1a: 9.10b tasya deśasya vistaraṃ; 9.63d bharagunandanaḥ (= bhṛgunandanaḥ).

7.4c. Examples of readings agreeing with unpreferred readings of other manuscripts.

With Ed: 9.1c tava, for bhavan°; 9.2d puṇyapāpa°, for pāyayasva; 9.3a janman, for brahman; 9.3d vividhāni ca, for vimalā*śa*ya; 9.13c kāraïtvātha (= kārayitvātha), for kārayām āsa; 9.55b āntarebhejapaṃ namuṃ (?), for †āre*bhe*† japam uttamaṃ.

With L1c: 9.5[1] śrīsūtaḥ, for sūtaḥ; 9.6c janamejayasya, for janmejayasya; 9.59c ākranditā, for ākranditāḥ; 9.62b °ātiduḥkhitān, for °ātiduḥkhitāḥ.

With L1a: 9.15d mahendrādā, for †mahendrādrau†.

With L1a and L1c: 9.63c vākyam, for vācā.

7.4d. Examples of readings agreeing with all other manuscripts to the exclusion of independent readings of L1a, L1c or Bm and M.

Against L1a: 9.11a tvayā; 9.11b sarvaṃ; 9.11c santīti; 9.52d pratasthe; 9.54b pracakrame; 9.62c hi.

Against L1c: 9.11b śrotuṃ; 9.12d jitendriyaḥ; 9.14a °mudrā°; 9.53c mandākinī°; 9.64c abhīpsitaṃ.

Against Bm and M: 9.2c ataḥ; 9.6b °kovidaṃ; 9.8a °nirato; 9.64cd brūta dattam ity; 9.65d aśru°.

7.5. Bm and M. Bm and M are very close to one another but it is impossible to state their exact genealogical relationship. They display independence from other MSS, but this is invariably in regard to points of spelling and declension. They also display a lack of knowledge of Sanskrit in their source and by their scribes. Often they disagree with one another on minor points. M displays a tendency for metathesis. Bm displays a tendency for misspelling, its mistakes often indicating that its source was in Telugu script. Both display a tendency to add or drop *anusvāras*. This latter is more prevalent in Bm than M. It must be noted that it is often impossible to decide which of the differing readings in these two MSS are the innovations. Bm and M agree with L1c very rarely, with L1a and L1c together very rarely, with L1a more frequently, with Br approximately the same number of times as with L1a, and much more often with Ed and L2. They agree with approximately the same number of L2's preferred readings as with Ed's preferred readings, but they agree more often with L2's unpreferred readings than with those of Ed.

7.5a. Examples of readings held independently by Bm and M.

9.7b °śravaṇo yutaḥ, for °śravaṇotsukaḥ; 9.8a niratāḥ, for nirato; 9.9d me, for na; 9.11c upagrāmāni, for upagrāmāṇi; 9.16c ato hy ātman, for ameyātmā; 9.53d °parivarjinī, for °parivarjinīṃ; 9.55a hṛdī, for hṛdi; 9.58a dadarśu (?), for dadarśur; 9.58a hṛṣṭaṃ, for hṛṣ*ṭāḥ*; 9.64cd brūtad (?) etat param, for brūta dattam ity; 10.1b garbhiṇyatānitatvavaḥ, for garbhiṇ-*yas* tā vitantavaḥ; 10.3d smuṣivire (?), for suṣuvire; 10.5d tān, for te.

7.5b. Examples of Bm and M disagreeing on minor points.

Readings due to metathesis: 9.58b M °āṅkitam, for °āntikam; 10.14a M deva°, for veda°.

Readings due to spelling errors: 9.5c Bm śruṇudhvam, for śṛṇudhvam; 9.52b Bm kṛtāñjuli°, for kṛtāñjali°; 9.57a Bm tapasvantaṃ, for tapasyantaṃ; 10.0[1] Bm śatānīkovāca, for śatānīka uvāca; 10.14b Bm mārta°, for smārta°.

Readings due to adding or dropping the *anusvāra*: 9.9c Bm vāgamṛta, for vāgamṛtaṃ; 9.71c M kriyatāmantra (?), for kriyatām atra; 9.74b Bm śivedirāmeṇa, for M śivendirāmeṇa; 10.4d Bm praprasṭuṇs (?), for M praprasṭus; 10.6a M saundarā (?), Bm saudarā (?), for sodarā; 10.13a Bm kṛpā, for kṛpāṃ.

7.5c. Examples of Bm and M agreeing with other manuscripts.

With L1c: Preferred. 9.68d niyater. Not preferred. 10.12d kṛpālu°, for kṛpāḷur.

With L1a: Not preferred. 9.10d °devatāni, for °daivatāni; 9.18a juṣṭa°, for juṣṭaṃ; 9.56d navākṛtiḥ, for navākṛti; 10.9a pravartamānasya, for pravartamānānāṃ.

With L1a and L1c: Preferred. 9.62c tathā; 9.67a bhartṛ°.

With Br: Not preferred. 9.12b adhidaivataṃ, for ādhidaivataṃ; 9.15b °kṣetra° (Bm only), for °kṣatra°; 9.54a mahābhāga, for mahābhāgas; 9.64b keśa (?), for kle*śaḥ*; 10.9b vyatiyu (M only), for vyatīyur;10.13c tathaity, for athety (Ed L2 K tathety).

With Ed: Preferred. 9.8d °bhaktir; 9.17c °tapo°; 9.56a viśvastāḥ; 10.3d sutān; 10.4b pīnonnata°. Not preferred. 9.5[1] sūta uvāca, for sūtaḥ; 9.17c °yogaṃ, for °yogair; 10.6b aghaughagāḥ, for athāghagāḥ; 10.7d tvāṃ, for tān.

With L2: Preferred. 9.2d bhavārtihaṃ; 9.9b °kovida; 9.15c °kāmena; 9.52c natvātha; 10.11b tadā. Not preferred. 9.4b graha°, for gṛha°; 9.14b nirmāyasya, for †*nigamya*† sva° (Ed L1c Br K nirmāya sva°); 9.52c tāṃ, for taṃ; 9.59c ākranditā, for ākranditāḥ; 10.6b cetaṃ (?), for cetthaṃ.

7.6. Br. Br is a fairly corrupt MS closer to Ed than to any other MS by itself, but usually sharing its readings with

with Ed when these agree with either L1a, L2, a combination of L2, Bm, M, and K, and rarely L1c. There are also many instances in which its readings agree with either Bm and M or with L2 alone, and a very few in which it agrees with almost every MS or combination of MSS possible. Many of its readings are independent of all other MSS, invariably in minor ways only. These are perhaps just corruptions of the other MSS. Other readings clearly are just corruptions of readings shared by all the other MSS together.

7.6a. Examples of readings shared with Ed.

With Ed and K alone: 9.1b viṃjitendriya (= vijitendriya), for vimalāśaya; 9.1c mukhendor galitaṃ, for °mukhenduvigaḷat; 9.2d bhayārtihaṃ, for bhavārtihaṃ; 9.5ab tac chrotum; 9.8d śiva°, for bhava°; 9.12a tāny ahaṃ, for tad ahaṃ; 9.15d mahendrādrau; 9.56d navasaṅkhyā navākṛti; 9.63c vācā.

With L1a, Ed and K: 9.9b °kovidaḥ, for °kovida; 9.54d bhāvayet, for bhāvayan; 9.62d kīrtayet, for kīrtaye.

With L2, Ed and K: 9.7b śravaṇe yutaḥ, for śravaṇotsukaḥ; 9.58a dadarśa, for dadṛśur; 9.62c tadā, for tathā.

With L2, Bm, M, Ed, and K: 9.2c śrotaṃ (= śrotuṃ), for puṇyaṃ; 9.2d puṇyapāpa°, for pāyayasva; 9.14d ninayed, for nināya; 9.59c procuḥ, for petuḥ; 9.62d mad abhāyata, for adabhrāya ca.

With L1c, Ed and K: 9.68c adhairyatvād; 9.71b bhaktir, for śaktir.

7.6b. Examples of readings shared with Bm and M.

9.8a °tīrtheka°, for °tīrthkaika°; 9.8b °karmas tathādaraḥ, for karma†kṛtādaraḥ†; 9.12b adhidaivataṃ, for ādhidaivataṃ; 9.54a mahābhāga, for mahābhāgas; 9.64b keśa (?), for kle*śaḥ*; 9.67c avasthā°, for avasthāṃ.

7.6c. Examples of readings shared with L2.

9.3c sakalānyad vā, for sakalāny addhā; 9.9d kathāṃ, for kathaṃ; 9.18c °mayai, for °mayaiḥ; 9.60d hatapriyaḥ, for hataśriyaḥ; 9.67a bhartu° (?), for bhartṛ°.

7.6d. Examples of miscellaneous readings.

With L1a: 9.52c daivaṃ, for devaṃ. With L1a L1c L2: 9.68b tapasvinyo. With L1a L1c L2 Bm M: 9.15c °kāmena. With L1a Bm M: 9.71d atindritaḥ (?), for atandritāḥ. With L1a M: 9.60d mṛtaprāya°, for mṛtaprāyā. With L1c: 9.55a °mūrti°, for °mūrtiṃ; 9.58a hṛṣṭā, for hṛṣṭās. With L1c L2: 9.63b kṛpālu°, for kṛpālur; 9.67a bālye. With L1c L2 Bm M: 9.61d °nandana; 9.62b °ātiduḥkhitān, for °ātiduḥkhitāḥ.

7.6e. Examples of 'independent' readings and corruptions.

9.1a °ārthaṃ, for °ārtha°; 9.2b hitaḥ, for hi naḥ; 9.3b varaḥ, for vara; 9.5a astiti, for astīti; 9.5b icchāmaheśvasaṃ (?), for icchāmahe vayaṃ; 9.5d catasaḥ, for cetasā; 9.7d bhārata°, for bhārataṃ; 9.10c nāni, for nāmāni; 9.10d ca, for tad; 9.17c °yoga°, for °yogair; 9.52c stutvā tatha, for natvātha; 9.53a śuktismatī, for śuktimatīṃ; 9.53d parivarjanī, for parivarjinīṃ; 9.59b bhaga° (?), for bhaṅga°.

7.7. K. K shows every sign of being either a direct copy of Ed, or a copy of such a copy. Several points indicate this to be the case, rather than *vice versa*. The *uttarārdha* in K begins with the same invocation as in Ed. From its layout on the page in Ed, and from a comparison of the beginning of the *uttarārdha* with the beginning of the *ādirahasya* in Ed, it appears that the invocation was introduced by

DaCunha. Also, the first chapter of the *uttarārdha* in K, as is the case with all chapters in Ed, begins with the formula '*atha* . . . .' Again, from the layout of this in Ed, it appears to be a retention in K of something introduced by DaCunha. It is to be noted that none of our other MSS proper read this way. In addition, in both K and Ed only, the *uttarārdha* is followed by the *Reṇukāmāhātmya*, the *Candracūḍamāhātmya*, etc. Again, this can be attributed to DaCunha as it follows his ordering of texts in Ed. Also, K preserves Ed's printing of '*hṛ*' with two '*d*'s, even though the resulting words are nonsense.

The readings in Ed and K are almost totally the same, and the differences, such as K's frequent reading of '*yāma*' for '*grāma*,' are few and generally insignificant. Some of K's very few differences from Ed, such as this one, are inexplicable. An assumption of another handwritten MS between Ed and K may explain some, but some can be due only to a conscious attempt to alter the text. Examples of these differences are 9.2c atraḥ (?), for ataḥ, and 9.6a iyaṃ, for idaṃ; the omission and addition of *anusvāras* as in 12.14d kuḍe (?), for kuṇḍe, and 12.14d kuntsita° (?), for kutsita°; the addition and omission of *visargas* as in 17.4d samadṛśyataḥ, for samadṛśyata, and 18.35a indranilai, for indranilaiḥ; the change of *anusvāra* to *visarga* as in 17.13d dhanaḥ, for dhanaṃ; and the change of the word °mārtaṇḍa° to °mātaṅga° in 14.34d, changing the expiation being noted to looking at many elephants rather than looking at the sun many times.

7.8. L3. L3 is a very good MS for the single chapter of our text that it contains (Skh.u. 15), despite Keith's note that this MS overall is not very accurate. It contains two verses of text not included in out other MSS for Skh.u. 15, and these most certainly belong. Also, in several instances it provides readings that support what were originally hypothesized to be the proper readings, but for which there was not enough evidence. In other instances, it provides us with a preferred reading. In the instance where village names are given, its readings seem to be more accurate. In Skh.u. 15.13ab its reading suggests how corrupt our other MSS are in this location, and seems to suggest that another ½ verse is missing in all our MSS. L3 also in instances gives a synonym or a paraphrase which, however, were not adopted here. Unlike our other MSS, *anusvāra* does not appear to have been written for '*n*' as a matter of course (see **§7.9a**), original final '*n*' having been maintained. Confusions that have crept into other MSS on this account do not occur here. Futher, in two instances, strictly correct euphonic combination appears, final '*m*' having been changed to '*n*' before a dental mute, instead of being changed to *anusvāra*. In one other instance, we may have an incorrect reading due to a possible hypercorrection. L3 often shares incorrect readings with L2, Bm and/or M. Sometimes, though, it shares correct readings with these MSS. In some instances, it agrees with Ed and K, usually when L2 agrees with these MSS as well. More than once, it seems to interpret a *Jainalipi* or non-standard *Devanāgarī* superscript vowel modification for '*ā*' as '*r*', indicating that L3 is most probably based on a *Devanāgarī* original. Lastly, *avagrahas* are not written. As negatives, toward the last few verses of Skh.u. 15, L3's readings appear to fall apart; and very occasionally a syllable is omitted.

7.8a. Insertions.

15.0[1]; 15.1; 15.9cd-15.10ab.

7.8b. Examples of readings that support earlier suppositions.

15.2c nāga°; 15.4a ullikhan; 15.4b ārarmakāriṇaḥ, for ārāmakāriṇaḥ; 15.8a śiṣṭān vipran, for śiṣṭān viprān; 15.12a grāma°.

7.8c. Examples of independent readings.

Preferred: 15.2c nāga°; 15.4a ta kṣitiṃ, for tat kṣitiṃ; 15.7d sva°.

Not preferred: 15.7b svapurīṃ , for medhāvī.

7.8d. Examples of readings shared with L2, Bm and/or M.

Preferred: 15.2a asty anyat, with L2; 15.4c °sūnyāḥ, with L2 Bm M; 15.11a bhavatu, with L2 Bm M.

Not preferred: 15.8d °nimitāḥ, with Bm for °nirmitāḥ; 15.10c katha, with Bm M for kathaṃ.

7.8e. Examples of readings shared with Ed and K.

Preferred: 15.2d °karma°, with Ed L2 K; 15.2d °kṛtaṃ, with Ed L2 K; 12.13a padikaṃ, with Ed L2 K.

Not preferred: 15.7c viprair, with Ed K for vipraiḥ.

7.8f. Grammatically final '*m*' changed to '*n*' by euphonic combination before a dental mute.

15.2a grāman [tam, for tad]; 15.9b bhūr iyan [nṛpa].

7.8g. Synonyms and paraphrases.

15.3a rāmena sṛṣṭās te pūrvaṃ, for rāmasṛṣṭās tu ye pūrvāḥ; 15.11c vāṇīṃ, for vākyam; 15.11c samārṇya (=

samākarṇya), for athākarṇya; 15.12c sa nṛpa, for nṛpatiḥ; 15.14d rājātarājā (= rājādhirājā) śavara (= iśvara), partial synonym based on misinterpretation of the text, for rājante bhuvaneśvara (L3 also fails to apply *saṃdhi*).

7.9. Errors, differences in readings, and unique features of the manuscripts. The types of errors and differences in readings between the MSS are very diverse. None are held exclusively by any one MS within the network of MSS described above. They include metathesis (see 10.12a, 11.5d), omissions and additions of syllables (see 10.41d, 11.7a) and simple spelling mistakes, some of which bridge gaps between two correctly spelled readings (see 9.7b, 9.67a). They also include synonyms, not only those held by L1a or L1c against all other MSS, but also those held by all MSS against preferred readings shared by L1a and L1c (see 9.13c, 9.62a). On a more complicated ground, they include differences in sentence structure (see 9.13-9.14) and differences in declension for nouns and in number for verbs (see 9.6b, 9.8a, 9.54b), as well as including different nouns, adjectives and verbs meaning different things (see 9.2d, 9.24c, 9.59c). Our main purpose here, however, is to discuss some of the implications of some spelling errors and some spelling peculiarities which cannot find their way onto our charts, and to note certain *saṃdhi* peculiarities shared by most MSS.

7.9a. Spelling errors. Charts of spelling errors which can be attributed to confusions due to *Devanāgarī* or to Telugu or Kanarese scripts, together with listings as to which MSS each confusion appears in, are given in Appendix G. The distribution of MSS on the charts is very similar to that in the critical apparatus. This can be viewed to reflect our editing of the text or, as we would maintain, to support the editing from a study of one aspect of the readings.

Of interest is that all MSS show corruption which can be attributed to either Telugu or Kanarese scripts. This indicates tangibly the possibility that all our MSS go back to a MS in one of these scripts, which possibility is virtually confirmed for Ed, L2, Bm, M, Br, and K in the readings for '*na kuryāṃ*' in 17.14b.

Not appearing in the charts is the point that all MSS except Ed and L3 indicate that *anusvāra* was written for '*n*' on a number of occasions almost as a matter of course. See 10.4d, 10.8b, 13.8c, 17.15b. Also, all MSS indicate that this led to confusion between '*m*' and '*n*.' See 12.8a, 15.4a.

Also not appearing are the following unexplained occurrences: e>ā, ṇ>n, t>c, th>t, dh>d, ś>s.

We have also located, but have not included in the appendix, the following listing of errors which would appear to be due to occasional readings of the MSS as if they were written in *Jainalipi* or a style of *Devanāgarī* different from the standardized *Devanāgarī* of today, and in one instance (see 9.62d, here asterisked) can be attributed only to a MS having been written in *Jainalipi* or such a style of *Devanāgarī*. The list is not included in the appendix because in most cases the instances of such occurrences are so few as to make them questionable. They are *a+C+e > i+C+a, in L2; ā+C+a > a+C+e, in Ed L2 Bm M Br K; c>tv, in L2; c>v, in Ed Bm M Br K; v>c, in Ed Bm M Br K; bh>t, in Ed L1a L1c L2 Bm M Br K[11]; ṣ>kh, in Ed Br K, and in one of the inserts, in Ed L2 Bm M; cch>tth, in Bm M (due to Telugu or Kanarese script ?); and tv>c, in Ed L1a L1c L2 Br K. In L3, we appear to

---

[11] See Levitt (1979a) with regard to this confusion.

have several instances in which C + *Jainalipi* or non-standard *Devanāgarī* superscript vowel modification for '*ā*' > Ca + superscript '*r*' before C as in *Devanāgarī* commonly.

It is also to be noted that one error which possibly may be due to a confusion in Malayalam script in a MS other than in our Malayalam script L3, specifically '*l*' for '*kh*,' was found in M. As it is the only example of a confusion due to Malayalam script, with the exception of L3 h>t in 15.14c, and as it appears in M only, which would have to be taken to indicate that it appeared in M after this MS's separation from Bm, we must conclude that it is probably not due to a Malayalam script MS of the text but rather to a point regarding script about which we just do not know. We therefore do not include it in Appendix G. Note, though, MS. L3 suggests that there may indeed have been Malayalam MSS of the PGN.[12]

Undoubtedly there are confusions due to script which we have not recognized. More research must be carried out on variations within given scripts and throughout the histories of these scripts before we are able to isolate with accuracy all the confusions which must be present.

7.9b. *Saṃdhi* peculiarities. There are two types of *saṃdhi* peculiarities in the MSS of our text. These have been included as variant readings in the critical apparatus.

The first is the insertion of a *visarga* before the normal *saṃdhi*. Examples of this are '*aiḥś* + *c*' and '*uḥs* + *t*.' This occurs three times in L1a, eight times in L1c, five times in L2, two times in Bm, two times in M, and four times in Br. It never occurs in Ed or K only. The text of L3

---

[12] Also note that Saletore's Puttige Maṭha MS was in Tulu script.

is too short for us to be able to say anything on this point with any degree of authority. Two of its occurrences are internally within a word beginning with '*dus*.' We are unable to explain this peculiarity. It clearly does not appear to be used for ornamental reasons, as I have been informed by Dr. Christopher George is the case for a symbol like the *visarga* at the end of lines in some *Newārī* MSS, nor does it appear to be due to a scribe's filling up the end of a line with a symbol like the *visarga*, as we have in *Jainalipi* MSS. It also is not due to writing the *anusvāra* on the line instead of over the preceding syllable, as is done for the corresponding symbol in Telugu, Kanarese and Malayalam scripts, but with a *virāma* below it. Dr. George informs me that such practice often results in *Newārī* MSS with a symbol that looks like a *visarga*. It does not explain the situation described here, however, though it might explain how neuter words, or accusative masculines, become nominative masculines, or *vice versa*. In the editing of the text, it has been chosen to omit the *visarga* for such readings.

The second *saṃdhi* peculiarity is the complete omission, disregarding all standard *saṃdhi* rules, of etymological final '*s*' from declensions in the nominative singular, nominative plural, instrumental plural, and dative-ablative plural on the affected base words. This includes '*as*' before a sonant becoming '*a*' instead of '*o*.' Indeed, there is no apparent consistency in breaking any one standard *saṃdhi* rule over another for the different types of combinations prescribed. This occurs in all MSS, Ed included. Some examples may be found under the variant readings for 9.8c °vindaikyaḥ; 9.18c °mayaiḥ; 9.21c mātaṅgair; 9.24c auṣadhibhiḥ; 9.29c rāmaḥ; 9.56a viśvastāḥ; 9.59c ākranditāḥ; 10.43a mūḍhāḥ; 11.2b vāhakebhyaḥ; 11.8c vidhair; 11.25d °saktās.

7.10. The impossibility of constructing a stemma codicum. The MSS, as described above, place themselves in a complicated network in which readings of any given MS agree with those of other MSS with different frequencies. Certain affinities display themselves, such as those of L2 with Bm and M, or that of Ed with Br, but these affinities never sharply delineate MS traditions. Large numbers of readings for any MS always agree with other MSS at variance with whatever MS it is being compared with. In short, we do not have recensions which differentiate themselves from one another by the uniformity of their divergent readings and by numerous discrepancies between their readings. Because of this it is impossible to establish clear cut relationships between MSS, and therefore lines of transmission.

Levitt (1977: 19-21, 1982: 129) tries to reconstruct historical levels of transmission on the basis of correlations between MS readings and chapter numberings in the different MSS: one, the latest with the most corrupt readings, numbering its chapters of the *uttarādha* as in DaCunha's edition (Bm M K); another (L2) numbering them in the 80's and 90's[13] – which numbering may just continue the numbering sequence started in the *ādi-rahasya*; and a third, found in MSS with some of our better readings and giving the *uttarārdha* more chapters than we have at present, numbering our present Skh.u. chapter 10 in the 20's and chapter 15 in the 30's (L1a L3). But this is very imperfect as L2's readings often agree with Bm and M; and Br, one of our worst MSS, also numbers its chapters in the 90's as does L2. As noted in **§1.3**, this is all very perplexing.

[13] See **§1.3** and Levitt (1977: 20-21) with regard to this.

7.11. Relationship of the manuscripts to the Puttige Maṭha manuscript of the *Grāmapaddhati* consulted by Saletore. From the passages of the *Grāmapaddhati* quoted in Saletore (1936a) certain observations can be made regarding the Puttige Maṭha MS. It is this MS which Saletore maintained was his best MS of the text. The observations, which are both of a general nature and of a more specific nature comparable with those given above for the MSS used for the present edition of the PGN, demonstrate that this MS displays limited independence from out MSS of the PGN both with regard to a minimal number of readings and with regard to certain types of errors. Overwhelmingly, however, its readings fall within the range of our present readings, errors are of a type similar to those in our MSS and across-the-board conflation with our MS sources is in evidence.

The Puttige Maṭha MS frequently disregards the requirements of meter, sometimes adding one or more syllables and sometimes omitting one or more syllables from a *pāda*.

It also displays standardly incorrect *saṃdhi* for etymological final '*s*.' Invariably this becomes *visarga* before a voiced sonant, and occasionally it becomes *visarga* before a dental surd mute. One cannot be certain, however, whether this is the result of the first *saṃdhi* peculiarity of our MSS described in **§7.9b** but "cleaned up" and perhaps standardized by Saletore, or whether it is a standard practice of the MS itself. Less invariably the second *saṃdhi* peculiarity of our MSS described in **§7.9b**, the complete omission of etymological final '*s*' from certain declensions, is the case. Often, but not standardly, final etymological '*t*' before a sonant does not become voiced.

In a large number of instances incorrect cases or impossible declensions occur. For example, 12.43d °vatsalaḥ, for °vatsala; lengthy commentary embedded in insertion between 12.46b and 12.46^2 etā, for ete; 14.27c tasyāḥ, for teṣāṃ; 14.30c °madheṣu, for °madhye tu; 17.53d mahātmanā, for mahājanāḥ.

The MS also contains instances in which the omission of *anusvāra* results in contextual nonsense. For example, insertion between 17.56d and 17.56^2 ity eva dvādaśa°, for ity evaṃ dvādaśa°.

In a large number of instances the MS contains nonsense words. For example, 12.45c tataṃ, for tataḥ; 14.29d dhṛdau vṛthāḥ, for dṛḍhavratāḥ.

In a larger number of instances the MS contains words or phrases which are correct Sanskrit, but nonsense contextually. In many cases these appear in our MSS and have been discarded by us. They have been accepted by Saletore, however, and have been translated by him, occasionally by utilizing meanings which are not lexicographically attested. For example, insertion between 12.41cd and 12.42ab gāyatam, for dhyāyantam; 12.45c taptamudrāṃ, for saptamud*rās*; 12.45d mataṃ, for †*mantraṃ*†; 14.28c galeṣu, for jaleṣu; 14.29b gomaya vāriṇā, for . . . †*tvaritaṃ*†.

From Saletore's translations of passages for which he did not give text, it can be seen that much of his best MS made little clear sense and that his other MSS apparently did not provide much help. And for those passages for which he did give text, it can be seen that he took great liberties with his translation, constructing sense from passages which make none and mistranslating passages in his text which do make sense. See, for example, Saletore (1936a: 312).

The Puttige Maṭha MS, however, does appear to contain a limited number of variant readings which prove to be better than any of the readings in the MSS which it was possible to use for the present edition. The one instance in which this proves to be the case in the passages for which text is given by Saletore is 14.26b nijamandiraṃ 'his house,' for nijapattanaṃ 'his native city.'

In another instance a line omitted in the insertion between 17.56d and 17.56^2 in the MSS used here, but surmised to exist and indicated in our text by periods (. . .) appears in the Puttige Maṭha MS and necessitates a change in the text adopted here: dakṣiṇe bāhumūle tu trīṇi padeti mantra taḥ / tathaiva vāmamūle tu . . . , 'at the base of the right arm the *mantra* "*trṇi pad*" (= RV 1.22.18), likewise at the base of the left . . .'.

In two instances, the readings of the Puttige Maṭha MS suggest improvements which might be made in our adopted text. In the passage of text held in common by the commentary embedded in the insertion between 12.46b and 12.46^2 and by the insertion between 17.56d and 17.56^2 phālādi, for bālādi (variant, thālādi) suggests *bhā*lādi, 'beginning with the forehead,' as the preferred reading. The confusion would have arisen out of Telugu script orthography. Likewise, in 17.55d, 17.56b and 17.56d mudrā°, for mṛdā 'with earth' in two instances suggests that our variant from M in 17.55d, mudā 'gladly,' should be the preferred reading in all cases and that the text should be emended accordingly in 17.56b and 17.56d. This would provide better sense. It also suggests that perhaps the reading mudrā° in the second *pāda* of the vs. referred to immediately above in the passage of text held in common by the commentary embedded in the insertion between 12.46b and 12.46^2 and the insertion between

17.56d and 17.56^2 should be emended to read mudā 'gladly.'

The Puttige Maṭha MS also contains two instances in which its readings support emendations made for the present edition. These are 12.18c tauryantrikena, for *taur*yatrikena; and 12.35a and 14.25c parityāgāparityāgaṃ, for †parityā*gā*parityāgaṃ†.

In a number of instances the MS contains true variants not among our present readings. Excluding the exceptions noted above, these are not preferred over our present adopted readings. For example, 12.25b bruve 'haṃ, for vraihe*yaṃ*; 12.34c asatya°, for asākṣi°; 14.25a ādāya, for svīkṛtya; 17.54b pālayām āsa, for pāvayām āsa.

The MS, however, contains an overwhelmingly large number of readings which either have been adopted for the present edition of the PGN or which are contained among our present variant readings. A significant number of these readings agree with L1c when L1c stands otherwise alone and contains readings which were not preferred. In a significant number of instances, however, the readings of this MS stand with those of our other MSS against L1c. A significant number of readings in this MS agree with L2 either when it stands otherwise alone or when it agrees with Bm M, Ed Br K or both Bm M and Ed Br K in various combinations. In a number of instances, however, the MS stands with Bm M and/or Ed Br K against L2.

In summary, the Puttige Maṭha MS of the *Grāmapaddhati* displays conflation with all our MS sources but appears to fall together most closely with our MSS. L1c and L2. It also displays independence from the MSS used for the present edition of the PGN. These instances of independence, however, usually are not preferred.

8. The Present Edition

8.1. Methods used for deciding preferred readings. **8.2.** Emendations. **8.3.** Uncertainty about text. **8.4.** Devices used. **8.5.** Peculiarities in the Sanskrit text. **8.6.** Normalization.

8.1. Methods used for deciding preferred readings. No one method was used consistently for deciding preferred readings in this edition of the PGN. Each situation was viewed individually on the basis of the evidence available. Generally, an easier reading was chosen over a more difficult one unless the difficult one was very unusual, the common denominator was always looked for in very confusing cases, and better MSS were gone along with once these were established if both the better and the not-so-good MS had readings which made sense. Better sense was always a criterion in choosing preferred readings. In cases where there were synonyms or paraphrases in one or more of the MSS, parallel readings or *testimonia*, these were utilized. In many cases it was two or more of these processes which decided the choice of a preferred reading. Noted here are a very few examples for the various types of situations which were encountered.

8.1a. *Lectio facilior*. 9.4a °saṃjñakaṃ, for °saṃjñikaṃ; 9.10a prabhāvaṃ ca, for pratāpena; 9.62c †tā*sām*$^{-}$, for teṣām; 10.22a °vivāda°, for °vicāra°; 12.2d vismayā°, for viṣayā°.

8.1b. *Lectio difficilior*. 9.3a addhā, for atra; 9.28a cāmaraiḥ svacchaiḥ, for cāmaracchatraiḥ, cāmarāśvatthai, cāmaracchatre; 10.6b athāghagāḥ, for aghaughagāḥ, athotkaṭāḥ.

8.1c. Common denominator. 9.7b °śravaṇotsukaḥ, for °śravaṇe yutaḥ, °śravaṇoditaṃ, °śravaṇo yutaḥ; 10.6b athāghagāḥ, for aghaughagāḥ, athotkaṭāḥ; 14.25c †parityā*gā*parityāgaṃ†, for parityāgāt sarītyāgaṃ (?), parityāgaṃ parityāgaṃ, parityāgan sarityāgaṃ (?), parityāgāt sarityāga° (?), parityāgāt saritya 'ga° (?), parityāgaparityāgaṃ, parityāgaparityāga°.

8.1d. Better manuscript. 9.0[1] ṛṣayaḥ, for ṛṣaya ūcuḥ; 9.4b gṛha°, for graha°; 9.20a °kokābhirutaṃ, for °kokilayutaṃ, °kekābhitantaṃ.

8.1e. Sense. 9.2b hi naḥ, for hitaḥ; 9.2d bhavārtihaṃ, for bhayārtihaṃ; 9.3a brahman, for janman; 9.8d °bhaktir, for °śaktir.

8.1f. Synonyms or paraphrases. 9.10a prabhāvaṃ ca, for pratāpena; 9.10b tasya deśasya vistaraṃ, for tad deśavibhavaṃ tathā; 9.13c svavaśaṃ, for svādhīnaṃ.

8.1g. Parallel readings. 17.14b na *kuryāṃ*, for kākriye (?), nākriye, na kriye, on the basis of 14.20b.

8.1h. *Testimonia*. 17.55c ā no bhadreti, 17.56a ā mandrair iti, 17.56c akṣībhyāṃ teti, on the basis of these *mantras* as listed in Bloomfield (1906).

8.2. Emendations. Emendations, or hypotheses as to what the text should read, were made, but only when they were clearly indicated by misspellings (9.3d vimalā*śa*ya, for vimalāśraya and vimalasaya) or by parallel readings (17.14b na *kuryāṃ*, as in the same context as 14.20b), or when they were clearly required for sense (15.4b †*ā*rāmakāriṇaḥ†; or 15.8a śiṣṭān *viprān*, for śiṣṭānvitān [forms as given in the 1973 dissertation]). In several cases these are fairly conjectural, and are to be understood as suggestions only, such as 15.6c †*a*nāhar*yā*maśākena†. These emendations have been kept to a minimum, and daggers have been placed around words with such emendations. Of note is that in the instances of †*ā*rāmakāriṇaḥ† and śiṣṭān *viprān*, readings in L3, which MS was consulted only recently, confirmed the earlier conjectures, and the text and critical apparatus have been changed accordingly.

8.3. Uncertainty about text. The text, as reconstructed here, is not to be taken as being the original text. It is only a reconstructed acceptable text which should be re-examined when further evidence becomes available. The unexplainable wide divergence between the readings of the different MSS, the incompleteness of our better MSS and the late date of the MS from which the MSS used for this edition have been derived, compared with the date at which the autographs must have been written, all indicate that we should regard the text as reconstructed here with proper reserve. The text is still uncertain.

8.4. Devices used. In the text as it has been reconstructed here certain devices have been used for the aid of the critical reader. Syllables in which an emendation was made have been italicized. Words which were viewed to be particularly suspect from the evidence we have available have been placed between daggers. The daggers have been used around the translation of these words as well. When a section of text was so uncertain that it was considered to be more advisable not to choose a reading, each syllable has been represented by a dot in the text. Three dots, indicating that something has been left out, were used in the translation to represent these passages or words. For devices used in the critical apparatus, see **§9.3** and **§9.5**.

8.5. Peculiarities in the Sanskrit text. There are certain peculiarities in the Sanskrit text which appear to have been in an autograph:

(1) The use of the neuter gender for words which are ordinarily masculine. This is the case consistently with the words '*grāma*,' '*vāda*' and '*saṃskāra*.'

(2) The usage in two instances of words cited in the dictionaries as being used in the *Veda* only, '*addhā*' in 9.3c and '*adabhra*' in 9.62d.

(3) The use of an ablative instead of an instrumental with '*parityakta*' in a construction which would seem properly to require an instrumental in 9.68a and 14.1a. This usage may be due to semantics.

(4) The usage of a nominative singular followed by '*iva*' in ascriptive statements which should properly use accusative singular feminines in 19.8b and 19.9ab.

There are also peculiarities which may have been in an autograph, or which may have been introduced into the MSS later on:

(1) The use of a nominal declension in the nominative plural for words ordinarily declined with a pronominal declension. This is the case in 15.3a with the word '*pūrvāḥ*,' and may be the case for the base form '*sarva*' in 14.23ab.

(2) The use of '*kvacid*' in the sense of '*kiṃcid*' and '*kecid*' in 10.3b and 10.6d.

Certain peculiarities certainly appear to have been introduced in the MSS themselves. One is the form '*adhairyatvād*' in 9.68c. Another is the usage of instrumental plurals in 13.4d. This seems clearly to be due to corruption. Others are *saṃdhi* peculiarities, for which see **§7.9b**.

8.6. Normalization. Normalization has generally been avoided as it was viewed that we should not be more consistent than the MSS and the author(s) seem to have been. This was particularly the case with regard to *saṃdhi*. Generally, though, the spelling of readings which agrees with that in Monier-Williams (1899) has been accepted. The one exception to this is that in cases where one of the readings contained a retroflex '*ḷ*,' the retroflex has been preserved. When a word was spelled with a retroflex '*ḷ*' in one place by a MS, but not elsewhere, though, the inconsistency has been preserved. Except for '*ch*'~'*cch*' and '*t*'~'*tt*' after '*r*', all variations in spelling have been shown in the critical apparatus as it was viewed that this was important sometimes in explaining variant readings proper. See **§9.3** below for this.

9. The Critical Apparatus.

9.1. DaCunha's edition treated as a manuscript. **9.2.** A new edition of the *uttarārdha* of the *Sahyādrikhaṇḍa*. **9.3.** All readings given. **9.4.** The ordering of the readings in the critical apparatus. **9.5.** The inclusion of additional material in the critical apparatus.

9.1. DaCunha's edition treated as a manuscript. As noticed in **§7.1** above, DaCunha's edition has been treated as a MS. It has not been given any more authority than any of the MSS proper in deciding the preferred readings. This course was decided on for two reasons: (1) We cannot ascertain how many MSS were utilized in the construction of the text for the PGN nor the rationale for deciding readings if more than one MS was used. (2) As described in **§3.3** and **§7.1**, the readings of the edition are not good. This suggests that it is perhaps only one MS, slightly 'cleaned up,' which is represented by the edition. Hereafter DaCunha's edition will be referred to as our MS. Ed when it is the text of the PGN in the edition which is being referred to.

9.2. A new edition of the *uttarārdha* of the *Sahyādrikhaṇḍa*. During the course of the preparation of this edition of the PGN an edition of the entire *uttarārdha*, together with translation into Marathi, was begun and to the best of my knowledge was completed by Gajanan Shastri Gaitonde of Bombay. Correspondence between myself and Mr. Gaitonde did make it apparent, though, that my approach to the text was different from Mr. Gaitonde's, and that reference to it in the critical apparatus here would be unnecessary if only because the undoubted value to be gained by such reference would not offset the undesirability of adding additional bulk to an already cumbersome and formidable apparatus. As it worked out, Mr. Gaitonde just adopted J. Gerson DaCunha's text for his edition – on the basis of my correspondence with him, with "corrections" and emendations here and there. See Gaitonde (pref. 1971).

9.3. All readings given. In the critical apparatus all readings of the collation have been given, spelling mistakes and peculiarities and *saṃdhi* irregularities included. The only readings omitted were '*ch*' for '*cch*,' as in '*gacchati*,' and double '*tt*' for '*t*' following an '*r*,' as in '*mārtaṇḍa*.' The reasoning behind such a comprehensive presentation is twofold. First, it was decided that this might be appreciated by the reader since the readings were so divergent and in many ways so bizarre, and since the readings which were chosen could nonetheless still entertain discussion. Secondly, it was decided that in several instances such detail was necessary since some readings which were nonsense words straddled two alternate readings and could therefore not be included very well as corruptions of either of those readings without presenting a picture which did not exist. It was then decided that comprehensiveness in listing the readings after L1a and L1c dropped out was necessary as a seeming nonsense reading might indicate that the present preferred reading was built on the nonsense word which had its source in another word which had given rise to the nonsense word, which in turn had given rise to the present chosen reading. A question mark in parentheses was used after the nonsense words. The use of parentheses around some of the readings indicates that these readings are almost certainly only easily explainable spelling mistakes which could in no way be taken to indicate that the text had, or which could in no way be taken to give the text itself, a different meaning or grammatical structure. The application of this principle, though, depended in large measure on the degree of difference between the reading in question and the other readings in any given entry. Whenever what was seen as a mistake had resulted in a new word, or a new possible position for that word in the sentence – this being due, for example, to a change of case or to the dropping of an ending so as to place that word in composition with the next, even if the word appeared to be nonsense, it was included as a separate reading.

9.4. The ordering of the readings in the critical apparatus. In the critical apparatus the readings have been ordered as follows: Ed L1a L1c L2 Bm M Br K L3. Ed has been placed first for purposes of easy reference for anyone who might want to compare it with the text as given in this edition. Following this are placed our two best MSS, keeping these in the order of their appearance in L1, and following these there is placed the last of the decent MSS. After this follow the more corrupt MSS with Bm and M, which fall together, following one after another. K, which is just a slightly corrupted copy of Ed, is place after Br. L3, which MS contains Skh.u. chapter 15 from our text only, and which MS was consulted at a later date than the other MSS, is placed last.

9.5. The inclusion of additional material in the critical apparatus. Also included in the critical apparatus is some information other than readings and sections of text omitted from this edition. There will be found there cross-references for parallel statements in the text, given with the chapter numbers agreeing with those in Ed, notices of the scriptual confusions which it was possible to isolate, and references to the introduction for spelling and *saṃdhi* peculiarities. The numbers referring to the introduction are indicated by the European number symbol and are in bold face type. It is hoped that these additions will be of help to the critical reader.

10. The Date of the Text

10.1. Multiple authorship of the *uttarārdha* of the *Sahyādrikhaṇḍa*. **10.2.** Previous attempts at dating the text. **10.3.** *Terminus post quem* for the text as represented by the manuscripts. **10.4.** *Terminus ante quem* for the text. **10.5.** *Terminus post quem* for the text.

10.1. Multiple authorship of the *uttarārdha* of the *Sahyādrikhaṇḍa*. As we have the text today, the four sections of the *uttarārdha* of the Skh appear to be stylistically distinct from one another. The second section of the *uttarārdha*, the MA (Skh.u. 7 and 8), which treats the introduction into the Sahyādri area of *brāhmaṇas* from Ahichatra in northern India by Mayūravarman, for example, is written in simple declarative sentences with simple Sanskrit vocabulary. The few vss. that describe the physical features of the area at the very beginning of this section (see Appendix D), however, demonstrate a different Sanskrit style of image heaped on image so as to form a lengthy hyperbole. This contrasts with the simple declarative style of the rest of these two chapters. The same description of the physical features of the area is found toward the beginning of the PGN, the third section of the *uttarārdha*. In this latter section, these vss. are somewhat disjunctive. This suggests that we have here a stock description that an author could draw on at will. Suggested as well is that these vss. may have been added in both contexts at the time of placing the second and third sections of the *uttarārdha* next to one another. It can be noted further that in the MSS, these sections appear to already have been placed next to one another by the time of our earliest numbering system for the chapters of the *uttarārdha*. This numbering system can be associated with out best MSS of the text.

The fourth section of the *uttarārdha*, which contains reference to Paraśurāma from the earlier sections, is composed of two chapters from the *Reṇukāmāhātmya* as in some MSS of that text. This *māhātmya*, or glorification, traditionally is attached to the Skh. The first of these chapters, as noted in **§1.3** above, also appears as the first chapter of the *Rāmakṣetramāhātmya*. The style of these two chapters is not one of simple declarative sentences, and it contrasts with the second section of the *uttarārdha* as much as it does with the PGN, the third section. It is clear that this section of the *uttarārdha* was attached to it for reasons of theme. It is not clear, however, at which point in the growth of the text it was so attached. MSS containing the text in its earliest stages of corruption are incomplete.

Within the PGN, we also have evidence that the last two histories, covering four chapters (Skh.u. 16-17, 18-19), are by a different hand than PGN chapters one through six (Skh.u. 9-14). For one thing, each of these histories is two chapters in length. While the first two PGN histories (Skh.u. 9 and 10) are so closely related that they can be understood to be a single history, they are nevertheless distinct in that each history discusses a different generation. In the case of the last two histories, however, neither chapter can stand without the other. The format of the last two histories is different.

Further, there is variation in the formulaic manners in which the histories begin and end.

And to note just one more point, there is a difference in vocabulary. The vocabulary of the last two histories contains far more retroflex consonants than the vocabulary of PGN chapters one through six.

Within the PGN, chapter seven (Skh.u. 15) also appears to be by a different hand. It is far shorter than the other chapters of the PGN. And its style appears to be more straightforward and simpler than that of the preceding PGN chapters. Verbal forms are simple; subordinate phrases are simple; sentence structure is simple. And its statements are brief. Its style is not as simple, though, as that found in Skh.u. 7 and 8, which chapters also treat

Mayūravarman introducing *brāhmaṇas* to the area from the north.

As well, within the PGN there are several short sections of text that contrast in style, content, or both style and content with surrounding sections of text.

One such section, the description of the land toward the beginning of the first history, has been noted above.

Another intance of a passage that contrasts contextually in style and content also occurs toward the beginning of the first history. In this section of text there is related in brief the origin of the Kroḍeśa *tīrtha*. The passage is juxtaposed with little connection to an account of Paraśurāma coming to the Sahyādri range of mountains, to which brief account of the description of the land is attached.

Further, after the description of the land in the first history, a 20-vs. *stotra* is spoken by Paraśurāma. This *stotra* breaks with the *śloka* meter of the rest of the text. It also differs in style from the rest of the text in that it is composed entirely of compounds that serve as laudations in the vocative case one on top of another. While the *stotra* follows contextually, as does the description of the land, it is not clear that its authorship is not as independent of the main narrative of the PGN as is the description of the land.

In instances such as these in the first chapter of the PGN, the juxtaposition of stylistically different sections of different authorship appears to have been effected by the author of the body of the PGN.

In other instances, though, this is not the case.

In the fourth history (Skh.u. 12), for example, there is a lengthy section of commentary within commentary, and elaborate and detailed ritual narrative that is not characteristic of the text. At some points, this section of text breaks with the standard *śloka* meter, breaking in fact with all meter. On account of the stylistic differences and contextual inappropriateness of these passages, they are clearly interpolations of later date than the text in which they are embedded. They are not integral to the text at any level. See Appendix B for these sections of text.

In another instance, in the second history (Skh.u. 10), brief scornful statements that are contextually inappropriate are added in a list of occupations practiced by the group with which the history is concerned. While they also are brief statements of occupation, they are clearly interpolations on account of the difference in tone between them and the text proper. These brief statements are given in the critical apparatus.

In such instances we have in the transmitted text of the PGN interpolations of spurious passages pure and simple.

This entire topic of multiple authorship of the *uttarārdha* of the Skh is discussed more fully in Levitt (1982).

Winternitz (1927: 462) wrote with regard to the *Mahābhārata* that "everything indicates that the *Mahābhārata* is not the work of one single author or of one time, but consists of earlier and later portions which belong to different centuries." He adds (1927: 469), "the date of each section, nay sometimes each single verse of the *Mahābhārata* must be determined separately ... ." What is true of *itihāsa* is also true of *purāṇa* (so also P. V. Kane, quoted above in **§5.1**).

10.2. Previous attempts at dating the text. Most previous attempts at dating sections of the Skh have focused themselves on the chapters of the *uttarārdha* of the Skh which treat the origins of the major brāhmaṇic groups in the area of the Sahyādri range of mountains. These have been on the whole less attempts at dating, however, than opinions attempting to establish these chapters as represented in poorly edited text as being of questionable authority.

The only attempt to date the specific text with which we are concerned here appears in Saletore (1936a: 342-347). This dating was based on an unedited text and did not distinguish between sections of the text which are discrete on stylistic and topical grounds and did not take into account the discontinuity between sections of the text.

Through a series of dubious correlations and identifications Saletore advances to a progressively later date the *terminus post quem* for his text as a unit. He states, however, that this does not preclude an earlier date for some of the material. His final decision is that those chapters which are here PGN chapters eight and nine (Skh.u. 16 and 17) were composed in the latter half of the fourteenth century A.D. He argues that the *Grāma-paddhati* as a unit must therefore be dated to the latter half of the fourteenth century A.D.

Saletore's most cogent arguments for the dating of those sections of the text which we refer to as the MA and PGN base themselves on four points which we will discuss in order.

(1) The first is that certain allusions to Mayūravarman and a narration of the distribution of thirty-two villages dates the text to after the fifth century A.D. With this date I have no argument. I hold reservations, however, about certain of the arguments advanced by Saletore.

(2) The second is that the king referred to in PGN chapter four (Skh.u. 12) as Vasu was the Ālupa king Vibudhavasu. This king ruled, by Saletore's dates, in

1244-1245 A.D. The text therefore must be dated after this.

Saletore's identification on the basis of one word which functions in one case as a name and in the other case as a member of a compound which is in its entirety the name is open to question. The name Vasu is not an uncommon one in Sanskrit literature. And it might very well be functioning here as an attributory or laudatory epithet. Saletore never offers a cogent argument for identifying the king Vasu of this story with the Ālupa king Vibudhavasu, despite Saletore (1936a: 124-125). Identification of the king Vasu of the story ought rest, I should think, on the identification of the time in which and king under whom the incident related occurred.

(3) The third point is that PGN chapters four and nine (Skh.u. 12 and 17) describe an ascetic who was probably Madhva, together with the method used by Madhva to convert people into the Vaiṣṇava fold. Therefore the text can be dated to Madhva's lifetime or after.

Saletore's identification here is based primarily on passages which clearly are interpolations in these two chapters. And the characater whom he identifies as Madhva in chapter four (Skh.u. 12) is clearly Paraśurāma on the basis of parallel descriptions elsewhere in the PGN. It is very probable that this is also the case in chapter nine (Skh.u. 17). Further, Saletore's identification of the character with Madhva is questionable even on the basis of the interpolations. The phrase in the interpolations which leads Saletore to identify the appearance of Paraśurāma with Madhva is in chapter four (Skh.u. 12). It reads, "ante yuge mādhvamatapracaṇḍam." This translates 'passionate about the thought of Madhva in the last *yuga*.' This passage clearly eliminates Madhva as the subject of the description. That the interpolations describes the way in which Madhva converted people into the Vaiṣṇava fold, and that Madhva's doctrines are specifically mentioned, does date the interpolations to after Madhva's lifetime, however.

(4) Finally, the fourth point is that PGN chapters eight and nine (Skh.u. 16 and 17) describe the judicial procedure in the court of a king named Vīra Bhūpa who is the Vijayanagar viceroy Vīra Bhūpati, son of Yuva Bukka, who was placed over a city in Karnataka, his "provincial capital," in 1386 A.D. The text therefore can be dated *in final form* [italics mine] to the latter half of the fourteenth century A.D. The judicial incident described in these chapters has been noted in Western sources regarding Mariāda-rāman (see **§12.4**). I have not been able to find any details regarding the life of this popular figure in Telugu and Tamil lore. In the translation here '*vīrabhūpa*' has been translated not as a personal name but rather as a very usual description of a king in general.

10.3. *Terminus post quem* for the text as represented by the manuscripts. The *terminus post quem* for the text as represented by all the MSS used for this edition, with the possible exception of L1a, cannot be before the middle of the thirteenth century A.D. This conclusion is based on the inclusion in all MSS except L1a of an insert between Skh.u. 12.41 and 12.42 which refers to the thought of the adherents of Madhva. Madhva, the expounder of the *Dvaita* doctrine, was a Kanarese *brāhmaṇa* born about 1200 A.D. In all probability the text as represented by MS. L1a can also be placed after the middle of the thirteenth century. I suggest this assumption because the text of L1a is not appreciably better than or different from that of L1c, which includes this insert. This cannot be stated with certainty, however, as the text of L1a ends with Skh.u. 10.

Further, L2 Bm M as they contain PGN chapters eight and nine (Skh.u. 16 and 17) which refers to an incident associated with Mariada-Ramen, and to the fate of his family after this, must be dated to at least two generations after Mariada-Raman. See **§10.5** below. Saletore implies that the date of Mariāda-rāman would be in the latter half of the fourteenth century A.D. So also, as Ed and K contain these two chapters, they too must be similarly dated. K, as noted in **§7.7**, is in the main a copy of Ed.

10.4. *Terminus ante quem* for the text. The *terminus ante quem* for the main body of the PGN would also be in the middle of the thirteenth century A.D. The argument is that the text existed already at a time when Madhva's philosophy was ascendent in the area. It is only such ascendency which can explain the unnecessary and marginal inclusion of a reference to this philosophy. Had the text itself been written at a time when Madhva's thought was ascendent, it could be argued that the same forces which led to the inclusion of a reference to it in what is judged to be an earlier text would have led to the inclusion of more integral references to it in the text proper.

This argument is strengthened by the fact that Madhva wrote a commentary on the *Jñānayogakhaṇḍa* of the Skp which as noted in **§4.3** is nearly identical with the *ādirahasya* of the Skh. It would appear from this that a case can be built for a close relationship between the Skh and the followers of Madhva starting in Madhva's lifetime, though as noted in **§4.3** the same forces that led Madhva to write his commentary may have also led to the transposition of the *Jñānayogakhaṇḍa* to the Skh, perhaps at a date anterior to Madhva.

Kane (1930-62/2.1[=1941]: 69), we should note, implies that at least chapter 26 of the *ādirahasya* of the Skh, as in DaCunha's edition, was written before 1000 A.D. This is one of the chapters of the *ādirahasya* that is not found in the *Jñānayogakhaṇḍa*. Should Kane's date stand, it lends additional support to a date prior to Madhva for the other regional material in the Skh as well.

And paleographically, it would seem that the main body of the PGN can be dated to a period before the modern form of *Devanāgarī* '*bh*' which made its appearance in the eleventh to twelfth centuries A.D. took on its more modern *Devanāgarī* distinctive features. See Levitt (1979a) and Bühler (1904: 74 [§24.24]), and **§7.9a** above.

An earlier *terminus ante quem* for the main body of the PGN and for chapter seven (Skh.u. 15) can be argued for here also on the basis that inscriptions indicate that when the Kadamas re-emerged from political obscurity in the tenth century A.D. they had lost sight of their origin (Rice 1886-1905/7[=1902]: Sk 117 and Sk 236, 8[=1902]: Sb 262, and 11[=1902]: Dg 35 regarding inscriptions in Shimoga District and Chitaldroog District; 1909: 27-28; 1931: 7-11). The PGN, and the MA preceding it in the *uttarārdha* of the Skh, however, both show realistic historical awareness of early Kadamba history. This may be taken to indicate that the two texts were composed before such awareness can be demonstrated to have been lost, which would be before the tenth century A.D. Standing with a later date is preferable, however, as it is possible that it is a social and cultural process that can explain what may be only a seeming ignorance of early Kadamba history. It could be that a mythological origin of the dynasty was required for purposes of legitimization.

10.5. *Terminus post quem* for the text. The only guide we have for the *terminus post quem* is the naming of kings in the different chapters of the PGN; and for the last four chapters of the PGN, the identification of the minister in chapters eight and nine (Skh.u. 16 and 17). Of the kings named, only one, Mayūravarman, can be identified with certainty. See **§10.2**, and below **§12.5** and **§12.5a**. His date is set by Rice (1909: 27) at the beginning of the fourth century A.D. Moraes (1931: 14) follows J. F. Fleet's dating of Kākusthavarman, Mayūravarman's great-grandson, for which see Fleet (1877: 23). He dates Mayūravarman at about 345-370 A.D. Both Rice and Moraes arrive at their dates for Mayūravarman in large through the date given to the Halsi plates of Kākusthavarman which state that they were written in the eightieth year of what Moraes (1931: 16-17) refers to as "an unknown era, called the year of victory." Rice (1909: 23) instead of postulating an unknown era, gives the term "*svavaijaika*," and notes that it has no explanation. For these plates, see Fleet (1877: 23). Both the gentlemen under discussion take the beginning of the eighty year period to be the independence of the Kadambas from Pallava control which is reputed to have been effected by Mayūravarman.

It can be postulated that the date of the body of our text and of chapter seven (Skh.u. 15) which we judge to be by a different hand is posterior to whatever date is decided on for Mayūravarman.

It further can be postulated that the body of our text must be dated to a period after Mayūravarman because of mention of the *brāhmaṇas* of the thirty-two villages. These were established finally by either Mayūravarman or his son. See **§12.6** for a discussion of the historical problem with regard to this. Their establishment is implicit in chapters one, four, and six (Skh.u. 9, 12 and 14). A certain amount of time between the settlement of the *brāhmaṇas* of the thirty-two villages and the expulsion of pregnant widows by these *brāhmaṇas*, as mentioned in chapter one (Skh.u. 9), must be allowed. Therefore we can be safe if we state that the date of the body of the PGN cannot be before the reign of Mayūravarman's son referred to as Kaṅgavarman in the inscriptions and as Candrāṅgada in Skh.u. 8, that is, in the MA, or before the reign of his son, referred to as Bhagīratha in the inscriptions. The dates for Bhagīratha would be the end of the fourth century A.D. according to Rice's dating, and in the end of the fourth century through the beginning of the fifth century according to Moraes' dating. Moraes would have Bhagīratha be a contemporary of Kālidāsa and would have it be Bharīratha's court that Kālidāsa visited in his capacity as ambassador of Chandragupta II.

Thus the *terminus post quem* for the main portion of the PGN and for PGN chapter seven (Skh.u. 15) can be set between the beginning of the fourth century A.D. and the beginning of the fifth century A.D.

As noted in **§10.1**, though, chapters eight through eleven (Skh.u. 16-17, 18-19) are by still a different hand than the body of the PGN and are most certainly a later addition. Here, in chapters eight and nine, we have mention of an incident that can be identified with a certain wise Mariāda-rāman, a figure popular in Telugu and Tamil lore. As noted in **§10.2**, Saletore places this incident in the court of the Vijayanagar viceroy Vīra Bhūpati, whom he dates to the late fourteenth century A.D. Also as noted, I have not been able to find any independent information regarding Māriada-rāman. As chapter nine refers as well to the fate of the son of Mariāda-rāman and his family, however, the *terminus post quem* for these four chapters, which would seem to have been incorporated into the text of the PGN at the same time, would be at least two generations after Mariāda-rāman.

11. The Shape of the Text.

11.1. The speakers. **11.2.** The mythological introduction. **11.3.** The *stotra*. **11.4.** Verses or penances at the end of chapters.

11.1. The speakers. The PGN, as all Purāṇic texts, is a discussion between speakers, here between Śatānīka and Śaunaka. This discussion is embedded in another between the *ṛṣis* and Sūta. In the course of the text the discourse of various persons within the stories is similarly embedded in Śaunaka's speech, though there is never any other discussion between two speakers. The four discussants in the PGN are identified here for the convenience of the reader and so that the reader will be able to put the text in the mythological framework intended by its author(s) or compiler.

11.1a. The *ṛṣis*. Many Purāṇic texts are conversations between the *ṛṣis*, or sometimes one *ṛṣi*, and another personage or personages. See, for example, the *Devīmāhātmya* in Agrawala (1963). It is often impossible to discover or know with certainty the identity of the *ṛṣi* or *ṛṣis*. In the present case, though, the discussion being between the *ṛṣis* and Sūta and the evidence of narration in chapter 20 of the *uttarārdha* of the Skh point to the identity of the *ṛṣis* with those who had assembled to attend the twelve year sacrifice of Śaunaka given in the Naimiṣa forest. This is the group to whom the *Mahābhārata* was related by Sūta. See the *Ādiparvan* of the *Mahābhārata* as in vol. 1 of the critical edition of the *Mahābhārata* (Sukthankar 1928-33: 5) and vol. 1 of the English translation of the Calcutta edition of the *Mahābhārata* (Roy 1893, 2nd ed. [1962 ?]: 1), or Pusalker (1955b: xxiii).

11.1b. Sūta. There is much confusion in the literature as to whether the speaker of *Purāṇas*, Sūta / *sūta*, is to be taken as another name of Lomaharṣana or Romaharṣana, and thus be the proper name of a pupil of Vyāsa, or is to refer merely to any bard or panegyrist, who would have served the function of being a charioteer also. Kane (1930-62/5.2[=1962]: 862-864) would have the term '*sūta*' refer to a bard and charioteer of *pratiloma* descent, but argues that he was deified by the time of Kautilya's *Arthaśāstra* because it was believed to be scandalous that great sages could have learned *Purāṇas* from someone of mixed descent. In the context of the PGN he is clearly an identifiable person who is the same as the narrator of the *Mahābhārata* to the *ṛṣis*. Dikshitar (1951-55/3[=1955]: 680) lists him to be versed in *Purāṇas*, *Itihāsas*, and *Dharmaśāstras* and to be the expounder of these who is addressed by *ṛṣis*, Śaunaka and others. He also notes that Sūta was insulted by Balarāma and identifies him as Romaharṣaṇa, the pupil of Vyāsa who narrated the *Purāṇa* to the sages assembled for the sacrifice at Kurukṣetra. For his various names see the critical apparatus for vs. 1.1.8 in vol. 1 of the critical edition of the *Mahābhārata* (Sukthankar 1928-33: 6).

11.1c. Śaunaka. Śaunaka is the son of Śunaka. His great-grandfather Pramathi is ascribed with the authorship of the 27th hymn of *maṇḍala* 2 of the *Ṛgveda* according to Devi ([n.d.]), who mentions Śaunaka on pp.54 and 69. We should note, though, that Aufrecht (1877/2: 472) lists the author of *Ṛgveda* 2.27-29 as Kūrma Gārtsamada, or Gṛtsamada. Śaunaka is listed by Dikshitar (1951-55/3[=1955]: 468) as having addressed Sūta as to the circumstances of the composition of the *Bhāgavata-purāṇa*. He is noted there to have had his residence in *Naimiṣālaya*, to have taught knowledge of *astra* and *kriyā* to Śatānīka, to have initiated Śatānīka into *ātmajñāna*, to have been a pupil of Pathya, to have divided the *Atharvasaṃhitā* between his two disciples Babhra and Saindhavāyana, to have formed four 'castes' under him, and to have asked Vaiśampāyana for a *śānti* ritual.

11.1d. Śatānīka. According to Devi ([n.d.]: 69) Śatānīka was a son of Janamejaya who was put on the throne when Janamejaya was dethroned. He was versed in the *trayī vidyā*, or triple sacred science of reciting hymns, performing sacrifices and chanting. Dikshitar (1951-55/3[=1955]: 377) notes that he was a pupil of Yājña-valkya and of Śaunaka, that he learned the science of arms from Kṛpa, that he was anointed by *brāhmaṇas*, that he performed an *aśvamedha*, that he was the father of Sahasrānīka, and that he realized *ātmajñāna* from Śaunaka and attained *nirvāṇa*.

11.2. The mythological introduction. Thus the PGN is introduced by placing the narration of its events in what by the time of its composition can have been no more than a mythological convention. Whether or not this was utilized to provide the text with authority is a moot point. We must assume that those who first heard it were aware of the discrepancy between the period of the events described in the text and whatever period their minds may have ascribed to the twelve year sacrifice given by Śaunaka and the time when Śatānīka studied under Śaunaka, and that this discrepancy did not matter.

There is also a mythological introduction to the events of the PGN as spoken by Śaunaka in chapter one (Skh.u. 9). This is the brief mention of the *muni* Kroḍa. Kroḍa brings under control Viṣṇu, goes to Kroḍeśa, sets up an *āśrama* there, and lives happily. At present it is perhaps best to view this as the mentioning of a situation somewhat parallel to that of the pregnant widows of chapter one (Skh.u. 9) which has been included in order to make this chapter into a glorification of Kroḍeśa, or to be the ending of a preceding story in the text's original (?) environment. It apparently did appear peculiar to the source of L1a and L1c or to a scribe who had copies of both MSS at hand as there is inserted a return to the story between Skh.u. 9.29b and c in both MSS. It must be added that we should not be surprised if future research into the PGN shows these few verses to be spurious.

Following this is another mythological section describing Paraśurāma's arrival in the Sahyādri range. This introduces the only recurrent protagonist in the PGN and serves to provide the author with an opportunity to glorify the land as well as to place the entire PGN in the framework of a glorification of Paraśurāma.

11.3. The *stotra*. In chapter one (Skh.u. 9) there is a *stotra* of twenty vss. in Vasantatilaka and Toṭaka meters praising Viṣṇu. It is spoken by Paraśurāma after doing *pūjā* in the land of the Tuḷus. For these vss. I have checked, but without success, both Vaidya (1967-71) and Bhatt (1961 and 1966). If the *stotra* is not original in the PGN, it is also not to be found in either of these works. But a good argument can be made that the *stotra*, though it may be an accretion as our MS. L1c does not contain it, is at least original in the PGN as we have it, on the grounds that there is precedent for the inclusion of such *stotras* in Purāṇic texts. The reader is referred to chapter 60 of the *ādirahasya* of the Skh as in DaCunha's edition, titled "*brahmakṛtaśivastuti*," 'The Praise of Śiva made by Brahman,' which also contains a *stotra*, though in *śloka* meter. The reader is also referred to *adhyāyas* 73 and 76 of the *Himavatkhaṇḍa* as in Naraharinath (1957: 160-164 and 168-171). We have there two *stotras*: the first in Bhujaṅgaprayāta meter, spoken by the *yogins*; the second in both Indravajra and Bhujaṅgaprayāta meters, spoken by Īśvara.

11.4. Verses or penances at the end of chapters. At the end of the first three chapters of the PGN (Skh.u. 9, 10 and 11) we find vss. which break the *śloka* meter of the rest of the text. The first of these is in Gīti meter, the second in Upendravajra meter and the third in Upajāti meter, this latter being a combination of Upendravajra and Indravajra meters. A comparison with the ends of the chapters of the Skh would lead us to believe these vss. are spurious. In the *uttarārdha*, for example, the only other chapter ending with such a vs. is chapter 7. The *Himavatkhaṇḍa*, though, as in Naraharinath (1957) has such vss. at the ends of its chapters more often than not. We might be justified therefore in assuming the inclusion of such vss. at the ends of chapters is firmly established within the Purāṇic tradition at some point in its development at least, and that therefore these vss. may very well not be spurious. An examination of the contents of these vss. and of the vss. immediately preceding them, indicates that in the case of the second and third chapters of the PGN (Skh.u. 10 and 11) these vss. are integral to the text. They are there formulas for expiation being recited by Śaunaka, and are clearly introduced by the vss. preceding them. Without these vss. the chapters would be incomplete. In the case of the vs. at the end of the first chapter of the PGN (Skh.u. 9), and of the vs. at the end of chapter 7 of the *uttarārdha*, this is not the case. They are laudatory. In every respect they are superfluous. We must accept them for the time being, at least, on the basis of precedent.

At the end of chapters four, five, six, and nine (Skh.u. 12, 13, 14, and 17) penances are mentioned. This is parallel to the providing of expiatory formulas at the end of chapters two and three (Skh.u. 10 and 11). These penances or expiatory formulas are provided for the person who sees the various communities discussed in the chapters. At the end of chapter eleven (Skh.u. 19) a penance is provided for one of the communities discussed in the chapter. This is unusual and therefore may be due to corruption which we cannot weed out given the state of preservation of our sources. Except for chapter seven (Skh.u. 15), the other chapters which do not end with expiations – chapters one, eight and ten (Skh.u. 9, 16 and18) – are the first halves of stories which cover two chapters each. This would explain why they do not end with expiations. The lack of an expiation at the end of chapter seven (Skh.u. 15), however, is an indication, together with its brevity and style, that the chapter is by a different hand

12. Historicity of the stories.

12.1. The mythological elements. **12.2.** Paraśurāma. **12.3.** Problem in deciding historicity. **12.4.** Incidents narrated in the *Pātityagrāmanirṇaya* as mentioned in Western sources. **12.5.** Proper names mentioned. **12.6.** Historical problems. **12.7.** Anthropological problems. **12.8.** Care should be taken in extracting historical and anthropological points.

12.1. The mythological elements. There are several clearly mythological elements in the stories proper. One is the usage in chapters two, four and nine (Skh.u. 10, 12 and 17) of a *deus ex machina*, a voice in the sky, to set things straight. In chapter two (Skh.u. 10) it announces to the *guru* Somapīṭhin where he is to set up villages for the purified *golakas*; in chapter four (Skh.u. 12) it announces to the king that the supposed voice of the earth which he had heard was that of a man; and in chapter nine (Skh.u. 17) it announces to the *brāhmaṇas* who had just discovered a wicker-work basket with a sacred Śālagrāma stone in it that they are to make a village at that spot. Another mythological element is the appearance in chapter five (Skh.u. 13) of the *ṛṣi* Kaṇva, an author of several hymns of the *Ṛgveda*, who tells the pregnant widows whom the story is about where to go to relieve their suffering. The fire which comes from the hand of the *brāhmaṇa* to burn down part of the assembly hall in chapter ten (Skh.u. 18), and perhaps also the portents, or *utpātas*, which are mentioned in the beginning of chapter nine (Skh.u. 17), may also be viewed as mythological elements. Clearly, though, the most significant mythological element is the appearance in chapters one, two, four, five, and perhaps nine (Skh.u. 9, 10, 12, 13, and 17) of Paraśurāma, and the mentioning of him as having established *brāhmaṇas* in chapter seven (Skh.u. 15).

12.2. Paraśurāma. Paraśurāma is the son of Jamadagni, a *ṛṣi* descended from Bhṛgu, and Reṇukā, and is reckoned to be the sixth *avatāra* of Viṣṇu. There are three major story complexes which center around him:

(1) At his father's request he consents to kill his mother, but as the reward for this he asks a boon. Jamadagni agrees and Paraśurāma kills Reṇukā. He then requests Jamadagni to bring Reṇukā back to life as part of his boon.

(2) He exterminates the *kṣatriyas* from the earth twenty-one times and gives the earth to the *brāhmaṇas*.

(3) He reclaims the Konkani and Malabar coasts from the sea and peoples the Konkan.

Paraśurāma is particularly venerated on the western coast of India, but his legend is very popular among groups throughout India. Most of the artisan castes reported in the various volumes of the 'Tribes and Castes' series, for instance, claim that they were once *kṣatriyas* who disguised themselves as artisans to escape destruction at Paraśurāma's hand. Considering the mythological importance of Paraśurāma, pitifully little work has been done on him.

In the PGN, his arrival in the Konkan is mentioned in the beginning of chapter one (Skh.u. 9) and is used as the framework for a lengthy listing of animals, plants and so forth in the area of the Sahyādri range of mountains. It is also used as an excuse for a twenty vs. *stotra* praising Viṣṇu, which is put in Paraśurāma's mouth.

After this, Paraśurāma figures mainly as a god of compassion – for unfortunate *brāhmaṇas*, at least. In chapters one and five (Skh.u. 9 and 13) he becomes the benefactor of pregnant *brāhmaṇa* widows and helps to settle them; in chapter two (Skh.u. 10) he becomes the benefactor of the *golakas* born to one of these groups of women and commands an established *guru* to perform *saṃskāras* for them and to establish them; and in chapters four and perhaps nine (Skh.u. 12 and 17) he purifies *brāhmaṇas* who have been excommunicated so that they can return to their proper dwellings. In short Paraśurāma appears in several chapters of the PGN as the resident deity of the area who is constantly performing *tapas* or traveling from one holy place to another and who, when called on to do so, performs acts of compassion.

12.3. Problem in deciding historicity. We should not dismiss the historicity of these stories, however, because of the intrusion of mythological elements. The function of mythology in the telling of history is a complex topic too involved to be gone into here in detail. Briefly, it may be said to legitimatize events, or to glorify a supernatural agency or supernatural agencies, or to serve a function in the community for whom the history is intended, and so forth. In stories of the type here it may also be used for purposes of literature or literary convention. In short, the incorporation of mythology into narratives of events does not vitiate the historicity of these narratives.

From the other side of the coin, though, we must keep in mind that it is also impossible to ascertain with certainty the historicity of the stories in the PGN, if only in their general outline, even should we account for mythological aspects of the stories in either an anthropological or literary fashion.

Several of the stories clearly appear to be historical, though. That of chapter seven (Skh.u. 15) certainly is in accord with what has been known for a long time – that Mayūravarman of the Kadamba dynasty brought *brāhmaṇas* into his kingdom from elsewhere in India. It has never been noted that he brought *brāhmaṇas* from Ballabhī, however. That of chapter four (Skh.u. 12) finds a parallel with regard to the cause of *pātitya* status among a small community of Kōtas in Karnataka reported by Thurston (1909/4: 31) and Anantakrishna Iyer (1928-36/2: 313-314). That of chapter two (Skh.u. 10) regarding areca nut cultivation has 'historical' parallels reported of the Kotippattans, a Kerala community, by Thurston (1909/4: 32) and of the Tirguls, or Trigarths, by Enthoven (1920-21/1: 249), both of which groups were polluted on account of cultivating betel vine. That of chapter one (Skh.u. 9) regarding pregnant widows also finds an 'historical' parallel in one of the stories told of the latter group as reported by Enthoven in the same place. The mentioning of the thirty-two villages in chapters one, four and six (Skh.u. 9, 12 and 14) may eventually prove to be important to historians of Karnataka. This is discussed below in **§12.6.**

Nonetheless, for the events noted in most of the stories of the PGN we have no historical evidence at present. This is probably more of an indication of the lack of research on this type of text, however, than of the lack of historicity for the events themselves. The lack of research on this type of text is what probably is responsible for the situation discussed in **§12.5**, **§12.5a**, **§12.5b**, and **§12.5c** below. It is noted there that in most cases the names of kings, etc., in these stories are not known from inscriptions. This does not mean that the kings, etc., are mythological, or original with our text, as elsewhere in the *uttarārdha* of the Skh we are presented with the same situation with regard to the name of a king. But there the event is one which we know of from inscriptions. The king's name in the inscriptions is different.

In short, the stories appear to have historical foundation, this opinion being based on the evidence we have for some of the stories and for some of the matters mentioned in the stories. We do not have enough corroboratory evidence for the stories, however. Without this evidence, even were we to accept general historicity for the stories, we cannot move that we have reliable histories. The mythological elements confound things even more as they often give cause rather than allowing situations and events to provide cause. Because of this we may get stories which function well in the social and cultural system of their day, or which helped glorify gods, but which certainly fall short of total acceptability for historical veracity for modern western world historiography.

12.4. Incidents narrated in the *Pātityagrāmanirṇaya* as mentioned in Western sources. The incident described in PGN chapter eight (Skh.u. 16) and the determination of guilt as described in chapter nine (Skh.u. 17), vss. 1-22 corresponds to a story told of the famous judge Mariadi-ramen [Mariyātai-rāmaṉ] by Father Jean Venant Bouchet in a letter written in 1714 A.D. from Pondicherry to a great man in France. See Rocher (1984: 22-24). Rocher points out that the story as told by Bouchet corresponds generally to the narration of "The Child Murderess Detected" in Ramachandra Rao (1902: 5-10): "details vary, but the solution is identical." See also Goonetilleke (1890: 11-13) which mentions the version of the story recounted by Father Bouchet (pp. 12-13), but which also recounts a version in which the father of Mariāda-rāman suspects his son's accepting the position of judge with the king would lead to his son's disgrace; and in which the child is killed because it awoke and cried while the wife was entertaining her paramour – which explains the comparable incident that leads to the downfall of our *brāhmaṇa*'s family in chapter nine (Skh.u. 17). See also, in this regard, **§10.2** (end of discussion).

Thurston (1909/4: 31) and Ananthakrishna Iyer (1928-36/2: 313-314), as noted in **§12.3** immediately above, refer to a small group in Mysore called Kōta, confined to the Kādur district and said to be immigrants from the northern part of Udipi taluk in South Canara. They are said to have been originally from the Kōta *brāhmaṇa* community, but were cursed to lose their rank for 700 years because their ancestors, or perhaps only one of their ancestors, committed perjury in a land case. The Kōta *brāhmaṇa* community, as such, takes its name from a village of that name in the northern part of Udipi taluk (Thurston 1909/1: 384). I correct here my earlier opinion (Levitt 1973: xliv, 111) that this community is to be identified with the *brāhmaṇas* who committed perjury in a land dispute in PGN chapter four (Skh.u. 12). Despite the similar cause for fallen status and a roughly similar name, it is not clear at all that they are the same as the *brāhmaṇas* of our story. These were from Koṭīśvara, and engaged in a land dispute with *brāhmaṇas* from Kūṭa. Kōta *brāhmaṇas* are an entirely different community. As noted in **§12.3** immediately above, all we can say is that the situation which led to *pātitya* status was comparable for the two communities.

12.5. Proper names mentioned. As noted in **§12.3**, many of the proper names in the stories of the PGN are not found elsewhere, even though there is indication from elsewhere in the *uttarārdha* of the Skh that this does not reflect on the historicity of the people and places themselves, but rather on our ignorance due to lack of familiarity with the specifics of this type of text. In some cases, because of the lack of corroboratory evidence, we cannot be certain of the names, usually when these are unusual. Such is the case in chapter two (Skh.u. 10) where the names of the newly consecrated *brāhmaṇa golakas* are given. Another is in chapter three (Skh.u. 11), where we cannot be sure of the names of the two *śūdra* chiefs. Listed here are the persons, places and rivers mentioned, as these have been made out, together with their identifications when this proved to be possible. Among the sources consulted were *The Imperial Gazetteer of India*, new ed. (1907-1909); Smith ([n.d.]); Bajpai (1967); Cunningham (1871); Sircar (1951); Mysore [State, India], *List of Villages in Mysore State* (1969); and many maps. Omitted from the list of places are all the names of the various polluted *brāhmaṇa* villages, with three exceptions which it may have been possible to locate using the sources available. Also omitted are the well-known geographical names listed in the beginning of chapter five (Skh.u. 13). A complete listing of the villages mentioned, of the well-known geographical names, and of all persons, places, rivers, etc., with their locations in the text, is given in the index. The reader is also referred to Appendix A where a map showing the modern-day locations of places and rivers mentioned in identifications below for the area under discussion in the PGN are given, and also for a map showing the locations of the ancient countries, regions and cities mentined in the PGN outside of this area.

12.5a. Persons.

Candradatta: An unidentified king, possibly of the Kadamba dynasty, ruling in the area of the thirty-two villages. Mentioned in chapter six (Skh.u. 14).

Guṇanidhi, Guṇavatī and Guṇamāliṇī: A *brāhmaṇa* of the city Vijaya and his two wives. Mentioned in chapters eight and nine (Skh.u. 16 and 17).

Hemamālin: An unidentified king of Kaliṅga. Mentioned in chapter ten (Skh.u. 18).

Ketu and Muddakunda (?): Two *śūdra* chiefs, perhaps agnates, ruling in the area of the thirty-two villages. Mentioned in chapter three (Skh.u. 11). See chapter three (Skh.u. 11), translation, n. 1.

Kroḍa (perhaps, Kroḍamuni): An unidentified *muni* who made an *āśrama* near Kroḍeśa and Kroḍapattana. Mentioned in chapter one (Skh.u. 9). See chapter one (Skh.u. 9), translation, n. 8.

Mayūravarman: Noted to be the founder of the Kadamba dynasty. Ruled in either the beginning or middle of the fourth century A.D. See **§10.5** above. Mentioned in chapter seven (Skh.u. 15).

Somapīṭhin: An unidentified *agnīdhra* priest dwelling on the shore of the western ocean near Kroḍeśa and Kroḍapattana. Mentioned in chapter two (Skh.u. 10).

Sunīta: A *brāhmaṇa* from Gorāṣṭra; son of the *brāhmaṇa* who is the subject of chapters ten and eleven (Skh.u. 18 and 19). Mentioned in chapter eleven (Skh.u. 19).

Vasu: An unidentified king, possibly of the Kadamba dynasty, ruling in the area of the thirty-two villages. For an alternate identification, which we find questionable, however, see **§10.2** above. Mentioned in chapter four (Skh.u. 12).

Vīrabhūpa (?): Possible name of a king ruling in Vijaya. See **§10.2** above. Possibly mentioned in chapter eight (Skh.u. 16).

12.5b. Places.

Avimukta: An unidentified *tīrtha* to the south of Gokarṇa. Mentioned in chapter nine (Skh.u. 17).

Ananteśa: An unidentified *tīrtha*. Bajpai (1967: 21) notes that an Anantaśaila is mentioned in the *Śaktisaṅgamatantra* as forming the boundary of the Kerala country and speculates that it may be Trivandrum which is known as Anantaśayana or Anantapura (modern-day Tiruvananthapuram). This identification is to be viewed with cautious reserve, however. Note *The Imperial Gazetteer of India* (1907-1909/5[=1908]: 350) where a village named Anantapura in Shimoga District, Mysore (modern-day Karnataka) is listed, albeit with a notation that the village's name has been changed from Anandapura. Mentioned in chapter nine (Skh.u. 17).

Ballabhī, or Vallabhī, Balabhī, Valabhī: An ancient city in Saurāṣṭra (Kathiāwār) which was a major center of Jaininsm. In the fifth century A.D., the Śvetāmbara Jain canon was settled and reduced to writing at a council at Ballabhī (Valabhī). The city is also mentioned in Daṇḍin's sixth century A.D. *Daśakumāracarita*, chapter nine ["Mitragupta's Adventure"] (Ryder 1927: 173). Cunningham (1871) notes it to have been founded possibly in 319 A.D., the starting date of the Balabhī era, and to have been sacked and destroyed in 658 A.D. *The Imperial Gazetteer of India* (1907-1909/25[=1909]: 607b) lists its dates as 480 A.D. to 790 A.D. Mentioned in chapter seven (Skh.u. 15).

Gokarṇa: A place of pilgrimage. *The Imperial Gazetteer of India* (1907-1909/12[=1908]) notes it to be a town in Kumta *tāluka* of North Kanara District, Bombay, situated in 14°32' N. and 74°19' E., 10 miles north of Kumta town. This is in modern-day Karnataka. It is noted there to be a place of pilgrimage frequented by Hindu devotees from all parts of India, and is noted to contain Mahābaleshwar temple. See Mahābaleśa below. At variance with this, Pusalker (1955a: 10) notes it to have been probably the southern limit of the Konkan coast. Mentioned in chapters one, two and nine (Skh.u. 9, 10 and 17).

Gorāṣṭra: An unidentified country on the Konkan coast not far from Vijaya. Gokarṇa appears to be within it. Often understood to be a Sanskrit name for Goa. Mentioned in chapters five, eight, nine, and ten (Skh. 13, 16, 17, and 18).

Kāñcanamālinī: An unidentified city in Kaliṅga. Mentioned in chapter ten (Skh.u. 18).

Koṭi / Koṭīśvara, Kūṭa and Koṭiliṅgeśa: Koṭi / Koṭīśvara and Koṭiliṅgeśa are the names of a village and perhaps a *tīrtha*. Koṭi / Koṭīśvara is noted in chapter four (Skh.u. 12) to have been, originally at least, near the village Kūṭa. The original village would seem to have been near the ocean, which is noted to be the place to which the *brāhmaṇas* of Koṭi / Koṭīśvara of our story travel and where they meet Paraśurāma after having been excommunicated. Just so, Koṭiliṅgeśa would seem to be near the ocean. Can we suggest that the villagers of Koṭi / Koṭīśvara have settled elsewhere after being ejected from the Koṭi of the text? The text is ambiguous as to whether they did settle elsewhere or whether they retuned to their original home. Kūṭa is the name of a village which, according to our lists of the thirty-two villages, was numbered as one of these. It shared a border with the village Koṭi / Koṭīśvara according to chapter four (Skh.u. 12). We should note that there is a modern-day village named Kōṭēshwar, the seat of the influential Kōṭēshwar *brāhmaṇas* in Coondapoor *tāluka*, Mysore (Karnataka). Could this be the original Koṭīśvara which the inhabitants of Kūṭa were given by the king? One point in favor of such identification is that modern Kōṭēshwar *brāhmaṇas* claim their village to be one of the original thirty-two villages. If their ancestors were originally inhabitants of Kūṭa, a village bordering on the original Koṭīśvara, and if this Kūṭa was the same as that of our lists of the thirty-two villages, then this may be taken as a somewhat plausible statement. There is not enough evidence yet to draw definite conclusions, however. Also to be kept in mind is that there is a festival in Kadod, about ten miles to the east of Broach, in honor of Mahādeo under the name Koteshwar or Kotilingeshwar. This is reported in *The Imperial Gazetteer of India* (1907-1909/14[=1908]: 260-261). See **§12.4** and **§12.6** for further discussion.

Kroḍapattana, Kroḍeśa / Kroḍeśvara and Kroḍa: Names of an unidentified city, *tīrtha* and mountain on the route from Mount Mahendra and the Tuḷu country to Gokarṇa. Mentioned in chapters one, two, five, and nine (Skh.u. 9, 10, 13, and 17).

Kuśasthalī: The name of a village in chapter seven in L3 (Skh.u. 15.13a). Kuśasthalī is the name of a village in Goa. It is also the ancient name of the city of Dvāraka in Saurāṣṭra. The name is not an uncommon place name. The *Rāmāyaṇa* and *Vāyupurāṇa* refer to it as the capital of the ancient north Indian country of Kosala, for instance. It is as well the ancient name of Kusinārā, where the Buddha's *nirvāṇa* took place (Damodara Nambiar 1973-79: 409). It too is the name of a community of Sārasvata *brāhmaṇas* who are said to have come to Kanara from Goa in the sixteenth century A.D. with the establishment of the inquisition in Goa, perhaps earlier with the coming of the Portuguese to Goa, or even with the fall of Goa to the Mohammedans in the mid-fifteenth century A.D. (Bombay [Presidency] 1883/15.1: 168). J. Kamat (2010) mentions that the Kuśasthalī *brāhmaṇas* migrated from northern India to Kuśasthalī in Saurāṣṭra and from there to Goa. As Ballabhī from where Mayūravarman is said to have brought *brāhmaṇas* is as well in Saurāṣṭra, this suggests that the Kuśasthalī of our story is the Goan village by this name. We cannot be sure, though, without identifying the Cakranadī river on the shores of which this *brāhmaṇa* community in our story is said to be found. See **§12.6** below for further discussion.

Mahābaleśa: Name of a *tīrtha* in Gokarṇa. It is on the Śuktimatī river. Mentioned in chapter nine (Skh.u. 17).

Mahendra: An unidentified mountain in the Sahyādri range. There is a famous Mount Mahendra in the northern section of the eastern ghats, but this cannot be the same. Various identifications of this mountain have been suggested, but none are convincing. See Janaki (1966: 168-169) for reference to these.

Nāgagrāma / Maṭināgapura: Abbott (1895) identifies the Nāgapura of a copper plate grant with the modern Nāgāṅv, situated southeast of Alibāg, in the Kōlābā District not very far south of Mumbai, on the basis of the location given for Nāgapura in the *Nāgāhvaya-māhātmya* attached to the Skh. See **§5.2**. This identi-fication is far too north to be the PGN town, however, which would be situated in Goa. Mentioned in chapter seven (Skh.u. 15). In the PGN references, it is on the Cakranadī river, and is near Kuśasthalī (see vss. 2 and 13).

Sahya / Sahyādri: Name of the western ghats. Variant readings in our MSS also give the name as Si̱nhādri and Sa̱nhādri. *The Imperial Gazetteer of India* (1907-1909/12[=1908]: 217) describes it as beginning at the Kundaibāri pass in the south-western corner of the Khāndesh District of Bombay Presidency. "From Kundaibāri (21°61' N. and 74°11' E.) the chain runs southward with an average elevation which seldom exceeds 4,000 feet, in a line roughly parallel with the coast, from which its distance varies from 20 to 65 miles

. . . [It terminates] at Cape Comorin, the southernmost extremity of India." Mentioned in chapters one, two, five, and eleven (Skh.u. 9, 10, 13, and 19).

Śailendra: An unidentified mountain in the Sahyādri range. Mentioned in chapter one (Skh.u. 9).

Tauḷavadeśa and Tauḷavamaṇḍaḷa: Probably Tuluva, the name of modern South Kanara according to Ananthakrishna Iyer (1928-36/2: 314) and Rice (1909: 21). Mentioned in chapters one and two (Skh.u. 9 and 10).

Vāñchatī (?): Possibly the name of a city. Mentioned in chapter eight (Skh.u. 16).

Vārāṇasī: The Sanskrit name for Benares. Mentioned in chapter eleven (Skh.u. 19).

Vijaya: Name of an unidentified city noted to be not far from Gorāṣṭra. Mentioned in chapter eight (Skh.u. 16).

12.5c. Rivers. The PGN mentions eight rivers, of which six are in the genral Karnataka region. These are the Cakranadī, the Caṇḍikā, the Sītā, the Śuktimatī, the Tuṅgabhadrā, and the Varāhī. Of these, only the Tuṅgabhadrā can be identified, its present name being the same. The Śuktimatī, which is noted in chapter nine (Skh.u. 17) to be near Gokarṇa, may be the modern-day Gaṅgāvali, which is today the only river near Gokarṇa, but we must be cautious with identifications. The Cakranadī may be in Goa. The seventh river, mentioned in an allusion in chapter one (Skh.u. 9), is the Mandākinī. This is the name of an arm of the Ganges which flows down through the valley of Kedāranātha in the Himālayas, but is employed here probably in its usage as a name of the heavenly Ganges. The eighth, mentioned in chapter eleven (Skh.u. 19) is the Ganges itself.

12.6. Historical problems. There are certain historical problems which are touched on in the PGN. One is the location and identification of the thirty-two villages. These villages are said to have been peopled by *brāhmaṇas* from Ahichatra, the capital of Pañcāla, who were brought south by Mayūravarman, his son Kaṅgavarman, or by a possibly legendary forbear named Mukaṇṇa. It is said that these are the ancestors of the modern-day Havik *brāhmaṇas*. The Havik *brāhmaṇas* today are located mainly in the west of Shimoga district in Mysore (Karnataka). As noted above, though, the *brāhmaṇas* of Kōtēshwar maintain that their village is one of the original thirty-two villages. Some would maintain that Ahichatra is used as the name of a more southern place. Govind Pai (1933: 367) maintains that this is the city mentioned by Ptolemy as Adisatroi, and through which the Godāvari river flows. Thus he would place Ahichatra in the western portion of what was in 1934 Hyderabad state, rather than in what was Rohilkhand. That southern cities were referred to by the names of northern cities we know. Rice (1886-1905/7: 34), for example, notes Kūḍali, at the junction of the Tuṅgā and Bhadrā rivers, to be the southern Vāraṇāsi. Nonetheless, Bhagīratha, Mayūravarman's grandson, does seem to have concluded a marriage alliance with Candragupta II. See Moraes (1931: 21-22) for this. This speaks against the argument of insurmountable distance, perhaps. Anantha-krishna Iyer (1928-36/2: 312) maintains Ahichatra, or its variant name Ahikṣetra, to be a reference to the ancient name of North Kanara. From chapter 8 of the *uttarārdha* of the Skh we obtain the impression that the area of the thirty-two villages was a rather restricted one. Warriar (1933), however, notes that the *Keralotpatti* refers to thirty-two *grāmas* of Canara being separated from the thirty-two *grāmas* of modern-day Kerala. This would speak for an older division of sixty-four *grāmas* from which the thirty-two in the north broke away, with these covering a fairly large territory. Too much weight should not be given to this text, though, as it has not been critically edited. The entire matter will be treated more fully elsewhere when we discuss chapters 7, 8 and the chapters interpolated by L1a and L1b. I prefer to reserve judgment on the various points raised until that time. A list of the thirty-two villages, as their names appear in our MSS, is given in Appendix E. These names, as they appear in Saletore's MSS, are given by Saletore (1936a: 598-604). To be kept in mind, of course, is that identification of all geographical areas and of all personal names presents a problem.

Another very peculiar matter is that in both instances in which the *brāhmaṇas* of the thirty-two villages exclude the other *brāhmaṇas* who have been judged to have sinned, they are noted to have taken a vow. In both chapters four and six (Skh.u. 12.38d and 14.29d) they are referred to as '*dṛḍhavratāḥ*,' 'firm in their vow,' and in chapter six (Skh.u. 14.32ab) they are futher noted to be '*pratijñāyuktāḥ satyavādināṃ*,' 'bound by the vow of speaking the truth.' What is behind this is hidden at present.

That Mayūravarman brought *brāhmaṇas* from Ballabhī is not noted in any of the sources to which I have referred. Can independent corroboration of this be found? Also, why is the village of Kuśasthalī given to the *brāhmaṇas* settled by Paraśurāma, and not to the *brāhmaṇas* brought by Mayūravarman from Ballabhī in Saurāṣṭra given the association of this name with Sārasvata *brāhmaṇas* who claim to have come to Goa from Saurāṣṭra – unless the local *brāhmaṇas* are themselves the Sārasvata *brāhmaṇas* brought from Trihotra by Paraśurāma? In this regard, see Thurston (1909/1: 391) who quotes the Cochin Census Report, 1901 with regard to the Konkani *brāhmaṇas*, "a branch of the Sarasvat sub-division of the Pancha Gaudas. . . . Trihotrapura, the modern Tirhut in Behar, is claimed as the original home of the community. According to their tradition, Parasu Rāma brought ten families, and settled them in villages in and around Gomantaka, the modern Goa, Panchrakosi, and Kusasthali. . . . With the establishment of the Inquisition at Goa, and the religious persecution set foot by the Portuguese, the community left Goa in voluntary exile." A further historical problem that requires clarification is that in the fourth century A.D. when Mayūravarman ruled, Goa seems to have been ruled by the Bhojas, though the early history of Goa is shrouded in darkness (P. P. Kamat 1990: 8-9).

The problem with regard to the identification of Koṭi / Koṭīśvara and Koṭiliṅgeśa has been referred to above in **§12.5b**. I repeat here that the *brāhmaṇas* of present-day Kōṭēshwar claim their village to be one of the original thirty-two, and add that in the *uttarārdha* of the Skh as in DaCunha's edition, chapter 8, vs. 10 refers to Koṭiliṅgeśa being to the north of one of the original thirty-two villages. This is as in DaCunha's edition, though, and not in a critically edited text.

Another problem is that the five villages of PGN chapter two (Skh.u. 10) appear to have been well-known. Why? And why is it that these *brāhmaṇas* are polluted on account of areca nut cultivation while present-day Havik *brāhmaṇas* and Citpāvan *brāhmaṇas* are not? How did an occupation which was considered to be polluting in the area come to be acceptable? As mentioned in **§12.3**, betel vine cultivation is also given as a reason for *pātitya* status for two communities in the 'Tribes and Castes' volumes.

Still another historical problem is how it was that *brāhmaṇas*, such as those of PGN chapter three (Skh.u. 11), resolved life under the governance of a *śūdra* with the prescriptions of the *Mānavadharmaśāstra* and similar texts. See n. 3 to the translation of chapter three (Skh.u. 11).

12.7. Anthropological problems. We are also presented with problems which, while they are historical certainly, verge into the interests of anthropologists.

One is the relation between *brāhmaṇas* of our stories and society at large.

Brāhmaṇas appear to form an insular community of which certain behavior is expected. While it appears that they can be punished only by *brāhmaṇas*, they are ostracized by the community at large if they do not live by the behavioral standards expected of them. If they fall from these standards or if they are excommunicated by *brāhmaṇas*, they become untoucable, which is to say of unclean *śūdra* status.

Another problem is the question of what rites were necessary and what requirements had to be met before *brāhmaṇas* could form villages. It appears from these stories that in most cases the *brāhmaṇas* had to have the permission of the people who dwelt in the area where the village was to be, and that their recognized ancestors were important from a ritual standpoint with regard to their setting up a village. The exact nature of the situation will depend on collation with material from other sources, though. The material on this in the PGN is too sketchy and incidental.

Still another problem of interest is the considerations of marriage mentioned in chapter three (Skh.u. 11). Was *jāti* (caste) ranking taken into account? Was locality a deciding factor? With regard to the *brāhmaṇas*, what are the prescriptions for being litter bearers? Related to this, perhaps of significance, perhaps not, is that *jāti* is never mentioned in the PGN. Of course, silence does not argue for nonexistence. It does indicate, though, that we should keep our minds open regarding the organization of the social structure. Perhaps the structure was more similar to that described in the Tamil *Caṅkam* literature rather than to that of contemporary India.

Also, does the brief mention of freeing slaves by the *brāhmaṇas* Sunīta in chapter eleven (Skh.u. 19) tell us anything about this institution when collated with other material?

A major point of interest should be the examples of legal deliberations, though these may be somewhat fictionalized.

For the convenience of readers with anthropological interests, the kinship terms which are mentioned are given in parentheses after their English translations.

12.8. Care should be taken in extracting historical and anthropological points. Extreme care should be taken in extracting historical and anthropological points from the PGN. This is not because of the mythological elements present, but because of the danger, and in fact the certainty, of the presence of mislections in the text as far as it has been possible to reconstruct it.

II. TEXT

CHAPTER ONE (Skh.u. 9)

ṛṣayaḥ /
sūta sarvapurāṇārthavijñāna vimalāśaya /
bhavanmukhenduvigaḷatkathāpīyūṣamaṅgalaṃ / 1 /
pītvā śrutipuṭair bhūyaḥ pipāsa vardhate hi naḥ /
ataḥ kathāmṛtaṃ puṇyaṃ pāyayasva bhavārtihaṃ / 2 /
rahasyaṃ vividhaṃ brahman tvayā matimatāṃ vara /
śrutāni sakalāny addhā dharmāṇi vimalā*śa*ya / 3 /
dvātriṉśadgrāmanāmāni gṛhabhedāni yāni ca /
pūrvam eva tvayaivoktaṃ pātityagrāmasaṃjñakaṃ / 4 /
yad astīti viśeṣaṃ tac chrotum icchāmahe vayaṃ /
sūtaḥ /
śṛṇudhvam ṛṣayaḥ sarve sāvadhānena cetasā / 5 /
idam eva purāpṛcchac chaunakaṃ dharmakovidaṃ
janmejayasya tanayaḥ śatānīko mahīpatiḥ / 6 /
vyāsopadeśāt satataṃ purāṇaśravaṇotsukaḥ /
kalināviṣṭam ālakṣya bhārataṃ khaṇḍam uttamaṃ / 7 /
kṣetratīrthaikanirato yajñakarma†kṛtādaraḥ† /
śivapādāravindaikyaḥ bhavabhaktir atandritaḥ / 8 /
śatānīkaḥ /
sarvavedāntatattvajña sarvaśāstrārthakovida /
tava vāgamṛtaṃ pītvā na tṛptir jāyate kathaṃ / 9 /
bhārgavasya prabhāvaṃ ca tasya deśasya vistaraṃ /
dvātriṉśadgrāmanāmāni tathā taddaivatāni ca / 10 /
vistareṇa tvayā brahman śrotuṃ sarvaṃ samagrataḥ /
upagrāmāṇi santīti purā yat kathitaṃ tvayā / 11 /
tad ahaṃ śrotum icchāmi grāmāṇām ādhidaivataṃ /

śaunakaḥ /
purā kroḍamunir nāma satyavādī jitendriyaḥ / 12 /
cirakālaṃ tapas taptvā śaṃkaraśrīśam avyayaṃ /
svavaśaṃ kārayām āsa svanāmnā kāritāṃ purīṃ / 13 /
svamudrāṅkitatīrthaṃ ca †*nigamya*† svamanoharaṃ /
āśramaṃ tatra kṛtvātha ninãya bahuvatsaraṃ / 14 /
kadā cid bhārgavaḥ śrīmān sarvakṣatrakulāntakaḥ /
gokarṇaṃ gantukāmena †mahendrādrau† jagāma saḥ / 15 /
tatra tatra ca tīrthāni ṛṣīṇām āśramāni ca /
śanaiḥ paśyann ameyātmā devatāyatanāni ca / 16 /
tataḥ sahyādriśikharam adūre dṛṣṭavān muniḥ /
divyauṣadhitapoyogair mantrasiddhair maharṣibhiḥ / 17 /
juṣṭaṃ kiṃnaragandharvair apsarobhiś ca cāraṇaiḥ /
nānāratnamayaiḥ sṛṅgair indranīlair vicitrakaiḥ / 18 /
nānāphalaprasravaṇair nānākandarasānubhiḥ /
†ruciraṃ viharantīnāṃ† ramaṇaiḥ siddhayoṣitāṃ / 19 /
mayūrakokābhirutaṃ madāndhāli sammūrchitaṃ /
ajasraṃ raktakaṇṭhānāṃ kūjitaiś ca patattriṇāṃ / 20 /
āhvayantam iva śrāntān pānthān kāmadu*gha*drumaiḥ /
vrajantam iva mātaṅgair gṛṇantam iva ṣaṭpadaiḥ / 21 /
mandāraiḥ pārijātaiś ca saraḷaiś copaśobhitaṃ /
tamālaiḥ sālatālaiś ca kovidārāsanārjunaiḥ / 22 /
cūtaiḥ kadambair nimbaiś ca nāgapuṃnāgacampakaiḥ /
pāṭalāśokabakulaiḥ kundaiḥ kurabakair api / 23 /
panasodumbarāśvatthaplakṣanyagrodhatindukaiḥ /
paṇyair auṣadhibhiḥ pūgai rājapūgaiś ca jambubhiḥ / 24 /
āmrātakair agniśikhaiḥ priyāḷair madhukāsanaiḥ /
drumajātibhir anyaiś ca rājitaṃ veṇukaṇṭakaiḥ / 25 /
śākhāmṛgaiḥ *krī*ḍitaiś ca mṛgendrair gajaśalyakaiḥ /
gavayaiḥ śarabhair vyāghrair urubhir mahiṣādibhiḥ / 26 /
mṛganābhibhir ākīrṇaṃ viśiṣṭaṃ camarīmṛgaiḥ /
kadaḷiṣaṇḍasaṃruddhanaḷinīpulinaśriyaṃ / 27 /
nikaraiś cāmaraiḥ svacchaiḥ kadaḷī†ketubhis tataḥ† /
virājamānaṃ śailendraṃ dṛṣṭvā hṛṣṭamanā muniḥ / 28 /
avatīrya dadarśātha tauḷavaṃ deśam uttamaṃ /
tatkṣetraṃ prāptavān rāmaḥ medhāvī bhṛgunandanaḥ / 29 /
īśanārāyaṇaṃ samyak pūjayām āsa śāstrataḥ /

kamalair lakṣasaṃkhyākaiḥ pūjayām āsa bhārgavaḥ / 30 /
nānopacārair vividhair vedoktair mantrarāśibhiḥ /
stotraṃ kartum samārebhe śaṃkaraśrīsam avyayaṃ / 31 /
śrībhārgavaḥ /
svārājapūrṇasurakoṭikirīṭarājan-
*nī*rājanīyanijapādasaroruhāya /
śastrāstratā*dhi*pataye varaśaṃkarāya
nārāyaṇāya vimalāya namaḥ śivāya / 32 /
mārāhitāya madhukaiṭabhadāraṇāya
dhārādharaprati . ka . tasuprabhāya /
sārāya sarvajagatām api śaṃkarāya
nārāyaṇāya vimalāya namaḥ śivāya / 33 /
dhārā . rāgadharaṇīdhararājakanyā-
vārākarendratanayāvaśamānasāya /
sūryenduvahninayanāya ca śaṃkarāya
nārāyaṇāya vimalāya namaḥ śivāya / 34 /
ārādhanapraṇayinām aniśaṃ janānāṃ
kārāgṛhe kalayate kalikalmaṣāni /
nārāyaṇāya narakacchidaśaṃkarāya
nārāyaṇāya vimalāya namaḥ śivāya / 35 /
. . . . mātra-
nāmāvaśeṣitasurārimahāpurāya /
nāthāya sarvajagatām api śaṃkarāya
nārāyaṇāya vimalāya namaḥ śivāya / 36 /
bhūvārivahnimarudambarapūruṣārka-
. . . . . vapuṣe daśavigrahāya /
nānācarācaramayāya ca śaṃkarāya
nārāyaṇāya vimalāya namaḥ śivāya / 37 /
kīnāśanakranigṛhītaraṭanmṛkaṇḍu-
bhūnāgabhītiharapādakarāmbujāya /
ārādhitāya sakalair api śaṃkarāya
nārāyaṇāya vimalāya namaḥ śivāya / 38 /
nānāvilāsanagarājanadīśakanyā-
narmā*yi*tāya naravāhanarapriyāya /
nāgadrumāya nama*tām* api śaṃkarāya
nārāyaṇāya vimalāya namaḥ śivāya /39 /
jaya śaṃkara paṅkajanābha vibho

vibhavaprada pādakṛpāmbunidhe /
nidhipālaka sevitadaityahara
hara mādhava mānavamāraripo / 40 /
ripudānava dānavacakradhara
dharajāpari . . . lolabhuja /
bhujagādhipa komalabhogaśaya
śayaśobhitaśūla viśālaga*da* / 41 /
gadabheṣajacitra vicitraga*ṇa*
gaṇanāyaka mānasatoṣakara /
karanīrajarājita śrīśava*ra*
varadābhayadāna nidhānapada / 42 /
padanamrasurāsura pūrṇakṛpa
kṛpaṇākhilakāmanakalpataro /
taruṇīmaṇibhūṣitarāmatano
tanukāntinirākṛtanīlamaṇe / 43 /
maṇimauḷivighaṭ*ṭi*tacandraka*la*
kalaveṇuravomadagopijana /
jananādivihīna gi*rīndra*dare
darikoṭinikāśavikāsaru*ce* / 44 /
ruci*man*navakaustubha kambugaḷa
gaḷalakṣitakālamahāgaraḷa /
garaḷāyudha mastaka . naṭana
naṭanasphaṭi*tāb*ja . . . ghaṭa / 45 /
ghaṭasaṃbhavadattamahās*tra*rate
rati . . . . jaga /
jagadīśa maheśa rameśa bhava
bhavasāgaratāraka . . . . / 46 /
. . . . rada
radanacchada , , tavidruma*bha* /
drumabhaṅgada laṅgada kundara*da*
radake*tana*rājitapadmamukha / 47 /
mukharīkṛtasadguṇa bhāgyavidhe
vidhivandya . . . . . hṛdaya /
hṛdayaṃgamakuṅkuma . . dhara
dharajākamalākucalolakara / 48 /
karajārditanirdayadaityapate
patitāghamahānagavajranute /

nutimuktida vedapurāṇagaṇa
gaṇanāviṣayānagha puṇyaguṇa / 49 /
guṇavarṇananiryu*ta*bhūmisura
sura bhūruhamūla lasadbhavana /
bhavanāśana bhāvitamaṅgaḷada
gaḷadujvaladivyataruprasava / 50 /
prasavāyudha tāpanakṛnnayana
nayanāmbuja sādhita . . jaya /
jaya kroḍapurīśa girīśa jaya
jaya digvijayī bhava deva jaya / 51 /
evaṃ stutvā tadā rāmaḥ kṛtāñjaliputaḥ sudhīḥ /
natvā natvātha taṃ devaṃ pratasthe vāruṇīṃ diśaṃ / 52 /
tatra śuktimatīṃ divyāṃ vihaṃgagaṇasevitāṃ /
mandākinīpratinibhām aghaughaparivarjinīṃ / 53 /
tāṃ dadarśa mahābhāgas tasyāṃ snātuṃ pracakrame /
vidhāya nityakarmāṇi haṉso 'ham iti bhāvayan / 54 /
mantramūrtiṃ hṛdi dhyāyann †āre*bhe*† japam uttamaṃ /
śaunakaḥ /
etasminn antare rājann ājagmur atiduḥkhitāḥ / 55 /
viśvastāḥ pūrṇagarbhiṇyaḥ kṣutpipāsātipīḍitāḥ /
nadīkulaṃ tataḥ prāpur navasaṅkhyā navākṛti / 56 /
avidūre tapasyantaṃ sākṣād vahniśikhopamaṃ /
koṭibhānupratīkāśaṃ nāsāgrakṛtalocanaṃ / 57 /
dadṛśur bhārgavaṃ hṛṣ*ṭḥ* tasyāntikam upāga*man* /
pāhi pāhi mahābāho sarvabhūtadayānidhe / 58 /
duḥkhān nas tāraya vibho bhaṅgabhūtān paraṃparāt /
uccair ākranditāḥ petuḥ pādayor bhārgavasya tāḥ / 59 /
tva*dāgatā* vayaṃ brahman ninditāḥ pāpadūṣitāḥ /
uddhāraya kṛpāmbhodhe mṛtaprāyā hataśriyaḥ / 60 /
śaunakaḥ /
kim etad idam āścaryaṃ vismayotphullalocanaḥ /
uddharann iva netrābhyāṃ dadarśa nṛpanandana / 61 /
yatante bhuvane dhīrāḥ pālanāyātiduḥkhitāḥ /
sahajaṃ hi tathā †tā*sām*† adabhrāya ca kīrtaye / 62 /
atha dṛṣṭvā bhayaṃ tāsāṃ kṛpālur dīnavatsalaḥ /
meghagambhīrayā vācā uvāca bhṛgunandanaḥ / 63 /

bhārgavaḥ /
dhairyam ālambyatāṃ nāryaḥ kle*śaḥ* saṃtyajyatām iti /
abhīpsitaṃ varaṃ brūta dattam ity avadhāryatāṃ / 64 /
tatas tadvākyam ākarṇya sudhārasam ivoditaṃ /
uttasthur atha viśvastā aśrupūritalocanāḥ / 65 /
trapāṃ tyak*tvā* svavṛttāntaṃ vyāhartum upacakramuḥ /
nāryaḥ /
dvātriṉśadgrāmamadhye tu śrotriyānvayin*yo* vayaṃ / 66 /
bālye bhartṛviyogena lalāṭalikhitena ca /
imām avasthāṃ saṃprāptāḥ janair ativigarhitāḥ / 67 /
grāmasthebhyaḥ parityaktāḥ tapasvinyo vayaṃ bata /
dehaṃ tyaktum adhairyatvād gacchāmo niyater vaśāt / 68 /
puṇyaleśaprabhāvena tvaddarśanam abhūd vibho /
kṛpāṃ kuru dayāsindho naḥ pālaya kṛpākara / 69 /
iti tāsāṃ vacaḥ śrutvā dattavān abhayaṃ muniḥ /
tābhiś ca saha saṃprāptaḥ kroḍeśaṃ bhadradāyakaṃ / 70 /
darśanaṃ kārayām āsa yathā śaktir bhaviṣyati /
kriyatām atra saṃvāsaṃ kiṃcit kālam atandritāḥ / 71 /
kramāc chaṃkaranārāyaṇa sa devaḥ karuṇānidhiḥ /
śaṃ tanoti na saṃdeho bhavitā kuladaivataṃ / 72 /
evam uktvā mahāyogī gokarṇaṃ prayayau tadā / 73 /
kiṃkarajanahitakaraṇaṃ
    saṃtatakaruṇaṃ śivendrirāramaṇaṃ /
paṅkajabhavanutacaraṇaṃ
    śaṃkaranārāyaṇaṃ sadā kalaye / 74 /

CHAPTER TWO (Skh.u. 10)

śatānīkaḥ /
kiṃ cakrur atha viprendra garbhiṇ*yas* tā vitantavaḥ /
vistareṇa vadasvādya pañcagrāmam abhūt kathaṃ / 1 /
śaunakaḥ /
saṃkṣepeṇātra vakṣyāmi śṛṇu pārthivasattama /
bhārgavasya prabhāvaṃ ca pañcagrāmasya vaibhavaṃ / 2 /
sūtimāsaś ca saṃprāptaḥ kvacid vasrād anantaraṃ /
nirbhītās tāś ca viśvastāḥ sutān suṣuvire tadā / 3 /
kramāt kanyāś ca saṃjātāḥ pīnonnatapayodharāḥ /
saṃtoṣam atulaṃ prāpuḥ pupuṣus tān sutān nṛpa / 4 /
teṣāṃ vyatīyur bālatvaṃ tathā kaumāravārṣikaṃ /
goḷakā †*yau*vanaṃ† prāpus tatas te manujeśvara / 5 /
sodarāvaraṇārthāya cetthaṃ cakrur athāghagāḥ /
kecij janāḥ karṣakatvaṃ lāṅgalatvaṃ kvacij janāḥ / 6 /
kecit prāpur bhāravidyāṃ kecit kurvanti vāṭikāṃ /
jaghanyajatvaprāyeṇa kim brūmas tān nareśvara / 7 /
vrātyān vivarṇān †vai*dhe*yān† piśunāṇs tān nirākṛtān /
netrahīnā yathā senā yathecchaṃ vicaranti hi / 8 /
itthaṃ pravartamānānāṃ vyatīyur bahavaḥ samāḥ /
śaunakaḥ /
bhārgavaḥ kṛtagokarṇas tathā tauḷavamaṇḍalaṃ / 9 /
mahendraṃ gantukāmena prapede kroḍapattanaṃ /
tato 'dūre samāyāntaṃ ghasrādhipasamadyutiṃ / 10 /
taṃ dṛṣṭvā bhārgavaṃ vadhvaḥ petuś caraṇayos tadā /
tathotthāya svavṛttāntam †uktvā khaṇḍaṃ punaḥ punaḥ† / 11 /
etān rakṣa mahābhāga dāserān pāpacāriṇaḥ /
tad ākarṇya vacas tāsāṃ kṛpāḷur bhṛgunandanaḥ / 12 /
kṛpāṃ cakāra kṛpayā pālayann iva bhūmipa /
athety āha mahābāhur agnīdhraṃ somapīṭhinaṃ / 13 /
vedavedāṅgatattvajñaṃ smārtakarmasuniṣṭhitaṃ /
†āgama*jña*mahāprājñaṃ† paścunābdhitaṭe sthitaṃ / 14 /
saṃskāraṃ kriyatām adya tvayā †cai*naḥ*sakāriṇaḥ† /
avaidikena mantreṇa nāmagrahaṇapūrvakaṃ / 15 /

sthānaṃ kuru tathā tebhyas tatra nikṣipyatām iti /
kuṭhārapāṇir ity uktvā māhendram agamat tadā / 16 /
śaunakaḥ /
guror vākyam athākarṇya somapīhī mahāmatiḥ /
goḷakān tān samāhūya mantrapūtair jalair api / 17 /
mṛdā ca bhasmanā cātha tadā śuktimatījalaiḥ /
vidhivat snāpayām āsa guror vākyasya gauravāt / 18 /
navānāṃ navaputrāṇāṃ navanāmāny akārayat /
. . . . ca vaidyavac . . . . . / 19 /
. . . . ca navaite †*kār*yamānavāḥ† /
. . . . paścāt saṃbhāvitābhavan / 20 /
caulopanītikarmāṇi udvāhādīni yāni ca /
laukikoktena mārgeṇa cākarod bhūsurāgraṇīḥ / 21 /
kāryākāyavivādajño nātikramya guror giraṃ /
grāmaṃ kutra kariṣye 'ham iti cintāparo 'bhavat / 22 /
etasminn antare rājan vyomi gīḥ samapadyata /
atraiva kārayasveti vismayaṃ vismayāvahaṃ / 23 /
tatas tad vākyam ākarṇya sa viprendro mudānvitaḥ /
upatyakāyāṃ kroḍādreḥ sahyaśailasya paścime / 24 /
uttare †kriyate† sīmā †yāmye sahyasamudbhavā† /
sītā nāma nadī puṇyā vartate vimalodakā / 25 /
kroḍādrer īśabhāge tu śuktimatyāś ca paścime /
. . . parataḥ †pāruśabdagrāmaṃ† cakāra saḥ / 26 /
tatrāste bhagavān śaṃbhuputro gajamukhas tadā /
śaṅkhacakragadāśārṅgapāṇinā saha vighnarāṭ / 27 /
tasya cottaradigbhāge kāraveleti viśrutā /
rājate tatra deveśaḥ śārṅgapāṇiś caturbhujaḥ / 28 /
atīva bhaktiyuktānāṃ vāñcchitārthapradāyakaḥ /
tasya paścimadigbhāge vāmanāḷeti viśrutaḥ / 29 /
tatrāste bhagavān pakṣirāṭdhvajam asurāntakaḥ /
anāratam hi sukhakṛt bhaktānām abhayapradaḥ / 30 /
śuktimatyāḥ purobhāge uḷḷugrāmeti viśrutaḥ /
karoti tatra sāṃnidhyaṃ devī bhagavatī hi sā / 31 /
mahiṣāsuranirnāśakāriṇī caṇḍadarpahā /
cāpaśūlagadākhaḍgadhāriṇī jagadambikā / 32 /
tatraiva puṇḍarīkākṣaḥ prabhuḥ sarvatra gocaraḥ /
sarvadā vāmabhāgastho lakṣmīsaṃśliṣṭavigrahaḥ / 33 /

tadvītihotradigbhāge . . . . †*ti viśru*tā† /
sthāpito 'bhūn mahāligaḥ carācarasukhapradaḥ / 34 /
adyāpi liṅgarūpeṇa dṛśyate dṛṣṭigocaraḥ /
evaṃ ca pañcagrāmān saḥ kārayitvā dvijāgraṇīḥ / 35 /
ekasminn ekam ājñāpya tatraivāṣṭau janāṇs tathā /
ubhāv ubhau pṛthaggrāme †nyadhāyī*tas*† tato narān / 36 /
sukhena sthāsyatām atra yāvac candradivākarau /
bhārgavasya prasādena tāvat tiṣṭhanti bālakāḥ / 37 /
atra gotrāṇi yuṣmākaṃ varddhantu kṛpayā vibho /
ity āśīrvādam ākāṅkṣan . . . . dvijottamaḥ / 38 /
bhūyo bhūyo namaskṛtry kroḍeśāya mahātmane /
gurave bhārgavāyātha prayayau svāśramaṃ prati / 39 /
śaunakaḥ /
tataḥ kālāntare rājan adrim āruru*hus* kvacit /
tatra vāṭaṃ prakurvanti †piṇḍabhṛt kuraro† yathā / 40 /
adhityakāyāṃ sahyādreḥ pūgīvāṭaṃ na saṃśayaḥ /
upatyakāyām eteṣāṃ lāṅgalatvaṃ vidhīyate / 41 /
eteṣāṃ goḷakānāṃ ca vāṭikāṃ ca praśasyate /
athavā bhāravidyāṃ ca sevāvṛttiṃ tathaiva ca / 42 /
pañcagrāmajanā mū*ḍhāḥ* karmahīnā nirākṛtāḥ /
tantumātrabrāhmaṇikā rājante rājaśekhara / 43 /
sahabhojyaṃ sahāvāsaṃ sahasaṃbhāṣaṇaṃ tathā /
sahayātrāprayāṇaṃ ca na †*he*ty† āhur vicakṣaṇāḥ / 44 /
teṣām annaṃ prabhuñjāno pātityam anugacchati /
agnihotraṃ ca saṃnyāsaṃ paurohityaṃ tathaiva ca / 45 /
śrautatvaṃ smārtakarmatvaṃ purāṇapaṭhanaṃ tathā /
svayaṃbhūliṅgasaṃsparśaṃ tāntrikatvaṃ tathaiva ca / 46 /
yamādyaṣṭāṅgayogatvaṃ nety āha bhṛgunandanaḥ /
naiva te goḷakā vrātyā vivarṇāś ca nirākṛtāḥ / 47 /
vipratvam anugacchantaḥ pracaranti kalau yuge /
bahunātra kim uktena kim anyac chrotum icchasi / 48 /
eteṣāṃ darśanāt puṇsāṃ pātityaṃ saṃbhaviṣyati /
prāyaścittavidhiṃ vakṣye mārtāṇḍasyāvalokanaṃ / 49 /
gaṇeśvaraṃ viṣṇum anādiśunyaṃ
viṣṇuṃ tathā viṣṇum udāravikramaṃ /
vedīm upendraṃ ca mahendraliṅgaṃ
namāmi bhūyaḥ praṇamāmi bhūyaḥ / 50 /

CHAPTER THREE (Skh.u. 11)

śauna*kaḥ* /
pātityagrāmam asty anyat śuktimatyāś ca dakṣiṇe /
modagrāmaṃ *tad* ity āhuḥ sarvasaṃ*yak*tvaraṃ śu*bhaṃ* / 1 /
śūdradattaṃ dvijebhyaś ca vāhakebhyaḥ †*svā*vāhakaṃ† /
purā tu pādajaiḥ †ketumuddakun*de*†ti viśrutau / 2 /
rūpayauvanasaṃpannau mahābalaparākramau /
śivapūjāparau niṣṭhau dvijabhaktiparāyaṇau / 3 /
tayos tu katicit kālaṃ vyatīyur nṛpanandana /
dvātriṇśadgrāmanilayāḥ śreṣṭhā vedavidāṃ varāḥ / 4 /
aṣṭau dvijāḥ samāyātāḥ sabhāryāḥ sahaputrakāḥ /
kiṃ vadan*taṃ* samākarṇya nirbhāg*yāḥ* dhanalobhayā / 5 /
tayoḥ samīpam ājagmur dāridryavinivṛttaye /
āśīrvādaṃ tataḥ kṛtvā samavetā dvijādhamāḥ / 6 /
āśāpūrvakavākyāni *tv* ūcus te dhanalolupāḥ /
yuvāṃ dhīrau yuvāṃ *āḍh*yau yuvāṃ pūjyau jagattraye / 7 /
bhavatoḥ sadṛśo nāsti rūpaudāryaguṇādiṣu /
stutim itthaṃ bahuvidhair vākyair vākyaviśāradaiḥ / 8 /
samāgatānām ālokya jyeṣṭho dharmaparāyaṇaḥ /
vidhivat pūjayām āsa sa tebhyo draviṇaṃ bahu / 9 /
athāṣ*ṭā*sakuṭumbibhyaḥ kṛtvā †*sahyā*ni† śūdrajaḥ /
tadā sarvasamṛddhāni paśudhānyāni yāni ca / 10 /
dāsījanayutā hy āśu dadau tebhyo mudānvitaḥ /
tena saṃmānitā viprāḥ vāsaṃ cakrur atandritāḥ / 11 /
śuśrūṣāṃ tasya kurvanto ninyur dvādaṣahāyanāḥ /
śaunakaḥ /
jaghanyajo 'tha saṃcintya putrahīno 'tha me 'ṅganā / 12 /
anyāṃ sulocanāṃ prāpsye pīnonnatapayodharāṃ /
rūpayauvanasaṃpannāṃ sarvalakṣaṇalakṣitāṃ / 13 /
asmatsantativṛddhyarthaṃ vṛṇe 'ha vanitāṃ śubhāṃ /
nāputrasya ca loko 'stīty āhur matimatāṃ varāḥ / 14 /
iti nirdhārya manasā vivāhe kṛtaniścayaḥ /
svajanair mantrayām āsa uktavān svamanorathaṃ / 15 /
kriyatāṃ mama cārvaṅgī sakhāyaḥ putrakāmi*naḥ* /

asminn arthe mahārājñaḥ jāt*yām* ākurutādhunā / 16 /
atha te bāndhavāḥ sarve samālocya parasparaṃ /
*kāṃ*cit kanyāṃ śubhaśroṇīṃ bimboṣṭhīṃ navayauvanāṃ / 17 /
dṛṣṭvā tam ūcus te sarve yoja*nār*dhe tu saṃsthitāṃ /
†*kāmyā*† tatra mahāprājñā tava bhāryā bhaviṣyati / 18 /
iti teṣāṃ vacaḥ śrutvā mene sa kṛtakṛtyatāṃ /
śvaḥkāle pariṇetavyā iti niścitya cetasā / 19 /
pāṇigrahaṇasaṃbhārān saṃpādya svajanaiḥ saha /
śibikāvāhakaḥ ko 'pi nāsty atra viṣaye bata / 20 /
kiṃ karomi kva gacchāmi iti cintāparo 'bhavat /
brāhmaṇān tān samāhūya vinayenābravīd vacaḥ / 21 /
ahaṃ ca bhavatāṃ bhṛtyaḥ mama kāryaṃ samagrataḥ /
manohitaṃ kulasyāsya bhavadbhiḥ kriyatāṃ laghu / 22 /
tadā tasya vacaḥ śrutvā viprāḥ premanimantritāḥ /
tathety ūcur dvijāḥ sarve †navaratne*nā*laṃkṛtāṃ† / 23 /
aṣṭapādena racitām aṣṭau te śivikāṃ dadhuḥ /
śaunakaḥ /
kiṃ kartavyaṃ narapate heḷayā vidhicoditān / 24 /
gurubandhujanān sarvān tyajanty arthaparā narāḥ /
veśyāsaktāḥ kulastrīṇāṃ dyūtāsaktās trayīm iva / 25 /
aśvāsaktā narā bhūpa satataṃ gāṃ tyajanti hi /
jaghanyaḥ sahasāgatya śibikām āruroha saḥ / 26 /
śanair vadhūgṛhaṃ prāpya kṛtodvāhaḥ sa śūdrajaḥ /
patnyā saha mudā yuktaḥ prapede nijamandiraṃ / 27 /
atha tebhyo dvijebhyaś ca vastrāṇy ābharaṇāni ca /
ekaikasya dvijasyātha pradadau sa mudānvitaḥ / 28 /
śataprasthāni niṣkāni kiṃ na deyaṃ mahīpate /
atha te brāhmaṇāḥ sarve dravyāny ādāya satvaraṃ / 29 /
bhadravarge samādāya grāmaṃ gantuṃ pracakramuḥ /
patitān āgatān dṛṣṭvā grāmasthāḥ krodhamūrchitāḥ / 30 /
daṇḍam ādāya hastena nijaghnus tān nareśvara /
te bhayāt sahasā jagmuḥ dāruṇaṃ †vṛṣa*lātma*jaṃ† / 31 /
tam ūcuḥ pāhi pāhīti kā gatir no vidhīyatāṃ /
atha teṣāṃ vacaḥ śrutvā kṛpayāviṣṭamānasaḥ / 32 /
jaghanyajāgra*ṇīr* bhūyaḥ tān uvāca bhayānvitān /
śūdraḥ /
śokaṃ tyajata he viprāḥ kimarthaṃ kleśakāraṇaṃ / 33 /

idaṃ grāmaṃ ca dāsyāmi navoḍhām aṅganām imāṃ /
gomahiṣyādisarvasvaṃ sthīyantām atra nirbhayāḥ / 34 /
śaunakaḥ /
atha tebhyo dvijebhyaś ca śūdro 'sau karuṇānvitaḥ /
kāntāṃ sva . . . . tāṃ navoḍhāṃ navayauvanāṃ / 35 /
vicitravasanopetāṃ vicitrābharaṇair yutāṃ /
gomahiṣyādisarvasvapūritaṃ bhavanaṃ tathā / 36 /
snātvā śuktimatītoye nṛsiṉheśasya saṃnidhau /
dharāpūrvaṃ dadau grāmaṃ sujanair abhinanditaṃ / 37 /
nirbhītāḥ saṃ*car*antv atra sthī*yan*tāṃ śāśvataṃ dvijāḥ /
ity uktvā tīrthayātrāyāṃ yayau sa vṛṣalātmajaḥ / 38 /
śaunakaḥ /
atha te brāhmaṇāḥ sarve hṛṣṭacittā 'bhavaṉs tadā /
tad grāmaṃ aṣ*ṭa*bhāgaṃ ca kṛtvā *svaṃ svaṃ* niveśanaṃ / 39 /
tathaiva bhāṣābhedāni tathā nāmāni yāni ca /
havyakavyaśubhādīni cakruḥ saṃketamārgataḥ / 40 /
tadāprabhṛti rajendra te viprā nyavasan sukhe /
dvātriṉśadgrāmasaṃsthānāṃ māhātmyaṃ vṛṣalasya ca / 41 /
navoḍhāyāś ca kāntāyāḥ kiṃ bravīmi nareśvara /
kulahīnāḥ parityaktāḥ gurubandhujanaiḥ saha / 42 /
dvātriṉśadgrāmavāsinyo ninditāḥ pāpacāriṇaḥ /
sadā śūdrānnaniratāḥ rājante bhūtaḷe bata / 43 /
eteṣāṃ darśanāt sadyaḥ pātityam anugacchati /
prāyaścittaviddhiṃ vakṣye caṇḍāṉśor darśanaṃ paraṃ / 44 /
bahunātra kim uktena nātra kāryā vicāraṇā / 45 /
hiraṇyahantāram anādipūruṣaṃ
jagattraye vyāptam udāravigrahaṃ /
surāsuraiḥ pūjitapādapaṅkajaṃ
bhaje nṛsiṉhaṃ ca bhaje nṛsiṉhaṃ / 46 /

CHAPTER FOUR (Skh.u. 12)

śaunakaḥ /
pātityagrāmam asty anyat koṭiliṅgeśasaṃnidhau /
tatra sthitānāṃ viprāṇāṃ pāpināṃ krūrakarmiṇāṃ / 1 /
asākṣivādināṃ teṣāṃ māhātmyaṃ pravadāmi te /
loke 'tivaicitryakaraṃ śrotṝṇāṃ vismayāvahaṃ / 2 /
purā tu pārthivaḥ kaścid āsīd varaguṇānvitaḥ /
nāmnā vasur iti khyāto yaṃ vidur bhūpuraṃdaraṃ / 3 /
tasmin śāsati bhūpāle kṣoṇīṃ sarvasamṛddhinīṃ /
anṛta*tva*moṣakatvaṃ nāstīty āhur manīṣiṇaḥ / 4 /
itthaṃ pravartamānasya vyatīyur bahavaḥ samāḥ /
kadācid abhavad vādaṃ kūṭasthānāṃ mahātmanāṃ / 5 /
tathā koṭīśvarasthānāṃ sīmavyatyastakāraṇaṃ /
tathā vrai*he*yasambandhaṃ ṣoḍaśāprasthahetukaṃ / 6 /
kṛtvā vivādaṃ bahudhā rājñe sarvaṃ nyavedayat /
atha rājā mahāprājñaḥ nītivākyavidāṃ varaḥ / 7 /
tadā koṭīśvarasthāṉs tān pracaṇḍān dhūrtapuṃgavān /
jalpataḥ sarvam anṛtaṃ sāntvayām āsa pārthivaḥ / 8 /
itthaṃ pravadatas tatra vākyaṃ ca nṛpateḥ śubhaṃ /
. . kṛtya nṛpasyāgre 'nya kurvanto babhāṣire / 9 /
nijagāda vicintyātha harṣann iva sa tāṃ sabhāṃ /
kāśyapīṃ prārthayiṣyāmo vadaty eṣā śubhāśubhaṃ / 10 /
kaluṣaṃ yatra yatrāsti tatra tatra †*vadiṣ*yati† /
iti niścitya manasā cārān ājñāpayat tadā / 11 /
dvātriṉśadgrāmanilayān sve sve dharma vyavasthitān /
bhṛśamānadhanān pūjyān kṣipram ānīyatām iti / 12 /
paraśvaḥ sādhayiṣye 'ham ā*viśan* nṛpatir gṛhaṃ /
śaunakaḥ /
tasminn eva kṣapām ardhe dhūrtāḥ koṭīśvare sthitāḥ / 13 /
sīmopāntaṃ samāgatya khanitrair ativegataḥ /
kṣo*ṇīṃ* khātvā vyomamātrāṃ kuṇḍe kutsitakarmaṇaḥ / 14 /
nikṣipya puruṣaṃ *kāṃ*cit sikatām te 'py apūrayan /
yathā *svaṃ svaṃ* gṛhaṃ prāpur ājñā eva vyavasthitāḥ / 15 /
atha cāraiḥ samānītā dvātriṉśadgrāmavāsinaḥ /

ājagmur nṛpasāṃnidhyam āśīrvādapuraḥsarāḥ / 16 /
tatkālocitavākyāni jaguḥ sarve nareśvaraṃ /
tadā †va*sur*† dvijaiḥ sārdhaṃ sīmaprāntaṃ yayau mudā / 17 /
saṃgṛhya pūjāsambhāraṃ daivajñais tāntrikaiḥ saha /
*taur*yatrikeṇa sahitaḥ kūṭakoṭīśvaraiḥ saha / 18 /
sthirāṃ pūjāṃ karoti sma gandhapuṣpākṣatādibhiḥ /
bhakṣabhojyais tathā dhūpadīpanaivedyavandanaiḥ / 19 /
prārthanām akarot tatra pārthivo manasepsitāṃ /
kṛtāñjalipuṭo bhūtvā vinayenābravīd vacaḥ / 20 /
rājā /
vidhehi devi kalyāṇaṃ kaluṣaṃ yan mayā kṛtaṃ /
ajñānato jñānato 'pi he kṣame kṣamyatāṃ tvayā / 21 /
kūṭasthānām idaṃ kṣetram koṭikṣetram athāpi vā /
vaktavyaṃ *yat* tvayā samyak śodhanāyedṛ*śāṃ nṝ*ṇāṃ / 22 /
evam uktvā mahīpālaḥ tatra tūṣṇīṃ babhūva saḥ /
śaunakaḥ /
śṛṇvatāṃ sarvabhūtānāṃ kuṇḍastho vidhicoditaḥ / 23 /
parityāgāya caiteṣāṃ svanāśāya tathaiva ca /
rājñaḥ kīr*tyās* tathākhyātyai gadati sma narādhamaḥ / 24 /
idaṃ koṭīśvarasthā*nāṃ* vraihe*yaṃ* nātra saṃśayaḥ /
idaṃ śabdaṃ samākarṇya piśunāḥ pāpakāriṇaḥ / 25 /
śrūyatāṃ manu*jaiḥ* sar*vair* bhavadbhir lokakaṇṭakaiḥ /
apahṛtyāsmadīyaṃ ca bhuvaṃ tebhyo dadāty asau / 26 /
iti saṃlāpayantas te menire kṛtakṛtyatāṃ /
śaunakaḥ /
etasminn antare vyomni janasyāścaryakāriṇī / 27 /
. . . . . . eva tathā koṭīśvarasya ca /
prāpnoti janatā*ghau*ghaṃ śaṅ*ka*yaivāmitaprabhā / 28 /
svaprabhāvaṃ darśayati bhāratī nijagāda tān /
nai*ṣā* gīr bhūmisambandhā jātā naramu*khād* dhruvaṃ / 29 /
koṭīśasthā janāḥ sarve vañcakāḥ pāpacāriṇaḥ /
tasminn arthe mahārā*jan* śapāmi śivopādayoḥ / 30 /
ity uktvā sā bhagavatī tatraivāntarhitābhavat /
tadā tad vākyam ākarṇya romāñcitakaḷevaraḥ / 31 /
tasthau muhūrtaṃ dharmātmā jaḍībhūtaḥ savismayaḥ /
grāmasthānāṃ purastāt tu bhūmiṃ khātvā pradṛṣṭavān / 32 /
*kri*misaṃkulitaṃ māṇsabhūtaṃ puruṣavigrahaṃ /

sa rājā vismay*ī*bhūtvā krodhāt saṃraktalocanaḥ / 33 /
grāmasthānāṃ puras*tāt* tu sarvasvam apahṛtya ca /
asākṣivādi*nāṃ* tatra grāmas*the*bhyaḥ pradattavān / 34 /
parityāg†*ā*parityāgaṃ† tair eva tu vidhīyatāṃ /
iti nirdiśya bhagavān gacchati sma puraṃ prati / 35 /
atha te brāhmaṇāḥ sarve vrīḷayā natamastakāḥ /
. . . . / 36 /
asākṣivādino yūyaṃ patitāḥ pāpayantritāḥ /
anāsthānāś cāgha . . sarvakarmabahiṣkṛtāḥ / 37 /
asmin grāme vivāhādir varjanīyo bhaviṣyati /
śaptvettham anṛtād bhūpa mahāprā*jñā* dṛḍhavratāḥ / 38 /
grāmam an*yat* samāsādya jagmus te svaṃ niketanaṃ /
parityaktās tataḥ sarve vārdhes tīram upāśritāḥ / 39 /
sthitāḥ ṣaṇmāsaparyantaṃ mandāk*ṣād* vyākulendriyāḥ /
śaunakaḥ /
yadṛcchayāgataḥ śrīmān vimatasthāpako mahān / 40 /
tato 'dūre samāyāntam ahaskara*samad*yutiṃ /
ūrdhvapuṇḍrāṅkitaṃ śāntaṃ lalāṭe cordhvapuṇḍrakaṃ / 41 /
taṃ dṛṣṭvā daṇḍavad bhūmau muniṃ mandarasaṃnibhaṃ /
vadantaś ca †*mantraṃ*† samyak petuś caraṇayor mudā / 42 /
ūcuḥ sveṣāṃ caritrāṇi hy asākṣitvena ninditāḥ /
pāhi pāhi mahābhāga kṛpāḷo dīnavatsala / 43 /
śaunakaḥ /
ity ākarṇya vacas teṣāṃ śokapūritadiṅmukhaṃ /
uddhariṣyāmy ahaṃ viprāḥ kṣaṇād eva na saṃśayaḥ / 44 /
kṛpākaraḥ sa bhagavān ity uktvā cābhayaṃ dadau /
saptamud*rās* tataḥ kṛtvā †*mantraṃ*† vaiśvambharānvitaṃ / 45 /
tathāṣṭākṣaramantraṃ ca viṣṇunāmāṅkitaṃ śubhaṃ /
śāsayitvā tato yogī prayayay taiś ca satkṛtaḥ / 46 /
niṣkaḷaṅkāś ca te viprāḥ guror vacanagauravāt /
tasmin grāme ni*vasantās* punaś ca nṛpaśāsanāt / 47 /
bahunātra kim uktena nirbhītāḥ saṃcaranty aho /
teṣāṃ darśanamātreṇa pātityaṃ labhate naraḥ / 48 /
prāyaścittavidhiṃ vakṣye ṣaṣṭhakāl†*āsanaṃ*† caret / 49 /

CHAPTER FIVE (Skh.u. 13)

śatānīkaḥ /
vicitram idam ākhyātaṃ vicitraṃ tvanmukhodgataṃ /
bhūyo 'pi śrotum icchāmi vada māhātmyam uttamaṃ / 1 /
śaunakaḥ /
śṛṇu rājan pravakṣyāmi . . . . /
purā śatavitantūnāṃ garbhiṇīnāṃ narottama / 2 /
nānādeśodbhavānāṃ ca vṛttāntaṃ pravadāmi te /
aṅgavaṅgakaliṅgebhyaḥ saurāṣṭrād gujja*rāt* tathā / 3 /
āndhradrāviḍakarṇāṭakāśmīrebhyas tathaiva ca /
mahārāṣṭrotka*ḷābh*yāṃ ca sindumāgadha . . . / 4 /
gauḍagorāṣṭradeśābhyāṃ parityaktā vitantavaḥ /
saṃjātāḥ pūrṇagarbhiṇyaḥ kṛtāśrāddhavigarhitāḥ / 5 /
ākalparahitā nāryaḥ kṣutpipāsātipīḍitāḥ /
mīḷitvā tāḥ samāyātāḥ tuṅgabhadrāntikaṃ nṛpa / 6 /
tīrastham advayaṃ śāntaṃ virūpākṣaṃ maheśvaraṃ /
nāryaḥ sarvāḥ samāviṣṭāḥ stutiṃ kartuṃ pracakramuḥ / 7 /
tatrāpaśyan mahābhāgaṃ nāsāgrakṛtalocanaṃ /
kaṇvaṃ nāma mahābhāgaṃ śataghasrādi*ka*prabhaṃ / 8 /
ūcuḥ prāñjalayaḥ sarvāḥ svavṛttāntaṃ pṛthak pṛthak /
kā gatir no vada muṇe ninditānāṃ ca mādṛśāṃ / 9 /
kiṃ kurmaḥ kutra gacchāmaḥ śreyo maraṇam eva naḥ /
garbhiṇyā vacanaṃ śrutvā kṛpāḷur vākyam abravīt / 10 /
kaṇvaḥ /
upatyakāyāṃ kroḍādreḥ āsāte śaṃkarācyutau /
tayoḥ samīpe vārāhī sahyaśailasamudbhavā / 11 /
tasyāḥ kūle tapasyantaṃ sarvakṣatrakulāntakaṃ /
bhārgavaṃ taṃ mahābhāgaṃ śaraṇaṃ vrajata drutaṃ / 12 /
iti tasya vacaḥ śrutvā muniṃ natvā punaḥ punaḥ /
yatrāste karuṇāsindhus tatraiva samupāgatāḥ / 13 /
nadīkule tapasyantaṃ vaiśvānarasamadyutiṃ /
*da*dṛśur bhārgavaṃ hṛṣṭāḥ tasyāntikam upāga*man* / 14 /
rakṣa rakṣa mahābāho sarvabhūtadayānidhe /

duḥkhān nas tāraya vibho . . . . . duḥsa*hāt* / 15 /
ittham ākranditāḥ petuḥ pādopānte nṛpātmaja /
tvad*āgatā* vayaṃ brahman dūṣitāḥ pāpakāriṇ*yaḥ* / 16 /
uddhāraya dayāsindho mṛtaprāyā hataśriyaḥ /
śaunakaḥ /
tāsāṃ vākyam athākarṇya kṛpāḷur bhṛgunandanaḥ / 17 /
darśayan svaprabhāvaṃ ca sāntvayan vākyam āha saḥ /
uddharann iva netrābhyā abhayaṃ dattavān muniḥ / 18 /
kā vipattiś ca samprāptā sarvaṃ vadata suvratāḥ /
kṣa*ṇār*dhe 'pi tathā na †*syād*† bhayaṃ mā kurutādhunā / 19 /
karābhyām añjalīkṛtvā procur bhārgavasaṃmukhe /
nāryaḥ /
bho bhārgava mahāprājña dayāḷo kṣatriyāntaka / 20 /
prāgjanmacaritaṃ vṛttaṃ bhujyate 'smābhir īdṛśaṃ /
svabandhubhyaḥ parityaktā mandabhāgya nirākṛtāḥ / 21 /
prāṇān moktum adhairyatvād gacchāmo niyater balāt /
pūrvapuṇyaprabhāvena tvaddarśanam abhūd vibho / 22 /
kṛpāṃ kuru bhṛguśreṣṭha pālayāsmān dvijottama /
iti tāsāṃ vacaḥ śrutvā abhayaṃ dattavān kila / 23 /
†*paraśurāmaḥ*† /
itaḥ ṣaḍyojanād dūre gokarṇeśasya saṃnidhau /
tatra nyagrodhavṛkṣo 'sti . . . . . maṇḍitaḥ / 24 /
tatra sthānaṃ prakurvantu nirbhītyā mama śāsanāt /
vihāya nāsābharaṇaṃ vinā pādāṅgulīyakaṃ / 25 /
dhāryatāṃ śrotrayoḥ samyag ākalpāntaṃ bhaviṣyati /
saṃjātānāṃ ca yuṣmabhiḥ saṃyutānāṃ ca lakṣaṇaiḥ / 26 /
tanujānāṃ tu tanujāṃ kāryaṃ vaivāhikaṃ śubhaṃ /
itthaṃ śatavitantūnāṃ varaṃ datvā mahāmuniḥ / 27 /
paśyatāṃ sarvalokānāṃ tatraivāntaradhīyata /
atha tasya vacaḥ śrutvā nyagrodhaṃ samupāviśan / 28 /
tatra sthānaṃ samāsādya grāmasthānām anujñayā /
sukhena nyavasan bhūpa bhārgavasyājñayā tadā / 29 /
kāścit kanyāḥ suṣuvire kāścit putrān mahābalān /
sveṣu sveṣu ca saṃbandhaṃ cakrur anyonyamārgataḥ / 30 /
tadā prabhṛti te sarve rājante bhuvane bata /
śaunakaḥ /
tāsu jātā mahābhāga śūdrā eva na saṃśayaḥ / 31 /

teṣāṃ saṃsargamātreṇa pātityam anugacchati /
tatpāpavinivṛttyarthaṃ mārtāṇḍam avalokayet / 32 /
bahunātra kim uktena punar anyaṃ vadāme te / 33 /

CHAPTER SIX (Skh.u. 14)

śaunakaḥ /
dvātriṇśadgrāmavāsibhyaḥ parityaktā narādhamāḥ /
kirātakanyāsaṃsargāt pracaranti nirākṛtāḥ / 1 /
caturviṇśatyarbhakānāṃ doḷānāṃ †sakuṭumbināṃ† /
satataṃ duścaritrāṇāṃ vibhavaṃ pravadāmi te / 2 /
purā dhvajotsave ramye candradatte narādhipe /
nānādeśāt samāyātāḥ nānāvarṇā †dvijā*da*yaḥ† / 3 /
brahmakṣat*ri*yaviṭśūdrā vivarṇāḥ śabarādayaḥ /
sarve te cotsavaṃ dṛṣṭvā jagmus tatra yathāgatāḥ / 4 /
janasammardataḥ kācit kanyā śabarasaṃbhavā /
vyastastābhūt tadā bhūpa sundarī pañcahāyanā / 5 /
gujjaragrāmagāḥ kecit vañcayitvātha bālakīṃ /
tasminn eva tadā rātrau tāṃ gṛhītvā yayur gṛhān / 6 /
duḥkhitā bāndhavās tasyāḥ mātṛbhrātrādayas tathā /
adṛṣṭvā bālakīṃ sarve duḥkham †avā*pire*† / 7 /
dinatrayam atho gatvā kleśayitvā puraṃ yayuḥ /
atīva dhūrtās te viprāḥ pupuṣus tāṃ puḷindajāṃ / 8 /
tām anyagrāmavaryasya sūnor udvāhaḥ kriyate /
śaba*rīṃ* te vidhānena cakradevena coditāḥ / 9 /
vyatīte ṣoḍaśe varṣe sā sutā śubhalakṣaṇā /
tanayā maṅgalāpāṅgī tārādhipanibhānanān / 10 /
putrān prāpa kramāt sā tu sarvāvayavasundarān /
itthaṃ pravartamānāyāḥ vyatīyur bahavaḥ samāḥ / 11 /
śaunakaḥ /
dhvajotsavaṃ punar draṣṭuṃ tadgrāmasthā dvijātayaḥ /
tayā nāryā samāyuktā tatputraiḥ pari*var*titāḥ / 12 /
nānādeśasthitā viprā utsavaṃ draṣṭum āgatāḥ /
vyādhaḥ so 'pi svabandhubhyaḥ sabhāryaḥ sahasāgamat / 13 /
tatrotsavadine rātrau tān bandhūn dṛṣṭavān kila /
sā tāvan mātaraṃ dṛṣṭvā rurodātīva duḥkhitā / 14 /
uraś ca tāḍayām āsa sā mātātīva duḥkhitā /
pitā . . . . / 15 /
etasminn antare martyāḥ hāhākāraṃ pracakramuḥ /

agrajasya vadhūr nīcā vañcayitvā †pra*yas*yati† / 16 /
iti te bāndhavāḥ sarve rājñe vārtāṃ nyaveda*yan* /
bhūpo 'tivismayo bhūtvā tām āhūya pulindajāṃ / 17 /
kimarthaṃ dvijapatnīṃ ca apahṛtya †pra*yas*yasi† /
iti rājavacaḥ śrutvā taṃ pratyāha puḷindajā / 18 /
puḷindajā /
eṣā madīyā bālā tu vinaṣṭābhūd dhvajotsave /
idānīṃ daivayogena prāptā mama kumārikā / 19 /
asminn arthe pramāṇāni kuryāṃ bhavad anugrahāt /
itthaṃ vijñapya rājñe tu sudhīrā sā sutānvitā / 20 /
putra*pa*tisamāyuk*tā* yayau vyā*dhā* svamandiraṃ /
tas*yā* vākyam athākarṇya nṛpatir vismayānvitaḥ / 21 /
nirdahann iva netrābhyāṃ krodhāt saṃraktavigrahaḥ /
abravīt tān sabhāmadhye tathyaṃ vadata bhūsurāḥ / 22 /
śaunakaḥ /
tadā dvijātayaḥ sarve nyūcur bhītātivihvalāḥ /
kṛtam asmābhir āgaś ca tatsarvaṃ kṣamyatāṃ vibho / 23 /
ity uktvā pādayos tasya petuḥ pāpanarādhamāḥ /
atha rājā mahāprājñaḥ satyadharmarataḥ sudhīḥ / 24 /
svīkṛtya teṣāṃ sarvasvaṃ grāmasthebhyaḥ pradattavān /
†parityā*gā*parityāgaṃ† tair eva tu vidhīyatāṃ / 25 /
ity uktvā nṛpatir dhīmān jagāma nijapattanaṃ /
dvātriṇśadgrāmavāsibhyo vrīḷāvanatamastakāḥ / 26 /
sametya sahasā tatra pāpināṃ grāmavāsināṃ /
teṣāṃ saṃparkiṇāṃ rājan caturviṇśatkuṭumbināṃ / 27 /
caturviṇśatyarbhakāṇāṃ ḍolāny ādāya satvaraṃ /
teṣāṃ jaleṣu nikṣipya †raktamālyāni† yāni ca / 28 /
teṣāṃ grāmād bahirdeśe tadvad . . . †*tvaritaṃ*† /
tathā visarjayām āsuḥ mahābhāgā dṛḍhavratāḥ / 29 /
tebhyaḥ śrāddhaṃ tataḥ kṛtvā vidhivat kumbhasaṃjñitaṃ /
dvātriṇśadgrāmamadhye tu na deyaṃ sthānam īdṛśāṃ / 30 /
ity ābhāṣya mahābhāgā yayuḥ sarve yathāgatāḥ /
śaunakaḥ /
kiṃ vaktavyaṃ mahārājan dvātriṇśadgrāmavāsināṃ / 31 /
itthaṃ pratijñāyuktānāṃ māhātmyaṃ satyavādināṃ /
tatas te patitāḥ sarve pracaranti narādhamāḥ / 32 /
sthānahīnāḥ parityaktāḥ sarvakarmabahiṣkṛtāḥ /

teṣāṃ darśanamātreṇa pātityaṃ prāpnuvanti hi / 33 /
prāyaścittavidhānaṃ tu mayā vaktuṃ na śakyate /
tatrāpi samakāle tu koṭimārtaṇḍadarśanāt / 34 /
tadā pūtā bhaviṣyanti nātra kāryā vicāraṇā /
bahunātra kim uktena grāmam anyaṃ vadāmi te / 35 /

CHAPTER SEVEN (Skh.u. 15)

śatānīkaḥ /
bhūyo 'pi śrotum icchāmi pātityagrāma*ge*hagaṃ /
ekād ekatamaṃ citraṃ lokanāṃ upakārakaṃ / 1 /
śaunakaḥ /
pātityagrāmam asty anyat cakranadyās taṭe śubhe /
nāgagrāmaṃ tad ity āhuḥ sarvakarmabahiṣkṛtaṃ / 2 /
rāmasṛṣṭās tu ye pūrvāḥ adhyūṣuḥ †saṃsth*āna*ṃ ca te† /
mayūravarmānītānāṃ viprāṇāṃ karadāyakāḥ / 3 /
ullikhan tatkṣitiṃ kecit kecid ā*rā*makāriṇaḥ /
vedabāhyāḥ karmaśūnyāḥ tantumātrā dvijātayaḥ / 4 /
gāyatrījapamātreṇa brāhmaṇā iti tad viduḥ /
khyātā lokeṣu sarvatra svagrāmābhidhayaiva te / 5 /
devatārādhane cāpi śrutismṛtyudite 'pi ca /
†anāhār*yā*maśākena† bhojane pratibhojane / 6 /
mayūravarmā sa purā medhāvī ballabhīṃ prati /
rāmeṇa nirmitair vipraiḥ vāhayitvā svavāhanaṃ / 7 /
śiṣṭān vipr*ān* samādāya punaḥ svapuram āyayau /
grāmapradānasamaye procur bhārgavanirmitāḥ / 8 /
purā bhārgavarāmeṇa sādhitā bhūr iyaṃ nṛpa /
sai 'va rāmeme hāte jāḥ satyasas yā dṛḍhavṛtāḥ / 9 /
asmabhyaṃ dattavāstū*nā*m asya dāyādharā ki*la* /
avahṛtya kathaṃ tebhyo dadāti vasudhām imāṃ / 10 /
tathā bhavatu medhāvī kā gatir no vidhīyatāṃ /
śaunakaḥ /
teṣāṃ vākyam athākarṇya sāntvayann āha pārthivaḥ / 11 /
grāmacatuṣṭayaṃ dāsye sthīyatāṃ tatra śāśvataṃ /
ity uktvā nṛpatiḥ śrīmān dadau grāmacatuṣṭayaṃ / 12 /
†kuśasthalīṃ tathā sāṣṭi maṭināgapur*aṃ ta*thā† /
āgatebhyo dvijebhyaś ca śeṣāṃ bhūmiṃ pradattavān / 13 /
śaunakaḥ /
rāmeṇa nirmitā viprāḥ sthitvā grāmacatuṣṭaye /
ṣaṭkarmarahitā ye tu rājante bhuvaneśvara / 14 /
bahunātra kim uktena sarvakarmabahiṣkṛtāḥ / 15 /

CHAPTER EIGHT (Skh.u. 16)

śaunakaḥ /
vakṣyāmi rājaśārdūla grāmam anyad bahiṣkṛtaṃ /
velañjīti tad ity āhuḥ sītāyāś cottararodhasi / 1 /
kṛtvā mithunahatyāṃ ca pracaranti narādhamāḥ /
vibhavaṃ pravadāmy adya sāvadhānamanāḥ śṛṇu / 2 /
āsīt purā vīrabhūpaḥ puraṃdarasamadyutiḥ /
dhanvinām agraṇīḥ śreṣṭhaḥ yaṃ vidur bhūpuraṃdaraṃ / 3 /
sarvakāmasamṛddhyāḍhyāṃ nagarīṃ ratnamālinīṃ /
. . . . śriyā dīd*ye* . . . . . saṃsthitāṃ / 4 /
jarāśokaklamaharāṃ niṣkalaṅkāṃ nirākulāṃ /
antaḥsalilayatnāḍhyāṃ utkṣiptadhvajatoraṇāṃ / 5 /
divyamūlaphalair vṛkṣaiḥ phalapuṣpopaśobhitāṃ /
nīlapītasitaiḥ śyāmair lohitaiś cāmarair mṛgaiḥ / 6 /
latāgulmaiḥ parivṛtāṃ raktamañjīradhāribhiḥ /
puṣpitā grāmahāśākhāḥ pravālāṅkuradhāriṇaḥ / 7 /
latāvitānasaṃchannā nadīṣu sarasīṣu ca /
vṛkṣā bahuvidhās tatra rājante ketavo yathā / 8 /
ketakāśokabakuḷāḥ puṃnāgatilakārjunāḥ /
cūtanimbāś ca badarī kadambabakuḷā dhavāḥ / 9 /
priyaṅgupāṭa*lās* jambuśālmalyaḥ plakṣavañjuḷāḥ /
sālatālatamālāś ca campakāś ca †manoramāḥ† / 10 /
saṃphullapuṣpaśikharā jvalitāgniśikhā iva /
āmrātakamadhūkāś ca lakuṭāḥ kuṭajāsanāḥ / 11 /
kharjūranārikeḷāś ca pūgāḥ saptaccha*dāś* chadāḥ /
ete cānye ca bahavaḥ śobhante paritaḥ purīṃ / 12 /
gandhavanti ca puṣpāṇi rasavanti phalāni ca /
. . . . tatra tatra sarāṇsi ca / 13 /
bhāsante puṇyatīrthāni ramyāṇi vimalāni ca /
merumadaratulyāni saudhāni bhavanāni ca / 14 /
nagarīṃ tāṃ viśeṣajñaḥ pālayām āsa bhūmipaḥ /
tasya rāṣṭre divjaḥ kaścid vedavedāṅgapāragaḥ / 15 /
yathārthanām*nā* bhagavān āsīd guṇanidhiḥ purā /
tasya jyeṣṭhā guṇavatī dvitīyā guṇamāliṇī / 16 /

rūpayauvanasaṃpanne bhārye bālamṛgekṣaṇe /
stanaṃdhayīṃ kaniṣṭhāyā rakṣaṇaṃ kurute sadā / 17 /
ādaratvāj jyeṣṭhabhāryā tāṃ kanyām aurasīm iva /
dvitīya cakrahṛdayā †madaṃ† bhartuś ca kurvatī / 18 /
atīva namrabhāvena cāste sā guṇamālinī /
śaunakaḥ /
itthaṃ pravartatas tasya dvijasya bhavanaṃ prati / 19 /
gorāṣṭranilayaḥ kaścid vipro vedavidāṃ varaḥ /
śayanārtham athāyātaḥ tanayāt khinnamānasaḥ / 20 /
duḥkhena rātrau śayanam akaroj jāgaraṃ muniḥ /
tasyāḥ kṣapāyā madhye tu kaniṣṭhā varavarṇinī / 21 /
utthāya śayanāt tūrṇam anvagāc chiśusaṃnidhaṃ /
mātsaryāt . . . . . arbha*ka*kaṃdharaṃ tadā / 22 /
babhañja nṛpaśārdula dhairyamālambhya cetasā /
taṃ śiśuṃ sahasā hatvā bhūyaḥ paryaṅkam āviśat / 23 /
kiṃ vaktavyaṃ durācārā sākṣād evābhavat tadā /
atha prabhāte jyeṣṭhā sā utthāya śayanāt tadā / 24 /
aṅkagāṃ bālakīṃ dṛṣṭvā rudhireṇārditāṃ tanuṃ /
āḥ kim etad idaṃ ghoraṃ hā hatāsmīty avocata / 25 /
udaraṃ tāḍayantī sā karābhyām ativihvalā /
jaḍībhūtvā kṣaṇenātha vilalāpātiduḥkhitā / 26 /
ārtasvaraṃ tadākarṇya kaniṣṭhātīvrabheṣajaṃ /
vaicitryeṇa †mahā*bhāga*† pralalāpa tathāvidhaṃ / 27 /
dvayor vivādaṃ śrutvā tu dvijaḥ khinnam *anva*bhavat /
rājñe nivedayām āsa vṛttāntaṃ vistarāt tayoḥ / 28 /
vipravākyam athākarṇya samrāḍ vismayam āpa saḥ /
tadānīṃ mantribhiḥ sārddhaṃ nirṇetuṃ na śaśāka ha / 29 /
samāhūya sa medhāvī bhūsuraṃ śayanārthinaṃ /
tathyaṃ vada yathādṛṣṭaṃ śaṅkāṃ mā kuru mā kuru / 30 /
nṛpater vākyam ābadhvā bhūsuraḥ prāha sasmitaṃ /
aho prāgabhyasiṇho 'yaṃ yuvatījanahāsyadaṃ / 31 /
mataṅgajaṃ vihāyādya maśakaṃ hantum udya*taḥ* /
dhyātvā muhūrtaṃ manasā dvijaḥ so 'pi dṛḍhīkṛtaḥ / 32 /
. . . . /
. . . . / 33 /
. . . . /
. . . . / 34 /

vipraḥ /
na jātam anayoḥ karma duṣkṛtaṃ cātigarhitaṃ /
tathāpy upāyaṃ vakṣyāmi rājaśreṇīśiromaṇe / 35 /
pratyagvārdhitaṭe ramye vikhyāte *vijayāntike* /
tasmin rāṣṭre dvijaḥ kaścit caturbhiḥ sūnubhiḥ saha / 36 /
jyeṣṭho vedavidāṃ śreṣṭho dvitīyaḥ śabdaśāstravit /
tṛtīyo līpiśāstrajñaḥ kaniṣṭho nyāya†*nipuṇaḥ*† / 37 /
gorāṣṭradeśādhipatiḥ sarvajño 'pi mahāmatiḥ /
. . tasya purobhāge nityaṃ nītijanaiḥ kṛtaṃ / 38 /
tam ānaya mahābāho prāgalbhyeṣv atikovidaḥ /
kaluṣākaluṣaṃ samyak sa kariṣyaty asaṃśayaḥ / 39 /
vinā tena tribhuvane nirṇetuṃ ko 'pi nāsti hi /
tathety uktvā narapatiḥ lekhayitvā supatrikāṃ / 40 /
cārān ājñāpayām āsa gorāṣṭranilayaṃ prati /
te prāpuḥ satvaraṃ dūtāḥ dadū rājñe *su*patrikāṃ / 41 /
lekhyam ālokayāṃ cakre gorāṣṭrādhipatiḥ svayaṃ /
taṃ tārkikaṃ samāhūya gadati sma nṛpottamaḥ / 42 /
idānīṃ sarvabhaumaś ca premṇā tvāṃ draṣṭum icchati /
†vijayākh*yā* purī ram*yā*† tvayā śvo gamyatām iti / 43 /
tathā sa bāḍham ity uktvā pratasthe vipranandanaḥ / 44 /

CHAPTER NINE (Skh.u. 17)

śaunakaḥ /
bhāvyavasthāmahājñāto helayā vidhicoditaḥ /
†*sa*gotrebhyaḥ *hā*tas† tūrṇaṃ nirjagāma śanaiḥ śanaiḥ / 1 /
tatrotpātāḥ samudbhūtāḥ divibhūmyantarikṣagāḥ /
. . prāptikarā ghorā dāruṇā romaharṣaṇāḥ / 2 /
nanādāntarhitā bhūmau pṛṣadaṉso jagarja ca /
anekaśākhāsaṃyuktā vṛkṣāḥ petuḥ samantataḥ / 3 /
viprasya dakṣiṇe bhāge śilā ghorā vavāśire /
rudanti vāyasās tasya śaśāṅkaḥ samadṛśyata / 4 /
etāny *ut*pātakādīni manasā na smaran yayau /
śaunakaḥ /
dināny aṣṭādaśātīte sārvabhaumaṃ dadarśa saḥ / 5 /
sa rājā matimān vipraṃ mānayitvā jagāda taṃ /
śiśuhatyām idaṃ samyak vicāraya mahāmate / 6 /
tac chrutvā dvijaśārdūlaḥ praviveśa sabhāṅgaṇaṃ /
dvijabhār*ye* samāhūya provāca dvijapuṃgavaḥ / 7 /
brāhmaṇaḥ /
vihāya vastrābharaṇaṃ tathā lajjāṃ vihāya yā /
pradakṣiṇaṃ karoty āśu sabhāṃ samyak sulocane / 8 /
sā niṣpāpā bhavaty evaṃ nātra kāryā vicāraṇā /
evam uktvā dvijavaraḥ tūṣṇīṃ tatrābhavat kila / 9 /
śaunakaḥ /
śrutvā jyeṣṭhā ca tad vākyaṃ hā kaṣṭaṃ prāptavaty ahaṃ /
manasā na kṛtaṃ karma durlabhyā niyater gatiḥ / 10 /
kathaṃ kāryaṃ pramāṇaṃ ca hṛdā smartuṃ na śakyate /
kaluṣaṃ *na* dhārayāmi na dhāryaṃ ninditaṃ mayā / 11 /
prāṇam eva parityaj*yaṃ* mānam evābhirakṣituṃ /
anityam adhruvaṃ prāṇaṃ mānam ācandratārakaṃ / 12 /
uttamā mānam icchanti dhanamānau hi madhyamāḥ /
adhamā dhanam icchanti māno hi mahatāṃ dhanaṃ / 13 /
tasmād ahaṃ pramāṇāni kadācid api na *kuryāṃ* /
paśyanti sarvabhūtāni tyakṣyāmīdaṃ kalevaraṃ / 14 /
ity uktvā sā guṇavatī tūṣṇīm evābhavat tadā /

dvitīyotthāya tvarayā vastrādyaiś ca vinā satī / 15 /
pradakṣinatrayaṃ kṛtvā tāṃ sabhāṃ varavarṇinīṃ /
tasthau tadā purobhāge nirlajjā bhayavarjitā / 16 /
tāṃ dṛṣṭvā manujāḥ sarve hāhākāraṃ pracukruśuḥ /
krūrayā pāparatayā bālakī cānayā hatā / 17 /
asminn arthe mahārājā śaṅkāṃ mā kuru mā kuru /
tasyāḥ sa *dhī*ratāṃ dṛṣṭvā rājā vismayam āgataḥ / 18 /
daṇḍayitvā śiśughnāṃ tāṃ mānayitvā dvijottamaṃ /
premṇā tasmai dhanaṃ gāś ca grāmadvayam adāt punaḥ / 19 /
anekavastrābharaṇaṃ vaijayantīṃ manoramāṃ /
datvā pradhānatāṃ rājā viśati sma niketanaṃ / 20 /
tadā prabhṛti loko 'sau prāvardhata dine dine /
śuklapakṣe śaśāṅkasya kaleva nṛpanandana / 21 /
grāmadvayaṃ sagotrebhyo dattaṃ dvijasattamaḥ /
sukhena nivasaṉs tasya mahatkālo nyavartata / 22 /
śaunakaḥ /
athainaṃ nigrahaṃ kartuṃ randhrānveṣaṇatatparāḥ /
sametya mantri*ṇaḥ* sarve prācīnā bandhavairiṇaḥ / 23 /
atīva mūrkhaḥ saṃjātaḥ sūnus tasya durātmavān /
tasya bhāryā varārohā rūpayauvanaśālinī / 24 /
āyatākṣā śubhaśroṇī pīnonnatakucadvayā /
bimbādharī suvadanā *viṇ*mārge ca pravartinī / 25 /
kadācij jāramartyeṇa vilāsaṃ kurvatī satī /
bhartā tathāvidhāṃ dṛṣṭvā tāṃ krodhād vivaśaṃ gataḥ / 26 /
khaḍgam udyamya hastena mithunīkṛtavigrahau /
smaragraheṇa vivaśau tau tadābandhayantritau / 27 /
kalābhijñau tu nipuṇau saṃbhāram akarot krudhā /
daivād ayaṃ samāyātaḥ kalas †*enaḥ*†śubhāptaye / 28 /
idānīṃ doṣam ā*rop*ya prācīnā mantrasattamāḥ /
rajñe nivedayām āsuḥ vārtāṃ mithunahatyakāṃ / 29 /
parityāgāya caiteṣām upāyaṃ cakrur añjasā /
gorāṣṭrajānāṃ mūrkhāṇāṃ pāpināṃ krūrakarmaṇāṃ / 30 /
āste mahābale*śe*ti gorāṣṭre sindhusaṃnidhau /
dakṣiṇasthā mahākṣetram avimuktaṃ vadanti hi / 31 /
yātrāṃ kṛtvā mahādevaṃ tathā kroḍeśvaraṃ vibhuṃ /
tathaiva darśanaṃ kṛtvā prāpnuvanti viśuddhatāṃ / 32 /

śaunakaḥ /
atha gorāṣṭrajāḥ sarve duḥkhān nirga*ma*tatpa*rāḥ* /
pātityavini*vṛt*tyartham tīrthayātrāṃ śanaiḥ śanaiḥ / 33 /
kurvantaḥ sahyam āsādya nānāmuniganair vṛtaṃ /
avatīrya gireḥ śṛṅgaṃ taulavaṃ deśam āviśan / 34 /
kramād gokarṇam adrākṣuḥ tatkṣetrasthaṃ mahābalaṃ /
gokarṇeśaṃ ca saṃpūjya vidhivan nṛpanandana / 35 /
snātvā śuktimatītoye sarvāghaughavināśini /
vidhivat pūjayām āsuḥ sveṣāṃ pāpanivṛttaye / 36 /
paścat tāpena saṃyuktā dakṣiṇāṃ diśam āyayuḥ /
dvābhyāṃ piśācarūpābhyāṃ suptaghnasya durātmanāṃ / 37 /
. . . . yatra yatra tatra tatra gamiṣyataḥ /
ananteśasamīpe tu tapasyantaṃ mahāmuniṃ / 38 /
śaṅkhacakragadāpadmamudrālāñchitavigrahaṃ /
taṃ dṛṣṭvā daṇḍavad bhūmau petuś caraṇayor mudā / 39 /
ū*cuḥ* sveṣāṃ caritrāṇi yugma*hatye*na dūṣitāḥ /
dhyātvā muhūrtaṃ dharmātmā kṛpayāviṣṭamānasaḥ / 40 /
dadau tīrthodakaṃ tebhyaḥ sūcayann iva maṅgaḷaṃ /
. . . tīrthamadhye tu guñjamātrāsthitaṃ śubhaṃ / 41 /
janārdana iti khyātaṃ śālagrāmam abhūt kila /
kṛtārtho '*stī*ti niścitya mañjūṣāṃ te †nibadhya† tāṃ / 42 /
āruhya sahyaśikharaṃ gantuṃ sarve pracakramuḥ /
mārge madhyāhnaveḷāyāṃ sītāyā uttare taṭe / 43 /
gaḷitaṃ panasaṃ dṛṣṭvā vṛkṣamūlam upāviśan /
phalaṃ tat sahasā bhittvā bubhukṣus te †narās tadā† / 44 /
vastreṇa mārjanaṃ kṛtvā †hastaman*tra*vivarji*taṃ*† /
te sarve gāḍham āgatya vṛkṣamūlaṃ vyalokayan / 45 /
tatra dṛṣṭvā mahāścaryaṃ kim etad iti śabditāḥ /
āsīt karaṇḍapī*ṭhe* ca śālagrāmo janārdanaḥ / 46 /
gantuṃ gṛhītvā taṃ mūḍhāḥ †khananāyo†pacakramuḥ /
etasminn antare bhūpa vyomni gīḥ samapadyata / 47 /
sthīyatām atra bho viprāḥ . . sthānaṃ bhaviṣyati /
eṣa eva na saṃdeho bhaviṣyati janārdanaḥ / 48 /
yuṣmākaṃ kuladaiva*taṃ* śreyaḥ prāptivivṛddhaye /
ity uktvā sā bhagavatī tatraivāntarhitā śivā / 49 /
kaiṣā sarasvatī kena kāraṇenoditā kila /
iti sarve samālocya harṣanirbharayantritāḥ / 50 /

asminn eva mahāgrāme pravāsaṃ kurmahe vayaṃ /
triṉśatsadmāni te cakrur grāmasthanām anujñayā / 51 /
ūṣus te katicit kālaṃ havyakavyavivārjitāḥ /
nāyātāḥ pūrvanilayāḥ eteṣāṃ bhavanaṃ prati / 52 /
kim etad iti niścitya sveṣāṃ pāpena śaṅkitāḥ /
munim ālokayām āsuḥ pūrvadṛṣṭaṃ mahājanāḥ / 53 /
so 'pi dṛṣṭvā mahātejāḥ pāvayām āsa śāstrataḥ /
taptamudāṅkitaḥ kṛtvā man*traṃ* vaiṣṇavasaṃjñitaṃ / 54 /
tathaivāṣṭākṣaraṃ mantraṃ paraṃ copadideśa saḥ /
ā no bhadreti mantreṇa mṛdāharaṇam ucyate / 55 /
ā mandrair iti sūktena mṛdā lepanam ucyate /
akṣibhyāṃ teti mantreṇa mṛdā snānaṃ viśiṣyate / 56 /
śaunakaḥ /
guror anujñaṃ svīkṛtya vāsaṃ cakrur atandritāḥ /
tadā prabhṛti tad grāmaṃ velañjīti vadanti hi / 57 /
tatra sthitān dvijān sarvān patitān pravadanti hi /
bahunātra kim uktena rājaśreṇiśiromaṇe / 58 /
teṣāṃ darśanamātreṇa pātityaṃ cānuyāsyati /
prāyaścittaṃ mayā vaktuṃ na śakyaṃ nṛpanandana / 59 /
sādhāraṇenaiva vakṣye kṛcchracāndrāyaṇaṃ caret / 60 /

CHAPTER TEN (Skh.u. 18)

śaunakaḥ /
anyad *grāmaṃ* pravakṣyāmi bhūdevasya mahātmanaḥ /
. . gorāṣṭrajasyātha sāvadhānamanāḥ śṛṇu / 1 /
abhūt kaḷiṅgadeśe tu nāmnā kāñcanamālinī /
nārīnarasamāyuktā hastyaśvarathasaṃkulā / 2 /
tasyāṃ puryāṃ jagattrātā ravigotrasamudbhavaḥ /
āsīt purā hemamālī yudhiṣṭhirasamadyutiḥ / 3 /
dhanvinām agrataḥ śreṣṭho mahābalaparākramaḥ /
yudhiprakhyāta†kīrtiś ca† rathakuñjaravājimān / 4 /
dordaṇḍamaṇḍalāgreṇa jitasāmantamaṇḍalaḥ /
udayādrisamārūḍhamārtāṇḍadyutimānayan / 5 /
so 'yaṃ kṣamāmaṇḍalasya cākhaṇḍalasamaprabhaḥ /
mahādāne copadāne jñāninam iti taṃ viduḥ / 6 /
yasya kīrtisukhābdheś ca saṃjātaś candramā iti /
yasya pratāpāt saṃbhūto dhanaṃjaya iti sphuṭaṃ / 7 /
kāmo 'py anaṅgatāṃ nīto rūpaṃ dṛṣṭvā jvalajjitaḥ /
gāmbhīryam asya dṛṣṭvātha . . . . bhayānvitaḥ / 8 /
†vṛddhikṣayatvaṃ† saṃprāptas . . . . /
itthaṃ guṇaviśiṣṭo yo dhīmān rājyaṃ praśāsati / 9 /
anāvṛṣṭibhayaṃ kiṃcit nāsti durbhikṣajaṃ bhayaṃ /
mlecchataskaraśārdūlabakasiṉhādijaṃ bhayaṃ / 10 /
evaṃ pravartatas tasya vyatīyur bahavaḥ samāḥ /
kadācid āgataḥ śrīmān vedavedāṅgapāragaḥ / 11 /
lalāṭanetrāt saṃbhūto vaiśvānarasamadyutiḥ /
tathāpi śāntisaṃyukto mūrtimāna*vo* lakṣyate / 12 /
sumatyā bhāryayā yukto śiṣyaiḥ satatam āvṛtaḥ /
agrajasyānurodhaṃ *yat* tad vākyaṃ prākṛte pade / 13 /
. . . . /
samāyātaṃ dvijaṃ vīkṣya madhuparkāsanādibhiḥ / 14 /
pūjayām āsa vidhivat hemamālī nṛpottamaḥ /
prāgalbhyaṃ cāsya paśyāma iti kṛtvā matiṃ dvijaḥ / 15 /
mantrapūtāny akṣatāni prayacchad vāmapāṇinā /
dṛṣṭvainaṃ rājaśārdūlaḥ kiṃcid vyākulitekṣaṇaḥ / 16 /

mantrākṣatam †*āna*yan*taṃ*† vākyaṃ praṣṭuṃ pracakrame /
bho bho deva dvijā loke santi †*sar*vo†ttamottamāḥ / 17 /
teṣāṃ dvijānāṃ madhye tu na hi ko 'pi bhavādṛśaḥ /
īdṛ*śa*karmakartāraṃ na dṛṣṭaṃ jagatītale / 18 /
tasya tad vākyaṃ ākarṇya bhi*yā*śūnyaṃ dvijāgraṇīḥ /
uvāca krodhatāmrākṣo vākyaṃ hetvarthasaṃyutaṃ / 19 /
asmābhiḥ pārthivā †dṛṣ*ṭā*† bahavo nṛpasattama /
na *dṛṣṭaṃ* triṣu lokeṣu vivekānāṃ bhavādṛśaḥ / 20 /
tathā bhavatu dāsyāmo dakṣiṇena kareṇa ca /
gṛhyatāṃ yadi śaktiś cen no cen mūrdhni kṣipāmy ahaṃ / 21 /
bhasmībhavantu tāṃ sarve paśyantv atra mahājanāḥ /
itthaṃ vadati viprendre pārthivas tu tadā nṛpa / 22 /
kirīṭamaṇidīpena pādapīṭhāntabhūtaḷaṃ /
tadā nīrājanaṃ cakre taṃ vipraṃ harṣayann iva / 23 /
uttiṣṭhottiṣṭha rājendra bhītiṃ tyaja mahāmate /
darśayāmo 'sya māhātmyaṃ paṭaṃ vis*tī*ryatām iti / 24 /
ukta*va*†*taś ca*† viprasya dūre tiṣṭhan nṛpottamaḥ /
paṭaṃ vistārayām āsa prabhāvaṃ draṣṭum utsukaḥ / 25 /
dvi*jaḥ* /
viprasya dakṣiṇe haste śikhāvān iti niścayaṃ /
paśyedānīṃ mahārāja jvalantaṃ havyavāhanaṃ / 26 /
ity uktvāsau tadā rājñe darśayām āsa bhūsuraḥ /
svīyaṃ prabhāvaṃ mantrasya sāraṃ sārānvitāya ca / 27 /
vaiśvānarāstraṃ saṃdhāya yat kṣiptaṃ cākṣataiḥ saha /
jājvalyamānas tejobhiḥ kśā*nuḥ* samudaikṣata / 28 /
tat paṭaṃ bhasmasāt kṛtya tāṃ sabhāṃ dagdhum udyataḥ /
śikhāvantaṃ tadālokya sarve saṃtāpayantritāḥ / 29 /
viprasyāntikam āgatya petuś caraṇayor mudā /
rājānam enam asmāṇś ca pāhi pāhi k*pāṃ* kara / 30 /
hara santāpam asmākam upasaṃhara pāvakaṃ /
teṣāṃ vākyam athākarṇya sasmitaḥ sa dvijottamaḥ / 31 /
taṃ kāraṃ . . . . . saṃmantrya . . . . . /
evaṃ kṛte bhagava*tā* śānto 'bhūd *hav*yavāhanaḥ / 32 /
atha bhūpo 'pi harṣābdhitaraṅgeṣu mamajja saḥ /
tadā dvijātaye premṇā cāṣṭau grāmāṇi dattavān / 33 /
asaṃkhyātasuvarṇāni vastrāṇy ābharaṇāni ca /
anarghyamaṇi†saṃyukta† graiveyakam adāt punaḥ / 34 /

indranīlaiḥ padmarāgaiḥ pratyuptaṃ cāṅgadaṃ dadau /
rūpaudāryaguṇair āḍhyaṃ tasmai dāsīśataṃ dadau / 35 /
tādṛgguṇaviśiṣṭasya kiṃ na deyaṃ mahīpate /
tena *saṃ*mānito vipraḥ ślāghayitvā guṇādikaṃ / 36 /
svasti te 'stu gamiṣyāmo yāvad ācandratārakaṃ /
ity uktvā tu dvijaḥ śreṣṭhaḥ pratasthe svapurīṃ prati / 37 /

CHAPTER ELEVEN (Skh.u. 19)

śaunakaḥ /
paredyur atha vipro 'sau saha śiṣyair mudānvitaḥ /
sopaskarāṇi saṃghṛya sthānaṃ gantuṃ pracakrame / 1 /
paśyan ramyāṇi tīrthāṇi kṣetrāṇi vividhāni ca /
kramād agād ameyātmā sahyaparvatam uttamaṃ / 2 /
sa tatra caṇḍikā nāma nadīṃ kalimalāpahāṃ /
vimalodakasaṃpūrṇāṃ siddharṣigaṇasevitāṃ / 3 /
ānīlotpalakalhāraśatapatrair alaṅkṛtāṃ /
cakoracakrakāraṇḍarathāṅgaiḥ pariśobhitāṃ / 4 /
tāṃ dadarśa mahābhāgas tasyāṃ snātuṃ pracakrame /
kṛtvā madhyāhnikaṃ karma pañcayajñadikāḥ kriyāḥ / 5 /
samāpya nityakarmāṇi sabhāryas taṭinītaṭe /
asmāt pa*rā*śu yātavyam iti cakre matiṃ dvijaḥ / 6 /
tataḥ sāyāhnasamaye samīro †mandam āvavau† /
sa tadā dṛṣṭavān *kāṃ*cit kāntādāsīṃ kadambake / 7 /
ṣoḍaśāb*dāṃ* . . . . smaraśaktir ivotthi*tāṃ* /
†lasan†nāsām āyatākṣīṃ tārādhipanibhānanāṃ / 8 /
dvitīyacandralekheva dṛśyamānalāṭikāṃ /
saṃprāptaṣaṭpadānīva vilasatkarṇakuṇḍalāṃ / 9 /
kambukaṇṭhāyatabhujāṃ pīnonnatapayodharāṃ /
sūkṣmamadhyāṃ śubhaśroṇīṃ namrāṅgīṃ navayauvanāṃ /10 /
sunitambojjvalāṃ subhrūṃ padminījātisaṃbhavāṃ /
dāsyāḥ putrīṃ ca tāṃ dṛṣṭvā sadyaḥ smaravaśo 'bhavat / 11 /
enāṃ dṛṣṭvā ratipatiḥ *sa*dṛdhīkṛtakārmukaḥ /
trilokīvijayaḥ so 'pi majjayā āsa saṃśaye / 12 /
yaśaḥ kīrtiṃ ca dhairyaṃ ca sāhasikyamano nṛpa /
tasyām eva kṣapāyāṃ tu yojayām āsa mārgaṇāt / 13 /
*hri*yānantarhitāṃ tanvīṃ śrīmantaṃ bhūsurāgrajaṃ /
yugapad daṃpatībhāvaṃ caṇḍikāyā nadītaṭe / 14 /
śaunakaḥ /
†kācit tanvī dvijaḥ ko 'yaṃ† citrā*dir* niyater gatiḥ /
sa tasyāṃ parṇaśālāyāṃ tayā saha mudānvitaḥ / 15 /
nināya gaṇarātraṃ ca cumbanāliṅganādibhiḥ /

atha tasyā viśālākṣyāḥ snehapātrādvijasya ca / 16 /
sukumārāḥ krameṇaiva cāṣṭau putrā 'bhavan kila /
tān vilokya mudā prājño grāmāny aṣṭau vibhajya ca / 17 /
putrebhyaḥ snehayuktebhyo dadau grāmāny anukramāt /
ekasyaikam athājñāpya śikṣām ittham cakāra saḥ / 18 /
yatra yatra śivāgāre tatra tatra mamājñayā /
śivanirmālyabhuñjāno chattravetrāṇi dhāra*ṇāḥ* / 19 /
saṃmārjanādikaṃ kṛtvā yathā gomayalepanaṃ /
apāṅkteyā viprasaṅghe saṃcarantu mamājñayā / 20 /
†*kālam*† ākrāntam ālokya tapase kṛtaniścayaḥ /
aurasaṃ putram āhūya sunītaṃ nāma kovidaṃ / 21 /
āgamajñam abhijñaṃ taṃ vākyam etad uvāca ha /
ete mama snehapātrāḥ putrāḥ snehaniyantritāḥ / 22 /
prajñena bhavatā samyak snehena paripāl*yan*tāṃ /
ity uktvā vipravaryo 'sau sabhāryas tapase yayau / 23 /
āgamoktena sa muniḥ pitur āj*ñāṃ* na laṅghi*tvā* /
caulopanītikarmāṇi kārayām āsa tān prati / 24 /
śatānīkaḥ /
katha †cakāra vipro 'sau† saṃskāra vidhipūrvakaṃ /
iti ceṭītanūjānāṃ śaṅkāṃ prāpnoti me manaḥ / 25 /
śaunakaḥ /
sādhu pṛṣṭaṃ tvayā rājan śaṅkāsthānam idaṃ khalu /
tā*dṛṅ* nivartayiṣyāmi saṃjātāṃ tava cetasi / 26 /
jaghanyajasya kṣetre tu yadi . . . . . . /
vipravaryāc ca saṃjāto gotrapravarapūrvakaṃ / 27 /
gotrasūtravihīnānāṃ kāśyapaṃ gotram iṣyate /
āśvalāyanasūtreṇa kāryā janmādisatkriyāḥ / 28 /
kārayitvātha yo janmasaṃskāraṃ vidhipūrvakaṃ /
kāśyapaṃ kauśikaṃ caiva tattatpravarabhedataḥ / 29 /
ity ādikaiś ca gotrāṇi saṃdideśa pṛthak pṛthak /
itarāsāṃ ca ceṭīnāṃ saṃjātānāṃ nṛpātmaja / 30 /
vivāham aṣṭakanyānāṃ kārayām āsa śāstrataḥ /
sāṅkaryakoṣavicchityai vibhāgaṃ kṛtavān ayaṃ / 31 /
purā parāśaraḥ sākṣāt nāvikān prāptavān kila /
sākṣāt kuṭhārapāṇis tu goḷakān uddadhāra ha / 32 /
evaṃ mahānubhāvānāṃ sahajaṃ guṇakīrtanaṃ /
ity ādivividhāḥ santi nātra kāryā vicāraṇā / 33 /

evaṃ kṛtvā sa bhagavān punaḥ prāha yathākramaṃ /
nātikramya guror vākyaṃ tathākuruta bhūtaḷe / 34 /
dāsīkadambam āhūya saṃbabhāṣe dvijātmajaḥ /
āgataṃ hi purād yasmāt puraṃ tad anugamyatāṃ / 35 /
ity uktvā dvijavaryo 'sau gacchati sma niketanaṃ /
tadā prabhṛhti te ceṭāḥ caranti pṛthivītaḷe / 36 /
sveṣāṃ vṛttim anādṛtya nirātaṅkā niraṅkuśāḥ /
eteṣāṃ darśanāt puṉsāṃ pātityam anugacchati / 37 /
karmaṣaṭkaṃ ca ṣaṭ . . upvītadvayaṃ tathā /
svapaṅktibhojanaṃ caiva purāṇaśravaṇaṃ tathā / 38 /
rudrākṣadhāraṇaṃ caiva tathoṣṇīṣanibandhanaṃ /
dvijasaṅghapraveśaṃ ca nety āha bhagavān guruḥ / 39 /
bahunātra kim uktena rājan rājendranandana /
apāṅkteyā*nām* eteṣāṃ narāṇāṃ nīcavartināṃ / 40 /
bhuñjānānām adharmāṉś ca gaṅgāsnānaṃ vidhīyate /
sadā teṣāṃ . . . . / 41 /
dvādaśāb*dān* pravastavyaṃ vārāṇasyāṃ na saṃśayaḥ / 42 /

III. TRANSLATION

CHAPTER ONE (Skh.u. 9)

The *ṛṣis* say that they want to hear still more of what was being told and ask to hear about the communities of polluted *brāhmaṇas*. Sūta replies that Śatānīka once asked Śaunaka the same thing. Śatānīka's request is given and the story as told by Śaunaka is begun. Once a *muni* named Kroḍa obtained spiritual release and went to dwell by the *tīrtha* of Kroḍeśa. The Bhārgava comes to the Sahādri range and sees its glories. These are described in detail. The Bhārgava praises Viṣṇu. The Bhārgava then reaches the Śuktimatī river and begins to perform austerities. He is approached by pregnant *brāhmaṇa* widows cast out from their native villages. The Bhārgava shows compassion for these, goes with them to Kroḍeśa and settles them near the *tīrtha* with the promise that their line will increase through the beneficience of Nārāyaṇa who has been made their family deity. The Bhārgava then leaves for Gokarṇa.

* * *

The *ṛṣis* said:
1-5b. Sūta, learned in the content of all the *Purāṇas*, you who have a stainless heart, our thirst increases still more after drinking with our ears the bliss of the nectar-like story which drips from your moon-like face. O *brāhmaṇa*,[1] because of this, have us drink the mysterious diverse nectar-like story which is auspicious and which destroys the pain of existence. O best of the intelligent, you who

have a stainless heart, most certainly we desire to hear everything that was heard by you – the names of the thirty-two villages,[2] the breaking of their housesites, the duties,[3] and also that which was spoken of previously by you as having the title *Pātityagrāma*.

Sūta said:
5c-8. All you *ṛṣis*, listen with attentive minds. This very same thing previously was asked Śaunaka, who was learned in duty, by king Śatānīka, son of Janamejaya, who was singly devoted to the *tīrthas* in the land, who had regard for sacrificial acts, who was one with the lotus-like feet of Śiva, who was devoted to the lord, and who, immediately after seeing that the principal book of the *Bhārata* (i.e., of the *Mahābhārata*)[4] was filled with discord, was eager constantly to hear the *Purāṇas* in accord with the instructions of Vyāsa.

Śatānīka said:
9-12b. O one who is learned in the entire *Vedānta*, who knows the object of all the *Śāstras*, why is there not satisfaction after drinking the nectar of your speech? O *brāhmaṇa*, I desire to hear from you the splendor of the Bhārgava, a detailed description of his land, the names of the thirty-two villages and their respective divinities,[5] and, at length, to hear everything about the presiding deity of the villages which were spoken of by you previously with the words 'there are outlying villages . . . .'

Śaunaka said:
12c-14. Once[6] there was a truthful *muni* with conquered senses named Kroḍa. After undergoing penance for a long time, he brought under control eternal, beneficient Śrīśa (i.e. Viṣṇu, lord of Śrī),[7] and became a person in his own

power. Pleasing himself, †he went† to the city bearing his own name and the *tīrtha* marked with his own *mudrā*.[8] After making an *āśrama* there, he spent many years.[9]

15-28b. Once the blessed Bhārgava who had put an end to all the *kṣatriyas*, desiring to go to Gokarṇa, went †to Mount Mahendra†. He who possessed extraordinary powers of mind saw everywhere *tīrthas*, *āśramas* of the *ṛṣis* and temples. Nearby the *muni* saw the peak of the Sahyādri range of mountains with great *ṛṣis* perfected by *mantras*, austerities and divine herbs, filled with *kiṃnaras*, *gandharvas*, *apsarases*, and *cāraṇas*, with peaks studded with different jewels, with wonderful sapphires,[10] with the tricklings of different fruits, with many caves and ridges, pleasant with the lovers of roaming female *siddhas*, resounding with the sounds of peacocks and cuckoos, entirely permeated with bees blind by drunkenness, always filled with the warbling of red-throated birds, inviting, as it were, wearied travelers with trees yielding whatever is desired, moving, as it were, with elephants, singing, as it were, with insects, adorned with outstretched Mandāra trees and Pārijāta trees, with Tamāla trees, with Sāla trees and Tāla trees, with Kovidāra trees, Asana trees and Arjuna trees, with Cūta trees, with Kadamba trees and Nimba trees and with Nāga, Puṃnāga and Campaka plants, with Pāṭala trees, Aśoka trees and Bakula trees, with Kunda trees, even with Kurabaka trees, with Panasa trees, Udambara trees, Aśvattha trees, Plakṣa trees, Nyagrodha trees, Tinduka trees, with marketable herbs, with Pūga trees, with Rājapūga trees and with Jambu trees, with Āmrātaka trees, with Agniśikha trees, with Priyāḷa trees, with honey-colored Kāsana trees, with other types of trees, embellished with Veṇu bamboo and Kaṇṭaka bamboo, with sporting (?) monkeys, with lions, with elephants[11] and porcupines, with Gayal oxen, with Śarabha deer, with tigers, with large buffaloes, and so forth, filled with musk deer, distinguished by its forest animals with bushy tails (?),[12] covered with thickets of plantain trees, and beautiful with islets of lotuses, with heaps of brightly colored chowrie shells, and †with the brightness of† the plantain trees' [blossoms] †in that place†.

28c-31. Upon seeing Śailendra mountain shining forth, the *muni* was filled with gladness. Descending, he then saw the excellent land of the Tuḷus.[13] Reaching the land, wise Rāma, the son of Bhṛgu, did *pūjā* to the lord Nārāyaṇa according to rule. The Bhārgava did *pūjā* with many different ceremonies, with a number of *mantras* spoken in the *Veda*, and with as many as a hundred thousand lotuses. He then began to eulogize eternal beneficient Śrīśa.

The holy Bhārgava said:[14]

32. 'Homage to the one whose lotus-like feet which themselves are shining[15] are shining [even further] with a thousand gods filled with their own splendor as a crown, to the lord of weapons and missiles, to the most excellent Śaṃkara, to Nārāyaṇa who is stainless and pure.

33. 'Homage to the enemy of Māra, to the destroyer of Madhu and Kaiṭabha, to . . . , to the essence of all the worlds, to Śaṃkara, to Nārāyaṇa who is stainless and pure.

34. 'Homage to the one mentally under the influence of the daughter of the lord of the ocean and the daughter of the king of the mountains . . . and to the one who has the sun, the moon and fire as his eyes, to Śaṃkara, to Nārāyaṇa who is stainless and pure.

35. 'Homage to the one who imprisons the sins of the *kali* age for those who are continuously intent on his worship, to Śaṃkara who cuts off hell, to Nārāyaṇa who is stainless and pure.

36. 'Homage to the one who has the great cities of the demons destroyed with only their names left . . . , to the

lord of all the worlds, to Śaṃkara, to Nārāyaṇa who is stainless and pure.

37. 'Homage to the one whose body consists of earth, water, fire, wind, atmosphere, *pūruṣa*, the sun, . . . , to the one who has ten *vigrahas* (components),[16] and to the one who consists of all which moves and does not move, to Śaṃkara, to Nārāyaṇa who is stainless and pure.

38. 'Homage to the one who took away the fear of earthworms from Mṛkaṇḍu while he was shouting when being held down by the crocadile of Kīnāśa (i.e., Yama)[17] and who has feet and hands like a lotus, to the one propitiated by everyone, to Śaṃkara, to Nārāyaṇa who is stainless and pure.

39. 'Homage to the one who spends his time with the daughter of Nagarāja (i.e., the Himālayas) and [the daughter] of the ocean in all sorts of pleasures, to the one who is fond of man and who carries man, to the one who is a tree of snakes for worshippers, to Śaṃkara, to Nārāyaṇa who is stainless and pure.

40. 'Śaṃkara, you who have a lotus-like navel, lord, conquer! You who give power (perhaps, wealth)! You who have a foot like an ocean of compassion! You who protect treasures! You who are the honored killer of the *daityas*! Hara! Mādhava! You who are the enemy of hindrances to men!

41. 'You who have the *dānavas* as your enemies! You who carry the *cakra* against the *dānavas*! You who . . . ! You who have a restless arm![18] You who are the lord of snakes! You who have the pleasing coils of a snake as your seat! You who have a spear beautified by snakes![19] You who have a broad club!

42. 'Splendid one who is a medicament for diseases! You who have multiform attendants! You who are leader of your attendants! You who give pleasure to the mind! You

who are adorned by lovers' hands (literally, hand-lotuses)! You who are the excellent lord of Śrī! You who grant wishes and give security! You who are a storehouse of treasure!

43. 'You who have gods and *asuras* bowing to your footsteps! You who are full of compassion! You who are a Kalpataru tree[20] who gives all delights to those in misery! You who have a pleasing body adorned with young maidens as its jewels! You who have a body which puts a sapphire to shame!

44. 'You whose crown of jewels disperses [the beams] of the digit of the moon! You who have cowherdesses who are intoxicated by the sound of your flute! You who are free from birth and so forth![21] You who cleft the high mountain! You whose splendor has an expanse similar to a thousand conchs!

45. 'You who have a splendid new *kaustubha* jewel! You who have a conch-like neck! You who have a dark blue strong poison marked on your neck! You who have the venom of a snake as a weapon! You who . . . on the top of your head! You who have a lotus expanded to dance on! . . . !

46. 'You who are fond of the great weapon given to you by the one born in a water-pot (i.e. Agastya)! . . . ! Be Jagadīśa (i.e., lord of the world), Maheśa (i.e., a great lord), Rameśa (i.e., lord of Ramā)![22] You who make the . . . cross the ocean of worldly existence!

47. '. . . ! You who have the splendor of a coral tree . . . on your lips! . . . ! You who have jasmine-like teeth! You who have your lotus-like face shining with a collection of teeth!

48. 'You who have good qualities proclaimed! You who have good fortune as your way! You who are to be worshipped according to the rules! You whose heart is . . . !

You who carry . . . marked with pleasant saffron! You who have a hand on Lola (i.e., Lakṣmī) as if it were on the rose-colored teat of the earth!

49. 'You who killed the pitiless lord of the *daityas* with your fingernails! You who are praised as the thunderbolt coming from the great mountain for the sins of those who have become polluted! You who have as your texts the *Vedas* and *Purāṇas* which praise and provide release! You who are faultless with regard to calculations! You who have pure qualities!

50. 'God of the earth who is not bound by any description of qualities! God! You who are at the root of trees! You who have a glittering radiance! Destroyer of worldly existence! You who give future auspiciousness! You who have as your offspring trickling delightful divine trees!

51. 'You whose weapons are flowers! You whose eyes chastise! You with lotus-like eyes! Conquer! God of Kroḍapurī, conquer! God of the mountain, conquer! You who have conquered the directions, conquer! Bhava! God! Conquer!'

52-55b. After making this eulogy wise Rāma, his hands in a reverential position, bowed again and again to the god and set out to the west. There the great lord saw the Śuktimatī river which abounds with flocks of birds, which resembles the Mandākinī river and which casts out masses of sins. He set about to bathe in it. After performing the *nitya* rites he thought about '*haṉso 'haṃ*,' meditated in his heart on Mantramūrti and uttered that highest *japa*.[23]

Śaunaka said:

55c-60. In the meantime, O king, distressed widows arrived, pregnant and afflicted by hunger and thirst. The nine women reached the bank of the river with its fresh appearance.[24] They were filled with joy because nearby in clear view they saw the Bhārgava performing austerities, resembling a flame of fire, shining like a million suns, his glance fixed on the tip of his nose. They approached him [and said,] 'Protect us mighty one, storehouse of compassion for all beings! O lord, save us, creatures of humiliation, from continual miseries!' They fell at the feet of the Bhārgava with loud lamentations, [saying,] 'O *brāhmaṇa*, we who are despicable and compromised by sin have come to you. O ocean of compassion, save us who are reduced to penury and are as good as dead!'

Śaunaka said:
61-63. He (the Bhārgava) thought, 'What is this?' O prince, he saw this wonder, while smiling, with his eyes opened in surprise.[25] They (the women), resolute and extremely distressed, fell to the earth for protection. Automatically the son of Bhṛgu, the one who is compassionate and kind to those in misery, after seeing their fear, spoke for †their† fame and strength with a voice deep as the rumbling of a cloud.
The Bhārgava said:
64. 'Women, compose yourselves! Distress is to be abandoned! Speak the desired boon and consider it granted.'
65-66b. The widows stood up, their eyes filled with tears upon hearing those words which had been spoken as if they were nectar. Abandoning their bashfulness, they set about to tell their story.
The women said:
66c-69. 'We[26] belong to the same families as the *brāhmaṇas* dwelling in the thirty-two villages. We have fallen to this position through separation, by fate, from our husbands when we were young. Censured by ordinary people and rejected from dwelling in the villages, we are poor wretched women who are wandering because we lacked

the self-command to abandon the body as is customary. Through a slight trace of merit, lord, we have seen you. O ocean of compassion, be compassionate! O very compasssionate one, protect us!'[27]

70-73. The *muni* provided comfort after hearing their words. He had them make a *darśana*, going with them to Kroḍeśa, grantor of good fortune, so that there would be efficacy. [He said,] 'You are to make a dwelling here for some time, without delay. In due course the god who is the family deity, beneficient Nārāyaṇa, an ocean of compasssion, will gladly extend it.' After saying this, the great *yogin* left for Gokarṇa.[28]

Śaunaka said:

74. I always laud beneficient Nārāyaṇa who is always well-disposed to servants, who is always compassionate, who is the delight of kind Indirā, and whose feet are worshipped by the one born of a lotus (i.e., Brahman).

NOTES

[1] It is unusual that Sūta should be referred to as a *brāhmaṇa*, but the readings leave no other choice. See **§11.1b**, particularly the reference to Kane (1930-62/5.2[=1962]: 862-864). Also note Rocher (1986: 54-56): "The term *sūta* has created a number of problems – and not a little speculation – on the part of modern scholars. . . . Some [few] scholars did not neglect to point out indications in the texts that the puranic *sūta* was indeed a brahman. For instance, Balarāma was accused of brahmanicide for killing the *sūta*. [Rocher cites here A. D. Pusalker. The textual references are *Bhāgavatapurāṇa* 10.78-79 and *Mārkaṇḍeyapurāṇa* 6.23-37. See, however, **§11.1b** with regard to Dikshitar's noting that Bālarāma, rather, *insulted* Sūta.] Other

sources seem to indicate that the puranic *sūta* was not a brahman. . . .”

[2] See **§12.6** for a discussion of the thirty-two villages, and **§12.5** hereafter for identification of persons, places and rivers mentioned within the text.

[3] This appears to refer to the preceding chapter in the *uttarārdha* of the Skh in which the *ṛṣis* hear what Skanda related to Nārada with regard to the thirty-two villages.

[4] Perhaps, the chief continent, Bhārata.

[5] This would seem to refer to the two preceding chapters in the *uttarārdha* of the Skh but with an important difference being that these two chapters do not contain information on the presiding deities of the thirty-two villages. Also to be noted in connection with continuity between the chapters of the *uttarārdha* is that neither Śaunaka nor Śatānīka have spoken previously in the *uttarārdha*, nor, for that matter, in the entire Skh.

[6] L1a and L1c each insert 1½ vss. of commentary before this. See Appendix B.

[7] See vs. 31d, where it is clearly Viṣṇu who is referred to in the same terms.

[8] The text, without the emendation here, would have a Kroḍa, or perhaps Kroḍamuni, build the city and *tīrtha*. This seems absurd to me. See 9.12² as an example of scribal changes of comparable magnitude, which I view as supporting the hypothesis here. There are other possible ways in which to construe the text without making a drastic emendation, but these involve the utilization of readings which are very peculiar. The city is Kroḍapattana, mentioned in 2(10).10b. The *tīrtha* is Kroḍeśa, mentioned in vs. 70 below. It has been impossible to identify either of these. We should note, though, that it is because of these names that I construe ‘*kroḍamunir nāma*’ in the grammatically more difficult way as ‘a *muni* named Kroḍa.’

[9] All MSS except L1c add: When the *kali* age arrived he attached himself to a Naimiṣa forest. I will speak briefly at this time. Listen with an attentive mind. L1c inserts: I will speak briefly

with regard to this. Listen with an attentive mind. O king, then at the end of time he obtained the highest station.

[10] L1a, L1c and L2 insert: . . . with various trees, creeping plants and shrubs, filled with various forest animals, . . .

[11] This is the second mention of elephants. Such repetition is not uncommon for lists of this type. See the double reference to Bakuḷa trees in 8(16).9 for another instance of such repetition in the PGN.

[12] The Sanskrit is '*camarīmṛgaiḥ*.' The simplest translation, 'with yaks and deer,' is not satisfying as we can be certain that the yak, a Himalayan animal, never lived in the western ghats. It is possible that '*camarī*' refers to another type of buffalo, but I view it to be more likely that the entire compound is the name of a type of deer or antelope.

[13] L1a and L1c insert: Once a person who was truthful speaking and who was not envious, a *muni* named Kroḍa, obtained the final aim at this best land after undergoing penance for a long time. See vss. 12c-14 above, and n. 8 and n. 9 above. See 9.12[2] in Appendix B. See **§11.2.**

[14] The usage of daggers around words and phrases which are extremely problematic has been suspended for the twenty vss. of the *stotra* as the unusual nature of much of the *stotra* removes any sound basis we might have for isolating unusually problematic points. The *stotra* appears to merge the personalities and mythologies of Nārāyaṇa (Viṣṇu) and Śiva. Thus, Śaṃkara is a name for Śiva, Nārāyaṇa for Viṣṇu. Madhu and Kaiṭabha, mentioned in vs. 33, are demons killed by Viṣṇu. So also, the one who carries a *cakra* against the *dānavas* in vs. 41 refers to Viṣṇu. But the lord of snakes, etc. in vs. 41 would refer to Śiva. In vs. 45, the one with a *kaustubha* jewel refers to Viṣṇu or Kṛṣṇa, whereas the one with a neck marked by dark blue poison refers to Śiva – both, referring to things obtained in the churning of the ocean by the gods and demons.

[15] The Sanskrit is '*svārājapurṇa*°.' The form '*svārāja*' is unusual. One might expect '*svarāja*,' which does not fit the meter, or '*svārājya*,' the meaning of which would not fit the play on

words. It is for this latter reason that both Dr. Rocher and myself have an objection against the normal translation of '*svārāja*,' 'self-rule.'

[16] It has not yet proved possible to determine what these ten *vigrahas* are.

[17] It is not clear what is being referred to here. Next to nothing is known of Mṛkaṇḍu, the father of Mārkaṇḍeya.

[18] Perhaps '*loka*' for '*lola*': 'you who have the world as your arm,' or 'you who are the arm of the world.'

[19] Perhaps, 'you who have a snake as your beautiful spear.'

[20] A Kalpataru tree is one of the five trees of Indra's paradise which is fabled to fulfil all desires.

[21] E.g., middle age, old age, ...

[22] Perhaps, 'Jagadīśa, Maheśa, Rameśa, Bhava!'

[23] For the *japa* '*haṉso 'haṃ*,' see *Brahmavidyopaniṣad* in Śrinivāsa Ayyaṅgar (1938: 198-216). Mantramūrti may apply here to this *japa* rather than be a name of Śiva, which is the usual usage. See *Brahmavidyopaniṣad*, vss. 60-63 (pp. 209-210), for support of this hypothesis.

[24] The L1c paraphrase would have us take '*navākṛti*' to refer to the nine women, which would then translate 'youthful.' The compound does not allow a proper declension for such a state of affairs, however, even though such would be preferable from the point of view of sense. '*navākṛti*' is therefore taken to modify '*nadīkulaṃ*,' as here translated.

[25] L1c inserts a defective ½ vs.: Hearing their words in this way, beaming with joy, ...

[26] Before this, L1c inserts: O Bhārgava, very wise one, compassionate one, you who caused the death of the *kṣatriyas*, . . .

[27] See Kane (1930-62/3[=1946]: 614-615. Kane here states, at variance with our text, that the ancient sages provide "that even women that are *patita* and have not yet performed the proper penance were not to be cast on the streets, but they were to be given a hut (near the house) for residence and bare maintenance that would keep body and soul together and were to be guarded against further lapses (Yāj[ñavalkyasmṛti] III.296)."

[28] L1c substitutes three *pādas* for vs. 72b. The reading of L1c would have the sentence translate: Then, after the blessed one said this and made good fortune for them, that intelligent one quickly went to the great lord Gokarṇeśa.

CHAPTER TWO (Skh.u. 10)

Śatānīka asks what happened to the pregnant widows and requests to know why there were five villages. Śaunaka relates that the widows gave birth to sons and daughters and that the sons engaged in various menial tasks in order to support their sisters. Many years pass. Paraśurāma passes nearby on this way to Mahendra mountain and the widows approach him about this state of affairs. Paraśurāma orders Somapīṭhin, an *agnīdhra* priest dwelling near the ocean, to purify them, perform the necessary *saṃskāras* and establish them. Somapīṭhin does so and establishes for the nine widows' bastards and their families a group of five villages. The location of the villages and the deities present near each are given. The sons eventually ascend the mountain and make an areca nut garden. They revert to gathering fruit and performing menial tasks. Because of this they lose their *brāhmaṇa* status. They become ostracized. Śaunaka then recites a formula for expiation should one see them. Such an encounter, it is stated, itself causes one to become polluted.

* * *

Śatānīka said:
1. O chief of *brāhmaṇas*, what did those pregnant widows do next? Speak in detail. How did there come into being five villages?

Śaunaka said:
2. I will speak briefly about this. O best of princes, listen to the splendor of the Bhārgava and the story (perhaps, glory or dignity)[1] of the five villages.[2]

3-9b. The last month of pregnancy arrived. Then, a few days later, the widows gave birth to sons free from fear. In the course of time daughters were born. The widows, with full and high breasts, obtained unequalled satisfaction. They reared the children. These passed through their infancy and childhood. O best of men, the widows' bastards[3] then became young men. And then, in order to support their sisters, they did as follows: some did ploughing and some gathered fruit, some became porters, some tended a garden.[4] Since they are basically low-born (*jaghanyajatva*), what can we call these despised, base, †fate-ridden† men of low condition (*vrātya*) who have lost their status (*vivarṇa*). As an army without a leader they move according to desire.[5] Many years passed while they lived like this.

Śaunaka said:
9c-16. The Bhārgava went to Gokarṇa and then, desiring to go to the country of the Tuḷus and Mahendra mountain, he went to Kroḍapattana.[6] The young women fell at his feet upon seeing nearby the Bhārgava, equal in radiance to the sun. Then rising up, †they told . . . † their story, [saying,] 'Great lord, protect these low-born sons living in sin.' O king, upon hearing their words the compassionate son of Bhṛgu, protecting with compassion, was compassionate. To Somapīṭhin, an *agnīdhra* priest who dwells on the shore of the western ocean, who is learned in the essence of the *Vedas* and *Vedāṅgas*, who is well-versed in acts enjoined by the *Smṛtis*, and who is wise with the knowledge of the *Āgamas*,[7] the long-armed one said this: 'You are to perform a *saṃskāra* for those engaged in sin.[8] Then perform first a giving of names with a non-Vedic formula and after make a dwelling for them. Establish it

there.' He (the Bhārgava) then went to Mahendra mountain with his axe in his hand, having spoken thus.[9]

Śaunaka said:
17-23. After hearing the words of the *guru* the very wise Somapīṭhin called together the widows' bastards and, out of respect for the words of the *guru*, purified them according to rule with sacred texts and with water, and then with earth, with ashes, and with water of the Śuktimatī river. He signified the new names of the nine new sons. According to rule these nine †men of occupation† . . . [10] were afterward esteemed. With ordinary speech the foremost of *brāhmaṇas* performed the tonsure and initiation ceremonies, and the others which begin with marriage.[11] Learned in the discussions about what is to be done and what is not to be done, he was filled with the worry of where to make a village without transgressing the words of his *guru*. At that moment there was a voice in the sky, wonderful and causing wonder, announcing, 'You are to make it here!'
24-35b. After hearing the voice the chief of *brāhmaṇas* was filled with joy.[12] The boundary was made to the north, west of the Sahya mountain range at the foot of Kroḍa mountain. To the south flowed the auspicious river named Sītā with its stainless water, arising in the Sahya range. He made Pāruśabdagrāma to the northeast of Kroḍa mountain and to the west of the Śuktimatī river, far off from . . . .[13] Vighnarāṭ, the blessed son of Śaṃbhu with the face of an elephant and holding in his hands the conch, the discus, the mace, and the bow, always dwells there. To the north of it is the one (i.e., village) called Kāravelā. There shines the lord of the gods with four arms and holding a bow, granting desired boons in excess to those bound by devotion. To the west of it is the one (i.e., village) called

Vāmanāḷa. There dwells the blessed lord who has Pakṣirāj as his symbol (i.e., Viṣṇu), the destroyer of *asuras*, continually causing happiness and giving safety to worshippers. To the east of the Śuktimatī river is the one (i.e., village) called Uḷḷugrāma (perhaps, Uḷḷagrāma). Present there is the goddess Bhagavatī, the mother of the world, holding a bow, a lance, a mace, and a sword, and destroying the *asura* Mahiṣa and the pride of Caṇḍa. At the same place, having his field everywhere, is the lotus-eyed one (i.e., Viṣṇu) always standing to the left and having his body embraced by Lakṣmī. To the southeast is †the one (i.e., village) called . . . .† Established there is a great *liṅga* giving good to all beings. Accessible to sight it is seen even today.

35c-39. The foremost of *brāhmaṇas*, having established the five villages, then settled the people here, directing one family to one and likewise eight families two by two to each remaining village. So long as the sun and moon exist, so long will the sons dwell there with good fortune through the kindness of the Bhārgava. Asking for a benediction, the best of *brāhmaṇas* . . . said, 'Compassionate lord, let their *gotras* increase here with your compassion.' He then went to his own hermitage after doing reverence again and again to the great lord of Kroḍa and to the Bhārgava *guru*.

Śaunaka said:

40-48b. O king, after some time some went up onto the mountain. They made a garden there, as if †an osprey procuring its subsistence†. On the land on the upper part of the Sahya range there was, without doubt, an areca nut garden. Gathering fruit was begun on their land at the foot of the Sahya range.[14] For these widows' bastards a garden, being porters and having work as their livelihood is prescribed. O best of kings, the foolish people of the five villages, censured, related to *brāhmaṇas* by dint of the thread only, shine without the duties of *brāhmaṇas*. The wise say that no one is to eat with them, live with them, talk with them, or set out on a journey with them. The one who eats their food becomes polluted. The son of Bhṛgu has said that for them there should not be the oblation to Agni and the renunciation of the world proper to a *purohita*, actions ordained by the *Veda*, actions enjoined by *Smṛti*, studying the *Purāṇas*, intimate contact with the self-existing *liṅga* which is taught in the *Tantras*, and the knowledge which is obtained through the *yoga* which has eight stages beginning with self-restraint. Those widows' bastards, men of low condition (*vrātya*), despised and having low status, should not attain to the status of *brāhmaṇas* in the *kali* age.

48c-49. What else is there to say? What else would you desire to hear? People become polluted from seeing these.[15] I will recite an appearance of Mārtāṇḍa, a formula for expiation.

50. To Viṣṇu who is the leader of all creatures, to Viṣṇu who has existed from eternity but is nonetheless absolute non-existence, also to Viṣṇu who has a lofty stride, who is the elevated altar, the younger brother of Indra, and the mark of great Indra, I bow very low, I bow down very low.

NOTES

[1] The Sanskrit is '*vaibhava*,' literally, 'glory.' Due to context, it is suggested that its meaning here is more general. See the usage of '*vibhava*' in 6(14).2d and 8(16).2c, and of '*māhātmya*' in 4(12).2b.

[2] L1c adds: . . . to a *māhātmya* of the Bhārgava and of the wives of their children.
[3] The Sanskrit term is '*goḷaka/golaka*.' This is defined in the *Mānavadharmaśāstra* 3.174 as a child born of a wife by a man other than the husband after a husband's death (Bühler 1886: 108). In 3.156-166 (pp. 104-107) it is said that *golakas* are to be avoided.
[4] After 'some became porters,' L1a inserts: some became keepers of prostitutes, some became thieves.
[5] They move according to desire with regard to how they make their living, that is, rather than following a prescribed path. Kane (1930-62/2.1[=1941]: 124-126) notes that there is a conflict of views in the *dharmaśāstra* texts as to whether agriculture is allowed to *brāhmaṇas*. Such is also the case today with regard to different groups of *brāhmaṇas* who engage in agriculture in different areas of India. It would appear from the statements here that an attitude similar to that stated in the *Mānavadharmaśāstra* 10.83-84 is being expressed, where it is stated: "But a Brāhmaṇa, or a Kshatriya, living by a Vaiśya's mode of subsistence, shall carefully avoid (the pursuit of agriculture), (which causes) injury to many beings and depends on others. (Some) declare that agriculture is something excellent, (but) that means of subsistence is blamed by the virtuous; (for) the wooden (implement) with iron point injures the earth and (the beings) living in the earth" (Bühler 1886: 420-421). With regard to their being porters, the *Mānava-dharmaśāstra* does not mention this as being an acceptable mode of existence for a *brāhmaṇa*. Kane (1930-62/3[=1946]: 483), however, notes that *Nāradasmṛti* 8.22-23 states that a porter is the lowest of the three kinds of hired servants.
[6] From the geographical information about these places given here and in chapter one (Skh.u. 9), it appears that in order to travel of Mahendra mountain from Gokarṇa, one must pass first through Kroḍapattana and Kroḍeśa, and then through the Tuḷu country.

[7] L1c inserts ½ vs. which would change the reading to: To Somapīṭhin, who was making a salutation, who was a very wise *brāhmaṇa* who dwelt nearby, who was an *agnīdhra* priest ....

[8] Kane (1930-62/3[=1946]: 646 n., writes that the *Laghu-Āśvalāyana* 21.14-15 states that *golakas* are not to have the *saṃskāras* performed on them in the *kali* age. It states that certain sages do provide for them to undergo the *saṃskāras*, but notes this to have been the practice before the *kali* age.

[9] L1c substitutes: O best of kings, after speaking just so, the Bhārgava went.

[10] It appears that it is the nine names that are mentioned here. The text, though, is very corrupt. Lacking *testimonia* it is necessary to omit the names. Before the names L1a inserts the commentary-like statement, 'In a list'; and after the names it inserts ½ vs. of commentary, for which see Appendix B.

[11] The standard twelve *saṃskāras*, as given by Monier-Williams in his dictionary, end with marriage. These are *garbhādhāna*, a ceremony performed before conception or after menstruation to insure conception; *puṃsavana*, the male production rite; *sīmantonnayana*, the parting or dividing of the hair, observed by women in the fourth, sixth or eighth month of pregnancy; *jātakarman*, a birth ceremony, consisting in touching a newly-born child's tongue three times with ghee after appropriate prayers; *nāmakarman*, name-giving; *niṣkramaṇa*, taking a child out of the house for the first time in the fourth month after birth to see the sun; *annaprāśana*, putting rice into a child's mouth for the first time; *cūḍākarman*, the tonsure ceremony, performed on a child in the first or third year; *upanayana*, the ceremony in which a *guru* draws a boy toward himself and initiates him into one of the three twice-born classes by investing him with the sacred thread and thus endowing him with a second, or spiritual, birth; *keśānta*, cutting off the hair finally, performed on *brāhmaṇas* at 16 years of age, *kṣatriyas* at 22, and *vaiśyas* at 24; *samāvartana*, the ceremony performed at the returning home of a *brāhmaṇa* student after completing his studies in the house of a preceptor; and *vivāha*, marriage. There

are, however, other lists of *saṃskāras*, such as Aṅgiras', which lists twenty-five, and Gautama's, which lists forty. These include *saṃskāras* after marriage. See Monier-Williams (1899: 1120b); Kane (1930-62/2.1[=1941]: 193-198, and 4[=1953]: 190); and Pandey (1949: 28-38).

[12] L1c substitutes: After hearing that, the best of *brāhmaṇas* [said,] 'I will make [it] quickly in this place.'

[13] The name of the village is taken from Ed, L2, Bm, and M. L1a would have it be Ruśatgrāma or Ruśadgrāma. The name of the place which it is noted to be far off from is too corrupt to chance even a guess at it.

[14] See discussion on areca nut cultivation and status in **§12.6**.

[15] This is a standard statement found at the end of almost every story in the PGN. See Kane (1930-62/3[=1946]: 614) where various texts are noted to state various types of association with *patita* people are themselves causing a person to become *patita*. The severest list noted is that given by Devala who declares that "sin is passed from one man to another by conversation (with a sinner), by touching him, by his breath (coming in close contact with one's nose), by occupying the same vehicle (horse) or seat, by eating (in this company), by being a priest, by being his teacher of the Veda or making him one's teacher, or by matrimonial alliance." The specific Sanskrit sources for this statement from the *Devalasmṛti* are given in **§2.3** above.

CHAPTER THREE (Skh.u. 11)

Śaunaka relates that eight poor *brāhmaṇas* together with their wives and sons approached two wealthy and devout *śūdras*. The *brāhmaṇas* praise the two *śūdras* in expectation of kind treatment and receive much wealth from the elder of the two. In consideration of this, they make a dwelling and serve the *śūdra* for twelve years. The *śūdra* decides to take a second wife so that he might have a son. As there are no litter-bearers for the marriage, he approaches the *brāhmaṇas*. They consent to carry his litter. Because of this the people of their village revolt against them and force them to flee. They go to the *śūdra* who realizes the offence he has caused them to commit and as a result gives them his wealth, his village and his newly married bride. The *śūdra* then goes on a pilgrimage to a *tīrtha*. The *brāhmaṇas* live happily and prosperously, but fallen in status. Śaunaka then adds that one becomes polluted by sight of these and provides as expiation a verse to Viṣṇu.

* * *

Śaunaka said:

1-2b. There is another village of polluted *brāhmaṇas* to the south of the Śuktimatī river. It is called Modagrāma, is perfect in every respect, and was given by a *śūdra* without any litter-bearer of his own for *brāhmaṇas* who carried a litter.

2c-8b. Previously, there were two people renowned by the *śūdras*, †Ketu and Muddakunda†,[1] who were endowed with youthful forms, were strong and courageous, were intent on the worship of Śiva as the highest goal, and who held reverence to *brāhmaṇas* to be the highest mode of behavior. The foremost of those dwelling in the thirty-two

villages, who were the best of those learned in the *Veda*, spent much time with the two. Eight unfortunate poverty stricken *brāhmaṇas* upon hearing what was said about those two and being covetous of wealth, approached them, along with their wives and sons, for the cessation of their poverty.[2] After reciting a benediction these lowest of *brāhmaṇas* who had come together with a desire for wealth spoke words full of hope. [They said,] 'You are brave! You are wealthy! You are revered in the threefold world! There is not character equal to that of your worships in beauty, generosity, virtues, and so forth.'
8c-12b. The older considered such praise with its eloquent phrases of many sorts and, as he had duty as his chief goal, honored them according to rule with much wealth. After providing †assistance† for the eight and their families, the *śūdra* rightaway gladly gave them female slaves and whatever cattle and grain that he was abundantly endowed with. The *brāhmaṇas*, treated with respect by him, immediately made a dwelling. They spent twelve years serving him.[3]

Śaunaka said:
12c-18. Then the *śūdra* thought, 'My wife has no son. I will take another with high and rounded breasts, endowed with a youthful form and marked with all the characteristics of beauty. I will marry a beautiful woman for the sake of extending my lineage. The best of the wise say, 'Heaven is not obtained without a son.'[4] Thus having made up his mind to get married, he informed his kinsmen (*svajana*) of his desire, [saying,] 'I am going to take a wife with a beautiful body in order to have a son. Summon someone born (*jātyā*) of noble family for this purpose.' Then all the relatives (*bāndhava*) looked at one another and, as they had seen a certain maiden in the bloom of

youth with beautiful hips and loins and red lips who dwelt within half a *yojana*, they said to him, 'The wife desired by you will be found there.'
19-24b. Upon hearing this he considered everything that had to be done. He thought, 'Tomorrow she will be married'; and then he and his kinsment brought together everything that was necessary for the marriage. Then he thought, 'There is not any litter-bearer in this area. What am I to do? How am I to proceed?' He called together the *brāhmaṇas* and spoke with educated words. 'I am your worships' servant. Consideration of this family is foremost in my mind. It must be done quickly by your worships.' Hearing his words, the *brāhmaṇas* deliberated with affection. The *brāhmaṇas* assented. They carried the litter fashioned with eight legs and adorned †with nine jewels†.[5]

Śaunaka said:
24c-26b. O king, what is to be done? Men intent on gaining wealth carelessly part from the laws handed down to all their venerable kinsmen. Men of virtuous women, as those fond of harlots, fond of gambling and fond of horses constantly abandon the threefold recitation.[6]
26c-29b. Arriving quickly, the *śūdra* mounted the litter. Gradually reaching the house of the bride the marriage was performed and the *śūdra*, happily joined with his wife, went to his own house. Then happily he gave each of the *brāhmaṇas* clothing, jewelry and a hundred *prasthas* of *niṣka* coins. O king, what is not to be given!
29c-33b. The *brāhmaṇas* quickly took the wealth, entrusted it to a prosperous family and set out to return to their village.[7] O king, the people of the village, having witnessed the fall in status, were filled with anger. They took punishment in their hand and attacked them (the *brāhmaṇas*). The *brāhmaṇas* immediately went to the

home of the *śūdra* out of fear. They said, 'Protect us! What happiness has been given to us?' Hearing their words and being very much the foremost of the *śūdras*, he spoke with extreme compassion to those filled with fear.
The *śūdra* said:
33c-34. '*Brāhmaṇas*! Abandon anguish! To what end is distress? I will give this village and this newly married woman with well-rounded limbs. All your property – cattle, buffaloes and so forth – is to be established here free from danger.'

Śaunaka said:
35-38. Then,[8] after bathing in the water of the Śuktimatī river near Nṛsiṉheśa, that *śūdra* who was filled with compassion, while being praised by the good men, gladly gave those *brāhmaṇas* his newly married wife in the bloom of youth . . . with her great amount of clothing and many jewels, the village filled with valuables, and his house together with all his property, beginning with cows and buffaloes. The *śūdra* then went on a journey to a *tīrtha*, saying, 'The *brāhmaṇas*, living here without fear, are to be established forevermore.'

Śaunaka said:
39-43. All the *brāhmaṇas* were filled with joy. They parcelled the village into eight divisions with a dwelling for each and sanctified the vernacular names for each. Then, according to convention, they did oblations to the gods and the ancestors, auspicious actions, etc., the names according with the divisions. O king, from then on the *brāhmaṇas* lived with good fortune. O king, what glorification can I speak of the wife, the newly married woman, of the people dwelling in the thirty-two villages, and of the *śūdra*? People dwelling in the region of the

thirty-two villages who are excluded from their community along with their venerable kinsmen, who have been censured, who are living in sin, and who have enjoyed the food of a *śūdra* are forever shining on the earth.

44-45. At the moment one sees these he becomes polluted. In order to provide expiation I will state the highest vision of the sun. What is there to say aside from this? There is no discussion to be made with regard to this.

46. I resort to Nṛsiṉha who has the lotus-like feet which are worshipped by the gods and *asuras*, and I resort to the imperishable destroyer (?), the one who has a soul without a beginning, the one who has a lofty form and pervades the threefold world.[9]

NOTES

[1] I have followed the reading of L1c for the names. All other MSS have an indefinite pronoun instead of the first name. The second name is given by Ed, Bm, M, Br, and K as Madvakanda and by L2 as Mandṛkanda. It is impossible to be certain about the names without *testimonia*.

[2] Kane (1930-62/2.1[=1941]: 110) notes that the third means of livelihood permitted to *brāhmaṇas* was to receive gifts from a worthy or unblemished person. Kane (1930-62/5.2[=1962]: 937) notes that the *Gautamadharmasūtra* advises *brāhmaṇas* to approach a king or a rich person for their livelihood. To be kept in mind with regard to this story, though, is that Kane notes the *Smṛticandrikā* to quote Yama as stating that the worthy person must be of the three highest *varṇas* and that the *Mānavadharmaśāstra* 10.109-111 states that receiving gifts from an unworthy person or a *śūdra* is worse than teaching him or officiating for him (Kane 1930-62/2.1[=1941]: 110). See *Mānavadharmaśāstra* 10.109-111 (Bühler 1886: 425) with

regard to the latter statement. Clearly our *śūdra* is not an unworthy person. Also, there may be a differentiation in the laws between receiving a gift for service and receiving it as an act of reverence toward *brāhmaṇas*.

[3] *Mānavadharmaśāstra* 4.61 (Bühler 1886: 138) notes that a *brāhmaṇa* is not to dwell in a country where the rulers are *śūdras*.

[4] See *Aitareyabrāhmaṇa* 33.2 and *Śaṅkhāyanaśrautasūtra* 15.17. References listed in Joshi (1937-41/1.2[=1938]: 1260.

[5] All MSS other than L1c translate 'with various jewels.' Considering the general good quality of L1c's readings, it was viewed to be advisable to prefer it here also over the other readings even though they make *more apparent* sense. With regard to the *brāhmaṇas* being litter-bearers, see the *Viṣṇupurāṇa* for the story of king Bharata in his rebirth as a contemplative *brāhmaṇa* who becomes a litter-bearer (Wilson 1840[1961]: 199-200). The description of how he became a litter-bearer on p. 200 is enlightening in that it implies certain regulations of status and remuneration with regard to who can carry a litter and also points out the demeaning nature of the task.

[6] The Sanskrit is '*trayī gā*,' probably a reference to the *Ṛgveda*, *Sāmaveda* and *Yajurveda*.

[7] See *Mānavadharmaśāstra* 10.111 (Bühler 1886: 425) where it is stated that the sin incurred by accepting gifts from unworthy men is removed by throwing them away and by austerities. Though our *śūdra* is not unworthy, he is a *śūdra*, and the gift was received not only for service, but for service of a specific demeaning type. To be kept in mind, perhaps, is the situation reported as the origin of the Sarjupari, or Sarwaria *brāhmaṇas* of Bengal as reported by Risley (1892/1: 156-157). Two *brāhmaṇas* from Kanauj were ordered by their father not to take any presents for helping perform a horse sacrifice for king Rāma of Ayodhya. The sacrifice, though, would have no effect unless the *brāhmaṇas* were rewarded. So, the king had diamonds hidden in the packets of betel which he gave to the

brāhmaṇas. When the *brāhmaṇas* got home their father asked them if they had taken any presents, which they had not. But on opening the packets of betel the diamonds were discovered, and they were excommunicated at once. The *brāhmaṇas* went back to the king, ready to curse him for his treachery. But he appeased them with smooth words and grants of land. Also to be considered is the quotation from *Yājñavalkyasmṛti* 1.213 in Kane (1930-62/5.2[=1962]: 936) where the text is noted to recommend that even if a *brāhmaṇa* be fit for receiving a religious gift he should refuse it.

[8] All MSS insert here 3½ vss. of commentary. See Appendix B.

[9] As in the *stotra* in chapter one (Skh.u. 9), it is impossible to know whether or not some of the descriptions of Viṣṇu translated here are to be taken as names proper. Parthasarathy (1966) was checked to see if some of these descriptions were used there as names, but without positive results.

CHAPTER FOUR (Skh.u. 12)

Śaunaka relates that there was a boundary dispute between the *brāhmaṇas* dwelling in Koṭīśvara and those dwelling in the village of Kūṭa when Vasu ruled. The dispute is referred to Vasu and he says that they will all question the earth on the matter. He commands spies to bring *brāhmaṇas* from the thirty-two villages to him. The *brāhmaṇas* of Koṭīśvara bury a man in the earth. Vasu and the *brāhmaṇas* from the thirty-two villages go to the boundary, worship the earth, and tell the earth that she must decide the dispute. The man in the ground says that the land belongs to the *brāhmaṇas* from Koṭīśvara. A voice in the sky informs everyone of the deceit. Vasu takes away the property of the lying *brāhmaṇas* and tells the *brāhmaṇas* of the thirty-two villages that they are to decide if the deceitful *brāhmaṇas* are to be excommunicated. The *brāhmaṇas* of Koṭīśvara are excommunicated and go to the ocean for penance. They meet the Bhārgava while they are staying there. The Bhārgava purifies them. They then make a dwelling with the approval of Vasu. Śaunaka adds that sight of these *brāhmaṇas* causes pollution. He states a penance for seeing them.

* * *

Śaunaka said:

1-2. There is another community of polluted *brāhmaṇas* near Koṭiliṅgeśa. I am speaking a *māhātmya* which is surprising to those who hear it and which causes excessive mental confusion in the world, [a *māhātmya*] of the lying evil *brāhmaṇas* who dwell there, performing evil.

3-5b. Once there was a certain king with the best of qualities, famous with the name Vasu and considered to be an earthly Indra. Men said that when he ruled over that section of the earth, the earth was prosperous in every respect and that there was neither lying nor thieving. Many years passed while he carried on in this way.

5c-13b. At one point there was a dispute between the great men dwelling in Kūṭa and those dwelling in Koṭīśvara concerning a change in a boundary. After quarreling for a long time over sixteen *prasthas* of a rice field, someone (perhaps, they) put the entire thing before the king. Then the very wise king, the best of those learned in the sayings of *nīti*, quieted down the terrible chieves among rogues who dwelt in Koṭīśvara and who spoke only falsehood. After, the king addressed them with his pure word. They did . . . and, doing another before the king, they spoke. Then, after thinking, he spoke to the assembly,[1] [thereby] gladdening it. [He said,] 'We will ask the earth. She will speak what is right and what is wrong to us.' After thinking in his mind that †she would say† where the sin is, he sent out spies, [saying,] 'Quickly bring men dwelling in the thirty-two villages who are very rich in honor and who adhere to their own duty. I will settle the thing the day after tomorrow.' The king entered his home.[2]

Śaunaka said:

13c-20. In the middle of that night the crafty men dwelling in Koṭīśvara, performing a contemptible act, quickly gathered near the boundary with shovels, dug up a hole of the proper length, put in a man, and filled in †some† sand.[3] As they went to their homes the [king's] orders [to the spies] were being executed. Thus the inhabitants of the thirty-two villages brought together by the spies went to the king along with benedictions. †Vasu†, not liking the words spoken at that time, gladly went to the edge of the boundary together with the *brāhmaṇas*. Having assembled the provisions for worship, together with the wise men learned in divine sciences and the people of Kūṭa and of Koṭīśvara, he did worship of the earth accompanied by song, dance and instrumental music, with fragrant flowers, unhusked barley grains (perhaps, winnowed rice) and so forth, as well as with food and drink to be enjoyed, incenses, lights, and the best of eatables to be presented to the deity. The king then made there the prayer desired in thought. Joining his palms together in proper fashion, he spoke with modesty.

The king said:

21-22. 'Goddess, you must decide! O earth, whatever sin is done by me through ignorance or even knowledge, let it be pardoned by you! Whether this land belongs to the dwellers of Kūṭa or is the land of Koṭi, that must be said correctly by you in order to purify these people.'

23a-23b. After saying this at that place the king was silent.

Śaunaka said:

23c-27b. When everyone was listening the low man in the hole, speaking in accordance with what he had been told, which was to lead toward their exclusion and also his destruction, all for the fame of the king, spoke: 'There is no doubt. This field belongs to the inhabitants of Koṭīśvara.' Upon hearing these words, the low, evil men thought they had succeeded, having made [the others] cry, 'Let it be heard by all men, by your worships and by the wicked men. Having taken away what is ours, the earth gives it for those.'

Śaunaka said:

27c-31b. Immediately after this, in the air, causing surprise to the people . . . and also of Koṭīśvara, she announced with unequalled splendor all the sins of the community, causing alarm. She caused her splendor to be seen. The voice addressed them: 'This voice was not that of the earth. It came clearly from the mouth of a man. All the men dwelling in Koṭīśa are fraudulent wrongdoers. For this reason, king, I curse them at the feet of Śiva.' After speaking thus, the goddess vanished.

31c-35. The king, hearing this, was stunned and astonished, the hair on his body stood on end, and he stood still a moment. Digging the earth in the presence of the villagers he saw the body of a man covered with worms as if he were bait. The king was dismayed and had a reddened glance due to anger, and right in front of the village dwellers (that is, the dwellers of the thirty-two villages) took all the property of the liars and gave it to the village dwellers. The lord said, 'Let them decide for themselves whether there is to be an exclusion or no exclusion';[4] and he went to his own city.

36-40b. Then all the *brāhmaṇas*, their foreheads bowed in shame, . . .[5] [and said]: 'You are liars, fallen, . . . sin (perhaps, fettered by sin), without dwellings, placed outside all brahmanical duties. Marriage and so forth are to be avoided with this community.' Cursing the liars in this way, O wise king, having obtained (perhaps, having arrived at) another village, they went to their own habitation firm in their vow. And all the abandoned ones, extremely agitated from their connivance, went to the shore of the ocean and dwelt there for six months.[6]

Śaunaka said:

40c-43. Accidentally there arrived the benefactor of those who have suffered offence. Then, forming a straight line on the ground, they saw with a splendour equal to the sun, free from passion, marked with the perpendicular mark, having the perpendicular mark on the forehead, the *muni* who resembled a coral tree who had come nearby.[7]

Speaking a *mantra* correctly they gladly fell at his feet. Censured because of lying, they spoke of their deeds [and said,] 'O great lord, protect us! Be compassionate, you who are kind to those in distress.'

Śaunaka said:
44-48b. After hearing their words he said, '*Brāhmaṇas*, I will take as my own the place filled with sorrow. The blessed lord is a mine of compassion without doubt.' He then provided comfort. The *yogin* made the seven *mudrās* and then taught the splendid eight syllable *mantra* (*aṣṭākṣaramantra*) marked with the name of Viṣṇu, the †*mantra*† which has Vaiśvambara as the essential part, and, treated with respect by those [*brāhmaṇas*], he went.[8] The *brāhmaṇas*, stainless, out of deference to the command of the *guru* dwell in that village once more according to the command of the protector of men. What else is there to say? They live without fear.
48c-49. Merely by seeing those a man becomes polluted. I will speak an expiation. Let one do an †*āsana*† at noon.

NOTES

[1] L1c and L2 insert ½ vs. which in all likelihood we would have included in the text could sense have been made out of it. The second *pāda* translates: . . . words always (?) aimed at the cause . . . . This is obviously the object of 'he spoke.'

[2] It is not clear which of the five kinds of boundaries mentioned in legal texts is here referred to. These boundary types are listed by Kane (1930-62/3[=1946]: 502-503) as *dhvajinī*, or indicated by trees; *matsyinī*, or indicated by rivers or tanks; *naidhānī*, or indicated by signs concealed in the earth, such as pots filled

with chaff, coal, bricks, bones, etc.; *bhayavarjitā*, or a boundary settled by agreement of the parties concerned; and a boundary which is laid down by the king. The boundary here would have to be either *naidhānī* or *bhayavarjitā*. If it is *naidhānī*, this would explain the king's statement in very concrete terms: he was intending to uncover the pot filled with chaff, or whatever, from the earth. The inhabitants of the thirty-two villages would be brought as boundaries are supposed to be decided, according to most of the legal texts cited by Kane, if not by witnesses of the adjoining villages, by neighbors in the presence of the king. Kūṭa is one of the thirty-two villages. See Kane (1930-62/3 [=1946]: 503-505).

[3] If the boundary was *naidhānī*, it would appear that the dwellers of Koṭīśvara were ignorant of this, and that they did not understand the king's intention!

[4] Perhaps, 'Let them decide a definite exclusion,' or 'Let them perform an exclusion forever!' The translation above is based on the principle of deriving a common denominator from the various readings both here and in 6(14).2, where the phrase is repeated, and on the principle of choosing the *lectio facilior*. It is possible that our text should read '*parityāgaṃ parityāgaṃ*,' or '*parityāgaparityāgaṃ*.' This would be unusual, however, and it is not certain as to how it should be construed. The alternate translations given here are suggestions.

[5] See 6(14).26cd. There is clearly at least one line omitted here in all MSS. 6(14).26cd, and sense, would appear to indicate the the it is the *brāhmaṇas* of Koṭīśvara whose heads are bowed with shame, which situation would probably require a case change from the nominative to the accusative. As we do not have the entire sentence we have refrained from postulating an emendation, though.

[6] Kane (1930-62/3[=1946]: 352) notes that *Yājñavalkyasmṛti* 2.81 and the *Smṛti* of Kātyāyana, as reconstructed by Kane, 407 prescribe that a *brāhmaṇa* guilty of perjury should be banished from the country, and that a *brāhmaṇa* frequently guilty of perjury should be fined and banished, or be degraded by being

carried naked through the streets or be deprived of his house. *Mānavadharmaśāstra* 8.380 (Bühler 1886: 320) states that no matter how heinous the offence done by a *brāhmaṇa*, he is only to be banished, leaving all this property to him and not physically harming him. See Kane (1930-62/2.1[=1941]: 141-142) for exceptions to this, however.

[7] All MSS add an extended description of Paraśurāma in *indravajra* meter, with two vss. in *upendravajra* meter. This appears to be an interpolation. The reconstruction, which is to be embedded in the preceding description, translatates: . . . marked with the *āmūla mudrā* on his powerful arm, with a tatter of cloth covering his loins, with a raised bamboo staff in his left hand, passionate about the thought of Madhva in the last *yuga*, his entire body, moreover, marked with *mudrās*, †holding† a water vessel in his left hand, his left eye looking with compassion, concentrating in his heart on the lord having a bird as his vehicle (i.e., Viṣṇu, whose vehicle is the *garuḍa*), a beautiful garland of lotuses firmly attached around his throat, meditating on the world with an offering of water (?), meditating on the Nṛsiṇ̱ha incarnation of Īśa, meditating in his heart on the primeval changeable form, ...

[8] The *aṣṭākṣaramantra* is '*oṃ nārāyaṇāya namaḥ*,' or '*oṃ namo nārāyaṇāya*.' Dr. Sanyukta Gupta of the Instituut voor Oosterse Talen, Utrecht, hypothesizes that this may be the *mūlamantra* of Paraśurāma, and suggests that the seven *mudrās* may refer to the *mūlamantramudrā* and the six *aṅgamudrās* of the *mūla-mantra*, although she notes that it is impossible to state this with certainty. Also, see Appendix B for two passages of commentary which are inserted in this sentence.

CHAPTER FIVE (Skh.u. 13)

Śatānīka requests to hear still more. Śaunaka relates a story of many pregnant *brāhmaṇa* widows coming from different countries in India. The widows meet at the Tuṅgabhadrā river. They see Kaṇva performing austerities. Kaṇva tells them to go to the Bhārgava who is performing austerities on the shore of the Varāhī river. The Bhārgava directs them to a Nyagrodha forest near the *tīrtha* Gokarṇeśa and provides a mark for their descendants to wear. They make a dwelling at the forest with the permission of the villagers and give birth to sons and daughters. Śaunaka adds that the children are *śūdras* and that one becomes polluted by association with them. He states an expiation for such association.

* * *

Śatānīka said:
1. I desire to hear still more of this remarkable story which is remarkable to be coming from your mouth. Speak the highest *māhātmya*.

Śaunaka said:
2-7. Listen king. I will speak . . . .[1] O best of men, I will tell you an old story of a large number of pregnant women coming from different countries. Abandoned widows from Aṅga, Vaṅga and Kaliṅga, from Saurāṣṭra and from Gujjara, from Āndhra, Drāviḍa, Karṇāṭa, and Kāśmīra, from Mahārāṣṭra and Utkalā, from Sindhu and Māgadha . . . ,[2] and from the countries of Gauḍa and Gorāṣṭra, pregnant women forsaken forever, despised because they had not performed the funeral rites (?), afflicted by hunger

and thirst, having met one another, O king, came together near the Tuṅgabhadrā river. Together all the women began to make a *stotra* to the kind great god Virūpākṣa who stood, unique, on the shore.[3]

8-10. They saw there a great lord with his glance fixed on his nose, the great lord named Kaṇva with the splendor of a hundred dawns. Each with a story of her own, they all joined their palms together and said, 'Say where people censured like us are to go, *muni*. What are we to do? Where are we to go? Better we were dead.' Upon hearing the words of the pregnant women he was filled with compassion and spoke.

Kaṇva said:

11-12. 'Śaṃkara and Acyuta are at the land at the foot of Kroḍa mountain. Near them, arising in the Sahya mountain range, is the Varāhī river. Quickly go to the great lord, the Bhārgava, who put an end to all the *kṣatra* families, who is undergoing austerities on its bank.'

13-17b. Upon hearing his words they bowed to the *muni* again and again and together went to that place where the river of compassion was. Filled with joy they saw the Bhārgava, equal in radiance to Vaiśvānara, undergoing austerities on the bank of the river. They approached him [and said,] 'Protect us, O mighty one, storehouse of compassion for all beings! O lord, ...' O prince, calling for help in this way they fell at his feet, [saying,] 'Being censured sinners, O *brāhmaṇa*, we have come to you. O ocean of compassion, save us who are reduced to penury and are as good as dead.'

Śaunaka said:

17c-20b. Hearing their words, the son of Bhṛgu was compassionate. Causing his splendor to be seen, he spoke kindly. With smiling eyes the *muni* provided comfort. [He said to them,] 'What misfortune has occurred? You who are strict in observing religious vows, speak everything! †Let such not be the case even for a moment.† Do not be afraid at this time.' They made a salutation with their hands and spoke before the Bhārgava.

The women said:

20c-23b. 'Bhārgava, wise one, compassionate one, you who put an end to the *kṣatriyas*, due to our previous lives such a situation is being endured: lacking the self-command to abandon the body as is customary we are wandering, rejected by our relations, ill-fated and repudiated. Because of previous virtue, lord, we have seen you. O best of the Bhṛgus, be compassionate! O best of *brāhmaṇas*, protect us!'

23cd. Hearing their words, most assuredly he provided comfort.

†Paraśurāma† said:

24-27b. 'In a place six *yojanas* from here, near Gokarṇeśa, there is a Nyagrodha forest adorned with . . . .[4] By my command, make a dwelling there free from fear, having removed nose ornaments and without toe rings. It is to remain on the ears.[5] Everything will be alright forever for the children adorned by us with the marks. Marriage by your sons and daughters will be happy.'

27c-28b. In this way the great *muni* gave a boon to the many widows. With everyone looking on, he disappeared on the spot.

28c-31b. They went to the Nyagrodha forest after hearing his words spoken thus. They approached a dwelling there and, with the assent of the villagers, they then dwelt there with fortune according to the command of the Bhārgava. They gave birth to daughters and strong sons. One by one they married together with one another. All went well in that place from then on.

Śaunaka said:
31c-33. O king, the children of those women are without a doubt *śūdras*. By association with them one becomes polluted. To put an end to that sin one should look up to Mārtāṇḍa (perhaps, look at the sun).[6] What else is there to say? I will speak still more to you.

NOTES

[1] L1c inserts a defective ½ vs. of commentary which attempts to clarify the meaning of 2b. It is too corrupt for us to make any sense out of it, however. See Appendix B.
[2] The two or three geographic names at this point are in the text in the instrumental case rather than the ablative. See **§8.5**. It seems most probable that the text has become corrupt here. Since there is no geographic order in the listing of the different countries and regions, it is impossible to ascertain what the text should read.
[3] L1c inserts a simple *stotra*, which clearly appears to be an addition, and 2½ lines of text ending the *stotra*. L2 inserts one line of this *stotra* and the last line of text, with one word changed. The text, as in L1c, translates: 'Virūpākṣa! Lord of all! Sadāśiva! One having many forms! Refuge! God who is the source of all existence! Śaṃkara! One who performs compassion! Hara! Śaṃbhu! Mahādeva! Viśveśa! Śiva! Śaṃkara! Sarvātma!' Those did homage to the one having a blue throat, to Śaṃbhu, to the immortal god Apaśarva, to Mahādeva. After praising Mahādeva thus, they began to leave.
[4] L1c inserts: 'They(!) are to make a dwelling there by the command of the village dwellers.'
[5] It would appear that something has been lost here. The source of L1c and L2 also had this impression as they insert: 'I will provide a bow-shaped mark bringing luck.' Then follows, 'It is

to remain on the ears.' This probably refers to a Vaiṣṇava sectarian mark. How it is to be placed on the ears, however, is problematic.

[6] See 6(14).33c-35.

CHAPTER SIX (Skh.u. 14)

Śaunaka relates the story of a tribal girl who becomes separated from her group at a banner festival which was held when Candradatta ruled. *Brāhmaṇas* from Gujjaragrāma find the child, take her home with them, raise her, and marry her to a *brāhmaṇa* of a family in a neighboring village. She gives birth to sons. All goes well until the family goes to another banner festival at the same place. The girl is recognized by her kinsmen. The king asks the mother why she is trying to take away the status of a *brāhmaṇa* woman. The mother informs the king of the situation. She leaves accompanied by the daughter, the daughter's *brāhmaṇa* husband and the sons. The king commands the *brāhmaṇas* to speak the truth. The *brāhmaṇas* of the thirty-two villages excommunicate them. Śaunaka adds that people become polluted by sight of these. He prescribes an expiation.

* * *

Śaunaka said:

1-2. Low men, banished from living in the thirty-two villages, live repudiated because of a connection with a Kirāta girl.[1] I will speak for all time the story (perhaps, more literally, glory or dignity)[2] of the cradles with the twenty-four children †of the householders†[3] who did bad deeds.

3-8b. Once, when Candradatta was king, the different classes †beginning with the *brāhmaṇas*† – *brāhmaṇas*, *kṣatriyas*, *vaiśyas*, *śūdras*, [and] low people such as Śabaras and so forth – came from different regions to the enjoyable banner festival.[4] After seeing the banner festival, all these went from there as they had come. O king, as a result of the confusion of people a certain girl of Śabara descent, a beautiful girl who was five years old, became separated. Some people on their way to Gujjaragrāma, having lured the little girl, took her on that same night and went to their homes. Not seeing the little girl all her distressed relatives – mother, brothers and so on – †were† unhappy. Nonetheless, traveling for three days and causing much grief [to the little girl], they (the *brāhmaṇas*) went to the city.

8c-11. The very crafty (perhaps, roguish) *brāhmaṇas* brought up the Pulinda girl. A marriage with the son of a prominent person of another village was arranged for her according to the *cakradeva* process.[5] That child with auspicious marks and auspicious looking eyes passed sixteen years as a daughter. In course she obtained sons with faces like the moon (Tārādhipa, lord of stars) and beautiful in all their limbs.[6] With her acting in this way many years passed.

Śaunaka said:

12-16b. The *brāhmaṇas* dwelling in that village again went to see the banner festival with that woman and her sons. *Brāhmaṇas* from different countries arrived to see the festival. Soon the low man with his wife and family also arrived. Under such circumstances, at the night on the day of the festival she saw her kinsmen and then, seeing her mother, wailed with extreme grief. With extreme grief her mother beat her breasts. Her father . . . , stepped forward. At this moment people, exclaiming 'aha,' stepped forward.

16c-18. All the kinsmen went to tell the story to the king, saying 'This low-born wife of the *brāhmaṇa* †is trying† to deceive us.' The king, very dismayed, called the Pulinda woman [and said,] 'Why do †you make an effort† to take

away the status of a *brāhmaṇa* woman?' Hearing the king's question, the Pulinda woman spoke to him.
The Pulinda woman said:
19-20b. 'This was my child who was lost at a banner festival. Now, by chance only, the young woman has met with me. With the consent of your worship, I could produce evidence for that fact.'
20c-22. Thus having informed the king, the resolute woman together with her daughter and taking along the children and the husband went to her house. The king, having heard her words and being full of dismay, burning up, as it were, [the people he looked at] with his eyes, his body red from anger, said to them (the *brāhmaṇas*) in the middle of the assembly, '*Brāhmaṇas*, speak the truth!'

Śaunaka said:
23-26b. Then all the *brāhmaṇas*, very much filled with fear, said, 'A sin has been done by us. O king, you must forgive us everything.' Saying this, those sinful low men fell at his feet. The wise king, a wise man delighting in truth and duty, then appropriated all their property, giving it to the village people. He said, 'Let them decide themselves whether or not there is to be †an exclusion or no exclusion†';[7] and he went to his native city.[8]
26c-31b. O king, having gathered together there with their heads bowed with shame before the dwellers of the thirty-two villages . . . [the latter forced them to leave] †quickly† because of the commingling of those sinful villagers, having taken the cradles of twenty-four children of the twenty-four householders, and having thrown whatever †red garlands† they had in the water.[9] In that way the eminent people who were firm in their vows sent them away. They performed a *śrāddha* called *kumbha*[10] for them according to rule and went as they had come, saying,

'A place should not be given in the thirty-two villages to people like that.'

Śaunaka said:
31c-33b. O king, what *māhātmya* is to be said of those dwelling in the thirty-two villages who, because of this, are bound by the vow of speaking the truth? Because of this all these low men live fallen in status, shut out from a proper dwelling and excluded from all brahmanical duties.
33c-35. People become polluted simply by looking at them. The only atonement I can prescribe [for these] is to look at the sun the same length of time, but a million (*koṭi*) times longer. Then they will be purified. There is not to be any discussion with regard to this. What else is there to say? I will speak to you of another village.

NOTES

[1] During the course of the story the girl is referred to as Kirāta, Śabara and Pulinda. Though names of separate groups of people, these words are used here most likely as generalized terms for someone of a mountain tribe. It was thought best to retain the actual names in the translation, however.
[2] See n. 1 to the translation to chapter two (Skh.u. 10).
[3] The word translated here as 'of the householders' is '*sakuṭumbinām*.' '*sa*°' is being taken here to signify a relationship between the householders and their children, though even so the word sits peculiarly. I view this to preferable to making an emendation at this point.
[4] The festival referred to as the banner festival, *dhvajotsava*, is in all probability the annual Indra festival, the *indramahotsava*, *dhvaja* being a reference to the *indradhvaja*, or banner or pole of Indra. See Gonda (1967) and Kane (1930-62/2.2[=1941]:

825-826). For literary descriptions of the festival see, for example, *Cilappatikāram*, *kāṇṭam* 1, *kātai* 5, in Dikshitar (1939: 110-121) and *Maṇimēkalai*, *kātai* 1, retold in Krishnaswami Aiyangar (1928: 114-116). To be sure, there are also other festivals in India which center their festivities around a *dhvaja*. For an example of one of these, see Oman (1908: 67-82). The participation of the king in the *dhvaja* festival described in our text, though, makes it more likely that it is the Indra festival which is being referred to rather than one of these.

[5] This form of marriage is not listed in any dictionaries, nor is it noted in A. L. Basham's discussion of marriage in Basham (1968: 166-171), nor in Dubois (1905), nor in Kane (1930-62/2.1) where marriage is dealt with extensively. See the dictionaries of Apte (1957-59), Böhtlingk and Roth (1855-75), and Monier-Williams (1899).

[6] The children of such a marriage would be referred to as *anuloma*, that is, descendents of a union in which the mother was of lower *varṇa* status than the father. For a standard discussion of *anuloma* and *pratiloma*, the latter being the inverse situation, see *Mānavadharmaśāstra* 10.5-42 (Bühler 1886: 402-412), etc.

[7] See n. 4 to the translation of chapter four (Skh.u. 12) above for a discussion of this phrase.

[8] Perhaps, 'and he went home.' See **§7.11**.

[9] What has been described from vs. 26c up to this point is perhaps an expiatory rite for the ominous event which has been revealed at this festival of rejuvenation. See Gonda (1967: 414b-415b).

[10] Kane (1930-62/4[=1953]) does not mention *kumbha* as the name of a *śrāddha* when dealing with the subject. He does mention in vol. 2.1[=1941] on p. 388 that if a sinner refused to undergo a prescribed *prāyaścitta*, "then a procedure called *ghaṭaspoṭa* (breaking a jar) was prescribed. In such a case the sinner's relatives (*sapiṇḍas*) made a slave girl whose face was turned to the south thrust aside with her foot an earthen jar full of water so that all water flowed out of it, then the relatives were to observe mourning for one day and night (as he was

deemed to be dead to them) and from that day they were to stop speaking or sitting with him, and all other social intercourse and he was to be given no inheritance (vide Manu XI.183-185, Yāj[ñavalkyasmṛti] III.294, Gaut. [=Dharmasūtra of Gautama] 20.2-7)." As the primary meaning of the word '*kumbha*' is 'waterpot,' we may not be too far astray in assuming that it was a ceremony such as this which was performed.

CHAPTER SEVEN (Skh.u. 15)

Śaunaka relates that Mayūravarman went to Ballabhī and returned with *brāhmaṇas* from there. *Brāhmaṇas* created by the Bhārgava object to giving these land. They say that the Bhārgava gave them the land. Mayūravarman gives these *brāhmaṇas* four villages and gives the remaining land to the *brāhmaṇas* whom he had just introduced to the area.

* * *

Śatānīka said:
1. I desire to hear still more with regard to the dwellings of polluted *brāhmaṇa* communities one-by-one individually for the benefit of mankind.

Śaunaka said:
2. There is another polluted community on the splendid shore of the Cakranadī river. Placed outside all duties it is called Nāgagrāma.
3-6. Those brought forth (possibly, created) previously by Rāma who settled at that dwelling place pay taxes to the *brāhmaṇas* brought by Mayūravarman, some dwelling there furrowing [the earth], others making groves.[1] Being excluded from the *Vedas* and being without proper duties, it is said that they are twice-born by dint of the sacred thread and *brāhmaṇas* by dint of the Gāyatrī *japa*. Those (i.e., *brāhmaṇas*) are known everywhere in the world by the name of their village, and are known for their performance of homage to the gods and for their practice of what is enjoined by *Śruti* and *Smṛti*, eating a prescribed diet †with uncooked vegetables being forbidden.†

7-11b. The learned Mayūravarman previously had his litter carried to Ballabhī by the *brāhmaṇas* who had been settled (perhaps, created) by Rāma.[2] Taking with him learned *brāhmaṇas*, he returned home. At the time of giving villages those who had been settled by the Bhārgava spoke: 'King, this land was previously given by the Bhārgava Rāma to us. These [villages] were set aside by Rāma, this [earth, our] descendants being endowed with which is certain according to sacred law, most assuredly fixed through inheritance of this which was given as dwellings for us. Disregarding this, how can you give this land to others? Wise one, it must be so! What shall we do?'

Śaunaka said:
11c-13. When the king heard their words he spoke consolingly. [He said,] 'I shall give [you] four villages. Stay there forever.' After the blessed king said this, that benefactor granted the *brāhmaṇas* four villages, †Kuśasthalī consisting just so of eight divisions [and] Maṭināgapura in the same way,†[3] and he gave the remaining land to the newly arrived *brāhmaṇas*.

Śaunaka said:
14-15. O king, once the *brāhmaṇas* settled (perhaps, created) by Rāma settled in the four villages they governed without practicing the six duties of a *brāhmaṇa*.[4] What else is there to say except that they were excluded from all brahmanical rites?

NOTES

[1] A translation 'brought forth,' rather than 'created,' is suggested as a possible translation of '*sṛṣṭa*' as Paraśurāma is reputed to have introduced *brāhmaṇas* from Trihotra in western Bengal into the area that appears to be discussed in this story. Note '*nirmita*,' also 'created,' but more probably to be construed as 'settled,' in vss. 7c, 8d and 14a.

[2] In the middle of this sentence L2 inserts a *pāda* of commentary and Ed and K insert ½ vs. of commentary of which *pāda* b is corrupt. See Appendix B.

[3] This is the reading of L3. It suggests that there may be two *pādas* missing here, with two more names. The other MSS appear to list four village names in the two *pādas* that we have, which text appears to reconstruct to '*kuḍālakaṃ ca padikaṃ madiṃ nāgābhidhaṃ tathā*,' 'Kuḍālaka, Padika, Madi, and that with the name Nāga.' The name of the third village here is Maṭṭī according to Ed, Maddi according to Bm and M, and according to K, the reading of which we need put no stock in, Maṭṭa. We have chosen the reading of L2. All MSS except Bm and M give the fourth name as Nāga. Bm and M give it as Nāma. See critical apparatus. Given the state of our MSS, we must emphasize that all these names are subject to question. See, though, Patil (2010: 178, 180-181) with regard to names mentioned in the *Koṅkaṇākhyāna*, an early eighteenth century Sārasvata text, of quarreling Sārasvata groups as including Kudaleshkars and Pednemkars, which names referred originally to their geographic location in Goa; and that based on copperplates issued by Vijayanagar's kings, the *Koṅkaṇākhyāna*'s author states that the town now known as Kuḍavāla was originally Kuśasthalī.

[4] The six duties of *brāhmaṇas* are generally recognized to be *adhyayana*, studying or repeating the *Veda*; *adhyāpana*, teaching the *Veda*; *yajana*, offering sacrifices; *yājana*, conducting sacrifices for others; *dāna*, giving gifts; and *pratigraha*, accepting gifts. According to the later law books, however, they are listed as *snāna*, religious bathing;

saṃdhājapa, repetition of prayers at the three *saṃdhyās*, religious services performed at sunrise, noon and sunset; *brahmayajña*, worship of the supreme being by repeating the first words of sacred books; *tarpaṇa*, daily oblations of water to the gods, sages and *pitṛs*, or ancestors; *homa*, oblations of fuel, rice, etc. to fire; and *devapūjā*, worship of the secondary gods either in the domestic sanctuary or in temples. See Monier-Williams (1891: 393-394).

CHAPTER EIGHT (Skh.u. 16)

Śaunaka relates the story of another village. First he describes Vijaya during the reign of a certain unnamed king. Then Śaunaka mentions a local *brāhmaṇa* family. A *brāhmaṇa* from Gorāṣṭra arrives at the house of this family for lodging. During the night he witnesses the youngest wife kill her infant. The elder wife, who had cared for the infant as if it were her own, is distressed. She cries out. She is accused of the murder. An argument arises and the king is informed. The *brāhmaṇa* from Gorāṣṭra has the king send for another Gorāṣṭrian *brāhmaṇa*, perhaps the *brāhmaṇa*'s son. This *brāhmaṇa* is noted to be expert in settling disputes. The king of Vijaya writes a letter to the king of Gorāṣṭra. The king of Gorāṣṭra informs the *brāhmaṇa* that he is to leave for Vijaya on the next day.

* * *

Śaunaka said:

1-2. O tiger-like king, I will speak of another cast out village. It is called Velañji.[1] The low men live on the northern bank of the Sītā river because of the murder of a couple. Now I will speak the story (perhaps, more literally, glory or dignity).[2] Listen carefully.

3-7b. There was once an heroic king[3] who was equal in radiance to Indra and who was the foremost of archers – the best was this wise terrestial Indra. With auspiciousness he pleased a city that was wealthy and thriving with everything to be desired, that was adorned with a necklace of jewels, . . . , that was established . . . ,[4] that removed weariness from the sorrows of old age, that was immaculate, that was not [socially] disarranged, that was rich with the activity that surged within, that had raised banners dercorating its gates, that was adorned with fruits and flowers by trees with heavenly fruits and roots, that was surrounded by red chowries, dark colored deer, light colored creeping plants, and dark green thickets,[5] and that of course had people who wore red anklets.

7c-14. Many different trees with flowering branches were resplendent as banners there, having as their beauty villages on rivers and on ponds which were surrounded by an abundance of creepers with both new and old sprouts. Ketaka, Aśoka and Bakuḷa trees, Puṃnāga plants, Tilaka and Arjuna trees, Cūta trees, Nimba trees and Badari trees, Kadamba and Bakuḷa trees,[6] Dhava trees, Priyaṅgu and Pāṭala trees, Jambu and Śālmalī trees, Plakṣa and Vañjula trees, Sāla trees, Tāla trees, Tamāla trees and †the pleasing† Campaka trees,[7] even the flaming Agniśikha trees with fully blossomed flowers at the top, Āmrātaka trees and Madhūka trees, Lakuṭa trees, Kuṭaja trees and Asana trees, Kharjūra trees and Nārikeḷa trees, Pūga trees, and also Saptacchada trees and Chada trees – these and many others were splendid surrounding the city. Fragrant flowers and succulent fruits[8] . . . , ponds were everywhere, as were beautiful and clean sacred *tīrthas*, and also there shone houses and stuccoed mansions comparable to those on Mount Meru.

15a-15b. A judicious king ruled that city.

15c-19b. In that country there was once a certain *brāhmaṇa* learned in the *Vedas* and *Vedāṅgas* named Guṇanidhi, a lord with a name according with truth,[9] his eldest wife Guṇavatī and his second wife Guṇamāliṇī. The two wives, endowed with beauty and youth, looked like young deer. Out of respect, the elder wife always protected the child of the younger wife as if it were her own daughter. The second wife, Guṇamāliṇī, the dearest of everyone (literally, the multitude), by her exceedingly gentle disposition filled her husband with †rapture†.

Śaunaka said:
19c-24b. With everything like this, a certain *brāhmaṇa* from Gorāṣṭra, the best of those learned in the *Veda*, then came to the house of that *brāhmaṇa* with the aim of sleeping. His mind distressed on account of family concerns, the *muni* was lying awake in the night, uneasy. In the middle of the night the younger wife, a woman with a beautiful complexion, got up from her bed and quickly went to the child. Out of envy (or perhaps, displeasure) and . . . she broke the neck of the child, courage having been gathered in her mind.[10] After quickly killing the child she went to her bed. What is to be said? She was most certainly an evil person.
24c- 26. When it became light the eldest wife got up from her bed, went quickly to the body and seeing the child, delicate, killed and with blood, said, 'Oh! What is this! This is terrible! Oh! I am lost!' Beating her belly she wailed, very much distressed, filled with grief, having been struck dumb all of a sudden.
27-30. Hearing the cry of pain which was due to the horrible medicine of the younger wife †the lord [of the house]† lamented likewise, filled with grief. Hearing a quarrel of both truth and falsehood, the *brāhmaṇa* became distressed. He told the story of the two in detail to the king. The ruler was astonished when he heard such a tale from the *brāhmaṇa*. Together with his ministers, the king could not come to a decision. He called the *brāhmaṇa* who had wanted lodging [and said,] 'Speak what is true as it was seen. Do not under any circumstances be afraid.'
31-32b. Adhering closely to the words of the king the *brāhmaṇa*, smiling, said, 'Alas! This proud lion is called

on to kill an elephant adjudged to be a mosquito, thereby causing the womenfolk to laugh.'[11]

32c-34. After reflecting in his mind for a moment, the *brāhmaṇa* became resolute. . . .[12]

The *brāhmaṇa* said:

35-40b. 'If a wickedly done act is not exceedingly contemned, bad conduct is produced. Therefore, I will speak a means of success, O jewel in a line of kings. In the land on the beautiful shore of the western ocean, near Vijaya, there shines a certain *brāhmaṇa* together with his four sons. The first is the best of those learned in the *Vedas*. The second is versed in grammar. The third is learned in the art of writing. The youngest †is expert in† deliberation. The king of the country of Gorāṣṭra is clever and understanding. O king who is very learned in what appears to be so, bring him who is in the forefront of the . . . , who is always appointed by people of moral conduct, and he will demonstrate sin and virtue without a doubt. Without him in the threefold world[13] there is not anyone who can make a decision.'

40c-44. Speaking his agreement, the king wrote a beautiful letter. He commanded spies to go to the [king's] residence in Gorāṣṭra. The messengers arrived quickly. They delivered the beautiful letter to the king. The king of Gorāṣṭra looked at the letter himself. The king summoned the wise man and then said articulately, 'At this moment a great king desires to see you. You are to go to the beautiful city called Vijaya tomorrow.' After agreeing, the best of *brāhmaṇas* arose.

NOTES

[1] Velañji, perhaps Belañji. See critical apparatus for 9(17).57d.
[2] See n. 1 to the translation of chapter two (Skh.u. 10).
[3] Saletore (1936a: 346-347) takes '*vīrabhūpa*,' translated here as 'heroic king,' to refer rather to the Vijayanāgara viceroy Vīra Bhūpati, who was placed over a city in Karnataka, his "provincial capital," in 1386 A.D. See **§10.2** (end of discussion) and **§12.5a** above. Saletore maintains that the judicial incident described in the beginning of chapter nine (Skh.u. 17), for which this chapter sets the stage, occurred in this figure's court. Regarding the association of the incident with a certain wise Mariāda-rāman, a figure popular in Telugu and Tamil lore, see **§10.2** (end of discussion), **§10.5** and **§12.4** above.
[4] All MSS read '*vāñchatīṃ iva saṃsthitāṃ*, which would appear to translate 'established like Vāñchatī.' As we cannot find any reference to a city of this name, however, we regard it to be very possibly a corruption. We therefore omit it from our text.
[5] The text lists first a series of adjectives and then a series of substantives. These are taken with the last adjective referring to the first substantive and the first adjective to the last substantive.
[6] Bakuḷa trees are mentioned here for the second time. As noted in n. 11 to the translation of chapter one (Skh.u. 9), this is not uncommon for lists of this sort.
[7] Perhaps, 'and Campaka and Manorama (or Manoratha) trees.' The structure of the vs. would certainly indicate this, but neither of these words are listed as the names of trees by any of the dictionaries consulted.
[8] Bm and M insert: . . . and a hundred beautiful forests comparable to those on mount Meru . . . .
[9] Literally Guṇanidhi means 'a treasury of good qualities,' i.e. 'an excellent man.'
[10] In the story as told by Father Bouchet narrated in both Rocher (1984: 22-24) and Goonetilleke (1890: 12a-13a), it is the elder wife who kills her own child and blames the younger out of jealousy, or envy. In the other version of this story told first by

Goonatilleke (1890: 11a-12a), it is the younger wife who kills *her* own child out of displeasure because it was crying while she was entertaining a lover. And she then blames the elder wife, saying the child was killed out of jealousy. This version of the story also explains why the *brāhmaṇa* lodger was lying awake with a troubled mind: his son had been made a judge by the local king, and the father suspected it would lead to his disgrace rather than his honor.

[11] I have consulted Böhtlingk (1870-73) for this vs., but without positive results.

[12] The text as presently constituted is not entirely clear. It seems, as we have translated, that first the *brāhmaṇa* father of the murdered child laments and reports the incident to the king. Then, when the king cannot decide the case, he speaks to the *brāhmaṇa* lodger who witnessed the crime. At this point, however, our text breaks down totally and all that can be ascertained is the jist of what is being narrated. It appears that the *brāhmaṇa* lodger lays the groundwork for the king to summon the *brāhmaṇa* lodger's son from Gorāṣṭra, and that he sets up some stipulation. The *brāhmaṇa* speaks in the course of this, but it is not clear as to what he says. He then speaks at length, for which see above.

[13] The threefold world refers to heaven, atmosphere and earth.

CHAPTER NINE (Skh.u. 17)

Śaunaka relates the portents boding calamity which occur during the trip to Vijaya made by the Gorāṣṭrian *brāhmaṇa* skilled in deliberation. The *brāhmaṇa* settles the dispute by an unusual strategem. The king punishes the younger wife and honors the *brāhmaṇa* with two villages, wealth, cattle, clothing, and eminence. Much time passes. The king's ministers are noted to be enemies of this *brāhmaṇa*'s family. The *brāhmaṇa*'s son kills his wife and her paramour while they are making love and reports this to the ministers himself. The family is told to travel on pilgrimage to holy spots in Gokarṇa. They meet a great *muni*. He gives them water from a certain *tīrtha*. They set firm a Śālagrāma stone which they find there. They go, and at noon come to a breadfruit tree. They eat. At the tree's roots they find the Śālagrāma stone in a basket. They get set to go. A voice in heaven tell them to stay and states that the Śālagrāma stone will become their family deity. They make a dwelling with the permission of the villagers. They live without performing oblations to the gods or their deceased ancestors. The villagers do not associate with them because of this. When they realize their sin they go to the *muni* whom they had seen before. He purifies them. Nonetheless, they are said to be polluted. Śaunaka adds that one becomes polluted by sight of these, but states that he cannot speak a specific expiation.

* * *

Śaunaka said:

1-5b. Informed at once of the direction the wise man with a great knowledge of future situations quickly †departed from his kinsmen† and went very slowly. Then, passing through heaven, earth and the intermediate region, there arose unusual events (*utpātas*) which boded calamity, which caused . . . , which were terrific, which were frightful, and which cause one's hair to bristle. †Hidden† in the earth Pṛṣadaṉsa[1] †thundered† and bellowed. Trees with many branches fell down all around. Terrific rock crags shrieked in a spot to the south of the *brāhmaṇa*. Crows cried out. He saw the moon. With his mind not disturbed by such unusual events (*utpātas*) as these, he went.[2]

Śaunaka said:
5c-7. After a period of eighteen days he saw the great king. The very wise ruler honored him and then said to him, 'Wise one! You must decide this killing of the child correctly.' Upon hearing this, the tiger-like *brāhmaṇa* entered into the court area of the assembly. After summoning the *brāhmaṇa*'s two wives the chief among *brāhmaṇas* spoke.
The *brāhmaṇa* said:
8-9b. 'Whichever one removes her clothing, in this way setting aside shame, and quickly walks around the courtroom in full view of the assembly, she is guiltless by dint of that. There is no doubt about this.'
9c-9d. When the best of *brāhmaṇās* had said this, he was quiet.

Śaunaka said:
10-15b. The eldest wife, having heard these words, [said,] 'Oh! I have met with a wrong. Even in one's mind one does not do such an act. The course of fate is difficult to overcome. How? The evidence to be produced cannot be conceived in my heart. I am not guilty of sin. I will not do something that is forbidden (perhaps, evil). To save my honor I must abandon life. Life is impermament. Honor lasts for as long as the moon and the stars. Those who are

highest desire honor. Those in the middle wealth and honor. The lowest desire wealth. Honor is the highest wealth. For this reason, I ought never †submit† to such evidence. While everyone is looking, I will surrender this body.' After saying this Guṇavatī became quiet.

15c-16. The second wife stood up quickly without any clothes and so forth, walked around the assembly of people of good *varṇa* three times and then stood in the front without fear or shame.

17-18b. After seeing her, all the men cried out in astonishment, 'The child was killed by an evil deed by this evil one disposed to sin. O king, do not have any doubt about this.'

18c-20. The king was astonished on seeing the uprightness of the one. He punished the one who killed the child and honored the *brāhmaṇa*. With affection for him he gave wealth, cows and two villages. Then, after giving much clothing and jewelry, a beautiful banner indicating victory, and eminence, the king went to his house.

21-22. O king, the country became more and more prosperous each day from then on, just as the moon increases as it approaches the full moon. Much time passed with the best of *brāhmaṇas* dwelling with good fortune, having been given two villages for his kinsmen.

Śaunaka said:

23. Then all the ministers, prior enemies of the family, came together in order to search for a fault which would allow them to chastise him accordingly.

24-28b. There had been born to him an exceedingly stupid son who was of mean nature. His wife had fine hips, was endowed with beauty and youth, had longish eyes, a beautiful middle part, two full and high breasts, a nether lip red like the Bimba fruit, and was engaged in the path of houselife, but as is human nature she sometimes enjoyed herself with a lover. The husband, seeing that she was doing this sort of thing, went to her with his self-control lost to anger, and with his sword raised in his hand in an excess of passion he put an end to the two who were very clever in deceit, their two bodies engaged in love, powerless by the grasp of love and compelled by their attachment to it.[3]

28c-32. As fate would have it, †the dumb one† came to obtain purification for †the sin†. In this case the old ministers, having declared him guilty, announced to the king the affair of the killing of the couple.[4] Immediately they devised a way to repudiate these foolish, cruel chieves of Gorāṣṭra. [They said,] 'There is near a river in Gorāṣṭra Mahābaleśa. There is a great spot situated to the south called Avimukta. If one makes a pilgrimage to the great god, and also to powerful Kroḍeśvara, and in this way makes a *darśana*, he obtains purity.'[5]

Śaunaka said:

33-34. Thus all the people of Gorāṣṭra, intent on getting out of their trouble and in order to put an end to their pollution, gradually made a pilgrimage to different *tīrthas*, and reaching the Sahya range of mountains filled with various groups of *munis*, and arriving at the summit of the mountain, they entered the land of the Tuḷus.

35-38b. In due course they saw Gokarṇa. O prince, after they did reverence in various ways to Mahābala, the lord of Gokarṇa who was in that place, and after they bathed in the Śuktimatī river which takes away an entire mass of sins, they performed reverence according to rule for the termination of their sin. Filled with repentence they went toward the south. Wherever . . . of evil Suptaghna with two *piśācas*, there they will go.[6]

38c-43b. When near Ananteśa they saw a great *muni* on earth, intent in austerity with a body marked by the signs of the conch shell, the discus, the mace, and the lotus, and seeing him they gladly fell at his feet in a straight line. Censured by the killing of the couple, they told of their deeds. The religious one, after thinking for a moment with a mind filled by pity, gave them water from the *tīrtha* as if to indicate auspiciousness. In the middle of the *tīrtha* . . . , standing with a Guñja plant as the measure of its holiness, splendid, there was a sacred Śālagrāma stone[7] called Janārdana. Having thought that they had obtained their goal, †they set firm† the stone, ascended the peak of the Sahya range, and all made ready to go.
43c-49b. At noon, while walking, they saw a fallen down breadfruit tree on the northern shore of the Sītā river and they approached the tree's root. †Then the men† quickly broke off its fruit, feeling hungry. Having done a cleaning with cloth †but without saying the *mantra* for the hands†, they gathered together closely and went to examine the root of the tree. They saw something astonishing there and cried out, 'What is this?' There was the sacred stone Janārdana in a wickerwork basket. Having taken it †for burying†, the foolish people got ready to go. In the meantime, king, a voice in heaven was heard [saying,] 'O *brāhmaṇas*! Stay here! This will be a dwelling [for you]! This Janārdana, without a doubt, will become your family deity in order for you to increase your welfare.'
49c-51. The stainless goddess became concealed after speaking there. They (the *brāhmaṇas*) were filled with much joy after they all thought, 'What goddess is this celestial voice? Why did she speak? We will make a dwelling in this great village.' They made thirty houses with the permission of the villagers.

42-56. For some time they dwelt there without performing oblations to either the gods or the spirits of deceased ancestors. Those dwelling there previously did not come to their dwelling. After reflecting on why this was so and then becoming alarmed at their own sin, the great men saw the *muni* whom they had seen before. After the one with much power looked into the matter, he did a purification according to rule. Marked with Viṣṇu's sign, he recited a *mantra* having the name of Viṣṇu and taught the highest *mantra* which has eight syllables (*aṣṭākṣaramantra*).[8] With the *mantra* '*ā no bhadra . . .*'[9] there was expressed a taking of earth. With the *mantra* '*ā mandrair . . .*' there was expresses a smearing with earth. With the *mantra* '*akṣībhyām te . . .*' there was specifically expressed a cleansing with earth.[10]

Śaunaka said:
57-60. Obtaining the permission of the *guru*, they made a dwelling without fear. Beginning then, that village was called Velañji (perhaps, Belañji). It is said that all the *brāhmaṇas* dwelling there are polluted. O jewel in a line of kings, what is there to say aside from this? Simply by looking at them one will become polluted. O prince, it is not possible to speak an expiation. I will speak generally. Let one perform a *kṛcchra* or *cāndrāyaṇa*.[11]

NOTES

[1] Apte (1957-59) lists '*pṛṣadaṇśa*' to be the same as '*pṛṣadaśva*,' which can be taken as an epithet of either the god of wind or Śiva. Böhtlingk and Roth (1855-75) and Monier-Williams (1899) keep these two words separate and give no

meaning for '*pṛṣadaṉśa*,' but note: *Kāśikā Vṛtti*, *pṛṣa*, *daṉśa*. "°*aṉsa*' must be taken as a normal variant for "°*aṉśa*.' All MSS read "°*aṉsa*.'

[2] Kane (1930-62/5.2[=1962]: 742) quotes Garga as stating "deities become unfavourable owing to the wrong doings of men and create extraordinary happenings in the sky, atmospheric region and on earth. These are the utpātas for all worlds created by gods; these utpātas sally forth for the destruction (of people) and they by their (terrific) appearances rouse people (to do what is proper)." See pp. 743-744, where Kane gives examples of such *utpātas* taken from the *Mahābhārata* and the *Rāmāyaṇa*.

[3] This incident suggests that it is the version of the story told first by Goonetilleke (1890: 11a-13a) that is at play here, in which the cause of Guṇamāliṇī's killing her infant child was that she was displeased with its crying while she was entertaining a paramour. By what one's family's status is raised, by that it will be lost. Such is the workings of karma.

[4] MSS Ed, L2 and Bm here insert a lengthy commentary on how an adultress is to be treated. See Appendix B. Also see Kane (1930-62: 2.1[=1941]: 571-573) where views on how to treat an addultress which are different from that inserted here are noted. The consensus, as deduced by Kane, is that ordinarily a woman who commits adultery can atone for this and restore herself to all the ordinary rights of wives, but for as long as she has not performed penance her punishment is that she is given starving maintenance in the house itself and is deprived of all her rights as wife. Certain situations do require different treatment, however, which treatment may be as rash as refusing the wife bare maintenance and residence near the house. Killing the wife, though, is not an acceptable treatment. Also, for the treatment to be dealt a *brāhmaṇa* accused of murder, see n. 6 to the translation of chapter four (Skh.u. 12) above. Kane does not note, incidentally, that a *brāhmaṇa*'s whole community is to be punished for a crime.

[5] All MSS insert ½ vs. which indicates that the king did something. The sentence, however, is incomplete, and is therefore impossible to translate properly.
[6] There appears to be a reference here to a mythological incident for which it has been impossible to find a reference. Suptaghna is mentioned is Gorresio's edition of the *Rāmāyaṇa* (1843-1858), in 1,4, 107; 5,80,1; 6,18,14; 6,69,11; and 7,5,36; but nowhere is light thrown on this allusion. Nor is Dikshitar (1951-55) of any help.
[7] The Śālagrāma is a sacred stone which is supposed to be pervaded with the presence of Viṣṇu. It is called Śālagrāma because it is found chiefly in the Gaṇḍakī river near the village of Śālagrāma. It is a black stone in which there is generally embedded a fossil ammonite.
[8] See n. 8 to the translation of chapter four (Skh.u. 12) above.
[9] RV 1.89.1. See Appendix C for this and the following two *mantras*, RV 3.45.1 and RV 10.163.1. On the basis of the context and the import of the three Ṛgvedic hymns being referred to, it would appear that it is the entire hymns that are being recited here
[10] L2 and M insert here a commentary type passage similar to the lengthy insertion in chapter 4(12). See Appendix B.
[11] All MSS add:

†Strife was caused to increase† by the great men dwelling at that spot, at that breadfruit tree, which is a place filled with compassion.

Sūta said:

Śaunaka, the best of *ṛṣis*, told this whole old story to king Śatānīka, O *brāhmaṇa*.

Śaunaka said:

He who hears here in this world even once this entire story and the tale of the bad people who killed the couple which when told correctly destroys every sin, becomes a realization for the sake of liberation among men.

These 4 vss. are omitted here because the end of the chapter, as it stands above, is more in keeping with the standard chapter endings of this text as seen in chapters 2(10), 3(11), 4(12), 5(13), 6(14), and 11(19).

CHAPTER TEN (Skh.u. 18)

Śaunaka says that he will relate a story of another Gorāṣṭrian *brāhmaṇa*. He describes king Hemamālin of the city of Kāñcanamālinī in Kaliṅga. A Gorāṣṭrian *muni* together with his wife and disciples comes to Hemamālin. Hemamālin honors the *brāhmaṇa*. The *brāhmaṇa* decides to test the king. He offers the king unhusked barley grains, or perhaps winnowed rice, which had been purified by *mantras* with the left hand. The king chides the *brāhmaṇa*. The *brāhmaṇa* displays anger and states his power. The king bows to the *brāhmaṇa* to placate him. The *brāhmaṇa* tells the king to stand. He demonstrates his power by throwing down the barley corns (?) from his right hand together with fire. The *brāhmaṇa* puts out the fire. The king gives the *brāhmaṇa* riches, female slaves, and eight villages. The *brāhmaṇa* praises and blesses Hemamālin and leaves for Gorāṣṭra.

* * *

Śaunaka said:

1. Now I will speak of another village of a revered Gorāṣṭrian *brāhmaṇa* . . . . Listen attentively.

2-11b. There was in the country of Kaliṅga Kāñcanamālinī by name, well-provided with men and women and filled with elephants, horses and chariots. Once there was in that city Hemamālin, a protector of the world born in the solar dynasty, equal in radiance to Yudhiṣṭhira, first among bowmen, very mighty, courageous with †his fame† in war well-known, possessing chariots, elephants and warriors, one who conquered the circle of neighboring princes by sword and a powerful arm and who honors the splendor of the sun mounted on the eastern mountain, this one who in the circle of the earth had a splendor equal to that of Ākhaṇḍala (i.e., Indra). He was considered to be one who knew about great gifts and small gifts. It is clear that out of his ocean of fame and happiness was born the moon and that out of his brilliancy was born fire. Kāma, himself, who had been brought to the condition of being without a body, upon seeing his form was conquered by fire (i.e., anger or jealousy ?) And . . .[1] having seen his depth, was filled with excessive fear. Having obtained the state of †a prosperous dwelling† . . . . When such an intelligent man who is distinguished by fine qualities in this way rules a kingdom there is not any fear of drought, any fear of famine, nor any fear of barbarians (*mlecchas*), thieves, tigers, herons, lions, and so forth. Many years passed with his continuing in this way.

11c-14b. Once there arrived a venerable master of the *Vedas* and *Vedāṅgas*. Through fate[2] he had become equal in radiance to Vaiśvānara, but nevertheless he appeared to be only an ordinary man who had obtained tranquility. Accompanied by a wife with a good disposition, always surrounded by pupils, . . . that speech in a Prākṛta foot which was pleasing to the *brāhmaṇa*.[3]

14c-18. After seeing the *brāhmaṇa* who had arrived, the best of kings did reverence by receiving the guest with milk and honey, by sitting with him and so forth. The *brāhmaṇa* decided, 'We should find out how resolute this one is.' With his left hand[4] he gave him unhusked barley grains (perhaps, winnowed rice) which had been purified with *mantras*. The best of kings, on seeing this, had a somewhat perplexed look. He decided to speak to †the one offering† the purified unhusked barley corns (?). 'Revered sir! In this world *brāhmaṇas* are the highest of †everything†. In the midst of these *brāhmaṇas* there is certainly not anyone like you. Noone has ever seen anyone doing such acts on earth.'

19-22b. After hearing his words which had been spoken without fear the foremost of the twice-born, his eyes red with anger, spoke words which had ascertainment as the goal: 'Many princes †have been seen† by us, O best of princes. There is not seen in the three worlds anyone like your honor among those making judgements. Let it be! I will give with the right hand. Let it be taken if you have the power. If not, I will throw it on your head. Let them (the barley corns or grains of rice) become ashes! Let all the great men here see it!'

22c-25. O king, while the *brāhmaṇa* was speaking in this way the lord (Hemamālin) did a waving of lights on the surface of the earth near the footstool with his crown being used as a lamp, but of jewels, so as to placate the *brāhmaṇa*. The *brāhmaṇa* †said†, 'Stand up, stand up, king! Wise one, abandon your fear! We will show the power of this [barley, or rice]. Let a cloth be spread!' The king stood at a distance. He spread out a cloth, desiring to see his (the *brāhmaṇa*'s) power.

The *brāhmaṇa* said:

26. 'There is a fixed opinion that in the right hand of a *brāhmaṇa* there is a lamp.[5] O king, look now at this burning fire.'

27-32. Having said this, the *brāhmaṇa* then showed the king his own power and the power of the *mantra* for one attended by power by putting together a bolt of fire, and this having been thrown down together with the barley (?), there appeared a fire flaming with brilliance. The good archer looked attentively. The woven cloth, reduced to ashes, was beginning to burn down the assembly hall. Everyone, seeing the fire and being restrained by the heat, came near the *brāhmaṇa* and gladly fell at his feet. [They said,] 'Please protect this king and us. Be compassionate! Take away the heat! Extinguish the fire!' The best of *brāhmaṇas*, hearing their words, smiling and deliberating that act (?) . . . .[6] This having been done by the blessed one, the fire was extinguished.

33-36b. Then the king plunged himself into a wave of the ocean of happiness. Out of affection he gave the *brāhmaṇa* eight villages. Moreover, he gave uncountable gold, cloth, ornaments, and a necklace with priceless jewels. He gave also a bracelet worn around the upper arm studded with sapphires and rubies. He gave him in addition a hundred female slaves richly endowed with the qualities of beauty and nobility. O great king, what should not be given to a man excelling in such qualities?

36c-37. The best of *brāhmaṇas*, honored by him and having praised his (Hemamālin's) good qualities, said, 'I am going. Let there be prosperity for you as long as there are the moon and the stars'; and he left for his own town.

NOTES

[1] It would appear that another god is mentioned here, but the name cannot be made out.

[2] Literally, 'from having his forehead as his guide.' At birth Brahman is said to inscribe one's future on the forehead. See Monier-Williams (1899: 739c, s.v. *brahmarekhā*).

[3] It is not clear what happened to the text at this point. The ½ vs. which has been indicated in our text by dots appears as if it may be a gloss indicating something about the name of the *brāhmaṇa*. It does not supply any verb which might connect the two sections of this sentence certainly. It is most probable that something has been lost here, and is possible that the two parts

of what is taken here to be one sentence may in fact be two separate sentences.

[4] Offering or eating food with the left hand is improper. This hand is reserved for performing one's toilet.

[5] Kane (1930-62/2.1[=1941]: 134-135), in writing on ideas of the sacredness and superiority of *brāhmaṇas*, quotes *Taittirīya-brāhmaṇa* 3.7.3 as stating that "one should sacrifice in the right hand of a brāhmaṇa; the brāhmaṇa indeed is Agni-vaiśvānara"; and makes reference in regard to this statement to *Mahābhārata*, *Śāntiparva* 343.13-14; *Mānavadharmaśāstra* 4.117; *Likhita* 311; and *Vasiṣṭhadharmasūtra* 30.2-5.

[6] Most of vs. 32ab cannot be made out. It does appear, in any event, that at least ½ vs. is missing here.

CHAPTER ELEVEN (Skh.u. 19)

Śaunaka continues the preceding story. The *brāhmaṇa* leaves and arrives at the Caṇḍikā river. There he performs the appropriate rites, some with his wife. At evening he sees one of his slaves and falls in love with her. These two dwell by the river and in time she gives birth to eight sons by him. The *brāhmaṇa* gives the eight villages to these sons, specifies their livelihood, summons his legitimate son, gives him directions as to what to do with these eight sons, and leaves with his wife to perform *tapas*. The son performs the tonsure ceremony and the initiation rites for the eight sons. Śatānīka expresses alarm and asks how such can be done for the sons of a female slave. Śaunaka explains. He states that raising non-*brāhmaṇas* to *brāhmaṇa* status is common. The legitimate son instructs the eight illegitimate sons as to their duties and instructs the female slaves to return to their native cities. He then returns home. Śaunaka adds that one becomes polluted from sight of these people. He provides an expiation for the sons (?).

* * *

Śaunaka said:

1-6. On the following day the *brāhmaṇa*, taking his belongings, happily set out together with his disciples to go to his place of residence. He saw pleasing *tīrthas* and different countries. Gradually that one who possessed immense powers of the mind approached the highest mountain of the Sahya range. There the great lord saw the river named Caṇḍikā which destroys discord and impurity, filled with pure water, frequented by groups of *siddhas* and *ṛṣis*, ornamented with the dark blue blossoms of the Utpala lotus and the hundred petals of the white esculent water lily, and beautified by groups of Cakora partridges, Kāraṇḍa ducks, and ruddy geese. He decided to bathe in it. After doing the midday observance, the rites of the five religious oblations of a householder[1] and so forth, and after accomplishing the *nitya* rites together with his wife on the bank of the river, the *brāhmaṇa* thought, 'We must go quickly from here.'

7-14. Then, at evening, †a gentle breeze blew†. He then saw a certain beautiful slave girl sixteen years old . . . near a Kadamba tree, standing as if she was a *śakti* of love with a †shining† nose, long eyes, a face similar to the moon (Tārādhipa, lord of the stars), her forehead appearing like the digit of a second moon (perhaps, like the second digit of the moon),[2] with earings glittering as if they had gathered bees, with a neck like a spiral shell and with long arms, with a full and high breast, a thin waist, splendid hips, a curving body in the bloom of youth, splendid buttocks, a beautiful brow, and having an origin of the *padminī* type.[3] On seeing this daughter of a slave woman he was overpowered by love. O king, on seeing this one Ratipati (the god of love), the one who has conquered the three worlds, with his bow made firm drowned in doubt fame, renown, courage, and a rapacious mind. On that same night, from an arrow, he joined together as husband and wife on the bank of the Caṇḍikā river that venerable best of *brāhmaṇas* and the slender woman who was not inhibited by modesty.

Śaunaka said:

15-16b. †Who is that woman? Who is this *brāhmaṇa*?† The ways of fate are mysterious. He spent a series of nights filled with joy in that arbor, kissing, embracing and so forth.

16c-20. Then, in due course, there were born eight sons, handsome youths, from her, with her long eyes, and from the *brāhmaṇa*, who was a worthy object of affection. Looking at them with joy, the wise man apportioned the eight villages and gave the villages, in proper order, to the sons bound [to him] by love. Thus having assigned [the villages] one by one, he instructed them thus: 'By my command they must live in the *brāhmaṇa* community but be inadmissible into society, performing sweeping wherever there is a house of Śiva, just so spreading on cow-dung, enjoying there the remains of offerings to Śiva, and bearing parasols and the the staffs of doorkeepers.'[4]
21-24. Seeing that it was †time† for him to do so, he decided to perform *tapas*. He summoned his legitimate son named Sunīta who was both learned in the sacred texts and wise and spoke these words to him: 'These sons are receptacles of my affection and are bound in love. They are to be protected with love properly by you, their eldest brother.' After saying this, that best of *brāhmaṇas* together with his wife went to perform *tapas*. According to the prescriptions of the sacred texts the *muni*, not transgressing the command of his father, performed for those the tonsure ceremony and the initiation rites.

Śatānīka said:
25. I ask myself how †did that *brāhmaṇa* do† a sanctifying ceremony according to rule, and my mind feels alarm because of the children of the female slave.

Śaunaka said:
26. This is a good question, king. It is indeed reason for alarm. I will cause to be brought to an end this alarm born in your mind in the following way:

27-28. In the land of the *śūdra*[5] . . . born of the best of *brāhmaṇas* according to *gotra* and *pravara*, he proclaimed the Kāśyapa *gotra* for those without rules to live by (? – *gotrasūtra*; perhaps, a list of *pravaras*), the purifying ceremonies beginning with birth having been done according to the *Āśvalāyanasūtra* (= *Āśvalāyanagṛhya-sūtra*).'[6]

29-31. Having thus done the birth *saṃskāra* according to rule, he assigned to each *gotras* beginning with the Kāśyapa and Kauśika with division into this and that *pravara*.[7] According to prescribed rule, prince, he performed a marriage of eight young girls born of different female slaves, having made this division in order to avoid the sin of mixing together (close relatives ?).

32-33. Once Parāśara (the destroyer [of the *kṣatriyas*], i.e. Paraśurāma) in clear view found sailors, it is well known.[8] In clear view, with axe in hand, he raised up widows' bastards most certainly.[9] Such is always the telling of the merits of the noble-minded one. There are many cases like this. There is no doubt about this.[10]

34. Having done thus, the blessed one named (them) again in due succession. Not transgressing the words of the *guru*, he did just so on the earth.

35-36b. Calling together the assemblage of female slaves, the son of the *brāhmaṇa* said, 'From wherever you came before, that city is to be sought.' After saying this, the best of *brāhmaṇas* went to his own home.

36c-37b. Beginning then, the (eight) slaves are dwelling on earth free from fear and independent regardless of their means of livelihood.

37c-39. One becomes polluted from sight of these people. The eminent *guru* (i.e., the Bhārgava; see 2[10].47b) has said that there is to be neither the six duties,[11] nor the six

. . . , nor the double sacred thread (?), nor any eating together, nor any learning of the *Purāṇas*, nor possession of a *rudrākṣa* rosary,[12] nor wearing an *uṣṇīṣa*, nor an entrance into the *brāhmaṇa* community.

40-42. O king, son of the best of kings, what is there to say aside from this? For these men with whom no meals can be eaten, living in a low condition and indulging in unrighteousness, a bath in the Ganges is prescribed. Always they . . . traveling to Vārāṇasī for twelve years, without a doubt.

NOTES

[1] The five religious oblations of a householder are the five *mahāyajñas*, or principle acts of devotion. These, according to the *Mānavadharmaśāstra* 3.69-71, are *brahmayajña*, homage to the supreme spirit and to that spirit present in the *Vedas*; *devayajña*, homage to the gods; *pitṛyajña*, homage to one's deceased ancestors; *manuṣyayajña*, homage to men; and *bhūtayajña*, homage to all beings, including animals. See Bühler (1886: 87-88) and Monier-Williams (1891: 411).

[2] The ascriptive part of the description, '*dvitīyacandralekheva*,' instead of agreeing with '*dṛśyamānalalāṭikāṃ*,' 'having a forehead appearing,' is put in the nominative. While this is grammatically incorrect, it appears to be the construction here. See '*smaraśaktir*,' 'a *śakti* of love,' immediately above.

[3] A woman belonging to the first of the four classes into which women are divided. The other three classes of women are the *citriṇī*, or woman of varied accomplishments; the *śaṅkhinī*, or conch-like woman; and the *hastinī*, or elephant-like woman. For descriptions of the *padminī* type similar to that given here see Kalyānamalla's *Anaṅgaraṅga* in the translation ascribed to Sir Richard F. Burton (and F. F. Arbuthnot) from [18-?] in *The Hindu Art of Love* ([19-?]: 8-9) and Kokkoka's *Ratirahasya* in

Comfort (1964: 103-104). For a rather comprehensive description of the *padminī* type taken from a large number of texts which discuss the matter see Schmidt (1902: 220-224). See also his table on pp. 234-241 for a tabular listing of the characteristics of the *padminī* type, as well as of the other three types, according to various sources.

[4] Perhaps, the rods (or maces) of officers. It is not altogether clear from our text here as to the nature of all the duties the *brāhmaṇa* is commanding his illegitimate sons to perform. Clearly, though, he is commanding them to be *patita* by stating that they are to live in the *brāhmaṇa* community but be inadmissible into society. To be noted is the discussion of Ambalavāsis in Thurston (1909/1: 28-31). In this discussion Thurston quotes the Madras Census Report, 1901, as stating that Ambalavāsi is "a generic name applied to all classes of temple servants in Malabar. There are many sub-divisions of the caste . . . which are assigned different services in the Hindu temples, such as the preparation of garlands, the sweeping of the floor, the fetching of firewood, the carrying of idols in procession, singing, dancing, and so on." The Travancore Census Report, 1901, is quoted as stating that Ambalavāsis occupy "an intermediate position between Brāhmans and the Brāhmanical Kshatriyas of Malabar on the one hand, and the Sūdras on the other. While according to one view they are fallen Brāhmans, others . . . would put them down as an advance from the Sūdras." From the Cochin Census Report, 1901, he quotes of the Ambalavāsis that "most of the castes have grown out of sexual relations between members of the higher and lower classes, and are therefore Anulomajas and Pratilomajas. They may be broadly divided into two classes, (1) those that wear the sacred thread, and (2) those that do not wear the same." Also to be noted are Thurston (1909/2: 208 and 5: 119-126) and Anantakrishna Iyer (1909/2: 125) where, under Mūssads, who are noted by some to be fallen *brāhmaṇas* and by others as the highest caste of Ambalavāsis, it is noted that some stories noting their fallen status say that they became so by eating the

offerings to Śiva. Anantakrishna Iyer (1928-36/4[=1931]: 185) notes under Mālerus, who are outcaste *brāhmaṇa* women who were excommunicated together with their children for conjugal infidelity and other communal offences, that one becomes a member of the group by eating the sacrificial rice cast in the alter of a Śiva temple. Our *brāhmaṇa* has commanded his children to sweep in Śiva temples; to prepare fresh flooring by spreading cowdung on the ground; to eat the remains of offering to Śiva, which apparently is in itself cause for fallen status; to bear parasols, probably over idols should we consider the duties of Ambalavāsis; and perhaps to be doorkeepers.

[5] 'The land of the *śūdra*' I take to be a euphemism for south India where the vast majority of the population are *śūdras*.

[6] The *saṃskāras* are household rites and the details of these would be in the *Āśvalāyanagṛhyasūtra* as opposed to the *Āśvalāyanaśrautasūtra*. And indeed, see *Āśvalāyanagṛhyasūtra* 1.15 ff. for reference to the birth *saṃskāra* and the following *saṃskāras*.

[7] It has proved impossible to clarify these statements regarding *gotra* and *pravara* through reference to Brough (1952). For lists of *pravaras* in the various *Śrautasūtras* see *Śrautakośah, Encyclopaedia of Vedic Sacrificial Ritual* (1958-62/1.2[=1962]: 979 ff.).

[8] This is reference to the history of Citpāvan *brāhmaṇas* narrated in the *uttarārdha* of the *Sahyādrikhaṇḍa*, chapter 1. In DaCunha's edition in chapter 1, the shipwrecked sailors are referred to as "fisherman" (see, for instance, Deshpande 2010: 37). Note, most Citpāvan *brāhmaṇas* have a fair complexion and greenish-gray eyes, which supports the argument that they are descended from shipwrecked sailors.

[9] This is a reference to the history in Skh.u. 9 and 10 (chapters one and two as in the PGN).

[10] In connection with this statement I would like to quote a lengthy passage from Enthoven (1920-22/1[=1920]: 214-215): "Once a Kshatriya always a Kshatriya was not by any means the case. We find numerous instances as late as the *Mahābhārata*

and *Purānic* period of Kshatriya and persons of lower classes becoming Brāhmans, and of Brāhmans marrying women of Kshatriya and even lower classes. Thus we find that descendants of Garga, although Kshatriyas by birth, became Brāhmans [Vishnu Puran]. Vishvāmitra, by the force of his austerities, became a Brāhman. From Ajāmidha, a Kshatriya, sprang Kanva, from whose son Medhātith the Kānvāyana Brāhmans descended. The great sage Vasishtha was born of the womb of a harlot, but became a Brāhman by religious austerities. Vyāsa, the celebrated author of the great Hindu epic *Mahābhārat*, was born of a fisher-woman, and Parāsara of a Chāndāl woman. The two sons of Nābhāgarishtha who were Vaishyas attained to the state of Brāhmans.

"Later still, in comparatively modern times, there are instances of the creation of certain classes of Brāhmans. 'Thus in Partābgarh there is a legend current that the celebrated Oudh chieftain Mānik Chand created Brāhmans wholesale out of various Kurmis, Ahirs and Bhars. A similar case occurred in Fatehpur. In Unāo, again, a story is told of Rāja Tilak Chand, that one day while hunting he was very thirsty, and having no attendant he asked a Lodha, who was present there, to fetch him some water, which he brought in his own drinking vessel. The Rāja after drinking the water discovered that the owner of the vessel was a low-caste man, and so he asked him to call himself a Brāhman under the title of Pāthak of Amtara, as he was watching the mango (*ām*) trees. This title still remains with his descendants, who are acknowledged as Brāhmans. . . .' [Crook's Tribes and Castes of the North-Western Provinces and Oudh, Volume II, p. 145.]"

See also the passage from the *Anuśāsanaparva* of the *Mahābhārata* referred to above in n. 9 to the translation of chapter three (Skh.u. 11). It is stated further in that passage that a *kṣatriya* or *vaiśya* who lives in the condition of a *brāhmaṇa* and who practices the duties of a *brāhmaṇa* becomes a *brāhmaṇa*, though, again, the intimation is that this is in the following lifetime. (Quoted in Muir 1872/1: 132-133.)

[11] See n. 4 to the translation of chapter seven (Skh.u. 15) above.
[12] L2 inserts ½ vs. of which only the first *pāda* can be deciphered: . . . nor a praising of Halagrāma, ...

IV. CRITICAL APPARATUS

CHAPTER ONE (Skh.u. 9)

9.0 Ed inserts: atha navamo ’dhyāyaḥ. L2 inserts:gaṇeśāya namaḥ.

9.0[1] ṛṣayaḥ: Ed L1a Bm M Br K ṛṣaya ūcuḥ (Bm uvāca, K ucuḥ).

9.1a °ārtha°: Br °ārthaṃ.

9.1b vimalāśaya: Ed Br K vijitendriya (Br viṃjitendriya); (L1a L2 Bm M vimalāśayā).

9.1c bhavan°: Ed L2 Bm M Br K tava. *Jainalipi*-nonstandard *Devanāgarī* bh>t. See **§7.9a**.

9.1c °mukhenduvigaḷat: Ed Br K mukhendor galitaṃ; L2 Bm M mukhendugalitaṃ; (L1a °mukhenduvigaḷa).

9.1d kathā° (L2 Bm M kathaṃ).

9.1d °maṅgaḷaṃ (L1a °sāgaḷaṃ). L1a different source?

9.2a °puṭair: L1a °pute (= °puṭe ?).

9.2b pipāsā vardhate: L2 Bm M pipāsāvaplute (L2 °āvalmutai). L2 due to *Devanāgarī* pl>lm.

9.2b hi naḥ: Br hitaḥ. Br due to *Devanāgarī* n>t.

9.2c ataḥ: Bm M atha; K atraḥ (?).

9.2c kathāmṛtaṃ (L1c kathāṃmṛtaṃ).

9.2c puṇyaṃ: Ed L2 Bm M Br K śrotuṃ (Br śrotaṃ).

9.2d pāyayasva: Ed L2 Bm M Br K puṇyapāpa°; L1a prāpayayasva (?). L1a extra syll.

9.2d bhavārthihaṃ: Ed Br K °bhayārthihaṃ.

9.3a brahman: Ed L2 Bm M Br K janmanaṃ (L1a brahma).

9.3b vara: Br varaḥ.

9.3c śrutāni (L2 śṛtāni). L2 due to Telugu or Kanarese script. See **§6.4**.

9.3c sakalāny addhā: L1c sakalāny atra; (L2 Br sakalānyad vā). L2 Br due to *Devanāgarī* ddh>dv.

9.3d dharmāṇi (L2 dharāṇi).

9.3d vimalā*śa*ya: Ed K2 Bm M Br K vividhāni ca (Br vividhāna ca); (L1a vimalāśraya, L1c vimalāsaya).

9.4b gṛha°: L2 Bm M graha°.

9.4c tvayaivoktaṃ (L1c tvayauvoktaṃ; L2 tvayaiyoktaṃ; Br tvayevoktaṃ).

9.4d °saṃjñakaṃ: Ed L2 Bm M Br K °saṃjñikaṃ.

9.5a astīti (Br astiti)

9.5ab tat chrotum: L1a tu chrotum; L1c ta chrotum; L2 Bm M tat śrotum.

9.5b icchāmahe vayaṃ: Br icchāmaheśvasaṃ (?). Source?.

9.5[1] sūtaḥ: Ed Bm M Br K sūta uvāca; L1c L2 śrīsūtaḥ.

9.5c śṛṇudhvam (Bm śruṇudhvam). Bm due to Telugu or Kanarese script ṛ>ru. See **§7.4**.

9.5d sāvadhānena: K sādhadhānena; (Br sāvanena). Br omits syll.

9.5d cetasā: Br cetasaḥ.

9.6a idam: K iyam.

9.6ab °āpṛcchac chaunakaṃ: L1c °āpṛcchach chaunakaṃ; L2 Bm M °āpṛcchan śaunako; Br °āpṛccha śaunakaṃ.

9.6b °kovidaṃ: Bm M °kovida.

9.6c janmejayasya: L1c L2 janamejayasya. L1c L2 extra syll.

9.7b °śravaṇotsukaḥ: Ed L2 Br K °śravaṇe yutaḥ; L1a °śravaṇoditaṃ; Bm M °śravaṇo yutaḥ.

9.7d bhārataṃ: Br bhārata°.

9.7d khaṇḍam (L1c 'khaṇḍam).

9.8a kṣetratīrthaika°: L1a kṣetre tathaiva; (Bm M Br kṣetratīrtheka°).

9.8a °nirato: Bm M Br °niratāḥ (Br °niratā). See 9.8c and d for Bm M, which attempt to put all endings in a pl. form.

9.8b °karma†kṛtādharaḥ†: L1a °karmasucādaraḥ (?); L1c °karmathādaraḥ (?); L2 °karma[-]thādaraḥ (?); Bm M Br karmas tathādaraḥ. Source? L1c omits syll. Bm M Br seem to have tried to make sense out of L1a L1c L2 readings.

9.8c śiva°: L1a bhava°.

9.8c °vindaikyaḥ: L1a °vindākyaṃ (?); L2 °vindaikya; Bm °vindhyaikā (?); M °vindhaikā. See 9.8a and d for Bm M pl. readings. See **§7.9b** for L2 final *saṃdhi*.

9.8d bhava°: Ed Br K śiva°; L1a L1c bhavad°; L2 bhaya°.

9.8d °bhaktir: L2 °śaktir. *Devanāgarī* bh>ś.

9.8d atandritaḥ (Bm M atandritāḥ; K atandritaṃ). See 9.8a and c for Bm M error.

9.8^1 śatānīkaḥ: Ed Bm M Br K śatānīka uvāca; L2 omits; (L1a śatānīka).

9.9a °jña: Ed K °jñaḥ.

9.9b śāstrārtha°: Br śāstra°. Br omits °artha°.

9.9b °kovida: Ed L1a Br K °kovidaḥ.

9.9c tava vāgamṛtaṃ (L1c tavagāmṛtaṃ; Br tava vāgāmṛtaṃ; Bm tava vāgamṛta). L1c omits one syll. and performs metathesis. Br seems to be derived from some such mistake. See **§7.5** for Bm omission of final *anusvāra*.

9.9d na: Bm M me.

9.9d tṛptir: Ed K vṛttir; Br tṛrsir (?).

9.9d kathaṃ: L2 Br kathā.

9.10a prabhāvaṃ ca: L1a pratāpena (= pratāpeṇa ?). Synonym.

9.10b tasya deśasya vistaraṃ: L1c tad deśavibhavaṃ tathā. Paraphrase.

9.10c nāmāni (Br nāni). Br omits syll.

9.10d tad°: Br ca; (K ta).

9.10d °daivatāni: L1a Bm M °devatāni (?).

9.11a tvayā: L1a tadā.

9.11b śrotuṃ: L1c śrutaṃ.

9.11b sarvaṃ: L1a sarva°

9.11c upagrāmāṇi (Bm M upgrāmāni; Br upagrāni). Br omits syll.

9.11c santīti: L1a saṃkhyāni (?); (Br satīti).

9.11d yat kathitaṃ: L1a L1c yad viditaṃ (L1c vaditaṃ). Source = uditaṃ? If so, this would be preferred.

9.12a tad ahaṃ: Ed Br K tāny ahaṃ; L1a kathahaṃ (?). L1a source = kathitaṃ?

9.12b grāmāṇām ādhidaivataṃ: Ed K grāmāṇāṃ cādhidaivataṃ; Bm M Br grāmānāṃ adhidaivataṃ (Br grāmānim adhidaivataṃ); (L1a grāmanām ānidaivataṃ; L1c grāmanām ādhidaivataṃ; L2 grāmanām ādhidevatāṃ). Construing L1a 'grāmanāmāni daivataṃ' is unlikely considering the contents which follow and which precede. All MSS except Ed and K have a dental 'n' in their readings for 'grāmāṇāṃ.'

9.12^{1} śaunakaḥ: Ed Bm M Br K śaunaka uvāca; L1c śrīśaunakaḥ.

9.12^{2} Between 9.12^{1} and 9.12cd L1a and L1c insert 1½ vss. of commentary. See Appendix B.

9.12d jitendriyaḥ: L1c jitendriya.

9.13a tapas°: K tatas.

9.13a °taptvā (L1c °tvaptā). Metathesis.

9.13b śaṃkara°: Ed L1a M K śaṃkaraṃ.

9.13c svavaśaṃ: Ed L2 Bm M Br K svādhīnaṃ. Synonym.

9.13c kārayām āsa: Ed L2 Bm M Br K kārayitvātha (L2 kāraïtvātha); (L1a kārayam āsa). See **§7.4** for L2.

9.13d svanāmnā kāritāṃ purīṃ: Ed L2 K svanāmākāritāṃ purīṃ (L2 svanāmākāritaṃ purīṃ); L1a svanāmnā kāritaṃ purī; L1c svanāmnākāri tatpurā; Bm svanāmā kāritā purī; M Br svanāmā kāritāṃ purī.

9.14a °mudrā°: L1c °mudā°; (Br °mudro°)

9.14bc L1c omits.

9.14b †*nigamya*† sva°: Ed L1c Br K nirmāya sva°; L2 Bm M nirmāyasya; (L1a nirmāyāsru°). All MSS show corruption due to Telugu or Kanarese script. L2 Bm M due to sv>sy. L1a due to sv or sy>sṛ>sru.

9.14c tatra kṛtvā°: L1a tatrākṛtvā°

9.14d See 9.71cd, 10.9ab, 11.4ab, 12.5ab, 14.11cd, 16.19c, 17.22cd, 17.52a, 18.11ab.

9.14d nināya: Ed Bm M Br K ninayed; L1a nirmāya; L2 ninaye (?). The reading of L2 suggests that the short 'a' and following 'e' in 'ninaye,' leading to the form 'ninayed,' may be due to a reading of 'nināya' as if it were written *pūrvamātra* fashion as in *Jainalipi*, Bengali script, or a style of *Devanāgarī* not conforming with the modern standardization. See **§7.9a**.

9.14[1] Between 9.14 and 9.15 all MSS except L1c insert:
kalau yuge ca saṃprāpte naimiṣāraṇyam āśritaḥ /
saṃkṣepenātra vakṣyāmi sāvadhānamanāḥ sṛṇu /
There are for this the following variant readings:
kalau: Ed Br K kali°; (L2 kalā°).
yuge (L2 °yugre).
ca: Bm tu.
naimiṣāraṇyam (L2 naimiṣāraṃnyam).
āśritaḥ: Ed K āśritān (K āśritāc ?); Bm M āśritaṃ.
saṃkṣepenātra: L2 Bm M Br saṃkṣepeṇātra (Br saṃkṣepaṇātra).
°manāḥ: L2 Br °manā.
śṛṇu: Bm śruṇu. Bm due to confusion of Telugu or Kanarese script 'ru' being written 'ṛ.' See **§7.4**.
L1c inserts:
saṃkṣepenātra vakṣyāmi sāvadhā[na] tayā śṛṇu /
tataḥ kālāntare rajan paraṃ padaṃ avāptavān /
L1c 'tayā' is obviously a misreading for the L2 Br variant 'manā.'

9.15a cid: Bm M cit.

9.15a bhārgavaḥ: L2 Bm M Br bhārgava.

9.15a śrīmān (L1c śrīmā).

9.15b °kṣatra°: L1a °kṣatri°; Bm Br °kṣetra°.

9.15c gokarṇaṃ: Br gokarṇa°; (Bm karṇaṃ). Bm omits syll.

9.15c °kāmena: Ed K °kāmaś ca; (Bm °mena). Bm omits syll.

9.15d †mahendrādrau†: L1a L2 Bm M mahendrādā; L1c mahadrājā. Source?

9.16c ameyātmā: Bm M ato hy ātman.

9.17a sahyādri°: L1c L2 siṉhyādri°.

9.17b muniḥ: L1c kila.

9.17c °tapo°: L2 °vato. Metathesis, followed by justification.
9.17c yogair: Ed Bm M K °yogaṃ; L2 °yoge; Br °yoga°.
9.17d maharṣibhiḥ: L1c maharṛṣibhihi. L1c reading indicates that somewhere in the geneology of the MS the text was read to the scribe, or written by the scribe as he would pronounce it when trying to elucidate distinctly.
9.18a juṣṭaṃ: L1a Bm M juṣṭa°.
9.18a °gandharvair: L1a L1c M °gandharvaiḥr; Br °gandharvairr. See **§7.9b** for L1a L1c M final *saṃdhi*.
9.18b apsarobhiś: L1c apsarobhiḥ. Final *saṃdhi* contingent on change of word following.
9.18b ca cāraṇaiḥ: L1c samāvṛtaṃ.
9.18c °ratna°: L1c °maṇi°. Synonym.
9.18c °mayaiḥ: L2 Br °mayai. See **§7.9b** for final *saṃdhi*.
9.18d L1c omits and substitutes:
nānādhātu[vicitra]kaiḥ.
See Appendix D, vs. 7.13b.
9.18d vicitrakaiḥ: L2 Bm M vicitritaiḥ. Synonym.
9.18[1] Between 9.18 and 9.19 L1a L2 insert:
nānātarulatāgulmaiś citrai mṛgavibhūṣitaiḥ /
L1c inserts:
nānādrumalatāgulmair nānāmṛgagaṇāvataḥ /
For L1c "°āvataḥ' read "°ānvitaḥ.' The differences between the two inserts are due to synonyms. See Appendix D, vs. 7.13cd.
9.19a nānāphala°: L1a nānāphalaiḥ.
9.19a °prasravaṇair: L1a Br °prasravaṇaiḥ (L1a prasravaṇaiḥ); (Bm M °prasavaṇair).
9.19c ruciraṃ: L1a racitaṃ.
9.19c viharantīnāṃ: L1a viharaṃ bhinnāṃ (?); (Ed vihirantīnāṃ). L1a variant source? Perhaps 'bh' reat for 't,' with other variations due to this. It is easy in *Jainalipi* to read 't' for 'bh.' See **§7.9a**.
9.19d siddha°: L2 siṃtvā (?). Source?
9.19d °yoṣitāṃ: L1c °yoṣitaṃ. Perhaps from yoṣitaḥ, pl. of yoṣit, which word is more common than yoṣitā.

9.20a °kokābhirutaṃ: Ed L2 Bm M K °kokilayutaṃ (Bm M °yutāṃ); L1a °kekābhitantaṃ. See 9.19d "°yoṣitāṃ' and §7.5 for explanation of Bm M reading.

9.20b madāndhāḷi: Ed K dhātubhiś ca; (L1a madāndhāni, L2 Bm M Br madānyāni).

9.20b sammūrchitaṃ (Ed L2 Br K samūrchitaṃ, L1a sumūrchitaṃ, L1c samurjitaṃ, Bm M samūrchitāṃ). See 9.19d °yoṣitāṃ and §7.5 for explanation of Bm M reading.

9.20c ajasraṃ raktakaṇṭhānāṃ: L1a ajasraṃ raktakarṇānāṃ; L1c tatra saṃraktakaṇṭhānāṃ; (Br °kaṭhānā).

9.20d kūjitaiś: L1a L1c kujaraiś. Source?

9.21a āhvayantam (Br āvayantam).

9.21a śrāntān (Bm M śrānt). Bm M omit syll.

9.21b pānthān: Ed L2 Bm M Br K kāntaiḥ; L1a kāntān.

9.21b °du*gha*drumaiḥ: Ed L2 Bm M Br K °dughair drumaiḥ (Br °dudhai drumaiḥ); L1a °dughodyamaiḥ; L1c °dughādrumaiḥ. L1a reading due to confusions from Telugu or Kanarese script, and indicates the *metricausa* reading of L1c.

9.21c mātaṅgair: L1c Br mātaṅgai; L2 M mātaṅgaiḥ. See §7.9b for L1c Br final *saṃdhi*.

9.21d ṣaṭpadaiḥ: L1c nirptaraiḥ (?). Source?

9.22ab L1a substitutes:
pārijātaiś ca saraḷaiś cāpiśobhihitaṃ mama /

9.22a mandāraiḥ: L1c mandaraiḥ; (Ed Bm M Br K māndāraiḥ).

9.22b saraḷaiś: Ed Br K rasālaiś (Br rasāleś); (Bm M saralaiś).

9.22b copaśobhitaṃ: Ed Bm M K copaśobhitaiḥ (Bm copasaubhitaiḥ); Br copaśobhitas.

9.22c sāla°: Ed Bm M Br K śāla°; L1c L2 sala° (?).

9.22c °tālaiś: L1c °tālaiḥś; Br tālai. See §7.9b for final *saṃdhi*.

9.22d °āsanā° (L1a °asanā°).

9.22d °ārjunaiḥ: Br °ārjunaḥ; (L1a °ājuraiḥ).

9.23a cūtaiḥ: Bm M cyūtaiḥ.

9.23a kadambair: Ed Bm M Br K kadamba°; L1c kadambai. See **§7.9b** for L1c final *saṃdhi.*

9.23a nimbaiś: L1c ṇipaiś (?); L2 nībhaiś (?). Different source from reading?

9.23b °campakaiḥ: Br °pañcakaiḥ. Metathesis.

9.23d kundaiḥ (Bm kudaiḥ; Br kubaiḥdaiḥ). Br extra syll.

9.23d kurabakair (L1a kuravakair; L1c karavakair; Bm M kūrabakair; Br kubarakair). Br metathesis.

9.24a panaso° (L1c Bm M phanasau°).

9.24a °āśvattha°: L1c °āśvakṣa° (?); Bm M °āśvatthair. L1c reading due to word following or orthography?

9.24b °plakṣa°: Bm M °nṛkṣa° (?); Br °vṛkṣa°. Variant readings due to mistake such as that of L1c in word preceding or orthography?

9.24b °tindukaiḥ: L1a °tiṭūkaiḥ (?); L1c °hiṅgukaiḥ (?). Source?

9.24c paṇyair: Ed L1a L2 Bm M Br K puṇyair.

9.24c auṣadhibhiḥ: L1c oṣadhibhiḥ; L2 auṣadhibhi; (L1a aiṣadhibhiḥ). See **§7.9b** for L2 final *saṃdhi.*

9.24c pūgai: L1a M Br pūgaiḥ.

9.24d rājapūgaiś ca: L1a rāgapūgaiḥś ca; Bm Br rajapūjaś ca (?); M rājapūrscajaṃ (?). See **§7.9b** for L1a final *saṃdhi.*

9.25a āmrātakair: L1a āmlātakair (?); Br āśramātakair. Br extra syll.

9.25a agniśikhaiḥ: L2 Br agniśikhai. See **§7.9b** for L2 Br final *saṃdhi.*

9.25b priyāḷair (Ed L2 Bm M Br K priyālair).

9.25b °kāsanaiḥ: Ed L2 Bm M Br K °kānanaiḥ.

9.25c druma°: Bm M dama°.

9.25d rājitaṃ: M rājita°.

9.25d °kaṇṭakaiḥ: Ed L1a L2 Bm M K °kīcakaiḥ (Bm M °vīcakaiḥ); Br °kiṃcakaiḥ (?). *Devanāgarī* k>v for Bm M readings.

9.26a śākhāmṛgaiḥ *krīḍitaiś* ca: Ed K sṛṅgair mṛgair mṛgendraiś ca; L1c mṛgaśākhāmṛgaiḥ kroḍaiḥr; L2 Br mṛgaiś ca camarīmṛgai; Bm M mṛgaiś camaribhṛṅgaiś ca; (L1a śākhāmṛtaiḥr krāḍitaiś ca). The reading is chosen on the basis of the best MS, best sense and parallel construction with 9.26b. The reading of Bm M appears to be a corruption of that of L2 Br, but is listed separately because of the acceptability of the reading "°bhṛṅgaiś," 'with fork-tailed shrikes,' though this does not fit the criterion of sense given the context. A good reason for not considering the reading of L2 Br is that 'camarīmṛgaiḥ' occurs again in 9.27b, though repetition of this sort in lists need not necessarily exclude the reading. See 9.26b and 16.9d, and nn. to the translations of same. See n. to translation of 9.27b for discussion of the meaning of 'camarīmṛga.' See **§7.9b** for discussion of the various final *saṃdhis* in these readings.

9.26b mṛgendrair: Ed K gajendrair; L2 Bm M mṛgendra°.

9.26b °śalyakaiḥ (M °vālyakaiḥ). *Devanāgarī* śa>vā.

9.26c gavayaiḥ (Bm M Br gavayaḥ).

9.26c śarabhair: Bm M śarabhaiś; (Br śarabher). Bm M *saṃdhi* conditioned by word following in Bm M.

9.26c vyāghrair: L1a L1c L2 vyāghraiḥr (L1a vyāghaiḥr); Bm M caiva. See **§7.9b** for L1a L1c L2 final *saṃdhi*.

9.26d urubhir mahiṣādibhiḥ: Bm M vyāghrair ūrumahīṣataḥ (?); (Br mamihiṣādibhiḥ). Br extra syll.

9.27a mṛganābhibhir (L1a mṛganābhigir; Bm M mṛgānābhibhir; Br mṛganābhībhir).

9.27b †viśiṣṭaṃ†: L1a L1c *niviṣṭaṃ* (L1a vinaṣṭaṃ, L1c viniṣṭan (?)). Metathesis, with L1a attempting to make some sense out of the result.

9.27b camarī°: L1a cāmarī°.

9.27c kadaḷi° (Ed Bm M Br K (kadali°).

9.27c °ṣaṇḍa°: Ed Br K °khaṇḍa°; L1c °bhaṇḍa° (?). *Devanāgarī* 'ṣ' = *Jainalipi* or nonstandardized *Devanāgarī* 'kh' sometimes. L1c due to Telugu or Kanarese script ṣ>bh. See **§7.9a** for Ed Br K reading.

9.27c °saṃruddha°: L1a °saṃru[?]°; L1c °saṃruhṛ° (?); (Br °sarudra°). L1a L1c different source?

9.27d °pulina°: Ed Br K °pulinas; L1a Bm M °pulinaḥ; L1c °pulana° (?).

9.27d °śriyaṃ: Ed Br K tathā; L1a śriyāṃ; Bm M śriyaṃ.

9.28ab L2 omits.

9.28a nikaraiś: Ed L1c Br K nirjharaiś; Bm M nirjaraiś (?).

9.28a cāmaraiḥ svacchaiḥ: Ed K cāmaracchkatraiḥ; L1c cāmarai svacchai; Bm M cāmarāśvatthai; Br cāmaracchatre. Bm M due to *Jainalipi*-nonstandard *Devanāgarī* or to Telugu or Kanarese script cch>tth. See **§7.9a**.

9.28b kadaḷī° (Ed L1a L2 Bm M Br K kadali°).

9.28b °†ketubhis: L1c °ketakis.

9.28b tataḥ†: L1a L1c tataiḥ (?); Bm M tathā. L1a L1c source?

9.28c virājamānaṃ: L2 Bm M virājamāna°.

9.28c śailendraṃ: K śailendra; (Br śailadraṃ).

9.28d hṛṣṭamanā: L2 dṛṣṭamanā. *Devanāgarī* h>d.

9.28d muniḥ: L2 munim.

9.29a avatīrya: L1c avantīrya (?).

9.29a dadarśā° (Br dadartthā°).

9.29b tauḷavaṃ (Ed L2 Bm M K taulavaṃ; Br caulavaṃ).

9.29[1] Between 9.29ab and 9.29cd L1a and L1c insert:
purā kroḍamunir nāma satyavāganasūyakaḥ /
cirakālam tapas taptvā sādhaya kṣetram uttamaṃ /
There are for this the following variants:
satyavāganasūyakaḥ: L1a satyaṃ gamanasūyakaḥ (?); L1c satyavāganusūyakaḥ (?).
tapas taptvā: L1c tatas taptā (?).
sādhaya: L1a sāddhitaṃ.
The first and third *pādas* of this vs. agree with 9.12c and 9.13a.

9.29c °kṣetraṃ: Ed Br K °kṣetre.

9.29c rāmaḥ: Ed K rāmo; L1a rāma. See **§7.9b** for L1a final *saṃdhi*.

9.29d medhāvī: L1c medhāvi°.

9.30a īśa°: Ed Bm M K īśan°; L1c L2 Br iśa° (?).

9.30a °nārāyaṇaṃ: L1a °nārāyaṇai; Bm M °nārāyaṇaḥ; Br °nairāyaṇaṃ (?). See **§7.9b** for L1a final *saṃdhi*.

9.30b pūjayām (L1c pujayām).

9.30[1] Between 9.30ab and 9.30cd Br inserts 9.31cd with the following variants:
śaṃkaraṃ: Br śakara°
avyayaṃ: Br avyaṃ (?). Omits syll.
It repeats the two *pādas* in place without these variants.

9.30cd L1a L1c L2 Bm M omit.

9.31a nānopa° (Br nānāpa°).

9.31b vedoktair: Ed Bm M Br K vedokta°; L2 vedoktaiḥ.

9.31b mantrarāśibhiḥ: L1a mantrar(?)ātmabhiḥ.

9.31cd L1c omits and skips to vs. 52c.

9.31c kartum: Bm M kurva (?); (L1a kartu).

9.31d śaṃkaraṃ: L1a śaṃkaraḥ; L2 śaṃkara°

9.31d śrīśam: L1a śrīyam.

9.31[1]-9.52b L1c omits. See 9.31cd above. The usage of daggers around words or phrases of unusual problematic nature has not been carried through for these vss. because of the apparent unusualness of many of its descriptions. Because of this unusualness the basis for questioning many problematic points is pulled out from under us.

9.31[1] śrībhārgavaḥ: Ed Br K paraśurāma uvāca; L2 śrīrāmaḥ; Bm M śrīparaśurāma uvāca (Bm śrīparaśurāmovāca; M śrīraparaśurāmovāca).

9.32a svārāja°: Bm M svārakta°; Br svarāja°.

9.32a °pūrṇasura°: Ed K °pūrtasura°; L2 °pūrṇāsura°; Br °purnasura° (?). Ed K synonym.

9.32a °kirīṭa°: L2 °kirīṇi° (?); Bm M °kirīṭi° (?).

9.32a °rājan°: L1a °rājña; Bm M °rāja°.

9.32b °*nī*rājanīya°: Ed Br K °nīrañjanīya°; L1a virājanīya°; (L2 °nirājanīyya°; Bm M °nirājanīya°). See **§7.4** for L2 spelling.

9.32b °nija°: Br °nida° (?).

9.32c śastrāstratā*dhi*pataye: Ed K śāstrāstravedapataye; L1a dārās tathā hi pataye; L2 śarāstratānipataye; Br śarāsutānipataye (?); (Bm M śastrāstratānipataye). L1a source?

9.32c °śaṃkarāya: Ed L2 Bm M K °śaṃkaraśrī°: L1a śaṃkarāya śri°. L1a extra syll.
9.33a mārā°: Br māra°.
9.33b dhārādhara°: Ed L2 K dhyānādara°; Bm M Br dhyānādaraḥ.
9.33b °prati . ka . tasu°: Ed L2 Bm M Br K °pratarakaṇṭhatanu° (L2 Bm M °prataru°); L1a pratinakaṃjitasu (?). L1a source?
9.33c śaṃkarāya: Ed Bm M Br K śaṃkaraśrī°; L1a śaṃkarāya śrī°; L2 śaṃkaraśrir (?). L1a extra syll.
9.33d nārāyaṇāya vimalāya namaḥ śivāya: Ed K °nārāyaṇāya°; L1a °[- - -]aṇāya°; Br °nārāya°. Br omits two syll.
9.34a dhārā . rāga°: Ed L2 Bm M Br K dhārānurāga°; L1a dhārāḷarāga°.
9.34a °dharaṇī°: Bm M °dharaṇi° (?).
9.34b °tanayā°: K °tamayā° (?).
9.34b °āvaśa°: L1a °āyaśa° (?).
9.34b °mānasāya (Bm M °mānasāyā).
9.34c sūryendu° (Br suryandu°).
9.34c °vahni°: L1a °vaṅki° (?).
9.34c śaṃkarāya: Ed L2 M K śaṃkaraśrī°; L1a śaṃkarāya śrī°; śaṃkaraṃ śrī; Br śaṃkaraśrīr. L1a extra syll.
9.34d nārāyaṇāya vimalāya namaḥ śivāya: Ed K °nārāraṇā°; L1a °nārāyaṇāya°; Bm °nārāyaṇāyaṇāya . . .; Br nārāya°. Bm adds two syll.
9.35a ārādhana°: Ed K ādhāraṇa°; L1a ārādhara (?); Br ādharana (?). Metathesis.
9.35a °praṇayinām: L1a °praṇayanām; L2 °praṇadhinām (?); (Bm praṇayināṃ).
9.35a aniśaṃ: L1a anijāṃ; Br aviśaṃ (?).
9.35b kārāgṛhe: Ed Br K kārāgrahai; L2 Bm M kārāgrahe.
9.35b °kalmaṣāni: Bm M °kalmaṣīni (Bm °kalmaṣīnī); (L2 Br °kalmaṣānī).
9.35c nārāyaṇāya: L1a ṣārāyaṇāya (?).
9.35c °cchida°: L1a °tīdi° (?); Br °ṭida° (?). L1a Br due to *Jainalipi*-nonstandard *Devanāgarī* ch>ṭ?

9.35c śaṃkarāya: Ed K śaṃkaraśrī°; L1a śaṃkarāya śrī°; L2 Bm M śaṃkaraśrīr. L1a extra syll.

9.35d nārāyaṇāya vimalāya namaḥ śivāya: Ed K °nārā°; L1a °nārāyaṇāya°; Br nā°.

9.36a Whole *pāda*, ending °mātra°: Ed L2 Br K namrasthitākulanapañcaladetimātā (?); L1a namāśritākulanalāñcalaṭetimātra°; Bm M nāmnā sthitāṃ kulanapāñcaladetimātā (?).

9.36b nāmāvaśeṣita°: L2 nāmāviśeṣita°.

9.36b °surāri°: Ed Br K °surā ca.

9.36b °mahāpurāya: L1a °mahāsurāya.

9.36c nāthāya (Br nāthā). Br omits syll.

9.36c °jagatām: L1a jvanakām (?). L1a source?

9.36c śaṃkarāya: Ed Br K śaṃkaraśrī°; L1a śaṃkarāya śrī°; L2 Bm M śaṃkaraśrīr. L1a extra syll.

9.36d nārāyaṇāya vimalāya namaḥ śivāya: Ed K °nārāyaṇā°; L1a ° only; Bm nā°; M nārā°; Br °nārāya°.

9.37a °vārivahnimarud°: L1a °vārttivad[?]imarud (?); L2 °varivan nāma rud° (?).

9.37a °ambara°: Ed K °ambuda°; L2 °ambura° (?); Bm M °umbara° (?); Br °akudava° (?). Br extra syll.

9.37a °pūruṣārka°: L1a pūruvārtā (?).

9.37b . . . . . vapuṣa: Ed K °jaivārakoṣṭavapuṣo (?); L1a °jaivāya rāṣṭravapuṣo (?); L2 vai vārakoṣṭavapuṣe (?); Bm M jaivārikoṣṭavapuṣo (?); Br jaivārakoṭavapuṣo (?). Source?

9.37c nānācarācaramayāya: Ed Br K tārācarācaramayāya; L1a nānācarāya umayāya (?); Bm M nārācarācaramayā. Bm M omit syll. Ed Br K n>t; L1a ra>u.

9.37c śaṃkarāya: Ed L2 K śaṃkaraśrī°; L1a śaṃkarāya śrī°; Bm M Br śaṃkaraśrīr. L1a extra syll.

9.37d nārāyaṇāya vimalāya namaḥ śivāya: Ed Br K °nārā° (Br nārā°); L1a Bm M °nā° (Bm M nā°).

9.38a kīnāśa°: L1a kīṇaśī°.

9.38a °nigṛhīta°: Ed Br K °tugrahīṭi° (?); L1a °nigṛhīka° (?); L2 °tagrahīti (?); Bm M °nagṛhītati° (?). Bm M extra syll.

9.38a °raṭan°: Br °ratan° (?); K °raran°; (L2 raṭan°; Bm °raṭaṃ°).

9.38a °mṛkaṇḍu° (L2 °mṛkaṇḍū; K °makaṇḍu°).

9.38b °bhūnāga°: L1a °bhūvāṭa°; Br °bhūnārā°.

9.38b °bhīti°: L1a °tīti. L1a due to *Jainalipi*-nonstandard *Devanāgarī* bh>t. See **§7.9a**.

9.38b °karāmbujāya (Br °karambujāya).

9.38c sakalair (Br salair). Br omits syll.

9.38c śaṃkarāya: Ed L2 K śaṃkaraśrī°; L1a śaṃkarāya śrī°; Bm M Br śaṃkaraśrīr. L1a extra syll.

9.38d nārāyaṇāya vimalāya namaḥ śivāya: Ed K °nārā°; L1a Bm M °nā° (Bm M nā°); Br nārāya°.

9.39a nānā°: Br mānā° (?).

9.39a °nadīśakanyā°: Ed Br K °sutapriyāya (K °sutapriyāya); L2 Bm M °nadīyakanyā° (?).

9.39b narmā*yi*tāya: Ed Br K bhogapriyāya; L2 Bm M nāmovitāya (?); (L1a narmājitāya).

9.39b °vāhanarapriyāya: Ed Br K °vāhanapuṣṭidāya; (Bm °vāharapriyāya). Bm omits syll.

9.39c nāgadrumāya nama*tām* api: Ed Br K nākar damāya namatīmati°; L2 nākadrumāya namatīmati°; Bm nānārkadagdhamadanāmati° (?); M nātārkadagdha[?]yadanāmati° (?); (L1a . . . namatīm . . .).

9.39c śaṃkarāya: Ed L2 K śaṃkaraśrī°; L1a śaṃkarāya śrī°; Bm M Br śaṃkaraśrīr. L1a extra syll.

9.39d nārāyaṇāya vimalāya namaḥ śivāya: Ed Br °nārāyaṇā° (nārāyaṇa°); L1a ° only; Bm M nā°; K nārā°.

9.40a °nābha (Br °nā). Br omits syll.

9.40b pādakṛpā°: L2 pādukapā° (?).

9.40b °āmbunidhe: L2 °āmbunidheḥ; Bm M °āmbunidhaiḥ (?).

9.40c nidhi°: Ed L2 Br K vidhi°.

9.40c °pālaka: Ed L2 Bm M Br K °pāvaka.

9.40c °daitya°: Ed L2 Bm M Br K °dainya°. *Devanāgarī* t>n.

9.40c °hara: K omits.

9.40d mādhava: L1a mādhara (?).

9.40d mānava°: L1a māmava° (?); Br mādhava°.

9.40d °ripo: L1a °pate.

9.41a °dānava dānava°: M repeats 'dānava' four times.
9.41a °dhara: Br °dhārā; (Ed L2 Bm M K °dharā).
9.41b dharajā° (Br dhara°). Br omits syll.
9.41b °pari . . . : Ed Br K paripūna (?); L1a paraśuhana (?); L2 Bm M pariyūnana (?). Ed Br K omit syll. Source?
9.41b lola°: L1a loka°.
9.41b °bhuja: Ed M Br K °bhūjā (?); (L2 Bm °bhujā).
9.41c bhujagā°: Ed Bm Br K bhūjagā (?); M bhujaṃgā (?).
9.41c komala°: L1a temala° (?).
9.41c °bhogaśaya (Ed L2 Bm M Br K °bhogaśayā; L1a °bhogayaśaya). L1a extra syll.
9.41d śayaśobhitaśūla: L1a śāṃtakaśūla (?); (L2 . . . śrūla; Br yaśobhitaśūla). L1a omits two syll. Br omits syll.
9.41d °ga*da* (All MSS °gadā).
9.42a gada°: L1a omits.
9.42a vicitra°: L1a caritra°; L2 viritra° (?). L1a metathesis.
9.42a °ga*ṇa*: L1a °guna; (Ed L2 Bm M Br K °gaṇā).
9.42b °nāyaka mānasa°: Bm M °mānasa nāyaka°. Bm M reverse word order.
9.42b °kara (Ed Br K °karā).
9.42c °nīraja°: L1a °nīvaya° (?); Br °niraja°.
9.42c °rājita: L2 °rokara (?); Bm M °rātita (?).
9.42c śrīśava*ra*: Ed Br K śrīkarā; L1a khavada; L2 śrīkara; Bm M śrīśakarā. All MSS except Bm and M omit syll.
9.42d vara°: L1a vada°; L2 kara°.
9.42d nidhāna°: Ed L2 Br K vidhāna°; Bm M vidhāya.
9.42d °pada (Ed L1a L2 Br K °padā).
9.43a padanamrasurāsura: Bm M padaämratasura (Bm padaäṃmra . . .). Bm M omit syll.
9.43a °kṛpa (Ed L2 Bm M Br K °kṛpā).
9.43c °rāma°: Ed L2 Bm M Br K °vāma°.
9.43c °tano: M °tato.
9.43d tanukāntinirākṛta°: Ed Br K tanukāntiranākṛti (? – Br tamnnu . . .); L2 tanukāntinarākṛti°; Bm M nanukāntinarākṛti.
9.44a °mauḷi°: Ed Br K °maili°; (Bm M °mauli°).

9.44a °vighaṭ*ṭi*ta°: Ed L2 Br K °viṣakaṇṭhita°; L1a °vighaṭita°; Bm M °viṣa ghaṭit° (?). Ed L2 Br K extra syll.

9.44a °ka*la* (All MSS °kalā).

9.44b kala°: Ed L2 K kara°; Bm M omit; Br karaḥ.

9.44b °veṇu°: Bm M vaṇu° (?).

9.44b °ravonmada°: Bm °revonmada°; M °kaunmada°. M omits syll.

9.44b °gopijana (Ed Bm M Br K °gopijanā).

9.44c jananā°: Ed Br K janatā°. Ed Br K *Devanāgarī* n>t.

9.44c °vihīna: Br vihir nāna (?). Br extra syll.

9.44c gi*rīndra*dare: Ed Br K niridere (?); L2 niridare (?); Bm M nirīdara (?); (L1a girīdudare). Ed L2 Bm M Br K omit syll. L1a *Devanāgarī* or Telugu or Kanarese script dra>du; Ed L2 Bm M Br K *Devanāgarī* g>n.

9.44d darikoṭi°: Ed Br K darakoṭi°; L2 [? ?]loṭi; Bm M daṃravikoṭi° (?). Bm M extra syll.

9.44d °nikāśa°: Ed Br K °vilāsa°; L2 Bm M °vikāśa°.

9.44d °vikāsa°: Ed L2 Br K °nikāsa°; Bm M °vikāśa°.

9.44d °ru*ce*: Ed L2 Br K °rupe; L1a °ruje; Bm M °rūpe. Emendation supported by first word of 9.45a.

9.45a ruci*man*°: Ed L2 Bm M Br K ruciraṃ; L1a ravimaṃ (?). See **§7.9a** for final ṃ = n.

9.45a °nava°: L1a °navi° (?).

9.45a °kaustubha (Ed K °kaistubha; L2 °kostubha).

9.45a kambu°: Ed Bm M Br K jambu°; L2 omits.

9.45a °gaḷa: Ed Br K °galaṃ; (Bm M °galā).

9.45b gaḷa° (Ed Bm M Br K gala°).

9.45b °lakṣita° (L1a °lakṣeta°; L2 °lakṣi°). L2 omits syll.

9.45b °garaḷa: Ed K °parala; L2 °yarala (?); Bm M °para (?); Br °rapala. Bm M omit syll. Br metathesis of Ed K.

9.45c garaḷā° (Ed Bm M Br K garalā°).

9.45c mastaka . naṭana: Ed L2 K mastakasaṃnaṭana (?); L1a mastakaghaṭana; Bm M mastakasaṃnaṭanaṃ (?); Br mastakasaṃnata (?). L1a Br omit syll.

9.45d naṭana°: Ed L2 Bm M K ṭana° (?); Br na° (?). Ed L2 Bm M K omit syll.; Br omits two syll.

9.45d °sphaṭi*tāb*ja: Ed Br °spāṭitakābja (?); L1a °sphaṭikāha (?); L2 °sphaṭikobja (?); Bm °sphṛtitaṃkābja (?); M °sphaṭitaṃkābja (?); K °spāṭitakābja (?). Ed Bm M Br K add syll.

9.45d . . . ghaṭa: Ed L2 Bm M Br K bhavāṉsaghaṭa (Bm M bhavāṉsaghaṭā); L1a bhakaṉsaghaṭa (?).

9.46a ghaṭasaṃbhava°: L1a ghaṭavasaṃtava° (?); L2 dharasaṃbhava°. L1a *Jainalipi*-nonstandard *Devanāgarī* bh> t. See **§7.9a**. L1a adds syll.

9.46a °datta° (Ed L1a Bm M K °data°).

9.46a °mahās*tra*rate: Ed L2 K °mahāstṛtato (?); Bm °mahāsṛtate (?); M °mahāsṛjatato (?); Br °mahāsmṛtato (?); (L1a mahāstarate). M adds syll.

9.46b All MSS omit.

9.46c jagadīśa: L2 Bm jayadīśa.

9.46c maheśa: Ed Bm M Br K rameśa.

9.46c rameśa: L1a omits.

9.46d °tāraka: L2 Bm M repeat two times.

9.46d . . . . . : Ed K kaṃvadhanāṃ; L1c katāraka; L2 omits; Bm M kaṃkavanāṃ; Br kaṃvadhavanāṃ. Source? Br extra syll.

9.47a Whole *pāda*, ending °rada: Ed K dhakitāṃdharaikakaṃdharada (?); L1a kadanāṃdha[- -]dakakaṃdara (?); L2 bhasāṃdhakatāṃdhakakaṃdara (?); Bm M dhakitāṃdhakaṃdarada (?); Br dhakitāṃdhakakaṃdarada (?). Source? Bm M omit four syll.; Br omits three syll. Ed K L2 omit two syll. L1a omits one syll.

9.47b radanacchada . . ta°: Ed Br K radanacchadavidhṛta°; L1a daranachadaviṭṭata (?); L2 danabhadanividhṛta° (?); Bm M radanachadābidatta° (?). Source?

9.47b °vidruma*bha*: Ed Br K °vidṛmabhaṭṭaṃ (? – Br vidamabhaṭṭaṃ); L1a °vidrumaja; L2 °vidrumābhā (?); Bm M °vidamabhaṃga (?). Ed Bm M Br K extra syll.

9.47c drumabhaṅgada laṅgada kundara*da*: Ed K mabhayadanagara[- - - - - - -]; L1a L2 . . . kundara (L2 °da naṃgada); Bm M danaṃgarapraraṃjitaniśubhaṃ (? – M °śrubhaṃ); Br mabhaṃyadanagara. Ed K indicate two syll. too many; Br omits five syll. See first syll. of L1a in 9.47d for final °da.

9.47d radake*tana*°: Ed Br K radakesara° (Br °keṃsara°); L1a daradakesara° (?); L2 radakenarakā (?); Bm M varadekasa° (?). L1a L2 extra syll.

9.47d °rājita° (L2 °rā ata°).

9.47d °padmamukha: L2 °sadmanudhākhā (?); (Bm M °padmamukhaṃ).

9.48a mukharī°: L2 muśakī° (?); Bm sukha°; M sukharī° (?); Br mukhari° (?). Bm omits syll.

9.48a °guṇa: L2 °huṇa.

9.48a °vidhe: Ed K °nidhe; (L2 °vidhi).

9.48b vidhivandya: L1a vidhivadya; L2 saṃdya (?). L2 omits two syll.

9.48b . . . . . hṛdaya: Ed L2 Bm M Br K vidhehipadaṃhṛdaye (? – L2 °hṛdaya; Br videhi . . hṛdayai); L1a videhapadaṃhṛdaye (?).

9.48c hṛdayaṃ°: Br hṛdaye.

9.48c ° . . dhara: Ed Bm M Br K °liptadhara (Br °liptadharaḥ); L1a °dharā; L2 taptadhara. L2 synonym. L1a omits two syll.

9.48d °kara (Ed L2 Bm M Br K °karā).

9.49a kara°: Ed L2 Bm M Br K tara°.

9.49a °jārdita°: Ed L2 Br K °jādrita° (?); L1a °jādhita°.

9.49a °nirdaya° (Bm M °nīrdaya°).

9.49a °daityapate: Ed K °daityapateḥ; L1a °paritā (?); L2 °daitṛpati (?); Br °daityapāteḥ. L1a omits syll. L2 due to Telugu or Kanarese script ya>ṛ.

9.49b patitā°: L1a paritā°. L1a due to *Devanāgarī* t>r.

9.49b °āgha°: Ed Bm M Br K °āsa° (?).

9.49b °mahānagavajranute: L2 manatavajramati (?); Bm M ° . . . tute (?). L2 omits syll.

9.49c nuti°: Bm M nati° (?).

9.49c °mukti° (Br °mukki°).

9.49c °da: L1a Bm M Br °ta (?); L2 omits.

9.49c veda°: Br deveda° (?). Br adds syll.

9.49c °purāṇagaṇa: Bm M °purāṇagaṇāḥ; Br purāgaṇagaṇāḥ (?). Br adds syll.

9.49d °ānagha: L2 °ānadhe (?).

9.49d puṇya°: Br ṣuṇya (?). *Devanāgarī* p>ṣ.

9.49d °guṇa: L1a °gaṇa; (L2 Bm M Br °guṇā).

9.50a °niryu*ta*°: Ed Br K °natīva; L1a °niryuti° (?); L2 °bhavarṇa°; Bm M °nītiva (?).

9.50a °bhūmisura: L2 °bhuma. L2 omits two syll.

9.50b-d All MSS preserve these three *pādas* as two *pādas*.

9.50b sura: Br sara (?).

9.50b °bhavana: Ed Bm M Br K °bhuvana; L2 °bhavanaṃ.

9.50c °āśana: L1a °āśina.

9.50c bhāvita°: Ed L1a L2 Br K bhāvin a°.

9.50c °maṅgaḷada: Ed °maṅgaladṛg (?); L1a °maṅgaḷadaṣṭala (?); L2 maṃgadmaḷamṛdu (?); Bm M °maṃgalamṛ (?); Br °maṅgaladag (?). L1a L2 add two syll.

9.50d gaḷadujvala°: Ed Br K galamṛdula° (?); L1a daṣṭaladujvala° (?); L2 jvala°; Bm M dvajalaṃjvala°. L1a adds syll.; L2 omits three syll.

9.50d °divyataru°: Ed K °divyataro; Bm °divyataru; M °divyadaru (?); Br divyataruḥ.

9.50d °prasava: Ed Bm M Br K omit; (L1a L2 °prasavā).

9.51a prasavā°: L2 omits.

9.51a °āyudha: L2 yada (?). L2 omits syll.

9.51a tāpana°: L1a tāni° (?); L2 tāsana° (?); Br tāpata° (?). L2 due to Telugu or Kanarese script p>s. Br due to *Devanāgarī* n>t.

9.51a °kṛn° (L1a °kṛṃ°). See **§7.9a** for ṃ = n.

9.51a °nayana: L1a °tanaya; Bm M °nayanaṃ. L1a due to *Devanāgarī* n>t.

9.51b °ja (Ed L2 Br K °jā).

9.51b sādhita . . : Ed Bm M Br K sādhitacakra; L1a sādhitajanta; L2 sādhitabhakra (?). Source? L2 due to Telugu or Kanarese script c>bh.

9.51b jaya: L1a bhaya; Bm M jayaḥ.

9.51c kroḍa°: Ed K kroda°.

9.51c °purīśa: L2 Bm M °pūrīśa.

9.51c girīśa: L2 Bm M omit.
9.51c jaya: Bm M jayaḥ.
9.51d: °vijayī: L2 °vijayā (?); Bm M °vijayi°; (Br vijaï).
9.51d jaya: Bm M jayaḥ.
9.51^{1} Bm M add:
tava pāda raje (?) vimalaṃ bhavame (?) /
9.52b kṛtāñjali° (Bm kṛtāñjuli°).
9.52b °puṭaḥ: L2 °puṭāḥ.
9.52b sudhīḥ: Br sudhiḥ (?).
9.52c natvātha: Ed L1a K stutvātha; Br stutvā tatha (?). Br extra syll.
9.52c taṃ: L2 Bm M tāṃ.
9.52c devaṃ: L1a Br daivaṃ.
9.52d pratasthe: L1a pratvaran (?). Source = prātvarat?
9.52d vāruṇīṃ: Bm Br varuṇī° (?); M varuṇīṃ.
9.53a śuktimatīṃ: L2 M śuktimatiṃ (?); Bm ṣuktimati (?); Br śuktimatī.
9.53b vihaṃgagaṇasevitāṃ: Ed L1a L2 Bm M Br K vimalodakapūritāṃ.
9.53c mandākinī°: L1a mandākinīṃ; Br mandākini° (?).
9.53d aghaugha°: L2 madyāgha°; (Bm M aghogha°).
9.53d °parivarjinīṃ: Ed L2 K °parivarjanīṃ; L1a °parivarjitaṃ; Bm M °parivarjinī; Br °parivarjanī.
9.54a mahābhāgas: L1a mahābhāgaṃ; L1c mahābhāgaḥ; Bm M Br mahābhāga.
9.54b tasyāṃ: L1c tatra. Synonym.
9.54b snātuṃ (Br sātuṃ).
9.54b pracakrame: L1a pracakramaḥ (= pracakramuḥ?).
9.54c °karmāṇi (Br °karmāṇī).
9.54d haṉso 'ham iti: Ed L1a L2 Bm M Br K so 'haṃ brahmeti.
9.54d bhāvayan: Ed L1a Br K bhāvayet.
9.55a °mūrtiṃ: L1c Br °mūrti°.
9.55a hṛdi (Bm M hṛdī).
9.55b †ā*rebhe*† japam uttamaṃ: Ed L2 Br K āntarebhejapaṃ namuṃ (? – Br ātarebhajapa namuṃ (?)); Bm M

āntarebhejapaṃ nabhūḥ (?); L1a āreha(?) japaṃ uttamaṃ; L1c anebhe(?) japaṃ uttamaṃ.

9.55[1] śaunakaḥ: Ed L2 Bm M Br K omit.

9.55d atiduḥkhitāḥ (L1c atidukhitāḥ; Br atiduḥkhitā).

9.56a viśvastāḥ: L1c avīrā; L2 Br viśvastā. L1c synonym. See **§7.9b** for final *saṃdhi*.

9.56a pūrṇagarbhiṇyaḥ: L1a pūrṇagarbhiṇyāḥ; L1c pūrṇāgarbhiṇyāṃ (?).

9.56b °pipāsātipīḍitāḥ: Ed K °pipāsena pīḍitāḥ; L1a °pipāsānipīḍitāḥ; L1c °pipāsāpirpatapīḍitāḥ (?); L2 °pipāsātipīḍitaḥ; Br °pipāsena pīḍitā. L1c extra syll. See 13.6b.

9.56c nadī°: L1a nadā° (?).

9.56c prāpur: L1c Br prāpuḥs. See **§7.9b** for final *saṃdhi*.

9.56d navasaṅkhyā navākṛti: L1a Bm M . . . navākṛtiḥ; L1c tā navā navayauvanāḥ; L2 . . . navākṛtiṃ. See n. to translation.

9.57-9.60 See 13.14-13.17b.

9.57a avidūre (L1a avindure; M avidūro).

9.57a tapasyantaṃ: L1a kapaśyantaṃ (?); L1c pastesyantaṃ (?); (Bm tapasvantaṃ, Br tapastyantaṃ). L1c metathesis? Bm due to Telugu or Kanarese script Cy>Cv.

9.57b sākṣād vahniśikhopamaṃ: L1a °opamāḥ: L1c vaiśvānarasamadyutiṃ; (Br °opama). L1c paraphrase. See 10.10c, 12.41b, 13.14b, 16.3b, 18.3d.

9.57c pratīkāśaṃ (L1c pratikāśaṃ).

9.57d See 13.8b.

9.58a-9.60d See 13.14c-13.17b.

9.58a dadṛśur: Ed L2 Br K dadarśa; Bm M dadarśu (?); (L1a dadarśur). Impossible to say whether Bm M reading due to omission of *Devanāgarī* superscript 'r' or misspelling of singular form.

9.58a hṛṣ*ṭāḥ*: Ed K hṛṣṭās (K ddaṣṭās); L1a dṛṣṭvā; L1c Br hṛṣṭā; L2 dṛṣṭvaḥ (?); Bm M hṛṣṭaṃ. See 13.14c for emendation. See **§7.9b** for L1c Br final *saṃdhi*. See **§7.7** for K error.

9.58b °āntikam: M °āṅkitam. Metathesis.

9.58b upāga*man*: Ed L2 K upāviśan; L1a L1c upāgamat; Bm M upāviśuḥ; Br upāviśat. Synonyms. Emendation based on a frequent alternation between 'n' and 't.' See Appendix G.

9.58cd See 12.43cd, 13.15ab.

9.58c pāhi pāhi: L1c trāhi trāhi. Paraphrase.

9.59a duḥkhān (L1c dukhānn).

9.59b bhaṅga°: Ed K hy aṅga°; M maṅga°; (Br bhaga°). M due to *Devanāgarī* bh>m?

9.59b paraṃparāt: Ed L1c L2 M K paraṃparān (?); L1a paraṃpadān (?); Br paraṃpatān (?).

9.59c uccair (Br ucair).

9.59c ākranditāḥ: L1c L2 Bm M ākranditā; (Br ākrānditāḥ). See **§7.9b** for final *saṃdhi*.

9.59c petuḥ: Ed L2 Bm M Br K procuḥ; L1c °mūṣa (?). L1c source?

9.59d pādayor bhārgavasya tāḥ: Ed L2 Bm M K paraprāntabhuvasthale (L2 pāropanta°, Bm paro . . . stheṃle); L1c pādayoḥ petur añjasā; Br paraprāntahitapriyaḥ /61/ śauna udvāraya bhavasthale (?).

9.60a tva*dāgata* vayaṃ: Ed L2 Br K tvadayetyāvayaṃ (L2 tvadaya°, Br °ayan) (?); L1a tvayādattā vayaṃ; L1c tvadāyattā(?) vayaṃ; Bm M tvayadetyāvayaṃ (M °āvanaṃ). L1a L1c metathesis. Bm M metathesis of Ed L2 Br K reading.

9.60a brahman: L1c rājan.

9.60b ninditāḥ (Br niditāḥ).

9.60c uddhāraya: Bm M uddharāya.

9.60c kṛpāmbhodhe: L1a kṛpāsindho. Synonym.

9.60d mṛtaprāyā: L1a M Br mṛtaprāya°; Bm mṛtapāya°.

9.60d hataśriyaḥ: Ed K hatapriyāḥ; L1a gatā striyaḥ; L2 Br hatapriyaḥ; Bm M hatāpriyaḥ.

9.60[1] śaunakaḥ: Ed L2 Bm M Br K śaunaka uvāca (Bm śaunakovāca).

9.61a kim etad idam āścaryaṃ: Ed kim etad ity hy āścaryaṃ; Bm M kim ecadītam(?) āścaryaṃ; Br kim etad itimāścaryaṃ(?); K kim . . . āścarya.

9.61[1] Between 9.61ab and 9.61cd L1c inserts:
vikasantaṃ tan rūhaṃ(?) tāsāṃ vākyam athākarṇyā /
The first *pāda* of this is missing a syll.

9.61c See 13.18c.

9.61c uddharann: L2 Bm M Br uddharān (?).

9.61d dadarśa (Br dadaśa).

9.61d °nandana: Ed L1a K °nandanaḥ.

9.62a yatante: Ed Br K patanti. Synonym.

9.62a bhuvane: Ed L2 Bm M Br K bhūtale; (L1c bhuvano). Ed L2 Bm M Br K synonym.

9.62a dhīrāḥ: L2 Bm M dhīrā. See **§7.9b** for final *saṃdhi*.

9.62b pālanāyā° (Bm pālayā°). Bm omits syll. in this *pāda*.

9.62b °ātiduḥkhitāḥ: L1c L2 Bm M Br °ātiduḥkhitān (L1c °ātidukhitān); (Ed K °ātidukhitāḥ).

9.62c hi: L1a ti.

9.62c tathā: Ed L2 Br K tadā.

9.62c †tā*sām*†: L1a L1c Bm M teṣām (L1a Bm M teṣāṃ); (Ed L2 K tāsāṃ, Br nāsāṃ).

9.62d adbhrāya ca: Ed L2 Bm M Br K mad abhāyata; L1a adṛṣṭvāya ca (?).

9.62d kīrtaye: Ed L1a Br K kīrttayet; L2 kīrtiya (?); Bm M kīrtayan. L2 due to final 'e' being written *pūrvamātra* fashion as in *Jainalipi*-nonstandard *Devanāgarī* or Bengali script. See **§7.9a**.

9.62[1] L1c inserts:
śrībhārgavaḥ.

9.63a dṛṣṭvā: Ed L1a L2 Bm M Br K datvā.

9.63a tāsāṃ: Ed L2 Br K tebhyaḥ (Br tebhya); L1c tebhyo; Bm M tābhyaḥ.

9.63b kṛpālur: L1c L2 Br kṛpālu°.

9.63c vācā: L1a L1c L2 vākyam; Bm M vācām.

9.63d uvāca: Ed K hy uvāca; (Br ubhāca).

9.63d bhṛgunandanaḥ: L1c narapuṃgavaṃ; (L2 bharagunandanaḥ).

9.63[1] bhārgavaḥ: Ed Br K bhārgava uvāca; L1c omits; Bm M śrīrāmovāca (= śrīrāma uvāca). See 9.62[1].

9.64a ālambyatāṃ (L1a Br ālambyatā).

9.64a nāryaḥ: Br nāryāḥ. Br tries to put a word which is already pl. into pl. form.

9.64b kle*śāḥ*, perhaps kleśaṃ: Ed L2 K keśaṃ; L1a kleśaṃ; L1c akleśaṃ; Bm M Br keśa (?). L1c extra syll. See **§8.5**.

9.64b saṃtyajyatām: L2 tyajadatām (?); (L1a samtyatām). L2 source? L1a omits syll.

9.64c abhīpsitaṃ: L1c abhīpsita°.

9.64c varaṃ: Bm omits.

9.64c Between 'varaṃ' and 'brūta' Br inserts:
prāptaṃ.

9.64cd brūta dattam ity: Bm M brūtad(?) etat param.

9.64d avadhāryatāṃ (L1a adhāryataṃ). L1a omits syll.

9.64[1] Between 9.64cd and 9.65ab L1c inserts:
śaunakaḥ.

9.65b °rasam ivoditaṃ: L1a °rasam idaṃ tataḥ; L1c °rasamayoditāṃḥ (?); Bm M °rasaśivoditaṃ; Br °ramās ivoditaṃ. Br metathesis.

9.65cd L1c omits.

9.65c viśvastā: L1a viśvastāḥ; M viśvasthā.

9.65d aśru°: Bm M aṣṭa°; Br aśva°.

9.65d °pūrita°: Bm M °bhūrita° (?).

9.65d °locanāḥ: L1a Bm M °locanaḥ; (L2 Br °locanā).

9.66ab Ed Br K omit. Bm M omit here, but insert below after 9.66[1], nāryaḥ.

9.66a trapāṃ: L1a tatra; L2 tapāṃ (?); Bm M tayāṃ (?).

9.66a tyak*tvā*: L1a Bm M tyaktā; L2 ta[ktrā ?].

9.66a sva°: L1a sma; Bm M sa°.

9.66b vyāhartum upacakramuḥ: L1c jagaduḥ pāpacāriṇaḥ; Bm M sahartum upacakramuḥ (Bm upacakrumuḥ).

9.66[1] nāryaḥ: Ed K nārya ūcuḥ; L1c omits; Br nāryuvāca (?). Bm M omit here, but insert between 9.66cd and 9.67ab.

9.66[2] L1c inserts:
bho bhārgava mahāprājña dayāḷo bāhujāntaka /

9.66[3] Bm M insert 9.66ab here. See above.

9.66c °triṉśad°: L1a °triṉśat°.

9.66d śrotriyānvayinyo: Ed L2 Br K śrotriyānvayino; L1a śrotriyas va[?]ino (?); L1c somapānvayino; Bm M śrotriyā cayino (?). L1c synonym.

9.66[4] Bm M insert:
nārya ūcuḥ.
See 9.66[1] above.

9.67a bālye: Ed L1a Bm M K balye.

9.67a bhartṛ°: Ed K bhartur; L2 Br bhartu (?). L2 Br due to *Devanāgarī* ṛ>u?

9.67b lalāṭa°: L2 Bm lalāte (?); M lalā[te/tā] (?).

9.67c avasthāṃ: L1c avasthāḥ; Bm M Br avasthā°.

9.67c samprāptāḥ: Ed L2 Br K samprāptā; L1a samprāpya; Bm M samprāptāṃ.

9.67d janair: L1c jānair.

9.67d ativigarhitāḥ: Bm M ativigarhitāṃ; Br ativigarhitā; (L1c ativirgahitāḥ). L1c metathesis.

9.68a grāmasthebhyaḥ: Ed L1a L2 Bm M Br K grāmaṇībhyaḥ (L1a °ṇebhyaḥ). Synonym. See 12.34d, 14.25b.

9.68a parityaktāḥ: Ed L2 Br K parityaktās; L1a Bm M parityaktā. See **§7.9b** for final *saṃdhi*.

9.68b tapasvinyo: Ed K tapasvinye; Bm M tapasvīno; (L1c tapanyo). L1c omits syll.

9.68b bata: L1a ca te. L1a due to Telugu or Kanarese script b>c.

9.68c-9.70d See 13.22a-13.23d.

9.68c adhairyatvād: L1a ayairyeva (?); L2 adhairya tvā; Bm M udhairya(?) tvā. See **§8.5**.

9.68d gacchāmo: Br gacchāmi.

9.68d niyater: Ed L2 Br K niyatair; L1a niyate.

9.68d vaśāt: L1a viśat.

9.69a puṇyaleśaprabhāveṇa: Ed L2 Bm M Br K puṇyaleśena mahatā (Br puṇaleśena mahatvā); L1c vṛṣaśeśaprabhāveṇa (?).

9.69b tvaddarśanam abhūd (L1c tvaddarśanabhūmad, Br tvadarśamacabhūd). L1c metathesis.

9.69c dayāsindho (Bm dayāṃśindho, M dayāśindho).

9.69d kṛpākara: Br K kṛpākaraḥ.

9.70b dattavān abhayaṃ: L1c reverses. See 12.45b, 13.18d, 13.23d.
9.70b muniḥ (Bm bhuniḥ). *Devanāgarī* m>bh.
9.70c tābhiś ca saha saṃprāptaḥ: L1c tadā taiḥ saha saṃgatya. Paraphrase.
9.70d kroḍeśaṃ (Br kroḍaśaṃ).
9.71 L1c substitutes:
darśanaṃ karayitvātha vrīḍayā natamastakāḥ /
ihāvāsaṃ catur gantu nibhītyā mad anudvaya /
This should be emended to the following:
darśanaṃ *kārayām āsur* vrī*ḷa*yā natamastakāḥ /
ihāvāsaṃ *prakurvan*tu *nir*bhītyā mad anu*jña*yā /
See 9.13c for situation parallel to that in a; 12.36b and 14.26d for readings parallel to that in b; and 13.25ab for reading parallel to that in cd.
9.71b śaktir: Ed L1c Br K bhaktir; L2 Bm M bhakti.
9.71cd See 9.14d, 10.9ab, 11.4ab, 12.5ab, 14.11cd, 16.19c, 17.22cd, 17.52a, 18.11ab.
9.71c kriyatām atra: M kriyatāmantra (?); Br kriyatīmantra (?).
9.71c saṃvāsaṃ: L2 kiṃ vāsaṃ.
9.71d atandritāḥ: L1a Bm M Br atindritaḥ (?).
9.72a kramāc chaṃkara°: L1c kramāt śaṃkarara° (= śaṃkara°); Bm M Br kramā chaṃkara°; (L2 kramāc bhaṃkara°). See **§7.9b** for Bm M Br final *saṃdhi*. L2 reading due to Telugu or Kanarese script ch>bh. L1c extra syll.
9.72a °nārāyaṇa: Ed Br K °nyāyena (Br °nyāyaina); Bm °nāyena; M °nāthena. Hypermetric. Bm M due to *Devanāgarī* y~th.
9.72b sa devaḥ: Ed L1a L1c Br K taṃ devaḥ; Bm M devāya.
9.72b °nidhiḥ: L1a °nidhe.
9.72c śaṃ tanoti: Bm M śaṃ satoti (?); (Br śa tanoti).
9.72c na (L1c naṃ).
9.72c saṃdeho: Br saṃdevo (?).
9.72d bhavitā: L1a bhavatāṃ.
9.72[1] L1c inserts:
śaunakaḥ.

9.73a uktvā: L2 ukta.
9.73a mahāyogī: L1c mahābhāgā.
9.73b L1c substitutes the following, with two syll extra:
tejā kṛtvā tebhyaḥ sukhaṃ tadā /
9.73b gokarṇaṃ: Br gokarṇa.
9.73b prayayau: Bm M taṃ prayau (?); Br yayau. Br omits syll.
9.73[1] L1c adds:
yayau sa dhīmātvarayā gokarṇeśaṃ mahābalaṃ /
dhīmātvarayā = dhīmān tvarayā?
9.73[2] śaunakaḥ: Ed Bm M Br K śaunaka uvāca; L1c omits.
9.74 L1c omits.
9.74b saṃtata°: Ed Br K saṃtati°; Bm M śaṃkara°.
9.74b °karuṇaṃ: Ed L2 Bm M Br K °karaṇaṃ.
9.74b śivendirāramaṇaṃ: Bm M śivendirāmeṇa (Bm śivedi°). Bm M omit syll.
9.74c paṅkajabhavanuta°: Ed Br K paṅkajavannūtana°; L1a paṅkajobhavanuta°; L2 paṅkajanutabhavanuta°. L2 two extra syll.
9.74d śaṃkara°: Bm M omit.
9.74d kalaye: Br kalpaye.

Colophons:
Ed K iti śrīskandapurāṇe uttararahasye sahyādrikaṇḍe śivagaṇeśasaṃvāde bhārgaveṇa kṛtā stutir (K stuti) nāma navamo 'dhyāyaḥ.
L1a iti śrīsaṇhyādrau uparibhāge grāmanirṇaye pātitya[- -] dhyāyaḥ.
L1c iti śrīsiṇhyādrikhaṇḍe dvātriṇśadgrāmanirṇaye pātityagrāmakathanaṃ.
L2 iti śrīsaṇhyādrikhaṇḍe aṣṭāśītitamo 'dhyāya[ḥ].
Bm M iti śrīsahyādre uttararahasye śaṃkaraśrīstutir navamaḥ.
Br iti śrīskandapurāṇe uttararahasye sahyādrikhaṇḍe śivagaṇeśasaṃvāde bhāraveṇa kṛtā stutir nāma navāśititamo 'dh[yā]yaḥ.

CHAPTER TWO (Skh.u. 10)

10.0 Ed inserts: atha daśamo 'dhyāya.
10.0[1] śatānīkaḥ: Ed Bm M Br K śatānīka uvāca (Bm śatānīkovāca, Br śatānīkauvāca).
10.1a cakrur (L2 cakṛr).
10.1a atha: L2 Bm Br apya (?).
10.1b garbhiṇ*yas* tā vitantavaḥ: Ed Br K garbhiṇyārtānitāṃtava (?); L1a garbhiṇyās tānitāntavaḥ (?); L1c garbhiṇyā tā vitantavaḥ; L2 garbhiṇyārtānitaṃtavaḥ (?); Bm M garbhiyatānitatvava (?).
10.1c vistareṇa: L1c vivistāreṇa (= vistāreṇa?). Extra syll.
10.1c °grāmam: L1c °grāmany (?)
10.1[1] śaunakaḥ: Ed Bm M Br K śaunaka uvāca; L1a L1c omit.
10.2a saṃkṣepeṇātra vakṣyāmi: L1a Bm M saṃkṣepeṇa pravakṣyāmi (L1a °ena); (Br saṃkṣepatra vakṣyāmi). Br omits syll. See 13.2a, 16.2c, 18.1a for support of L1a Bm M reading, and 9.12[2] (L1c reading) and 16.1a for support of our preferred reading.
10.2b °sattama: L1a °nandana. Synonym.
10.2c bhārgavasya prabhāvaṃ: Bm M bhārgavaṃ svaprabhāvaṃ. Bm M due in part to Telugu or Kanarese script sya>sva.
10.2d pañca°: Bm M omit.
10.2[1] L1c inserts:

tāsāṃ garbhavadhūnāṃ ca māhātmyaṃ bhārgavasya ca /

10.3a sūti°: Bm M sūkṣmi°.
10.3b kvacid vasrād: Ed L2 Bm M Br K śucivastrād; L1a kicit prastrād (?). L1a due to Telugu or Kanarese script v>p? See **§8.5** and 10.6d for 'kvacid.'
10.3c nirbhītās tāś ca: Ed K nirmitān tāś ca; L1a nirbhīrtāś(?) cāpi; L2 Br nirbhītā tā ca; Bm M nirbhītā tāś ca. See **§7.9b** for L2 Br and Bm M final *saṃdhi*.

10.3c viśvastāḥ: L1c viśvastās; L2 Br viśvastā; Bm M viśvaś ca (?). L1c final *saṃdhi* conditioned by word following.

10.3d sutān: L1c tu tān; L2 sutāḥ.

10.3d suṣuvire: Bm M smuṣivire (?); (Br suṣuviret). Br reading perhaps due to doubling of following 't.'

10.3d tadā: L1a mudā.

10.4a kanyāś (L2 kaṃnyāś, Br katyāś). Br due to *Devanāgarī* n>t.

10.4a saṃjātāḥ: Ed L1c Br K saṃjātā; L1a saṃjātaḥ. See **§7.9b** for Ed L1c Br K final *saṃdhi*.

10.4b pīnonnata°: L2 pīnainṛta (?).

10.4b °payodharāḥ: Br °payodharā; (L2 °payādharāḥ). L2 reading probably due to confusion of Telugu or Kanarese modifications for 'ā' and 'o.'

10.4c atuḷaṃ prāpuḥ: L1c janayām āsuḥ; (Ed L2 Bm M Br K atulaṃ prāpuḥ).

10.4d pupuṣus: Ed L2 K papracchus; L1c pupuṣuḥs; Bm prapraṣṭuṃs; M prapraṣṭus; Br praprṣṭas. Bm M Br, and probably Ed L2 K also, indicate confusion of Telugu or Kanarese modification for 'u' with subscript for 'r' and/ or modification for 'ṛ.'

10.4d tān sutān nṛpa: Ed Br K tā nṛpottama; L1c tān śiśun (= śiśūn) nṛpa; L2 tāṃ nahittamā (?); Bm M tāṃ nacottama (?); (L1a sutāṃ = sutān). See **§7.9a** for L1a ṃ = n. L1c synonym.

10.5a teṣāṃ vyatīyur: Ed Br K teṣānyatīyur (?); Bm tāsāṃ nyatīyur (?); M tāmānyatīyur; (L1a vyatiyur). Variants due to Telugu or Kanarese script v>n.

10.5a bālatvaṃ: L1a bālānāṃ.

10.5b tathā (Br tathe).

10.5b kaumāra°: Br komāsa° (?).

10.5c goḷakā †*yau*vanaṃ† prāpus: Ed Br K golakā iti tān prāhus; L1a tatas tu yavanaṃ(?) prāpus; L1c goḷakā yavanaṃ(?) prāpuḥs; L2 goḷakā yovanaḥ(?) prāptuḥ(?); Bm M golakāyaiva naḥ prāpus. See **§7.9b** for L1c final *saṃdhi*.

10.5d te: Ed K cen; Bm M tān; Br can (?).

10.5d manujeśvara: L1a Bm M K manujeśvaraḥ.

10.6ab L1c omits.

10.6a sodarā°: L1a sodaraṃ (?); L2 Bm saudarā° (?); M sauṃdarā° (?).

10.6a °āvaraṇā°: L1a °aṃ bharaṇā°. Synonym. See 10.7b 'vāṭikāṃ' for v~bh.

10.6b cakrur (L2 cakṛr). See **§7.4**.

10.6b cettham: Ed K cetaś; L2 Bm M Br cetaṃ (?).

10.6b athāghagāḥ: Ed Bm M Br K aghaughagāḥ (Bm M aghaighagāḥ); L1a athotkaṭāḥ. *Devanāgarī* th>gh.

10.6c kecij janāḥ karṣakatvaṃ: Ed Br K . . . karṣataṃ ca; Bm M . . . karṣayanti (M ke jjanāḥ kaṣayanti ti); (L1a L1c . . . karṣikatvaṃ).

10.6d lāṅgalatvaṃ: Ed L2 Br K lāṅgalaṃ ca; Bm lāṅgalaṃ; M lāṅgalaṃ[?]; (L1a [- -]latvaṃ). Bm omits syll.

10.6d kvacij: Bm kvācij (?); M kvācit (?).

10.7a bhāravidyāṃ: L2 bhāravidhyāṃ (?); Bm M bharīvindyāṃ (?). *Devanāgarī* nd>dh?

10.7b kecit (Br kacit).

10.7b kurvanti: Ed K kurvati; Bm M kurvantir (?).

10.7b vāṭikāṃ: Ed L2 Br K bhaṭṭikāṃ; Bm M bhādakāṃ. See 10.6a "°āvaraṇā°" for v~bh.

10.7^1 Between 10.7ab and 10.7cd L2 adds:
kecit vrāpur bhandigatvaṃ moṣakatvaṃ kvacij janāḥ /
vrāpur = prāpur.
bhandigatvaṃ = bhujaṃgatvaṃ.
See 10.7^2 below, where L1a adds the same two *pādas*.

10.7c °tvaprāyeṇa: Ed L2 Bm M Br K °tvaṃ prajñāya; L1a °tvaṃ prāyeṇa.

10.7^2 Between 10.7c and 10.7d L1a adds:
kecid trāpu[r] bhujaṃgatvaṃ mo[- -]tkkvacij janāḥ /
kecid = kecit.
trāpu[r] = prāpur.
mo[- -]t = moṣakatvaṃ.
kkvacij = kvacij.
See 10.7^1 above, where L2 adds the same two *pādas*.

10.7d kiṃ brūmas: L1c kica[?]s.

10.7d tān: Ed L1a Bm M Br K tvāṃ; L2 tvā.

10.7d nareśvara: Ed vareśvara.

10.8a vrātyān: Ed Br K vṛttyā; L2 vṛtyān; Bm M mṛtyān (?).

10.8a vivarṇān: L1a vivartān; L2 vivarnyan (?); Bm M vivarṇa°; (Br vivarṇāṃn = vivarṇān).

10.8a †vai*dhe*yān†: Ed K vaidāyān (?); L1a vedheyān (?); L1c vaidhoyān (?); L2 vaidyayān (?); Bm M °vaidhavyān (?); Br vaidhāyān.

10.8b piśunān̲s: Ed Br K paśūnās (?); L1a L2 piśunās; Bm M piśūnāṃs (?); (L1c piśunāns).

10.8b tān: Ed Br K tā; L1a L2 Bm M tāṃ.

10.8b nirākṛtān: L1c tirākrane (?). Different source?

10.8c netra°: L1c tṛ°. Omits syll.

10.8c senā: L1c sevā. Telugu or Kanarese script n>v?

10.8d yathecchaṃ: L1a patheṣu; Br yacha. Br omits syll. L1a reading, in part, from *Devanāgarī* y>p?

10.8d vicaranti hi: L1c viharantā (= viharanti) te.

10.8^{1} L1a L2 insert: śaunakaḥ. Bm M Br insert: śaunaka uvāca (Bm śaunakovāca).

10.9ab See 9.14d, 9.71cd, 11.4ab, 12.5ab, 14.11cd, 16.19c, 17.22cd, 17.52a, 18.11ab.

10.9a pravartamānānāṃ: Ed Br K pravṛttamānasya (?), L1a L2 Bm M pravartamānasya.

10.9b vyatīyur (M Br vyatiyu).

10.9b bahavaḥ samāḥ: Ed L2 Bm M Br K bahuvatsarāḥ (Br bahuvatsarā); L1c bahuhāyanāḥ. Synonyms.

10.9^{1} Ed L1a L2 Bm M Br omit 'śaunakaḥ,' all except Ed having inserted it above at 10.8^{1}.

10.9c °gokarṇas: Ed L1a Br K °gokarṇaṃ; L2 Bm M °gokarṇaḥ.

10.9d °maṇḍalaṃ: Ed Bm K °maṇḍanaṃ; L1c °maṇḍalaḥ; Br °mandaṇaṃ (?).

10.10a mahendraṃ: L1a māhendraṃ (?).

10.10b prapede: L1c jagāma; (L1a prāpade). L1c synonym. L1a reading is almost certainly due to a *pūrvamātra* writing of 'e' as in *Jainalipi*-nonstandard *Devanāgarī* or Bengali script. See **§7.9a**.

10.10c 'dūre (Br 'dū). Br omits syll.

10.10c samāyāntaṃ: Ed Bm M Br K samāyātaṃ.

10.10d See 9.57b, 12.41b, 13.14b, 16.3b, 18.3d.

10.10d ghasrādhipa°: Ed L2 Bm M Br K bhāskarasya (L2 bhārasya); L1a ahaskarā° (= ahaskara°). Synonyms. L2 omits syll.

10.10d °samadyutiṃ: L1c °samaprabhaṃ; (Ed L2 M Br K samadyutiṃ, L1a °samadyutīṃ, Bm samadyuti). L1c synonym.

10.11a taṃ (Bm M ta).

10.11a vadhvaḥ: L1a vandyaḥ.

10.11b tadā: Ed Br K tathā.

10.11c tatho°: L1a tato° (?); L1c atho°.

10.11c svavṛttāntam: M svavṛ[kṣ ?]ttāntam (?).

10.11d khaṇḍaṃ: L1c daṇḍaṃ; (Br khaṇḍa). Perhaps d>ś>>kh? See 9.27c above.

10.12a etān (Br etāt). *Devanāgarī* n>t.

10.12a rakṣa: Ed Br K kṣetra°; L1a aha; Bm M kṣatra°. Ed Br K Bm M metathesis.

10.12a mahābhāga: L2 mahābhāgā (?); (Ed Bm M Br K °mahābhāga).

10.12b dāserān: Ed L2 Bm M Br K trāhi māṃ; L1a dāśeyān. L1a synonym.

10.12b dāserān pāpa°: Before 'pāpa°' L2 inserts, 'bhavan ākaraḥ.'

10.12b °cāriṇaḥ: Ed Br K °cāriṇāṃ.

10.12^{1} Between 10.12ab and 10.12cd L1c inserts: śaunakaḥ.

10.12d kṛpāḷur: L1c Bm M kṛpālu°; L2 kṛpāluḥr; (Ed Br K kṛpālur). See **§7.9b** for L2 final *saṃdhi*.

10.13a kṛpāṃ: Bm kṛpā (?).

10.13a cakāra kṛpayā: Bm M kṛtvā callapayā (?). Source?

10.13b pālayann: L1a pāvann. Omits syll. Source?

10.13^{1} Between 10.13ab and 10.13cd L1c inserts: bhārgavaḥ.

10.13c athety: Ed L2 K tathety; Bm M Br tathaity (?).

10.13c āha (Bm aha).

10.13c mahābāhur: L1a mahābāhu; (Br māhābāhūr).

10.13d agnīdhraṃ: L1a Bm M āgnīdhraṃ. Synonym.

10.13d somapīṭhinaṃ (Br somapīṭhanaṃ).

10.13^{2} L1c inserts:
pārśvasthitaṃ mahāprājñaṃ kṛtāñjaliputaṃ dvijaṃ /

10.14a veda°: M deva°. Metathesis.

10.14a °jñaṃ: Bm M K °jña.

10.14bc L1c omits.

10.14b smārta° (Bm mārta°).

10.14b °niṣṭhitaṃ: Bm M °niṣṭhita.

10.14c †āgama*jña*°: Ed L Br K aṅgajñaṃ ca; L1a āgamajñaṃ; Bm M āgacha(?) ca.

10.14c °mahāprājñaṃ†: Bm M K mahāprājña; (Ed L2 Br K mahāprājñaṃ).

10.14d paścimā° (M taścimā°).

10.14d °ābdhi°: Ed L2 Bm M Br K °ābdhau.

10.15a saṃskāraṃ, or saṃskā*raḥ*: Ed L1a K saṃskāra; L2 saṃskārā. L1c Bm M Br read 'saṃskāraṃ.' See **§8.5**. The only other place in which the word appears is 19.29b, where it is in the accusative. Because of this we cannot ascertain whether it is a masculine or neuter in that place.

10.15a kriyatām (Bm krīyatām).

10.15a adya: L1c āśu; L2 atradya (?). L1c synonym. L2 adds syll.

10.15b †cai*naḥ*sakāriṇaḥ†: Ed L2 Bm M Br K cainasakār^{c}; L1a caiva sakār°; L1c enasakār°. L1a reading probably due to Telugu or Kanarese script n>v.

10.15c avaidikena (Bm M avaidikaṃna). *Devanāgarī* e>aṃ.

10.15d °pūrvakaṃ: Bm M °pūrvakaḥ.

10.16a sthānaṃ: L1c grāmaṃ.

10.16a tebhyas: L1c Br tebhyaḥ.

10.16b iti: L1a ime.

10.16cd L1c substitutes:
evaṃ uktvā sa bhagavān payau nṛpatinandana /
payau = yayau.

10.16d māhendram (Bm M mahendram).

10.16d agamat (L1a agat). Omits syll.

10.16[1] śaunakaḥ: Ed Bm M Br K śaunaka uvāca (Bm śaunakovāca).

10.17a L1c substitutes:
tathety uktvā sa bhagavān.
A rough paraphrase.

10.17a guror: Ed Bm M Br K guru°.

10.17b somapīṭhī: Ed K somapīṭhir; L1c M Br somapīṭhi (Br sopīhi); Bm somapīṭha. Br omits syll.

10.17b mahāmatiḥ: L1c mahāmuniḥ, and then adds 'matiḥ.'

10.17c golakān: L1a golakās; L2 golakā; (L1c Br golakāṃ = golakān). L2 either omits *anusvāra* or is an example of the *saṃdhi* treatment referred to in **§7.9b**. See **§7.9a** for final ṃ = n.

10.17c tān: L1a tu.

10.17c samāhūya: L1a samādāya; (L2 camāhūya).

10.17d °pūtair: Br °pūtrai (?). Metathesis. See **§7.9b** for final *saṃdhi*. This, however, is probably a case of *Devanāgarī* superscript 'r' being omitted and then compensated for.

10.18ab L1c omits.

10.18a mṛdā ca: Ed K mṛtsnānaṃ; L2 Bm M mṛtsnāca (?); Br mṛtsnāna°.

10.18a bhasmanā cātha: Ed Br K bhasmasnānaṃ ca (Br °bhasmasnā°); L2 bhasmanā nātha.

10.18b tadā: Ed L2 Bm M Br K tathā.

10.18b śuktimatī°: Bm śuktimati°; M śuktimatir (?); Br śrutimatī° (?).

10.18b °jalaiḥ: Br °jalaḥ.

10.18c snāpayām āsa (Br snāpayābhāsa). *Devanāgarī* m>bh.

10.18d guror vākasya gauravāt: Ed K guruvākyaṃ sugauravaṃ (?); L1c guror vacanagauravāt; Bm M guruvākyasugauravāt; Br suruvākyasugauravaṃ (?); (L1a gauravān). L1c praphrase of L1a L2. L1a due to *Devanāgarī* t>n. Ed K, Bm M and Br due in part to Telugu or Kanarese script Cy>Cu.

10.19ab L1c substitutes:

navaṃ ca navanāmāni saṃpakāra saṃbhūsuraḥ /
saṃpakāra = saṃcakāra.
saṃbhū° = śaṃbhū°.
Paraphrase.

10.19a navānāṃ: Bm M navārṇaṃ (?).

10.19b akārayat: Bm M Br akārayet (?).

10.19^{1} Between 10.19ab and 10.19cd L1a inserts:
saṃgrahe.

10.19c-10.20d L1c omits.

10.19cd L1a has 14 dashes for these two *pādas*.

10.19cd Ed reads:
gāsīlayaḥ kaṃnataṃ ca vaidyavac cānicātaraḥ /
There are for this the following variant readings:
gāsīlayaḥ: L2 gārsālayaḥ; Bm gośālayaḥ; M gāśālayaḥ.
L2 due to *Devanāgarī* ī > r+C+ā?
ca: Br omits.
cānicātaraḥ: L2 cāṇikārakāḥ; Bm M cāṇicātaraḥ.

10.20a Ed reads:
heraṃbāraye ledālaś.
There are for this the following variant readings:
heraṃbāraye: L1a hebāreya; L2 Bm M hebāraye (M hevāraye).
ledālaś: L1a ḍaheḷāś; Bm M ledaulāś.
L1a L2 Bm M add 'ca' to their readings, which would otherwise be omitting a syll. in this *pāda*.

10.20b ca: Ed Br K add as they would othersise be omitting a syll in this *pāda*.

10.20b navaite †*kārya*°: Ed K navaikerya° (?); L1a navaite cārya°; L2 navaite kerya° (?); Bm M navaite karma°; Br navekairya° (?). Br metathesis on Ed K reading.

10.20c Ed reads:
koügīhemṇakalkūrā.
There are for this the following variant readings:
L1a koḍagṛhema[- -]rāḥ; L2 koḍakīheṇyakalkūrāḥ; Bm M goḍagīhemṇakalkūrāḥ; Br koḍagīhemṇakalkūrā.

10.20d saṃbhāvitā°: Ed Bm M Br K saṃbhāvatā (?).

10.20d °ābhavan: Ed Bm M Br K °ā bhavān; L2 °ābhavat. L2 due to *Devanāgarī* n>t.

10.20¹ L1a inserts ½ vs. of commentary. See Appendix B.

10.21a °opanīti°: L1c °panītya° (?); L2 °opanīta° (?).

10.21b udvāhādīni: Ed L1a L2 Br K tathodvāhāni; Bm M tatodvāhāni (?).

10.21c laukikoktena: L1c laukikoktu na (?).

10.21c mārgeṇa: L1c mārge; L2 mantreṇa. L1c omits syll.

10.21d cākarod: Ed K cakrur vai; L1c akarod; L2 Bm M cakrod (?); Br cakāra. L2 Bm M omit syll.

10.21d °surāgraṇīḥ: Ed M Br K °surādayaḥ; L1c °surāgrajaḥ; L2 Bm °surādajaḥ (?).

10.22ab L1c omits.

10.22a kāryākārya°: L1a kāryākāryaṃ.

10.22a °vivāda°: Ed Br K °vicāra°; L2 Bm M °viveka°. Ed Br K and L2 Bm M synonyms.

10.22b See 19.34c.

10.22b nātikramya: Ed Br K nātikarmya (?); Bm M nātikarma (?).

10.22b guror: Bm M Br guro (?).

10.22b giraṃ: Ed L2 Bm M Br K girāṃ.

10.22c grāmaṃ: L1c kramaṃ (?); (Br grāma).

10.22c kutra: L1a tatra; L1c kratu; L2 kuru.

10.22c kariṣye 'ham: L1a kariṣyāmi.

10.22d 'bhavat: Bm M 'bhavan. *Devanāgarī* t>n.

10.22¹ L1a L2 insert: śaunakaḥ; Bm M Br insert: śaunaka uvāca (Bm śaunakovāca).

10.23a rājan: L1c bhūpa. Synonym.

10.23b vyomni: L1c vyomna°; Br vyognir (?). Br due to *Devanāgarī* mn>gn?

10.23b gīḥ: Bm M giḥ (?); Br gāḥ. Br due to *Devanāgarī* ī>ā.

10.23b samapadyata: Br samapadyate.

10.23c atraiva: Ed M Br K atreyaṃ; L1c L2 atraivaṃ (L1c ataivaṃ); Bm ātreyaṃ (?). See L1c substitution for 10.24b.

10.23c kārayasve° (L1c kārayāsve°; Br kārayaṃsve°).

10.23d vismayaṃ: L1c adrutaṃ (?). Source?

10.23d vismayāvahaṃ: Ed L1a K vismayavahaṃ; L2 vistaram āvahaṃ. L2 extra syll.

10.24ab L1c substitutes:
tad ākarṇya dvijaśreṣṭho karomy atraiva satvaraṃ /

10.24b viprendro: L1a viprāṃnṛ (?).

10.24b mudā°: Bm M madā°.

10.24c upatyakāyāṃ: Bm upadhyakāyā (?); M upakāyā (?); (L1a L2 upatyakāyā). M omits syll.

10.24c kroḍādreḥ: Ed Bm K kopādreḥ; L1c kroḍāgreḥ; L2 M kopāde; Br kopādeḥ. See 10.26a where L1c repeats its mistake. The choice of the mountain's name is based on the occurrence of this name in 10.26a, 10.39b and 9.12c-14, and on its occurrence in both MSS. L1a and L1c.

10.24d sahya°: L1c L2 saṉhya°.

10.24d °śailasya: L1a Br °śailaś ca.

10.24[1] L1a inserts, but then crosses out:
kuśagrāmāt parataḥ rusadgrāmaṃ cakā[ra] /

10.25a kriyate: L1a krīṇī (?); L1c L2 cakriṇī (?); Bm cakrur ṇā (?); M cakraṇī. Source? L1a omits syll.

10.25a sīmā: L1c śrīma (?); L2 hīmā; (Br sībhā). Br due to *Devanāgarī* m>bh.

10.25b †yāmye sahyasamudbhavā†: L1a bhūtā yāmye samudbhavā; L1c bhūtā yāmye saṃghasamudbhavā (= saṉhya°); Bm M . . . samudbhavaḥ.

10.25c sītā: Ed L1c L2 K sitā; Br satā (?). See 16.1d.

10.25c nāma nadī: Between 'nāma' and 'nadī' L1c inserts: da (?).

10.25d L1c substitutes:
āste janamanoharā.

10.25d vartate: Ed Br K parvate.

10.25d vimalodakā: L1a Br vimalodakāḥ.

10.26a kroḍādrer: L1c kroḍāgrer. See 10.24c.

10.26a īśabhāge: L1c īśadigbhāge; M īśabhage. L1c extra syll.

10.26b śuktimatyāś ca: L1a suktimatyās tu (= śukti° tu).

10.26c . . . parataḥ: Ed Bm M Br K kṛśābdāt parataḥ; L1a kṛśa[- -]sarataḥ (?); L1c kṛśabrāt kṛśataḥ parataḥ; L2 kṛśādvātyarataḥ (?). L1c three extra syll. See 10.24[1] above and see n. to translation.

10.26cd †pāruśabdagrāmaṃ†: L1a pāruruśatgrāmaṃ; L1c pārasabdāgrāmaṃ. See 10.24[1] above.

10.27a tatrāste: L1a tatra sthe (?); (Br tatraste). See 10.30a, where L1a repeats its mistake.

10.27a śaṃbhu°: M śaṃbhu.

10.27b gajamukhas tadā: Ed L2 Bm M K gajamukhaḥ sadā (Bm M jamukhaḥ sadā); L1a gaṇapatis tadā; Br gajamudha sadā. L1a synonym. Bm M omit syll.

10.27cd L1c omits.

10.27c °śārṅga°: L1a Bm M Br °śārṅa° (?); L2 °śārṅaṃ (?). See 10.28d where not only Br repeats the mistake, but where L1c has it.

10.27d saha: L2 sa°. Omits syll.

10.28b kāraveleti: Bm M kāravelīti; Br kāravelati (?).

10.28b viśrutā: Ed Br K viśrutaḥ; L1c viśrutāḥ; Bm vismṛtāṃ; M vismṛtaṃ; (L2 viśṛtā). Bm M synonym. For probable origin of this see 10.31b variant reading.

10.28c L1c substitutes:
karotu tatra sāṃnidhyaṃ.
See 10.31c where the other MSS have this reading and where L1c carries the reading given here in 10.28c.

10.28c deveśaḥ: Bm M veśasya.

10.28d śārṅga°: L1c Br śārṅa (?); L2 śāndra°; Bm M indra°. Telugu or Kanarese script śā>i-?

10.28d caturbhujaḥ (Bm caturbhugaḥ).

10.29ab L1c omits.

10.29a atīva: Bm M ataivaṃ (?). Bm M source = tatraiva as in 10.33a?

10.29a bhaktiyuktānāṃ: Ed L2 Br K ca svabhaktānāṃ; Bm M ca subhaktānāṃ. Synonym. Bm M due to Telugu or Kanarese script Cv>Cu.

10.29b vāñcchitā° (L2 vāñcitā°, vāchitā°).

10.29b °ārtha°: Br °ārthaḥ.

10.29d vāmanāḷeti: Ed K vāmaneti ca; L2 vāmanāceti (?); Bm M vāmaceti (?); Br vāmanoti ca (?). Bm M omit syll.

10.29d viśrutaḥ: Ed L2 Br K viśrutā (L2 viśṛtā); Bm M vismitāṃ (= vismṛtāṃ). Bm M synonym. See 10.28b for Bm M reading. For probable origin of this reading see 10.31b variant reading.
10.30a tatrāste: L1a tatra sthe (?). See 10.27a for same mistake.
10.30ab pakṣirāṭdhvaja asurāntakaḥ: Ed Br K sākṣād asurāntakaro vibhuḥ; L1a pakṣi[- - -]muragāntakaḥ (?); L1c viṣṇuśaṅkhacakru(= cakra)gadādharaḥ; L2 pakṣīrāṭdvajamagurā(= asurā)ntakaḥ; Bm M pakṣīrāṭdvajasurāntakaḥ. Bm M omit syll.
10.30cd L1c omits.
10.31a śuktimatyāḥ: L1a śuktimatyaḥ; Bm M Br śuktimatyā. See **§7.9b** for Bm M Br final *saṃdhi*.
10.31a purobhāge (L1a purābhāgem, Bm parobhāge). L1a due to Telugu or Kanarese script o>a?
10.31b uḷḷugrāmeti: Ed Br K ulūnāmeti; L1a uḷagrāmeti; L2 [?]urtāmeti; Bm M ulunāmaiti (?).
10.31b viśrutaḥ: Ed K viśrutā; Bm M viśṛtā (?); (L2 viśṛtaḥ). See 10.28b and 10.29d for Bm M reading. Bm M due to Telugu or Kanarese script 'ru' written 'ṛ,' in part.
10.31c L1c substitutes:
rajate(= rājate) devadeveśi.
See 10.28c.
10.32a-10.32d L1c omits.
10.32a nirnāśa: Br ninaṃśa (?). Probably, *Devanāgarī* superscript 'r' is read as *anusvāra*.
10.32b °kāriṇī (L1a °kāraṇī).
10.32cd °khaḍgadhāriṇi: L2 °vadri(?)dhā[ri]ṇi. Source of first member? L2 omits syll.
10.33a tatraiva: Bm tatraivaṃ.
10.33b °gocaraḥ: L1c °gopuraḥ.
10.33cd L1c omits.
10.33c sarvadā (L1a sarvedā, Br sarvāda).
10.33c vāma°: Bm M rāma°.
10.33c °stho: L2 Bm M Br °sthaḥ.
10.33d °saṃśliṣṭa°: L1a °saṃsthita°; (M °sāṃśliṣṭa°, Br °saṃślīṣṭa°).

10.34a Ed L2 Bm M Br K substitute:
kapitthānātra triṣagaiḥ.
There are for this the following variants:
kapitthā° (L2 kapittha°).
triṣagaiḥ: L2 Br triṣagai; Bm M triṣaḍgaiḥ (?). See **§7.9b** for L2 Br final *saṃdhi*.

10.34a °vīti° (L1c °viti°).

10.34b . . . . †*ti viśru*tā†: Ed Br K purāradrena(?) dhīmatā; L1a L1c purāraṭṭena(?) dhīmatā; L2 purāradaina(?) dhīmatā; Bm M purā rāmena dhīmatā. Emendation required for sense, and in order to make statement parallel to those in 28ab, 29cd and 31ab of this chapter. See above. The name of another village is needed in order to make five.

10.34c mahāliṅgaḥ: Ed L1a Bm M Br K mahāliṅgaṃ; L2 mahānīlāḥ.

10.34d L1c omits.

10.34d °pradaḥ: Ed L2 Bm M Br K °pradaṃ.

10.35a L1c omits.

10.35b dṛṣṭigocaraḥ: L1a dṛṣṭigocarāḥ; L2 dakṣiṇicaraḥ.

10.35cd L1c substitutes:
pañcagrāmavarān samyak kṛtvā nṛpa bhūsūraḥ /
Paraphrase.

10.35d dvijāgraṇīḥ: Br dvi[jā]graṇī. Br omits syll.

10.36a-10.36d L2 omits.

10.36a ekasminn (Br evasminn). *Devanāgarī* k>v.

10.36a ekam: Ed Bm M Br K evam. *Devanāgarī* k>v.

10.36a ājñāpya: Bm M āsāpya; (L1a ajñāpya, L1c ā[?]āpya).

10.36b tatrai°: Ed L1c Bm M Br K tathai°.

10.36b janāṉs: L1a L1c Bm M Br janān (L1a janāṃ, L1c janā[?]ṃn, Br jānāṃn). See **§7.9a** for ṃ = n.

10.36b tadā: Ed Br K tathā; L1c yadā.

10.36cd L1c substitutes:
ubhāv ubhau tu saṃsthāpya śoṣagrāmacatuṣṭayo /
śoṣa° = śeṣa°.
Paraphrase.

10.36c ubhāv ubhau: L1a udvā ubhe (?); (Br ubhā ubhau).

10.36c pṛthag°: L1a Br pṛthu°; Bm M pṛthak°.
10.36d †nyadhāyī*tas*† tato: Ed K nyadhāyīta(?) tato; L1a nyathāyita tene (?); Bm nyadhāyīpatata (?); M nyadhīyīpatane (?); Br jñādhātā(?) tato. Sources? Br omits syll.
10.36d narān: L1a ta (?). Omits syll.
10.37a sthāsyatām: L1a sthāpitām
10.37a atra: M antra. The scribe who inserted the *anusvāra* was probably reading the final 'm' of the previous word with this word, i.e. reading the word 'mantra.'
10.37b-10.39d L1c omits, but inserts:
yāsyāmīti yayau dvijaḥ.
10.37b °divā°: K °divya°.
10.37d tāvat (Bm tāva).
10.37d tiṣṭhanti: L1a L2 tiṣṭhantu.
10.38a atra: Ed M Br K atri°.
10.38a yuṣmākaṃ (Br yuṣmāka).
10.38b vibho: Bm M vibhoḥ.
10.38c ity (Br īty).
10.38c āśīr°: Ed L1a Br K āsīr; Bm ārśīr° (?).
10.38c ākāṅkṣan: Bm M ākāṅkṣyan.
10.38d . . . . dvijottamaḥ: Ed K tair nutaḥ siddhayottamaḥ; L1a tai nṛ(?) tatra dvijottamaḥ; L2 tair nutaḥ sadhyajottamaḥ; Bm M tair nutaḥ siddhijottamaḥ; Br tair nṛta(?) siddhayottamaḥ.
10.39b kroḍeśāya (Br kroḍaśāya).
10.39c bhārgavāyātha (L1a bhargaveyāya). L1a due to *Devanāgarī* th>y.
10.39[1] śaunakaḥ: Ed Bm M Br K śaunaka uvāca (Bm śaunakovāca).
10.40ab rājan adrim: Ed L2 Bm M K rājan nadīm; Br rājannadim (?). Ed L2 Bm M K due to misinterpreting final *saṃdhi* of 'rājan.'
10.40b āruru*hus*: Ed L2 M Br K āruruhaḥ; L1a aruru[-]; L1c āhururuḥ; Bm āruruha.
10.40c vāṭaṃ: Bm repeats 'vā' twice, then drops a syll. in the following word to compensate.

10.40c prakurvanti: Ed Br K prakurvantī (?); L2 prakurvantaḥ; Bm kurvanti. Bm omits syll. See 'vāṭaṃ' above.
10.40d †piṇḍa°: Br pīṇḍa° (?).
10.40d °bhṛt: L1a °buk (?); L1c °bhṛk (?); L2 °bhut (?); Bm M Br °bhūt (?).
10.40d kuraro†: L1a ku[-]ro; L1c kukuro; L2 kururo (?); Bm M karuro (?). Bm M metathesis.
10.41a adhityakāyāṃ (L1a adhītyarāyāṃ, Bm M ādhityakāyāṃ).
10.41a sahyādreḥ: L1a L2 saṉhyādreḥ (L2 saṉhādreḥ); L1c siṉhādreḥ; Bm M sahyādre.
10.41b °vāṭaṃ: L1c °vāṭo; Br °vāṭa.
10.41c upatyakāyām: L2 Bm M upatyatāyām (?); Br upatatāyām (?).
10.41d lāṅgalatvaṃ: L1a laṅgulatvaṃ (?); (L1c lāṅgatvaṃ). L1c omits syll.
10.41d vidhīyate: Ed Br K vidhāryate.
10.42a goḷakānāṃ: L1c koḷakānāṃ; (Ed L2 Bm M K golakānāṃ, Br golokānāṃ).
10.42b vāṭikāṃ ca: Ed L2 Br K vāṭikā ca; L1c pūgīvāṭaṃ; Bm M vātakā(?) ca. See **§7.9b** for Ed L2 Br K and Bm M possible final *saṃdhi*.
10.42b praśasyate: L1a praśāsyate; Bm M prakāśyate.
10.42c °vidyāṃ ca: Bm M vidyāyāṃ (?).
10.42d °vṛttiṃ: Ed L1a L2 Bm M Br K °vṛttis.
10.43a mū*ḍhāḥ*: Ed L1c L2 Bm M K mūṭhāḥ (?); L1a murkhāḥ; Br mūḍhā. L1a synonym. See **§7.9b** for Br final *saṃdhi*.
10.43c tantu°: Ed Br K teṣāṃ.
10.43c °mātra°: Ed K mātā; L1a Br °mātrā.
10.43c °brāhmaṇikāḥ: Ed L1a Bm K °brāhmaṇīkā (Ed L1a K brāhmaṇīkā); L1c °brāhmaṇikaḥ; M Br °brāhmaṇikā (Br brāhmaṇikā). See **§7.9b** regarding final *saṃdhi*.
10.43d rājante: Ed L2 Br K rājate; L1a rājyante; Bm M sajato (= sajāto?).
10.43d rājaśekhara: L1a rājya°; Bm M °sekharāḥ.
10.44b °saṃbhāṣaṇaṃ: L1c °saṃbhāṣayāṃ.

10.44cd L1c omits.

10.44c °prayāṇaṃ: Br °prayāṇe. Br due to *Devanāgarī* aṃ>e.

10.44d na †*he*ty†: Ed L1a L2 Bm M Br K na cety. See 10.47b and 19.39d.

10.44d āhur: L2 ādmur (?).

10.44d vicakṣaṇāḥ: L2 vicakṣaṇaṃ; Br vicekṣaṇaṃ (?).

10.45ab L1c substitutes:
tasya nnabhuktamātreṇa pātityaṃ labhate naraḥ /
tasya = teṣāṃ?
nnabhukta° = prabhukta°.
Paraphrase.

10.45a teṣāṃ: K teṣaṃm (?).

10.45a annaṃ: L1a aṃna (?); (Br annuṃ).

10.45a prabhuñjāno: Bm M prapūjānāṃ (?).

10.45[1] L1c inserts here its reading for 10.47cd, which it omits in that place:
navaite goḷakā brātyāḥ vivarṇāś ca nirākṛtāḥ /

10.45d paurohityaṃ: Br purohityaṃ (?).

10.46a śrautatvaṃ: Ed K śrautaṃ ca; Br protaṃ(?) ca. Ed K and Br due to *Jainalipi*-nonstandard *Devanāgarī* tv>c? See 12.47c, 15.12a for c > tv/t. See **§7.9a** for tv>c.

10.46a °karmatvaṃ: Ed K °karma ca; L1c L2 Br °karmaṃ ca. See **§7.9b** for Ed K final *saṃdhi*. The reading here, however, is probably due to an omitted *anusvāra*. Ed K and L1c L2 Br due to *Jainalipi*-nonstandard *Devanāgarī*? See **§7.9a** for tv>c.

10.46b °paṭhanaṃ: L1c Bm M °paṭhaṇaṃ (?).

10.46c °bhūliṅgasaṃsparśaṃ: L2 bhuliṅgaṃtsaṃsparśaṃ (?); (Br °liṅgasparśaṃ). Br omits syll.

10.47a °yogatvaṃ: L1a L2 °yogaṃ ca. See 10.46a.

10.47b āha: Ed L1a L2 Bm M Br K āhur.

10.47cd L1c omits here, having substituted its reading for these two *pādas* between 10.45ab and 10.45cd. See 10.45[1].

10.47c naiva te: Ed Bm M Br K na caite; L2 navaite. Ed Bm M Br K due to *Jainalipi* or perhaps *Devanāgarī* v>c. See **§7.9a**.

10.47c vrātyā: Ed Bm M Br K vṛttyo; L2 vṛtyor (?).

10.47d nirākṛtāḥ: L2 nirākṛtaḥ.

10.47[1] Between 10.47cd and 10.48ab L1a inserts: narādhamāḥ.

10.48ab L1c omits.

10.48a anugacchantaḥ: Bm anugaṃcchanta (?); M anugacchanta (?).

10.48b pracaranti: Ed Br K pracarantu.

10.48c bahunātra kim uktena: L1a kim atra bahunoktena; (Br . . . vim . . .). Br due to *Devanāgarī* k>v.

10.49a-10.50d L1c omits.

10.49a eteṣāṃ (Br eteṣā).

10.49b saṃbhaviṣyati: L1a ca bhaviṣyati; Br sabhaviṣyati (?).

10.49c °citta°: Bm °citya° (?).

10.49c °vidhiṃ: Br °vidhi.

10.49c vakṣye (Br vakṣe).

10.49d mārtāṇḍasyā°: Ed Br K mārtaṇḍasya; Bm M martaṇḍasyā° (?).

10.49d °syāvalokanaṃ: Ed Br K °sya vilokanaṃ.

10.50b tathā: L2 tadā.

10.50b viṣṇum: Bm M kṛṣṇam.

10.50c upendraṃ: Bm M uprendraṃ (?).

10.50d praṇamāmi (Br praṇamābhi). Br due to *Devanāgarī* m> bh.

10.50d bhūyaḥ: Ed L1a L2 K bhuyaḥ.

Colophons:

Ed K iti śrīskandapurāṇe uttararahasye sahyādrikhaṇḍe pātityagrāme pañcagrāmanirṇayo nāma daśamo 'dhyāyaḥ.

L1a iti śrīsaṇhyādrau uparibhāge pātityapañcagrāmanirṇaye pañcaviṇśatitamo 'dhyāyaḥ.

L1c iti śrīskande sahyādrikhaṇḍe pāti[tya]grāmakathkanaṃ.

L2 iti saṇhyād*rau* uparibhāge pātityagrāmapañcagrāmanirṇayaṃ nāma ekonanavatitamo 'dhyāyaḥ.

Bm M iti śrīsahyādre pātityapañcagrāmanirṇayaṃ daśamo 'dhyāyaḥ.

Br iti śrīskandapurāṇe uttararahasye sahyādrikhaṇḍe pātityagrāme pa[ñ]cagrāmanirṇayo nāma navatitamo 'dh[yā]yaḥ.

CHAPTER THREE (Skh.u. 11)

11.0 Ed inserts: atha ekādaśo 'dyāyaḥ. Bm inserts: śrīgaṇeśāya (= śrīgaṇeśāya) namaḥ.

11.0[1] śauna*kaḥ*: Ed L2 Br K śaunaka uvāca; Bm M śrīśaunaka uvāca (Bm śrīśaunakovāca); (L1c śaunaka).

11.1a °grāmam asty anyat: Ed K . . . anyac (K onyac); L1c grāmasyanyat (?); Bm M grāmam anyānyat; Br . . . anyan. L1c omits syll.

11.1b śuktimatyāś: Ed K chuktimatyāś; L1c śuktimatyaś.

11.1cd Ed L2 Bm M Br K omit.

11.1c *tad* : L1c tam.

11.1d °saṃ*yak*tvaraṃ: L1c °saṃpaktvaraṃ (?).

11.1d śu*bhaṃ*: L1c śubhaḥ.

11.2a śūdradattaṃ: L1c śūdraddattaṃ (?). Different source?

11.2b vāhakebhyaḥ: L1c vāhakebhya; (Br vāhaṃkebhyaḥ, K vahakebhāḥ). See **§7.9b** for L1c final *saṃdhi*.

11.2b †*svā*vāhakaṃ†: Ed L1c Bm M Br K svavāhanaṃ; L2 svavāhakaṃ.

11.2[1] L1c inserts:
dvātriṉśagrāmamadhye tu.
dvātriṉśa° = dvātriṉśad°.

11.2c pādajaiḥ: Ed L1c Br K pādajai. See **§7.9b** for final *saṃdhi*.

11.2cd †ketumuddakun*de*†ti: Ed Bm M Br K kaścit madvakandeti (Bm M kaścin . . .); L1c kektumuddakundaiti; L2 kaścit madṛkandety.

11.2d viśrutau: L1c viśrutaṃ.

11.3a °saṃpannau: Bm saṃpanno.

11.3c °parau: Bm M °parā°; Br °purau.

11.4ab See 9.14d, 9.71cd, 10.9ab, 12.5ab, 14.11cd, 16.19c, 17.22cd, 17.52a, 18.11ab.

11.4a kālaṃ: Ed Br K kālo; L2 Bm M kālaḥ.

11.4b vyatīyur: Bm M vyatiya (?); (L2 vyatīryur).

11.4b nṛpanandana: Bm M rājanandana (Bm rājandana); Br rājanandanaḥ. Bm M synonym. Bm omits syll.
11.4c dvātriṉśad° (Bm M dvātriṉśa°).
11.4c °grāma°: Br °vima° (?).
11.4c °nilayāḥ: L1c °madhye tu; L2 °nilayaḥ; Bm M °nilayaṃ; Br °nilayā. L1c synonym.
11.4d śreṣṭhā: Br śreṣṭā (?).
11.4d vedavidāṃ: L1c vedavatāṃ.
11.4d varāḥ: Bm M Br varaḥ.
11.5a dvijāḥ: L2 dvija; Bm M Br dvijā.
11.5a samāyātāḥ: L1c samāyātā; L2 samāyataḥ.
11.5b sabhāryāḥ: L2 sabhāryaḥ; Bm M sabhāryā.
11.5c kiṃ: Ed L2 Bm M Br K taṃ.
11.5c vadan*taṃ*: Ed L2 M Br K vadanti; L1c vadantīṃ (?); Bm vandanti.
11.5d nirbhāg*yāḥ*: Ed Bm M Br K nirbhāgyo; L1c nirbhāgyā; L2 nibhārgo (= nirbhāgo). L2 metathesis.
11.5d °lobhayā: L1c °lobhaye (?).
11.6a tayoḥ: L2 tayos.
11.6a ājagmur: L1c ājagmuḥr; L2 Bm M Br ājagmuḥ. See §**7.9b** for L1c final *saṃdhi*.
11.6b dāridrya°: Ed Bm M Br K daridra° (?); L1c dāridra°.
11.6b °vinivṛttaye: Ed K °vinivṛttayaḥ; L1c °vinivartaye (?); Br °vinitavṛttayaḥ. Br extra syll.
11.6c-11.9b L1c omits, but inserts:
tayor jyeṣṭhaḥ samāk[arṇ]ya āgatān dvijapuṃgavān /
11.6d samavetā (Bm M samevetā).
11.7a °vākyāni: L2 repeats 'ni' twice.
11.7b *tv*: Ed Br K hy; L2 Bm M ty. L2 Bm M reading probably due to Telugu or Kanarese script v>y.
11.7b ūcus: Br ūcuḥs. See §**7.9b** for final *saṃdhi*.
11.7c yuvāṃ: Br yuvā (?).
11.7c *āḍh*yau: Ed K āḍathau; L2 ānyo (?); Bm āḍhyo; M āḍh[?]yo; Br ādyau (?). Ed K extra syll.
11.7d yuvāṃ: Bm M yuyaṃ (?).
11.7d pūjyau: Br pūjyo.

11.7d jagattraye (L2 Bm M jagatraye, Br jagatre). Br omits syll.

11.8a bhavatoḥ: Ed K bhavantaḥ; L2 bhavatāḥ (?); Br bhavanto.

11.8a sadṛśo: Ed L1c L2 K sadṛśau.

11.8b rūpaudārya°: L2 M rūpo dārya° (?); Bm Br rūpo dāya°.

11.8b °guṇādiṣu: Ed K °guṇānvitau; Bm °guṇādipu (?); Br °guṇānvitā. Bm reading probably due to *Devanāgarī* ṣ> p.

11.8c itthaṃ: L2 ithyaṃ (?).

11.8c °vidhair: Bm °vidhai. See **§7.9b** for final *saṃdhi*.

11.9a ālokya: Bm M alokya (?).

11.9b jyeṣṭho: Br jaṣṭhau (?).

11.9b °parāyaṇaḥ: Br °parāyaṇā.

11.9d sa: L1c omits.

11.9d tebhyo draviṇaṃ: L1c inserts 'dīr' (?) after 'tebhyo.'

11.9d draviṇaṃ: Br draviṇe. Probably due to *Devanāgarī* aṃ> e.

11.10a athā°: Ed L2 Bm M Br K tathā°.

11.10a °āṣ*ṭā*°: Ed L1c L2 Bm M Br K °āṣṭau.

11.10a °sa°: Ed L2 Bm M Br K °sat°.

11.10a °kuṭumbibhyaḥ: Br kuṭumbībhya (=kuṭumbibhya); (L1c kuṃṭumbibhyaḥ). See **§7.9b** for Br final *saṃdhi*.

11.10b †*sahyā*ni†: Ed Br K sadmāni (?); L1c saṃjñani (= saṃjñāna?); Bm M saprāni (?). Sources?

11.10b śūdra°: L2 repeats 'śū' twice.

11.10c sarva°: L1c repeats 'sarva' twice.

11.10d-11.11a L1c omits.

11.11b dadau: Bm tadau.

11.11b mudānvitaḥ: Br mudānvitāḥ.

11.11c sanmānitā (Br samnānitā). Metathesis.

11.11c viprāḥ: Ed K viprā.

11.11d vāsaṃ: Br vārsa (?).

11.11d cakrur (L2 Br cakṛr). Reading due to Telugu or Kanarese script. See **§7.4**.

11.11d atandritāḥ: Br atandritaḥ.

11.12a tasya: L2 tatra.

11.12a kurvanto: L1c kurvato; L2 kurvantā (?); Bm M kurvajño (?).
11.12b ninyur: Ed L2 K ninyu; L1c yayur; Bm ninyar (?).
11.12^1 śaunakaḥ: Ed L2 Bm M Br K omit.
11.12c °jo 'tha: Ed Br K °josya.
11.12c saṃcintya: Bm M saṃcitya (?).
11.12d L1c substitutes:
aputrā mama vallabhā.
Paraphrase.
11.12d °hīno 'tha: Ed K °hīnāś ca; Br °hīnā ca.
11.12d me 'ṅganā: Ed K me 'ṅganāḥ; L2 Br maṃganā (= me 'ṅganā?); Bm M aṅganāṃ.
11.13a-11.16d L1c omits as presented in the other MSS, but continues the story in three instead of four vss., utilizing assorted *pādas* and paraphrases of *pādas* from these vss., most in order. From this point L1c reads as follows:
nāputrasya ca loko 'sti vadantīti manīṣiṇaḥ /
anyāṃ sulocanāṃ prā[bhi?] pīnonnatapayodharāṃ /
rūpayauvanasaṃpannāṃ sarvalakṣaṇasaṃyutāṃ /
iti niścitya manasā vivāhe kataniśrayaḥ(?) /
svajanair mantrayām āsa uktavān svamanoratham /
putrārthaṃ mama cārvaṅgīm udvāhaṃ kriyatām iti /
The *pādas* are or correspond to, in order, 14cd; 13ab; 13cd; 15ab; 15cd; 16ab. The readings are noted together with the other readings of these vss. as they occur.
11.13a anyāṃ: Br anyā (?).
11.13a prāpsye: L1c prā[bhi?]; Br prāśye (?).
11.13b pīno°: Ed M Br K pino° (?).
11.13b °onnata° (L2 °onata°).
11.13c °yauvana° (L2 °yauvvana°).
11.13c °saṃpannāṃ: K °saṃpannā; (L2 °saṃpaṃnnāṃ).
11.13d °lakṣitāṃ: L1c °saṃyutāṃ; (Bm °kṣitāṃ). L1c synonym. Bm omits syll.
11.14a asmat°: L2 Bm M asmāt° (?); Br asmā° (?).
11.14a °santati°: Bm °saṃpati° (?); M °saṃpatti°. M synonym.
11.14a °arthaṃ: Br °arthe. Br probably due to *Devanāgarī* aṃ>

e.

11.14b vanitāṃ: Bm M vanatāṃ (?).

11.14cd 'stīty āhur: L1c 'sti vadan°; L2 Bm M Br 'sti ty āhur (?).

11.14d °ty āhur matimatāṃ varāḥ: L1c vadantīti manīṣiṇaḥ. Paraphrase.

11.14d matimatāṃ: L2 mativatāṃ (?); Bm matamatāṃ (?).

11.14d varāḥ: Br varaḥ.

11.15a nirdhārya: L1c niścitya; Bm M nirdhāya. L1c synonym.

11.15b kṛtaniścayaḥ: L1c kata(?)niśrayaḥ.

11.15c āmantrya bāndhavaiḥ sārdham: L1c svajanair mantrayām āsa. Paraphrase, with finite verb.

11.15c bāndhavaiḥ: Ed K bāṅghavaiḥ (?).

11.15d uktavān (Bm uktuvān). *Devanāgarī* a>u.

11.15d svamanorathaṃ: L2 Bm M Br K sa manorathān.

11.15[1] Ed Br K insert: śūdrjāyā(?) uvāca; Bm śūdrajo uvāca; M śūdrajovāca (?); L2 śūdrajā[-]cuḥ.

11.16ab L1c substitutes:
putrārthaṃ mama cārvaṅgīm udvāhaṃ kriyatām iti /
Paraphrase.

11.16a kriyatāṃ: L2 Br kriyatā (?); Bm krīyātāṃ (?).

11.16a cārvaṅgī: Ed K cārvaṅgi (?).

11.16b °kāmi*naḥ*: Ed Br K °kāminī; L2 Bm M °kāmini.

11.16c arthe: Br artheṣv. Br extra syll.

11.16c mahārājñaḥ: Ed Br K mahārājā (Br māhārājā); L2 mahānajñaḥ (?).

11.16d jāt*yām* ākurutā°: Ed Br K jātam ākurutā°; L2 jātyaṃmākurucā (?); Bm jātyaṃ māṃ kurutā°; M jātyamākurutā°.

11.17a te: Bm tāṃ.

11.17b samālocya: Bm M samālokya.

11.17c *kāṃ*cit: Ed L2 Br K kācit (Br kāci); Bm M kvacit.

11.17c kanyāṃ: Ed L1a Br K kanyā; (L1c L2 Bm M kaṃnyāṃ).

11.17c śubha° (Bm śubhrā°, M śubhra°)

11.17c °śroṇīṃ: Ed K °śreṇī; L1c °śreṇīṃ; Bm M °śroṇi; Br °śroṇī.

11.17d °oṣṭhīṃ: Ed L1c Bm M Br K °oṣṭhī.

11.17d navayauvanāṃ: Ed Br K navayauvanā.

11.18a dṛṣṭvā: Bm daṣṭvā (?). *Devanāgarī* ṛ>a.

11.18a tam: Ed M K tām.

11.18a ūcus: L1c L2 Br ūcuḥs. See **§7.9b** for L1c L2 Br final *saṃdhi*.

11/18b yoja*nār*dhe tu saṃsthitāṃ: Ed L2 Bm M Br K yojanārdhārdhasaṃsthitāḥ; (L1c yojanardhe . . .).

11.18c †*kāmyā*†: Ed L1c L2 Bm M Br K kāpyas (?). Source?

11.18c mahāprājñā: L1c mahābhāga; Bm M māhauprājñaḥ (= mahāprājñaḥ). See 11.16c.

11.19a L1c substitutes:
tad ākarṇya vacas teṣāṃ.
Paraphrase.

11.19a śrutvā (L2 Br śṛtvā). Telugu or Kanarese script ru>ṛ.

11.19b mene: L1c mehe; Br mena (?).

11.19b sa: Bm M sā.

11.19cd L1c omits.

11.19c śvaḥkāle: Ed L2 Br K sva(?) kālo.

11.19d niścitya: L2 Bm M niścintya (?).

11.19d cetasā: Bm cesā (?); M tejasā; Br cetasāṃ. Bm omits syll.

11.20b svajanaiḥ: K svajanai. See **§7.9b** for final *saṃdhi*.

11.20d bata: L2 tava; Bm bataḥ (?).

11.21a gacchāmi: L1c yāsyāmi. Synonym.

11.21b Ed Br substitute:
kathaṃ cintāṃ tariṣyasi.
L2 Bm K substitute:
kathaṃ cintāṃ tariṣyati.

11.21c K reads:
brāhmaṇājān(?)somāhūya(?).

11.21c tān: L1c tat; Bm tām.

11.21c samāhūya: Bm āhya (?). Bm omits syll.

11.21d vinayenā°: K vilayenā° (?).

11.22a bhṛtyaḥ: Ed Br K bhṛtya.

11.22b kāryaṃ: Br kāya (?).

11.22b samagrataḥ (Bm samāgrataḥ).

11.22c manohitaṃ: L1c manonatiṃ.

11.22c kulasyāsya: L1c kalasyāsya.

11.22d bhavadbhiḥ: Br bhadbhiḥ (?). Br omits syll.
11.22d laghu: L2 Br laghuḥ.
11.23a śrutvā (L2 śṛtvā). See **§7.4** for L2 ru>ṛ.
11.23b viprāḥ: Ed K viprā. See **§7.9b** for final *saṃdhi*.
11.23cd L2 omits.
11.23c °ty: Ed M Br K °ti. This reading adds an extra syll. to this *pāda* for Ed M Br K.
11.23c ūcur (Br ūcūr).
11.23d †navaratne*nā*laṃkṛtāṃ†: Ed K nānāratnair alaṃkṛtaḥ; Bm M Br nānāratnair alaṃkṛtāḥ; (L1c navarathenalaṃkṛtāṃ).
11.24a °pādena: L2 °padena; Bm M °padīna (?).
11.24a racitāṃ: Bm M racitā; (Br racittāṃ).
11.24b aṣṭau te: Bm M aṣṭataiḥ (?).
11.24b śibikāṃ: L2 śibikaṃ (?).
11.24b dadhuḥ: M daduḥ.
11.24[1] śaunakaḥ: Ed Br K śaunaka uvāca; Bm M omit. See 11.24[2].
11.24c kartavyaṃ: Ed L2 Bm M Br K vaktavyaṃ (Br vaktaṃvyaṃ).
11.24d heḷayā (Ed L2 M Br K helayā, Bm halayā).
11.24d °coditān: Ed L2 K °coditāḥ; Bm M Br °coditā.
11.24[2] Bm M insert: śaunaka uvāca (Bm śaunakovāca). See 11.24[1].
11.25a guru°: Ed L2 Br K gurūn.
11.25a sarvān: L1c sarvā.
11.25b tyajanty: Bm tyajaty.
11.25b °parā: K °padā.
11.25c veśyā°: Br vaiśyā.
11.25c °saktāḥ: L2 Bm M °saktā; Br sakta. See **§7.9b** for L2 Bm M final *saṃdhi*.
11.25c kula°: Ed L2 Bm M Br K para°.
11.25d dyūtā°: Bm ghutā° (?).
11.25d °saktās: Bm M Br °saktā. See **§7.9b** for L2 Bm M Br final *saṃdhi*.
11.25d trayīm: L2 trayam.
11.26a aśvā°: L1c āśvā°.

11.26a bhūpa: Ed K bhūya.
11.26b satataṃ: Bm satata°.
11.26c jaghanyaḥ: L1c sajanyaḥ; Br jaghanya. See **§7.9b** for Br final *saṃdhi*.
11.26d saḥ: Bm M sā. *Devanāgarī* aḥ>ā?
11.27a śanair: Bm [?]anair.
11.27a vadhū°: Bm Br vadhu°.
11.27a °gṛhaṃ: Bm M °grahaṃ.
11.27b kṛtodvāhaḥ: Bm kṛtodvāha.
11.27b śūdrajaḥ: Bm M śūdrajāḥ; (L1c śūjaḥ). L1c omits syll.
11.27c patnyā: Bm M paṭanyāṃ (?). Bm M add syll. See 'mudā yuktaḥ' below.
11.27c mudā yuktaḥ: Ed Br K mudaṃ(?) yuktaṃ; L2 mudā yuktaṃ; Bm M mudrāyuṃ (?). Bm M omit syll. See 'patnyā' above.
11.27d °mandiraṃ: Ed Br K °mandire.
11.28c ekaikasya (Bm M ekaikasyā).
11.28d mudānvitaḥ: L1c madānvitaḥ.
11.29a niṣkāni (Bm M niṣkāṇi).
11.29b kiṃ na (L1c kiṃ nna).
11.29b mahīpate (Br mahipate).
11.29c sarve: Bm sarva°.
11.29d dravyāny ādāya: Br dravānmādāya (?).
11.29d satvaraṃ: L2 Br satvaraḥ.
11.30a L1c substitutes:
uksāvagreṣu nikṣipya.
Paraphrase.
11.30a bhadra°: Ed K bhrātṛ°; Br bhrāta° (?).
11.30a °varge: Ed K °vargaṃ; Br °varga.
11.30a samādāya: Br samādāstha (?).
11.30b grāmaṃ gantuṃ: L1c L2 M grāmān gantuṃ (M gantu); Bm grāmānāṃ tu.
11.30b pracakramuḥ (L1c pracamuḥ). L1c omits syll.
11.30c āgatān (L2 āgatāṃ, Bm āgatāṃn). See **§7.9a** for ṃ = n.
11.30d grāmasthāḥ: L1c grāmasthaḥ; M grāmasyā (= grāmasthā?). M probably due to *Devanāgarī* th>y.

11.30d °mūrchitāḥ: Br °bhūchitaḥ (?). Br due, in part, to *Devanāgarī* m>bh.

11.31b nijaghnus: L1c nijaghas (?); Br nijaghnuḥ.

11.31b tān: L2 Bm tāṃ. See **§7.9a** for ṃ = n.

11.31b nareśvara: Bm M nareśvaraḥ; (Br neraśvara). Br metathesis.

11.31c te: Bm to (?).

11.31c jagmuḥ: Ed Br K jagmur; Bm M jagmu (?).

11.31d śaraṇam: Ed L2 Bm M Br K dāruṇam. Probably *Devanāgarī* śa>dā.

11.31d †vṛṣa*ḷātma*jaṃ†: Ed Bm Br K vragalāṅgajaṃ (?); L1c vṛṣaḷāgrajaṃ; L2 bradyalāṅgajaṃ (?); M vrajalāghajaṃ (?). See 11.38d. Or perhaps we should read 'vṛṣaḷāgra*ṇī*.' See 11.33a.

11.32a ūcuḥ: Br ṛcuḥ (?).

11.32ab °ti kā gatir: Br omits three syll., writing only 'tir'; K . . . gati.

11.32b See 13.9c, 15.11b.

11.32b vidhīyatāṃ: Br vidhīyatā (?).

11.32c atha: Ed L2 Bm M Br K tadā.

11.32c śrutvā (Br śṛtvā). Telugu or Kanarese script ru>ṛ. See **§7.4**.

11.32d °manasaḥ: Ed Br K °cetasā; L2 Bm M °cetasaḥ.

11.33a °āgra*ṇīr*: All MSS °āgraṇī.

11.33a bhūyaḥ: Ed Br K bhūya. See **§7.9b** for Ed Br K final *saṃdhi*.

11.33[1] śūdraḥ: Ed L2 Bm M Br K omit.

11.33c he: L1c bho.

11.33c viprāḥ: L1c vipraḥ; Br vipra.

11.34a idaṃ: Ed Br K imaṃ.

11.34b navoḍhām: Ed L1c K navodām (?); L2 navodhām (?); (Br navoḍhaṃm).

11.34b aṅganām: Br agam (?). Br omits syll.

11.34b imāṃ: L1c imāḥ.

11.34c gomahiṣyādi (Br gohiṣyādi). Br omits syll.

11.34d sthīyantām: Ed L2 Bm M Br K sthīyatām.

11.34d atra: Bm M yatra.

11.34[1] śaunakaḥ: Ed Bm M Br K śaunaka uvāca (Bm śaunakovāca).
11.34[2] All MSS here add three *ślokas* of commentary. See Appendix B.
11.35a tebhyo divjebhyaś: L2 inserts 'śrutvā' after 'tebhyo.'
11.35a dvijebhyaś: Ed L2 K dvijebhyas.
11.35b °ānvitaḥ: Ed L2 Bm M K °ārditaḥ (L2 °ārdītaḥ); Br °ārdita. Synonym.
11.35c kāntāṃ: L2 kāntāṉś; Bm M kāntā. L2 *saṃdhi* due to word following.
11.35c sva . . . . tāṃ: Ed K svakāṃcatāntāṃ tu (?); L1c svakārāṃtaṃtāṃ taṃ (?); L2 ca kā ca tāṃtāṃ tāṃ (?); Bm M svakāṃtākāṃtānāṃ (?); Br svakāṃcatāṃtā tu (?).
11.35d navoḍhāṃ: L1c tān navothān (?); Bm M navoḍhā. L1c extra syll. See 'navayauvanāṃ' below.
11.35d navayauvanāṃ: L1c na yauvanāṃ. L1c omits syll. See 'navoḍhāṃ' above.
11.36a vicitra°: Br vici°. Br omits syll.
11.36a °vasano°: L1c °vāhano°.
11.36b °ābharaṇair: Br °ābharaṇai. See **§7.9b** for final *saṃdhi*.
11.36c °sva°: Ed L2 Bm M Br K °svaṃ.
11.36d bhavanaṃ: K bhavana.
11.37a śuktimatī°: L2 śuktimato (?). Probably *Devanāgarī* ī>o.
11.37a °toye: L1c °toya.
11.37c dharā°: L1c L2 Bm M dhārā°.
11.37c °pūrvaṃ: Bm °pūraṃ; Br °pūrva.
11.37c abhinanditaṃ: L2 abhinanditāṃ; Bm M abhinandanaṃ.
11.38a saṃ*car*antv atra: Ed K saṃcaranty atra; L2 Br saṃcaran tatra; Bm M saṃcaraṉs tatra; (L1c saṃparantv atra).
11.38b sthī*yan*tāṃ: Ed L1c Br K sthīyatāṃ; L2 Bm M sthāyatāṃ. See 11.34d.
11.38b śāśvataṃ: L2 śāśvatāṃ.
11.38b dvijāḥ: M dvijaḥ.
11.38cd °yātrāyāṃ yayau: L1c Bm M yātrāya(?) yayau; (L2 yātrāyāyaṃyau). L2 metathesis.
11.38d vṛṣalātmajaḥ: L1c vṛṣalātmanaḥ; Br vṛṣalātmaja.

11.38[1] śaunakaḥ: Ed Bm M Br K śaunaka uvāca (Bm śaunakovāca).

11.39b hṛṣṭa°: L2 duṣṭa°; (K ddaṣṭa°). L2 reading probably due to *Devanāgarī* hṛ>du. See **§7.7** for K reading.

11.39b °cittā: Br °citta.

11.39b 'bhavaṉs: L1c 'bhavaṃ (?); L2 M Br 'bhavat; Bm bhavatā (?). Bm extra syll.? See 'tadā' below.

11.39b tadā: Bm [smudge]dā.

11.39c tad grāmaṃ: Ed K grāmaṃ ca hy; L2 grāmaṃ tam; Bm M Br grāmaṃ mat (?).

11.39c aṣ*ṭa*bhāgaṃ ca: Ed L2 Bm M Br K aṣṭau bhāgāni; L1c aṣṭau bhāgaṃ ca.

11.39d *svaṃ svaṃ*: Ed K svaiḥ svair; L1c sve only; L2 Bm M svai svair; Br svai svai. See **§7.9b** for *saṃdhi*.

11.39d niveśanaṃ: L1c omits.

11.40a bhāṣābhedāni: Ed Br K bhāvayety āsaṃ (?); L2 bhāṣatety āsaṃ (?); Bm M bhāṣayety āsaṃ (?). Telugu or Kanarese script ṣ>v.

11.40d cakruḥ (L2 cakṛḥ). See **§7.4** for L2 ru>ṛ.

11.41b nyavasan (L2 nyavasaṃn). See **§7.9a** for ṃ = n.

11.41b sukhe: Ed Br K sukhaṃ; M mukhe.

11.41c °grāma°: °grāmaṃ.

11.41c °saṃsthānām: Ed Br K °saṃsthānam.

11.41d māhātmyaṃ: L2 māhātmya; Br mahātmya (?).

11.42a navoḍhāyāś: L2 navodhāyāś (?).

11.42b bravīmi: Bm M bravīma (?).

11.42c °hīnāḥ: Ed Br K °hīnā; Bm M °hīnāt. See **§7.9b** fir Ed Br K final *saṃdhi*.

11.42c parityaktāḥ: Ed Bm M Br K parityaktā.

11.43a dvātriṉśad° (L1c dvātriṉśa°).

11.43a °vāsinyo: L1c °vāsibhyo; (L2 °vāsiṃnyo). See **§7.9a** for ṃ = n.

11.43b °cāriṇaḥ: L1c °kāriṇaḥ; L2 M °cāriṇā (?); Br °cārini (?).

11.43c sadā: L1c sayaḥ (?).

11.43c °niratāḥ: Ed Br K °niratā.

11.43d rājante: L2 Bm M Br rājate.

11.43d bata: L1c L2 cata (?); Bm M 'bhavet. L1c L2 probably due to Telugu or Kanarese script b>c.
11.44b pātityam (L1c M patityaṃ).
11.44c prāyaścitta°: Br prāyaścittaṃ.
11.44d caṇḍāṉśor: Ed K candrāṉśor; M caṇḍāṉśo; Br caṇḍāṉśo (?).
11.44d darśanaṃ (L2 daśanaṃ).
11.45a bahunātra (L2 bahunātrā).
11.45b kāryā: Bm M kārya.
11.46a °hantāram: Ed Br K °hatāram.
11.46a anādi°: Br atādi° (?).
11.46b jagattraye: L1c jagatrayaṃ (= jagattrayaṃ); L2 Bm M jagatraya° (= jagattraya°); (Br jagatraye).
11.46b vyāptam: Ed Br K vyāptas.
11.46d bhaje: Ed Br K bhajan°; Bm bhajen.
11.46d ca bhaje nṛsiṉhaṃ: Bm M substitue 'suhṛdā prabhuṃ taṃ.'
11.46d bhaje: Ed Br K bhajen.

Colophons:

Ed K iti śrīskandapurāṇe uttararahasye sahyādrikhaṇḍe ekādaśo 'dhyāyaḥ.
L1c iti śrīskandapurāṇe saṉhyādrau uparibhāge pātityagrāmanirṇaya[ḥ].
L2 iti śrīs*kan*de sahyādrau uparibhāge navatitamo 'dhyāyaḥ.
Bm iti śrīsahyādrikhaṇḍe uttarār*dhe* ekādaśo 'dhyāyaḥ.
M iti śrīsa° uttara° ekādaśo 'dhyāyaḥ.
Br iti śrīskandapurāṇe uttararahasye sahyādrikhaṇḍe ekanavatitamo 'dhyā[ya]ḥ.

CHAPTER FOUR (Skh.u. 12)

12.0 Ed inserts: atha dvādaśo 'dhyāyaḥ. Bm inserts: śrīgaṇeśāya namaḥ.

12.0[1] śaunakaḥ: Ed M Br K śaunaka uvāca; Bm śrīśaunakovāca (= śrīśaunaka uvāca); (L1c śaunaka).

12.1a pātitya°: M pātityaṃ.

12.1a asty: Ed L2 Br K astv. Probably Telugu or Kanarese subscript y>v.

12.1b koṭiliṅgeśa°: L2 Bm M koṭiliṅgasya.

12.1b °saṃnidhau (Ed M Br °sannidhau, L1c L2 Bm °saṃnnidhau).

12.1c sthitānāṃ (Br sthi[-]ānāṃ, K sthitānā).

12.1c viprāṇāṃ: Ed L2 Br K martyānāṃ; Bm M atyānāṃ (?). Ed L2 Br K and Bm M source?

12.1d pāpināṃ (M pāpīnāṃ).

12.1d krūrakarmiṇāṃ: Ed L2 Bm M Br K krūrakarmaṇāṃ. Synonym.

12.2a asākṣi°: Ed Br K asatya°; L2 asākṣya°; Bm M asākṣa°. Ed Br K part of paraphrase. See 12.34c.

12.2a teṣāṃ (Br teṣā).

12.2b māhātmya: Bm M Br mahātmya (Bm M mahātya).

12.2b pravadāmi: Ed M Br K ca vadāmi.

12.2c °karaṃ: L1c °kaṃ ca.

12.2d śrotṝṇāṃ (Bm śrotṛṇāṃ).

12.2d vismayā°: Ed L2 Bm M Br K viṣayā° (Br viṣā°). Br omits syll.

12.3a pārthivaḥ (Bm pāthivaḥ).

12.3a cid: L2 Bm M Br cit.

12.3b āsīd: Bm M āsīt.

12.3c nāmnā: L2 snātvā.

12.3d yaṃ: L2 yāṃ.

12.4a bhūpāle: L2 bhūpālaiḥ; Br bhūpālai. See **§7.9b** for Br final *saṃdhi*.

12.4b kṣoṇīṃ: L1c koī; Bm M kṣoṇiṃ.

12.4b °samṛddhinīṃ: L1c Br °samṛddhinī.

12.4c anṛta*tva*°: Ed L1c L2 Bm M Br K anṛtatvaṃ.

12.4c °moṣakatvaṃ: Ed Br K °poṣakatvaṃ (?); L1c °taskaratvaṃ; M °mokṣakatvaṃ. L1c synonym. Ed Br K probably due to *Devanāgarī* m>p.

12.4d nāstīty: L1c nāst[?]ty; Br nāstiky (?).

12.4d āhur: Br āghur (?).

12.5ab See 9.14d, 9.71cd, 10.9ab, 11.4ab, 14.11cd, 16.19c, 17.22cd, 17.52a, 18.11ab.

12.5a itthaṃ (Br ityaṃ). *Devanāgarī* tth>ty.

12.5b vyatīyur: L2 vyatīta; (Br vyatiryur).

12.5b bahavaḥ: Br bavaha (?). Metathesis.

12.5c kadācid (Bm kādācid).

12.5c vādaṃ, or vādaḥ. See **§8.5**.

12.6a tathā: Ed Bm M Br K tadā.

12.6a koṭīśvara° (Br koṭiśvara°).

12.6a °sthānāṃ: Bm °sthānaṃ.

12.6b sīma°: Ed L2 Br K sīmā°; Bm M samā°. Ed L2 Br K synonym.

12.6b °vyatyasta° (M °vyatasta°).

12.6c tathā: Ed Bm M Br K tadā.

12.6c vrai*he*ya°: Ed Br K vaineya°; L2 vainyeya° (?); Bm M vainyeva° (?); (L1c vraihaya°). See 12.25b.

12.6d ṣoḍaśā°: Ed Bm M Br K ṣoḍaśa°.

12.6d °hetukaṃ: Ed Br K °hetuke.

12.7a vivādaṃ: Bm M vivāhaṃ; Br vivādha (?).

12.7b rājñe: L1c rājye.

12.7b sarvaṃ: L1c L2 Br sarva.

12.7b nyavedayat, perhaps nyavedayan: Ed Bm M Br K nyavedayet (?); L2 nyaveśayat. Ed Bm MBr K dependent on someone reading a *Devanāgarī* version of L2 as if it were in *Jainalipi* or nonstandard *Devanāgarī*, with *Devanāgarī*, śa>dā. See **§7.9a**.

12.7c mahāprājñaḥ: Ed L2 Bm M Br K mahāprājño.

12.7d °vidāṃ varaḥ: L1c viśāradaḥ. Synonym.

12.8a koṭīśvara° (Br koṭiśvara°).

12.8a °sthāṉs tān: L2 °sthān tān; Bm M °sthānāt; Br °sthā tān; K sthās tān.

12.8b pracaṇḍān (Br pracaṇḍīn).

12.8c jalpataḥ: Ed M Br K jalpantaḥ; L2 Bm jalyantaḥ (?). L2 Bm *Devanāgarī* p>y.

12.8d sāntvayām āsa: Ed L2 Bm M Br K sāntvayann āha (L2 sāntvayaṃn, Bm sātyayann, Br sātvayaṃn); (L1c santvayām). See **§7.9a** for ṃ = n.

12.9a ittham (Br ityam). *Devanāgarī* tth>ty.

12.9a pravadatas (Br pravadas). Br omits syll.

12.9c . . kṛtya: All MSS tiras(?)kṛtya.

12.9c nṛpasyā°: Bm M bhupasyā° (= bhūpasyā°); Br nṛpaśyā° (?). Bm M synonym.

12.9[1] L1c and L2 here insert a half *śloka* which we would have included in the text in all likelihood if any definite sense could have been made out of any of it. L1c reads:
sarātānīti mānvagmī vākyaṃ hetvarthasaṃtutaṃ /
°saṃtutaṃ = °saṃtataṃ.
L2 variants:
hetvarthasaṃtutaṃ: hetva saṃjñayataṃ.

12.10a vicintyā°: Ed Br K vicinvā (?); L2 vicitvā°; Bm M vicinyā° (?)

12.10b harṣann iva sa: Ed L2 Bm MBr K harṣayann iva (Br harṣayaṃnn iva).

12.10c kāśyapīṃ: Br kāśyapī.

12.10c prārthayiṣyāmo: Bm Br prārthaïṣyāmo (Br pārtha°). Bm Br due to the dropping of 'y' in such environments when the text is written in Telugu or Kanarese script. See **§7.4**.

12.10d vadaty eṣā: Ed L2 Bm M K vadaty eṣāṃ; Br vada teṣāṃ.

12.10d °āśubhaṃ: L1c Bm M °āśubhāṃ.

12.11a yatrāsti: L1c yatrārsā[?] (?); Bm M yastita (?); Br yatrāstī (?). Different sources?

12.11b tatra tatra (M tra tatra). M omits syll.

12.11b †*vadiṣ*yati†: Ed L2 Bm M Br K dahiṣyati; L1c bhaviṣyati. Emendation required for sense.

12.11c niścitya: Bm M niścintya.
12.11d cārān ājñāpayat: L1c cārān ājñāpayaṭ (?); L2 Bm M cārāṇājñāpayat (?). L2 Bm M synonym, but grammatically incorrect.
12.11d tadā: Br tadāṃ (?).
12.12a dvātriṉśad° (M dvātriṉṣad°).
12.12b dharme: L2 Bm M Br dharma°.
12.12b vyavasthitān (L2 vyavasthitānṃ). See §**7.9a** for ṃ = n.
12.12c bhṛśamāna°: Ed Br K bhṛṣamāna° (?); L1c bhṛṣaṃ māna°.
12.12d ānīyatām (L2 ānīyyatām). See §**7.4**.
12.12d iti: M ite (?).
12.13a paraśvaḥ: Ed K paścāc ca; Bm paraśva; Br paśvaḥ (?). Br omits syll.
12.13a sādhayiṣye° (L2 sādhaïṣye°). See §**7.4**.
12.13b *āviśan*: Ed Br K ādiśya; L1c ādiśyan; L2 ādiśa[?]; Bm M ādiṣya. *Devanāgarī* v>d?
12.13¹ śaunakaḥ: Ed Br K śaunaka uvāca; Bm M omit here. See 12.13².
12.13c kṣapām ardhe: Ed L2 Br K kṣapāmadhye (Br kṣayāmadhye); Bm M sabhāmadhye. Br *Devanāgarī* p>y.
12.13d dhūrtāḥ: L1c dhūrtāṃ.
12.13d koṭīśvare (Br koṭiśvare).
12.13² Bm M insert: śaunaka uvāca (Bm śaunakovāca).
12.14a sīmo°: L2 Bm M Br simo°.
12.14a °opāntaṃ: Ed K °opāntyaṃ; L2 Br °opānta; Bm M °pāntya.
12.14b ativegataḥ: L1c ati[?]taḥ
12.14c kṣo*ṇīṃ* khātvā: Ed L1c L2 K kṣoṇiṃ khātvā; Bm kuṇḍera; M kuṇḍe khyātvā; Br kṣoṇī khātvā (?). See 12.4b.
12.14c vyomamātrāṃ: L1c yāma°; L2 Bm M °mātraṃ.
12.14d kuṇḍe: Bm kṣoṇi; M kṣoṇiṃ; K kuḍe (?).
12.14d kutsita°: K kuntsita° (?).
12.15a *kāṃ*cit: All MSS kaścit.
12.15b sikatām: Ed K sthīyante; L2 Br sthīyataṃ; Bm M sthīyate.

12.15b 'py apūrayan: Ed L1c K prapūrayet; L2 Bm vyapūrayan (?); Br 'py apurayet (?). Ed L1c K and L2 Bm due to p~v and Cy~Cr in Telugu and Kanarese scripts.
12.15c *svaṃ svaṃ*: Ed L2 Bm M Br k svasva°; L1c sve sve.
12.15c gṛhaṃ: Ed L2 Bm M Br K °gataṃ.
12.15c prāpur ājñā: Ed L1c Bm K prāpū rājñā; Br prāpuḥr ājñā. See **§7.9b** for Br final *saṃdhi*.
12.15d vyavasthitāḥ: L1c sthitaṃ tadā.
12.16a cāraiḥ: L1c pāraiḥ; Bm cauḥ (?). Bm omits syll.
12.16a samānītā: L2 Bm M samānītāḥ.
12.16b dvātriṉśad° (Bm M dvātriṉṣad°)
12.16b °vāsinaḥ: Bm M °bhedataḥ (?). Bm M source?
12.16c °sāṃnidhyam (Br °sānnidhyaṃ). See **§7.9a** for ṃ = n.
12.15d āśīr°: Bm Br āsir°.
12.16d °vāda°: L1c °vādaḥ.
12.16d °puraḥ°: L2 °puras°.
12.16d °sarāḥ: Ed Br K °saraṃ; Bm M °saraiḥ.
12.17a °kālocita°: L1c °kālopita°.
12.17a °vākyāni: L1c °vākyā. L1c omits syll.
12.17b jaguḥ sarve: Ed L2 M K jugupsur vai; Bm jagupsu(?) vai; Br jagupsur vair (?).
12.17b nareśvaraṃ: Ed K nareśvara.
12.17c †va*sur*†: All MSS vasu°.
12.17c dvijaiḥ: Ed Bm M K janaiḥ; L2 janais; Br janai. See **§7.9b** for Br final *saṃdhi*.
12.17d sīma°: Ed Br K sīmā°; Bm M simā° (?).
12.17d yayau: Ed L2 Bm M Br K yayur.
12.18a saṃgṛhya: Bm M sagṛhya (?).
12.18a pūjā°: Bm M pūjāṃ.
12.18a °sambhāraṃ: Bm sabhāraṃ (?).
12.18b daivajñais: L1c L2 daivajñaiḥs; Bm M vedajñais. See **§7.9b** for L1c L2 final *saṃdhi*.
12.18b tāntrikaiḥ: Bm M tyāntrikaiḥ (?).
12.18c *taur*ya°: Ed Bm M Br K tairya° (?); L1c toya°; L2 tārya°. See **§7.11**.
12.18c °trikeṇa: L1c °ti[?]a (?); L2 Bm M °trikoṇa.

12.18c sahitaḥ: Ed K sahitāḥ; L1c saṃyuktāḥ; Br sahito. L1c synonym. Br incorrectly changes final *saṃdhi* to that before voiced initial.
12.18d kūṭa°: Ed Bm M Br K kuṭa°.
12.18d °koṭīśvaraiḥ (L1c °koṭeśvaraiḥ, Bm M °kotiśvaraiḥ).
12.19a L1c substitutes:
pūjāṃ cakāra dharaṇīṃ.
Paraphrase.
12.19a karoti: Bm M karotī (?).
12.19b °ākṣatā°: M °ākṣyatā°
12.19c bhakṣa°: Bm M bho bho.
12.19c °bhojyais: L2 °bhojyaiḥs; Bm M bhojyas. See **§7.9b** for L2 final *saṃdhi*.
12.19d dhūpadīpanaivedyavandanaiḥ: Ed Br K dhūpair dīpair naivedyacandanaiḥ (Br dhūpai dīpai); (Bm dhyūpa°). Ed Br K 'candanaiḥ' probably due to the type of confusion in *Jainalipi* between 'c' and 'v'. See **§7.9a**. See **§7.9b** for Br final *saṃdhi*.
12.20a prārthanām akarot tatra: L1c akarot prārthanāṃ tatra; Bm M prārthanāmaṃ (= °mānaṃ ?) karoty atra; (Br . . . akarot tra). Br omits syll.
12.20b °epsitāṃ: L2 Bm M Br °epsitaṃ.
12.20[1] rājā: Ed Bm M Br K rājovāca.
12.21a devi: Ed Bm M K dehi; Br dahi (?).
12.21c ajñānato jñānato 'pi: Ed Br K ajñānājñānato vāpi; Bm M ajñānatājñānato 'pi.
12.21d he kṣame: Ed Br K kṣamyatāṃ; L2 nakṣoma (?); Bm M nekṣyomat (?). L2 Bm M different source?
12.21d kṣamyatāṃ: L1c kṣama tāṃ; Br kṣakṣmatī (?).
12.22a kūṭa°: L1c kūṭaṃ.
12.22a °sthānām: Ed L2 Bm M Br K °sthānam.
12.22a idaṃ: L2 Br imaṃ; Bm M amuṃ.
12.22a kṣetram (L2 K kṣetraṃm, M Br kṣetraṃ).
12.22b koṭikṣetram: Ed L2 Br K anyasthānam; Bm M anyat sthānam.
12.22c vaktavyaṃ: Ed Bm M Br K vāstavya; L2 tasyasya (?).

12.22c *yat* tvayā, or *tat* tvayā: Ed Br K te tvayā; L1c Bm M ya(?) tvayā; L2 sa tvayā.

12.22c samyak: L1c samyag.

12.22d śodhanāyedṛ*śāṃ*: Ed L2 Br K bodhanāya imāṃ (Br bodhanāma); Bm M bodhanāya ime; (L1c śodhanāyedṛśā). ś~b probably due to confusion from Telugu or Kanarese script. Br *Devanāgarī* y>m.

12.22d *nṝ*ṇāṃ: Ed L2 Bm M Br K nṛṇāṃ; L1c nṛpāṃ (?).

12.23a evam: Ed L2 Bm M Br K ittham.

12.23a uktvā: Br uktā (?); (L2 utkvā). L2 mistake in reading *Devanāgarī* script.

12.23a mahīpālaḥ: Ed K mahīpālas; Br mahīpālo. Br incorrectly changes final *saṃdhi* to that before voiced initial.

12.23b tūṣṇīṃ (Br tūṣṇiṃ).

12.23b babhūva saḥ: Bm M babhūvahaḥ (?).

12.23^{1} śaunakaḥ: Ed Br K śaunaka uvāca; Bm M omit here. See 12.23^{2}.

12.23c sarvabhūtānāṃ: Br sarvatānāṃ. Br omits syll.

12.23d kuṇḍa°: Bm M kuḍa° (?).

12.23d °stho: L2 °sthe.

12.23^{2} Bm M insert: śaunaka uvāca (Bm śaunakovāca). See 12.23^{1}.

12.24a caiteṣāṃ: Bm M ceteṣāṃ (?).

12.24b tathaiva ca: Ed Br nṛpātmajāḥ; L2 nṛpātmajā; Bm M nṛpātmajaḥ.

12.24c rājñaḥ: Ed Br K rāja°; Bm omits; M rājaḥ (?).

12.24c kīr*tyās*: Ed Br K °kīrtis (= °kīrtes ?); L1c L2 Bm M kīrtyai. See **§7.9b** for L1c L2 Bm M final *saṃdhi*.

12.24c °ākhyātyai: Bm M °ākhyātai.

12.24d gadati: L1c jagādo (= jagāda); Bm M gadatī (?).

12.24d sma: L1c svair.

12.24d narādhamaḥ: Bm M narādhipa; Br narādhamāḥ.

12.25a koṭīśvara°: Ed Bm M Br K koṭīśvaraṃ (Br koṭiśvaraṃ).

12.25a °sthā*nāṃ*: All MSS sthānaṃ (L1c L2 °sthānaṃ).

12.25b vraihe*yaṃ* nātra: Ed L2 Bm M Br K jñātavyaṃ nātra; L1c vraiheyaṇātra (?).

12.25c idaṃ: Ed K imaṃ.

12.25c śabdaṃ: Bm M śabda. Bm M probably omit *anusvāra*. See **§7.5**.

12.25c samākarṇya: Bm M tad ākarṇya.

12.25d piśunāḥ: Bm M piśunā.

12.25d °kāriṇaḥ: Bm M °karmaṇā; Br °kariṇāḥ (?).

12.26a śrūyatāṃ: L1c śrūyantāṃ; L2 śrūyatā (?).

12.26a manu*jaiḥ* sar*vair*: All MSS manujāḥ sarve.

12.26b bhavadbhir: L2 vādadbhir (perhaps, hadadbhir); Bm bhavadbhi; Br vāvadbhir. See **§7.9b** for Bm omission of *Devanāgarī* superscript 'r,' perhaps here a *saṃdhi* irregularity.

12.26c apahṛtyāsmadīyaṃ: Ed Bm M Br K apahṛtya madīyaṃ; L2 apahṛtyasmadīyaṃ (?).

12.26d bhuvaṃ tebhyo: Ed L2 Bm M Br K bhavantebhyo (?); L1c bhuvantebhyo (= bhuvaṃ tebhyo). See **§7.9a** for n = ṃ.

12.27a saṃlāpayayantas te, or L1c L2 sallāpayantas te: Bm sallāpayatas te; M sallāpayattas(?) te; Br saṃlāpayan tasmai.

12.27b kṛta°: Bm kṛtat° (?).

12.27[1] śaunakaḥ: Ed Br K śaunaka uvāca; Bm M omit here; (L1c śaunaka). See 12.27[2].

12.27c etasminn (Bm M itesminn).

12.27c vyomni: Bm vyomnī (?); M reads both 'i' and 'ī' vowel modifications for 'mn.'

12.27d janasyāścarya°: Ed Br K janam āścarya°; L1c janavismaya°. L1c paraphrase.

12.27d °kāriṇī: Bm M °kāriṇi (?).

12.27[2] Bm M insert: śaunaka uvāca (Bm śaunakovāca). See 12.27[1].

12.28a Ed reads:
nijabhartṛsneha eva.
There are for this the following variant readings:
nija°: Br ni° (?). Br omits syll.
°bhartṛ°: L2 °bhartuḥs; Bm bhatṛ (?). See **§7.9b** for L2 final *saṃdhi*.
sneha: L2 omits.

12.28b koṭīśvarasya: L1c koṭīśvara. L1c omits syll.
12.28c janatā*ghau*ghaṃ: Ed K janatāpaughaḥ (?); L2 janapāpaugha; Bm M Br janatāpaugha (? – M janatāyaugha, Br janatāpaudya). L2 synonym. *Devanāgarī* p>y in M reading, gh>dy in Br reading.
12.28d śaṅ*ka*yaivā°: Ed L2 Bm M Br K śaṅkāyaivā°; L1c śaṅka evā°.
12.28d °prabhā: Ed K °prabhau; L2 Bm M Br °prabho.
12.29a °prabhāvaṃ: L1c °prabhāva.
12.29a darśayanti: L1c dadarśayantī (?); Bm dṛśaiveti (?); M darśaiveti (?). Bm M source? L1c extra syll.
12.29b bhāratī nijagāda tān: Ed Bm M Br K nijagādātha tān prati (M tāṃ); L2 nijagādādṛtān mati (?). See **§7.9a** for use of *anusvāra* in M.
12.29c nai*ṣā*: Ed L2 Bm M Br K natvā; L1c naiśā.
12.29c gīr: Bm gī (?).
12.29c °saṃbandhā: L1c °saṃmandhā (?); M saṃbandhāḥ.
12.29d °mu*khād*: Ed L2 Bm M Br K °sukhā; L1c mukhā.
12.29d dhruvaṃ (Bm M dhṛvaṃ). See **§7.4** on Telugu or Kanarese script ṛ = ru.
12.30b °cāriṇaḥ: Bm °cāriṇiḥ.
12.30c tasminn: Ed L2 Bm M Br K asminn.
12.30c mahārā*jan*: All MSS mahārājā.
12.30d śapāmi: Br śaṃpāmi.
12.31a uktvā: Br uktā.
12.31a bhagavatī: Br bhagavataṃ.
12.31b tatrai°: Br trai° (?). Br omits syll.
12.31d kaḷevaraḥ: L2 kaḷeciraṃ (?); Bm M Br kalevaraṃ; (Ed K kalevaraḥ). L2 due to *Jainalipi*-nonstandard *Devanāgarī* confusion between 'v' and 'c'? See **§7.9a**.
12.32a muhūrtaṃ: L1c Bm M Br muhūrta (Br muhurta).
12.32a dharmātmā: Br dharmātmā: Br dharmā. Br omits syll.
12.32c grāmasthānāṃ (L1c masthānānāṃ). L1c omits syll. and then compensates.
12.32c purastāt tu: Ed K purobhāge; L2 purasthātuṃ (?); Bm M purastātu (?). Ed K synonym. L2 builds on a mistake such as that of Bm M.

12.32d bhūmiṃ: L1c Br bhūmi; Bm M bhūtiṃ.

12.32d pradṛṣṭavān: Bm M prahṛṣṭavān. Bm M due to *Devanāgarī* d>h.

12.33a *krimi*°: Ed Br K kṛmi°; L1c kimi° (= krimi°?); L2 krama°; Bm M krimī° (?).

12.33a māṉsa°: Ed Bm M K māṉsaṃ; Br māsaṃ.

12.33b °vigrahaṃ: Br °vigrahaḥ.

12.33c visma*yī*°: All MSS vismayo.

12.33d saṃrakta°: Br sa rakta°.

12.34a °sthānāṃ: Bm °sthānā; K °sthāno.

12.34a puras*tāt* tu: Ed L2 Bm M Br K purobhāge; L1c purastattu (= purastāt tu). Ed L2 Bm M Br K synonym. See 12.32c.

12.34b sarvasvam apahṛtya: Ed Br K sarvasvapadahatya; Bm M sarvasya padahatya (Bm savasya . . .). *Devanāgarī* m>p?

12.34c °vādi*nāṃ*: All MSS °vādinas (Bm M repeating 'vādi' twice).

12.34d grāmas*the*bhyaḥ: Ed L1a L2 Bm M K grāmas tebhyaḥ; Br grāmas tebhyo (?). The masculine form for 'grāma' would be extremely unlikely in this text. See **§8.5**.

12.35ab See 14.25cd.

12.35a parityā*g†ā*parityāgaṃ†: Ed Br K parityāgāt sarītyāgaṃ (?); L1c parityāgaṃ parityāgaṃ; L2 parityāgan sarityāgaṃ (?); Bm parityāgāt sarityāga° (?); M parityāgāt sarityā 'ga° (?). p~s due to Telugu or Kanarese script. See **§7.11**.

12.35ab °gaṃ tair eva tu: L1c °gaṃ raiva[- -] (?); Bm gatair eva tu; M 'gatair eva tu.

12.35b vidhīyatāṃ (L2 vidhīyyatāṃ). See **§7.4**.

12.35c nirdiśya: Bm nirdviśya (?); Br niddiśya (?).

12.35c bhagavān (L1c bhagavā).

12.35d L1c substitutes:
jagāma svaniveśanaṃ.
Paraphrase.

12.35d gacchati: Bm M gacchatī (?).

12.35d sma: Bm M sva°.

12.36ab See 14.26cd.
12.36b vrīḷayā natamastakāḥ: Ed L2 Br K kīlayānatamastakāḥ; Bm M kilīyā(?)nantaṃ astakaḥ; Br . . . mastakā (?).
12.36cd All MSS omit. See n. to translation at this point.
12.37a asākṣi°: Ed L2 Br K asākṣa°.
12.37a yūyaṃ: Ed Br K yūnaṃ.
12.37b patitāḥ: L1c pati 'tāḥ.
12.37b pāpayantritāḥ: L1c pātayanti tāḥ; L2 pāpayantitāḥ (?); Bm M pāpayantitaḥ (?).
12.37c anāsthānāś: Ed K anasthānāḥ (?); L1c anāsthānaś; L2 Bm anāsthānā; M anāsthānāsthāś (?); Br anasthānā (?). M extra syll.
12.37c cāgha . . : Ed K ślāghanīyāḥ; L1c cāghanīyaḥ (?); L2 Br ślāghanīya (L2 ślāghanīyya); Bm bhthāghā(?)nīyā; M chāghanīyā (?) Bm due to Telugu or Kanares script c> bh and subscript l>th. See **§7.4** for L2 reading.
12.37c °bahiṣ (Bm °hiṣ°). Bm omits syll.
12.37d °kṛtāḥ: M °kṛtaḥ; Br °kṛtā.
12.38a asmin (K asmiṃ). See **§7.9a** for ṃ = n.
12.38a grāme: Br rāme.
12.38a vivāhādir: L1c L2 Bm M Br vivāhādi.
12.38b varjanīyo (L2 varjanīyyo). See **§7.4**.
12.38c śaptvettham: L2 śapedyam (?); Bm M svaptvetham (= °ettham).
12.38c anṛtān: Ed L2 Bm M Br K anṛtād.
12.38d mahāprā*jñā*: Ed K mahāprajñā; L1c Bm M mahāprājño (M hāprājño); L2 māhaprājña (?); Br mahāprajño. L2 metathesis. M omits syll.
12.39a an*yat*: All MSS anyaṃ.
12.39a samāsādya: L2 M samākhyāta; Bm samākhyata (?).
12.39b niktanaṃ: Ed L2 Bm M Br K niveśanaṃ. Synonym. *Devanāgarī* k>v, probably.
12.39c parityaktās: L2 Bm M parityaktā. See **§7.9b** for final *saṃdhi*.
12.39d vārdhes: Bm M Br vārdhaṉs (Bm vārddhaṉs); (L1c vārddhes).
12.39c upāśritaḥ: Bm upaśritāḥ (?); M uśritāḥ (?). M omits syll.

12.40a sthitāḥ: L2 sthātiḥ; Bm M sthāti. L2 Bm M metathesis.
12.40a °paryantaṃ: Ed °paryata (?); Bm M °paryanta; K °paryattaṃ (?)
12.40b mandākṣād: Ed madakṣā (?); L1c māndākṣā; L2 mandākṣo; Bm M mandakṣyo (?); Br madakṣo (?).
12.40b °endriyāḥ: Bm M Br °endriyaḥ (Bm °edriyaḥ).
12.40[1] śaunakaḥ: Ed Br K śaunaka uvāca; Bm M omit.
12.40c yadṛcchayā°: Bm M yadṛcchaya (?); Br yadacchayā.
12.40c °āgataḥ: L2 Br °āgata; Bm M gatā.
12.40d °sthāpako: Ed Br K °sthāpito.
12.41a-12.41d Bm M omit.
12.41b °*samad*yutiṃ: Ed K °maha(?)dyutiṃ; L1c °sadyutiṃ; L2 samṛ[?]dhṛtiṃ (?). L1c missing syll. L2 probably due, in part, to Telugu or Kanarese script dyu>dh. See 9.57b, 10.10d, 12.14b, 16.3b, 18.3d for emendation.
12.41c ūrdhva°: L1c Br ūrdhvaṃ.
12.41c °puṇḍrāṅkitaṃ: L1c puḍrāṅki (?). L1c missing syll.
12.41c śāntaṃ: L1c omits; L2 śānta.
12.41d lalāṭe cordhva°: L1c gālepordhva° (?). L1c omits syll.
12.41d °puṇḍrakaṃ: Br °puḍrakaṃ (?).
12.41[1] Between 12.41cd and 12.42ab the following three vss. mainly in Indravajra meter, but with *pādas* 1 and 3 of vs. 2 in Upendravajra meter, are inserted:

āmūlamudrāṅkitabāhudaṇḍaṃ
madhye samāveśitacelakhaṇḍaṃ /
vāme karevoddhṛtaveṇudaṇḍam
ante yuge mādhvamatapracaṇḍaṃ //
punaś ca mudrāṅkitasarvagātraṃ
vāme kare saṃsthitanīrapātraṃ /
kṛpāsamālokitavāmanetraṃ
dhyāyantam īśaṃ hṛdi pakṣipatraṃ //
kaṇṭhe samāśliṣṭasupadmamā*laṃ*
brahmāṇḍapiṇḍīkṛtapiṇḍajālaṃ /
dhyāyantam īśasya nṛsiṇhalīlāṃ
dhyāyantam ādyaṃ hṛdi lolarūpaṃ //

There are for these vss. the following variant readings:
daṇḍaṃ: Ed Br K daṇḍa°: L2 kaṇṭha°.

madhye: L1c kaṭau. Synonym.
samāveśita°: L1c L2 samāveṣita° (?); Br sabhāveśita° (?). Br due to *Devanāgarī* m>bh.
°cela°: Ed Bm M Br K °caila° (Br °cai°). Br omits syll.
karevoddhṛta°: Ed Br K kare praudgata°; L2 kare prauddhṛta°; Bm M paripraudrata (?). Bm M due in part to Telugu or Kanarese script ṛ >ra.
°daṇḍam (L2 °daṇḍaṃm, Bm M °daṇḍaṃ).
ante: L1c kalau; L2 antye (?); Bm M ate (?). L1c synonym.
°mata°: Bm M Br °mataḥ.
°pracaṇḍaṃ: L2 pracaṇḍaḥ (?); (Br praṃcaṇḍaṃ).
punaś (Br munaś). Br due to *Devanāgarī* p>m.
°āṅkita°: Bm °ānvita°.
kare: L1c L2 Br tare (?). L1c L2 Br probably due to *Devanāgarī* k>t.
saṃsthita°: L1c taṃstita° (?). L1c probably due to *Devanāgarī* s>t.
°nīra°: Ed Br K °nīla°.
°pātraṃ: Ed Bm M Br K °patraṃ.
kṛpā°: L1c kṛtā°.
kaṇṭhe: Bm kaṇṭe.
samāśliṣṭa°: L1c masāśliṣṭa° (?). L1c metathesis.
°mā*laṃ*: Ed L1c L2 M Br °mālāṃ; Bm °mālā; K °māloṃ (?).
brahmāṇḍa° (L2 braṃhmāṇḍa°, Bm brahmāḍa°).
°piṇḍa°: L1c °piṇḍu° (?); Br °pīḍa° (?).
°jālaṃ: Br °jvālaṃ.
dhyāyantam: Ed K dhyāyanti; L1c gāyantam; Br dhyāyanhtim (?).
īśasya: Ed K ceśasya.
ādyaṃ: Bm M āddyaṃ (?); Br ādya°.
hṛdi: Bm M sida° (?).
lola°: Ed K loka°; L2 Bm M kola° (Bm M °kola°). Possible that L2 Bm M due to metathesis of Ed K reading, or *vice versa*.

12.42a See 17.39c.

12.42b munim: Bm M Br muni°.
12.42b mandara°: Ed Bm MBr K mandāra°. Synonym.
12.42b °saṃnibhaṃ (Br °saṃnnibhaṃ).
12.42c vadantaś: Ed Bm M K vadantaṃ; L1c vadataṃ (?); Br vadanta (?).
12.42c ca: Ed L1c Bm M Br K sva°.
12.42c †*mantraṃ*†: All MSS mataṃ. See 12.45d.
12.42d See 17.39d.
12.42d petuś: Br yetuś (?). *Devanāgarī* p>y.
12.43a ūcuḥ sveṣāṃ: Ed K ūcus teṣāṃ; L1c L2 ūcusveṣāṃ (?); Br brūcuḥs(?) teṣāṃ.
12.43a caritrāṇi: L1c paritrāṇi (?).
12.43b hy: L2 Br omit.
12.43b asākṣitvena: L1c āsākṣitvena (?); Bm M astakṣitvena (?).
12.43cd See 9.58cd, 13.15ab.
12.43d kṛpāḷo: Bm kṛlola (?); M kṛlo (?); (Ed Br K kṛpālo). M omits syll.
12.43d dīna°: Bm vidi° (?); M dī° (?). Bm metathesis of reading based on Telugu or Kanarese script n>v. M omits syll.
12.43d °vatsala: L1c L2 °vatsalā.
12.43[1] śaunakaḥ: Ed Bm M Br K śuanaka uvāca (Bm śaunakovāca).
12.44a ākarṇya: M ākarṇa.
12.45a kṛpā°: Br kapā° (?).
12.45b See 9.70b. 13.18d, 13.23d.
12.45b dadau: L1c dādau (?).
12.45c saptamudr*ās* tataḥ: Ed L2 Bm M Br K taptamudrāṅkitaṃ; L1c saptamudrāṃ tataḥ.
12.45d †*mantraṃ*†: All MSs mataṃ. See 12.42c.
12.45d vaiśvambharānvitaṃ: Ed K vetyaṃ(?) harābhidhaṃ; L2 tyaṃ(?) harābhidhaṃ; Bm M vai tvaṃ mahāvibho; Br vaityaṃ(?) harābhidha. L2 omits syll.
12.46b °āṅkitaṃ: Ed Br K °āhnikaṃ; L1c °āntikaṃ.
12.46[1] Between 12.45ab and 12.46cd all MSS insert three vss. which make only partial sense and which most certainly are commentary. There is after the first of these vss. another more lengthy commentary. See Appendix B.

This is followed in all MSS except Bm M by the addition: śaunakaḥ. There is for this the usual variation of Ed Br K reading: śaunaka uvāca. For Bm M insertion of 'śaunaka uvāca,' see 12.46[2] below.

12.46c śāsayitvā: Ed K sthāpayitvā; Bm M śāpayitvā; Br śāyayitvā (?); (L2 śāsaïtvā). The development of the readings appears to be L1c L2 > Bm M (+Br) > Ed K. Ed K Bm M 'p' probably due to Telugu or Kanarese script s~p. Br variation due to *Devanāgarī* p>y. See **§7.4** for L2 reading.

12.46d satkṛtaḥ: L1c sār(?)kṛtaḥ; Br satkṛtā.

12.46[2] Bm M insert: śaunaka uvāca (Bm śaunakovāca). See 12.46[1] above.

12.47a niṣkalaṅkāś: M kiṣkalaṅkāś (?).

12.47a viprāḥ: Ed Br K viprā.

12.47b °gauravāt: L2 Bm M °gauravān. L2 Bm M due to *Devanāgarī* t>n.

12.47c ni*vasantās*: All MSS nivāsaṃ ca. See 10.46a, 15.12a for tv/t>c. See also **§7.9a**.

12.47d punaś ca: Bm omits.

12.48a Ed L2 Bm M Br K substitute:
vedavākyāt parityaktāḥ.
There is for this the following variant reading:
parityaktāḥ: Ed Br K parityaktā.

12.48a bahunātra: L1c vadganātrā (?).

12.48b nirbhītāḥ: L2 nirbhītās.

12.48b saṃcaranty: L2 Br saṃcaraty.

12.48c darśana°: M dar'śana (?).

12.48d pātityaṃ: L1c pāpātityaṃ. L1c extra syll.

12.49a °citta°: Ed L2 Bm M Br K °cittaṃ.

12.49a °vidhiṃ: Ed L2 Bm M Br K ahaṃ.

12.49b ṣaṣṭha°: Bm ṣaṣṭa° (?).

12.49b kal†*āsanaṃ*†: Ed Bm M K kālaśataṃ; L1c kālaśanaṃ; L2 kālāśataṃ; Br kāleśataṃ.

Colophons:

Ed K	iti śrīskandapurāṇe uttararahasye sahyādrikhaṇḍe śivagaṇeśasaṃvāde pātityagrāmakathanaṃ nāma dvādaśo 'dhyāyaḥ.
L1c	iti śrīskande sahyādrau uparibhāge pātityagrāmakathanaṃ.
L2	iti śrī*skan*de saṉhyādrau uparibhāge pātitya (!) ekanavatitamo 'dhyāyaḥ.
Bm	iti śrīsahyādre pātitya uttaravibhāgo nāma (!) dvādaśo 'dhyāyaḥ.
M	iti śrīsa° pātitya uttaravibhāgo nāma (!) dvādaśaḥ.
Br	iti śrīskandapurāṇe uttararahasya sahyādrikhaṇḍe pātityagrāmakathanaṃ nāma dvinavatitamo 'dhyā[ya]ḥ.

CHAPTER FIVE (Skh.u. 13)

13.0 Ed inserts: atha trayodaśo 'dhyāyaḥ. Bm inserts: śrīgaṇeśāya namaḥ.
13.0[1] śatānīkaḥ: Ed Bm M K śatānīka uvāca; L2 śaunakaḥ.
13.1b vicitraṃ (M vicintraṃ).
13.1b tvan°: L1c tvaṅ.
13.1b °mukhodgataṃ: L1c mukhād gataṃ.
13.1d māhātmyam: Bm mahātmyam (?).
13.1[1] śaunakaḥ: Ed Bm M K śaunaka uvāca (Bm śaunakovāca).
13.2b Ed reads:
sakalatrapurapunaḥ.
There are for this the following variant readings:
L1c saka[?] 'tra kaḷaṃ puraṃ; L2 Bm M sakalatrapuraṃ punaḥ.
13.2[1] Between 13.2ab nad 13.2cd L1c inserts a half vs. of commentary, apparently in an attempt to clarify 13.2b. See Appendix B.
13.2c śata°: L1c śāta°.
13.2d L1c omits.
13.2d garbhiṇīnāṃ: L2 garbhīṇīnāṃ (?).
13.2d narottama (Bm rottama). Bm omits syll.
13.3a °deśodbhavānāṃ ca: L1c °deśasamudbhavāṃ.
13.3b L1c omits.
13.3c aṅgavaṅga°: L1c saṃkate tu.
13.3d saurāṣṭrād: L2 saurāṣṭrān; Bm M saurāṣṭraṃ.
13.3d gujja*rāt*: Ed K gurjarās; L1c gujurāt; L2 gujjarān; Bm M gurjaras.
13.4a āndhra°: L2 [?]dhra.
13.4a °drāviḍa°: Bm °drāvīḍa°; M °ḍāvīḍa°. *Devanāgarī* dr>ḍ?
13.4a °karṇāta°: Ed K °karnāta°.
13.4c mahārāṣṭrotka*ḷābh*yāṃ ca: Ed K karahāṭamahārāṣṭra°; L2 mahārāṣṭrau karoḍāś ca; Bm M mahārāṣṭrau karāṭaṃ ca; (L1c mahārāṣṭrotkaḷākhyāṃ ca).

13.4d māgadha . . . : Ed K māgadha tair naraiḥ; L1c māgadha tai ttirāḥ (?); L2 māgadha taiḥr naraiḥ; Bm M māgadhanirjarāḥ. See **§7.9b** for L1c and L2 final *saṃdhi*.

13.5a gauḍa°: L2 goḍā°; Bm M gauḍā°.

13.5a °gorāṣṭra°: L1c °gauraṣṭa°; Bm M °gaurāṣṭra°.

13.5a °deśābhyāṃ: Bm M °veśābhyāṃ. Probably *Devanāgarī* d>v.

13.5b parityaktā: L2 parityaktvā. See 9.68a.

13.5b vitantavaḥ: L2 Bm vitantuvaḥ (?).

13.5c saṃjātāḥ: L2 Bm M saṃjātā. See **§7.9b** for L2 Bm M final *saṃdhi*.

13.5c pūrṇa°: Ed L2 Bm M K pūrva°. See 9.56a.

13.5d kṛtā°: Ed K kṛtāḥ; L2 Bm M kṛta°.

13.5d kṛtāśrāddhavigarhitāḥ: Ed K kṛtāḥ śrāddha°; L1c kṛtāśrāddhā°; L2 kṛtaśrāddhā°; Bm M kṛtaśrāddhavigarhitaṃ.

13.6a ākalparahitā: Ed Bm M K kalpanārahitā; L2 ākalparahitāṃ.

13.6b See 9.56b.

13.6b °ātipīḍitāḥ: L2 °ātipīḍitaḥ.

13.6c mīḷitvā: Ed L2 K militvā; (Bm M mīlitvā).

13.6c tāḥ: L2 tās.

13.6c samāyātāḥ: Ed K samāyātās.

13.7c sarvāḥ: Bm M sarvā. See **§7.9b** for Bm M final *saṃdhi*.

13.7c samāviṣṭāḥ: L1c samāviṣṭā. See **§7.9b** for L1c final *saṃdhi*.

13.7d stotraṃ: Ed K stutiṃ.

13.7[1] Between 13.7cd and 13.8ab L1c inserts the following three crude vss. in *śloka* meter:
viśveśvara virūpākṣa viśvarūpa sadāśiva /
śaraṇaṃ bhava bhūteśa karuṇākara śaṃkara //
hara śaṃbho mahādeva viśveś†āmakhallabha† /
śiva śaṃkara sarvātma nīlakaṇṭhāya śaṃbhave //
amṛteśāpaśarvāya mahādevāya te namaḥ /
iti stutvā mahādevaṃ gantuṃ samupacakramuḥ //
L2 inserts the first, tenth, eleventh, and twelfth *pādas* of

this with only one change. Thus L2 inserts the following:
viśveśvara virūpākṣa mahādevāya te namaḥ /
iti stutvā mahādevaṃ stotuṃ samupacakramuḥ //

13.8a tatrā°: L2 yatrā°.

13.8b See 9.57d.

13.8b nāsāgra°: L2 nāsāgraṃ.

13.8c kaṇvaṃ: L1c kaṇvan. See **§7.9a** for L1c final nasal.

13.8d śataghasrādi*ka*°: Ed K śataghastrādikaṃ (?); L1c śataghastrādhipa°; L2 śatadyastrādikaṃ (?). L2 due to *Devanāgarī* gh>dy.

13.8d °prabhaṃ (L2 prabhuṃ).

13.9a sarvāḥ: Bm M sarvā. See **§7.9b** for Bm M final *saṃdhi*.

13.9b svavṛttāntaṃ: L1c savṛtāntaṃ; (Bm svavṛtāntaṃ).

13.9c See 11.32b, 15.11b.

13.9c gatir: L2 gatiṃ.

13.9c no: Ed L2 Bm M K bho.

13.9d ninditānāṃ: Bm niditānāṃ (?).

13.9d ca mādṛśāṃ: Ed K ca māṭṭaśāṃ (?); L1c mamādṛśāṃ; Bm M mahādṛśāṃ

13.10b naḥ: Bm M taḥ. Bm M due to *Devanāgarī* n~t.

13.10[1] Ed K insert: śaunaka uvāca. L1c inserts: kaṇvaḥ. L2 inserts: śaunakaḥ. See 13.10[2].

13.10c garbhiṇyā: L1c gārbhiṇyaṃ.

13.10d kṛpāḷur (Ed Bm M K kṛpālur).

13.10[2] kaṇvaḥ: Bm M śaunaka uvāca (Bm śaunakovāca). See 13.10[1].

13.11a upatyakāyāṃ (Bm M utpatyakāyāṃ).

13.11a kroḍādreḥ: Ed K kroḍādre; L2 kroḍādreḥr; Bm M kroḍādrer. Ed K might be explained best perhaps by peculiar final *saṃdhi*. See **§7.9b**.

13.11b āsāte: L2 Bm M āsate.

13.11b śaṃkarācyutau: L2 śaṃkaracyutau; M śaṃkarācyute.

13.11d sahya°: L1c saṇhyā°.

13.11d °samudbhavā: L2 °samudbhavaṃ; Bm M °samudbhavāṃ.

13.12a tasyāḥ: L2 Bm M tasya.

13.12a tapasyantaṃ: L1c tapasyastaṃ.
13.12b °kulāntakaṃ: M °kulāṅkante (?). Metathesis.
13.12d vrajata: L2 vrajataṃ.
13.13a śrutvā (L2 śṛtvā). See §**6.4** for L2 Cru>Cṛ.
13.13b muniṃ: L1c munin; L2 munir. See §**7.9a** for L1c ṃ~n.
13.13c °sindhus: L2 Bm M °sindhuḥ.
13.14b See 9.57b, 10.10d, 12.41b, 16.3b, 18.3d.
13.14c-13.17b See 9.58a-9.60d, 12.43cd.
13.14c *da*dṛśur: Ed L2 Bm M K īdṛśaṃ; L1c idṛśur. Emendation>L1c>Ed L2 Bm M K. *Devanāgarī* da>i in L1c.
13.14c hṛṣṭāḥ: Ed L2 Bm M K dṛṣṭvā.
13.14d tasyāntikam: M tasyāṅkitam. Metathesis.
13.14d upāga*man*: Ed L1c K upāviśan; L2 upāgamat; Bm M upāyayuḥ. Emendation based on *Devanāgarī* alternation of 'n' and 't.'
13.15a mahābāho: Ed L2 Bm M K mahābhāga.
13.15c duḥkhān (L1c duḥkhāṃ). See §**7.9a** for L1c final ṃ = n.
13.15c nas: Bm M naḥs. See §**7.9b** for Bm M final *saṃdhi*.
13.15c vibho: L1c mune.
13.15d . . . . . duḥsa*hāt*: Ed L2 K bhaṅgamān(?) eva duḥkhadāt; L1c bhaṅgamāleva(?) duḥsahān; Bm M bhaṅgamān(?) eva duḥkhadān.
13.16a ittham: L1c ikṣam (?).
13.16a ākranditāḥ: L2 ākranditā. See §**7.9b** for final *saṃdhi*.
13.16a petuḥ: L1c petu. See §**7.9b** for final *saṃdhi*.
13.16b pādopānte: L2 M pādaupānte (?); Bm pāndaupānte (?).
13.16c tvad*āgatā*: Ed Bm M K tvayā dattā; L1c tvad āyattā (?); L2 tvad avāttā (?).
13.16d °kāriṇ*yaḥ*: All MSS °kāriṇaḥ.
13.17b hataśriyaḥ: L1c hatastriyaḥ; L2 hataśriyaṃ; Bm M hataḥ śriyaṃ.
13.17[1] śaunakaḥ: Ed K śaunaka uvāca; Bm M omit. See 13.17[2].
13.17d kṛpāḷur (Ed Bm M K kṛpālur).
13.17[2] Bm M insert: śaunaka uvāca (Bm śaunakovāca). See 13.17[1]

13.18a svaº: L2 omits, and makes up for the missing syll. in following *pāda* (13.18b).
13.18b sāntvayan vākyam āha saḥ: Ed sāntvayām āsa bhārgavaḥ; (L1c sāntvāyan . . . , L2 sāntvayaṃn āvakyam . . .).
13.18c See 9.61c.
13.18c uddharann iva: Ed Bm M K udvahann iva; L2 uddharaṃ naiva; (L1c uddharaṃn iva). See **§7.9a** for L1c (+L2) final ṃ = n.
13.18c netrābhyām (K netrābhyāṃm).
13.18d See 9.70b, 12.45b, 13.23d.
13.19a saṃprāptā: Bm M saṃprāpta.
13.19b sarvaṃ: L1c sarva.
13.19b suvratāḥ: L2 suvrata.
13.19c kṣa*ṇār*dhe 'pi: Ed L2 Bm M K kṣaṇārdhena; L1c kṣaṇāddhe 'pi (?).
13.19c na †*syād*†: Ed L1c K naśye (?); Bm nasyad (?); L2 M nasyed (?).
13.19d kurutāº: L1c rutāº (?). L1c omits syll.
13.19d ºādhunā: K ºadhunāḥ.
13.19[1] L1c L2 insert: nāryaḥ. Bm M insert: nārya ūcuḥ. See 13.20[1].
13.20a karābhyām (L1c karābhyāṃm).
13.20a añjalīº: Ed L2 K añjaliṃ; Bm M añjuliṃ (?).
13.20a ºkṛtvā: L1c ºkṛtya.
13.20b ºsaṃmukhe: Bm M ºsanmukhe.
13.20[1] nāryaḥ: All MSS omit. See 13.19[1].
13.20c mahāprājña: L2 mahāprājñā.
13.20d dayāḷo (Ed Bm M K dayālo).
13.21a ºjanmaº: L1c ºjamaº (?).
13.21a vṛttaṃ: L1c vṛtta; Bm omits.
13.21b bhujyate: Ed K bhuñjyate (?); L1c bhujyante.
13.21b īdṛśaṃ: L1c L2 īdṛśāṃ.
13.21c parityaktā: L2 Bm M parityaktāḥ.
13.21d mandaº: L1c mandada[?]. L1c two or three extra syll.
13.21d ºbhāgyā: Bm M ºbhāgya.
13.22a-13.23d. See 9.68c-9.70b.

13.22a prāṇān: L2 Bm M praṇā° (?).
13.22a moktum: K mo[-]m.
13.22a adhairyatvād: Bm M adhairyatvāt; (L2 ayairyatvād). L2 due to *Devanāgarī* dh>y.
13.22b niyater: L1c viyate; Bm M niyate.
13.23b pālayāsmān: Bm M pālayāsma.
13.23^{1} Ed K insert: śaunaka uvāca. L1c inserts: śaunakaḥ. L2 Bm M omit. See 13.23^{2}.
13.23c śrutvā (L2 śṛtvā). See **§7.4** for L2 ru>ṛ.
13.23d See 9.70b, 12.45b, 13.18d.
13.23d abhayaṃ: Ed K cābhayaṃ.
13.23^{2} †*paraśurāmaḥ*†: Bm M śaunaka uvāca (Bm śaunakovāca). See 13.23^{1}. It seems more likely that if there is the introduction of a speaker's name it be that of our emendation rather than 'śaunakaḥ' at 13.23^{1}. Statements beginning like 13.23cd are frequent after direct quotes, but they always follow the quote directly without the interpolation of the speaker's name. See 9.70ab, 14.17ab and 14.18cd for examples.
13.24a ṣaḍyojanād: L1c ṣaḍyojanā; Bm ṣaṣṭhojanā (?); M ṣaṣvyojanā (?). Difference between Bm and M due to *Devanāgarī*?
13.24b gokarṇeśasya: L2 gorkarṇeśasya.
13.24d . . . . . maṇḍitaḥ: Ed L2 Bm M K yojanadvaya°; L1c yojanahaya°. Sense?
13.24^{1} L1c inserts:
tatra sthānaṃ prakurvantyaḥ grāmasthānāṃ praśāsanāt /
13.25a sthānaṃ: L1c vāsaṃ.
13.25a prakurvantu: M prakurvanti; K prakurvantā (?).
13.25b nirbhītyā: L1c nirbhityā (?).
13.25c vihāya: Ed Bm M K vivāha°; L2 vidhāya.
13.25d vinā: M vitā (?). *Devanāgarī* n>t.
13.25d °yakaṃ (L2 °yyakaṃ).
13.25^{1} L1c L2 insert:
dāsyāmi dhanurākāralañchanaṃ śubhahetukaṃ /
L2 has one variant reading for this half vs.:
°ākāra°: L2 °ākāraṃ.

See n. to translation at this point.
13.26a śrotrayoḥ: Ed śreṣṭha yo; Bm M śreṣṭha yoḥ.
13.26a samyag: L2 Bm M samyak
13.26b ākalpāntaṃ: L1c L2 ākalpāntad (?); Bm M ākalpante.
13.26c saṃjātānāṃ (Bm saṃjātānā).
13.27a tu tanujāṃ: L1c tanujānā; L2 tantujānāṃ; Bm M manūjānāṃ (?).
13.27bc Ed Bm M K omit.
13.27b kāryaṃ (L2 kārya).
13.27c itthaṃ: L1c ikṣaṃ (?).
13.27d varaṃ datvā: L1c va[?]ṃtvā (?). L1c omits syll.?
13.28a paśyantāṃ: L1c paśyatāḥ tāḥ (?).
13.28b °adhīyata: K °adhīyataḥ (?); (L2 °adhīyyata).
13.28c śrutvā (L2 śṛtvā). See **§7.4** fir K2 ru>ṛ.
13.28d samupāviśan: L1c K samupāviśat. *Devanāgarī* n~t.
13.29a sthānaṃ: L1c sthānāṃ.
13.29b sthānām: L1c sthānam
13.29b anujñayā: Ed L2 Bm M K arājñayā.
13.29c nyavasan: Ed Bm M K nyavasad; (L2 nyavasaṃn). Probably L1c L2>nyavasat>Ed Bm M K. *Devanāgarī* t~n.
13.30a kāścit: L2 kaścit.
13.30a kanyāḥ: L1c L2 Bm M kanyāṃ (L2 kaṃnyāṃ).
13.30b kāścit: Ed K kāṉścit.
13.30b putrān (K putrāṃ).
13.30b mahābalān: Ed L2 Bm M K prapedire.
13.30d cakrur (L2 cakṛr). See **§7.4** for L2 ru>ṛ.
13.31b rājante: L1c rājānta; L2 rājate; Bm M rāreta (?).
13.31b bhuvane bata: L1c bhuvaner cata (?); L2 bhuvane cata (?); Bm M bhuvaneva tat. Ed K>L1c L2. Ed K or L1c L2>Bm M.
13.31[1] śaunakaḥ: Ed K omit; Bm M śaunaka uvāca (Bm śaunakovāca).
13.31c tāsu: L2 Bm M tat su°.
13.31c mahābhāga: Ed L2 K mahābhāgāḥ.
13.32c tatpāpavinivṛtty°: L1c tasya pāpanivṛtty°.
13.32d mārtāṇḍam: Ed L2 Bm K mārttaṇḍam.

13.33b punar anyaṃ: Ed K purenyaṃ (?) na.

Colophons:

Ed K	iti śrīskandapurāṇe sahyādrikhaṇḍe uttararahasye śūdrotpattir nāma trayodaśo 'dhyāyaḥ.
L1c	iti śrīskande sahyādrau pātityakathanaṃ.
L2	iti śrīsaṉhyādrau uparibhāge dvanavatiśatatamo 'dhyāya[ḥ].
Bm	iti śrīsahyādre trayodaśo 'dhyāyaḥ.
M	iti śrīsahyādre° trayodaśo 'dhyāyaḥ.

CHAPTER SIX (Skh.u. 14)

14.0 Ed inserts: atha caturdaśo 'dhyāyaḥ. Bm inserts: śrīgaṇeśāya namaḥ.
14.0[1] śaunakaḥ: Ed Bm M K śaunaka uvāca.
14.1b parityaktā: Bm parityāya; M parityā. M omits syll.
14.1c °kanyā° (L2 Bm M °kaṃnyā°).
14.2a °viṉśaty°: Bm °viś°. Bm omits syll.
14.2a °arbhakānāṃ (Bm °arbhakānā).
14.2b See 14.27c-14.28b.
14.2b ḍoḷānāṃ: Ed K ḍolanā (?); Bm M ḍolānā (?).
14.2b †sakuṭumbināṃ†: Ed K sakuṭumbinī; Bm M sakuṭumbini (?).
14.2c satataṃ: L2 satatraṃ (?); Bm satata°.
14.2c duś°: Bm M duḥś°. See §**7.9b** for Bm M reading.
14.2d vibhavaṃ: L2 vipravaṃ (?). See 10.2d
14.3a dhvajotsave: Bm M dhvajove (?). Bm M omit syll.
14.3b narādhipe: Bm nadhipe (?). Bm omits syll.
14.3c samāyātāḥ: Ed Bm M K samāyātā (Bm masāyātā). Bm metathesis.
14.3d †dvijā*da*yaḥ†: Ed L2 M K dvijātayaḥ; Bm dvijātayā.
14.4a brahmakṣat*ri*ya°: Ed K brāhmaṇakṣatra°; Bm M brāhmaṇakṣatri° (Bm bāhmaṇa°); (L2 °kṣatraya°).
14.4b vivarṇāḥ: Bm M vivarṇā. See §**7.9b** for Bm M final *saṃdhi*.
14.4c cotsavaṃ: L2 cotsa[n+?+ḥ]vaṃ (?).
14.5a kācit: Ed Bm M K kāścit.
14.5b kanyā: Ed K kanyāḥ; (L2 kaṃnyā).
14.5b °saṃbhavā: Ed K °saṃbhavāḥ.
14.5c vyastastā°: Ed L2 K vyatyastā°.
14.6a gujjara°: Ed K gurjara°; Bm M gurjarā (?).
14.6a °gāḥ: Bm °gā.
14.6b vañcayitvātha: Bm M vañcayitvā yathā (Bm vañcaïtvā). Bm M extra syll. See §**7.4** for Bm spelling.
14.6b bālakīṃ: L2 bālakī; Bm M bali (?). Bm M omit syll.

14.6[1] L2 inserts: bālakā.
14.6d yayur: L2 yayau; Bm yayu (?).
14.6d gṛhān: L2 gṛhāt; Bm M gṛhaṃ. L2 due to *Devanāgarī* t~n.
14.7a bāndhavās: L2 bāndhavāḥs. See **§7.9b** for L2 final *saṃdhi*.
14.7a tasyāḥ: Ed Bm M K tasyā.
14.7b mātṛ°: L2 Bm M mātā.
14.7b °bhrātrādayas: L2 M bhrātādayas (?); Bm bhrātāyas (?). Bm omits syll.
14.7c bālakīṃ: Bm M bālakiṃ (?).
14.7d duḥkhaṃ: L2 Bm M khinnaṃ (L2 kiṃnaṃ). See **§7.9a** for L2 reading.
14.7d †avā*pire*†, or avāpuste: Ed K avāpa te; L2 Bm M ivābhavat. L2 Bm M different source?
14.8b kleśayitvā (Bm kleśaïtvā). See **§7.4** for Bm spelling.
14.8c dhūrtās: Bm M dhūtāṉs. *Devanāgarī* superscript 'r' read as *anusvāra* for following syll.
14.8d puḷindajāṃ (Ed Bm M K pulindajāṃ).
14.9b udvāhaḥ kriyate: L2 udvāhakīṃ kr[i/ī]yāṃ (?); Bm udvāhaḥ kiṃ kriyaḥ (?); M udvāha kiṃ kriyāḥ (?). L2 Bm M source?
14.9c śaba*rīṃ*: All MSS śabarī.
14.9d cakradevena: L2 caturdevena.
14.9d coditāḥ: Ed Bm K coditā.
14.10c °āpāṅgī: Bm °āpāgī (?).
14.10d tārādhipanibhānanān: Ed K tārādhipakalānanā; Bm M tārādhipatim ānanāṃ; (L2 tārādhipanibhānanāṃ [= °nān]). See **§7.9a** for probable explanation of L2 declension, specifically ṃ = n.
14.11a prāpa: Bm M prāyaḥ.
14.11cd See 9.14d, 9.71cd, 10.9ab, 11.4ab, 12.5ab, 16.19c, 17.22cd, 17.52a, 18.11ab.
14.11c itthaṃ: Bm ityaṃ (?). *Devanāgarī* tth>ty.
14.11c pravartamānāyāḥ: Ed Bm K pravartamānāyā.
14.11[1] śaunakaḥ: Ed K omit. Bm M śaunaka uvāca.
14.12a °otsavaṃ (Bm °otsaṃva). Bm metathesis.

14.12b °sthā: Bm °stā (?).
14.12c nāryā: Ed K nāryaḥ; Bm M nāryāḥ.
14.12c samāyuktāḥ: Ed Bm M K samāyuktās.
14.12d pari*var*titāḥ: Ed Bm M K parivāritāḥ; L2 parivārtitāḥ (?). parivartitāḥ>L2>Ed Bm M K.
14.13a viprāḥ: Ed Bm M K viprā.
14.13b utsavaṃ: Bm utsava (?).
14.13c vyādhaḥ: L2 vyādhaḥs. See **§7.9b** for L2 final *saṃdhi*.
14.13c 'pi svabandhubhyaḥ: Ed M K 'pi sabandhubhyaḥ; Bm pīvabadhubhyaḥ (?).
14.13d sahasāgamat: Bm M sahamāgaman (?). *Devanāgarī* s> m, t>n.
14.14b bandhūn: K badhūn (?).
14.14b dṛṣṭavān: L2 draṣṭavān (?).
14.14d duḥkhitā: M duḥkhitāḥ.
14.15b duḥkhitā: L2 duḥkhitāḥ.
14.15cd Ed Bm M K omit. L2 reads:
pitā jaṃnamanābhūtvā tāṃ gataṃ tu pracakrame /
14.16a martyāḥ: Ed K martyā.
14.16b °kāraṃ: Bm °kāra (?).
14.16c vadhūr: L2 Bm vadhū; M vadhūṃ.
14.16c nīcā: L2 n[? ?]ā; Bm M nico.
14.16d vañcayitvā (L2 Bm vañcaïtvā). See **§7.4** for L2 Bm spelling.
14.16d †pra*yas*yati†: Ed Bm M K prahāsyati; L2 prayāsyati.
14.17a te: Bm M tā.
14.17b rājñe: L2 rājñāṃ.
14.17b vārtāṃ: Bm M vārtā.
14.17b nyaveda*yan*: Ed K nivedayan; L2 Bm nyavedayat; M nyavedayet. *Devanāgarī* n>t.
14.17c bhūpo: M bhūyo. *Devanāgarī* p>y.
14.17c 'tivismayo: Bm M 'tivismito.
14.17d tām: L2 Bm tam.
14.17d āhūya: Bm āhaya.
14.17d pulindajāṃ: Bm pulidinaṃ (?); M pulindinaṃ (?).
14,18a °patnītvam: L2 pa[?]tvam; Bm M patnīṃ ca.
14.18b pra*yas*yasi: Ed Bm K prayāsyasi; L2 M prayāsyati.

14.18c rāja°: L2 rājñā; Bm M rājñi,
14.18c śrutvā (L2 śṛtvā). See **§7.4** for L2 ru>ṛ.
14.18d puḷindajā: L2 puḷindajāḥ; pulindajaḥ; (Ed Bm K pulindajā).
14.18[1] puḷinda*jā*: Ed K pulindajovāca; L2 puḷindaḥ; Bm M omit. See 14.19[1].
14.19a madīyā: L2 madīyya.
14.19a bālā: L2 Bm M bāle.
14.19b °ābhūd: L2 M °ābhū (?); Bm °āmū (?). Bm due to *Devanāgarī* bh>m.
14.19b °otsave: Ed K °otsavaiḥ.
14.19[1] Bm M insert: pulindajovāca. See 14.18[1].
14.19c idānīṃ: Bm idānī (?).
14.20ab See 17.14ab.
14.20b kuryāṃ: Bm M kuryād (?).
14.20b anugrahāt: L2 Bm M anujñayā. Synonym.
14.20d sudhīrā: L2 su[? ?]; Bm M sudhīraḥ.
14.20d sā sutānvitā: L2 sutayānvitaḥ; Bm sutayānỵitaḥ. Bm due to Telugu or Kanarese subscript Cv>Cy.
14.21a-14.21d M omits here, leaving a mark only to represent this vs., but inserts the vs. after 14.22ab.
14.21a putra°: L2 Bm M putraiḥ.
14.21a °*pa*tisamāyuk*tā*: Ed K °brātṛsamāyukto; L2 pratibhir(?) yutayā; Bm M paribhir(?) yutayā.
14.21b vyā*dhā*: Ed Bm M K vyādha; L2 vyādha. See **§7.9b** for L2 final *saṃdhi*.
14.21c tas*yā*: All MSS tasya.
14.21c °ākarṇya: Bm °ākarṇa.
14.21d nṛpatir: Bm nṛpati°
14.22a nirdahann (L2 nirdahaṃn). See **§7.9a** for ṃ = n.
14.22[1] M inserts 14.21ab. See above.
14.22c abravīt: Bm K abravī (?).
14.22d vadata: L2 vadatu
14.22d bhūsurāḥ: Bm bhūsuraḥ.
14.22[2] śaunakaḥ: Ed K śaunaka uvāca; Bm M omit. See 14.23[1].

14.23a-14.23c K omits from 'dvijātayaḥ' in 14.23a to 'rājā' in 14.24c.
14.23ab sarve nyūcur, or perhaps sarvā nyūcur: Ed sarvānyūcur (?); L2 sarvān nyucu (?); Bm sarve trucu (?); sarve trūcur. See 15.3a and see **§8.5** for the possibility of reading 'sarvā.'
14.23b bhītā°: L2 bhītyā° (?).
14.23b °ātivihvalāḥ: Ed °ātivihvalaḥ.
14.23[1] Bm M insert śaunaka uvāca. See 14.22[2].
14.23c āgaś ca: Ed āgaccha.
14.24a pādayos: Bm M yādayo (?). *Devanāgarī* p>y.
14.24b petuḥ: Bm patuḥ (?).
14.24b °narādhamāḥ: Ed Bm M °ratādhamāḥ (Bm M °ratāṃdhamāḥ). Ed Bm M K probably due to *Devanāgarī* n>r and r>t.
14.24c °prājñaḥ: Bm M °prājño.
14.25a svīkṛtya: L2 svī/svā (both vowel modifications are written) or hvī° (?); Bm svākūtya (?).
14.25b °sthebhyaḥ (Bm °stebhyaḥ).
14.25cd †parityāg*ā*parityāgaṃ† tair eva tu: Ed L2 K partyāgaparityāgaṃ . . . ; Bm M parityāgaparityāgatyāgavairair (?). See 12.35ab. Bm M extra syll. See **§7.11**.
14.25d vidhīyatāṃ (L2 vidhīyyatāṃ). See **§7.4** for L2.
14.26b nijapattanaṃ. Read nijamandiraṃ? See **§7.11**.
14.26cd See 12.36ab.
14.26c °vāsibhyo: L2 Bm M °vāsibhyaḥ.
14.26d vrīḷā°: Ed K vrīḍā°; (L2 Bm vrīlā°).
14.26d °āvanata°: Bm M °āvana°. Bm M omit syll.
14.26d °mastakāḥ: Ed K °mastakaḥ.
14.27a sahasā: L2 sadasā (?); Bm M sadṛśa. Bm M + L2 due to *Devanāgarī* h>dṛ.
14.27a pāpināṃ: M pāpīnāṃ (?).
14.27c saṃparkiṇāṃ: Bm saparkaṇāṃ (?); M saṃparkaṇāṃ (?).
14.28a °arbhakāṇāṃ: Bm °arbhakāṇaṃ (?).
14.29a teṣāṃ: L2 steṣāṃ (?).
14.29a grāmād: L2 grāma°.

14.29a bahir°: L2 °cahir°. L2 due to Telugu or Kanarese script b>c.

14.29b tadvad . . .†*tvaritaṃ*†: Ed Bm M K tadvad no maya vāriṇā; L2 tadvad gomaya vāriṇā. Verb needed.

14.29c āsuḥ: Ed K āsa; Bm M āsur.

14.29d mahābhāgā: Ed Bm M K mahābhāga.

14.29d dṛḍha°: L2 dṛḍhī° (?).

14.30a tebhyaḥ śrāddhaṃ: L2 tebhyaś cadhaṃ (?).

14.30b kumbha°: Bm M kumbhi° (?).

14.30d deyaṃ: Bm deya (?).

14.30d īdṛśāṃ: Bm M īdṛśaṃ.

14.31a mahābhāgāḥ: Ed K mahābhāgā; Bm M mahābhāga.

14.31[1] śaunakaḥ: Ed Bm M K śaunaka uvāca (Bm śaunakovāca).

14.31d °triṉśad°: Bm °priṉśad° (?); K °triṉśat°.

14.31d °vāsaināṃ: Bm M °vāsinaḥ.

14.32a °yuktānāṃ: K °yuktānā (?).

14.32b māhātmyaṃ: Bm mahāmyaṃ.

14.32d narādhamāḥ: Bm narādhamā. See **§7.9b** for Bm final *saṃdhi*.

14.33a Bm M substitute 14.34c:
tatrāpi samakāle tu.

14.33b °karma°: Bm M °dharma°.

14.33b °bahiṣ°: L2 °cahiṣ. L2 due to Telugu or Kanarese script b>c.

14.33d prāpnuvanti hi: Bm M anugacchati.

14.34a prāyaścitta° (Bm prāyaścita).

14.34a °vidhānaṃ tu: L2 °vidhānāni; Bm M °vidhānena.

14.34c Bm M substitue 14.33a with one *saṃdhi* change:
sthānahīnāḥ parityaktā.
For change in final *saṃdhi* see **§7.9b**.

14.34d °mārtaṇḍa°: K °mātaṅga°.

14.35b kāryā: Bm M kārya.

14.35b vicāraṇā: L2 vicāraṇī.

14.35c bahunā°: L2 cahunā° (?). L2 due to Telugu or Kanarese script b>c.

14.35d grāmam anyaṇ: K grāmabhanyaṇ (?). K due to *Devanāgarī* m>bh.

Colophons:

Ed K iti śrīskandapurāṇe sahyādrikhaṇḍe uttararahasye pātityagrāmanirṇayo nāma caturdaśo 'dhyāyaḥ.

L2 iti śrīsaṇhyādrau uparibhāge pātityagrāmnirṇayaṃ nāma trinavatiśatatamo 'dhyāyaḥ.

Bm iti sahyādrikhaṇḍe pātityagrāmanirṇaya *nā*ma caturdaśaḥ.

M iti śrīsahyādrikhaṇḍe pātityagrāmanirṇaya nāma caturdaśaḥ.

CHAPTER SEVEN (Skh.u. 15)

15.0 Ed inserts: atha pañcadaśo 'dhyāyaḥ. Bm inserts: śrī-gaṇeśāya namaḥ.

15.0[1] śatānīkaḥ: All MSS except L3 omit.

15.1 All MSS except L3 omit.

15.1b °*ge*ha°: L3 °gaiha° (?).

15.1[1] śaunakaḥ: Ed Bm M K śaunaka uvāca (Bm śaunako-vāca); L2 omits.

15.2a asty anyat: Ed K anyas ti (?); Bm M anyat tu.

15.2c nāga°: All MSS except L3 read 'nānā°.' See 15.13b variant readings. *Devanāgarī* g>n.

15.2c grāmaṃ: Ed K °grāmāt; Bm M °grāma; L3 grāman. See **§7.9b** for possible Bm M final *saṃdhi*. See **§7.8** for L3 strictly correct *saṃdhi* (Whitney 1889: 71[213c]).

15.2c tad: L3 tam.

15.2d °karma°: Bm M °dharmād; L3 °karmma°.

15.2d °kṛtaṃ: Bm °kṛtāḥ; M °kṛtaḥ.

15.3a L3 reads: rāmeṇa sṛṣṭās te pūrvaṃ. Paraphrase.

15.3a °sṛṣṭās: L2 °śṛṣṭā (?); Bm M °sṛṣṭas. See **§7.9b** for L2 final *saṃdhi*.

15.3a pūrvāḥ, or pūrve: Ed K pūrvār. See 14.23a and see **§8.5** for L2 Bm M form.

15.3b ahyūṣuḥ: Bm M adhyuṣuḥ (?); L3 hy addhyūṣuḥ.

15.3b †sasth*āna*ṃ ca te†: Ed L2 K saṃsthalaṃ ca te; Bm M sasthalaṃ ca te; L3 seṃsthāḷa ca te. *Devanāgarī* Cān> Cal?

15.3c mayūravarmā°: L2 L3 mayūravarma° (L3 mayūravar-mma°).

15.3c °nītānā: L3 °nītebhyo.

15.3d viprāṇāṃ: L3 viprebhyaḥ.

15.3d kara°: L2 phara°; Bm M gara°.

15.3d °dāyakāḥ: Ed K °dāyakaḥ; Bm M °dāyakān.

15.4a ullikhan: All MSS except L3 read 'ullikhaṃ.' Incorrect interpretation of final nasal. See **§7.9a**.

15.4a tatkṣitiṃ: Ed L2 M K tatkṣaṇāḥ (= takṣaṇāḥ?); Bm tatkṣaṇā; (L3 ta kṣitiṃ). See **§7.9b** for Bm final *saṃdhi.*

15.4b ār*ā*makāriṇaḥ: Ed L2 K dārāma(?)kāriṇaḥ; Bm rāmam akāriṇaḥ; M grāmam akāriṇaḥ; (L3 ārarmakāriṇaḥ). L3 due to *Jainalipi*-nonstandard *Devanāgarī* superscript ā> superscript r. See 15.6c and **§7.9a**.

15.4c °sūnyāḥ: Ed K °sūnyās.

15.4d tantumātrā: Bm M saṃtu(?)mātṛ°; L3 tumātṛ°. L3 skips syll.

15.5b tad viduḥ: K ta[?]dhaḥ (?); L3 taṃ viduḥ.

15.5d °grāmābhidhayaiva: Ed K °grāmā vidhayaiva; L3 °grāmābhidhayeva.

15.6b śruti° (L2 śṛti°). See **§7.4** for L2 ru>ṛ.

15.6c †anāhār*yā*maśākena†: Ed K teṣāṃ hārāmāṉsakena; L2 M enārhārā(?)maśākena; Bm enāharimaśākhena (?); L3 anarhārāmaśākhena. L3 *Jainalipi* or nonstandard *Devanāgarī* superscript ā>superscript r. See 15.4b and **§7.9a**.

15.7b medhāvī: Bm medhāvi (?); L3 svapurīṃ.

15.7b ballabhīṃ: Ed K balabhī; Bm M balibhī.

15.7b prati: L2 pratī (?).

15.7[1] Ed K insert ½ vs. o f commentary of which the second *pāda* is corrupt. L2 inserts the first *pāda* of this commentary and substitutes the words 'tv ardhaḥ' for the second *pāda*. See Appendix B.

15.7c rāmeṇa: L3 rameṇa.

15.7c vipraiḥ: Ed K L3 viprair.

15.7d vāhayitvā (L2 Bm vāhaïtvā). See **§7.4** for L2 Bm reading.

15.7d sva°: All MSS except L3 read 'ca.'

15.8a śiṣṭān vipr*ān*: All MSS except L3 read 'śiṣṭānvitān'; (L3 śiṣṭān vipran).

15.8a samādāya: L3 samādaya.

15.8b punaḥ: L2 L3 puna (?).

15.8b āyayau: Bm M āyayauḥ (?).

15.8d bhārgavanirmitāḥ: L2 bhāgavinirmitāḥ; Bm L3 °nimitāḥ (?).

15.9b sādhitā: Bm sādhitāṃ.

15.9b bhūr iyaṃ: Bm hariyaṃ (?); (L3 bhūr iyan [nṛpa]). See **§7.8** for L3 strictly correct *saṃdhi*. See 15.2c above.
15.9cd-15.10ab All MSS except L3 omit.
15.10a datta°: L3 darta°. Hypercorrection.
15.10a °vāstū*nā*m (L3 °vāstūnam).
15.10b ki*la* (L3 kilā).
15.10c avahṛtya: Ed Bm M K āhṛtya tat; L2 ādṛtya tat. *Devanāgarī* h>d.
15.10c kathaṃ: Bm M L3 katha (?).
15.11a bhavatu: Ed K vadatu.
15.11a medāvī: Bm M medhāvi (?).
15.11b See 11.32b. 13.9c.
15.11b vidhīyatāṃ: Bm M vidhīyate; L3 vidhiyatāṃ; (L2 vidhīyyatāṃ).
15.11[1] śaunakaḥ: Ed Bm M K śaunaka uvāca (Bm śaunakovāca).
15.11c vākyam: L3 vāṇīṃ. Synonym.
15.11c athākarṇya: L3 samārṇya (for samākarṇya). Synonym. L3 omits syll.
15.11d sāntvayann: L2 sātvayaṃn (?). See **§7.9a** for ṃ = n.
15.12a grāma°: All MSS except L3 read 'grāmaṃ.'
15.12a °catuṣṭayaṃ: L2 °tvatuṣṭayaṃ (?). L2 due to *Jainalipi*-nonstandard *Devanāgarī* c>tv? See 10.46a, 12.47c. See **§7.9a**.
15.12c nṛpatiḥ: L2 nṛpati; L3 sa nṛpa. L3 synonym.
15.12d dadau: L3 tai(?)dā.
15.13ab This is the reading of L3. The other MSS appear to reconstruct to:
kuḍālakaṃ ca padikaṃ madiṃ nāgābhidhaṃ tathā /
There are for this the following variants:
padikaṃ: Bm M yadikaṃ. Bm M due to *Devanāgarī* p> y.
madiṃ nāgābhidhaṃ: Ed maṭṭīnāgābhidhaṃ; L2 madiṃ nāmābhidaṃ (?); Bm M maddināgābhidaṃ (?); K maṭṭanāgābhidhaṃ. See 15.2c.
15.13c dvijebhyaś (Bm dvijabhyaś).
15.13d śeṣāṃ: Ed M K śeṣaṃ.

15.13d bhūmiṃ pradattavān: Bm bhūmipradattavān; L3 viśvajarāmakān (?).

15.13[1] śaunakaḥ: Ed Bm M K L3 omit.

15.14a viprāḥ: Bm M viprā; L3 vipra. See **§7.9b** for Bm M final *saṃdhi*.

15.14b sthitvā grāma°: L3 āsa te te (?).

15.14c °rahitā ye tu: L3 °tiratās (for °rahitās) te tu (?). L3 metathesis. Malayalam script h>t.

15.14d rājante bhuvaneśvara: Bm M rājante bhuvaneśvarāḥ; L3 rājātarājā (for rājādhirājā) śavara (for īśvara). L3 partial synonym based on misinterpretation of text. L3 fails to apply *saṃdhi*.

15.15b L3 substitutes: grāmam anyaṃ vadāmi te.

Colophons:

Ed K iti śrīskandapurāṇe sahyādrikhaṇḍe uttararahasye pātityagrāmanirṇayo nāma pañcadaśo 'dhyāyaḥ.

L2 iti śrīsaṉh[y]ādrau uparibhāge pātityagrāmanirṇayaṃ catuḥsaptatiśatamo 'dhyāyaḥ.

Bm iti śrīskandapurāṇe pātityagrāmanirṇayaṃ nāma pañcadaśo 'dhyāyaḥ.

M iti śrīskandapurāṇe pātityagrāmanirṇayaṃ nāma pañcadaśaḥ.

L3 ity uparibhāge grāmanir*ṇa*ye pātitye ṣaṭtriṉśa*d a*dhyāyaḥ.

CHAPTER EIGHT (Skh.u. 16)

16.0 Ed inserts: atha ṣoḍaśo 'dhyāyaḥ. Bm inserts: śrīgaṇeśāya namaḥ.

16.0[1] śaunakaḥ: Ed Bm M K śaunaka uvāca (Bm śaunakovāca).

16.1b anyad: Ed L2 K anyaṃ.

16.1c āhuḥ: L2 Bm M āhu. See **§7.9b** for L2 Bm M final *saṃdhi*.

16.1d Hypermetric. Nine syll.

16.1d sītāyāś cottara°: Bm M sītāyottara° (?).

16.2a °hatyāṃ: L2 °hantyāṃ (?).

16.2d °manāḥ: Bm °manā. See **§7.9b** for Bm final *saṃdhi*.

16.3a āsīt purā: Bm M āsīsurā (?). Bm M due to *Devanāgarī* tp>s.

16.3a bhūpaḥ: Bm bhūyaḥ. *Devanāgarī* p>y.

16.3b See 9.57b, 10.10d, 12.41b, 13.14b, 18.3d.

16.3b °dyutiḥ: L2 °dyatiḥ (?).

16.3c dhanvinām: Bm M dhanvīm (?). Bm M omit syll.

16.3c agraṇīḥ: L2 agraṇī. See **§7.9b** for L2 final *saṃdhi*.

16.3c śreṣṭhaḥ: Ed Bm M K śreṣṭho.

16.3d vidur: L2 vidu.

16.4a °samṛddhyāḍhyāṃ: L2 °samṛddhānyāṃ; Bm °samūddhāḍhyo (?); M °samṛddhāḍhyo. Bm due to ṛ>ū in either *Devanāgarī* or Telugu or Kanarese script.

16.4b nagarīṃ: Bm M nagarī.

16.4b °mālinīṃ: Bm °mālirnā (?); M °mālinī. Bm due to *Devanāgarī* ī>rCā.

16.4c . . . . śriyā: Ed K prajvālayan śriyā; L2 prajvalantyāṃ śriyā; Bm M prajvalatyā śriyā. Source?

16.4c dīdy*e*: Ed K dīptyā; Bm M dīptvā; (L2 dīdyā). See **§7.9a** for L2 e>ā.

16.4d All MSS read:
vāñchatīm iva saṃsthitāṃ.
See n. to translation of this vs.

16.5a °klama°: Ed K °kṛmi°. *Devanāgarī* kla>kṛ.
16.5b niṣkalaṅkāṃ: Bm M tīṣkakaṃpāṃ (?).
16.5b nirākulāṃ: Bm nitikulāṃ (?).
16.5c antaḥ°: L2 Bm ataḥ.
16.5c °yatnāḍhyāṃ: L2 °yatyānyāṃ.
16.5d °toraṇāṃ: Bm M °toraṇī (?). Bm M probably due to *Devanāgarī* ā>ī.
16.6a vṛkṣaiḥ: Bm vakṣaiḥ (?).
16.6c °pīta°: L2 °pītā°
16.6c °sitaiḥ śyāmair: L2 Bm M sitaśyāmaiḥ.
16.6d lohitaiś: Bm M lohitaś.
16.6d cāmarair: Ed K camarair; L2 Bm cāmarai. See **§7.9b** for L2 Bm final *saṃdhi*.
16.7a latāgulmaiḥ (Bm latāgulyaiḥ). *Devanāgarī* m>y.
16.7c °śākhāḥ: Ed Bm M K °śākhā. See **§7.9b** for Ed Bm M K final *saṃdhi*.
16.7d °āṅkura°: L2 Bm M °āṅkuśa°.
16.8a °saṃchannā: Bm M °saṃchinnā; (L2 saṃchaṃnnā).
16.8b nadīṣu: K nadīṣa (?).
16.8d yathā: Bm yathāḥ.
16.9a ketakā°: Bm M ketakyā° (?).
16.9a °bakuḷāḥ: L2 °bakuḷā; Bm M °bakulaiḥ; (Ed K °bakulāḥ). See **§7.9b** for L2 final *saṃdhi*.
16.9b °ārjunāḥ: Bm M °ārjunaiḥ.
16.9c cūta°: Bm cyūta°.
16.9c °nimbāś: L2 °nīpāś (?).
16.9c badarī: Bm repeats twice.
16.9d kadamba°: Bm kamandha°; M kamanda° (?).
16.9d °bakuḷā (Ed Bm M K °bakulā).
16.9d dhavāḥ: Ed K druvaṃ; Bm M druvaiḥ.
16.10a °pāṭa*lās*: Ed K °pāṭalau; L2 Bm M °pāṭalī.
16.10b °śālmalyaḥ: Bm M °śālmakyaḥ (?). Bm M due to *Devanāgarī* ly>ky?
16.10b °vañjuḷāḥ: Ed K °vañjulau; Bm M °vañculāḥ (?). Bm M due to Telugu or Kanarese script j>c.
16.10d †manoramāḥ†: Bm M manorathāḥ.
16.11a saṃphulla°: Bm M saphalaiḥ.

16.11c °madhūkāś ca: Bm M °madhūś caiva.
16.11d kuṭajā°: L2 kuṭaśā° (?); Bm M kuṭacā° (?).
16.11d °āsanāḥ: Ed K °āsanau.
16.12a °nārikeḷāś (Ed Bm M K °nārikelāś).
16.12b saptaccha*dāś* chadāḥ: Ed K saptacchadās tathā; L2 saptaladā(?) chadāḥ; Bm M saptachadaṉś cadhā (?).
16.12d śobhante: L2 śobhate; Bm śrobhitaiḥ (?); M śobhitaiḥ.
16.12d purīṃ: L2 Bm M purī.
16.13a gankdhavanti: Bm gandhavati.
16.13b phalāni: K phatāni (?). *Devanāgarī* l>t?
16.13[1] Bm M insert 16.14c and another *pāda*:
merumāndāratulyāni suvanāni śatāni ca /
16.13c Ed K read: niśitāni tato dyāni. L2 reads: nasitāni nacoṣṭhāṇī (?). Bm reads: naśtāni ca tatra stha (?). M reads only: niśitāni. Bm omits syll. Source?
16.13d sarāṉsi: Bm sarāsi (?).
16.14a bhāsante: Bm bhāsate.
16.14a °tīrthāni: L2 °tīrthāś ca.
16.14c °mandara°: Ed M K °māndara°; Bm °māndāra°. Synonyms.
16.14d bhavanāni: Ed Bm M K bhuvanāni. Synonym.
16.15a nagarīṃ: L2 Bm M nagarī.
16.15c-16.16b. Bm omits.
16.15d °vedāṅga°: M °vegāṅga° (?).
16.16a °nām*nā*: Ed M K °nāmno; L2 °nāmne.
16.16b purā: M paraḥ.
16.16c jyeṣṭhā (K jyeṣṭā).
16.16d guṇamāliṇī: Bm M guṇamāliṇi (?).
16.17a °yauvana° (L2 °yauvvana°).
16.17a °saṃpanne: Ed K °saṃpannā; Bm M °saṃpannau; (L2 °saṃpaṃnne).
16.17b bhārye: Ed K bhāryā.
16.17b °ekṣaṇe: Ed K °ekṣaṇā.
16.17c stanaṃdhayīṃ: L2 stānaṃdhuyo (?); Bm M stanaṃdhayi (?).
16.17c kaniṣṭhāya: Ed K kaniṣṭhāyāṃ; M kaniṣṭhāra (?). M reading probably due to omitting one consonant and

writing in the first consonant of the following word in its stead.

16.17d rakṣaṇaṃ: L2 rakṣaṇīyaṃ; Bm M rakṣaṇyaṃ (?). L2 extra syll.

16.17d kurute: L2 kurutā (?).

16.18a ādaratvāj jyeṣṭha°: Ed K ādaratvāj jeṣṭha° (?); L2 M ādaratvājyeṣṭha°; Bm ādaratvajveṣṭha° (?). Bm due, in part, to Telugu or Kanarese subscript y>v in 'jyeha.'

16.18b kanyām (Ed L2 K kaṃnyām).

16.18b aurasīm, or L2 Bm M aurasām.

16.18c dvitīyā: L2 dvitīyya (?).

16.18c cakra°: Bm M cakru° (?). Bm M probably due to Telugu or Kanarese script reading 'cakṛ.' See **§7.4**.

16.18d †madaṃ†: L2 [?]ṛdaṃ; K marda (?).

16.18d bhartuś: Ed K bharttuś; Bm M bhartṛś (?). Bm M perhaps due to *Devanāgarī* or Telugu or Kanarese script u>ṛ?

16.18d kurvatī: L2 Bm M kurvati.

16.19b guṇamāliṇī: Bm m guṇamālini (?).

16.19[1] śaunakaḥ: Ed K śaunaka uvāca. Bm M omit. See 16.19[2].

16.19c See 9.14d, 9.71cd, 10.9ab, 11.4ab, 12.5ab, 14.11cd, 17.22cd, 17.52a, 18.11ab.

16.19c itthaṃ: Bm ityaṃ (?). Bm due to *Devanāgarī* tth>ty.

16.19c pravartatas tasya: Bm pravartatasyātha (?).

16.19[2] Bm M insert: śaunaka uvāca (Bm śaunakovāca). See 16.19[1].

16.20a gorāṣṭra°: Ed K bhorāṣṭra°. Place?

16.20a kaścid: L2 kaścit.

16.20c athāyātaḥ: Ed K athāyātas.

16.20d tanay*āt* khinnamānasaḥ: Ed L2 M K tanayān khinnamānasaḥ (L2 khiṃna°); Bm tanayā enivana(?)mānasaḥ. Ed L2 M K due to *Devanāgarī* t>n. Bm adds two syll.

16.21b jāgaraṃ: Bm M jāgarakaṃ (?). Bm M add syll.

16.21c tasyāḥ: L2 tasyā. See **§7.9b** for L2 final *saṃdhi*.

16.21d °varṇinī: Bm M °varṇini (?).

16.22a śayanāt tūrṇam (Bm śayanā tū°).

16.22a tūrṇam: K tūrṇas.

16.22b °saṃnidhaṃ: Bm °saṃhati (?); M °saṃhitiṃ.

16.22^{1} Bm M insert 16.23cd:
taṃ śiśuṃ sahasā hatvā bhūyaḥ paryaṅkam āviśat /
śiśuṃ: Bm śiśu.
hatvā: Bm 'tvā' only.
bhūyaḥ: M bhuyaḥ.
They then repeat the half vs in its proper place.

16.22c mātsaryāt . . . . . : Ed K mātsaryatvātidīyatvād (?); L2 mātsaryātvātidīyyad; Bm M utsāryam atidīyatvād. L2 omits syll. Source?

16.22d arbha*ka*kaṃdharaṃ tadā: Ed K arbhakasya ca kaṃdharāṃ; L2 arbhakaṃ . . . ; Bm M arbhakāṃ . . . .

16.23b °ālambhya: Bm M °ālambye.

16.23b cetasā: Bm catasā (?); M tecesā (?). M metathesis.

16.23cd See 16.22^{1} above.

16.22c taṃ: Ed K tān; L2 tāṃ.

16.23d bhūyaḥ: L2 M bhuyaḥ.

16.24a °ācārā: Ed K °ācāraḥ; Bm °ārā (?). Bm omits syll.

16.24d utthāya: Ed K cotthāya; Bm M utsārya.

16.24d śayanāt tadā (Bm M śayanā ta°).

16.25a bālakīṃ, or bālakāṃ: Bm M balakā (?).

16.25b °ārditāṃ: L2 °arditaṃ (?).

16.25c āḥ: Bm M ā (?).

16.25d hatāsmīty avocata: L2 hatāsmi vidhe(?) bata; Bm hatāsmi vidhe(?) vataṃ; M hatāsmi vidhe(?) cataṃ. L2 Bm M source?

16.26a tāḍayantī: L2 tāḍayātī (?).

16.26c kṣaṇenātha: Bm kṣaṇīnātha (?); M kṣaṇinātha (?).

16.26d vilalāpāti°: Bm M lalāpātiva°.

16.27b kaniṣṭhātīvra°: Bm M kaniṣṭhātīva°.

16.27b °bheṣajaṃ: Bm °bheṣaja.

16.27c vaicitryeṇa: L2 Bm M vaicitreṇa.

16.27c †mahā*bhāgaḥ*†: Ed Bm M K mahārāja; L2 mahārājā.

16.27d pralalāpa: Ed K pralāpa ca; Bm M prayāyata (?).

16.27d °vidhaṃ: Bm M °vidhāṃ.

16.28a śrutvā (L2 śṛtvā). See **§7.4** for ru>ṛ.

16.28b khinnam *anva*bhavat: Ed L2 khinnamanābhavat (? – L2 khiṃna°); Bm M khinnamanā abhūt; K khinnananābhavat (?).
16.28d vṛttāntaṃ: Bm vṛttānta.
16.28d vistarāt tayoḥ (Bm vistarā tayoḥ).
16.29b samrāḍ vismayam āpa saḥ: Ed K samrāṭ smayam avāpa saḥ; (Bm vismayam āya). Bm due to *Devanāgarī* p>y.
16.29c tadānīṃ: Bm M tadāni (?).
16.29d na śaśāka: L2 na śaśāna (?).
16.30a samāhūya: Bm tam āhaya (?); M tam āhūya.
16.30a medhāvī: Bm M medhāvi°.
16.31a nṛpater (Bm nṛparter).
16.31a ābadhvā: Ed K ākarṇya; Bm ārbudhvā (?); M ābudhvā.
16.31c prāgalbhya°: Bm M prāgasta (?),
16.31c °siṉho: Bm M siṅkyo (?)
16.31d yuvatī°: Bm M yuvati°.
16.31d °hāsya°: Bm M °sasya°.
16.31a vihāyādya: Bm vivāhasya; M vibāhasya (?). M due to *Devanāgarī* v>b.
16.32b maśakaṃ: Bm aśaṅkaṃ; M āśaṅkaṃ (?).
16.32b udya*taḥ*: Ed L2 K udyate; Bm M iha te.
16.32c muhūrtaṃ (Bm muhurtaṃ).
16.32d dṛḍhī°: Bm M dalī° (?).
16.33a-16.34d Ed reads:

maya prabhodhitaṃ vākyam atikramitum añjasā /
rājeva śikṣayiṣyāmi narakṣaṇaphalaṃ yathā //
itthaṃ nirdhārya vipro 'sau sūnum aurasikaṃ tadā /
yadā bhavatu me putraś cet kṛtaṃ yadi nirṇayaṃ //

There are for this the following variant readings:
atikramitum: Bm M atikrāmitum.
añjasā (Bm ajasā).
rājeva: Bm M rājñeva. Perhaps 'rājānaṃ'?
śikṣayiṣyāmi (L2 śikṣaïṣyāmi). See **§7.4**.
narakṣaṇaphalaṃ: L2 narapeṇa phalaṃ; Bm M naraṃ phalāphalaṃ. Source?
itthaṃ: M ityaṃ (?) M due to *Devanāgarī* tth>ty.
nirdhārya: L2 nidhārya; Bm nidhāya.

putraś: Bm M putra. Bm M *saṃdhi*? See **§7.9b**.
kṛtaṃ: Bm M kathaṃ.
See n. to translation for these vss.

16.34[1] vipraḥ: Ed Bm M K vipra uvāca.

16.35b duṣkṛtaṃ: Bm duḥṣkṛtaṃ; K duṣkṛta. See **§7.9b** for Bm *saṃdhi*. See **§7.7** for K.

16.35c tathāpy upāyaṃ: Bm tathāpy upāya (?); M tathāyuyāya (?).

16.35c vakṣyāmi: Ed K vakṣyāmo; L2 vakṣyāmuḥ (?).

16.35d rāja°: Bm rājaḥ; M rājñaḥ.

16.35d °śreṇī°: Bm M °śroṇī°.

16.35d °śiromaṇe: Bm M °śiromaṇi (?).

16.36a °vārdhitaṭe ramye: L2 °vābdhitaṭe ramyā (?); Bm °vārdhitaṭe myā (?); M °vārdhitataṭe myā (?); (K °vādhi°). Bm omits syll.

16.36b vikhyāte: Bm M vivikhyāte (?). Bm M add syll.

16.36b *vijayāntike*: All MSS °ti jayanti kā (?).

16.36c kaścit: Ed Bm M K kaścic.

16.36d sūnubhiḥ: Bm sūnubhi. See **§7.9b** for Bm final *saṃdhi*.

16.36d saha: Bm M sahaḥ (?).

16.37a vedavidāṃ: K vedavidā.

16.37b dvitīyaḥ (L2 dvitīyyaḥ).

16.37b °śāstravit: M repeats 'śāstra' twice.

16.37c tṛtīyo (L2 tṛtīyyo).

16.37d †°*nipuaḥ*†: Ed K °vistaraḥ; L2 °nirnayaḥ (= nirṇayaḥ); Bm M °vistarāt. L2 source?

16/38c . . tasya: Ed L2 K karot(?) tasya; Bm M karā tasya.

16.38c purobhāge: Bm purobhoge.

16.38d nityaṃ: Bm M nitya°.

16.38d nīti° (Bm niti°).

16.38d kṛtaṃ: L2 Bm M kṛtāṃ.

16.39b prāgalbhyeṣv: Bm M prāgalbhyeṣy (?). Bm M due to Telugu or Kanarese subscript v>y.

16.39b atikovidaḥ: Ed K atike viduḥ.

16.40b nirṇetuṃ (L2 nirnetuṃ).

16.40b nāsti hi (Bm nāstī hi).

16.40c tathety: L2 tathyety; (Bm tayety). Bm due to *Devanāgarī* th>y.
16.40c narapatiḥ: Ed K narapatir.
16.40d ledhayitvā su°: Ed K lekhayām āsa; M lelayitvā(?) su°; (L2 lekhaïtvā su°). See §**7.4** for L2.
16.41a cārān: L2 carān. Synonym. See 'cārān' in 12.11d for choice of reading here.
16.41b °nilayaṃ: Ed K °nagaraṃ; Bm M °milayaṃ (?).
16.41c prāpuḥ: M prāyuḥ. M probably due to *Devanāgarī* p>y.
16.41c dūtāḥ: Ed K dūtā.
16.41d dadū rājñe *su*patrikāṃ: L2 rājñe duḥpatrikāṃ nṛpa; Bm rājñendruḥ pannikāṃ(?) nṛpa; M rājñenduḥpatrikāṃ(?) nṛpa; (Ed K . . . tu patrikāṃ). L2 Bm M source?
16.42a lekhyam: Bm M lekhyām (?).
16.42a ālokayām: L2 ālokayā (?); Bm M olokayaṃ (?).
16.42a cakre: Bm tra tve (?); M tve tve (?).
16.42b gorāṣṭrādipatiḥ (L2 gorāṣṭradhipatiḥ).
16.42c taṃ (Bm M ta).
16.42c samāhūya: Bm samāhūyaṃ (?).
16.42d gadati (Bm M gadatī).
16.43a idānīṃ: Bm M dadāti.
16.43a sarvabhaumaś ca: Ed K sārvabhaumasya; Bm M sarvabhomaś(?) ca.
16.43b premṇā (L2 premmnā).
16.43b tvāṃ: Ed L2 K tvaṃ.
16.43b icchati: Ed K icchasi.
16.43c †vijayākhy*ā* purī ramy*ā*†: Ed L2 M K vijayākhyāṃ purīṃ ramyāṃ; Bm vijayākhyāṃ purī ramyāṃ.
16.43d śvo (M śco).
16.43d gamyatām: L2 gamyagām.
16.44a bāḍham: M vāḍham. Synonym.

Colophons:

Ed K iti śrīskandapurāṇe uttararahasye sahyādrikhaṇḍe (K sahyādrikhaṇḍe uttararahasye) ṣoḍaśo 'dhyāyaḥ.

L2 iti śrīsaṉhyādrau uparibhāge pañcasaptatiśatamo 'dhyāyaḥ.

Bm M iti śrīskandapurāṇe ṣoḍaśo 'dhyāyaḥ (Bm 'dhyāya).

CHAPTER NINE (Skh.u. 17)

17.0 Ed inserts: atha saptadaśo 'dhyāyaḥ. Bm inserts: śrīgaṇeśāya namaḥ.

17.0[1] śaunakaḥ: Ed Bm M K śaunaka uvāca (Bm M śaunakovāca).

17.1a °mahājñāto: Ed K mahājñātau.

17.1b vidhicoditaḥ: L2 Bm M vidhicoditāḥ (Bm vidhivoditāḥ). Bm due to *Devanāgarī* c>v.

17.1c †*sa*gotrebhyaḥ *hā*tas†: Ed L2 M K gotrebhyaḥ sahitas; Bm gotrebhya sahitas. Emendation > gotrebhyaḥ sahātas > Ed L2 M K + Bm. See **§7.9b** for Bm final *saṃdhi*.

17.1c tūrṇaṃ: L2 turṇīṃ (?); K tūrṇa (?).

17.2a samudbhūtāḥ: Ed Bm M K samudbhūtā. See **§7.9b** for Ed Bm M K final *saṃdhi*.

17.2b divi°: L2 diva°.

17.2b °antarikṣagāḥ: Bm antarakṣigāḥ. Metathesis.

17.2c . . prāpti°: Ed L2 K pipat(?)prāpti°; Bm M vipraprāpti°.

17.2d dāruṇā: Bm dāruṇo. Bm perhaps due to confusion between vowel modification for 'ā' and 'o' in Telugu and Kanarese scripts.

17.2d romaharṣaṇāḥ: L2 romaharṣaṇa; Bm M vomaharṣaṇa (?).

17.3a nanādā°: L2 nanāndā° (?).

17.3a bhūmau: Bm M mūnau. Bm due to *Devanāgarī* bh>m.

17.3b pṛṣadaṇso: Bm M pṛṣadaṇsau.

17.3d petuḥ: Bm petu. See **§7.9b** for Bm final *saṃdhi*.

17.4b śilā: L2 Bm M śivā.

17.4b ghorā vavāśire: Ed K ghorā ca vāsire (?); Bm ghorā pravāśire (?); M ghorātra vāśire (?). Ed K due to *Devanāgarī* v>c. Bm due most probably to Telugu or Kanarese script v>p. Both readings have attempted to justify themselves by additional changes.

17.4c rudanti: L2 rundyanti (?).

17.4c vāyasās: L2 Bm M vāyasaṃ.

17.4d samadṛśyata: K samadṛśyataḥ. See §**7.7**.

17.5a etāny *ut*pātakādīni: Ed L2 M K etānyotpātakādīni (?); Bm etānyotpātakadīni (?).

17.5b manasā na: Bm M manasānyat.

17.5b smaran (M smaraṃn).

17.5[1] śaunakaḥ: Ed K śaunaka uvāca. Bm M omit.

17.5d sārvabhaumaṃ: L2 sārvabaupaṃ (?); Bm sārvabhauma.

17.6b mānayitvā: L2 procaïtvā (= procayitvā). See §**7.4**.

17.6b jagāda: L2 jagādṛ (= jagādur). See §**7.4**.

17.6b taṃ: L2 tāṃ.

17.6c °hatyam: Ed Bm M K °hatyām.

17.6d vicāraya: Bm M vicārāya.

17.7a tac: L2 ta (?).

17.7a chrutvā (L2 chṛtvā). See §**7.4**.

17.7a °śārdūlaḥ: K °śārdūlāḥ.

17.7b sabhā°: K samā°. *Devanāgarī* bh>m.

17.7b °aṅgaṇaṃ: L2 āṅkaṇaṃ (?); Bm M °ākaṇaṃ (?).

17.7c °bhār*ye*: Ed L2 Bm K °bhāryāṃ; M °bhāryā.

17.7d provāca (Bm provaca).

17.7[1] brāhmaṇaḥ: Ed Bm M K brāhmaṇa uvāca (Bm brāhmaṇovācaḥ, M brāhmaṇovāca); (L2 brāṉhmaṇaḥ).

17.8b yā: Ed K yaḥ; L2 ca.

17.8d sulocane: Bm M sulocanā.

17.9a niṣpāpā: Bm M niṣyāpa (?); K niṣppāpā (?). Bm M due to *Devanāgarī* p>y.

17.9a bhavaty: Bm bhavety.

17.9a evaṃ: L2 eva.

17.9b kāryā: L2 Bm M kārya; K kāyā.

17.9c evam (K evaṃm).

17.9c °varaḥ: Ed K °varas.

17.9d tūṣṇīṃ: Bm tūṣṇī (?).

17.9[1] śaunakaḥ: Ed Bm M K śaunaka uvāca (Bm śaunakauvāca).

17.10a śrutvā (L2 śṛtvā). See §**7.4**.

17.10a ca tad vākyaṃ: Ed K tadā vākyaṃ; Bm M tathā vākyaṃ.

17.10b prāptavaty: Ed K prāptavān.

17.10d durlabhyā: Ed Bm M K durlaṅghyā.
17.10d niyater: Bm M niyate (?).
17.10d gatiḥ: Bm gati.
17.11a kāryaṃ: Ed Bm M K kārya.
17.11b hṛdā: Ed K hṛdi.
17.11b smartuṃ: Bm M smartu (?).
17.11c kaluṣaṃ: L2 kaṭhuṣaṃ; Bm kaluṣa. L2 due to Telugu or Kanarese script l>ṭh.
17.11c *na*: All MSS vā.
17.11d dhāryaṃ: Ed K dharye; (M dhādharyaṃ). M repeats syll.
17.11d ninditaṃ: Ed nidhanaṃ; K nidhana.
17.11d mayā: K na yā.
17.12a parityaj*yaṃ*: Ed L2 K parityajya; Bm M parityajye.
17.12b °ābhirakṣituṃ: L2 Bm M °ābhirakṣati; (K °ābhirakṣitu).
17.12c anityam: Ed Bm M K anṛtyam.
17.12c adhruvaṃ: Bm adhruvat (?); M adhruvan (?); (L2 adhṛvaṃ). Bm and M due to *Devanāgarī* n~t. At some time the *anusvāra* of the preferred reading must have been written as 'n.' See **§7.9a** for n = ṃ. See **§7.4** for L2.
17.12c prāṇaṃ: Ed Br K prāṇān; Bm M prāṇā. See variants and n. for 'adhruvaṃ' immediately above, as well as **§7.9a**.
17.13b dhanamānau: Bm M dhanavāno.
17.13b madhyamāḥ: Ed L2 K madhyamaḥ.
17.13d dhanaṃ: M dhānaṃ; K dhanaḥ.
17.14a pramāṇāni: Bm M prāṇamāni. Metathesis.
17.14ab See 14.20ab.
17.14b na *kuryāṃ*: Ed K kākriye (?); L2 nākriye; Bm M na kriye. See 14.20 b for emendation. Probably, Telugu or Kanarese script 'ṛ' for 'ru' was read as 'ṛ' for 'ri,' pronouncing the vowel 'ṛ' as in north India rather than as in south India. See **§7.4**.
17.14cd °bhūtāni tyakṣyāmī°: Bm M °bhūtād yat pakṣāmī°. *Devanāgarī* ty>tp.
17.15a guṇavatī: Bm M guṇavati.
17.15b tūṣṇīm: L2 Bm M tūṣṇim.

17.15b °ābhavat: Bm °āvhavaṃ. Bm due to *Devanāgarī* t>n>ṃ. See **§7.9a**.
17.15c °otthāya: L2 °oyāya (?); Bm M °otsāya (?). L2 due to *Devanāgarī* th>y. Bm M due to *Devanāgarī* tth>ts.
17.15c tvarayā: Bm tvarā (?). Bm omits syll.
17.15d vastrādyaiś ca vinā: Ed Kvastrādirahitā. Synonym.
17.15d satī: Bm sati.
17.16ab Ed Bm M K omit.
17.17a manujāḥ: Bm m[ā/u]nujāḥ (?).
17.17b pracukruśuḥ: L2 pracakṛśuḥ (= pracakruśuḥ) (?); M K pracukrumuḥ (?).
17.18a mahārājā: Ed Bm M K mahārāja (?).
17.18c sa *dhī*ratāṃ: Ed K sa dairyatāṃ (K sardheryatāṃ); L2 Bm M sa dīratāṃ (?). K due to misreading *Devanāgarī* 'ai.' See **§7.9a** for L2 Bm M.
17.19a daṇḍayitvā (L2 daṇḍaïtvā, Bm daṇḍayitva). See **§7.4** for L2.
17.19a śiśu°: Bm śibhu°. *Devanāgarī* ś>bh.
17.19b mānayitvā (L2 mānaïtvā). See **§7.4**.
17.19c premṇā: Bm premṇo. Bm perhaps due to Telugu or Kanarese script vowel modification ā>o.
17.19c gāś: L2 gaṃś. Telugu or Kanarese scripot ā>aṃ?
17.19d grāma°: K yāma°.
17.19d °dvayam adāt punaḥ: Bm M °dvaya mudā tadā.
17.20b vaijayantīṃ: Bm M vaijayanti° (?).
17.20b manoramāṃ: K manoramā.
17.20d viśati sma: Bm M viśāti(?) sva°.
17.21a-17.22b Bm M omit.
17.21a prabhṛti: L2 prabhṛtī (?).
17.21d °nandana: K °nandanaḥ.
17.22b °sattama: L2 °sattamaḥ.
17.22cd See 9.14d, 9.71cd, 10.9ab, 11.4ab, 12.5ab, 14.11cd, 16.19c, 17.52a, 18.11ab.
17.22c nivasaṇs: L2 nivasaṃ.
17.22d mahatkālo: L2 mahāṅkāle (?); Bm M mahākālo.
17.22d nyavartata: Bm M vyavartata. Bm M due to Telugu or Kanarese script n>v.

17.22[1] śaunakaḥ: Ed K śaunaka uvāca. Bm M omit. See 17.23[1].

17.23b randhrā°: Bm M radhrā°.

17.23b °tatparāḥ: Ed Bm M K °tatparaḥ.

17.23[1] Bm M insert: śaunaka uvāca (Bm śaunakovāca). See 17.22[1].

17.23c mantri*ṇaḥ*: All MSS mantriṇaṃ.

17.23d bandhavairiṇaḥ: Ed Bm M K buddhijīvinaḥ.

17.24a saṃjātaḥ: Bm sajātaḥ; M saṃjātāḥ.

17.24b durātmavān: Ed K durātmavat.

17.24d śālinī: Bm M śālini (?).

17.25a āyatā° (Bm āthatā°). Bm due to *Devanāgarī* y>th.

17.25d *viṇ*°, or less correctly viṭ°: Ed L2 K viṭ°; Bm M vīṭ° (?).

17.25d °mārge: L2 Bm M °mārga°

17.25d ca pravartinī: L2 Bm M °pravartanī. L2 Bm M omit syll.

17.26a jāramartyeṇa: Ed K jārabhartrā vai; M jāgaramartyeṇa. M extra syll.

17.26b vilāsaṃ: L2 viśālaṃ. L2 metathesis?

17.26b satī: Bm M sati.

17.26c °vidhāṃ: L2 °vidāṃ; Bm °vidhā. See **§7.9a** for L2.

17.26d krodhād vivaśaṃ: L2 krodhāṃ dvivaśāṃ.

17.26d gataḥ: M gatāḥ.

17.27a khaḍgam udyamya: L2 khaḍham(?) udyamya; Bm M khaḍgamusṛjya (?).

17.27c tau tadābandha°: Ed K tadā nirbaddha°; L2 tau tadabandha°.

17.28a tu nipuṇau: L2 sinda(?)nipuṇau; Bm M sunipuṇau. L2 extra syll.

17.28b saṃbhāram: Bm M saṃhāram.

17.28b akarot: Bm M akaro (?).

17.28b krudhā: L2 kadhā (?); Bm M kṛdhā. Bm M due to Telugu or Kanarese script 'ṛ' for 'ru.'

17.28d kalas†*enaḥ*†°: Ed K kālaḥsvenā° (?); L2 kalasvenāṃ° (?); Bm kalasvenā (?); M kalaḥsvenā. See **§7.9b** for 'ḥs' as a *saṃdhi* final.

17.28[1] L2 Bm M insert lengthy commentary. See Appendix B and 17.29[1].

17.29a idānīṃ: Bm idānī (?).

17.29a ā*rop*ya: Ed Bm M K āroṣya; L2 ārosya. Emendation > Ed Bm M K > L2. Ed Bm M K due to *Devanāgarī* p>ṣ.

17.29b mantrasattamāḥ: L2 mantregattamāḥ (?); M °sattamaḥ; K matra°.

17.29c āsuḥ: Ed Bm M K āsa.

17.29d vārtāṃ: Bm vārtā.

17.29[1] Ed footnotes the syllable 'thu' in 17.29d 'mithunahatyakāṃ' with the lengthy commentary inserted by L2 Bm M in 17.28[1]. See Appendix B.

17.30a caiteṣām: Ed Bm K sarveṣām; (L2 ceteṣāṃm, M caiteṣāṃ).

17.30b cakrur (L2 cakṛr). See **§7.4**.

17.30c gorāṣṭra°: Bm gorāṣṭva° (?). Bm due to Telugu or Kanarese subscript Cr>Cv.

17.30c mūrkhāṇāṃ (L2 Bm M mūrkhānāṃ).

17.30d pāpināṃ: Bm pāpīnā (?); M pāpīnāṃ (?).

17.31a āste: Bm aste (?).

17.31a mahābale*ś*eti: Ed L2 K mahābaleneti; Bm M mahābalineti. Emendation required for sense.

17.31b gorāṣṭre: Bm gorāṣṭve (?). Bm due to Telugu or Kanarese subscript Cr>Cv.

17.31b °saṃnidhau (Ed Bm M K °sannidhau, L2 °saṃnnidhau).

17.31c °sthā: Bm M °staṃ.

17.32a mahādevaṃ: Bm matyadevaṃ (?). Bm due to *Devanāgarī* h>ty.

17.32b vibhuṃ: Bm vibhu (?).

17.32d viśuddhatāṃ: L2 Bm M viśudhyatāṃ (?). L2 Bm M probably due to *Devanāgarī* ddh>dhy.

17.32[1] All MSS insert:
śāsayitvā nṛpeṇaivaṃ mantriṇair mantrakovidāḥ /
There are for this the following variant readings:
śāsayitvā (L2 śāsaïtvā). See **§7.4**.
nṛpeṇaivaṃ: Ed Bm M K nṛpeṇaiva.
mantriṇair: L2 Bm mantriṇai; M mantrinai. See **§7.9b** for L2 Bm and M final *saṃdhi*.
°kovidāḥ: Bm M °kovidaiḥ.

See n. to vs. 32 in the translation.

17.32^2 śaunakaḥ: Ed Bm M K śaunaka uvāca (Bm śaunakovāca).

17.33a gorāṣṭra°: Bm gorāṣṭva°. Bm due to Telugu or Kanarese subscript Cr>Cv.

17.33a °jāḥ: Bm M °jā. See **§7.9b** for Bm M final *saṃdhi*.

17.33b duḥkhān: L2 duḥkhā.

17.33b nirga*ma*°: All MSS nirgatya°. Emendation required for sense.

17.33b °tatpa*rāḥ*: Ed K °tatparāt; L2 Bm M tat puraṃ. Emendation required for sense.

17.33c °vini*vṛt*ty°: Ed K °vinikṛty° (?); L2 Bm M °vinivṛty° (?). Emendation required for sense. Ed K perhaps due in part to *Devanāgarī* v>k.

17.33d °yātrāṃ: Bm °yātrā.

17.34a kurvantaḥ: L2 kurvantyaḥ (?); Bm M kurvataḥ.

17.34a sahyam: L2 saṇhyam.

17.34a āsādya: Bm ādya (?). Bm omits syll.

17.34c avatīrya: M avatīrtha (?). M due to *Devanāgarī* y>th.

17.34d taulavaṃ: Bm tālavaṃ (?).

17.34d āvisan: L2 Bm āvisat. *Devanāgarī* n~t?

17.35a adrākṣuḥ: Ed K adrākṣīt.

17.35b °kṣetra°: Bm °kṣetraṃ.

17.35c saṃpūjya: L2 saṃphukhya (?); Bm sapūjya (?). L2 due to Telugu or Kanarese script j>kh.

17.35d vidhivan (L2 vidhivaṃ). See **§7.9a** for ṃ = n.

17.35d °nandana: Bm M °nandanaḥ.

17.36a śuktimatī°: L2 śuktimatīṃ.

17.36b °vināśini: Ed L2 K °vināśinī; Bm vināśani (?).

17.36c pūjayām: L2 pūjyayām (?).

17.36d sveṣāṃ: Ed K svasya; L2 teṣāṃ. See 17.53b.

17.36d pāpa°: Bm M pati°.

17.37b diśam: Ed K diśim (?).

17.37b āyayuḥ: Bm āyuyuḥ (?).

17.37d durātmanaḥ: Ed K durātmanāṃ; Bm durātmana (?).

17.38a . . . . yatra yatre: All MSS pṛṣṭhabhāge yatra yatra. Sense?

17.38b tatra tatra: L2 'tatra' only. L2 omits two syll.
17.38b gamiṣyataḥ: Bm M gamiṣyata (?).
17.38d tapasyantaṃ: Bm M te paśyanti.
17.39b °lāñchita°: L2 °lāñchite; Bm °lāchitaṃ (?).
17.39cd See 12.42a and 12.42d.
17.40a ū*cuḥ* sveṣāṃ: Ed L2 K ūcus teṣāṃ; (Bm M ūcu sveṣāṃ)
17.40b °*hatye*na: All MSS °hastena. Emendation necessary for sense. *Devanāgarī* ty>st?
17.41b maṅgaḷaṃ (Ed Bm M K maṅgalaṃ).
17.41c . . . tīrthamadhye: All MSS kasyāpi tīrthamadhye.
17.41d °mātrā°: L2 Bm M °mātra°. Synonym.
17.42b śālagrāmam: L2 M śāligrāmam; K śālayāmam.
17.42c kṛtārtho: Bm kṛtātho (?).
17.42c '*stī*ti: All MSS 'smīti. Emendation required for sense.
17.42d †nibadhya† tāṃ: Ed Bm K nibaddhya(?) tāṃ; M nibadhyata(?). Sense?
17.43a āruhya: Bm aruhya (?).
17.43b gantuṃ (Bm gantu).
17.43c madhyāhnaveḷāyāṃ: Bm mādhyann avelāyāṃ; (Ed M K °velāyāṃ).
17.43d sītāyā uttare: Ed K sītāyāś cottare.
17.44a gaḷitaṃ (Ed Bm M K galitaṃ). See 9.1c.
17.44b upāviśan: L2 Bm M upāviśat. L2 Bm M due to *Devanāgarī* n>t?
17.44[1] L2 inserts 17.46ab with 'eta' for 'etad.'
17.44d †narās tadā†: L2 narottamaḥ. Perhaps *nṛpot*tama?
17.45b †hastaman*tra*vivarji*taṃ*†: Ed K hastamanta(?)vivarjitāḥ; L2 hastīṃ mativivarjitāḥ; Bm M hastaṃ mativivarjitāḥ.
17.45d vyalokayan: L2 vyalokayat. *Devanāgarī* n>t?
17.46c āsīt: Bm asīt (?).
17.46c °pī*ṭhe*: Ed L2 M K °pīṭhaṃ; Bm °pīṭha. *Devanāgarī* e> aṃ?
17.46d śālagrāmo: Ed Br K śālagrāma°; M śālagrāmaṃ; (L2 sālagrāmo). L2 ś>s. See **§7.9a**.
17.47a gantuṃ: Bm gatu (?).
17.47a taṃ: Bm te. *Devanāgarī* aṃ>e?

17.47b °opacakramuḥ (M °opacakrumuḥ). M due to Telugu or Kanarese 'ṛ' for 'ru'? Cra>Cṛ>Cru. See **§7.4**.
17.47c etasminn (L2 etasmiṃn). See **§7.9a** for ṃ = n.
17.47d samapadyata: K sabhapadyataḥ (?).
17.48a viprāḥ: Ed K viprās.
17.48b . . sthānaṃ: All MSS tebhyaḥ sthānaṃ (Bm tebhya sthānaṃ). Sense should be, 'for you (pl).'
17.49a kuladaiva*taṃ*: Ed K kuladaivatvaṃ (?); L2 Bm kuladevatva (?); M kuladevatvaṃ (?). See 9.10d.
17.49b prāpti°: Ed L2 M K prāpta°.
17.49c ity uktvā (Bm iy uktvā).
17.49c bhagavatī: Bm M bhagāvati (Bm bhabhagāvati). Bm extra syll.
17.49d °āntarhitā śivā: Bm M °āntaradhīyata.
17.50b kāraṇeno°: Bm M kāraṇeto°. *Devanāgarī* n>t.
17.50c samālocya: Bm M samālokya.
17.50d °nirbhara°: Bm °nibhara° (?).
17.51a mahāgrāme (Bm mahāgrame).
17.51b kurmahe: L2 kurvahe.
17.51b vayaṃ: K vaye. *Devanāgarī* aṃ>e.
17.51c te: Ed K ye.
17.51c cakrur: L2 Bm cakruḥ (L2 cakṛḥ); M cakru. See **§7.9b** for L2 Bm final *saṃdhi* and **§7.4** for L2 ṛ>ru. M may be due to the positioning of the word at the end of a MS line.
17.52a See 9.14d, 9.71cd, 10.9ab, 11.4ab, 12.5ab, 14.11cd, 16.19c, 17.22cd, 18.11ab.
17.52a ūṣus: Bm uṣus (?).
17.52b havyakavya°: M havyahakavya° (?). M extra syll.
17.52c nāyātāḥ: Ed L2 K na yātāḥ.
17.52cd pūrvanilayāḥ eteṣāṃ: Ed K pūrvanilayā eteṣāṃ; Bm pūrvanilaye yeteṣā (?); M pūrvanilaye yeteṣāṃ (?). See **§7.9b** for Ed K final *saṃdhi*. Bm M dialectical?
17.52d bhavanaṃ: M bhavaneṃ (?).
17.53b sveṣāṃ: Ed K svasya; L2 teṣāṃ. See 17.36d.
17.53c munim: Bm M muninn (?).
17.53c āsuḥ: Bm M āsu. See **§7.9b** for Bm M final *saṃdhi*.

17.35d °dṛṣṭaṃ: Bm °dṛṣṭa; M °daṣṭaṃ.
17.54a mahātejāḥ: Ed Bm M K mahātejā. See **§7.9b** for Ed Bm M K final *saṃdhi*.
17.54c °mudrāṅkitaḥ: L2 °mudrāṃ tataḥ.
17.54d mant*raṃ*: Ed Bm M K mataṃ; L2 mantra•.
17.54d °saṃjñitaṃ: Ed K °saṃmataṃ; L2 °saṃjitaṃ; Bm °sajñitaṃ (?). L2 due to *Devanāgarī* jñ>j.
17.55a °āṣṭākṣaraṃ (Bm M °āṣṭāṣṭākṣaraṃ). Bm M extra syll.
17.55b saḥ: L2 saṃ (?).
17.55c ā no bhadreti: Ed K ānebhireti (?); L2 ānobhareti (?).
17.55d mṛdā°: M mudā°. Read 'mudā°' as in M? See **§7.11**.
17.56a ā mandrair iti: L2 āmandreriti (?); Bm āmadrairiti (?).
17.56b mṛdā. Read 'mudā'? See **§7.11**.
17.56c akṣibhyāṃ teti: L2 ākṣibhyāntveti (?); M akṣībhyāṃ(?) teti.
17.56d mṛdā. Read 'mudā'? See **§7.11**.
17.56[1] L2 Bm insert lengthy passage. See Appendix B.
17.56[2] śaunakaḥ: Ed Bm M K omit. See 17.57[1].
17.57b vāsaṃ: Bm vāsāṃ (?);l M vāmāṃ. M due to *Devanāgarī* s>m?
17.57b cakrur: L2 catur.
17.57[1] Bm M insert: śaunaka uvāca (Bm śaunakovāca). See 17.56[2].
17.57c grāmaṃ: K yāmaṃ.
17.57c velañjīti: All MSS belañjīti.
17.58b pravadanti: Bm pravadati.
17.58d °śreṇi°: Bm M °śroṇī°.
17.59b cānuyāsyati: Bm M anuyāsyati.
17.59d śakyaṃ: Ed K śaktaṃ; Bm M śakye. Ed K synonym. Bm M due to *Devanāgarī* aṃ>e.
17.60b caret: Bm carat (?).
17.60[1] All MSS add four vss., the last two in Mālinī meter. For justification for ending the text proper at this point rather than including these vss. see 10.48c-10.49, 11.47-11.48, 12.47c-12.48, 13.32-13.33, 14.33c-14.35. The vss. are:
tasmin panasavṛkṣe tu mahākāruṇike sthale /

†dvandvam āropayām āsa† kūṭasthaiś ca mahātmabhiḥ //
sūtaḥ /
idam eva purākhyātaṃ śaunako ṛṣisattamaḥ /
śatānīkāya rājñe tu uktavān sakalaṃ dvijaḥ //
śaunakaḥ /
caritam idam aśeṣaṃ durvṛtānāṃ ca vṛttaṃ /
mithunaharajanānāṃ samyag uktaṃ narendra //
sakalakaluṣanāśaṃ yaḥ śṛṇotīha loke /
sakṛd api janamadhye sādhanaṃ muktihetoḥ //
There are for these vss. the following variant readings:
stale: Bm sthile (?).
āsa: L2 āsuḥ
mahātmibhiḥ (Bm °bhi). See **§7.9b**.
sūtaḥ: Ed K sūta uvāca; Bm M śrīśaunaka uvāca.
śatānīkāya: L2 śatānīkaiś ca.
uktavān: Ed K hyuktavān
dvijaḥ: Ed K dvija.
śaunakaḥ: Ed Bm M K śaunaka uvāca (Bm śaunakovāca).
aśeṣaṃ: L2 Bm aśeṣa°.
durvṛtānāṃ (Bm duvṛtānāṃ).
°janānāṃ: L2 °jananāṃ.
°īha: Bm °īda. Bm due to *Devanāgarī* h>d.
°hetoḥ: Bm M °hetau.

Colophons:

Ed K iti śrīskandapurāṇe sahyādrikhaṇḍe uttararahasye mithunaharabrāhmaṇakathanaṃ (= mithunahatya°?) nāma saptadaśo 'dhyāyaḥ.

L2 iti śrīsaṉhyādrau uparibhāge caturnavatiśatatamo 'dhyāyaḥ.

Bm M iti śrīskandapurāṇe sa° (Bm omits 'sa°') saptadaśo 'dhyāyaḥ.

CHAPTER TEN (Skh.u. 18)

18.0 Ed inserts: atha aṣṭādaśo 'dhyāyaḥ.

18.0[1] śaunakaḥ: Ed Bm M K śaunaka uvāca (Bm śaunakauvāca).

18.1a *grāmam*: All MSS vrataṃ.

18.1c . . gorāṣṭrajasyā°: Ed K kaścid gorāṣṭrakasyā°; L2 kaścit gorāṣṭrajasyā°; Bm M kaścid gorāṣṭrajasyā°.

18.1c °ātha: Bm M °ārthe.

18.1d °manāḥ: L2 °manā.

18.2a kaḷiga° (Ed Bm M K kaliga°).

18.2a °deśe: Bm °deśa.

18.2b nāmnā: Bm nāmnāṃ.

18.2b kāñcamālinī: Bm kācanamālini (?); M kāñcanamālini (?).

18.2c °nara°: M °naraḥ.

18.2c samāyuktā: L2 samāyuktāḥ.

18.3a tasyāṃ: Bm tasyā (?).

18.3a puryāṃ: K puryā.

18.3a jagattrātā (Bm M jagatrātā).

18.3b °gotra°: Bm M °vaṉśa°. Synonym.

18.3b °samudbhavaḥ: L2 M °samudbhavā.

18.3c hemamālī: Bm M hemamālir. Bm M probably due to *Devanāgarī* vowel modification for 'ī' being misplaced in part, or misread, followed by justification.

18.3d See 9.57b, 10.10d, 12.41b, 13.14b, 16.3b.

18.3d °dyutiḥ: Ed K °prabhaḥ. Synonym.

18.4b mahābala°: K mahāvala° (?). K due to *Devanāgarī* b>v.

18.4c yudhi° (Bm yuddhi°).

18.4c °†kīrtiś ca†: L2 °padāta (?); Bm °padāṃta; M °yadānta (?) M due to *Devanāgarī* p>y?

18.4d ratha°: L2 stha°. L2 omits syll. L2 due to *Devanāgarī* ra>s before 'th'?

18.4d vājimān (Bm vāmān). Bm omits syll.

18.5a dor°: K daur°.

18.5b jita°: Ed K jitaṃ; L2 jitān.

18.5b °maṇḍalaḥ: Ed K °maṇḍalaṃ; (Bm °maḍalaḥ).

18.5c udayādri°: Bm M udayādrī° (?).

18.5d °mārtāṇḍa°: Ed Bm M K °mārtaṇḍa°. Synonym.

18.5d °mānayan: Bm M °mānayāṃ (?); (Ed L2 K °mānayaṃ = °yan). See **§7.9a** for final ṃ = n.

18.6a so 'yaṃ: L2 yo 'yaṃ; Bm M yo mā (?)

18.6b °prabhaḥ: Bm M °prabhāḥ.

18.6d jñāninam iti: Ed K jñāninaṃ coti (?); L2 Bm jñānīnam(?) iti; M jñānam iti. M omits syll.

18.7a kīrti°: L2 Bm M kīrtiḥ.

18.7a °ābdheś: Bm M °ābdhai. See **§7.9b** for final *saṃdhi.*

18.7b saṃjātaś: Bm saṃjātaḥś. See **§7.9b** for final *saṃdhi.*

18.8a kāmo 'py: Bm M kāmyopy (?).

18.8a anaṅgatāṃ: Bm M anaṅgatā.

18.8b jvalajjitaḥ: Ed L2 K ca lajjitaḥ; M jvālajjitaḥ.

18.8c gāmbhīryam asya: K gāmbhīryayasya (?); (Bm gābhīryam asya).

18.8c °ātha: M °āpya.

18.8d . . . . bhayānvitaḥ: Ed K kṛpāloti(?) bhayānvitaḥ; L2 kṛpāḷoti(?) bhayānvitaḥ; Bm kṛpāloti cayānvitaḥ (?); M kṛpāloti yānvitaḥ (?). M omits syll. Bm due to Telugu or Kanarese script bh>c. See n. to translation at this point.

18.9a saṃprāptas: L2 saṃprāptaḥ; Bm M saṃprāpte.

18.9b Ed reads:
taraṅgaiḥ saha kūjati.
There are for this the following variant readings:
taraṅgaiḥ: L2 turagaiḥ.
kūjati: Bm kuḍāti (?); M kuñjati (?).

18.9c °viśiṣṭo: K °viśiṣṭā.

18.10a kiṃcin: L2 kiṃcit.

18.10b durbhikṣajaṃ (M durbhikṣpajaṃ).

18.10c mleccha° (M mleṃcha°).

18.10c °baka°: L2 °caka°. L2 due to Telugu or Kanarese script b>c.

18.11ab See 9.14d, 9.71cd, 10.9ab, 11.4ab, 12.5ab, 14.11cd, 16.19c, 17.22cd, 17.52a.
18.11b vyatīyur: Bm vyatīvyur (?).
18.11b bahavaḥ: L2 cahavas (?); K vahavaḥ (?). L2 due to Telugu or Kanarese script b>c. K due to *Devanāgarī* b>v.
18.11c āgataḥ: L2 āgata. See **§7.9b** for L2 final *saṃdhi*.
18.11d °pāragaḥ: M °pāragāḥ.
18.12a saṃbhūto: Ed K saṃbhūta. See **§7.9b** for Ed K final *saṃdhi*.
18.12c śānti°: L2 Bm M K śānta°.
18.12d mūrti°: L2 mūrtī° (?).
18.12d °māna*vo*: All MSS °mānava. See **§7.9b** for final *saṃdhi*.
18.13a sumatyā: K samutpāṃ (?).
18.13a yukto: Ed K yuktaḥ.
18.13b āvṛtaḥ: L2 āvṛtāḥ.
18.13c °ānurodhaṃ: Ed K °ānurodho; Bm M °ānurodhair.
18.13c *yat*: Ed L2 K yan; Bm M ya.
18.14ab Ed reads:
prāguktāt tārakāc chabdāt paraśabdā sa nāmavān /
There are for this the following variant readings:
°uktāt: L2 °ukta; Bm M °uktvā.
tārakāc: L2 tārala; Bm M tvarakā (?).
chabdāt: L2 Bm M chabdān.
18.14c samāyātaṃ: L2 samāyāntaṃ.
18.15b nṛpottamaḥ: Bm nṛpottama.
18.15c paśyāma: L2 paśyāmaḥ; Bm M paśyāmo.
18.15d matiṃ: L2 matīṃ (?).
18.16a akṣatāni: Ed K akṣatāś ca; (Bm akṣatāṇi).
18.16b prayaccad: L2 prayabhad (?). L2 due to Telugu or Kanarese script ch>bh.
18.16b °pāṇinā: L2 °pāṇīnā (?).
18.16c °ainaṃ: Bm M °aivaṃ.
18.16c °śārdūlaḥ: L2 Bm M °śādūla (= śārdūla?). See **§7.9b** for L2 Bm M final *saṃdhi*.
18.16d °ekṣaṇaḥ: L2 Bm M °endriyaḥ.

18.17a †*āna*yan*taṃ*†: All MSS aṇīyantraṃ. Emendation requireed by sense.
18.17b vākyaṃ: Bm vākya.
18.17b praṣṭuṃ: Bm M pṛṣṭaṃ.
18.17c bho bho: M bhu bhu (?).
18.17d santi: L2 sati.
18.17d †*sar*vo†ttamottamāḥ: Ed K saṃvittamottamāḥ (?); L2 saṃvottamottamāḥ (?); Bm M sevitamottamāḥ (M sevitamotamāḥ). Emendation>L2>saṃvīta°(?)>Ed K>Bm M?
18.18b bhavā°: Bm M bhavān.
18.18c īdṛ*śa*°: Ed K īdaśaṃ (?); L2 Bm M īdṛśaṃ. Emendation yields better sense.
18.18d jagatītale: L2 jagatāṃ pate. See 18.23b, 19.34d, 19.36d for examples of 'ḷ' for 'l' in '°tale.'
18.19b bhi*yā*°: Ed K bhita°; L2 bhijñā°; Bm M bhinyā°. Emendation required for sense.
18.19c krodha°: Bm M kro° (?). Bm M omit syll.
18.19c °tāmrākṣo: Bm M °tāmrāṅkṣo (?); (L2 °tāṃmrākṣo).
18.20a pārthivā: L2 Bm M pārthivo.
18.20a †dṛṣ*ṭā*†: Ed L2 M K dṛṣṭvā; Bm dṛṣṭyā (?). Bm due to Telugu or Kanarese subscript Cv>Cy.
18.20b °sattama: L2 °sattamāḥ.
18.20c na *dṛṣṭaṃ*: Ed L2 Br K na dṛśaṃ; Bm M nedṛśaṃ. See 18.18d for emendation.
18.20c triṣu: Bm priṣu (?).
18.20d vivekānāṃ: L2 M vivekāntāṃ; Bm vivekāntā.
18.20b bhavā: Bm bhāvān; M bhavām (?).
18.21a tathā: L2 tayā; M tasyā. L2 due to *Devanāgarī* th>y.
18.21a dāsyāmo: Bm M dāsyamo (?).
18.21c cen: L2 ce (?).
18.22a °bhavantu: L2 °bhavanta; Bm M °bhavata.
18.22a te: L2 Bm M tāṃ.
18.22b mahājanāḥ: Bm mahājanaḥ.
18.22c viprendre (Bm vipredre).
18.22d pārthivas: L2 Bm M pārthive.
18.22d nṛpa: L2 Bm M nṛpaḥ.

18.23a kirīṭa°: L2 kiriṭi° (?).

18.23a °maṇi°: M °bhaṇi°. M due to *Devanāgarī* m>bh.

18.23a °dīpena: M °dīyena (?). M due to *Devanāgarī* p>y.

18.23b pāda°: Bm M pāta°.

18.23b °taḷaṃ (Ed Bm M K °talaṃ).

18.23c nīrājanaṃ: L2 nīrājanāṃ (?); Bm M nīrācanaṃ (?).

18.23d iva: Bm ivā (?).

18.24a rājendra: Bm rājendraṃ.

18.24b bhītiṃ: Bm M pīta.

18.24c māhātmyaṃ: Bm māhātma.

18.24d paṭaṃ: Bm paṭha; K paṭhaṃ.

18.24d vis*tīr*yatām: Ed Bm M K vistāratām; L2 vistāryatām (?). L2 due to *Devanāgarī* vowel modification ī>ā? Emendation>L2>Ed Bm M K.

18.25a uktava*†taś ca*†: All MSS uktavan tasya (L2 Bm uktavaṃ tasya). See **§7.9a** for ṃ = n. Emendation required for sense.

18.25b tiṣṭhan (Bm tiṣṭhaṃn). See **§7.9a** for Bm final.

18.25b nṛpottamaḥ: L2 nṛpottama.

18.25c paṭaṃ: Ed K paṭe; Bm paṭhaṃ.

18.25d prabhāvaṃ: Bm prabhāva.

18.25[1] dvi*jaḥ*: Ed K dvija uvāca; L2 Bm M omit.

18.26a-18.29d L2 omits.

18.26b niścayaṃ: Bm M niścitaṃ (?).

18.26c paśyedānīṃ: Bm paśyadānīṃ (?).

18.26d jvalantaṃ: Bm M jājvalaṃ (?).

18.27a uktvāsau: Ed Kuktvā sā.

18.27b bhūsuraḥ: Bm bhūsurā.

18.27c svīyaṃ: Bm M svasya.

18.27d sāraṃ: Bm sāra°.

18.27b yat: Bm M ya.

18.28b kṣiptaṃ cākṣataiḥ: Bm M kṣiptavātkṣataiḥ (?). Bm M due to *Devanāgarī* c>v and insertion of 't.'

18.28b saha: Bm sahā (?).

18.28c jājvalyamānas: Bm M jājvalyamānaṃ.

18.28c tejo 'bhūt: Bm M tejobhiḥ.

18.28d kṛśa*nuḥ*: Ed K kṛśānaḥ (?); Bm kṛśāna (?); M kṛśā (?). M omits syll. Emendation required to make proper word.
18.28d samudaikṣata: Bm sadaihyatā (?); M sadaihyata (?). Bm M omit syll.
18.29a paṭaṃ: Bm paṭhaṃ.
18.29a °sāt kṛtya: Bm M sākṛtyaṃ.
18.29b udyataḥ: Bm M udhatāḥ (= uddhatāḥ?). Bm probably due in part to *Devanāgarī* dy>dh.
18.30a viprasyāntikam: L2 vipraś cāntim (?); Bm vipratyāntikam (?). L2 omits syll. Bm due to *Devanāgarī* sy>ty.
18.30c asmāṇś: L2 asyāṇś (?). L2 due to *Devanāgarī* m>y.
18.30d kṛ*pāṃ*: All MSS kṛpā.
18.31a santāpam (Bm satāpam).
18.31a asmākam: Bm M askākam (?).
18.31b pāvakaṃ: Ed K pāṃvakaṃ (?); L2 pāvaka (?).
18.32ab Ed reads:
taṃ kāraṃ bhojakuhare saṃmantrya prāharaṃ yathā /
There are for this the following variant readings:
kāraṃ: L2 karāṃ.
saṃmantrya: L2 samantrya; (Bm saṃmatrya).
18.32c bhagava*tā*: All MSS bhagavati.
18.32d 'bhūd *hav*ya°: Ed L2 M K 'bhūd dhavya°; Bm muddhavya (?). See 18.26d for emendation. Emendation>'bhūdhavya>Ed L2 M K? Bm due in part to *Devanāgarī* bh>m.
18.33a bhūpo: L2 bhūyo. L2 due to *Devanāgarī* p>y.
18.33a 'pi: Ed Bm M K hi.
18.33b mamajja (M mamaja).
18.33c dvijātaye: K dvijāyate (?). Metathesis.
18.34b ābharanāṇi: Bm abharanāṇi.
18.34c °†saṃyukta†: L2 saṃvītta (?); Bm M saṃvitta (?). L2 Bm M source?
18.35a indranīlaiḥ: K indranīlai. See **§7.9a** and **§7.7** for K final *saṃdhi*.
18.35b pratyuptaṃ: Ed K prataptaṃ; Bm pratyatpaṃ. Bm reads 'pt' as 'tp.'

18.35b cāṅgadaṃ: Bm cāgada (= cāṅgada?).
18.35c āḍhyaṃ: Bm āḍhya; M āḍhyaḥ.
18.35c dāsī°: Bm M dāsi°.
18.36a tādṛg°: L2 tvādṛg° (?).
18.36b kiṃ na: Bm M kin na (?), perhaps 'kinn a°.' See **§7.9a** for Bm M ṃ = n.
18.36c *saṃ*mānito: Ed Bm M K sanmānito; L2 sanmārgino. Ed Bm M K due to ṃ = n? See **§7.9a**.
18.36c vipraḥ: Bm M vipro.
18.36d ślāghayitvā (L2 Bm ślāghaïtvā). See **§7.4**.
18.37b °tārakaṃ: Bm M °tārakaḥ.
18.37c uktvā (Bm aktvā).
18.37c dvijaḥ: Bm M muni.
18.37c śreṣṭhaḥ: Bm śreṣṭho; M śreṣṭhā. M variance from Bm due to Telugu or Kanarese vowel modification o>ā?
18.37d pratasthe: Bm M prayayau. Synonym.
18.37d svapurīṃ: Bm svā purī; M svā purīṃ.

Colophons:

Ed K iti śrīskandapurāṇe uttararahasye sahyādrikhaṇḍe pātityagrāmakathkanaṃ nāma aṣṭādaśo 'dhyāyaḥ.

L2 iti saṇhyādrikhaṇḍe uparibhāge pātityagrāmanirṇayaṃ nāma caturviṇśatiśatatamo 'dhyāya[ḥ].

Bm iti śrīskandapurāṇe sahyādrikhaṇḍe ādirahasye (!) pātityagrāmāhatyaṃ (= °grāmamāhātmyaṃ?) aṣṭādaśo 'dyāyaḥ.

M iti śrīsahyādrikhaṇḍe ādirahasye pātityagrāmamāhātmyaṃ aṣṭādaśaḥ.

CHAPTER ELEVEN (Skh.u. 19)

19.0 Ed inserts: atha ekonaviṉśatitamo 'dhyāyaḥ. Bm inserts: śrīgaṇeśāya namaḥ.

19.0[1] śaunakaḥ: Ed Bm M K śaunaka uvāca (Bm śaunakovāca, M śaunakovācaḥ).

19.1c sopaskarāṇi: Bm M sopaskārāṇi.

19.1c saṃgṛhya (Bm saṃgṛdya). Bm due to *Devanāgarī* h>d.

19.1d gantuṃ (L2 gantu).

19.2a tīrthāṇi (Ed K tīrthāni, L2 tīrthāṇinī). L2 extra syll.

19.2c kramād agād: L2 kramāyāgād (?).

19.2d sahya°: L2 saṉhya°.

19.3a sa: Ed K sā.

19.3b nadīṃ: Ed K nadī.

19.3b °āpahāṃ: Ed K °āpahā.

19.3c °saṃpūrṇāṃ: Ed K °saṃpūrṇā.

19.3d °sevitāṃ: Ed K °sevitā.

19.4a ānīlo°: Bm M anilo°; K anīlo°.

19.4a °kalhāra°: Bm °kalhārai; M °kalhāraiḥ. See **§7.9b** for Bm final *saṃdhi*.

19.4b alaṅkṛtāṃ: Ed K alaṅkṛtā; Bm M alaṅkṛtaṃ.

19.4d pariśobhitāṃ: Ed pariśobhitā; (Bm ppariśobhitāṃ).

19.5a mahābhāgas: L2 mahābhāgā; Bm mahābhāga.

19.5c mādhāhnikaṃ: Bm māhnikaṃ; M tu māhnikaṃ. Bm omits syll. Probably mādhyāhnikaṃ>Bm>M.

19.5d °yajñadikāḥ: Bm M °yajñādika°.

19.6b taṭinī°: Bm taṭanī° (?).

19.6c par*ā*śu: Ed K paru śu; L2 Bm M paraśur.

19.6c yātavyam: Ed K pātavyam. Ed K due to *Devanāgarī* y> p.

19.7a sāyāhna° (L2 sāyāṃhna°).

19.7b †mandam āvavau†: L2 Bm M mandarāvayuḥ. Source?

19.7c dṛṣṭavān: Ed L2 K pṛṣṭavān.

19.7c *kāṃ*cit: Ed L2 Bm M kācit; K kāścit.

19.7d kāntādāsīṃ: Ed K kāntāsi (?); Bm M kāntāṃ dāsīṃ. Ed K omit syll.

19.7d kadambake (Bm kadabake).

19.8a °āb*dāṃ* . . . . : Ed L2 K °ābdān samānītān; Bm M °ābdāt samānītān. See **§7.9a** for ṃ = n. 'samānītān' source?

19.8b °otthi*tāṃ*: All MSS °otthitān. See **§7.9a** for ṃ = n.

19.8c †lasan°† (L2 lasaṃn°).

19.8c °nāsām: L2 °māsām.

19.8c °ākṣīṃ: Bm M °ākṣiṃ.

19.8d tārādhipanibhā°: Bm M tārādhipatibhā° (?). Bm M due to *Devanāgarī* n>t.

19.9a-19.10d L2 omits.

19.9a dvitīya°: K dvitīyaṃ.

19.9a °candra° (Bm °cadra°).

19.9a °eva: Bm M °ena.

19.9b dṛśyamāna°: Bm M dṛśyamānā.

19.9c °ṣaṭpadānīva, perhaps "°ṣaṭpadām iva.' See **§7.9a**, **§8.5** and 19.12c ''pi' variant below.

19.10a °kaṇṭhā°: Bm °kantā°.

19.10c śubhaśroṇīṃ: Bm M suraśreṇīṃ.

19.10d nāmrāṅgīṃ: Bm M namnāṅgīṃ. Bm M probably due to *Devanāgarī* Cr>Cn.

19.11a °ojjvalāṃ: L2 °ojvalā (= °ojjvalā?); (Bm M °ojvalāṃ).

19.11a subhrūṃ (Bm subhruṃ, M subhraṃ).

19.11b padminī°: Bm padmani; M padmāni.

19.12a enāṃ: K etāṃ (?). K due to *Devanāgarī* n>t?

19.12b *sa*dṛdhī°: All MSS saṃdṛdhī° (?).

19.12b °kṛta°: L2 °kṛtya°.

19.12c 'pi (L2 Bm 'pī).

19.13a kīrtiṃ: Bm K kīrti. See **§7.9b** for a possible Bm K final *saṃdhi*.

19.13a dhairyaṃ: Bm dhairya. See **§7.9b** for a possible Bm final *saṃdhi*.

19.13b sāhasikya° (Bm M sāhasikma°). Bm M due to *Devanāgarī* y>m.

19.13d mārgaṇāt: Ed Bm K mārgaṇān; (M mārgaṇātt). Ed Bm K due to *Devanāgarī* t>n.

19.14a *hri*yā°: Ed L2 K hviyā°; Bm M hīyā°.

19.14a °ānantarhitāṃ: Ed K °ānantāhitāṃ; Bm °ānataṃ hitāṃ; M °ānantaṃ hitāṃ.

19.14a tanvīṃ: Bm M tanviṃ.

19.14c yugapad: Bm M pagapad (?); K yugapard (?). Bm M in part due to *Devanāgarī* y>p.

19.14c daṃpatī° (Bm M dapatī°).

19.14c °bhāvaṃ: Bm °bhāvāṃ.

19.14d caṇḍikāyā: M caṇḍikāyāṃ.

19.14[1] śaunakaḥ: Ed Bm M K śaunaka uvāca.

19.15a tanvī: Bm M anvi (?).

19.15b °*ādir*: Ed Bm M K °ādi; L2 °ādvi° (?).

19.15b niyater: Ed K °nayanair; Bm M °niyamair.

19.15b gatiḥ: L2 gataḥ.

19.15c tasyāṃ: L2 tasvyā (?).

19.16a-19.16d Bm omits.

19.16a ninaya (M nināya).

19.16a °rātraṃ: M °rātriṇś.

19.16b °āliṅga°: M °āliṅgya°.

19.16c tasyā: Ed M K tasya.

19.16d °pātrā°: Ed M K °pātra°.

19.17a-19.17d Bm M omit in proper order, inserting after 19.18.

19.17a sukumārāḥ: L2 sukumāraḥ; Bm M sukumāra. See **§7.9b** for Bm M final *saṃdhi*.

19.17b 'bhavan: L2 M 'bhavat. *Devanāgarī* n>t.

19.18a putrebhyaḥ: Bm M putrebhyo.

19.18b grāmāny anukramāt: L2 Bm M cakram asikramāt (?).

19.19c-19.20d M omits.

19.19d dhāra*ṇāḥ*: Ed Bm K dhārakāḥ; (L2 dhāranāḥ). See **§7.9a** for ṇ>n.

19.20c apāṅkteyā (Bm apānteyā).

19.20d saṃcarantu: Bm saṃcaranta.

19.21a †*kālam*† ākrāntam: Ed L2 K kalinākrāntam; Bm M kalim(?) ākrāntam..

19.21d sunītaṃ: K sunīta.

19.21d nāma: Bm M mama.

19.22a °jñam abhijñaṃ taṃ: Bm M °jñamam(?) ābhijñaṃ.

19.22c °pātrāḥ: Bm M °putrāḥ.
19.22d putrāḥ: L2 putrā; Bm M putra°. See **§7.9b** for L2 final *saṃdhi*.
19.22d sneha°: Ed K snehe.
19.23a prajñena: L2 Bm M prājñena.
19.23b paripāl*yan*tāṃ: Ed L2 K paripālyatāṃ; Bm M pratipālyatāṃ. Emendation required by sense.
19.23d sabhāryas: L2 sabhāryaḥs. See **§7.9b** for L2 final *saṃdhi*.
19.24b āj*ñāṃ*: All MSS ājñā. Emendation required by sense.
19.24b laṅghi*tvā*: Ed Bm M K laṅghitā; L2 laṅghitaḥ. Emendation required by sense.
19.24c °opanīti: L2 °opanita (?).
19.24^{1} śatānīkaḥ: Ed K śatānīka uvāca; Bm M śrīśatānīka uvāca.
19.25a vipro 'sau†: Ed L2 K vipreṇa.
19.25b saṃskāraṃ: K saṃskāra.
19.25c ceṭī°: Ed K dāsī°; M cedī° (?). Ed K synonym.
19.25d śaṅkāṃ: Ed K saṅkām.
19.25d prāpnoti: Ed K āpnoti.
19.25d me: L2 te.
19.25^{1} śaunakaḥ: Ed Bm M K śaunaka uvāca (Bm śaunakovāca).
19.26a sādhu: L2 sādhaṃ.
19.26c tā*dṛṅ*, or 'tādṛg': Ed K tādṛg; L2 Bm M tādṛk.
19.26d saṃjātāṃ: Bm M saṃjātā. See **§7.9b** for possible final *saṃdhi*.
19.27b yadi . . . . . . , perhaps 'yadi bhūmispṛ*śo na* vā: Ed K yadi bhūmispṛśaḥ śivaḥ; L2 yadi bhūmispṛśāś ca vā: Bm M bhūmipṛpāchivaḥ (?). Source? With the suggested emendations this passage would translate, 'whether or not there is a touching of the earth.' But what does this mean in the context here?
19.27c vipravaryāc (Bm viprayāc, M vipraryāc). Bm M omit syll.
19.28a gotra°: Bm M gotraṃ.
19.28a °vihīnānāṃ (M °vihīnāṃ). M omits syll.

19.28b kāśyapaṃ gotram: Ed K gotraṃ kāśyapam (K gotraṃ kaśyapam). Ed K transpose words.
19.28b iṣyate: Ed K ucyate.
19.28c āśvalāyana° (Bm aśvalāyana°).
19.28c kāryā: L2 kāryaṃ.
19.28d °satkriyāḥ: L2 °saṃnkriyāṃ (= ?); Bm M °satkriyā.
19.29a kārayitvā° (L2 kāraïtvā°). See **§7.4**.
19.29c kāśyapaṃ (K kaśyapaṃ).
19.29d tattat° (K tatat°).
19.30a ādikaiś ca: L2 ādikai cid; Bm M ādikāni. See **§7.9b** for L2 final *saṃdhi*.
19.30b saṃdideśa (Bm M sadideśa).
19.30b pṛthak pṛthak: Bm 'pṛthak' only. Bm omits two syll.
19.30d saṃjātānāṃ: L2 saṃjātāṃ ca.
19.30d nṛpātmaja: L2 nṛpātmajāṃ.
19.31a °kanyānāṃ (L2 °kaṃnyānāṃ).
19.31c sāṅkarya°: Bm M sākalpa°.
19.31c °vicchityai: M °vichityair (?).
19.31d ayaṃ: Bm ayāṃ (?).
19.32a parāśaraḥ: L2 parāśaras.
19.32a sākṣāt: L2 sākṣā (?).
19.32b nāvikān: Ed L2 K nāvikāṃ. See **§7.9a** for ṃ = n.
19.32c kuṭhāra°: Bm akuṭhāra°. Bm adds syll.
19.32d goḷakān (Ed Bm M K golakān).
19.32d uddadhāra (L2 udadhāra, Bm M udvadhāra). Bm M due to *Devanāgarī* dd>dv.
19.33a mahā°: M māhā°.
19.33b °kīrtanaṃ: Bm M °kīrtitaṃ.
19.33c °vividhāḥ: L2 °vividhāḥs. See **§7.9b** for L2 final *saṃdhi*.
19.33cd santi nātra: Bm satitātra; M santitatra. Bm M due to *Devanāgarī* n>t.
19.33d kāryā: L2 Bm M kārya.
19.34c See 10.22b.
19.34c nātikramya: Ed K nātikrāmad; Bm M nātikrama° (M nāttikrama°).
19.34c guror: M guro.

19.34d °taḷe (Ed Bm M K °tale).
19.35b saṃbabhāṣe dvijātmajaḥ: L2 inserts 'ta' after 'saṃbabhāṣe.' L2 extra syll.
19.35c āgataṃ: Ed K āgatā.
19.35c purād: Ed L2 K purā.
19.36a dvijavaryo: Bm dijarkyo (?). Bm omits syll.
19.36b sma: Ed Bm M K sva°.
19.36c ceṭāḥ: Ed K dāsyāś; M ceṣṭāḥ. Ed K synonym.
19.36d °taḷe (Ed Bm M K °tale).
19.37a anādṛtya: Bm anādatya (?). Bm probably due to *Devanāgarī* vowel modification ṛ>a.
19.38a °ṣaṭkaṃ (M °ṣaṭṃ). M omits syll.
19.38a ca ṣaṭ . . : Ed K ca ṣaṭpuccham (?); L2 ca ṣaṭpuchaṃ; Bm ṣaṭkapuchaṉs (?); M ṣaṭpucchaṉs (?). Source? M omits syll.
19.38b upavīta°: Bm ūpavītta (?); M ūyanīta (?). M in part due to *Devanāgarī* p>y and probably Telugu or Kanarese script v>n.
19.38c sva°: L2 Bm M sa.
19.39a rudrākṣadhāraṇaṃ: M rudrākṣādhāraṇaṃ.
19.39[1] Between 19.39a and 19.39b L2 inserts:
halagrāmārcanaṃ tathā tri[? ? ?]ṛṇṭradhāraṇaṃ /
19.39c °saṅgha°: Bm M °saṃdha° (?). Bm M due to *Devanāgarī* gh>dh.
19.40c apāṅkteyā*nām* eteṣāṃ: Ed L2 K apāṅkteyān ime teṣāṃ; Bm M apāṅkteyān iye(?) teṣāṃ. Emendation required for sense. Bm M due to *Devanāgarī* m>y.
19.40d narāṇāṃ (Bm narāṇā).
19.40d °vartināṃ: Bm M °vartināḥ; K °vartinā.
19.41a bhuñjānānām (Bm M bhuñjāṃnānām).
19.41a adharmāṉś: Bm M adharmāś.
19.41b gaṅgā° (Bm gagā°).
19.41cd Ed reads:
sadā teṣāṃ samāśritya varttate te narādhamāḥ /
There are for this the following variant readings:
teṣāṃ (Bm M teṣā).

varttate te: L2 varttate yo; Bm varttayatto; M vartayanto.

19.42a °āb*dān*: Ed L2 K °āṣṭān; Bm M °ābdā.

19.42a pravastavyaṃ: Ed K pravastavye. Ed K due to *Devanāgarī* aṃ>e.

19.42b vārāṇasyāṃ: L2 vārāṇasyā.

Colophons:

Ed K iti śrīskandapurāṇe sahyādrikhaṇḍe uttararahasye pātityagrāme ekonaviṉśatitamo 'dhyāyaḥ.

L2 iti śrīsaṉhyādrau uparibhāge pātityagrāme pañcaviṉśa[ti]śatatamo 'dhyāyaḥ.

Bm M iti śrī-uttararahasye pātityagrāme ekonaviṉśati[ta]mo 'dhyāyaḥ.

V. APPENDIXES

APPENDIX A: MAPS

Map A. Map of Southwestern India.

The boundaries of Shimoga district, South Kanara district and Udipi *tāluka* are approximate as these boundaries have changed often and as the calibration of the maps used as the sources for this map differed from one another. The boundaries are those of the British period from the late 1800's to the early 1900's, and not those of modern India, as the sources mentioning them were of this time span. The state boundaries shown are those of modern India, however. It is hoped that this will make the discussion of the areas under consideration easier to follow.

Sources:

1907-1909. *The Imperial Gazetteer of India*, new ed. 26 vols. Oxford: Clarendon Press.

India. Great Trigonometrical Survey. [19 -]. *An Atlas of the Southern Part of India, Including Plans of All the Principle Towns and Cantonments. Reduced from the Grand Trigonometrical Survey of India Shewing Also the Tenasserim Provinces*. Madras: Pharoah and Co.

India. Ministry of Scientific Research and Cultural Affairs. 1962. *India: Waterways and Airways*, for *National Atlas of India*, 1st ed. Prepared under the direction of S. P. Chatterjee. [Map.]

India. Surveyor General. [Surveyed 1929-32]. *Bombay, Goa and Mysore: North Kanara District, Goa, Shimoga District*. Published under the direction of Brigadier H. J. Couchman, Surveyor General of India. Marked, 'For Official Use Only.' [Map.]

Rice, Benjamin Lewis. 1876. *Mysore and Coorg. A Gazetteer Compiled for the Government of India*. Vol. II: *Mysore, by Districts*. Bangalore: Mysore Government Press.

Rice, Benjamin Lewis. 1897. *Mysore. A Gazetteer Compiled for Government*, rev. ed. Vol II: *Mysore, by Districts*. Westminster: Archibald Constable and Company.

Map B. Map of the Regions of Ancient India mentioned in the PGN.

Included on this map are the sites of the two identifiable major cities mentioned in the PGN and of Ahichatra, from which the *brāhmaṇas* of the thirty-two villages are alleged to have come.

Sources:

Davies, Cuthbert Collin. 1944. *An Historical Atlas of the Indian Peninsula*. [Bombay]: Geoffrey Cumberlege, Oxford University Press.

Monier-Williams, Monier. 1899. *A Sanskrit-English Dictionary*, new ed. Oxford: Clarendon Press.

Spate, Oskar Hermann Khristian. 1957. *India and Pakistan: A General and Regional Geography*, 2nd ed. London: Methuen and Co. Ltd.

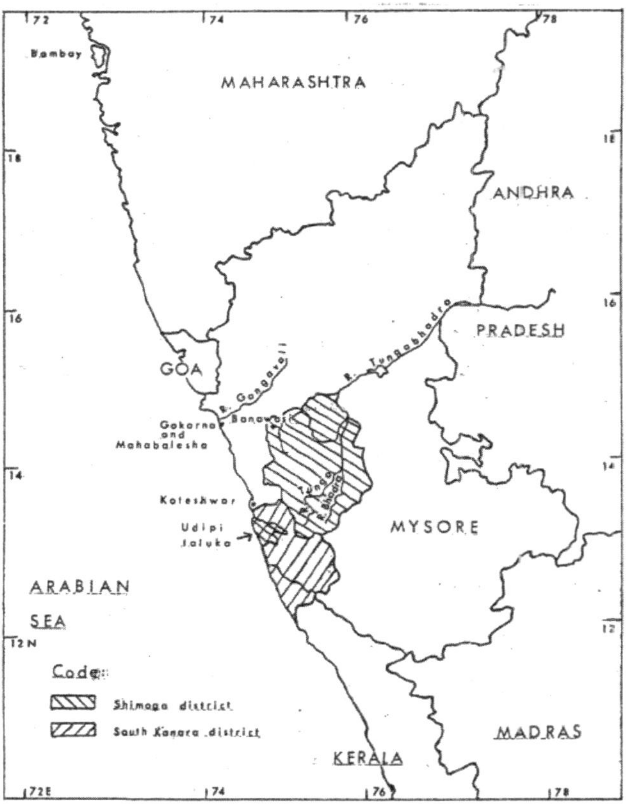

MAP A. MAP OF SOUTHWESTERN INDIA.
[Mysore State = Karnataka. Madras State = Tamil Nadu.
Bombay = Mumbai.]

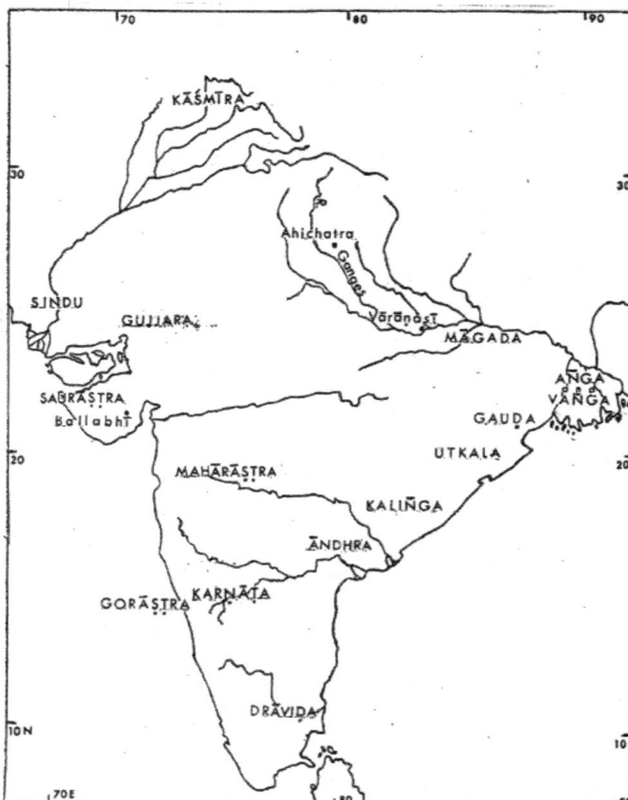

MAP B. MAP OF THE REGIONS OF ANCIENT INDIA MENTIONED IN THE PGN.

APPENDIX B: GLOSSES

9.12[2] Insertion between 9.12[1]and 9.12cd in L1a and L1c.
L1a inserts:
ākarṇya nṛpater vākyaṃ kiṃcit smaramukhāmbujaḥ /
śrutvā kroḍeśapādābjayugaḷaṃ sa dvijāgraṇīḥ /
harṣayaṃ nṛpate svāntaṃ jagāma madhurāṅgiraṃ /
It then repeats:
śaunakaḥ /
harṣayaṃ = harṣa*yan*. See **§7.9a** for ṃ = n.
These 1½ vss. are not translatable.
L1c inserts:
ākakarṇye nṛ[pa]ter vākyaṃ kiṃcit smara[n] mukhāmbujaḥ /
natvā kroḍeśvarapadaṃ jagāda madhurāṃ giraṃ /
pātityagrāmnāmāni vakṣyāmi nṛpanandana /
ākarṇye = ākarṇ*ya*.
°padaṃ = °*pā*daṃ.
Translation:
After hearing the king's words the one with a lotus-like face remembered something, bowed to the feet of Kroḍeśvara, and spoke sweet words. 'O king, I will speak the names of the villages of those who are polluted.'
This appears to be a gloss which both introduces the PGN and attempts to explain the beginning story about the *muni* Kroḍa. It can in no way be construed as a continuation of chapter 8 of the *uttarārdha* of the Skh as this is presently constituted. The readings in L1c for L1a śrutvā/L1c natvā, L1a jagāma/L1c jagāda and L1a madhurāṅgiraṃ (name of a place)/L1c madhurāṃ giraṃ appear to be preferable to those of L1a, though under such circumstances the word 'svāntaṃ,' 'one's own country, etc.' in L1a would present a problem.

10.20[1] Insertion between 10.20d and 10.21a in L1a:
idaṃ purāṇavākyāni nāmāni kavivākyataḥ /
The grammar is defective. The sense would seem to be: These are the names mentioned in the *purāṇa* as spoken by the *kavi*.

11.34[2] Insertion between 11.34[1] and 11.35a in all MSS:
yasya drohaṃ ca kurute †yadā yaḥ† karuṇānvitaḥ /
atīva duḥkhasaṃtaptas tam eva śaraṇaṃ vrajet /
manasānusmaran so 'pi drohaṃ ten kṛtaṃ punaḥ /
uddhariṣyati dharmātmā rāmaḥ śastrabhṛtāṃ varaḥ /
teṣām asau drohadṛtaṃ caturthe narapuṃgavaḥ /
. . . vismayaḥ kāryo na kaścit karuṇātmanāṃ /
This passage is extremely confusing, even with whatever editing is possible. It appears to be perhaps two glosses, one embedded in the other, both incomplete. It cannot be translated in full.
Partial translation:
I. When one who is filled with compassion does an offence to someone, he should go to that one for shelter when he is consumed by exceeding sorrow, again remembering in his mind the offence done by him. . . . There is not to be any doubt . . . about one filled with compassion.
II. Dutiful Rāma, the best of those who bears arms, will lift up . . . .
Critical apparatus:
ca kurute: L1c cakrur ure (?). There seems to be little doubt that the reading of L1c here comes from that of the other MSS, with *Devanāgarī* t>r.
†yadā yaḥ†: Ed L2 Br K yadāpaḥ; L1c yaśatha (?). Probably, *Devanāgarī* dā>śa, *Devanāgarī* y>p
°ānvitaḥ: Ed L2 Br K °ānvitāḥ; L1c °ānitaḥ.
°saṃtaptas: L1c °saṃtaptaḥs; L2 °saṃtaptās; Bm M °saṃtaptaḥ; Br °saṃtap (?). See **§7.9b** for L1c final *saṃdhi*. Br omits syll.

°ānusmaran: Ed Br K dusmarat (?); L2 °ānasmarat; Bm M °ānusmṛtaḥ. *Devanāgarī* n>t.
droham: Ed K drohas.
tena kṛtaṃ punaḥ: Ed Br K tena kṛtaḥ punaḥ; L1c tanakapunapuṃgavaḥ (?). L1c two extra syll.
uddhariṣyati . . . narapuṃgavaḥ: L1c omits.
nara°: Ed Br K para°. Telugu or Kanarese script n>p?
°puṃgavaḥ: L2 °puṃgava.
. . . vismayaḥ: Ed L2 Br K te gātra vismayaḥ; L1c netrātra vismayaḥ; Bm M vegātra(?) vismayaḥ. Source?
kāryo: Br rko (?). Br omits syll.
kaścit: L2 kasmit (?).
karuṇā°: L1c karaṇa°.
°ātmanāṃ: Ed Br K °ātmanaḥ; Bm M °ātmanāḥ.

12.46^1 Insertion between 12.46b and 12.46^2 in all MSS:
ṛṣiś ca vāmadevākhyaś chando 'nuṣṭup prakīrtitaḥ /
tathā nārāyaṇo devaḥ kaivalyārthapradāyakaḥ /
purā cakradharaḥ śrīmān bhūtaṃ māṃ uktavān kila /
kaṇṭhe ca tuḷasīdāma lalāṭe cordhvapuṇḍrakaṃ /
mukhe cāṣṭākṣaraṃ yasya viṣṇur eva na saṃśayaḥ /
bahunātra kim uktena kurvantu mama śāsanaṃ /
This appears to be layer upon layer of commentary, and appears to be quite confusing because of this.
Translation:
I. The ṛṣi is called Vāmadeva. The meter is called Anuṣṭup. Nārāyaṇa, bestowing the object of perfect isolation of the soul, is the god.
II. The blessed one who carries a *cakra* (i.e. Viṣṇu) previously told me what actually occurred.
III. One who has a garland of Tuḷasī on the throat, the bow-shaped mark on the forehead, and the eight syllables in the mouth, he indeed is Viṣṇu without a doubt.
IV. What else is there to say? They must do according to my command.
Critical apparatus:

devākhyaś: L1c devārtva (?); L2 devākhyā; Bm M devākhyo; Br devāthyo (perhaps, devāyyo).
chando 'nuṣṭup prakīrtitaḥ: L1c L2 chando 'nuṣṭuprakīrtitaṃ (?).
°ārtha°: Br °ārthe.
cakradharaḥ: L1c cakradhara.
śrīmān: L1c śrīmā.
bhūtaṃ: Ed L2 Bm M Br K hita.
tuḷasī°: L2 tulaśī° (?); (Ed Bm M Br K tulasī°).
lalāṭe cordhva°: L1c bhuvor madhyordhva°; L2 Bm M lalāṭe urdhva° (L2 urdva°); Br lalāṭe vurdhva (?).
cāṣṭā°: Ed L2 Bm M Br K pañcā°.
bahunātra: L1c bahunātṛ (?). L1c probably due to Telugu or Kanarese script usage of 'ṛ.' See **§7.4**.
kim: Br vim (?). Br due to *Devanāgarī* k>v.
After the first vs., L1c inserts a lengthy commentary:
asya śrīnārāyaṇāṣṭākṣaramahāmantrasya vāmadeva *ṛṣi* a*nuṣṭup* chandaḥ śrīnārāyaṇo devatā mahāviṣ*ṇor prāgrya*jape viniyogaḥ /
oṃ krāṃ aṅguṣṭhābhyāṃ namaḥ /
oṃ krī tarjanībhyāṃ namaḥ /
oṃ krū madhyamābhyāṃ namaḥ /
oṃ kraiṃ anāmikābhyāṃ namaḥ /
oṃ krauṃ kaniṣṭhikābhyāṃ namaḥ /
oṃ kraḥ karataḷakarapṛṣṭhābhyāṃ namaḥ /
dhyānaṃ /
śaṃkaraṃ bhujagaśayanaṃ padmanābhaṃ sūre*śaṃ* viśvādhāraṃ gaganasadṛśaṃ meghavarṇaṃ śu*bhaṃ* gaṃ /
lakṣmīkāntaṃ kamalanayanaṃ yogibhir dhyānavandyaṃ sagamyaṃ vande viṣṇuṃ bhavabhayahara viśvavan*dyaṃ* kundaṃ /
oṃ namo nārāya*ṇāya* /
*bā*lādi dvādaśsthāne mudrālakṣaṇam āha saḥ /
śaṅkhacakragadāpadmadhvajaiś ca pariśobhi*taiḥ* /
ete praśastā loke 'smin pañcacudrāḥ prakīrtitāḥ /
lalāṭe keśavāyeti tathā nārāyaṇeti ca /
hṛdaye dhāraṇaṃ kāryaṃ *par*śvayos tad anantaraṃ /

tadvan mādhavagovindau dakṣiṇe viṣṇaveti ca /
vāme madhu*sūdaneti bāhvau mūle* viśiṣyate /
tatas trivikramāyeti kapole dakṣiṇe smṛtaṃ /
anyasmin vāmanāyeti śrīdharāyeti *mūr*dhani /
hṛṣīkeśā*yeti* . . . . kaṇṭhe vidhīyate /
padmanābhāyeti kakṣau pṛṣṭhe dāmodareti ca /
lalā*ṭe* tu dhvajākāraṃ hṛdaye . . . . . /
bāhvau padmadalākāram ūrdhvapuṇḍrasya lakṣaṇaṃ /
ity evaṃ *dvāda*śā*n*śe*ṣu* pañcamudrāṃ vidhīya*te* /
idaṃ pavitraṃ paramaṃ gopanīyaṃ prayatnataḥ /
kadā cin nopadeṣṭavyaṃ kṛtaghnāya durātma*ne* /
mayā †yuṣmākam† uktaṃ yat sādhitaṃ . . . . . /
For *testimonia* see the insertion of L2 and M given below under 17.56¹.

Translation:

For the great *mantra* of eight syllables to holy Nārāyaṇa the *ṛṣi* is Vāmadeva, the meter is Anuṣṭup, the god is holy Nārāyaṇa, the use is in the foremost *japa* of great Viṣṇu.

Oṃ krāṃ. Homage to the two thumbs.[1]
Oṃ krī. Homage to the two forefingers.
Oṃ krū. Homage to the two middle fingers.
Oṃ kraiṃ. Homage to the two ring fingers.
Oṃ krauṃ. Homage to the two little fingers.
Oṃ kraḥ. Homage to the backs of the hand and to the palms of the hand.

Meditation.

Śaṃkara, having a snake as his sleeping place, lotus-naveled, lord of the sun, mainstay of all, with an appearance similar to that of a sky with the hue of a cloud, splendid, the third consonant of the alphabet.
Husband to lotus-eyed Lakṣmī, worthy of praise by devotees, Viṣṇu who is accessible to men when they are extolling [him], lord of the fear of worldly existence, Kunda who is worthy of praise by all.

---

[1] It has been impossible to locate this series of *mantras* to date.

Beginning with the children[2] he pronounced the marks of the *mudrās*[3] on the twelve places. When they were adorned by the conch shell, the discus, the mace, the lotus, and the emblem, these five consecrated marks which are celebrated in the world, he specified [the *mantra*] "*keśavāya*"[4] on the head, likewise "*nārāyaṇa*" to be carried in the heart, and after that on the two sides "*mādhava*" and "*govinda*" in the same way, and on the right shoulder blade [the *mantra*] "*viṣṇave*" and on the left "*madhusūdana*." Then he bestowed on the right cheek the *mantra* "*trivikramāya*" as prescribed by law, on the other "*vāmanāya*," on the head "*śrīdharāya*," . . . on the throat "*hṛṣīkeśāya*," on the belly "*padmanābhāya*, and on the back "*damodara*." He prescribed the shape of the emblem on the forehead, on the heart . . . , [and] on the shoulder the sign of the perpendicular sectarian mark with the appearance of a lotus leaf. In this way he bestowed the five *mudrās* on the twelve sections. This highest mean of purification is to be protected diligently. It is in no way to be advised for the ungrateful of wicked nature. What I speak †of you† is accomplished . . . .

Critical apparatus:
°deva *ṛ*ṣi: °devarṣiḥ.
a*nuṣṭup*: anraṣṭapra (?).

---

[2] Perhaps, 'Beginning with the forehead . . . .' See **§7.11**.

[3] Perhaps, '. . . he pronounced the marks gladly . . . .' See **§7.11**.

[4] All the *mantras* mentioned here are from the *Baudhāyanadharmasūtra* and constitute most of 2.5.9.10 as in Hultsch (1922: 64). This reads: oṃ keśavaṃ tarpayāmi / oṃ nārāyaṇaṃ tarpayāmi / oṃ mādhavaṃ tarpayāmi / oṃ govindaṃ tarpayāmi / oṃ viṣṇuṃ tarpayāmi / oṃ madhusūdanaṃ tarpayāmi / oṃ trivikramaṃ tarpayāmi / oṃ vāmanaṃ tarpayāmi / oṃ śrīdharaṃ tarpayāmi / oṃ hṛṣīkeśaṃ tarpayāmi / oṃ padmanābhaṃ tarpayāmi / oṃ damodaraṃ tarpayāmi / etc. This is part of a long list of gods to be satiated, and constitute part of a *tarpaṇa* ceremony introduced in 2.5.8.14. A *tarpaṇa* is a satiation of either the gods or deceased persons by presenting to them libations of water.

°viṣ*ṇor*: °viṣṇur.
prāgrya°: prātya°
sūre*śaṃ* : sūresaṃ.
śu*bhaṃ*: śubhā.
van*dyaṃ*: vandyamu (?).
nārāya*ṇāya*: nārāyayāāyā (?).
*bā*lā°: thālā° (?). Read '*bhā*lā°'? See **§7.11**.
mudrālakṣaṇam. Read 'mu*dā* lakṣaṇam"? See **§7.11**.
*par*śvayos: ph[?]arśvayos.
madhu*sūdaneti bāhvau mūle*: madhubhide tubhyaṃ bābādgamule (?).
*mūr*dhani: murdhani.
hṛṣīkeśā*yeti* . . . . : hṛṣīkeśāyate tubhyaṃ iti.
lalā*ṭe*: lalāte.
hṛdaye . . . . . : hṛdaye śvakṣapatravat (?).
bāhvau: bādko (?).
*ūr*dhva°: ūdhva° (?).
*dvā*da*śaṇśe*ṣu *pañ*camudrām: pādaśāṅgeṣu ghañcamudrāṃ (?).
vidhīya*te*: vidhīyakaḥ (?).
durātma*ne*: durātman.
sādhitaṃ . . . . . : sādhitaṃ svapravavataḥ (?).

13.2[1] Insertion between 13.2b and 13.2c in L1c:
ity ukte sakalakalatraputram ity arthaḥ /
This half-*śloka* is defective and corrupt, and is not translatable, though it seems to fall into the outline: 'In saying . . . , . . . is the meaning.'

15.7[1] Insertion between 15.7b and 15.7c in Ed L2 K.
Ed K insert:
balabhī nāma nagarī tasyāṃ kirvanta(?) nāmataḥ /
Pāda 2 is corrupt and is not translatable. K reads 'nāmanaḥ' for 'nāmataḥ.'
L2 inserts:
balabhī nāma nagarī tv ardhaḥ /
Translation:

The city named Balabhī is a place.
This usage of '*ardha*' is Vedic.

17.28[1] and 17.29[1] Insertion between 17.28d and 17.29a in L2 Bm M and n. to the second syllable of 'mithuna°' in Ed:

svabhāryāṃ śikṣāṃ kṛtavān asya kathaṃ doṣam āropaṇīyaṃ / śikṣā nāryaḥ sarvathaiva vacanāt / iti cec chaṅkāyām āha / ahiṉsa paramo dharma iti bhagavadvacanāt / brāhmaṇasya sarvathaiva hiṉsā niṣiddhā / evaṃ tāvat tatrāpi strīhatyaṃ mithunahatyaṃ ca / evaṃkṛtasya puruṣasya kathaṃ doṣaṃ nāropaṇīyaṃ ca / evaṃkṛtasya puruṣasya kathaṃ doṣaṃ nāropaṇīyaṃ / bhāryādaṇḍaṃ pṛthakśayyeti parityājyā duṣṭabhāryeti vā / ayaṃ puruṣaḥ sarvathā duḥ*khya* / evaṃ arthaḥ / prakṛtim anusarāmaḥ //

Translation:

How is there guilt for one who has punished his wife? The wife is to be punished under all circumstances according to express teaching. If such an objection is raised, then I answer, because of the text of the lord which says 'non-violence is the highest duty.' Under any circumstances, violence is forbidden of a *brāhmaṇa*. In the same way, then, here also, killing one's wife and killing the paramour.[1] For a man who has acted thus, how can guilt not be ascribed? 'The punishment of a wife is sleeping separately,' or 'A bad wife should be abandoned.' Such a man causes pain in every possible way. This is the meaning. Let us return to the subject.

After 'bharyādaṇḍaṃ pṛthakśayyeti,' the unidentified quotation 'The punishment of a wife is sleeping separately,' Ed inserts the half-*śloka*:

pṛthakśayyā ca nārīṇām aśastravadham ucyate /

[1] From context the word '*mithuna*' clearly means 'paramour' here – not 'couple.'

Translation:
Sleeping apart is said to be the weaponless killing of a wife.
Critical apparatus:
svabhāryāṃ: Ed Bm M svabhāryā°.
śikṣāṃ: L2 sikṣaṃ.
śikṣāṃ kṛtavān: Ed kṛtavān śikṣām.
After 'kṛtavān' L2 inserts: ayaṃ.
kathaṃ: Ed omits.
doṣam āropaṇīyaṃ: Ed doṣo na kārayeti; L2 doṣam aropaṇīyyaṃ.
nāryaḥ: Ed nāryāḥ; M naryaḥ.
vacanāt: Ed karttavyā.
After 'iti' Ed inserts: śāstrataḥ iti.
cec chaṅkāyām: L2 cebhaṃ kāyām (?); Bm M cetthaṃ kāyām.
dharma iti: L2 M dharmo dharmeti (?); Bm dharmo dharmati (?).
bhagavad: Ed omits.
vacanāt: Bm vacāt (?).
brāmaṇasya: L2 brāhmaṇyasya.
hiṉsā: L2 omits.
tatrāpi: Ed atra.
strīhatyaṃ: Ed Bm M strīhatyāṃ (Bm M strīhatyā).
mithunahatyaṃ ca: Ed maithunahatyāṃ; Bm M mithunaṃ ca.
doṣaṃ: Ed doṣo; M doṣa°; (L2 doṣam).
nāropaṇīyaṃ: Ed nāropaṇīyaḥ; Bm nāṃropaṇīyaṃ (?); M ṇaropaṇīyaṃ (?); (L2 nāropaṇīyyaṃ).
°daṇḍaṃ: Bm °daṇḍa.
°śayyeti: Bm °śauyyeti (?).
After '°śayyeti' Ed inserts the half-*śloka* noted above.
parityājya: L2 parityage; Bm parityajyā.
ayaṃ: Ed atha.
puruṣaḥ: Ed puruṣāḥ.
duḥ*khya*: Ed 'dūṣyā; L2 Bm M duḥṣya (?). All MSS due to *Jainalipi*- nonstandard *Devanāgarī*, etc. ṣ = kh.

evety: L2 patīty; Bm M evam. L2 due to *Jainalipi-Devanāgarī* e>p?
prakṛtim: Ed L2 Bm prakṛtam.

17.56^{1} Insertion between 17.56d and 17.56^{2} in L2 and M:
bālādi dvādaśasthāne mudrālakṣaṇam āha saḥ /
śaṅkhacakragadāpadmadhvajaiś ca pariśobhitaiḥ /
ete pañcapraśastaś ca loke mudrāḥ prakīrtitāḥ /
lalāṭe dhāraṇaṃ kāryaṃ ato deveti mantra taḥ /
idaṃ viṣṇur ṛcā nityaṃ hṛdaye dhāraṇaṃ smṛtaṃ /
. . . . /
dakṣiṇe *bāhvau mūle* tu viṣṇoḥ karmā*ṇi* mantra taḥ /
tad viṣṇor iti mantreṇa kapole dakṣiṇe smṛtaṃ /
tad viprāseti mantreṇa kapole vāmake śubhe /
viṣṇor nu keti mantreṇa uttamāṅge vidhīyate /
pra tad viṣṇuḥ *kaṭa*de*śe* mudrayā cakrasaṃjñayā /
pra viṣṇaveti mantreṇa kuk*ṣau* sam*yag vi*dhīya*te* /
yasya *trīt*īti manteṇa *pṛṣṭha*deśe vidhīyate /
tad asya priyamantreṇa vāmapārśve vidhīyate /
tā vāṃ vāstv iti mantreṇa dakṣiṇe pārśvake śubhe /
ity evaṃ dvādaśāṇ̱śeṣu vedamantrair vidhīyate /
idaṃ pavitraṃ paramaṃ gopanīyaṃ prayatnataḥ /
kadā cin nopadeṣṭavyaṃ kṛtaghnāya durātmane /
bahunātra kim uktena kurvantu mama śāsanaṃ /
śāsayitvā mahāyogī prayayau taiś ca satkṛtaḥ /
For *testimonia* see the insertion of L1c at 12.46^{1} given above.
Translation:
Beginning with the children[1] he pronounced the marks of the *mudrās*[2] on the twelve places. When they were adorned with the conch shell, the discus, the mace, the lotus, and the emblem, these five consecrated marks which are celebrated in the world, he bestowed the

[1] Perhaps, 'Beginning with the forehead . . . .' See **§7.11**.
[2] Perhaps, '. . . he pronounced the marks gladly . . . .' See **§7.11**.

mantra "*ato devā*"[3] [to each one] to be carried on the forehead, with the sacred verse "*idaṃ viṣṇur*"[4] [to each one], as prescribed by law, to always be worn in the heart, . . . ,[5] to the right shoulder blade[6] the *mantra* "*viṣṇoḥ karmāṇa*,"[7] with the *mantra* "*tad viṣṇor*,"[8] always to be worn on the right cheek, with the *mantra* "*tad vipraso*"[9] to the splendid left cheek, with the *mantra* "*viṣṇor nu kaṃ*"[10] to the head. With clear understanding of the sign of the discus, he provided [the *mantra*] "*pra tad viṣṇuḥ*"[11] to the region of the hips and loins, and the *mantra* "*pra viṣṇave* "[12] to the belly. With the *mantra* "*yasya trītīti*"[13] he bestowed on the back. With the *mantra* "*tad asya priyam*"[14] he bestowed on the left side, [and] with the *mantra* "*tā vāṃ vāstūni*"[15] on the splendid right side. Just so, with *mantras* from the *Veda*, he bestowed on twelve places. This highest means of purification is to be preserved diligently. It is in no way to be advised for the ungrateful of wicked nature. Aside from this, what is there to say? "They must obey my orders." Having made this recommendation, the great *yogin* went, treated with respect by those.

Critical apparatus:

bālādi: M bālādir. Read '*bhā*lādi'? See **§7.11**.

---

[3] RV 1.22.16.

[4] RV 1.22.17.

[5] 'at the base of the right arm . . . [RV 1.22.18].' See **§7.11**.

[6] Perhaps, 'likewise at the base of the left . . . .' See **§7.11**.

[7] RV 1.22.19.

[8] RV 1.22.20.

[9] RV 1.22.21.

[10] RV 1.154.1.

[11] RV 1.154.2.

[12] RV 1.154.3.

[13] RV 1.154.4.

[14] RV 1.154.5.

[15] RV 1.154.6.

dvādaśa°: M vādaśa (?).
mudrālakṣaṇam: Read '*mudā* lakṣaṇam'? See **§7.11**.
pariśobhitaiḥ: L2 pariśobhitaḥ.
kāryaṃ: M kāyaṃ.
viṣṇur ṛcā: L2 viṣṇutṛcā (?).
dhāraṇaṃ smṛtaṃ . . . dakṣiṇe *bāhvau mūle* tu. See **§7.11**.
dakṣiṇe *bāhvau* . . . dakṣiṇe smṛtaṃ: M omits.
bāhvau mūle: L2 cāhumotetu (?).
karmā*ṇi*: L2 karmāṇa.
nu keti: M anuketi. Adds syll.
uttamāṅge vidhīyate: M uttamāṅge dhīyate (?). Omits syll.
pra tad . . . *pṛṣṭha*deśe vidhīyate: M omits.
pra: L2 reads just 'a' or 'e.'
*kaṭa*de*śe*: L2 kantadeśa.
kuk*ṣau*: L2 kukṣaṃ.
sam*yag*: L2 samṛ (?).
*vi*dhīya*te*: L2 [?]dhīyyatāṃ.
*tritī*ti: L2 tṛteti.
pṛṣṭha°: L2 dṛṣṭa°.
vidhīyate (L2 vidhīyyate).
vāmapārśve vidhīyate: L2 vāmapārśve viśasyate.
vāstv iti: L2 vāṃ stviti (?).
°āṉśeṣu: L2 °āṅgeṣu.
vedamantrair vidhīyate: L2 vedamantrair vidhīyyatāṃ.
gopanīyaṃ (L2 gopanīyyaṃ).
prayatnataḥ: M prayatrataḥ (?).
śāsayitvā (L2 śāsaïtvā).

APPENDIX C: *ṚGVEDA* PASSAGES CITED IN THE PGN AND ATTACHED COMMENTARIES

For the convenience of the reader the hymns which contain the *Veda* passages cited in the text of the PGN and in the commentary passages are given here with translations and a few notes, though such is marginal to the work at hand. This presentation is not to be understood as a study of these hymns in any way. Such a study could easily involve very lengthy articles for each hymn alone, *Veda* scholarship being a highly developed and refined discipline. It would be both out of place and improper to attempt such a study here. The hymns are presented solely for the reader's convenience, retranslation having been attempted only to provide the reader with a readable text in contemporary English.

It is my contention that seeing the hymns in context as used in the Hindu tradition helps us understand better their import. For instance, it is clear from the usage of RV1.89 that it has to do with communal well-being and longevity. Such an understanding of the hymn may lead to a modification in the way in which RV 1.89.10 has been generally interpreted – which interpretation has presented scholars with problems (see n. 3 to RV 1.89).

RV 1.89, RV 3.45, and RV 10.163 are used in ritual as mentioned in chapter nine (Skh.u. 17), vss. 55cd and 56. As noted in a n. in place, it would appear that it is the entire hymns that are being recited here on the basis of context and the content of each of the hymns. RV 1.22.16-21, the vss. of this hymn that refer to Viṣṇu, and RV 1.154.1-6, which hymn also refers to Viṣṇu, are used in ritual as mentioned in an insertion in chapter nine (Skh.u. 17) immediately following the above in MSS. L2 and M. It is the individual vss. referred to that are being used in the ritual here, one by one.

Below, the Sanskrit text of the hymns is given first. This is followed by a translation and notes for each hymn in the same order.

The various translations that have been consulted are:

Geldner, Karl Friedrich, trans. 1951[i.e. 1952]-57. *Der Rig-Veda, aus dem Sanskrit ins Deutsche übersetzt und mit einem laufenden Kommentar versehen*, 4 vols. Harvard Oriental Series 33-36. Cambridge, Massachusetts: Harvard University Press.

Grassmann, Hermann, trans. 1876-77. *Rig-Veda, übersetzt und mit kritischen und erläutenden Anmerkungen versehen*, 2 vols. Leipzig: F. A. Brockhaus. [Consulted here for only RV 1.89.]

Griffith, Ralph Thomas Hotchkiss, trans. 1889. *The Hymns of the Ṛgveda*. New rev. edition, ed. J. L. Shastri. Delhi: Motilal Banarsidass, 1973.

Maurer, Walter H., trans. 1986. *Pinnacles of India's Past, Selections from the Ṛgveda*. University of Pennsylvania Studies on South Asia 2. Amsterdam and Philadelphia: John Benjamins Publishing Company.

O'Flaherty, Wendy Doniger, trans. 1981. *The Rig Veda, An Anthology*. Rpt. Harmondsworth, Middlesex, England: Penguin Books, 1983.

Wilson, Horace Hayman, trans. 1850-88. *Rig-Veda Sanhita, A Collection of Ancient Hindu Hymns of the Rig-Veda, The Oldest Authority on the Religion and Social Institutions of the Hindus*, 7 vols. Rpt. New Delhi: Cosmo Publications, 1977.

Witzel, Michael and Toshifumi Gotō, trans. 2007. *Rig-Veda, das heiligen Wissen; erster und zweiter Liederkreis*. Frankfurt am Main: Verlag der Weltreligionen.

Ṛgveda 1.89

ā no bhadrā́ḥ krátavo yantu viśvátó 'dabdhāso áparītāsa udbhídaḥ / devā́ no yáthā sádam íd vṛdhé ásann áprayuvo rakṣitā́ro dive-dive / 1 /
devā́nām bhadrā́ sumatír ṛjūyatā́ṃ devā́nāṃ rātír abhí no ní vartatām / devā́nāṃ sakhyám úpa sedimā vayáṃ devā́ na ā́yuḥ prá tirantu jīváse / 2 /
tā́n pū́rvayā nivídā hūmahe vayám bhágam mitrám áditiṃ dákṣam asrídham / aryamáṇaṃ váruṇaṃ sómam aśvínā sárasvatī naḥ subhágā máyas karat / 3 /
tán no vā́to mayobhú vātu bheṣajáṃ tán mātā́ pṛthivī́ tát pitā́ dyaúḥ / tád grā́vāṇaḥ somasúto mayobhúvas tád aśvinā śṛṇutaṃ dhiṣṇyā yuvám / 4 /
tám ī́śānaṃ jágatas tasthúṣas pátiṃ dhiyaṃjinvám ávase hūmahe vayám / pūṣā́ no yáthā védasām ásad vṛdhé rakṣitā́ pāyúr ádabdhaḥ svastáye / 5 /
svastí na índro vṛddhásravāḥ svastí naḥ pūṣā́ viśvávedāḥ / svastí nas tā́rkṣyo áriṣṭanemiḥ svastí no bṛ́haspátir dadhātu / 6 /
pṛ́ṣadaśva marútaḥ pṛ́śnimātaraḥ śubhaṃyā́vāno vidátheṣu jágmayaḥ / agnijihvā́ mánavaḥ sū́racakṣaso víśve devā́ ávasā́ gamann ihá / 7 /
bhadráṃ kárṇebhiḥ śṛṇuyāma devā bhadrám paśyemākṣábhir yajatrāḥ / sthiraír áṅgais tuṣṭuvā́ṃsas tanū́bhir vy àśema deváhitaṃ yád ā́yuḥ / 8 /
śatám ín nú śarádo ánti devā yátrā naś cakrā́ jarásaṃ tanū́nāṃ / putrā́so yatra pitáro bhávanti mā́ no madhyā́ rīriṣatā́yur gántoḥ / 9 /
áditir dyaúr áditir antárikṣam áditir mātā́ sá pitā́ sá putráḥ / víśve devā́ áditiḥ páñca jánā áditir jātám áditir jánitvam / 10 /

Ṛgveda 3.45

ā́ mandraír indra háribhir yāhí mayū́raromabhiḥ / mā́ tvā ké cin ní yamam víṃ nā́ pāśínó 'ti dhánveva tā́m̐ ihi / 1 /
vṛtrakhādó valaṃrujáḥ purā́ṃ darmó apā́m ajáḥ / sthā́tā ráthasya háryor abhisvará índro dṛḷhā́ cid ārujáḥ / 2 /
gambhīrā́m̐ udadhī́m̐r iva krátum puṣyasi gā́ iva / prá sugopā́ yávasaṃ dhenávo yathā hradáṃ kulyā́ ivāśata / 3 /
ā́ nas tújaṃ rayím bharā́ṇśaṃ ná pratijānaté / vṛkṣám pakvám phálam aṅkī́va dhūnuhī́ndra sampā́raṇaṃ vásu / 4 /
svayúr indra svarā́ḷ asi smáddiṣṭiḥ sváyaśastaraḥ / sá vāvṛdhāná ójasā puruṣṭuta bhávā naḥ suśrávastamaḥ / 5 /

Ṛgveda 10.163

akṣī́bhyāṃ te nā́sikābhyāṃ kárṇābhyāṃ chúbukād ádhi / yákṣmaṃ śīrṣaṇyàm mastíṣkāj jihvā́yā ví vṛhāmi te / 1 /
grīvā́bhyas ta uṣṇíhābhyaḥ kī́kasābhyo anūkyā̀t / yákṣmaṃ doṣaṇyàm áṇsābhyām bāhúbhyāṃ ví vṛhāmi te / 2 /
āntrébhyas te gúdābhyo vaniṣṭhór hṛ́dayād ádhi / yákṣmam mátasnābhyāṃ yaknáḥ plāśíbhyo ví vṛhāmi te / 3 /
ūrúbhyāṃ te aṣṭhīvádbhyām pā́rṣṇibhyām prápadābhyām / yákṣmaṃ śróṇibhyām bhā́sadād bháṇsaso ví vṛhāmi te / 4 /
méhanād vanaṃkáraṇāl lómabhyas te nakhébhyaḥ / yakṣmaṃ sárvasmād ātmánas tám idáṃ ví vṛhāmi te / 5 /
áṅgād-aṅgāl lómno-lomno jātám párvaṇi-parvaṇi / yákṣmaṃ sárvasmād ātmána tám idáṃ ví vṛhāmi te / 6 /

Ṛgveda 1.22

prātaryújā ví bodhayāśvínāv éhá gachatām / asyá sómasya pītáye / 1 /
yā́ suráthā rathī́tamobhā́ devā́ divispŕ̥śā / aśvínā tā́ havāmahe / 2 /
yā́ vāṃ káśā mádhumaty áśvinā sūnŕ̥tāvatī / táyā yajñám mimikṣatam / 3 /
nahí vām ásti dūraké yátrā ráthena gáchathaḥ / áśvinā somíno gr̥hám / 4 /
híraṇyapāṇim ūtáye savitā́ram úpa hvaye / sá céttā devátā padám / 5 /
apā́ṃ nápātam ávase savitā́ram úpa stuhi / tásya vratā́ny uśmasi / 6 /
vibhaktā́raṃ havāmahe vásoś citrásya rā́dhasaḥ / savitā́raṃ nr̥cákṣasam / 7 /
sákhāya ā́ ní ṣīdata savitā́ stómyo nú naḥ / dā́tā rā́dhāṇsi śumbhati / 8 /
ágne pátnīr ihā́ vaha devā́nām uśatī́r úpa / tváṣṭāraṃ sómapītaye / 9 /
ā́ gnā́ ihā́vase hótrāṃ yaviṣṭha bhā́ratīm / várūtrīṃ dhiṣáṇāṃ vaha / 10 /
abhí no devī́r ávasā maháḥ śármaṇā nr̥pátnīḥ / áchinnapatrāḥ sacantām / 11 /
ihéndrāṇī́m úpa hvaye varuṇānī́ṃ svastáye / agnā́yīṃ sóma-pītaye / 12 /
mahī́ dyaúḥ pr̥thivī́ ca na imáṃ yajñáṃ mimikṣatām / pipr̥tā́ṃ no bhárīmabhiḥ / 13 /
táyor íd ghr̥távat páyo víprā rihanti dhītíbhiḥ / gandharvásya dhruvé padé / 14 /
syonā́ pr̥thivi bhavānr̥kṣarā́ niveśanī / yáchā naḥ śárma sapráthaḥ / 15 /
áto devā́ avantu no yáto viṣṇur vicakramé / pr̥thivyā́ḥ saptá dhā́mabhiḥ / 16 /

idáṃ víṣṇur ví cakrame tredhā́ ní dadhe padám / sámūḷham asya pāṉsuré / 17 /
trī́ṇi padā́ vícakrame víṣṇur gopā́ ádābhyaḥ / áto dhármāṇi dhār-áyan / 18 /
víṣṇoḥ kármāṇi paśyata yáto vratā́ni paspaśé / índrasya yújyaḥ sákhā / 19 /
tád víṣṇoḥ paramám padáṃ sádā paśyanti sūráyaḥ / divī̀va cákṣ-ur ā́tatam / 20 /
tád viprāso vipanyávo jāgṛvā́ṉsaḥ sám indhate / víṣṇor yát para-mám padám / 21 /

Ṛgveda 1.154

víṣṇor nú kaṃ vīryā̀ṇi prá vocaṃ yáḥ pā́rthivāni vivamé rájāṉ-
si / yó áskabhāyad úttaraṃ sadhásthaṃ vicakramāṇás tredhóru-
gāyáḥ / 1 /
prá tád víṣṇu stavate vīryeṇa mṛgó ná bhīmáḥ kucaró giriṣṭhā́ḥ /
yásyaorúṣu triṣú vikrámaṇeṣv adhikṣiyánti bhúvanāni víśvā / 2 /
prá víṣṇave śūṣám etu mánma girikṣíta urugāyā́ya vṛ́ṣṇe / yá id-
áṃ dīrghám práyataṃ sadhástham éko vimamé tribhír ít padé-
bhiḥ / 3 /
yásya trī́ pūrṇā́ mádhunā padā́ny ákṣīyamāṇā svadháyā mádan-
ti / yá u tridhātu pṛthivī́m utá dyā́m éko dādhā́ra bhúvanāni víś-
vā / 4 /
tád asya priyám abhí pā́tho aśyāṃ náro yátra devayávo mádan-
ti / urukramásya sá hí bándhur itthā́ viṣṇoḥ padé paramé mádh-
va útsaḥ / 5 /
tā́ vāṃ vā́stūny uśmasi gámadhyai yátra gā́vo bhū́riśṛṅgā ayā́-
saḥ / átrā́ha tád urugāyásya vṛ́ṣṇaḥ paramám padám áva bhāti
bhū́ri / 6 /

Ṛgveda 1.89

1. Let good judgments free from deception and unobstructed come to us, manifesting themselves in all places. In this way may the gods, being diligent guardians each day, provide success to us.

2. Let the auspicious kindness of the gods to those who espouse proper behavior, let the grace of the gods, come down to us. We have requested the friendship of the gods. May the gods promote our long life so that we may endure.

3. With an old proclamation we call upon those (the gods) – Bhaga, Mitra, Aditi, Dakṣa who never fails, Aryaman, Varuṇa, Soma, the Aśvins.[1] May wealthy Sarasvatī give pleasure to us.

4. Let Vāta blow to us that medicament which causes pleasure. Let the mother Pṛthivī give it. Let the father Dyaus give it. Let the stones which press the Soma and cause pleasure give it. Benevolent Aśvins, you must hear it.

5. For assistance we call on the one who reigns over men, the immovable ruler who excites devotion. In this way may Pūṣan, the guard, the benevolent protector of prosperity bring an increase of wealth to us.

6. Let Indra, illustrious far and wide, bestow success on us. Let Pūṣan, who knows all things, bestow success on us. Let Tārkṣya, the felly of whose wheel is undamaged, bestow success on us. Let Bṛhaspati bestow success on us.

7. Maruts, you who have piebald horses,[2] who have Pṛṣṇi as your mother, who fly swiftly – hastening to the assembly of the gods, [you] who are sages with Agni as your tongues and Sūra as your eyes, let all the gods come here for our assistance.

8. Gods, we should hear with our ears what is correct. You who deserve adoration, we should see with our eyes what is correct. Extolling, with firm-limbed bodies, may we obtain the duration of life appointed by the gods.

9. Gods, assuredly there are a hundred autumns yet wherein you will have brought our bodies to old age, wherein sons will become fathers. Do not destroy the course of life in the middle.

10. Heaven is boundless.[3] The *antarikṣa* is boundless. The mother is boundless. Such is the father. Such is the son. All the gods are boundless. The five groupings of beings[4] are boundless. Those born and to be born are boundless.

NOTES

[1] Five of the deities mentioned here, Bhaga, Mitra, Dakṣa, Aryaman, and Varuṇa are figured as Ādityas, or sons of Aditi, also mentioned here. The Ādityas are all abstract deities and are noted by Brereton (1981: viii, 8) to be gods of social relationships, avengers of evil-doing and guardians of those who act according to the principles they uphold. It is in this context no doubt, given the usage of this hymn in the PGN, that they are called on here. Dakṣa and Bhaga are figured as minor Ādityas, though Brereton (1981: 299-300) notes that to figure Dakṣa as such is misleading and has little justification.

[2] Perhaps, 'antelopes as horses.'

[3] Or 'unending.' Brereton (1981: 248-249) finds this vs. difficult to interpret, and considers it a late addition to this hymn, as had Grassmann (1876-77/2: 445). Similarly, Maurer notes that this vs. has nothing to do with the rest of the hymn, from whose tenor it differs markedly. The term translated here as 'boundless,' perhaps 'unending,' is translated in the various translations consulted, though, simply as reference to the goddess 'Aditi.' Thus, "Aditi is heaven, Aditi is mid-air, . . . " (Griffith 1889 [1973]: 57a). Such a translation would seem to be prohibited,

however, by the usage of the masculine form of the demonstrative pronoun in parallel constructions within the vs., e.g. 'aditiḥ mātā, saḥ pitā, . . .' . Grassmann (1873: 36, *s.v.* 2.á-diti) construes it as 'das *Unendliche*,' in this location, as opposed to the name of the goddess, not unlike the way we translate it here. (In Grassmann [1876-77/2: 445], though, he translates it as 'Aditi,' the name of the goddess, as in the other translations.) Translated as we translate it here, the vs. makes perfect sense in the context of the emphasis in this hymn on communal well-being and longevity. I might mention that Wilson's 1850 translation of this hymn makes it abundantly clear that this hymn is a prayer for communal well-being and longevity.

[4] The five groupings of beings may possibly be gods, men, *gandharvas* and *apsarases*, serpents, and the fathers (see Monier-Williams 1899: 576a [s.v. *pañca-janá*]). Wilson (1850-88/1: 230 n. *c*, 20 n. *a*) as well notes Yāska, in *Nirukta* 3.7 as listing the five groupings of beings as being *gandharvas*, the fathers, the gods, the *asuras*, and the *rakṣas* (or demons); and speculates, following Sāyaṇa, that it may refer instead to the four classes of men – *brāhmaṇas*, *kṣatriyas*, *vaiśyas*, and *śūdras*, to which are added the *niṣādhas* (non-Aryan barbarians). More modern opinion would have this locution refer rather to a listing of five tribes mentioned in some hymns of the *Ṛgveda* – the Anus, Druhyas, Yadus, Turvaśas, and Pūrus, who may be considered as comprising the Vedic grouping of peoples. See, for instance, Maurer (1986: 110 n. 8) and Witzel (2007: 631 n. 9, 414-415). Bharata and Kuru are descended from Pūru. Kṛṣṇa is descended from Yadu. The Yadus, or Yādavas – the descendants of Yadu, are generally considered to be non-Vedic Aryans.

Ṛgveda 3.45

1. Come here, Indra, with pleasing horses that have peacock-like hairs. May none stop you as bird-catchers stop a bird. Pass those as you would pass a desert.

2. Destroying Vṛtra, cleaving Vala, demolishing strongholds, the mover of waters, the driver of the chariot at the call of his two bay horses, Indra destroys even what is set.

3. Just as deep waters and just as cows, you cherish your strength.[1] In this way milch cows go to fodder[2] well-protected just as rivulets reach deep water.[3]

4. Bring us offspring and possessions as if a bestowal of inheritance by one who has given his consent.[4] Indra, as if possessing a hook, shake down ripe fruit from a tree, leading to wealth.

5. Indra, you are self-ruling, ruling from your own right; you are well-practiced, being most glorious through your own acts. You who are praised by many, thrive with strength. Be most kind to us.

NOTES

[1] Strictly speaking, what is here translated as 'deep waters' is 'a deep water recepticle.' Whether this refers to 'the seas' or 'the oceans,' as Wilson, Geldner, and Maurer translate, or 'pools of water' as Griffith translates, or to 'large rivers ["Ströme"]' as Grassmann (1873: 252 s.v. *uda-dhi*) suggests as another possibility, is problematic. Clearly, though, the usage is metaphorical. Geldner translates, "Du begest Weisheit, tief wei die Meere,

. . . [You cherish wisdom deep as the seas . . .].” With regard to such a translation as Geldner’s, see Griffith’s n. to this vs.

[2] Perhaps, ‘pasturage.’

[3] Again here, the term translated ‘deep water’ which certainly refers back to the term used above, is problematic. The term translated here as ‘rivulets’ is also problematic. Just like the term translated above as ‘fodder,’ referred to in n. 2, the meaning depends on whatever the cultural reality was. Strictly speaking, the term may refer to both small streams and irrigation canals.

[4] This line has been translated variously by the various translators. It is the commentator Sāyaṇa who explains the line as referring to a father giving a share of his wealth to his son who has come of age.

Ṛgveda 10.163

1. I tear away the sickness in your head from your head, from your eyes, from both nostrils, from both ears, from the chin, and from the tongue.

2. I tear away the sickness in your arms from both shoulders, from both arms, from your neck, from the nape of the neck, from the ribs, and from the backbone.

3. I tear away the sickness from your entrails, from the bowels, from the *vaniṣṭhu*,[1] from the heart, from the *matasna*,[2] from the liver, from the *plāśi*.[3]

4. I tear away the sickness from both thighs, from both knees, from both heels, from the forepart of both feet, from both hips, from the buttocks, and from the *bhaṉsas*.[4]

5. I tear away the sickness from the urethra, from the bladder, from the hair, from your nails, from your entire self, top to bottom.

6. I tear away the sickness from every limb, from every hair, from every joint in which it is generated, from your entire self, top to bottom.

NOTES

[1] A part of the entrails. According to the commentator Sāyaṇa either 'the rectum' or 'a particular part of the entrails near the omentum.

[2] Unidentified internal organs. According to the commentator Sāyaṇa, the kidneys.

[3] Unidentified part of the intestines. According to the commentator Sāyaṇa, 'the lungs.' Grassmann (1873: 895 s.v. *plāçí*) defines it as "etwa die *Milz* oder ein anderes Eingeweide [approximately the *spleen* or another of the innards]." Wilson translates it as 'thy (other) viscera,' Griffith as 'the spleen,' and Geldner as "dem Gekröse (?) [the mesentery (?)].

[4] Unidentified part of the intestines or abdomen. Wilson and Geldner translate this as 'private parts,' Geldner so translating it with question ["der Scham (?)"]. Griffith translates it as 'groin.' Grassmann (1873: 921) defines *bhaṉsas* as "ein Theil des Unterleibes, wahrscheinlich = bhasád *Hintertheil, After* [a part of the lower abdomen, probably = bhasád *hinderpart, anus*]." Monier-Williams (1899: 750a) defines *bhasád* 'the hinder or secret parts, (esp.) pudendum muliebre'; also 'glans penis.' Also, instead of translating *bhā́sada*, preceding *bhaṉsas*, as 'buttocks,' as do Wilson, Grassmann, and Geldner, Griffith translates here 'stomach.'

Ṛgveda 1.22

1. Wake up the two Aśvins who yoke at dawn. Let them come here to drink this Soma.

2. We summon the two Aśvins, who have a good chariot, who are the best of charioteers, who are the two gods who reach heaven.

3. Aśvins, your whip is sweet and glorious. Prepare[1] the sacrifice with it.

4. Aśvins, no matter where you are going with the car, the home of one offering Soma is not far off from you.

5. I call up golden-handed Savitṛ for kindness. That divinity knows the station.

6. We invoke Savitṛ, the son of the waters, for assistance. We long for his laws.[2]

7. We summon Savitṛ, who watches men, the one who distributes wealth and excellent bounty.

8. Friends, sit down. Savitṛ, who is worthy of a hymn of praise by us, the bestower of gifts, is gleaming.

9. Agni, bring here the obedient wives of the gods, and Tvastṛ, for a draft of Soma.

10. Here, O newly-born Agni,[3] bring the wives of the gods – Hotrā, Bhāratī, Varūtrī, Diṣanā,[4] for [their] assistance.

11. Goddesses, wives of heroes, with undiminished wings be favorable to us with great assistance and with protection.

12. Indrāṇī, Varuṇānī and Agnāyī I invite here for a draught of Soma.

13. Great Dyaus, and Pṛthivī, prepare this sacrifice for us. Further us with nourishments.

14. At the *gandharva*'s permanent station the inspired ones taste through their devotions[5] the liquid[6] rich with ghee which belongs certainly to those two.

15. Pṛthivī, be pleasant, thornless, and prove a dwelling place. Show shelter to us far and wide.

16. Gods, for this reason[7] favor us from where Viṣṇu strode through the seven domains of the earth.[8]

17. Viṣṇu strode through the world. He put down his foot in three places. Everything became arranged in the dustiness of what was then the world.

18. Viṣṇu, the trusty guardian, strode three steps, in that way establishing the laws.

19. Look at Viṣṇu's works, from which[9] the friend closely associated with Indra let proper practices be seen.

20. Sages always see that highest step of Viṣṇu as if it were an eye in heaven, but spread out widely.

21. The watchful praising singers kindle that which is the highest step of Viṣṇu.

NOTES

[1] The word translated here as 'prepare' is often used in this sense in connection with an oblation to Soma. It may also mean "ausgiessen [pour out]," more specifically "besprengen, beregnen, schmachhheft macken (mit Süssigkeit) [sprinkle (2x), make tasty (with sweetness)]," as it is taken by Grassmann (1873: 1043-1044 s.v. *mih, migh . . . mimikṣa*). Griffith trans-lates it as 'sprinkle,' having taken the word translated here as 'sweet' very literally as 'dripping honey.' So also, both Geldner and Witzel take the latter as "honighaltige [containing honey]," Geldner translating Griffith's 'sprinkle' as "wurzet [season]" and Witzel translating this as "vermischt [mix]." Wilson translates 'stir up,' and notes that *mimikṣatam* means to mix inti-mately the juice of the Soma, but that it is not clear how this is to be done with the whip. See also Witzel's comment on this.
[2] Perhaps, 'duties,' i.e. 'we desire to perform in accord with duties.' Geldner translatges "seinen Dienste [his duty]" here. Witzel translates "Sein Gebot [his law]." Wilson translates, "We desire to celebrate his workings." Griffith translates, "Fain are we for his holy ways."
[3] The word '*yaviṣṭha*' is translated 'newly-born' as it is especially applied to Agni when just produced from wood or when placed on the altar after everything else.
[4] For identification of these goddesses see Wilson's or Griffith's n. to this vs., or see Monier-Williams (1899) under the different names.
[5] Perhaps, more specifically, 'prayers.'
[6] Perhaps, 'water(s),' as Wilson and Griffith translate, Griffith explaining it as the fertilizing rain sent by Dyaus and Pṛthivī; or, 'milk.'
[7] Perhaps, 'from now on.' Geldner and Witzel interpret it as 'from heaven.'
[8] For a discussion of the problematic nature of this vs. see the comments of Wilson, Griffith, and Witzel. Sāyaṇa interprets it as referring to the three steps of Viṣṇu in his Trivikrama

incarnation in which he encompassed the three regions of the universe – earth, atmosphere, and sky, in three steps.

[9] Perhaps signifying a particular place in the layout of the sacrifice.

Ṛgveda 1.154

1. It is the heroic deeds of Viṣṇu that I will proclaim, [the deeds] of he who measured out[1] the earthly regions and fixed the highest place of meeting[2] with three widely spaced strides.

2. Praised aloud because of his heroic deed, done as if he were a fearful wild beast that roams about dwelling in the mountains, is Viṣṇu, in whose three wide strides all living beings are settled.

3. Let the petition go forth with efficacy for Viṣṇu, he of might[3] who lives on high[4] and makes large strides: alone he has measured out this long far-extending home with just three steps.

4. His three imperishable steps, filled with what is delightful,[5] delight in his power.[6] Furthermore, he is the one who has alone supported the threefold world, the earth itself, and heaven – all creatures.

5. May I reach that well-loved place of his where men who long for the gods delight. There one draws near to the one who makes wide strides; there is the fountain of sweetness[7] at Viṣṇu's highest step.

6. We wish to go to the dwellings of you two[8] where oxen have many horns[9] and are agile. Certainly there the highest step of he of might[10] who makes large strides shines down mightily.

NOTES

[1] The Vedic term also allows the meaning 'passed over.' The mythological import is that by passing over the terrestrial regions Viṣṇu measures them out. See Keith (1925/1: 108-109).

[2] A problem occurs as to whether 'the highest home' is the place of meeting of the gods above or the home referred to with the same word in vs. 3 below. Should we take 'the highest home' to mean the place of meeting of the gods then it would seem that in vs. 3 the land of Dīrghatamas, the author of the hymn, is being likened to the place of meeting of the gods.

[3] Perhaps, 'bull,' as all translators consulted translate, with the exception of Wilson who takes it to refer to Viṣṇu's vigor, not unlike the way we take it here; or, perhaps, the male of any animal.

[4] All translators consulted, with the exception of Wilson, view this to refer to dwelling in the mountains. Wilson takes the locution here to mean either 'who dwells in speech' or, as we take it here, to mean 'who dwells in high places.'

[5] All translators consulted, except Wilson, translate 'honey' here, Wilson translating instead 'ambrosia.'

[6] Perhaps 'delight in the law,' or 'delight in the home.' Geldner translates "nach ihren Art schwelgen [indulged in according to his nature]." O'Flaherty translates, "rejoice in the sacrificial drink." Maurer translates simply "rejoice," taking Viṣṇu's three steps to be "undecaying *by nature* [italics mine]." Witzel translates this line still differently.

[7] All translators consulted, except Wilson, translate here 'honey' or 'meath' – Griffith qualifying his 'meath' with the comment "or nectar, or honey; meaning celestial Soma."

[8] All the translations consulted, except Wilson's, take 'you two' to refer to Indra and Viṣṇu, Viṣṇu being closely associated with Indra. Wilson takes it to refer to the sacrificer and his wife and construes the vs. differently.

[9] What is meant by 'many horns' is problematic. Keith (1925/1: 108) notes "the many-horned swiftly moving cows, doubtless the clouds." Both O'Flaherty and Maurer take the bovines with many horns to refer to 'rays of light' or 'the rays of the sun,' following Sāyaṇa. O'Flaherty suggests further that 'rays of light' may perhaps refer to the stars. She adds, though, that "many-horned cattle" may refer to "just what the verse says, the

cattle who abound in heaven." Maurer translates here, "cows lusty-horned and unwearied." Geldner and Witzel both interpret bovines with many horns to refer to "die Sterne [the stars]." So also Griffith, who comments,"the stars with their ever-twinkling rays."

[10] See n. 3 above.

APPENDIX D: DESCRIPTION OF THE LAND IN SKH.U. 7 (Ed 7.10c-7.18b)

Text:

caran sa vasudhāṃ kṛtsnāṃ saśailavanakānanāṃ /
kramād āgatvā cādrākṣīt sahyaparvatam uttamaṃ /
nānāgamataponiṣṭhaiḥ mantrasiddhair maharṣibhiḥ /
abhakṣair vāyubhakṣaiś ca śīrṇaparṇ*āśi*nair api /
juṣṭaṃ kiṃnaragandharvair apsarobhiś ca cāraṇaiḥ /
nānāmaṇimayaiḥ śṛṅgair nānādhātuvicitrakaiḥ /
nānādrumalatāgulmair nānāpakṣigaṇair api /
nānāmṛgagaṇaiś cāpi nānāprasravaṇair api /
jambubhiḥ panasaiś caiva kapitthaiś ca rasāḷakaiḥ /
phalabhārān namraśākhāśikharair bahubhir vṛtaṃ /
cāṃpeyair *rāja*pūgaiś ca bakuḷair ghrāṇatarpaṇaiḥ /
satataṃ raktakaṇṭhānāṃ kūjitaiś ca patattriṇāṃ /
āhvayantam iva śrāntān . . . . /
vrajantam iva mātagair gṛṇantam iva *bhrama*raiḥ /
krandantam iva pañcāsyair gāyantam iva ṣaṭpadaiḥ /
āruhya sa gireḥ śṛṅgaṃ dadarśārād a*pāṃ*nidhiṃ /

Translation:

Wandering the entire earth with its mountains, forests and groves, in due course he (Paraśurāma) arrived and saw the highest mountain of the Sahya range with its great *ṛṣis* perfected by *mantras*, devoted to different *Āgamas* and austerities, and fasting – eating only air and withered leaves, filled with *kiṃnaras*, *gandharvas*, *apsarases*, and *cāraṇas*, with peaks studded with different jewels, with various wonderful ores, with clusters of different trees and creepers, with flocks of different birds, with flocks of different forest animals and with different streams, with Jambu trees, with Panasa trees, with Kapittha trees, and with Rasālaka trees, covered with the tips of branches bowing under the weight of fruit, with fragrant Cāṃpeya trees, Rājapūga trees and Bakuḷa trees, always filled with the cries of red-throated birds, summoning, as it were, the wearied; . . . [1]; moving, as it were, with elephants; humming, as it were, with bees; calling out, as it were, with lions; singing, as it were, with bees. Having ascended the peak of the mountain, he saw the ocean nearby.

Critical apparatus:
caran: L1a carant (?).
sa: Br saṃ (?).
kṛtsnāṃ: L1a kṛtvā.
kramād (Br kramad).
āgatvā: Ed L1c Bm M Br K āgatya.
cādrākṣīt: L1a Bm M cāndrākṣī (?); L1c cādrājan (?). L1c source?
sahya°: Ed Br K sahyaṃ; L1a saṉhyā°.
L1c inserts 'oṃ' before 'nānā°.'
°āgama°: L1a °āgatat (?).
°niṣṭhaiḥ: Ed Bm M K °niṣṭhair; L1a °niṣṭhe; Br °niṣṭhaṃ.
°siddhair: L1a °siddhir.
maharṣibhiḥ (Bm mamaharṣibhiḥ). Bm adds syll.
abhakṣair: Ed Br k abbhakṣair; L1c abhabhar (?).
śīrṇaparṇā*śi*nair: Ed L1a Br K śīrṇaparṇāśanair; L1c śīrṇacarn-āśanair (?); Bm M śīrṇapatrāśanair.
juṣṭaṃ: L1a L1c juṣṭa°.
°gandharvair: L1a °gandharva.
ca cāraṇaiḥ: L1a carācaraiḥ.
nānāmaṇi° . . . rasāḷakaiḥ: Br runs through incompletely and then returns to beginning to give 'nānāmaṇi° . . . °pakṣigaṇair api.'
°maṇi°: Br² °marṇi° (?).
°mayaiḥ: L1c Br¹ Br² °mayai. See **§7.9b** for L1c Br¹ Br² final *saṃdhi*.

---

[1] All MSS giving this ½ vs. insert a *pāda* of commentary here instead of giving the *pāda* proper. Ed L1c K note: 'And it yields results.' L1a notes: 'And it gives rise to a competent person (?).'

śṛṅgair: L1c śṛgai (?); Bm M śṛṅgaiḥs; Br[1] śṛṅgaiś. See **§7.9b** for L1c and Bm M final *saṃdhi*.
nānādhātuvicitrakaiḥ: Ed L1c nānādhātuvicitritaiḥ; Bm M varṇānāṃ dhātucitritaiḥ; Br[1] omits; Br[2] varṇānāṃ dhātucitritaḥ.
nānādruma° . . . °gaṇair api: Br[1] omits.
°gulmair: Bm M °gulyair (perhaps, °gulpair (?)); Br[2] °gulyai. See **§7.9b** for Br[2] final *saṃdhi*.
nānāmṛgagaṇaiś: Br[1] omits.
°mṛga°: L1c °mṛgair.
°prasravaṇair (Bm M °praśravaṇair, Br °pratśravaṇair).
panasaiś: L1a panasai. See **§7.9b** for L1a final *saṃdhi*.
caiva: L1a ceva; Bm cava (?).
kapitthaiś: L1a kapitthaś.
rasāḷakaiḥ: Bm rasālakai; (Ed L1a M Br K rasālakaiḥ). See **§7.9b** for Bm final *saṃdhi*.
°bhārān namraśākhaiḥ: L1a °bhārāṅgatāśākhā; L1c °hārā namachākhā° (?); Bm M °bhārā namraśākhā°; (Br °bhārān naśākhaiḥ). Br omits syll.
vṛtaṃ: Ed Br K vṛttaṃ; Bm M vṛtaḥ.
cāmpeyair: Ed L1a M campakair; Bm campakai; (L1c cāmpeyaiïr, Br cāpaiyair). See §7.9b for Bm final *saṃdhi*.
*rāja*pūgaiś ca: Ed L1a Bm K nāgapuṃnāgair (K nāgapunnāgair); L1c nāgapūgaiś ca; M nāgapuṃnāgai; Br jāgapuṃnāgair (?). See Skh.u. 9.24d for emendation. See **§7.9b** for M final *saṃdhi*.
L1c inserts 'baku' before 'bakuḷair.'
bakuḷair: Bm bakulai; Br bakule; (Ed L1a M K bakulair). See **§7.9b** for Bm final *saṃdhi*.
ghrāṇa°: L1c ghāṇa° (?).
°tarpaṇaiḥ: Br °tarpana (?).
raktakaṇṭhānāṃ: L1a dantakañjānāṃ; (Br raktakaṭānāṃ).
patattriṇāṃ: Bm M Br patatriṇaḥ.
'āhvayantaṃ,' to end of following *pāda*: Bm M Br omit.
āhvayantaṃ: Ed K āhūyantaṃ.
After 'śrāntān' Ed L1c K insert: phalam āharateti ca. L1a inserts: pātram āharateti ca.
vrajantam iva: M vrajattamatta (?); M vrajanta iva.

mātaṅgair: L1c mātaṅgai; Br mattaṅgair (?); (Bm mātagair). See **§7.9b** for L1c final *saṃdhi*.
gṛṇantam: L1c śṛṇantam.
*bhramara*iḥ: Ed nirjarais; L1a K nirjaraiḥ; L1c vibharaiḥ; Bm M kiṃnnaraiḥ (Bm kinnaraiḥ); Br nirptaraiḥ (?).
krandantam (Br kradantam).
pañcāsyair: L1c pañcāsyaiḥ.
sa gireḥ: Bm M sāgarāt; Br parvate.
śṛṅgaṃ: L1a śṛṅgair; M śṛṅga; Br śṛṅge.
dadarśā°: Ed dadarśa; L1a L1c Bm daddarśā° (?); M darddarśā° (?); Br dadaśaṃ (?); K dadarśaṃ (?).
°ārād a*pāṃ*nidhiṃ: Ed hy uddadhiṃ hariḥ; L1a °ārād apānidhiḥ (?); Bm M °ārād apāṃnidhiḥ; Br udadhiṃ hariḥ; K hādadhiṃ(?) hariḥ; (L1c °ārād apānidhiṃ).

APPENDIX E: THE THIRTY-TWO VILLAGES

The Villages to the West (16)

Ed	L1a	L1c	L1a (*extra*)[1]
Kareurū	Kareūru	Kareiru	Kareūru
Karkāḍi	Ūrkāḍi	Kārkāsi	Karkāḍi
Maraṇa	Maraṇa	Maraṇa	Maraṇe
Kānuvī	Kolavināḍ	Konavināḍu	Kolavināḍu
Pāḍi		Pāḍī	Pāḍi
Koḍīla	Kuḍelu		Kudeḷu
Māgava	Mugerubailu	Magebayalu	Mogebailu
Mitranāḍu	Mittanāḍu	Mittanāḍu	Mittanāḍu
Nirmārgaka	Nirmārga	Nimāgra	Nirmārga
Sīmantura	Sīmantūru	Sīmantūru	Simantūru
	Tinakaḷa	Teṇakaḷe	Tenakāḷa
	Majerūru	Vomañjuru	Mañjūru
Śivabalī	Śivabaḷī	Śivabaḷī	Antaraśivabeli
			Brahmapura
Ajapūrī	Ajapūrī	Ajapuru	
Nīlāvara	Nīrāvara	Nīlāvara	Nilāvara
Kūṭa	Kūṭa	Kuṭa	Koḍa
Skandapura	Skandapura	Skandapura	Skandapura

[1] L1a (*extra*) = a list of the names of the thirty-two villages given by one of the inserted chapters in L1a.

The Villages to the West, continued.

Bm	M	Br	K
Kārāruḍa	Kāroruḍa	Kareurū	Kareurū
Karkāḍi	Karkāḍi	Karkāḍi	Karkāḍi
Maraṇa	Maraṇa	Maraṇa	Maraṇa
Komavī	Komavī	Konuvī	Kānuvī
Pāḍi	Pāḍi	Pāḍi	Pāḍi
Koḍilu	Koḍilu	Koḍīla	Koḍīla
Nāgabelu	Nāgabelu	Māgava	Māgava
Mitranāḍu	Miranāḍu	Mitranāḍu	Mitranāḍu
Nirmārgaka	Nirmārgaka	Nirmārgaka	Nirmārgaka
Sīmanturaṃ	Sīmanturaṃ	Sīmanturaṃ	Sīmantura
Śaivabelī	Śaivabelī	Śivabalī	Śivabalī
Ajapūrī	Ajapūrī	Ajapūrī	Ajapūrī
Nīlāvara	Nīlāvara	Nīlāvara	Nīlāvara
Kuṭa	Kuṭa	Kuṭa	Kūṭa
Skandhapura	Skandhapura	Skandapura	Skandapura

The Villages to the East (16)

Ed	L1a	L1c	L1a (*extra*)
Śrīpāḍi		Śrīpādi	Śrīpādi
Kaundila	Voḍilu	Oḍilu	Oṃulu
			Nāḷa
Karamūru	Kārandūru	Kāramharu	Kāramūru
Ujjaya	Ujira	Ujjara	Ujjire
Kartumārga	Kunnimārga	Kutramārga	Kuntamārga
Cīrkodī	Kokkaḍa	Kokkoḍu	Kokkaḍa
Vāmījurū	Rāmañjūra	Rāmiñjuru	Rāmiñja
Pura	Pude	Pude	Pude
Ballamañja	Baḷḷamañja	Baḷḷamāñja	Baḷḷa
Haināḍu	Airnāḍu	Bhaināḍu	Ernāḍu
Icuka	Iḍuka	Iḍaka	Iḍakeḍu
Komiñja	Kemmiñja	Keṃmiñja	Kemmiñja
Pāliñja		Pāliñja	Pāliñja
Śiripāḍi	Siryādiñca	Śiripāḍi	Śiriyaḍi
Kodipāḍi	Kodipāḍi	Koḍipāḍi	Kaḍipāḍi

The Villages to the East, continued.

Bm	M	Br	K
Śrīpādī	Śrīpāḍi	Śrīpāḍi	Śrīpādi
Koḍilu	Koḍilu	Kaundila	Kaudila
Kāramuru	Kāramuru	Kāramūrū	Kāramūru
Ujjara	Ujjara	Ujjaya	Ujjaya
Kartu	Kartu	Kartumārga	Kartumārga
Cirkoḍī	Cirkoḍī	Cīrkodī	Cīrkodī
Vāmijuru	Vāmiñjuru	Vāmījuru	Vāmījurū
Pura	Pura	Pura	Pura
Baḷḷamañja	Baḷḷamañja	Ballamañja	Ballamañja
Hainādu	Haināḍu	Heṇāḍu	Haināḍu
Icuka	Icuka	Icuka	Icuka
Kemiñja	Kemiñja	Komiñja	Komiñja
Pāliñja	Pāliñja	Pālija	Pāliñja
Śiripādi	Śiripādī	Śiripāḍi	Śiripāḍi
Koḍīpādi	Koḍīpāḍī	Kodipāḍi	Kodipāḍi

APPENDIX F: REPRODUCTIONS OF THE FIRST FOLIO SIDES GIVING TEXT OF THE PGN FOR EACH MS

Following are reproductions of the first folio sides giving text of the PGN for each MS used. It is hoped that this will aid in giving the reader a clearer insight into the MSS themselves.

For example, the reproduction from MS. L1 shows how careful the scribe was not to misrepresent the MSS from which he was copying. If he was not able to read a syllable, it seems, he left a dash instead. We can say that this was an innovation on the part of the scribe of L1 becauose it holds true for more than one section of the MS, which appears to be a compilation of several MSS. This latter would not hold true if the scribe of L1 was using as his source a MS which was already a compilation. But nevertheless, it would indicate why our MSS L1a and L1c have better text than our other MSS.

The reproduction from MS. M might give the reader an idea of the concern for a neat and grandiose looking copy which seems to have been held by its scribe. That the first chapter of the PGN begins at the top of a new folio side is a fluke, however, and is not meant by the scribe to indicate its separateness as an individual unit from the other parts of the Skh.u. In the case of MS. L2, which also begins with a fresh folio side, this is not a fluke. The separate sections of the MS, of which the PGN alone is one, all begin in this way.

The reproduction from MS. Bm shows an inkling of the concern of its scribe for layout, though not as clearly as might two folio sides from many of the other chapter beginnings. The scribe of Bm tended to start each chapter on a new folio side, filling up a line or two at the end of a chapter with the standard practice of using the letter 'cha' as a filler. Using the beginning of the text of the PGN uniformly for all MSS for the purpose of reproduction was believed to be better than picking folio sides at random, however, for several reasons, even though this latter point cannot be seen with the total clarity which might have been obtained by showing the two folio sides.

It is hoped that these reproductions will also be of help to the person wanting to try his hand at reading *Devanāgarī*, Telugu, or Malayalam scripts in their MS forms, which I know from experience takes some readjustment from reading these scripts in their printed forms.

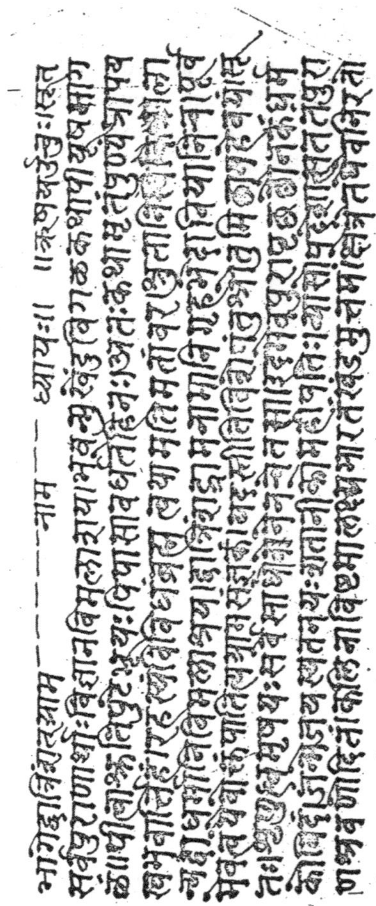

MS. L1, folio 156 recto.

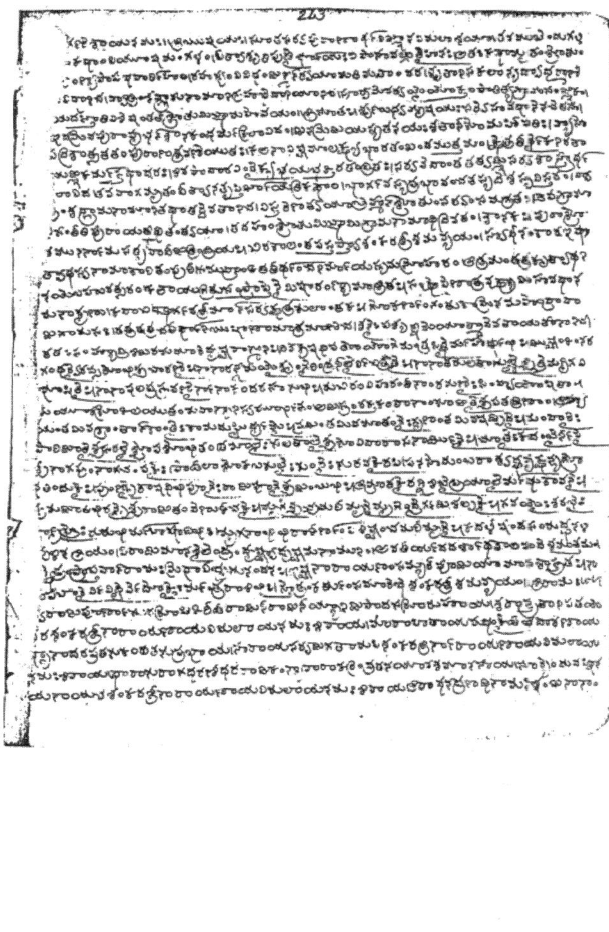

MS. L2, page 243.

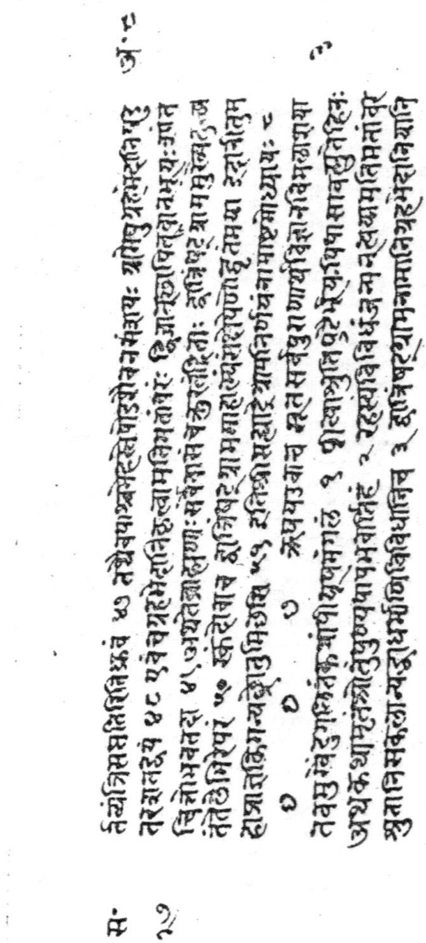

MS. Bm, folio 27 verso of Skh.u.

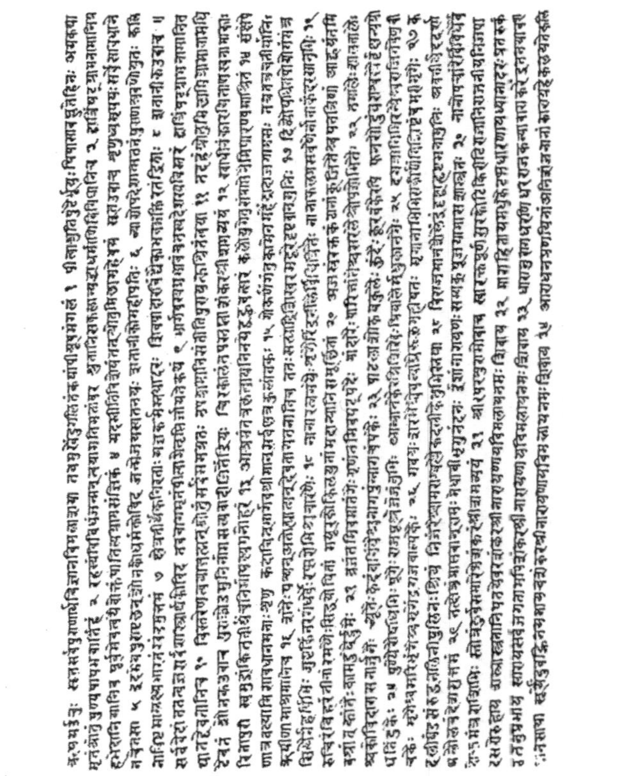

MS. M, folio 7 verso of Skh.u.

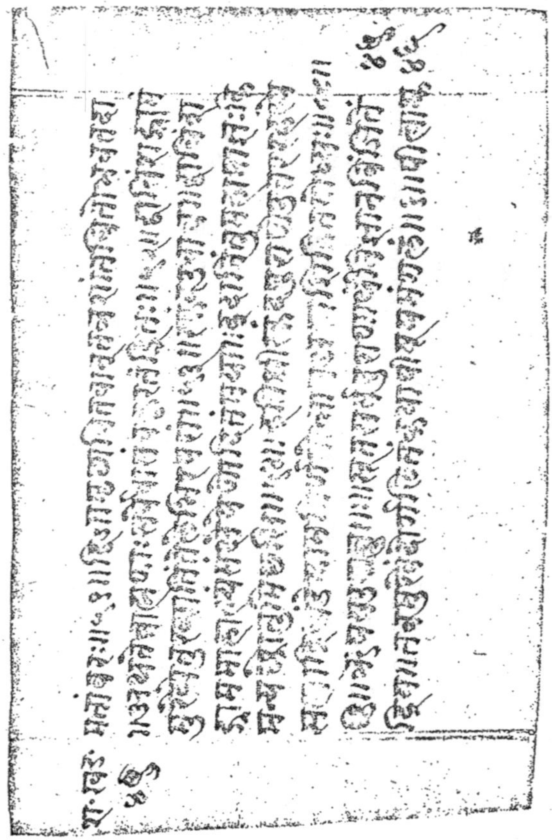

MS. Br, folio 46 verso.

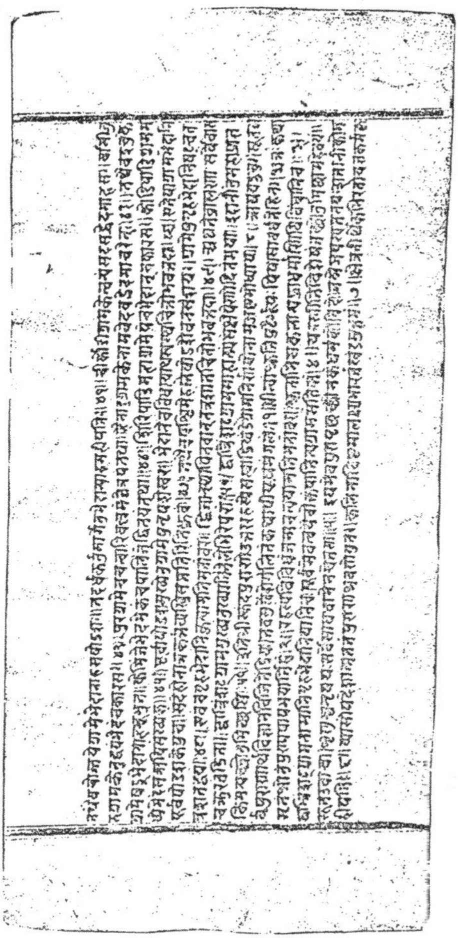

MS. K, folio 12 verso of section 2.

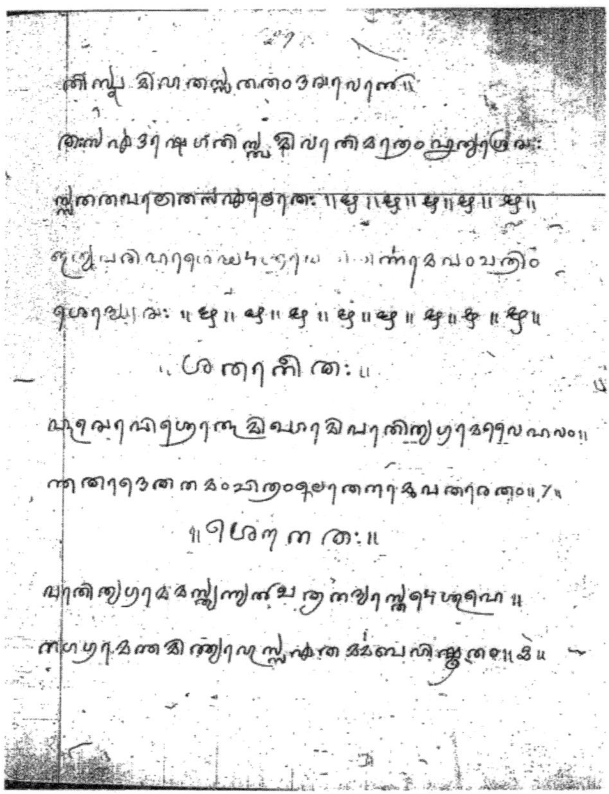

MS. L3, folio 29 recto.

APPENDIX G: PRINCIPAL LETTER CONFUSIONS[1]

1. PRINCIPLAL LETTER CONFUSIONS DUE TO *DEVANĀGARĪ* SCRIPT

Confusion	MSS in which present	Comments
a > u	Bm	
aṃ > e	Ed Bm M Br K	
aḥ > ā	<u>L2</u> Bm M <u>Br</u>	
āṃ > ī	Bm M	
ā > aḥ	Br	
Cān > Cal	Ed L2 Bm M K	
ī > ā	<u>Ed</u> <u>L1a</u> <u>L2</u> Br <u>K</u>	
ī > o	L2	
ī > ir	Bm M	
ī > rCā	Bm	
u > ṛ	<u>Bm</u> <u>M</u>	(Telugu or Kanarese script?)
ṛ > a	Bm	
ṛ > u	L2 Br	(Telugu or Kanarese script?)

[1] For additional confusions see **§7.4** and **§7.9a**. Underlining under MS *sigla* indicates that there is question as to whether or not the confusion in question occurs in that MS. Capital 'C' stands for an unspecified consonant.

Confusion	MSS in which present								Comments
	Ed	L1a	L1c	L2	Bm	M	Br	K	
ṛ > ū					Bm				(Telugu or Kanarese script?)
e > aṃ	Ed			L2	Bm	M	Br	K	
e > p				L2					
k > t			L1c	L2			Br		
k > v	Ed			L2	Bm	M	Br	K	
g > n	Ed			L2	Bm	M	Br	K	
gh > th		L1a							
gh > dy				L2			Br		
gh > dh					Bm	M			
c > v	Ed				Bm	M	Br	K	
t > n	Ed	L1a	L1c	L2	Bm	M	Br	K	
t > r		L1a	L1c						
th > y		L1a		L2	Bm	M			
d > v	Ed		L1c	L2	Bm	M	Br	K	
d > h					Bm	M			
da > i-			L1c						
dā > ś			L1c						
dh > y				L2					
n > t	Ed	L1a	L1c	L2	Bm	M	Br	K	
n > r	Ed				Bm	M	Br	K	

Confusion	MSS in which present							Comments
p > m						Br		
p > y			L2	Bm	M	Br		
p > v		L1a	L2	Bm				(Telugu or Kanarese script?)
p > ṣ	Ed			Bm	M	Br	K	
b > v	Ed					Br	K	
bh > m				Bm	M			
bh > ś			L2					
m > p	Ed			Bm	M	Br	K	
m > bh				Bm		Br	K	
m > y			L2	Bm				
y > th				Bm	M			
y > p	Ed	L1a	L2	Bm	M	Br	K	
y > m				Bm	M	Br		
r > t	Ed			Bm	M	Br	K	
ra > u		L1a						
ra > s			L2					(Before 'th')
Cr > Cn				Bm	M			
rC > Cṃ				Bm	M			
l > t							K	

Confusion	MSS in which present								Comments
	Ed	L1a	L1c	L2	Bm	M	Br	K	
v > k	Ed						Br	K	
v > c	Ed				Bm	M	Br	K	
v > p		L1a			Bm				(Telugu or Kanarese script?)
v > b						M			
ś > dā	Ed			L2	Bm	M	Br	K	
ś > bh					Bm				
ś > vā						M			
ṣ > p					Bm				
s > t			L1c						
s > m					Bm	M			
h > ty					Bm				
h > d				L2	Bm				
h > dṛ					Bm	M			
hṛ > du				L2					
kt > tk				L2					
kla > kṛ	Ed						Br	K	
jñ > j				L2					
tp > s					Bm	M			
ty > tp					Bm	M			
ty > st	Ed			L2	Bm	M	Br	K	

Confusion	MSS in which present					Comments
tth > ts			Bm	M		
tth > ty			Bm	M	Br	
dd > dv		L2	Bm	M	Br	
ddh > dv		L2			Br	
ddh > dhy		L2	Bm	M		
dy > dh			Bm			
dr > ḍ				M		
dra > du	L1a					
nt > tt				M		
nd > dh		<u>L2</u>				
pt > tp			Bm			
pt > s					Br	
pl > lm		L2				
mn > gn					Br	
ly > ky			<u>Bm</u>	<u>M</u>		
sy > ty			Bm			

2. PRINCIPAL LETTER CONFUSIONS DUE TO TELUGU OR KANARESE SCRIPTS

Confusion	MSS in which present								Comments
ā > aṃ				L2					
ā > o					Bm				
u > ṛ					Bm	M			(*Devanāgarī?*)
u > ṛ > ra	Ed			L2	Bm	M	Br	K	
ṛ > u				L2			Br		(*Devanāgarī?*)
ṛ > ū					Bm				(*Devanāgarī?*)
ṛ > ru				L2	Bm		Br		
o > ā		L1a		L2		M			
c > bh				L2	Bm				
ch > bh				L2					
j > kh				L2					
j > c					Bm	M			
n > p	Ed						Br	K	
n > v		L1a	L1c		Bm	M			
p > v		L1a		L2	Bm				(*Devanāgarī?*)
p > s	Ed			L2	Bm	M	Br	K	
b > c		L1a	L1c	L2					
bh > c					Bm				
l > ṭh				L2					

Confusion	MSS in which present								Comments
	Ed	L1a	L1c	L2	Bm	M	Br	K	
v > n	Ed				Bm	M	Br	K	
v > p		L1a			Bm				(*Devanāgarī*?)
ś > b	Ed			L2	Bm	M	Br	K	
śā > i-					Bm	M			
ṣ > bh			L1c						
ṣ > v	Ed						Br	K	
s > p	Ed				Bm	M		K	
cch > tth					Bm	M			(*Jainalipi*?)
dyu > dhṛ				L2					
Cy > Cu	Ed				Bm	M	Br	K	
Cy > Cr	Ed		L1c					K	
Cy > Cṛ > Cru		L1a							
Cy > Cv	Ed			L2	Bm	M	Br	K	
Cr > Cv	Bm								
Cra > Cṛ > Cru						M			
Cru > Cṛ				L2	Bm	M	Br		
Cl > Cth					Bm				
Cv > Cu					Bm	M			
Cv > Cy					Bm	M			
Cv > Cr					Bm				

APPENDIX H: CONTENTS OF THE *SAHYĀDRIKHAṆḌA*

1. PRELIMINARY OUTLINE OF THE *SAHYĀDRIKHAṆḌA* AS IN DA CUNHA'S EDITION.[1]

Ādirahasya

Topic or Title	Chapter Numbers	Discussants A	Discussants B
Pañcalakṣaṇa	1-36		
First four topics of *Pañcalakṣaṇa*?	1	Vyāsa (Q) and Sanatkumāra (N)	
	6		Various occasional speakers (Q and N?)
	19		
	20		Devī (Q) and Maheśvara (N)
	25		
History of *kṣatriyas*, etc.	26		Gaṇeśa (Q, sometimes N) and Maheśvara or Mahādeva (N)
	36		
Topic(s) uncertain	37		

[1] Abbreviations: Q=Questioner; N=Narrator. The speech of discussants B is related by the N of discussants A.

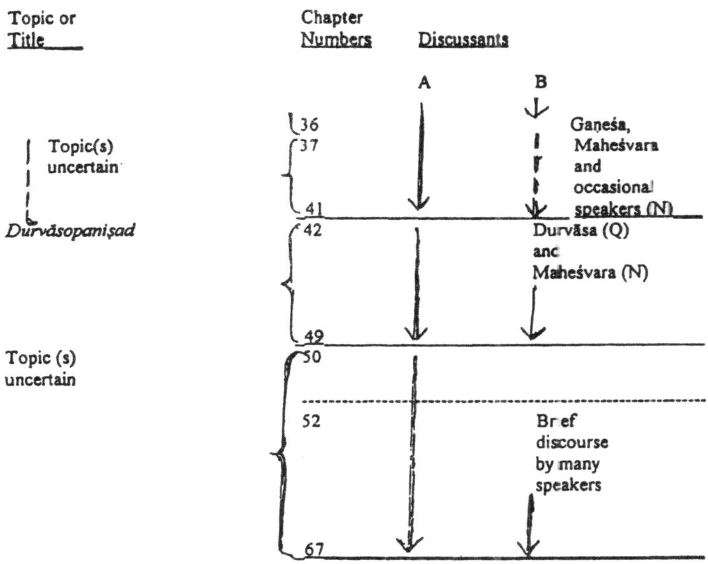

Topic or Title
Chapter Numbers
Discussants
A
B
36
37
41
Topic(s) uncertain
Gaṇeśa, Maheśvara and occasional speakers (N)
Durvāsopaniṣad
42
49
Durvāsa (Q) and Maheśvara (N)
Topic (s) uncertain
50
52
67
Brief discourse by many speakers

Uttarārdha

Topic or Title	Chapter Numbers	Discussants A	Discussants B
Origin of various *brāhmaṇa* communities and creation of Konkan	1 6	Skanda (Q) and Mahādeva (N)	
Creation of Konkan and introduction of *brāhmaṇas* by Mayūravarman	7 8	*Ṛṣi* (Q) and Sūta (N)	Nārada (Q) and Skanda (N)
Origin of various polluted *brāhmaṇa* communities	9 19	*Ṛṣis* (Q) and Sūta (N)	Śatānīka (Q) and Śaunaka (N)
Topic(s) uncertain but including arrival of Śaunaka at 7-year sacrifice	20 20	?Śaunaka (N)	
	21 21	?Śaunaka (Q) and ?Śatānīka (N)	

2. LISTING OF THE CHAPTERS OF THE *SAHYĀDRIKHAṆḌA* AS IN DA CUNHA'S EDITION

Chapter Number	Title Given in the Colophon[1]	Number of Verses	Page Reference
	Ādirahasya		
1	Brahmāṇḍotpatti	29	pp. 1-4
2	Sṛṣṭikrama	54	pp. 4-9
3	Bhūmivistāra	11	pp. 9-10
4	Narakavarṇana	83	pp. 10-17
5	Saptalokākhyāna	41	pp. 17-21
6		19	pp. 21-22
7	Brahmagītākathkana	18½	pp. 23-24
8	Brahmagītā	33	pp. 24-27
9	Śivapuravarṇana	166	pp. 27-42

[1] Blank spaces are used to indicate chapters which do not carry titles in their colophons.

Chapter Number	Title Given in the Colophon	Number of Verses	Page Reference
10		28	pp. 42-44
11		18	pp. 44-46
12		64	pp. 46-51
13	Pralayotpattikathana	92	pp. 52-59
14	Pañcāyatana	34	pp. 60-62
15	Śivamāhātmya	45	pp. 63-66
16	Liṅgodbhava	78	pp. 66-73
17	Puṣpādidānamāhātmya	30	pp. 73-75
18		19	pp. 76-77
19		3	pp. 77-78
20	Upavāsavidhi	142	pp. 78-89
21		71	pp. 89-95
22		23	pp. 95-97
23	Dānamahimakathana	81½	pp. 97-103

Chapter Number	Title Given in the Colophon	Number of Verses	Page Reference
24	Dharmopadeśa	62½	pp. 103-108
25	Niyamopadeśakathana	74	pp. 108-114
26	Śaṃkarajātivarṇana	70½	pp. 114-120
27	Pāṭhārīyajātikathana	68	pp. 120-126
28	Pāṭhārīyajātikathana	16½	pp. 126-127
29	Kṣatriyotpatikathana	20½	pp. 127-129
30	Kṣatriyotpatikathana	46	pp. 129-133
31	Somavaṉśotpattikathana	59½	pp. 133-137
32	Somavaṉśotpatti	51½	pp. 138-142
33	Kṣatriyotpatikathana	175	pp. 142-155
34	Kṣatriyotpatikathana	78½	pp. 155-161
35	Candrajanmakathana	37	pp. 162-164
36	Pāṭhārīyadharmotpattikathana	13½	pp. 165-166
37	Bhūtimāhātmyakathana	54	pp. 166-170
38	Liṅgārcanavidhi	74	pp. 170-176

Chapter Number	Title Given in the Colophon	Number of Verses	Page Reference
39		69	pp. 176-181
40	Nandīśvarayoga	35	pp. 182-184
41	Yogopaniṣat	32½	pp. 185-187
42	Durvāsopaniṣat	15	pp. 187-189
43	Durvāsopaniṣat	17½	pp. 189-190
44		19½	pp. 190-192
45		6	p. 192
46		24	pp. 193-194
47		9½	p. 195
48	Durvāsopaniṣat	8½	p. 196
49	Prāṇayajanakathana	12	pp. 196-197
50		36½	pp. 198-200
51	Avimuktamāhātmyakathana	26½	pp. 201-203
52	Daṇḍapāṇivarada	82	pp. 203-210
53	Pañcāyatanavarṇana	119	pp. 210-219

Chapter Number	Title Given in the Colophon	Number of Verses	Page Reference
54	Daṇḍapāṇivarada	149	pp. 219-231
55	Nandyutpattivarṇana	73	pp. 231-237
56	Nandivarapradāna	86	pp. 237-243
57	Devasamūhāgamana	60	pp. 244-248
58		33½	pp. 248-251
59	Nandivarapradāna	58½	pp. 251-256
60	Brahmakṛtaśivastuti	102	pp. 256-264
61	Śaṃkarastuti	43½	pp. 264-270
62		89	pp. 270-277
63		60	pp. 277-282
64		65	pp. 282-287
65	Yogavidhi	46	pp. 288-291
66		46	pp. 291-295
67		62	pp. 295-300

Chapter Number	Title Given in the Colophon	Number of Verses	Page Reference
	Uttarārdha		
1	Citpāvanabrāhmaṇotpatte	54½	pp. 301-305
2	Sūrpārakakṣetramāhātmya ca Brāhmaṇotpatti (Title given above chapter: Kārāṣṭrabrāhmaṇotpatti)	32½	pp. 305-308
3	Gomāñcalakṣetramāhātmya	35½	pp. 308-311
4	Brāhmaṇotpatti	51	pp. 311-315
5	Brāhmaṇavicāra	92½	pp. 315-322
6	Pṛthvīdānapraśaṉsā	82	pp. 323-329
7	Paraśurāmakṣetrotpatti	53	pp. 329-333
8	Grāmanirṇaya	51	pp. 334-338
9	Bhārgavakṛtastuti	73	pp. 338-344
10	Pañcagrāmanirṇaya	50	pp. 344-348

Chapter Number	Title Given in the Colophon	Number of Verses	Page Reference
11		48	pp. 348-352
12	Pātityagrāmakathana	54	pp. 352-356
13	Śūdrotpatti	32	pp. 356-359
14	Pātityagrāmanirṇaya	34½	pp. 359-362
15	Pātityagrāmanirṇaya	13	pp. 362-363
16		43½	pp. 363-366
17	Mithunaharabrāhmaṇakathana	62	pp. 367-372
18	Pātityagrāmakathana	37	pp. 372-375
19	Pātityagrāma	42	pp. 375-378
20	Kṣetramāhātmya	36	pp. 378-381
21	Mahāliṅgeśamahimāvarṇana	66	pp. 381-387

* * *

Chapter Number	Title Given in the Colophon	Number of Verses	Page Reference
	Reṇukāmāhātmya		
1		27	pp. 389-391
2	Aditivarapradāna	21	pp. 391-393
3	Reṇukāvaradāna	23	pp. 393-395
4		22½	pp. 395-397
5	Bhṛguvaṉśānukathana	25	pp. 397-399
6		21	pp. 399-401
7		18	pp. 401-402
8		8	pp. 402-403
9		16½	pp. 403-404
10		26	pp. 405-407
11		20	pp. 407-408
12		19	pp. 409-410

Chapter Number	Title Given in the Colophon	Number of Verses	Page Reference
13	Paraśurāmotpatti	56	pp. 410-415
14		14	pp. 415-416
15		15	pp. 416-418
16		23	pp. 418-420
17		16	pp. 420-421
18	Nāradāgamana	27½	pp. 422-424
19		27½	pp. 424-426
20		20	pp. 426-428
21		24	pp. 428-430
22		24	pp. 430-432
23		22½	pp. 432-434
24		15½	pp. 434-436
25		32	pp. 436-438
26	Jamadagnikrodhasaṃvāda	22	pp. 439-440
27	Rāvaṇaparājaya	91	pp. 441-448

Chapter Number	Title Given in the Colophon	Number of Verses	Page Reference
28		35½	pp. 448-451
29		9½	pp. 451-452
30		38½	pp.452-455
31		119	pp. 455-465
32		9	pp. 465-466
33		15	pp. 467-468
34	Jamadagnivadha	25	pp. 468-470
35		22	pp. 470-472
36	Jamadagnisaṃskāra	20	pp. 472-474
37		22	pp. 474-476
38		62½	pp. 476-481
39		61	pp. 481-486
40	Sahasrārjunavadha	39	pp. 486-490

Chapter Number	Title Given in the Colophon	Number of Verses	Page Reference
	Candracūḍa- (Candreśvara-) māhātmya		
1		23½	pp. 491-493
2	Candracūḍaprādurbhāva	12½	pp. 493-494
3	Tīrthapraśaṉsa	17	pp. 494-496
4	Ambaṣṭhātīrthamahimavarṇana	17	pp. 496-497
5	Tīrthamahimavarṇana	17	pp. 498-499
6	Tīrthamahimāna	24½	pp. 499-501
7	Tīrthamahimāna	16½	pp. 501-503
8	Parvatopākhyāna	15	pp. 503-504
	Nāgāhvayamāhātmya		
1	Nāgabhayadūrīkaraṇa	40½	pp. 505-508
2	Śāntādurgāprādurbhāva	38½	pp. 508-512

Chapter Number	Title Given in the Colophon	Number of Verses	Page Reference
	Varuṇāpuramāhātmya		
1	Devīsthāpana	40½	pp. 513-516
2	Mahālasāprabhāvakathana	13	pp. 516-518
	Kāmākṣīmāhātmya		
1		37½	pp. 519-523
2		32	pp. 523-526
3	Mahiṣasaunyādivadha	30	pp. 526-529
4		31	pp. 529-532

Chapter Number	Title Given in the Colophon	Number of Verses	Page Reference
	Māṅgīśamāhātmya		
1		27	pp. 533-535
2	Śaṃkaratapaḥpraśaṇsākathana	29	pp. 536-538
3	Saptakoṭīśākhyāna	46	pp. 539-543
4	Grāhavadha	52½	pp. 543-547
5	Vyāghrarūpadhāraṇa	36	pp. 548-551
6	Śaṃkarapūjanādimāhātmyakathana	39	pp. 551-554
7	Kapilāmāhātmya	27	pp. 554-557
8	Aghanāśinīmāhātmyakathana	43	pp. 557-561
9	Siddheśvaraprādurbhāva	33	pp. 561-563
10	Śaṅkhāvalivarṇana	49	pp. 564-567
11	Śaṅkhavalyākhyānakathana	38	pp. 568-573
12	Vijayādurgākhyāna	47½	pp. 573-576

3. ALPHABETICAL INDEX TO THE CHAPTERS OF THE *SAHYĀDRIKHAṆḌA* AS IN DA CUNHA'S *EDITION*

Chapter Title[1]	Section and Chapter Number
Aghanāśinīmāhātmyakathana	Māṅgīśamāhātmya 8
Aditivarapradāna	Reukāmāhātmya 2
Ambaṣṭhātīrthamahimavarṇana	Candracūḍa- (Candreśvara-) māhātmya 4
Avimuktamāhātmyakathana	Ādirahasya 51
Upavāsavidhi	Ādirahasya 20
Kapilāmāhātmya	Māṅgīśamāhātmya 7
Kārāṣṭrabrāhmaṇotpatti[2]	Uttarārdha 2
Kṣatriyotpattikathana	Ādirahasya 29
	Ādirahasya 30
	Ādirahasya 33
	Ādirahasya 34

[1] Not all the chapters in the edition carry titles in their colophons. Because of this, this list is not an index to all the chapters of the *Sahyādrikhaṇḍa* and its attached *māhātmyas*, but only to those for which titles are given.

[2] This title is given by the editor at the head of the chapter. For the title carried in the colophon, see Brāhmaṇotpatti and Sūrpārakakṣetra° below.

Chapter Title	Section and Chapter Number
Kṣetramāhātmya	Uttarārdha 20
Gomāñcalakṣetramāhātmya	Uttarārdha 3
Grāmanirṇaya	Uttarārdha 8
Grāmavadha	Māṅgīśamāhātmya 4
Candracūḍaprādurbhāva	Candracūḍa- (Candreśvara-) māhātmya 2
Candrajanmakathana	Ādirahasya 35
Citpāvanabrāhmaṇotpatti	Uttarārdha 1
Jamadagnikrodhasaṃvāda	Reṇukāmāhātmya 26
Jamadagnivadha	Reṇukāmāhātmya 34
Jamadagnisaṃskāra	Reṇukāmāhātmya 36
Tīrthapraśaṇsā	Candracūḍa- (Candreśvara-) māhātmya 3
Tīrthamahimavarṇana	Candracūḍa- (Candreśvara-) māhātmya 5
Tīrthamahimāna	Candracūḍa- (Candreśvara-) māhātmya 6

Chapter Title	Section and Chapter Number
	Candracūḍa- (Candreśvara-) māhātmya 7
Daṇḍapāṇivarada	Ādirahasya 52
	Ādirahasya 54
Dānamahimakathana	Ādirahasya 23
Durvāsopaniṣat	Ādirahasya 42
	Ādirahasya 43
	Ādirahasya 48
Devasamūhāgamana	Ādirahasya 57
Devīsthāpana	Varuṇāpuramāhātmya 1
Dharmopadeśa	Ādirahasya 24
Nandīvarapradāna	Ādirahasya 56
	Ādirahasya 59
Nandīśvarayoga	Ādirahasya 40
Nandyutpattivarṇana	Ādirahasya 55
Narakavarṇana	Ādirahasya 4
Nāgabhayadūrīkaraṇa	Nāgāhvayamāhātmya 1

Chapter Title	Section and Chapter Number
Nāradāgamana	Reṇukāmāhātmya 18
Niyamopadeśakathana	Ādirahasya 25
Pañcāyatana	Ādirahasya 14
Pañcāyatanavarṇana	Ādirahasya 53
Pañcagrāmanirṇaya	Uttarārdha 10
Paraśurāmotpatti	Reṇukāmāhātmya 13
Paraśurāmakṣetrotpatti	Uttarārdha 7
Parvatopākhyāna	Candracūḍa- (Candreśvara-) māhātmya 8
Pāṭhārīyajātikathana	Ādirahasya 27
	Ādirahasya 28
Pāṭhārīyadharmotpattikathana	Ādirahasya 36
Pātityagrāma	Uttarārdha 19
Pātityagrāmakathana	Uttarārdha 12
	Uttarārdha 18
Pātityagrāmanirṇaya	Uttarārdha 14
	Uttarārdha 15

Chapter Title	Section and Chapter Number
Puṣpādidānamāhātmya	Ādirahasya 17
Pṛthvīdānapraśaṇsā	Uttarārdha 6
Pralayotpattikathana	Ādirahasya 13
Prāṇayajanakathana	Ādirahasya 49
Brahmakṛtaśivastuti	Ādirahasya 60
Brahmagītā	Ādirahasya 8
Brahmagītākathana	Ādirahasya 7
Brahmāṇḍotpatti	Ādirahasya 1
Brāhmaṇavicāra	Uttarārdha 5
Brāhmaṇotpatti (full title: Sūrpārakakṣetramāhātmya ca Brāhmaṇotpatti)	Uttarārdha 2
Brāhmaṇotpatti	Uttarārdha 4
Bhārgavakṛtastuti	Uttarārdha 9
Bhūtimāhātmyakathana	Ādirahasya 37
Bhūmivistāra	Ādirahasya 3
Bhṛguvaṇśānukathana	Reṇukāmāhātmya 5

Chapter Title	Section and Chapter Number
Mahālasāprabhāvakathana	Varuṇāpuramāhātmya 2
Mahāliṅgeśamahimāvarṇana	Uttarārdha 21
Mahiṣasaunyādivadha	Kāmākṣīmāhātmya 3
Mithunaharabrāhmaṇakathana	Uttarārdha 17
Yogavidhi	Ādirahasya 65
Yogopaniṣat	Ādirahasya 41
Rāvaṇaparājaya	Reṇukāmāhātmya 27
Reṇukāvaradāna	Reṇukāmāhātmya 3
Liṅgārcanavidhi	Ādirahasya 38
Liṅgodbhava	Ādirahasya 16
Vijayādurgākhyāna	Māṅgīśamāhātmya 12
Vyāghrarūpadhāraṇa	Māṅgīśamāhātmya 5
Śaṃkarajātivarṇana	Ādirahasya 26
Śaṃkaratapaḥpraśaṇsākathana	Māṅgīśamāhātmya 2
Śaṃkarapūjanādimāhātmyakathana	Māṅgīśamāhātmya 6
Śaṃkarastuti	Ādirahasya 61
Śaṅkhāvalyākhyānakathana	Māṅgīśamāhātmya 11

Chapter Title	Section and Chapter Number
Śaṅkhāvalīvarṇana	Māṅgīśamāhātmya 10
Śāntādurgāprādurbhāva	Nāgāhvayamāhātmya 2
Śivapuravarṇana	Ādirahasya 9
Śivamāhātmya	Ādirahasya 15
Śūdrotpatti	Uttarārdha 13
Saptakoṭīśākhyāna	Māṅgīśamāhātmya 3
Saptalokākhyāna	Ādirahasya 5
Sahasrārjunavadha	Reṇukāmāhātmya 40
Siddheśvaraprādurbhāva	Māṅgīśamāhātmya 9
Sūrpārakakṣetramāhātmya ca Brāhmaṇotpatti	Uttarārdha 2
Sṛṣṭikrama	Ādirahasya 2
Somavaṉśotpatti	Ādirahasya 32
Somavaṉśotpattikathana	Ādirahasya 31

4. PRELIMINARY CORRELATION OF CHAPTERS OF THE *SAHYĀDRIKHAṆḌA, ĀDIRAHASYA* (ED. DA CUNHA) AND THE *JÑĀNA[YOGA]KHAṆḌA* AS IN MANUSCRIPT NO. 129 IN THE BODLEIAN LIBRARY, OXFORD.[1]

Sahyādrikhaṇḍa, Ādirahasya	*Jñāna[yoga]khaṇḍa*
1. Brahmāṇḍotpatti	1. Material analagous to that of the
2. Sṛṣṭikrama	2. first 5 chapters of Skh.ā. according
3. Bhūmivistāra	3. to Latin description given by
4. Narakavarṇana	4. Aufrecht in his catalog of Bodleian
5. Saptalokākhyāna	5. Library Sanskrit MSS.
6. = ?	
7. Brahmagītākathana	6.
8. Brahmagītā	7. Brahmagītā
	8.
	9.
9. Śivapuravarṇana (= Jñkh 56)	
10.	10.
11.	11.
12.	12.
13. Pralayotpattikathana	13. Vibhīṣaṇamaheśvarasaṃvāda
14. Pañcāyatana	14. Nāmasaṃkīrtana
15. Śivamāhātmya	15. Sthānamāhātmya
	16. Guhyākhyāna
	17. Maheśvaradarśana
16. Liṅgodbhava	18. Liṅgodbhava
17. Puṣpādidānamāhātmya	19 Puṣpādidānamāhātmya
18. (= Jñkh 20-21?)	20. Puṣpasamuddeśa
19.	21. Puṣparasārasamuccaya

[1] Abbreviations: Skh.ā. = *Sahyādrikhaṇḍa, Ādirahasya*; Jñkh = *Jñāna[yoga]khaṇḍa*. Chapter numbers and titles are indented in each column if the material placed parallel to one another in the two texts does not appear to correspond. The only instance in which the ordering of the seemingly identical material is not parallel in the two texts is in the case of Skh.ā. 9 and Jñkh 56, in which case the chapter is marked off in both texts by broken horizontal lines in order that the reader may correlate them clearly despite their radically different placement. In all other cases, horizontal lines indicate the divisions suggested in Table 1 (Preliminary Outline of the *Sahyādrikhaṇḍa* as in Da Cunha's Edition) above.

Sahyādrikhaṇḍa, Ādirahasya	*Jñāna[yoga]khaṇḍa*
* { 20. Upāsavidhi	* { 22. Dānavidhi
21.	23. Nāmavidhi
22.	24. Nāmāṣṭamīvidhāna
23. Dānamahimakathana	25. Dānadharmavidhi
24. Dharmopadeśa }	26. Vratavarnana }
25. Niyamopadeśakathana	27. Yamopadeśa
{ 26. Śaṃkarajātivarṇana	
27. Pāṭhārīyajātikathana	
28. Pāṭhārīyajātikathana	
29. Kṣatriyotpattikathana	
30. Kṣatriyotpattikathana	
31. Somavaṃśotpattikathana	
32. Somavaṃśotpatti	
33. Kṣatriyotpattikathana	
34. Kṣatriyotpattikathana }	
35. Candrajanmakathana	28. Candrajanmakīrtana
36. Pāṭhārīyadharmotpattikathana	
37. Bhūtimāhātmyakathana	29. Bhūtikīrtana
38. Liṅgārcanavidhi	30. Liṅgārcanaphala
{ 39.	{ 31.
	Nandīśvarayogopākhyāna
40. Nandīśvarayoga }	32. }
41. Yogopaniṣat	33. Yogopaniṣat
{ 42. Durvāsopaniṣat	{ 34.
43. Durvāsopaniṣat	35.
44.	36.
45.	37. Durvāsopaniṣat
46.	38.
47.	39
48. }	40.
49. Prāṇayajanakathana (= Jñkh 41?)	41. }
50. = ?	42. Nāḍisaṃcāra
51. Avimuktamāhātmyakathana	43. Avimuktamāhātmya

* Common source from another MS of Jñkh or from a third source?

Sahyādrikhaṇḍa, Ādirahasya	*Jñāna[yoga]khaṇḍa*
52. Daṇḍapāṇivarada	
53. Pañcāyatanavarṇana	44. Daṇḍapāṇivarapradāna
54. Daṇḍapāṇivarada	
55. Nandyutpattivarṇana	45.
56. Nandivarapradāna	46.
57. Devasamūhāgamana	47. Nandyupākhyāna
58.	48.
59. Nandivarapradāna	49.
	50.
60. Brahmakṛtaśivastuti (= Jñkh 51?)	
61. Śaṃkarastuti (= Jñkh 51?)	51. Nīlakaṇṭhastava
62.	52.
63. = ?	53. Tripuropākhyāna
64.	54.
65. Yogavidhi	55. Yogavidhi
	56. Śivapuravarṇana (= Skh.ā. 9)
66. = ?	
67. = ?	

APPENDIX I: GLOSSARY[1]

adhyāya, a chapter.
ādirahasya, literally, the first teaching.
Āgama, a traditional doctrine or precept; a collection of such doctrines.
agnīdhra, the priest who kindles the fire.
agnihotra, oblation to Agni, chiefly of milk, oil and sour gruel. There are two kinds – one is of constant obligation, the other is optional.
aṅgamudrā, a subordinate *mudrā*. See *mudrā*.
anuloma, descendents of a relationship in which the woman is of lower social status than of the man with whom she is connected.
anusvāra, the nasal sound which is marked by a dot above the line in north Indian scripts such as *Devanāgarī*, and which always belongs to a preceding vowel.
apsaras, a class of female divinities who inhabit the sky but sometimes visit the earth. They are the wives of the *gandharvas*. See *gandharvas*.
āsana, sitting in a peculiar posture according to the custom of devotees. Five, and in places as many as eighty-four, are enumerated.
āśrama, a hermitage; the abode of ascetics.
astra, name of a *mantra* pronounced, for instance, before reading a book or while kindling a fire. See *mantra*.
asura, an evil spirit, demon, enemy of the gods.

---

[1] This glossary is meant to provide easy reference to terms used in the text of the work for readers not familiar with the Indian terminology. For this reason it is in English alphabetical order and includes words which anyone familiar with Indology might consider to be included unnecessarily. It is hoped that the list will serve its purpose for those for whom it is intended.

aśvamedha, the horse-sacrifice, the efficacy of which became greatly exaggerated in comparatively late times.

ātmajñāna, knowledge of the soul or supreme spirit.

avatāra, appearance of any deity upon earth, but more particularly the incarnations of Viṣṇu in his ten principal forms.

brāhmaṇa, a member of the first of the three twice-born classes, generally considered to be the priestly class. See *varṇa*.

cakra, a discus or sharp circular missile weapon, especially that of Viṣṇu.

cakradeva, an unidentified form of marriage.

cāndrāyaṇa, a fast regulated by the moon, the food being diminished every day by one mouthful for the dark fortnight and increased in like manner during the light fortnight.

Caṅkam (Tamil, generally pronounced '*Śaṅgam*'), a convocation of learned men at Madurai. There are said to have been three, the third ending in the third century A.D. It is only from this last *Caṅkam* that we have literary works.

cāraṇa, a celestial singer.

daitya, a son of Diti; a demon.

dānava, a class of demons often identified with the *daityas* or *asuras* and held to be implacable enemies of the gods. See *daitya* and *asura*.

darśana, a seeing, an observation. Great merit is acquired from obtaining *darśana* of gods, holy people, holy objects, etc.

deśa, a province, a country, or a kingdom.

deva, a god.

Devanāgarī, name of the character in which Sanskrit is usually written, particularly in northern India, and in which modern Hindi is written.

danuṣka, a measure of length.

dharmaśāstra, the science of law.

dhvaja, a banner, flag, or standard.

Dvaita, the doctrine of dualism, which asserts the existence of the human soul to be separate from the supreme being.

dvāpara, the name of the third of the four ages of the world.

gandharva, a mythical being with a long developmental history in India. In epic times *gandharvas* are the celestial musicians or heavenly singers who form the orchestra at the banquets of the gods and who belong, together with the *apsarases*, to Indra's heaven.

garuḍa, a mythical bird which is the vehicle of Viṣṇu.

golaka, a widow's bastard.

gotra, a family, or lineage.

grāma, a village, referred to by A. Govinda Warriar (see Bibliography) as a canton in the British sense of the word. Also, a community.

guru, any venerable or respectable person. Also, the spiritual parent or preceptor.

Jainalipi, or *Jainanāgarī*, the script used by Jains in Jain texts in western India. The script is closely related to *Devanāgarī*.

japa, a muttered prayer or spell.

jāti, position assigned by birth, rank, *varṇa*, family, race, and lineage. The modern term for caste. See *varṇa*.

kali, the last and worst of the four ages, our present age, which is an age of vice.

kaustubha, name of a celebrated jewel obtained with thirteen other precious things at the churning of the ocean and suspended on the breast of Kṛṣṇa or Viṣṇu.

khaṇḍa, a section of a work, a book.

kiṃnara, a mythical being with a human figure and the head of a horse, or with a horse's body and the head of a man. They are reckoned as being among the *gandharvas*. See *gandharva*.

kṛcchra, a particular kind of religious penance.

kriyā, a sacrificial act, in general.

krośa, a measure of distance, literally the range of the voice in calling.

kṛta, the first of the four ages of the world, the golden age.

kṣatra, or *kṣatriya*, a member of the military, or reigning, order or *varṇa*; the second *varṇa*. See *varṇa*.
kumbha, name of an unidentified *śrāddha*. Literally the word means 'water-pot,' or 'the urn in which the bones of a dead person are collected.' See *śrāddha*.
liṅga, a mark, sign, token; or the male sexual organ, especially that of Śiva worshipped in the form of a stone or marble column.
māhātmya, a work giving an account of the merits of any holy place or object. The term seems to be used more loosely in the PGN as a class of literature which gives accounts.
maṇḍala, literally, a circle. Used in reference to a district, territory, or country; and to the circle of a king's near and distant neighbors.
mantra, a sacred formula addressed to any individual deity.
manu, literally, man, but especially applied to fourteen successive mythical progenitors and sovereigns of the earth described in various works as creating and supporting this world through successive long periods of time.
marut, a storm god. *Ṛgveda* 8.96.8 maintains there are three times sixty of these. Later literature maintains them to be either seven, or seven times seven, in number.
mudrā, a sign, a token or mark of divine attributes impressed upon the body; a hand pose.
mūlamantra, a principle or primary or fundamental text, or spell.
muni, an inspired person; a saint, sage, seer, devotee.
Newārī (Nepali), a script used in Nepal since medieval times and which was the prevailing script at the time of the Gurkha conquest in the eighteenth century. After the Gurkha conquest *Devanāgarī* gradually became the prevalent script, superseding *Newārī*.
nirvāṇa, extinction or annihilation of individual existence or of all desires and passions.
niṣka, a particular coin varying in value at different times.
nīti, political ethics, or moral philosophy; right or wise conduct.

nitya [rites], constant and indispensable rites or acts such as observance of the five great acts of worship, for which see n. 1 to the translation of chapter eleven (Skh.u. 19); particularly the *śrāddha* consisting of offerings of water to one's ancestors, generally performed at the daily *tarpaṇa* ceremony during the *saṃdhyā*. See *tarpaṇa* and *saṃdhyā*.

pāda, a foot, or fourth part of a verse.

padminī, a woman belonging to the first of the four classes into which women are divided.

patita, fallen in social and ritual status; ritually polluted; excommunicated.

pātitya, a polluted or excommunicated *brāhmaṇa* or community of *brāhmaṇas*.

piśāca, name of a class of demons. They are mentioned in the *Veda* along with *asuras* and *rākṣasas*. In later times they are figured to be the children of Krodā.

prastha, a particular weight and measure, calculated variously at different times.

pratiloma, born in an inverse order of the classes, in which case the woman is of higher status than the man.

pravara, an invocation of Agni at the beginning of a sacrifie; a series of ancestors – so called because Agni is invited to bear the oblations to the gods as he did for the sacrificer's progenitors, the names of the four or five most nearly connected with the ancient *ṛṣis* then being added.

prāyaścitta, atonement, expiation.

pūjā, honor, worship, adoration of the gods.

Purāṇa, literally, a thing or event of the past, or an ancient tale or legend. It is the name of a class of sacred works supposed to have been compiled by Vyāsa and to treat five topics, for which see **§4.1**.

purohita, literally, one holding a charge or commission, e.g. a family priest; a domestic chaplain.

purūṣa, the individual personal soul.

ṛṣi, an inspired poet or sage.

rudrākṣa, a rosary, or the berries of the *Elaeocarpus ganitrus*, used for rosaries.

saṃdhi, euphonic junction of final and initial letters in grammar; modifications of final and initial letters of separate words and in the final letters of roots and stems when combined with terminations to form such words due to euphonic coalition.

saṃdhyā, religious acts performed by *brāhmaṇas* and other twice-born men at the juncture of the three divisions of the day, morning, noon and evening.

saṃhitā, any methodically arranged collection of texts or verses.

saṃnyāsa, renunciation of the world, the profession of asceticism.

saṃskāra, a sacred or sanctifying ceremony. Twelve are generally enjoined on the first three classes. See n. 11 to the translation of chapter two (Skh.u.10) of the PGN.

saṃvat, a year, especially of the Vikrama era, beginning in 56 B.C., in later times.

śānti, peace or calmness of mind.

Śāstra, any religious or scientific treatise, or any sacred book or work of divine authority. The word '*śāstra*' is often found in final composition with words denoting the subject of a book, and is often applied collectively to whole departments of knowledge, such as *steyaśāstra*, the science of theft.

satī, ritual self-immolation by a widow on her husband's funeral pyre.

siddha, any holy personage or great saint, especially one who has attained to one of the states of beatitude; any adept who has acquired supernatural powers.

śloka, a stanza, especially a particular kind of common epic meter, also called *Anuṣṭubh*, which consists of four *pādas* or quarter verses of eight syllables each, each line allowing great liberty except in the 5th, 13th, 14th, and 15th syllables which should be unchangeable as in the following scheme, ... ˘ . . . / . . . . ˘ ¯ ˘ . , the dots denoting either long or short syllables, with the 6th and 7th syllables being long, though if the 6th is short the 7th should be short also.

Smṛti, the whole body of sacred tradition remembered by human teachers, as opposed to *Śruti* which is directly heard or revealed by the *ṛṣis*. In its widest sense it includes the six *Vedāṅgas*, the *Śrauta*- and *Gṛhya-sūtras*, the law books, the *Itihāsas* (e.g. the *Mahābhārata* and the *Rāmāyaṇa*), the *Purāṇas*, and the *Nītiśāstras*.

śrāddha, a ceremony in honor of and for the benefit of dead relatives observed with great strictness at various fixed periods and on occasions of rejoicing and of mourning by the surviving relatives. It is an act of reverential homage to a deceased person performed by relatives, and is supposed to supply the dead with strengthening nutriment after the performance of the funeral ceremonies has endowed them with ethereal bodies.

Śruti, sacred knowledge orally transmitted by the *brāhmaṇas* from generation to generation. It is properly only applied to the *mantra* and *Brāhmaṇa* portion of the *Vedas*, but came to be extended to the *Upaniṣads* and other Vedic works. It is opposed to *Smṛti*, which see.

stotra, a praise, a eulogy, a hymn of praise.

śūdra, the lowest of the four classes, whose business is to serve the higher classes.

tāluka (Arabic derivation, through Persian), in south and west India, the subdivision of a district. The term has different shades of meaning in different areas of India.

Tantra, doctrine, rule, scientific work; or a class of works teaching magical and mystical formularies, mostly in the form of dialogues between Śiva and Durgā.

tapas, religious austerity.

tarpaṇa, the satiation of gods and deceased persons by presenting to them libations of water.

tīrtha, a place of pilgrimage on the banks of sacred streams, etc.; also, an object of veneration.

tretā, the name of the second age of the world.

Upaniṣad, a class of philosophical writings the aim of which is the exposition of the secret meaning of the *Veda*.

uparibhāga, the upper portion, the later portion.

uṣṇīṣa, anything wound around the head, such as a turban.

utpāta, an unusual or startling event boding calamity; a portent.

uttarakhaṇḍa, the later book, the concluding book.

uttararahasya, literally, the later teaching, the concluding teaching.

vaiśya, a man of the third class, whose business was primarily agriculture, but also trade.

varṇa, a class, usually referring to the four principle classes, or estates – the *brāhmaṇas*, *kṣatriyas*, *vaiśyas*, and *śūdras*.

Veda, the name of certain celebrated works which constitute the basis of the first period of the Hindu religion. Primarily there are three; the *Ṛgveda*, the *Yajurveda* and the *Sāmaveda*. These are sometimes referred to collectively as the *trayī vidyā* or triple knowledge, but the *Ṛgveda* is really the only original work of the three, and is much more ancient. Subsequently a fourth *Veda* was added, called the *Atharvaveda*, but this was probably not completely accepted till after the time of the *Mānavadharmaśāstra*. Each of the four *Vedas* has two distinct parts: *mantra*, words of prayer and adoration; and *Brāhmaṇa*, directions for the details of the ceremonies at which the *mantras* were to be used, together with explanations of the legends, etc. connected with the *mantras*.

Vedāṅga, literally, a limb of the *Veda*; the name of certain works or classes of works regarded as auxiliary to and even in some sense as part of the *Veda*. Six are usually enumerated: *śikṣā*, the science of proper articulation and pronunciation; *chandas*, meter; *vyākaraṇa*, linguistic analysis or grammar; *nirukta*, explanation of difficult Vedic words; *jyotiṣa*, astronomy, or rather, the Vedic calendar; and *kalpa*, ceremonial considerations. The first and second are said to be intended to secure the correct reading and recitation of the *Veda*, the third and fourth the understanding of it, and the fifth and sixth its proper employment at sacrifices.

Vedānta, name of the second and most important part of the *Mīmāṉsā* or third of the three great divisions of Hindu philosophy. It is called *Vedānta* either as teaching the ultimate scope of the *Veda* or simply as explained in the *Upaniṣads*, which comes at the end of the *Veda*.

vigraha, component, of which there appear to be ten. See n. 16 to the translation of chapter one (Skh.u. 9) of the PGN.

virāma, a cessation, termination, stop; the name of a small oblique stroke placed under a consonant in north Indian scripts to denote that the consonant has no vowel inherent in it or otherwise pronounced after it.

visarga, name of a symbol in grammar, usually marked by two perpendicular dots and transliterated 'ḥ,' representing a hard and distinctly audible aspiration. It generally, but not always, occurs at the end of a word, often taking the place of final 's' and 'r.' In some parts of India the preceding vowel is pronounced after it, as well.

yoga, abstract meditation and mental abstraction; or any simple act or rite conducive to such.

yogin, a follower of the *yoga* system of philosophy, or a contemplative saint, devotee or ascetic.

yojana, a measure of distance, figured variously.

yuga, an age of the world, of which there are four.

BIBLIOGRAPHY

[19-?]. *Catalogue of Sanskrit Manuscripts in the Sanskrit College Library, Benares, with full index*. Allahabad: Printed at the Government Press.

[19-?]. *The Hindu Art of Love* [= translation ascribed to Richard F. Burton (and F. F. Arbuthnot) of *The Anaṅgaraṅga* and *The Ratirahasya*]. Classics Library No. 2. Cleveland: Connoisseur Publishing Company.

1902. "Obituary [for J. Gerson da Cunha]." *The Journal of the Bombay Branch of the Royal Asiatic Society* 20: lxxvi-lxxvii.

1907-1909. *The Imperial Gazetteer of India*, new ed. 26 vols. Oxford: Clarendon Press.

1924. *Hand-Book of Castes and Tribes Employed on Tea Estates in North-East India*. Calcutta: Tea Districts Labour Association, printed by A. Rome at the Catholic Orphan Press.

1958-62. *Śrautakośaḥ, Encyclopaedia of Vedic Sacrificial Ritual Comprising Two Complimentary Sections, Namely, the Sanskrit Section and the English Section*, Vol. 1, Pts. 1 and 2 (English Section; by Ramachandra Narayan Dandekar). Poona: Vaidika Samsodhana Mandala.

Abbott, J. E. 1895. "Identification of Nagapura in the Konkan." *Indian Antiquary* 24: 83.

Agrawala, Vasudeva S., ed. and trans. 1963. *Devī Māhātmya, The Glorification of the Great Goddess*. Varanasi: All-India Kashiraj Trust.

Anantakrishna Iyer, L. K. 1909. *The Cochin Tribes and Castes*. 2 vols. Madras: Higginbotham and Co.

Anantakrishna Iyer, L. K. 1928-36. *The Mysore Tribes and Castes*. 4 vols. + Index. Mysore: Published under the auspices of the Mysore University.

Apte, Vaman Shivaram. 1957-59. *The Practical Sanskrit-English Dictionary*, rev. and enl. ed., eds.-in-chief Parshuram Krishna Gode and Cintāmaṇa Gaṇeśa Karve. 3 vols. Poona: Prasad Prakashan.

Aufrecht, Theodor. 1877. *Die Hymnen des Ṛigveda*, 2. Aufl. 2 vols. Bonn: Adolph Marcus.

Aufrecht, Theodor. 1891, 1896, 1903. *Catalogus Catalogorum, An Alphabetical Register of Sanskrit Works and Authors*. Rpt., 3 vols. in 2, Wiesbaden: Franz Steiver Verlag GMBH, 1962.

Bajpai, K. D., chief ed. 1967. *The Geographical Encyclopaedia of Ancient and Medieval India*, Pt. 1. Varanasi: Indic Academy.

Basham, Arthur Llewellyn. 1968. *The Wonder That Was India*, 3rd ed. New York: Taplinger Publishing Co.

Bayly, Susan. 1999. *Caste, Society, and Politics in India from the Eighteenth Century to the Modern Age*. The New Cambridge History of India, Vol. 4, Pt. 3. Cambridge: Cambridge University Press.

Bendall, Cecil. 1902. *Catalogue of the Sanskrit Manuscripts in the British Museum*. London: [Gilbert and Rivington].

Betham, G. K. 1895. "Specimens of Modern Brahmanical Legends, No. 1 – *Mañjgunī-Purāṇa* (= Veṅkateśa-Mahātmya from the Mahāpurāṇa Sahyādrikhaṇḍa)." *Indian Antiquary* 24: 231-242.

Betham, G. K. 1897. "Specimens of Modern Brahmanical Legends, No. 2 – the Vanavāsī Mahātmya." *Indian Antiquary* 26: 33-39.

Bhatt, Govindlal Hargovind. 1961 and 1966. *Pāda-Index of Vālmīki-Rāmāyaṇa*. 2 vols. Gaekwad's Oriental Series 129 and 153. Baroda: Oriental Institute.

Bhattacharya, Jogendra Nath. 1896. *Hindu Castes and Sects, An Exposition of the Origin of the Hindu Caste System and the Bearing of Sects Towards Each Other and Towards Other Religious Systems*. Calcutta: Thacker.

Birwé, Robert. 1976. "The *Amarakośa* and the Lexical Chapters of the *Agnipurāṇa*." *Journal of the American Oriental Society* 96.3: 383-403.

Bloomfield, Maurice. 1906. *A Vedic Concordance*. Harvard Oriental Series 10. Rpt. Delhi: Motilal Banarsidass, 1964.

Böhtlingk, Otto. 1870-73. *Indische Sprüche, Sanskrit und Deutsch*, 2., verm. u. verb. Aufl. 3 vols. St. Petersburg: Commissionare der Kaiserlichen Akademie der Wissenschaften.

Böhtlingk, Otto and Rudolf Roth. 1855-75. *Sanskrit-Wörterbuch*. 7 vols. Rpt. Wiesbaden: Harrassowita, 1966.

Bombay [Presidency]. 1883. *Gazetteer of the Bombay Presidency*, Vol. 15, Pt. 1: *Kanara*. Bombay: Printed at the Government Central Press.

Brereton, Joel Peter. 1981. *The Ṛgvedic Ādityas*. American Oriental Society 63. New Haven, Connecticut: American Oriental Society.

Brockhaus, Hermann, ed. 1839. *Katha Sarit Sagara. Die Märchensammlung des Sri Somadeva Bhatta aus Kaschmir; erstes bin fünftes Buch, Sanskrit und Deutsch*. Leipzig: F. A. Brockhaus.

Brough, John, trans. 1953. *The Early Brahmanical System of Gotra and Pravara, A Translation of the Gotra-Pravara-Mañjarī of Puruṣottama-paṇḍita with an Introduction*. Cambridge: Cambridge University Press.

Bühler, Georg, trans. 1886. *The Laws of Manu*. The Sacred Books of the East 25. Rpt. New York: Dover Publications, Inc., 1969.

Bühler, Georg. 1904. *Indian Paleography*. Rpt. Calcutta: Indian Studies – Past and Present, [1959].

Burnell, Arthur Coke. 1880. *A Classified Index to the Sanskrit Manuscripts in the Palace at Tanjore*. London: Trübner and Company.

Burrow, Thomas and Murray Barnson Emeneau. 1984. *A Dravidian Etymological Dictionary*, 2nd ed. Oxford: Clarendon Press. [1st ed., 1961.]

Cāminātaiyar, U. Vē. 1944. *Cilappatikāra mūlamum arumpatavuraiyum Aṭiyārkkunallāruraiyam*, 4. *patippu*. Ceṉṉai: Kapir Accukkūṭam. [1st ed., 1892.]

Coleman, Tracy. 2010. "Viraha-Bhakti and Strīdharma: Re-Reading the Story of Kṛṣṇa and the Gopīs in the *Harivaṃśa* and the *Bhāgavata Purāṇa*." *Journal of the American Oriental Society* 130.3: 385-412.

Comfort, Alex. 1964. *The Koka Shastra*. New York: Stein and Day, 1964.

Crooke, William. 1890. *Ethnographical Hand-Book for the North-West Provinces and Oudh*. Allahabad: North-Western Provinces and Oudh Government Press.

Cunningham, Alexander. 1871. *The Ancient Geography of India*, 1. *The Buddhist Period, Including the Campaigns of Alexander, and the Travels of Hwen-Thsang*. London: Trübner and Company.

Damodaran Nambiar, K. 1973-79. *Nārada Purāṇa: A Critical Study*. Issued as supplements to *Purāṇa* 15.2 (pp. 1-56), 16.1 (pp. 57-120), 17.1 (pp. 121-168), 17.2 (pp. 169-232), 18.2 (pp. 233-272), 19.2 (pp. 273-336), 20.2 (pp. 337-408), 21.1 (pp. 409-503). [= Doctoral Dissertation, Poona University.]

Daniélou, Alain, trans. 1965. *Shilappadikaram (The Ankle Bracelet) By Prince Ilangô Adigal*. New York: New Directions.

Davies, Cuthbert Collin. 1949. *An Historical Atlas of the Indian Peninsula*. [Bombay]: Geoffrey Cumberlege, Oxford University Press.

Deshpande, Madhav M. 2010. "Pañca Gauda and Pañca Drāviḍa: Contested Borders of A Traditional Classification." *Studia Orientalia* 108: 29-58.

Devi, Akshaya Kumari. [n.d.]. *A Biographical Dictionary of Puranic Personages*. Calcutta: Vijaya Krishna Brothers.

Dikshitar, V. R. Ramachandra. 1939. *The Śilappadikāram*. Madras: Humphrey Milford, Oxford University Press.

Dikshitar, V. R. Ramachandra. 1951-55. *The Purāṇa Index*. 3 vols. Madras University Historical Series 19. Madras: University of Madras.

Dubois, Jean Antoine. 1905. *Hindu Manners, Customs and Ceremonies*, 3rd English ed.; trans. from French, ed., and annotated by Henry K. Beauchamp. Rpt. Mineola, New York: Dover Publications, Inc., 2002. [Original, 1806; rev. by author in 1821.]

Eggeling, Julius. 1899. *Catalogue of the Sanskrit Manuscripts in the Library of the India Office*, Pt. 6. London: Printed by order of the Secretary of State for India in Council.

Emeneau, Murray Barnson. 1935. *A Union List of Printed Indic Texts and Translations in American Libraries*. American Oriental Series 7. New Haven, Connecticut: American Oriental Society.

Enthoven, Reginald Edward. 1920-22. *The Tribes and Castes of Bombay*. 3 vols. Bombay: Printed at the Government Central Press.

Fleet, J. F. 1877. "Sanskrit and Old Canarese Inscriptions." *Indian Antiquary* 6: 22-32.

Gaitonde, Gajanan Shastri [Gāyatoṇḍe, Gajānanaśāstrī], trans. [pref. 1971]. *Śrī Skandapurāṇa, Sahyādrikhaṇḍa, Dō. Jarsana da Kunhā sampādita granthācī saṃśodhita, saṃvardhita āvṛtti, Marāṭhī arthāsaha* [The text of the *Sahyādri-khaṇḍa* as established by J. Gerson da Cunha, with a Marāṭhī translation]. Mumbai: Shri Katyayani Publications.

Geldner, Karl Friedrich, trans. 1951[i.e. 1952]-57. *Der Rig-Veda, aus dem Sanskrit ins Deutsche übersetzt und mit einem laufenden Kommentar versehen*. 4 vols. Harvard Oriental Series 33-36. Cambridge, Massachusetts: Harvard University Press.

Gonda, Jan. 1967. "The Indra Festival According to the Atharvavedins." *Journal of the American Oriental Society* 87: 413-429.

Goonetilleke, William. 1890. "The Judgment of Solomon." *The Orientalist, A Journal of Oriental Literature, Arts and Sciences, Folklore, &c., &c., &c.* 4: 6-16.

Gorresio, Gaspare, ed. and trans. 1843-58. *Ramayana, Poema Indiano di Valmici*. 10 vols. Parigi: Stamperia Reale.

Govinda Pai, Manjeshwar. 1933. "The Geneology and Chronology of the Early Kadambas of Banavasi." *Journal of Indian History* 12: 354-373.

Grassmann, Hermann. 1873. *Wörterbuch zum Rig-veda*, 4., unveränderte Aufl. Wiesbaden: Otto Harrassowitz, 1964.

Grassmann, Hermann. 1876-77. *Rig-Veda, übersetzt und mit kritischen und erläuternden Anmerkungen versehen*. 2 vols. Leipzig: F. A. Brockhaus.

Griffith, Ralph Thomas Hotchkiss, trans. 1889. *The Hymns of the Ṛgveda*, new rev. ed., ed. by J. L. Shastri. Delhi: Motilal Banarsidass, 1973.

Hayavadana Rao, Conjeevaram. 1930. *Mysore Gazetteer, Compiled for Government*, new ed. Vol. 5: *Gazetteer*. Bangalore: Printed at the Government Press.

Hazra, Rajendra Chandra. 1940. *Studies in the Purāṇic Records of Hindu Rites and Customs*. University of Dacca Bulletin 20. Calcutta: University of Dacca.

Hultsch, Eugen, ed. 1922. *Das Baudhāyanadharmasūtra*, 2., verb. Aufl. Abhlandlungen für die Kunde des Morgenlandes herausgegeben von der Deutschen Morgenländischen Gesellschaft, 16. Band, No. 2. Leipzig: In kommission bei F. A. Brockhaus.

India. Great Trigonometrical Survey. [19-?]. *An Atlas of the Southern Part of India, Including Plans of All the Principle Towns and Cantonments. Reduced from the Grand Trigonometrical Survey of India Shewing Also the Tenasserim Provinces*. Madras: Pharoah and Co.

India. Ministry of Scientific Research and Cultural Affairs. 1962. *India: Waterways and Airways, for National Atlas of India*, 1st ed. Prepared under the direction of S. P. Chatterjee. [Map.]

India. Surveyor General. [Surveyed 1929-32]. *Bombay, Goa and Mysore: North Kanara District, Goa, Shimoga District*. Published under the direction of Brigadier H. J.

Couchman, Surveyor General of India. Marked, 'For Official Use Only.' [Map.]

Joshi, Laxman Shastri, ed. 1937-41. *Dharmakośa*. Vol. 1: *Vyavahārakhaṇḍa*, Pts. 1-3. Wai, District Satara: Prājña-pāthaśālā Maṇḍala.

Kamat, Jyotsna. 2010. "We the People of Dwaraka! *Amma's Column*, Monday, June 28, 2010. Accessed on June 28, 2013 at www.kamat.am/jyotsna/blog/blog.php?BlogID=1426.

Kamat, Pratima P. 1990. "Historical Geography and Natural Resources." *Goa Through the Ages,* Vol. 2: *An Economic History*, ed. Teotonio R. De Souza. Goa University Publication Series 6. Rpt. New Delhi: Concept Publishing Company, 1999. Pp. 1-54.

Kane, Panduranga Vamana. 1930-62. *History of Dharmaśāstra*. Government Oriental Series, Class B, No. 6. 5 vols. Poona: Bhandarkar Oriental Research Institute.

Karmarkar, A. P. 1944. "Human Sacrifice in Proto-India." *Annals of the Bhandarkar Oriental Research Institute* 25: 109-115.

Karve, Irawati. 1932. "The Paraśurāma Myth." *Journal of the University of Bombay* 1: 115-139.

Karve, Irawati. 1961. *Hindu Society – An Interpretation*. Poona: Deccan College.

Karve, Irawati. 1965. *Kinship Organization in India*, 2nd rev. ed. Bombay: Asia Publishing House. [1st ed., 1953.]

Keith, Arthur Berriedale. 1925. *The Religion and Philosophy of the Veda and Upanishads*. 2 vols. Harvard Oriental Series 31 and 32. Cambridge, Massachusetts: Harvard University Press.

Keith, Arthur Berriedale. 1928. *A History of Sanskrit Literature*. Oxford: The Clarendon Press; 1st Indian ed., Delhi: Motilal Banarsidass Publishers Private Limited, 1993.

Keith, Arthur Berriedale. 1935. *Catalogue of the Sanskrit and Prākrit Manuscripts in the Library of the India Office*, Vol. 2. Oxford: Published by order of the Secretary of State for India in Council at the Clarendon Press.

Kosambi, Damodar Dharmanand. 1962. *Myth and Reality, Studies in the Formation of Indian Culture*. Bombay: Popular Prakashan.

Krishnaswami Aiyangar, S. 1928. *Manimekhalai in Its Historical Setting*. London: Luzac and Company.

Levitt, Stephan Hillyer. 1973. *The Pātityagrāmanirṇaya, A Puranic History of Degraded Brahman Villages*. Available from Xerox University Microfilms, Order No. 74-14,100 as listed in *Dissertation Abstracts International*, Vol. 34/12 (June 1974), p. 7711A. [= Doctoral Dissertation, University of Pennsylvania.]

Levitt, Stephan Hillyer. 1976. "A Note on the Compound *pañcalakṣaṇa* in Amarasiṉha's *Nāmaliṅgānuśāsana*." *Purāṇa* 18.1: 5-38 + foldout.

Levitt, Stephan Hillyer. 1977 and 1979b. "The *Sahyādrikhaṇḍa*: Some Problems Concerning a Text-Critical Edition of a Purāṇic Text." *Purāṇa* 19.1: 8-40, 21.1: 77-79.

Levitt, Stephan Hillyer. 1979a. "Orthographic Confusion Between 'bh' and 't' in *Devanāgarī* Manuscripts." *Journal of the Asiatic Society, Calcutta* 21: 27-30.

Levitt, Stephan Hillyer 1982. "The *Sahyādrikhaṇḍa*: Style and Context as Indices of Authorship in the *Pātityagrāmanirṇaya*." *Purāṇa* 24.1: 128-145.

Levitt, Stephan Hillyer. 1992. "An Origin of Some Brahmans According to the *Pātityagrāmanirṇaya*." *The Journal of Sanskrit Academy, Osmania University* 14: 1-18.

Levitt, Stephan Hillyer. 1993. "Pollution and *karman* in the *Pātityagrāmanirṇaya*." *Purāṇa* 35.1: 88-105.

Levitt, Stephan Hillyer. 2011. "McKim Marriott's Theory of 'Coded Substance' as an Explanation of Formulaic Turns of Phrase in Certain Vedic and Hindu Prayers, and Its Relationship to Mircea Eliade's Theory of 'The Sacred'." *Anthropos* 106.1: 49-55.

Levitt, Stephan Hillyer. 2015. *The Veṟṟi Vēṟkai, or The Hand with a Victorious Spear: A Popular Book of Maxims Attributed to the 15th Century South Indian King Ativīrarāma Pāṇṭiyaṉ*. Chennai: Kaviri Pathippakam.

Mandlik, V. N. 1875. "Saṅgameśvara Māhātmya and Linga Worship." *The Journal of the Bombay Branch of the Royal Asiatic Society* 11: 99-114.

Mankad, D. R. 1941-42. "The Yugas." *Poona Orientalist* 6: 206-216.

Monier-Williams, Monier. 1891. *Brāhmanism and Hindūism; or, Religious Thought and Life in India*, 4th ed. New York: Macmillan and Co.

Monier-Williams, Monier. 1899. *A Sanskrit-English Dictionary*, new ed. Oxford: Clarendon Press.

Moraes, George M. 1931. *The Kadamba Kula, A History of Ancient and Medieval Karnataka*. Studies in Indian History of the Indian Historical Research Institute, St. Xavier's College, Bombay, No. 5. Bombay: B. S. Furtado and Sons.

Moraes, George M. 1964-65. "Dr. José Gerson DaCunha, 1844-1900." *Journal of the Asiatic Society of Bombay*, n.s. 39-40: 1-50.

Maurer, Walter H., trans. 1986. *Pinnacles of India's Past, Selection from the Ṛgveda*. University of Pennsylvania Studies on South Asia 2. Amsterdam and Philadelphia: John Benjamins Publishing Company.

Muir, John. 1872-74. *Original Sanskrit Texts on the Origin and History of the People of India, Their Religion and Institutions*, 2nd ed. 5 vols. Rpt. Amsterdam: Oriental Press, 1967.

Mysore [State, India]. 1969. *List of Villages in Mysore State*. Bangalore: Printed by the Director of Printing, Stationery and Publications at the Government Press.

Naraharinath, Yogi, ed. 1957. *Himavatkhaṇḍa, Skandapurāṇamadhye*. Kathmandu: Jagadamba Prakasha.

O'Flaherty, Wendy Doniger, trans. 1981. *The Rig Veda, An Anthology*. Rpt. Harmondsworth, Middlesex, England: Penguin Books, 1983.

Oldenberg, Hermann, trans. 1885. *The Grihya-Sūtras, Rules of Vedic Domestic Ceremonies*, Part 1 (*Sāṅkhāyana-grihya-sūtra, Āsvalāyana-grihya-sūtra, Pāraskara-grihya-sūtra,*

Khādira-grihya-sūtra). Sacred Books of the East 29. Oxford: Clarendon Press.

Oman, John Campbell. 1908. *Cults, Customs and Superstitions of India*. London: T. F. Unwin.

Padmanabha Menon, Krishnat P. 1924-37. *History of Kerala*. 4 vols. Ernakulam: Printed at the Cochin Government Press.

Pandey, Raj Bali. 1949. *Hindu Saṃskāras, A Socio-religious Study of the Hindu Sacraments*. Badaini, Banaras: Vikrama Publications.

Parajuli, Buddhisagar. *Saṃvat* 2020 [= A.D. 1963]. *Nepālarājakīyavirapustakālayasthahastalikhitasamastapustakā nāṃ Saṃkṣiptasūcīpatraṃ*. Kakthmandu: Virapustakālayataḥ.

Parthasarathy, K. E., ed. 1966. *Śrī Viṣṇu Sahasranāman, with the Commentaries of Śrī Śāṅkarācārya and Śrī Parāśara Bhattar*. Madras: Ganesh and Co. (Madras) Private Ltd.

Patil, Urmila Rajshekhar. 2010. *Conflict, Identity and Narratives: The Brahman Communities of Western India from the Seventeenth through the Nineteenth Centuries*. Published online at *https://repositories.lib.utexas.edu/bitstream/handle/2152/ETD-UT-2010-12-2082/PATIL-DISSERTATION.pdf*. Accessed on November 2, 2015. [= Doctoral Dissertation, University of Texas at Austin.]

Poleman, Horace Irvin. 1938. *A Census of Indic Manuscripts in the United States and Canada*. American Oriental Series 12. New Haven, Connecticut: American Oriental Society.

Pusalker, A. D. 1955a. "Paraśurāma and the Konkan." *Kerala Studies, Prof. A. Gopala Menon Commemoration Volume*, ed. P. K. Narayana Pillai. Trivandrum: University of Travancore. Pp. 1-13.

Pusalker, A. D. 1955b. *Studies in the Epics and Purāṇas*. Bombay: Bharatiya Vidya Bhavan.

Raghavan, Venkatarama et al. 1966. *New Catalogus Catalogorum, An Alphabetical Register of Sanskrit and Allied Works and Authors*, Vol. 2. Madras University Sanskrit Series 26. Madras: University of Madras.

Raghavan, Venkatarama et al. 1988. *New Catalogus Catalogorum, An Alphabetical Register of Sanskrit and Allied Works and Authors*, Vol. 12. Madras University Sanskrit Series 38. Madras: University of Madras.

Ramachandra Rao, P. 1902. *Tales of Mariada Raman, 21 Amusing Stories*. Madras: G. A. Natesan and Co.

Rice, Benjamin Lewis. 1876. *Mysore and Coorg, A Gazetteer Compiled for the Government of India*, Vol. 2: *Mysore, by Districts*. Bangalore: Mysore Government Press.

Rice, Benjamin Lewis. 1886-1905. *Epigraphica Carnatica*. 12 vols. Bangalore: Mysore Government Central Press.

Rice, Benjamin Lewis. 1897. *Mysore, A Gazetteer Compiled for the Government of India*, rev. ed., Vol. 2: *Mysore, by Districts*. Westminster: Archibald Constable and Company.

Rice, Benjamin Lewis. 1909. *Mysore and Coorg from the Inscriptions*. London: Archibald Constable and Company, Ltd.

Risley, Herbert Hope. 1892. *Tribes and Castes of Bengal, Ethnographic Glossary*. Calcutta: Printed at the Bengal Secretariat Press.

Rocher, Ludo. 1984. "Father Bouchet's Letter on the Administration of Hindu Law." *Studies in Dharmaśāstra*, ed. Richard W. Lariviere. Calcutta: Firma KLM Private Ltd. Pp. 15-48.

Rocher, Ludo. 1986. *The Purāṇas*. A History of Indian Literature, ed. Jan Gonda, Vol. 2, Fasc. 3. Wiesbaden: Otto Harrassowitz.

Rose, Horace Arthur. 1911-19. *A Glossary of the Tribes and Castes of the Punjab and North-West Frontier Province*. 3 vols. Lahore: Printed at the Civil and Military Gazette Press by Samuel T. Weston.

Row, B. Suryanarain. 1905. *History of Vijayanagar, The Never to be Forgotten Empire*, Pt. 1. Madras: Printed by Addison and Co.

Roy, Pratap Chandra, trans. 1893. *The Mahabharata of Krishna-Dwaipayana Vyasa*, rev. by Hirala Haldar, Vol. 1: *The Adi Parva*. 2nd ed., Calcutta: Oriental Publishing Co., [1962?].

Russell, Robert Vane, assisted by Rai Bahadur Hīra Lāl. 1916. *The Tribes and Castes of the Central Provinces of India.* 4 vols. London: Macmillan and Co., Ltd.

Ryder, Arthur W., trans. 1927. *The Ten Princes.* 3rd impression, Chicago: University of Chicago Press, 1960.

Saletore, Bhasker Anand. 1936a. *History of Ancient Karṇātaka*, Vol. 1: *History of Tuḷuva*. Poona Oriental Series 53. Poona: Oriental Book Agency.

Saletore, Bhasker Anand. 1936b. "The Tuluva Grama-paddhati." *S. Aiyangar Commemoration Volume*. Madras: The Committee. Pp. 116-117.

Śāstri, Hrīshikeśa and Siva Chandra Gui. 1902. *A Descriptive Catalogue of Sanskrit Manuscripts in the Library of the Calcutta Sanskrit College*, Vol. 4. Calcutta: Printed by J. N. Banerjee and Son, Banerjee Press.

Schmidt, Richard. 1902. *Beiträge zur indischen Erotik, das Liebesleben des Sanskritvolkes nach Quellen dargestellt.* Leipzig: Lotus-Verlag.

Sharma, Aryendra, Khanderao Deshpande, D. G. Padhye, and Sundara Sharma. 1964. *A Catalogue of the Sanskrit Manuscripts in the Osmania University Library*. Hyderabad: The Sanskrit Academy, Osmania University.

Sircar, Dines Chandra. 1951. "Text of the Purāṇic List of Rivers." *The Indian Historical Quarterly* 22: 215-238.

Śiromaṇi, Raghavan Nambiyar. 1950. *An Alphabetical List of Manuscripts in the Oriental Institute, Baroda*, Vol. 2. Baroda: Oriental Institute.

Smith, Vincent Arthur. [n.d.]. *General Index to the Reports of the Archeological Survey of India, Vols. 1 to 23*. Rpt. Varanasi: Indological Book House, 1969.

Söhnen-Thieme, Renate. 2009. "Buddhist Tales in the *Mahābhārata*?" *Parallels and Comparisons: Proceedings of the Fourth Dubrovnik International Conference on the Sanskrit Epics and Purāṇas, September 2005*, ed. Petteri Koskikallis. Zagreb: Croatian Academy of Sciences and Arts. Pp. 349-372.

Spate, Oskar Hermann Khristian. 1957. *India and Pakistan: A General and Regional Geography*, 2nd ed. London: Methuen and Co. Ltd.

Spellman, John W. 1964. *Political Theory of Ancient India*. Oxford: Oxford University Press.

Śrivivāsa Ayyaṅgar, T. R., trans. 1938. *The Yoga Upaniṣads*. Adyar, Madras: The Adyar Library.

Sukthankar, Vishnu Sitaram, ed. 1928-33. *The Mahābhārata*, Vol. 1: *The Ādiparvan*. Poona: Bhandarkar Oriental Research Institute.

Talekar, Śrīkrishna Śāstri. 1876. "Karhāḍa Brāhmaṇs." *Indian Antiquary* 5: 25.

Thurston, Edgar, assisted by K. Rangachari. 1909. *Castes and Tribes of Southern India*. 7 vols. Madras: Government Press.

United States of America. The Library of Congress Processing Department. 1964. *Transliteration, Languages of India and Pakistan*. Cataloging Service Bulletin No. 64.

Vaidya, Parashuram Lakshman. 1967-71. *The Pratīka-Index of the Mahābhārata*. 5 vols. Poona: Bhandarkar Oriental Research Institute.

Velankar, Hari Damodar. 1928. *A Descriptive Catalogue of Saṃskṛta and Prākṛta Manuscripts in the Library of the Bombay Branch of the Royal Asiatic Society*, Vol. 2. Bombay: Dr. Edward Parker.

Vidyāratna, Rāmanārāyana, ed. 1874. *The Śrauta Sūtra of Āśvalāyana with the Commentary of Gārgya Nārāyaṇa*. Bibliotheca Indica, n.s. 55, 61, 66, 69, 71, 80, 84, 89, 90, 93, and 299. Calcutta: Printed at the Baptist Mission and the Vālmiki Presses.

Wagle, Narendra K. 1970. "The History and Social Organization of the Gauḍa Sāraswata Brāhmaṇas of the West Coast of India." *Journal of Indian History* 48: 7-25, 295-333.

Warriar, A. Govinda. 1933. "The Keralotpatti, An Historical Study." *Bulletin of the Sir Rama Varma Research Institute* 2: 9-41.

Whitney, William Dwight. 1889. *Sanskrit Grammar*. Rpt. Cambridge, Massachusetts: Harvard University Press, 1960.

Wilson, Horace Hayman, trans. 1840. *The Vishnu Purāna, A System of Hindu Mythology and Tradition*. 3rd ed., Calcutta: Punthi Pustak, 1961.

Wilson, Horace Hayman, trans. 1850-88. *Rig-Veda Sanhita, A Collection of Ancient Hindu Hymns of the Rig-Veda, The Oldest Authority of the Religious and Social Institutions of the Hindus*. 7 vols. Rpt. New Delhi: Cosmo Publications, 1977.

Winternitz, Moriz. 1927. *A History of Indian Literature*, Vol. 1: *Introduction, Veda, National Epics, Purāṇas, and Tantras*, trans. S. Ketkar, and rev. by the author. Rpt. New York: Russell and Russell, 1971. [Original, 1905-1908.]

Witzel, Michael and Toshifumi Gotō, trans. 2007. *Rig-Veda, das Heiligen Wissen; erster und zweiter Liederkreis*. Frankfurt am Main: Verlag der Weltreligionen.

Zvelebil, Kamil V. 1995. *Lexicon of Tamil Literature*. Handbuch der Orientalistik. 2. Abteilung, *Indien*, ed. J. Bronkhorst, Vol. 9. Leiden / Köln: E. J. Brill.

INDEX[1]

Names of Gods, Goddesses and Demons

[1] This is a listing of names as in the text as edited here. See also the critical apparatus and the commentary passages in Appendix B. Not included are the names of Viṣṇu repeated formulaically in the first eight vss. of the *stotra*. The chapter numbers used are those of Skh.u.

Names of Countries and Regions

Names of Cities

Names of Villages

Nāgagrāma	15.2c
Nāga[grāma] (variant reading)	15.13b
Padika (variant reading)	15.13a
Pāruśabdagrāma (?)	10.26cd
Maṭināgapura	15.13b
Madi (variant reading)	15.13b
Modagrāma	11.1c
Vāmanāḷa	10.29d
Velañji (Belañji ?)	16.1c, 17.57d

Names of Holy Places

Name	Location in Text
Ananteśa	17.38c
Koṭiliṅgeśa (?)	12.1b
Kroḍeśa	9.70d
Gokarṇeśa	13.24b
Nṛsiṉheśa	11.36d
Mahābaleśa	17.31a

Names of Mountains

Name	Location in Text
Kroḍādri	10.24c, 10.26a, 13.11a
Nagarāja	9.39a
Mahendra	9.15d, 10.10a, 10.16d
Merumandara	16.14c
Śailendra	9.28c
Sahya / Sahyagiri / Sahyaparvata / Sahyādri / Sahyaśaila	9.17a, 10.24d, 10.25b, 10.41a, 13.11d, 17.34a, 17.43a, 19.2d

Names of Rivers

Name	Location in Text
Gaṅgā	19.41b
Cakranadī	15.2b
Caṇḍikā	19.3a, 19.14d
Tuṅgabhadrā	13.6d
Mandākinī	9.53c
Varāhī	13.11c
Śuktimatī	9.53a, 10.18b, 10.26b, 10.31a, 11.1b, 11.36c, 17.36a
Sītā	10.25c, 16.1d, 17.43d

Names of Plants

Name	Location in Text
Agniśikha	9.25a, 16.11b
Arjuna	9.22d, 16.9b
Aśoka	9.23c, 16.9a
Aśvattha	9.24a
Asana	9.22d, 16.11d
Āmrātaka	9.25a, 16.11c
Utpala	19.4a
Udumbara	9.24a
Kaṇṭaka	9.25d
Kadamba	9.23a, 16.9d
Kadambaka	19.7d
Kadaḷī / Kadalī	9.27c, 9.28b
Kamala	9.30c
Kalhāra	19.4a
Kāsana	9.25b
Kīcaka	9.26d
Kuñjara	18.4d
Kuṭaja	16.11d
Kunda	9.23d
Kurabaka	9.23d
Ketaka	16.9a

Kovidāra	9.22d
Kharjūra	16.12a
Guñja	17.41d
Campaka	9.23b, 16.10d
Cūta	9.23a, 16.9c
Chada	16.12b
Jambu	9.24d, 16.10a
Tamāla	9.22c, 16.10c
Tāla	9.22c, 16.10c
Tinduka	9.24b
Tilaka	16.9b
Dhava	16.19d
Naḷinī / Nalinī	9.27d
Nāga	9.23b
Nārikeḷa / Nārikela	16.12a
Nimba	9.23a, 16.9c
Nyagrodha	9.24b, 13.24c, 13.28d
Paṅkaja	11.45c
Panasa	9.24a, 17.44a
Pāṭala	9.23c, 16.10a
Pārijāta	9.22a
Puṇḍarīka	10.33a
Puṃnāga	9.23b, 16.9b
Pūga	9.24c, 16.12b
Pūgī	10.41b
Priyaṅgu	16.10a
Priyāḷa / Priyāla	9.25b
Plakṣa	9.24b, 16.10b
Bakuḷa / Bakula	9.23c, 16.9a, 16.9d
Badarī	16.9c
Bimba	11.17d
Madhūka	16.11c
Mandara	9.22a, 12.42b
Rājapūga	9.24d
Lakuṭa	16.11d
Vañjuḷa / Vañjula	16.10b
Veṇu	9.25d, 12.42a

Names of Birds, Animals and Insects

Siṉha	16.31c, 18.10d
Hastin	18.2d

Personal Names

Name	Location in Text
Kaṇva	13.8c
Ketu (?)	11.2c
Kroḍa (perhaps, Kroḍamuni)	9.12c
Guṇanidhi	16.16b
Guṇamāliṇī	16.16d, 16.19b
Guṇavatī	16.16c, 17.15a
Candradatta	14.3b
Janamejaya	9.6c
Muddakunda (?)	11.2d
Mṛkaṇḍu	9.38a
Mayūravarman	15.3c, 15.7a
Yudhiṣṭhira	18.3d
Vasu	12.3c
Vyāsa	9.7a
Śatānīka	9.6d
Śaunaka	9.6b
Sunīta	19.21d
Suptaghna	17.37d
Sūta	9.1a
Somapīṭhin	10.13d, 10.17b
Hemamālin	18.3c

Names of Mythical Beings

Name	Location in Text
Apsaras	9.18b
Asura	9.43a, 10.30b, 10.32a, 11.45c
Kiṃnara	9.18a
Gandharva	9.18a
Caṇḍa	10.32b
Cāraṇa	9.18b

Names of Precious or Sacred Stones

HINDU TRADITION SERIES

General Editor

Johannes Bronkhorst

Editorial Board

Shrikant Bahulkar, Greg Bailey, Alf Hiltebeitel, Raffaele Torella, Michael Witzel

The Hindu Tradition Series aims to bring together books of the highest academic standard that critically interrogate Hindu tradition in the widest sense. Its focus is on cultural and religious history, including relevant political and social developments. The interaction with other traditions, whether originally from inside or outside the Indian subcontinent, will figure prominently among its volumes.

1. *The Mahābhārata and Greek Mythology* — **Fernando Wulff Alonso** [978-81-208-3791-1]
2. *Viraha-Bhakti : The Early History of Kṛṣṇa Devotion* — **Friedhelm Hardy** [978-81-208-3616-1]
3. *Classical Hindu Mythology : A Reader in the Sanskrit Purāṇas*— Ed. and Tr. by **Cornella Dimmitt** and **J.A.B. Van Buttenan** [978-81-208-3972-4]
4. *India and the Hellenistic Word* — **Klaus Karttunen** [978-81-208–4100-0]
5. *Engaged Enancipation : Mind, Morals and Make- Believe in the Mokṣopāya (Yogavāsiṣṭha)* —Edited by **Christopher Key Chapple** and **Arindam Chakrabarti** [978-81-208–4093-5]
6. *The Pātityagramanirnaya : A Purāṇic History of Some Brahman Communuties* — **Stephan Hillyer Levitt**
7. *Mythology of Brahma* — **Greg Bailey**